NATIONAL GEOGRAPHIC

CONCISE HISTORY OF THE
WORLD

AN ILLUSTRATED TIME LINE

NATIONAL GEOGRAPHIC

CONCISE HISTORY OF THE
W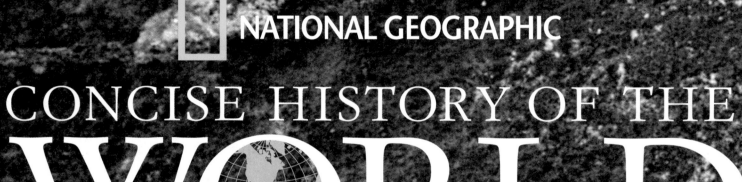RLD
AN ILLUSTRATED TIME LINE

EDITED BY NEIL KAGAN
FOREWORD BY JERRY H. BENTLEY AND J. R. MCNEILL

REVISED EDITION

NATIONAL GEOGRAPHIC
WASHINGTON, D.C.

PREVIOUS PAGE: *Cave paintings, discovered in the Drakensberg Range, South Africa, symbolize how hunters gained power from the animals they killed.*

OPPOSITE: *Some 25 million light-years away, in the Hunting Dogs constellation, luminous young stars and glowing hydrogen swirl in the Whirlpool galaxy. This spiral galaxy was first spotted in 1773 by French astronomer Charles Joseph Messier.*

CONTENTS

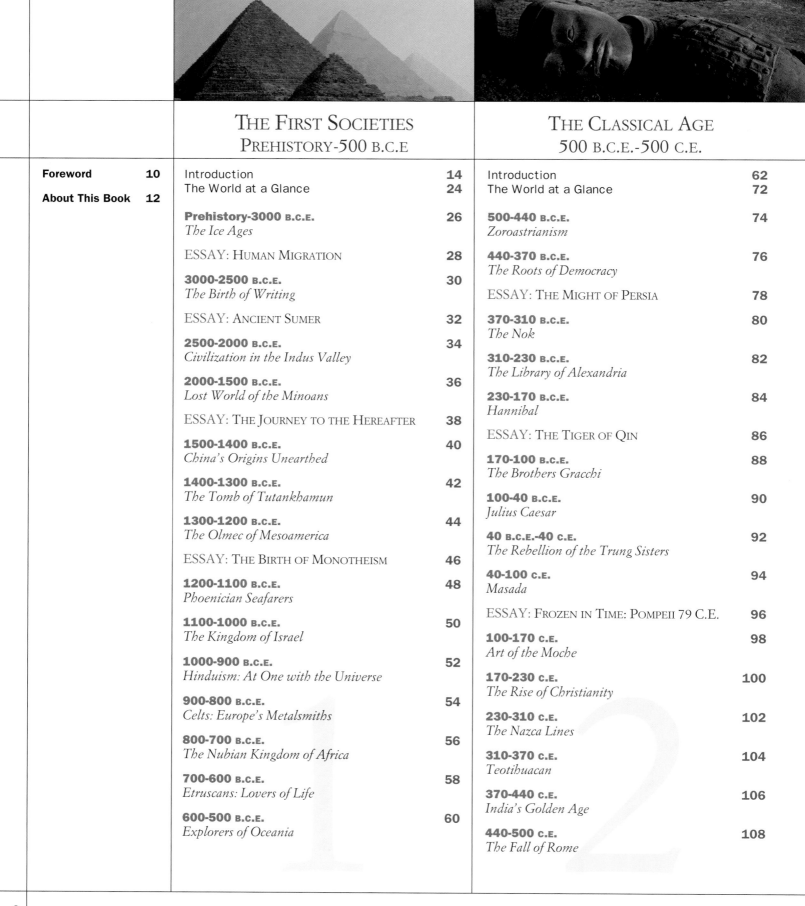

THE FIRST SOCIETIES
PREHISTORY-500 B.C.E

THE CLASSICAL AGE
500 B.C.E.-500 C.E.

FAITH AND POWER
500-1000

INVASIONS AND ADVANCES
1000-1500

CONTENTS

Converging Worlds
1500-1750

Empires and Revolutions
1750-1900

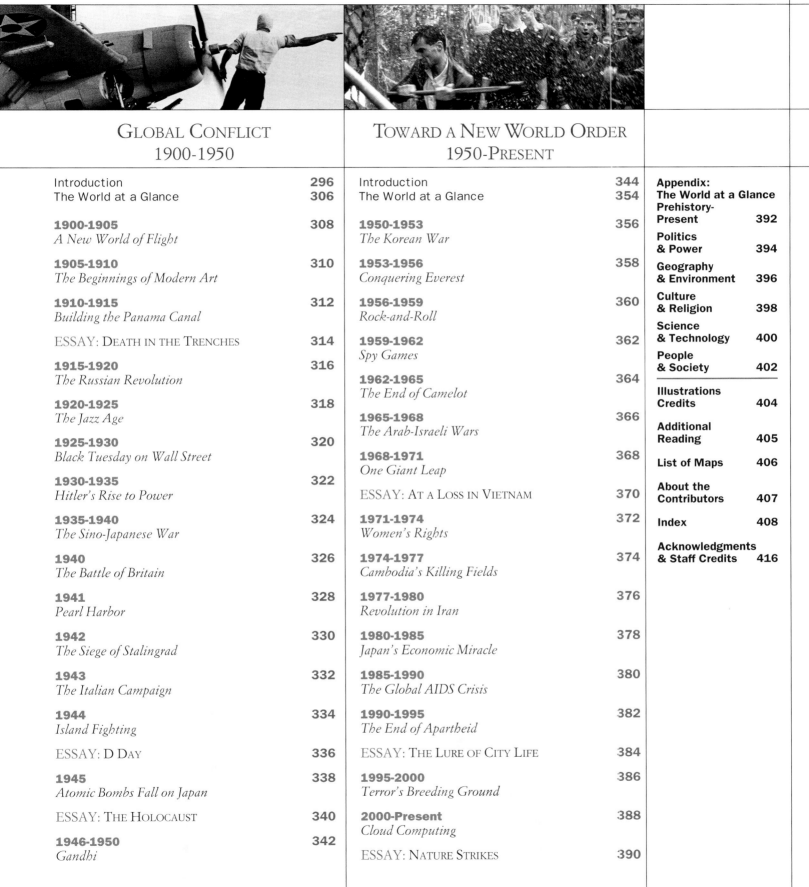

GLOBAL CONFLICT
1900-1950

TOWARD A NEW WORLD ORDER
1950-PRESENT

FOREWORD

IN HIS ORATION "DE ORATORE" (55 B.C.E.), THE ROMAN PHILOSOPHER AND ORATOR CICERO STATED THAT "history is the witness that testifies to the passing of time; it illuminates reality, vitalizes memory, provides guidance in daily life, and brings us tidings of antiquity." Cicero's words aptly characterize the *National Geographic Concise History of the World: An Illustrated Time Line*. Since its establishment in 1888, the National Geographic Society has worked to promote "the increase and diffusion of geographical knowledge," including historical knowledge of the world and its regions. Many of the Society's maps and publications have been devoted to particular lands or peoples, sometimes even to specific individuals who made important contributions to furthering geographical knowledge. In so doing, the Society has brought all corners of the world into welcome geographical and historical focus.

The National Geographic Society has served its members and readers well by focusing not just on local and regional issues but also on global developments in publications such as this one. It has been clear since the early 20th century, if not before, that it is impossible to understand any region in isolation from its neighbors and the larger global community, that understanding the world requires adopting global as well as local or regional perspectives. Scholars have become increasingly attentive to historical processes that have transcended national or cultural boundaries and influenced affairs on transcultural, transcontinental, and transoceanic scales. These processes include climatic changes, economic fluctuations, the diffusions of food crops and animal stocks, the spread of diseases, mass migrations, transfers of technology, campaigns of imperial expansion, long-distance trade, the spread of ideas and ideals, and the expansion of religious faiths and cultural traditions. In combination, these processes have shaped the world we inhabit—an interconnected, interdependent world linked by networks of travel, trade, communication, and cultural exchange. Examining global historical processes in past times can throw light on the dynamics of current events and place the experiences of individuals or societies in a larger context.

The purpose of this illustrated time line is precisely to provide global perspectives on the human past. Each chapter of the time line deals with a distinct era of world history and opens with an essay outlining major trends and events during the era under review. Each chapter also features illustrated essays that focus on significant developments that linked societies, such as travel and trade over the silk roads, or on the contributions of a particular society, such as the Anasazi in the American Southwest. The time line itself offers a global view of history by placing concurrent events in the world's major regions together in one column.

"*History is the witness that testifies to the passing of time . . .*"

Illustrated sidebars on subjects such as Marco Polo or the giant stone statues of Easter Island concisely examine notable individuals, cultures, and social developments within each time period.

By providing global perspectives on the past, this illustrated time line will help readers make sense of today's headlines and the seemingly chaotic course of current affairs. Many of today's boundary disputes, power struggles, and armed conflicts have their origins in events that occurred hundreds or even thousands of years ago. This book goes well beyond political and military affairs to explore the historical roots of social, religious, cultural, economic, scientific, technological, and environmental issues that challenge the modern world.

The National Geographic Society enjoys a well-earned reputation for the power of the photographs and the precision of the maps that accompany its various publications. This illustrated time line has benefited from the remarkable wealth of resources at the Society's disposal. The time line has also benefited from the advice of a sterling Board of Advisers who have provided expert guidance and counsel on the book. All of the advisers are recognized scholars in their field of historical expertise who have distinguished themselves through their efforts to view that field from a global perspective and to communicate their insights to students and popular readers. Working as a team, the National Geographic Society and the Board of Advisers have produced a world history that is not only concise but attractive, authoritative, and informed by the latest scholarly findings.

Since this book was first published in 2006, the world has continued to spin and history to unfold. The global economic meltdown, the election of an African-American president in the United States, the Arab Spring, and Japan's nuclear disaster were just some of the many events of recent years. In the 21st century, as never before, responsible citizenship requires understanding of the larger world. In this rapidly changing and interconnected age, it is vital to comprehend the political, social, and cultural traditions of peoples in regions beyond our borders and to grasp the nature of the networks that link societies. That understanding begins with the study of our shared global past. The *National Geographic Concise History of the World* provides a unique framework for comprehending the global past and its ongoing impact on the present.

— JERRY H. BENTLEY (1949-2012)
Professor of History, University of Hawaii
Editor, Journal of World History

— J. R. MCNEILL
Professor of History, Georgetown University

DEFINING TIME PERIODS

Scholars and editors working today in the multicultural discipline of world history use terminology that does not impose the standards of one culture on others. As recommended by the historians who make up our Board of Advisers, this book uses the terms **B.C.E.** (before the Common Era) and **C.E.** (Common Era). B.C.E. refers to the same time period as B.C. (before Christ), and C.E. refers to the same time period as A.D. (anno Domini, a Latin phrase meaning "in the year of the Lord").

ABOUT THIS BOOK

NATIONAL GEOGRAPHIC CONCISE HISTORY OF THE WORLD: AN ILLUS-trated Time Line brings the sweeping story of humanity over the ages into sharp focus through a versatile design that allows readers to use this book as a handy reference to learn more about a particular time or region or to follow events continuously from ancient to modern times. The book is divided into eight chapters covering major historical eras from prehistory to the present. Each chapter begins with an Introduction that sums up global developments during the era, followed by The World at a Glance, a chronological overview region by region. The core of each chapter is a time line that divides the era into 15 periods over 15 spreads, with entries arranged by subject and region. Supplementing the time line are picture essays, sidebars, and boxes that explore significant topics such as the rise of Islam, the end of apartheid, and the devastating Indian Ocean tsunami of late 2004.

Simply browsing through the time line will offer readers countless surprises and insights, as in this sampling drawn from the thousands of entries compiled here:

1792 B.C.E. Hammurabi's Babylonian code of laws states that men can sell their wives and children into slavery to pay debts.

436 B.C.E. Rome is struck by a famine so severe that thousands commit suicide by throwing themselves into the Tiber River.

670 C.E. The folding fan is invented in Japan based on the structure of a bat wing.

1692 Witch trials in Salem, Massachusetts, condemn 19 people to death for trafficking with Satan.

1830s Opium imports from British traders outstrip Chinese exports of tea and silk.

1905 An obscure Swiss patent clerk, Albert Einstein, formulates the theory of relativity, $E = mc^2$, and ushers in the atomic age.

1943 Hitler orders the mobilization of all children in Germany over the age of ten.

1967 Both sides in the Nigerian civil war agree to a 48-hour cease-fire so they can watch Pelé play in an exhibition soccer match in Lagos.

— NEIL KAGAN
Editor

INTRODUCTION

Each chapter opens with an introductory essay that surveys the major events and historical trends of the era. The example here, covering the years 1500-1750, begins by discussing European expansion, a process that transformed both the Old World and the New World as people, plants, livestock, and viruses were exchanged. Over 40 National Geographic maps, portraying the spread of ideas and cultures and the interactions of societies, appear throughout the book.

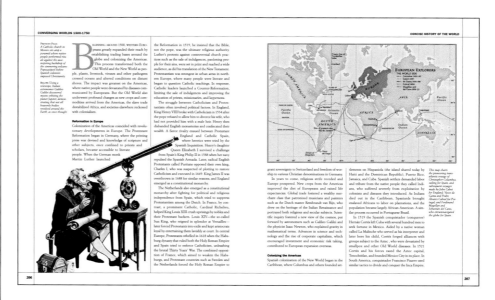

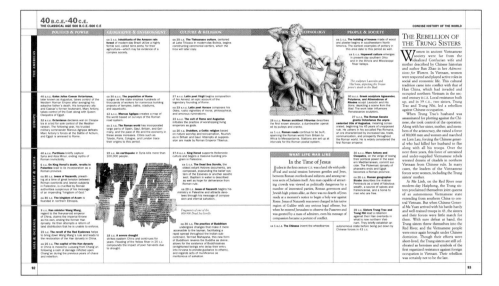

THE WORLD AT A GLANCE

The World at a Glance displays the era's key events chronologically from left to right and regionally from top to bottom. The four regions defined here—**The Americas** (North and South America), **Europe**, **Middle East & Africa**, and **Asia & Oceania**—appear in the same order in the time line. This overview allows for quick comparison of concurrent events in different regions. The first vertical column here, for example, reveals that between 1500 and 1525 slaves were first brought to the New World by the Spanish, Martin Luther instigated the Protestant Reformation, and the Ottoman Sultan Selim conquered the Arab world.

TIME LINE

Each time line spread offers a global view of events during the period defined in red at top left. (Time spans may vary in length, depending on the length of the era covered in each chapter.) The five vertical columns cover major historical themes—**Politics & Power**, **Geography & Environment**, **Culture & Religion**, **Science & Technology**, and **People & Society**. Developments within those areas are listed chronologically from top to bottom within each of the four regions. Sidebars at the far right of each spread highlight significant individuals or events, and boxed features entitled **What Life Was Like** and **Connections** describe how people lived or how societies interacted.

PICTURE ESSAY

Each chapter contains three picture essays that explore the unique contributions made by a particular society during the era or the interactions of societies through such means as trade, warfare, or immigration, as in this example. Over 245 illustrations appear throughout the book documenting the epic story of humanity. Quotes here and throughout the chapter define the era in the words of poets, philosophers, politicians, and others who embodied their times.

HUMAN HISTORY IS THE STORY OF A species so skilled at exploiting and altering its environment that it now has the power to create new life forms genetically or destroy life on a vast scale and extinguish many species. As builders, colonists, and conquerors, humans have shown an astonishing capacity to invent, transform, and lay waste. "Wonders are many, but none is more wonderful than man," wrote the Greek playwright Sophocles. "Cunning beyond fancy's dream is the fertile skill which brings him, now to evil, now to good."

Humans owe their phenomenal ability to alter the world for good or ill to a process of evolution that began in Africa more than four million years ago with the emergence of the first hominids: primates with the ability to walk upright. Early hominids stood only three or four feet tall on average and had brains roughly one-third the size of the modern human brain, which limited their capacity to reason or speak. But their upright posture and opposable thumbs (used to grip objects between fingers and thumb) allowed them to gather and carry food and process it using simple tools.

Over time, other species of hominids evolved that possessed larger brains and the ability to fully articulate their thoughts, craft ingenious tools and weapons, and hunt collectively. *Homo sapiens,* or modern humans, emerged in Africa perhaps 250,000 years ago, and they had a talent for adapting to changing circumstances that allowed them to occupy much of the planet. By clothing themselves in animal hide and living in caves warmed by fires, they survived winters in northern latitudes during the most recent phase of the Ice Age, which came to an end around 12,000 years ago. That glaciation lowered sea levels and enabled people to walk from Siberia to North America and reach Australia and other previously inaccessible land masses.

During the Ice Age, humans gathered wild grains and other plants, but they owed their survival and success largely to hunting. So skilled were they at hunting in groups and killing large animals that they probably contributed to the extinction of such species as the mammoth and mastodon. Hunters paid tribute to the animals they stalked in wondrous cave paintings that may have been intended to honor the spirit of those creatures so they would offer up their bounty. From early times, the destructive power of humans as predators was linked to their creative power as artists and inventors.

Putting Down Roots

The warming of the planet that began around 10,000 B.C.E. forced humans to adapt, and they did so with great ingenuity. Many of the larger animals people had feasted on during the Ice Age died out as a result of global warming and over-hunting. At the same time, edible plants flourished in places that had once been too cold or dry to support them. Based on the behavior of hunter-gatherers in recent times, women did much of the gathering in ancient times and probably used their knowledge of plants to domesticate wheat, barley, rice, maize (corn), and other cereals. That allowed groups who had once roamed in search of sustenance to settle in one place.

The domestication of animals also contributed to a more settled way of life. Dogs were probably the first animals tamed by humans. People later succeeded in domesticating other useful creatures such as cattle and sheep, which furnished meat, milk, wool, and hide. This was most likely accomplished by men, who did most of the hunting and learned gradually how to control animals.

That in itself did not cause people to settle down. Nomadic herders continued to follow grazing animals such as sheep and goats from place to place long after other people had settled in villages. The most productive societies, however, were those that practiced agriculture by controlling animals and cultivating plants. Agriculture provided food surpluses that allowed people to specialize in other pursuits and devise new tools and technologies.

Some of the earliest advances in agriculture

occurred in the Middle East, where sizable towns such as Jericho developed. By 7000 B.C.E., Jericho had around 2,000 inhabitants, or more than ten times as many people as in a typical band of hunter-gatherers. To protect their community from raiders, the people of Jericho built a wall that became legendary. Within Jericho and other such towns lived many people who specialized in nonagricultural trades, including merchants, metalworkers, and potters. The demand for pots to hold grain and other perishables led to development of the potter's wheel, which may in turn have inspired the first wheeled vehicles. Farmers here and elsewhere used wooden plows pulled by cattle or other draft animals to cultivate their fields and exchanged surplus food for clay pots, copper tools, and other crafted items.

By 5000 B.C.E. agriculture was being practiced in large parts of Europe, Asia, and Africa. Few animals were domesticated in the Americas because they had few domesticable species. (Horses had died out and would not be reintroduced until Europeans reached what they called the New World.) But the domestication of corn and other crops in the Americas led to the growth of villages and complex societies, marked by a high degree of specialization.

Dawn of Civilization

By 3500 B.C.E., the stage was set for the emergence of societies so complex and accomplished they rank as civilizations, a word derived from the Latin *civis,* or citizen. All early civilizations had impressive cities or ceremonial centers adorned with fine works of art and architecture. All had strong rulers capable of commanding the services of thousands of people for public projects or military campaigns. Many but not all used writing to keep records, codify laws, and preserve wisdom and lore in the form of literature.

People in these highly complex societies possessed

superior technology, but they were no better or wiser than those in simpler societies. Civilizations embodied the contradictions in human nature. They were enormously creative and hugely exploitative, enhancing the lives of some people and enslaving others. Their cities fostered learning, invention, and artistry, but many were destroyed by other so-called civilized people. The glory and brutality of civilization was recognized by philosophers and poets, who knew that anything a ruler raised up could be brought down. "When the laws are kept, how proudly his city stands!" wrote Sophocles. "When the laws are broken, what of his city then?"

Hominids in Tanzania left these 3.6-million-year-old footprints in volcanic ash that hardened after they passed. As shown in the chart at left, early hominids, who had much smaller brains than modern humans, endured for over three million years. They coexisted with two archaic human species with larger brains—Homo habilis and Homo erectus—but died out before the evolution of Homo sapiens, or modern humans.

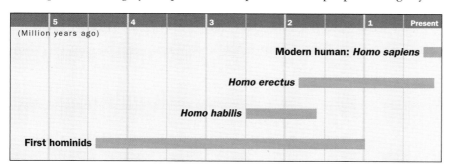

(Million years ago)	5	4	3	2	1	Present
Modern human: *Homo sapiens*						
Homo erectus						
Homo habilis						
First hominids						

Corridors of Power

Several ancient civilizations arose along rivers: the Tigris and Euphrates in Mesopotamia, the Nile in Egypt, the Indus in what is now Pakistan, and the Yellow River in China. People living in these fertile corridors needed strong leaders to coordinate irrigation projects or flood-control efforts and collect surplus food for those engaged in public works and other vital tasks. Leaders often demanded heavy sacrifices from people in labor and taxes or required a portion of the harvest, but communities as a whole grew more productive and powerful as a result.

In this way, towns developed into cities that controlled outlying farms and villages. The world's first cities emerged in Mesopotamia around 3200 B.C.E. and grew to contain as many as 50,000 people. Surplus grain was stored at temple complexes, and scribes there developed writing called cuneiform, inscribed on clay tablets, to keep track of goods received and distributed. When conflicts arose with outsiders over access to land or water, the city appointed a chief to wage war. Successful chiefs clung to power and became kings. Some royal families built palaces near temples and demanded human sacrifices. At the Sumerian city of Ur around 2500, some people lost their lives and were buried with deceased rulers to serve them in the next world.

Around 2330 Ur, Uruk, and other prosperous cities of Sumer, situated near the Persian Gulf, fell to a conqueror from northern Mesopotamia named Sargon. His successors lost control of that empire, but the region was later reunited under Hammurabi, who ruled at Babylon. He issued the law of his realm in writing, making it clear and consistent. Writing also enabled Babylonian scribes to transform legends into literature such as the *Epic of Gilgamesh,* the story of a fabled king who sought immortality.

In Egypt cities were slower to develop, but the Nile helped unify the country. People rode boats downstream to the Mediterranean and used sails or oars to travel upstream. Rains falling in the highlands far to the south caused the Nile to overflow its banks in summer and replenish what would otherwise have been a desert. The miraculous emergence of fertile land from the flood waters helped instill in Egyptians hope that they too might return to life after they died. Their early kings, or pharaohs, who consolidated power around 3000 B.C.E and ruled at Memphis, were preserved after death through mummification and buried in tombs that grew grander over time. The Great Pyramid of Khufu, built at Giza in the 26th century B.C.E., required tens of thousands of laborers and symbolized the lofty aspirations of Egypt's rulers, who identified with the sun god Re. One text promised that the pharaoh's spirit would rise from the pyramid and "ascend to heaven as the eye of Re" (an image that endures today on the American dollar).

Monumental architecture was not confined to Egypt or other centers of civilization. Construction of the Great Pyramid was preceded by the building of Stonehenge in Britain, which may have been used for religious ceremonies related to phases of the sun and moon. Such massive stone monuments in Europe demonstrate that agricultural societies there were capable of concerted efforts under the direction of priests or other authorities. But Europe had no cities as yet and no rulers who held sway over vast areas and left their mark on history as the pharaohs did. Around 2000 B.C.E. power in Egypt shifted from Memphis to Thebes, whose kings expanded their domain southward into Nubia (present-day Ethiopia).

Along the Indus River and its tributaries, irrigation efforts fed the growth of remarkable cities that were flourishing by 2500 B.C.E. and reflected careful planning, with broad streets, large granaries to store surplus crops, and elaborate sewage systems. The two largest cities were Mohenjo Daro, which had almost 40,000 inhabitants, and Harappa, for which this Harappan civilization is named. Artisans in the cities produced cotton fabric and jewelry, and merchants shipped crafted goods and raw materials to Mesopotamia. Harappan writing has not been deciphered and may have been rudimentary. But this was one of the most-well-organized societies in the world before its cities declined after 2000 B.C.E., most likely as a result of flooding or other natural causes.

This imposing bronze figure with braided beard represents the ideal Mesopotamian ruler. It may be a likeness of Sargon, who forged the first empire in Mesopotamia by sweeping down from Akkad and conquering the cities of Sumer, on map opposite.

In China, agricultural and technological innovation took place in many areas, including the lower Yangzi River, where rice was cultivated as early as 5000 B.C.E. Food surpluses in communities there and elsewhere helped support Chinese artisans skilled at crafts such as pottery, the sculpting of jade objects, and the casting of bronze—an alloy of copper and tin that provided ancient societies in various parts of the world with stronger weapons and tools than those made of copper alone.

Around 2200 B.C.E. crucial political developments occurred along the Yellow River. Villagers there did not have much need for irrigation. They usually received adequate rainfall and raised millet and other grains in loess: fertile yellow soil deposited by winds blowing from the north. That same soil, however, clogged the Yellow River and caused floods. Chinese chronicles credit a legendary king named Yu with taming the river's floods and bringing order to the world. Rulers of the Xia dynasty founded by Yu mobilized laborers for flood-control projects such as dredging the river or building dikes and gained power and prestige in the process.

Around 1750 B.C.E. the Xia dynasty was succeeded by the Shang dynasty, whose rulers built defensive walls of rammed earth around their capitals and raised armies, expanding their domain to embrace a large area in northeastern China. Veneration of ances-

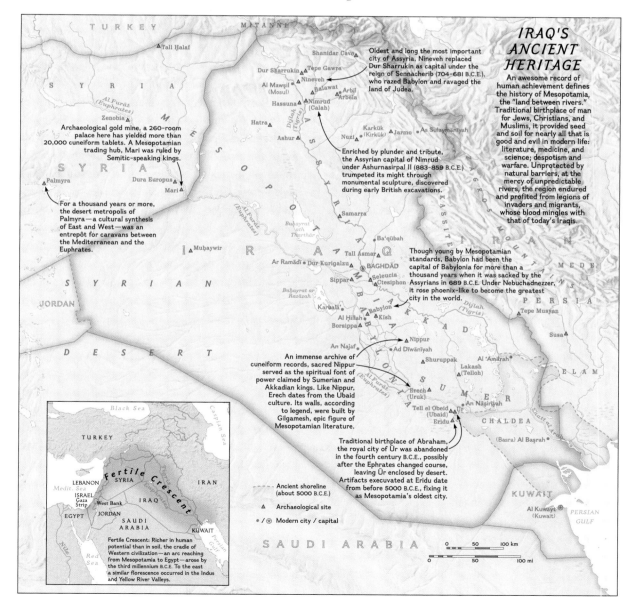

IRAQ'S ANCIENT HERITAGE

An awesome record of human achievement defines the history of Mesopotamia, the "land between rivers." Traditional birthplace of man for Jews, Christians, and Muslims, it provided seed and soil for nearly all that is good and evil in modern life: literature, medicine, and science; despotism and warfare. Unprotected by natural barriers, at the mercy of unpredictable rivers, the region endured and profited from legions of invaders and migrants, whose blood mingles with that of today's Iraqis.

tors was an ancient tradition in China. Shang rulers made offerings to their ancestors in ritual vessels of bronze and tried to divine the future by communicating with their ancestors using oracle bones, which cracked when heated, revealing answers to their questions. Those questions were inscribed on oracle bones using an elaborate writing system involving thousands of characters. Here as in other ancient civilizations, society became highly stratified, with great differences in wealth and power between rulers or nobles and peasants or slaves. Slaves captured in battle were sometimes put to death and buried with deceased Shang kings in their tombs.

Invasions and Innovations

Beginning around 1600 B.C.E., invaders from the north swept down into Egypt, Mesopotamia, the Indus Valley, and other parts of the ancient world. Most of these invaders were of Indo-European origin. Over the centuries, wave after wave of Indo-Europeans migrated from the Eurasian steppes above the Black Sea and Caspian Sea, where they were among the first to domesticate horses and use them to haul vehicles. Their horse-driven chariots made them formidable warriors. Through their migrations, they influenced the development of many languages, including Sanskrit (the classical language of India), Persian, Greek, Latin, and English, all of which belong to the Indo-European family of languages.

By 1600 B.C.E. one group of Indo-Europeans called Mycenaeans had descended into Greece, where they built hilltop fortresses and majestic tombs for their kings, who were buried amid hoards of gold. Before long those restless Mycenaeans took over the island of Crete and ousted its Minoan rulers, who had grown rich through maritime trade and constructed palaces decorated with vibrant wall paintings. In centuries to come, Celts of Indo-European origin would spread westward across Europe as far as the British Isles, building lofty strongholds like the Mycenaeans and burying their nobility amid treasure.

In the Middle East, an Indo-European people called the Hittites invaded Mesopotamia and used war chariots to conquer Babylon in 1595 B.C.E., shattering the empire founded by Hammurabi. Assyrians later dominated the Middle East by adopting chariots and war horses, perfecting the use of cavalry, and crafting sturdy weapons of iron, which was cheaper than bronze and stronger when combined with carbon from charcoal during forging—a process that led eventually to the production of steel. Assyrians boasted of their cruelty to enemies. "I put out the eyes of many of the soldiers," one king proclaimed in writing after a victory. Those who submitted to the Assyrians became part of their empire and provided fresh recruits for their army.

After centuries of conquest, these masters of war were overthrown by Medes and Babylonians, who regained Babylon only to lose that prize to invading Persians in 539 B.C.E. Persian rulers identified with the god Ahura Mazda, a supreme deity engaged in a cosmic struggle with the forces of evil, according to the teachings of the Persian holy man Zarathustra, who inspired Zoroastrianism.

Those Persians descended from Indo-Europeans who called themselves Aryans (noble people) and had occupied Iran (meaning Aryan) more than a thousand years earlier. Some had remained in Iran while others had swept on through Afghanistan into the Indus Valley, arriving around 1500 B.C.E. By then, Harappan civilization had collapsed. The local villagers were no match for the invaders, who imposed a strict hierarchy in which Aryan priests and chieftains, aided by merchants and landowners, dominated a vast underclass of peasants and laborers. In time, they expanded southeastward toward the Ganges River. Their class system hardened into a caste system, which gave people almost no chance for advancement. Their rituals and teachings, however, were challenged and modified as priests came in contact with beliefs native to the Indian subcontinent. From that great religious ferment arose Hinduism, Buddhism, and Jainism, whose followers practiced nonviolence.

During this tumultuous era in which many kingdoms collapsed, China and Egypt endured, but not without struggle. The Chinese acquired horses and chariots through contact with nomadic people to their north and west and learned to forge iron. These developments spelled trouble for rulers of the Zhou dynasty, which supplanted the Shang dynasty around 1100 B.C.E. The Zhou were unable to prevent local rulers under their authority from amassing iron weapons and other assets. By 700, those lords were rebelling and China was fragmenting. But the old

King Tutankhamun of Egypt is anointed with perfume by his wife, Queen Ankhesenamun, in a scene portrayed on his Golden Throne, one of many treasures buried with the young pharaoh when he died in the late 14th century B.C.E.

ideals of unity and harmony were kept alive by Confucius, a philosopher born around 550 B.C.E. whose teachings inspired later rulers of China.

Egyptian rulers, for their part, overcame a fierce challenge from invaders called the Hyksos by adopting their weapons and horse-drawn chariots. This victory, achieved around 1550 B.C.E., marked the rise of the New Kingdom, during which Egypt reached the height of its power. Some of that authority was exercised by women, including priestesses of the goddess Hathor, who symbolized fertility and motherhood. One Egyptian queen, Hatshepsut, ruled on behalf of her young stepson and clung to power after he reached maturity. But here as in most ancient kingdoms, men generally dominated society. One ruler who personified this patriarchal trend was Ramses II, who fathered more than 100 children by his various wives and flexed his muscle abroad by leading his forces into Syria, where they clashed with Hittites in an epic chariot battle at Kadesh in 1285 B.C.E.

Among those who came under Egypt's influence or control during this era were Hebrews of nomadic heritage who told in their scriptures of being enslaved in Egypt before Moses led them to the promised land of Canaan, where they forged the kingdom of Israel around 1000 B.C.E. Those Hebrews traced their origins to the patriarch Abraham, from Ur in Mesopotamia, and some of their customs and legends were influenced by Sumerian or Babylonian traditions.

Unlike the Babylonians, however, they rejected all other gods in favor of Yahweh, who entered into a covenant with Abraham and his descendants and revealed his laws to them through Moses. Among those laws, recorded in Hebrew scripture, was the commandment: "You shall have no other gods before me." Theirs was not the first kingdom devoted to monotheism, or the worship of one god. Around 1350 B.C.E., the pharaoh Akhenaten had proclaimed the supremacy of the solar god Aten and outlawed the worship of other deities. But while that cult died with Akhenaten, Judaism endured and inspired both Christianity and Islam.

Egyptians also had a strong impact on the Lybians to their west and the Nubians and other black Africans to their south. Nubians adopted the Egyptian writing system, worshiped Egyptian gods, and built Egyptian-inspired pyramids to house the remains of their kings. Over time, Nubian rulers grew stronger and bolder and stopped paying tribute in gold to Egyptian kings. Around 750 B.C.E., Nubians took power in Egypt and ruled as pharaohs until Assyrians invaded the country in the following century.

Olmec artists sculpted massive stone heads like this one from huge blocks of basalt transported from distant quarries. The heads probably represent Olmec rulers, who commanded the labor of thousands of people and oversaw the construction of temples and earthen pyramids at ceremonial centers near the Gulf of Mexico.

An Increasingly Complex World

Contacts with civilizations sometimes hastened cultural development, but many complex societies evolved largely on their own. Such was the case in Southeast Asia, where prolific rice harvests helped support expert potters and bronze workers employed by nobles who grew rich through trade and warfare. In the Americas, complex societies emerged in complete isolation from the established civilizations of the Old World. In the Andes, the cultivation of potatoes, corn, and other crops yielded food surpluses that allowed people to devote great energy and skill to building ceremonial centers such as Chavín de Huántar, where work began on temples around 850 B.C.E. Along the Gulf Coast of Mesoamerica, meanwhile, the Olmec people were performing similar architectural feats at sites such as San Lorenzo and La Venta under the direction of strong rulers, whose stern features may appear on the great stone heads carved by Olmec artists. Olmec achievements laid the foundations for Maya civilization.

Some of the world's most dramatic cultural advances occurred where complex societies interacted. Around the Mediterranean between 1000 and 500 B.C.E., Phoenicians from what is now Lebanon and Greeks from rising city-states such as Athens founded scores of colonies and spread literacy through phonetic alphabets consisting of only two dozen or so characters, compared to the hundreds or thousands of characters that scholars elsewhere had to master. This enabled men and women who were not priests, rulers, or scribes to learn to read and write. The growth of literacy helped transform people such as the Romans, who ousted their Etruscan overlords around 500 B.C.E., from subjects into citizens, capable of governing themselves. Literacy did not alter the combative nature of humans, for whom words could be deadly weapons. But it enhanced their capacity to cultivate fields of knowledge and create works of literature, philosophy, and science that would outlast the triumphs of conquering armies. ■

	Prehistory	3000 B.C.E	1500 B.C.E	1200 B.C.E	1100 B.C.E	
THE AMERICAS	**16,000** Humans cross the Bering Strait to Alaska. Native Americans are likely present. **14,000** Humans arrive in South America. By 11,000 they reach Chile. **11,500** The Clovis culture begins in North America's Great Plains. **3750** Fishing villages are established in Peru. **3500** The Haida culture begins in Canada.	**ca 3000** People settle in the Great Lakes region and Louisiana in North America. **ca 3000** Agricultural villages appear in Mexico, Honduras, El Salvador. **ca 3000** Fishing villages become established along the Peruvian coast. By 1800 they build ceremonial centers. **2800** Farm villages form in the Amazon region.	**ca 1500** Olmec culture develops in the modern states of Veracruz and Tabasco in Mexico. **ca 1500** Nomadic Chichimeca people expand in northern Mexico. **ca 1300** People at Poverty Point in the Mississippi Valley construct a complex of earthworks, in the center of which is a plaza for ceremonies. Traders and artisans work there.	**ca 1200** People along the California coast sustain their communities through marine life. **1200** Olmec civilization is at its peak with a monumental ceremonial complex of huge pyramids, temples, and palaces at San Lorenzo.	**ca 1100** The Chavín de Huántar people in the Andes in South America organize in a complex society around a religious cult and construct a large temple.	
EUROPE	**230,000** Neanderthals—*Homo erectus*—appear in Europe. **40,000** Modern humans—*Homo sapiens*—arrive in Europe, living alongside Neanderthals. **28,000** Neanderthals become extinct in Spain. **7000** Farming tribes spread from Anatolia into Greece and northward. **5400** Bandkeramik culture develops in Europe.	**ca 3000** Passage graves are built throughout England, Ireland, and northern France. **ca 3000** Danubian cultures flourish in central Europe. **ca 3000** Lake Dwellers settle along lakes in an alpine arc from France to Slovenia. **ca 2000** The Minoans on Crete emerge as a civilization.	**1450** Mycenaeans on mainland Greece establish settlements in Anatolia, Sicily, and southern Italy. They also take control of Crete, ending Minoan civilization.	**ca 1200** Proto-Celtic people of Indo-European origin settle in central Europe. **ca 1200** Dorian-speaking Greeks arrive on the Peloponnesus. **1150** The Mycenaean civilization declines in mainland Greece.	**ca 1100** Indo-Europeans stream into Italy from the north, among them the Latin, the Sabine, and the Samnite tribes.	
MIDDLE EAST & AFRICA	**250,000** Modern humans emerge in Africa. **100,000** Modern humans migrate to the Middle East. **7250** Çatal Hüyük in Anatolia reaches a population of 6,000. **3200** Sumer, the first civilization, emerges in modern-day Iraq. **3100** Menes unites Upper and Lower Egypt.	**ca 3000** Phoenicians settle the Syrian coast. **ca 3000** The Hittites migrate into Anatolia. **2660-2180** Egypt's Old Kingdom period. **2080-1640** Egypt's Middle Kingdom period. **1960** Egypt invades Nubia. **1792** Hammurabi expands Babylon to include Sumer.	**1505** Queen Hatshepsut becomes ruler of Egypt. **ca 1500** Ugarit's ships rule commerce in the Mediterranean. **1490-1436** Tutmosis III of Egypt expands the empire to Palestine, Syria, and Nubia. **ca 1300** The Hebrews establish the kingdom of Israel. **1298-1232** Ramses II rules Egypt.	**ca 1180** The Hittite homeland in Anatolia is invaded, ending the empire. **1174** The 12 tribes of Israel, ruled by judges, meet at the sanctuary of Shiloh to agree on a united front. **1173** The Elamites sack Babylon. **1125** Israelites fight against the Canaanites in the Battle of Megiddo.	**ca 1100** Incursions by Aramaeans into Assyria and Babylon destroy both countries. **1075** Chaos marks the end of the New Kingdom period in Egypt. **1050** Samuel, the prophet and last of the judges, becomes ruler of Israel. **1025** Saul becomes king of Israel.	
ASIA & OCEANIA	**75,000** Modern humans arrive in Southeast Asia and China. **60,000** Modern humans reach New Guinea and Australia by boat. **28,000** The Solomon Islands are settled. **12,000-8,000** Ceramic arts begin in Japan. **10,000** Agriculture develops in the Yellow River Valley and other sites in China.	**ca 3000** Neolithic villages along the Indus River of modern-day Pakistan and western India develop into large cities. **ca 3000** Austronesian people migrate from Taiwan to the Philippines. **ca 3000-1750** Village life is established in China along the Yellow River, the Yangtze River Delta, and the southeast coast. Xia, Shang, and Zhou dynasties emerge.	**ca 1500** Aryan-speaking Indo-Europeans move into India. Harappan civilization declines, perhaps because of drought, and its cities are abandoned. **ca 1500** The Jomon period in Japan reaches its peak. **ca 1500** The Lapita exchange network in the western Pacific is formed.	**ca 1200** The Shang dynasty in China is showing signs of turmoil.	**ca 1100** Austronesians settle the islands of Tonga and Samoa. **1045** The Shang dynasty is toppled by a challenger from northwestern China, who founds the Zhou dynasty.	

1000 B.C.E	900 B.C.E	800 B.C.E	700 B.C.E	600-500 B.C.E
ca 1000 The Pinto Indians establish settlements in California. **ca 1000** In the Ohio River Valley, the Adena people form an agricultural society. **ca 1000** The Cochise culture dominates the area of modern-day New Mexico and Arizona.	**ca 900** The Olmec capital of San Lorenzo in Mexico is destroyed; a ceremonial complex at La Venta becomes the new focal point of Olmec civilization. **ca 900** People on the Paracas Peninsula of Peru develop ceremonial centers.	**ca 800** The Chavín culture in Peru reaches a high point as a religious center and as a market center in the long-distance-trade network developing in the Andes.	**ca 700** Reliefs at Monte Albán in Oaxaca, Mexico, show far-ranging Olmec influence. **ca 700** Maya begin to organize into 50 separate religious-political entities in the diffuse civilizational network they are known for.	**ca 600** The Arctic Dorset people construct housing of stone and driftwood and semi-subterranean sod shelters along the Hudson Strait of Canada.
ca 1000 Proto-Etruscans develop independent city-states between the Arno and Tiber Rivers in Italy. **ca 1000** Greeks migrate across the Aegean Sea and colonize parts of Asia Minor.	**ca 900** The Etruscans develop a rich culture, spreading farther out along present-day Tuscany, Latium, and Umbria in Italy. **ca 900** Greek traders, the Euboeans, found colonies on the west coast of southern Italy. **ca 885** Lycurgus creates the laws and institutions of Sparta in Greece.	**ca 800** The Celts move into England. **800** The city of Rome is founded in central Italy by Romulus and Remus. **800** Independent city-states develop in Greece; foremost among them are Sparta and Athens. **750** Scythian horsemen sweep in from the east, moving into the Crimea and the Dnieper and Danube River regions.	**ca 700** Athens and other city-states in Greece become centers of learning. Maritime trade brings riches to Athens. **ca 700** Etruscans in northern Italy become prosperous because of their mineral wealth, trading with Egypt, Syria, Asia Minor, and Greece. **616** The Etruscan Tarquinus Priscus becomes king of Rome.	**594** Solon of Athens, Greece, introduces reforms that allow all free citizens to participate in government. He is called "the father of democracy." **509** The Romans drive the Etruscans out of Rome, establish the Roman Republic, and conquer Etruscan cities.
1000 David becomes king of Israel, uniting Judah and Israel. **1000** Indo-European Medes and Persians migrate from Central Asia to Iran. **960-925** Solomon succeeds his father David. At his death, his sons split Israel in two. **920** The Assyrians begin to reconquer lost territories.	**ca 900** The Nubian kingdom of Kush establishes its capital at Napata. **883-859** Under King Ashurnasirpal II, Assyria regains its lost land and becomes again a great power in Mesopotamia. **876-869** King Omri rules in Samaria, Israel. **859-824** Assyrian King Shalmaneser III invades Syria. He is stopped by a coalition including Israel.	**ca 800** Assyria embraces Mesopotamia, Syria, Palestine, and parts of Anatolia. **750** The Phoenician colony of Carthage in North Africa develops into a hub of trade for the western Mediterranean. **750** The Nubian kingdom of Kush conquers Egypt and rules for 100 years. **721** Israel falls to Assyria. Hebrews are exiled.	**ca 700** Mounted horsemen—Cimmerians and Scythians—sweep into the Middle East. Assyrian king Sargon II falls in battle. **664** Assyrians drive Nubians out of Egypt. Nubian kings move their capital from Napata south to Meroe. **647** Assyrians vanquish the Elamites in Iran. **614** Assyria collapses.	**587** Nebuchadrezzar II sacks the kingdom of Judah. Many people are carried off as captives to Babylon. **558-529** Cyrus the Great rules Elam and Persia and conquers Media, Asia Minor, and Babylon. The Jews are permitted to return to Jerusalem. Cyrus's son Cambyses gains Egypt. **522** Darius I succeeds as ruler of Persia.
ca 1000 Aryans in India settle into permanent communities between the Himalayan foothills and the Ganges River. Regional kingdoms form in northern India. **ca 1000** Zhou kings rule the "central kingdom" and apportion rule of outlying territories to their kin, granting titles of nobility as they confer the right to rule.	**ca 900-800** During the Zhou dynasty, craftsmen excel in producing artistic bronze wares, which are prized and traded beyond China's borders.	**771** Nomads attack the Zhou, forcing them to move their capital east to Luoyang, and dividing China into the eastern Zhou and western Zhou kingdoms.	**ca 700** With the decline of the Zhou dynasty, China is torn by a power struggle between rival semi-autonomous states in what becomes known as the Spring and Autumn states.	**ca 600** Small kingdoms vie for power in India, but none achieves domination. **ca 560** Siddhartha Gautama is born in the foothills of the Himalaya; he is later known as the Buddha and introduces Buddhism. **520** Northwestern India is conquered by Persia.

POLITICS & POWER	GEOGRAPHY & ENVIRONMENT	CULTURE & RELIGION

THE AMERICAS

16,000 Humans cross the Bering Strait and reach the far north of the Americas. Indigenous Americans live alongside.

14,000 Humans begin to arrive in South America; they reach modern-day Chile by about 11,000.

11,500 The Clovis culture begins in the Great Plains of North America, the Cochise in the Southwest. By 5000 the Folsom culture replaces the Clovis culture. The Chumash inhabit California.

3750 Permanent fishing villages are established in the Chilca Valley in Peru.

3500 Haida culture begins in Canada.

10,000 The last worldwide glaciation ends, and humans successfully adapt.

9,000 The Great Bison Belt—grasslands—reaches from Alaska to the Gulf of Mexico.

4000 Pottery first comes into use in Guyana, South America.

3372 The first date in the Maya calendar, as the later civilization calculates back to the beginning of time.

WHAT LIFE WAS LIKE

In the Stone Age

The Stone Age, the first known period of prehistoric human culture, is so named for the use of stone tools. Striking one stone against another to shape a chopping instrument, early hominids fashioned the oldest known tools more than two million years ago in Africa. In time they chipped and struck off flakes to produce sharp points. They made scrapers and blades for food preparation, spear points and arrowheads for the hunt. Once hominids understood how to cultivate plants, they made agricultural tools such as axes to fell trees, sickle-like blades to cut cereal grasses, and hoes to till the soil. Some tools also served as protection against large animals and other predators.

EUROPE

230,000 Neanderthals—*Homo erectus*, but not yet *Homo sapiens*—appear in Europe.

40,000 Modern humans—*Homo sapiens*—arrive in Europe. They live alongside Neanderthals, but don't seem to interbreed.

28,000 The last Neanderthals become extinct in southern Spain.

7000 Farming tribes wander from Anatolia into Greece and farther west into Europe.

5400-4500 The Bandkeramik culture of farmers and potters develops in central Europe.

4500 Indo-Europeans roam the steppes of eastern Europe and Central Asia on horses.

3500 Farming is well established throughout Europe, spreading from the Ukraine to France.

32,000-14,000 Humans express themselves with cave art in southern Europe. Cave paintings in Lascaux, France, and Altamira, Spain, in particular, have artistic merit.

5000 Early pottery decorated with linear bands, for which the Bandkeramik culture is named, is found throughout Transdanubia—western Hungary and adjacent regions along the Danube.

4300 The first megalithic tombs are built in western Europe.

MIDDLE EAST & AFRICA

4,500,000 Hominids begin to appear.

250,000 Modern humans (*Homo sapiens*) emerge in Africa.

100,000 Modern humans, subsisting as hunter-gatherers, migrate to the Middle East.

8000 Jericho in present-day Israel becomes a large city.

7250 Çatal Hüyük, a town in Anatolia (Turkey), reaches a population of 6,000.

3200 Sumer, the first civilization, emerges between the Tigris and Euphrates Rivers.

3100 Menes unites Upper and Lower Egypt.

120,000-90,000 Heavy rainfall makes the Sahara in Africa habitable for humans.

75,000 Glaciation turns Africa's Sahara arid; it becomes a nearly impassable desert.

12,000 Abundant crops of wild cereals grow in the Fertile Crescent, which ranges from Egypt to Iraq.

8000-7700 Wheat and barley are cultivated in the Fertile Crescent. Irrigation agriculture begins ca 5000; cattle are domesticated.

6500 Ugarit in modern Syria is settled.

5000 Farming spreads into the Indo-Iranian borderlands.

45,000 The flute, the oldest-known instrument, is used in North Africa.

24,000 Rock paintings at the Apollo site in Namibia, Africa, can be dated to this period.

4000 People along the coast of Ghana, West Africa, develop pottery.

3760 The Jewish calendar counts the dates from this year on.

3500 Sumerians invent a form of writing and numbering called cuneiform, incised in clay, to keep track of trade transactions and taxes.

3100 Hieroglyphic script appears in Egypt.

ASIA & OCEANIA

95,000 *Homo floresiensis,* a small species of *Homo erectus*, exists in Indonesia.

75,000 Modern humans arrive in Southeast Asia and China.

60,000 Modern humans reach New Guinea and Australia by boat.

35,000 Aboriginal hunter-gatherers establish traditions in Australia.

35,000 Hunting tribes move deep into Central Asia.

28,000 The Solomon Islands are settled.

30,000 Humans move across the land bridge from Korea to Japan.

10,000 Rising ocean waters separate Australia and New Guinea, Korea and Japan.

10,000 Agriculture develops along the Yellow River and other sites in China.

7000-5000 Rice cultivation is developed in Southeast Asia and southern China.

6500 Farming begins in the Indus Valley in modern-day Pakistan and western India.

6000 Millet is grown in the Yellow River Valley in China.

45,000 The first rock art in Australia is dated to this time.

18,000 The first sculptures are crafted in Asia.

12,000 Jomon hunter-gatherers in Japan make the first pottery. Jomon means "cord pattern" and describes the ceramic ware.

12,000-8000 Ceramic arts begin in Japan.

5000 Yangshao culture in China produces fine, painted pottery with geometric patterns, and designs of animals and humans.

SCIENCE & TECHNOLOGY

9000 Flint arrowheads and spear points, known as Clovis points, are made by the Clovis culture in North America.

8000 The Folsom people develop sophisticated tools, enabling them to clean animal hides and make effective weapons.

Ice Age carving of a bison, found at La Madeleine, France

26,000 Hunter-gatherers in central Europe build houses roofed with clay.

16,000 On the steppes of Russia, some shelters are built of mammoth bones.

6000 Along the Danube in central Europe, people build sturdy huts made of poles thatched with grasses. Plaster floors hold sunken fireplaces.

ca 100,000 Middle Stone Age flake-tool technology is established in Africa.

35,000 A simple counting device is invented in South Africa.

6200 Copper smelting and textile manufacture begins in Çatal Hüyük, Anatolia.

4000 Egyptians begin to use a sail on their Nile River boats.

3800 The earliest bronze work is produced in the Middle East, using copper and arsenic.

3500 The potter's wheel and the kiln are invented in Mesopotamia, modern-day Iraq.

8000 The boomerang is invented in Australia.

4000 Bronze objects, made of a combination of 90 percent copper and 10 percent tin, are produced in Thailand. This is the first use of bronze worldwide.

Australian Aborigine rock painting

PEOPLE & SOCIETY

3500 The discovery of corn cobs in New Mexico suggests that the Cochise culture was influenced by Mesoamericans.

12,000 Social hierarchies are evident in varied European burial practices.

ca 3200 The Sumerians, tribes settled between the Tigris and Euphrates Rivers (called Mesopotamia by the Greeks, meaning "land between the rivers"), develop the first civilization. Their fertile valley produces a surplus of food early on, leading to population growth. Cities like Nippur and Ur develop, with leaders organizing large-scale construction projects such as public buildings, temples, and defensive walls. Religion is organized and laws are established, which allow this culture to develop rapidly into a stratified society.

THE ICE AGES

From the formation of the earth five billion years ago to modern times, there have been at least four major Ice Ages, periods when ice sheets covered at least part of the northern and southern hemispheres.

The present Ice Age began 40 million years ago with the growth of an ice sheet in Antarctica and intensified about three million years ago with the spreading of more ice in the Northern Hemisphere. From the south, ice sheets eventually stretched over large parts of South America, covering Patagonia and the Andes; from the north, they reached across Greenland, northern Europe, Canada, and as far south as Pennsylvania, along the Ohio and Missouri Rivers to North Dakota, Montana, Idaho, and Washington. Because the Greenland and Antarctica ice sheets still exist, we are still technically in this Ice Age.

During this time, however, the earth has undergone several cycles of glaciation, where the ice sheets advance, and interglacial periods, where milder climates cause the ice sheets to retreat. These cycles generally occur in 40,000-100,000 year periods. The most recent period of glaciation ended about 12,000 years ago, at the end of which the climate was much colder and wetter than at present—as much as 27°F cooler—so that areas that are now desert were lush with vegetation. Large lakes and rivers also formed as ice melted.

This last glaciation made possible the spread of modern humans to all the world's habitats. Because glaciation lowers sea levels, humans were able to move not just from Africa to the Middle East, Asia, and Europe, but also to previously isolated Oceania and North America across temporary land bridges. Once the ice retreated, climate change created favorable conditions for a great variety of food stuffs, and humans adapted both their diet and lifestyle to this abundance. The beginning of agriculture was soon to come, and with it the development of more permanent human settlements.

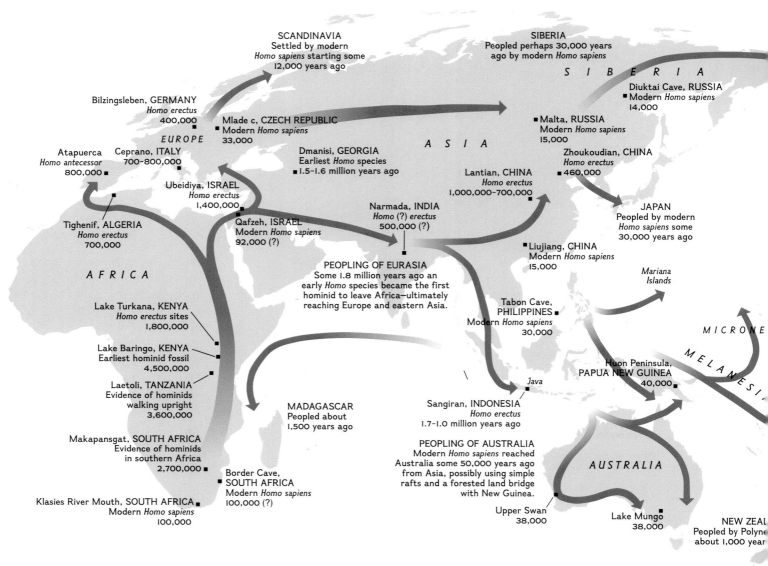

SCANDINAVIA
Settled by modern
Homo sapiens starting some
12,000 years ago

SIBERIA
Peopled perhaps 30,000 years
ago by modern *Homo sapiens*

S I B E R I A

Diuktai Cave, RUSSIA
■ Modern *Homo sapiens*
14,000

Bilzingsleben, GERMANY
Homo erectus
400,000

Mlade c, CZECH REPUBLIC
■ Modern *Homo sapiens*
33,000

■ Malta, RUSSIA
Modern *Homo sapiens*
15,000

E U R O P E

A S I A

Zhoukoudian, CHINA
Homo erectus
■ 460,000

Atapuerca
Homo antecessor
800,000 ■

Ceprano, ITALY
700-800,000

Dmanisi, GEORGIA
Earliest *Homo* species
■ 1.5-1.6 million years ago

Lantian, CHINA
Homo erectus
1,000,000-700,000

Ubeidiya, ISRAEL
Homo erectus
1,400,000

Narmada, INDIA
Homo (?) erectus
500,000 (?)

JAPAN
Peopled by modern
Homo sapiens some
30,000 years ago

Tighenif, ALGERIA
Homo erectus
700,000

Qafzeh, ISRAEL
Modern *Homo sapiens*
92,000 (?)

Liujiang, CHINA
Modern *Homo sapiens*
15,000

*Mariana
Islands*

A F R I C A

PEOPLING OF EURASIA
Some 1.8 million years ago an
early *Homo* species became the first
hominid to leave Africa—ultimately
reaching Europe and eastern Asia.

M I C R O N E

Lake Turkana, KENYA
Homo erectus sites
1,800,000

Tabon Cave,
PHILIPPINES ■
Modern *Homo sapiens*
30,000

M E L A N E S I

Lake Baringo, KENYA
Earliest hominid fossil
4,500,000

Huon Peninsula,
PAPUA NEW GUINEA
40,000 ■

Laetoli, TANZANIA
Evidence of hominids
walking upright
3,600,000

Java

Makapansgat, SOUTH AFRICA
Evidence of hominids
in southern Africa
2,700,000

MADAGASCAR
Peopled about
1,500 years ago

Sangiran, INDONESIA
Homo erectus
1.7-1.0 million years ago

A U S T R A L I A

Border Cave,
■ SOUTH AFRICA
Modern *Homo sapiens*
100,000 (?)

PEOPLING OF AUSTRALIA
Modern *Homo sapiens* reached
Australia some 50,000 years ago
from Asia, possibly using simple
rafts and a forested land bridge
with New Guinea.

Klasies River Mouth, SOUTH AFRICA ■
Modern *Homo sapiens*
100,000

Upper Swan
38,000

Lake Mungo
38,000

NEW ZEAL
Peopled by Polyne
about 1,000 year

HUMAN MIGRATION

LTHOUGH THE STORY OF HUMAN EVOLUTION AND THE PEOPLING OF THE PLANET
still holds many mysteries, the most widely accepted theory states that modern
humans came out of Africa. Piecing together humanity's history from clues
found in rocks and bones, paleontologists and archaeologists have come to
the general agreement that Homo erectus, or upright-walking humans,
evolved in Africa from other more primitive ancestors about 1.7 million years ago. From
this precursor, modern humans—Homo sapiens—evolved about 250,000 years ago and
eventually replaced the earlier species.

An increase in population and competition and the ability to shape sophisticated
tools, hunt big game, and build permanent shelter may have spurred the first wave of
migration of *Homo sapiens* from Africa to the Middle East about 100,000 years ago.
From there, people slowly made their way into Central Asia and onward. A new push
into Southeast Asia occurred about 75,000 years ago, and as Ice Ages cooled the earth
and water was concentrated in massive glaciers, the earth's oceans receded and exposed

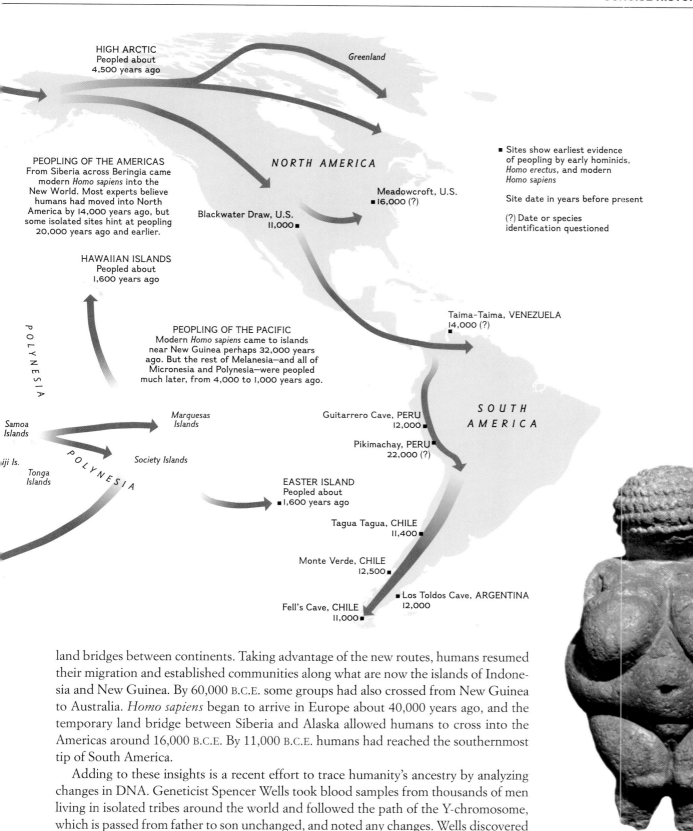

HIGH ARCTIC
Peopled about
4,500 years ago

Greenland

NORTH AMERICA

PEOPLING OF THE AMERICAS
From Siberia across Beringia came
modern *Homo sapiens* into the
New World. Most experts believe
humans had moved into North
America by 14,000 years ago, but
some isolated sites hint at peopling
20,000 years ago and earlier.

■ Sites show earliest evidence
of peopling by early hominids,
Homo erectus, and modern
Homo sapiens

Site date in years before present

(?) Date or species
identification questioned

Meadowcroft, U.S.
■ 16,000 (?)

Blackwater Draw, U.S.
11,000 ■

HAWAIIAN ISLANDS
Peopled about
1,600 years ago

POLYNESIA

PEOPLING OF THE PACIFIC
Modern *Homo sapiens* came to islands
near New Guinea perhaps 32,000 years
ago. But the rest of Melanesia—and all of
Micronesia and Polynesia—were peopled
much later, from 4,000 to 1,000 years ago.

Taima-Taima, VENEZUELA
14,000 (?) ■

*Samoa
Islands*

*Marquesas
Islands*

Guitarrero Cave, PERU
12,000 ■

*SOUTH
AMERICA*

P O L Y N E S I A

Society Islands

Pikimachay, PERU ■
22,000 (?)

iji Is.

*Tonga
Islands*

EASTER ISLAND
Peopled about
■ 1,600 years ago

Tagua Tagua, CHILE
11,400 ■

Monte Verde, CHILE
12,500 ■

■ Los Toldos Cave, ARGENTINA
12,000

Fell's Cave, CHILE
11,000 ■

land bridges between continents. Taking advantage of the new routes, humans resumed
their migration and established communities along what are now the islands of Indonesia and New Guinea. By 60,000 B.C.E. some groups had also crossed from New Guinea
to Australia. *Homo sapiens* began to arrive in Europe about 40,000 years ago, and the
temporary land bridge between Siberia and Alaska allowed humans to cross into the
Americas around 16,000 B.C.E. By 11,000 B.C.E. humans had reached the southernmost
tip of South America.

Adding to these insights is a recent effort to trace humanity's ancestry by analyzing
changes in DNA. Geneticist Spencer Wells took blood samples from thousands of men
living in isolated tribes around the world and followed the path of the Y-chromosome,
which is passed from father to son unchanged, and noted any changes. Wells discovered
that all humans alive today can be traced back to a tribe in Africa. He established a map
of the spread of the Y-chromosome and its mutations, mirroring the map of human
migration that paleontologists and archaeologists have established.

*The Venus of Willendorf, found in Austria,
can be dated to 24,000-22,000 B.C.E., one of
the earliest pieces of art found in Europe.*

POLITICS & POWER	GEOGRAPHY & ENVIRONMENT	CULTURE & RELIGION
THE AMERICAS **ca 3000 Archaic people** settle in the Great Lakes region of North America. Others settle near Poverty Point, Louisiana. **ca 3000 Agricultural villages** begin to appear in Mesoamerica—the region between central Mexico, Honduras, and El Salvador. **ca 3000 Fishing villages** become established along the Peruvian coast of South America. **2800 Farming groups** in the Amazon region form villages.	**3000 Meso-americans** begin intensive cultivation of maize, beans, chilies, avocados, and squash and other gourds. *Stonehenge, on England's Salisbury Plain*	
EUROPE **ca 3000 Danubian cultures** flourish in central Europe. **ca 3000 So-called Lake Dwellers** settle in communities along lakes in an alpine arc from France to Slovenia. **ca 3000 The Bronze Age**, called the Early Minoan Period, begins on Crete.	**ca 3000 Milled grain** forms an important part of central European diet. **ca 2700 The horse** is domesticated in the Ukraine.	**ca 3000 Megalithic temples** are constructed on the island of Malta.
MIDDLE EAST & AFRICA **ca 3000 Sumer, the first civilization,** grows in power as Nippur and other city-states begin to form a political federation. **ca 3000 Phoenicians** settle the Syrian coast. **ca 3000 The Hittites** migrate into Anatolia. **2700 King Enmebaragisi** of Kish in northern Sumer engages in wars against neighbors in the east, the Elamites of present-day Iran. **2675 Gilgamesh** rules as the Sumerian king of Uruk. **2660 Pharaoh Sanakht** founds Egypt's third dynasty, beginning the Old Kingdom period.	**ca 3000 Camels** are domesticated in the Middle East. **ca 3000 Sorghum** is first cultivated in Ethiopia. **ca 2900 The Deluge or Great Flood** described in the Bible and Sumerian epics may have happened at this time. **ca 2600 Egyptians** trade along the Mediterranean and the Red Sea, importing cedar wood from Lebanon and gold, ebony, ivory, cattle, and slaves from Africa, while exporting linen, gold, leather, wheat, and lentils.	**ca 3000 Sumerians** develop a complex society with urban centers built around multi-level temples, known as ziggurats, presided over by priests. **2685 The sophisticated arts of Sumer** include the Standard of Ur, a two-sided mosaic of shell, lapis lazuli, and carnelian, depicting daily life at peace and war. **2650 The pyramid of Djoser** is built as a royal tomb, the first of many, culminating in the massive pyramids at Giza. They are a manifestation of the pharaoh's power as a divine ruler to marshal enormous resources for such building projects.
ASIA & OCEANIA **ca 3000 Neolithic villages** along the Indus River of modern-day Pakistan and western India develop into large cities. **ca 3000 Austronesian people** migrate from Taiwan to the Philippines. **ca 3000 Village life** is established in China along the Yellow River, the Yangtze River Delta, and the southeast coast.	**ca 3000 China** cultivates soybeans. **ca 3000 People in New Guinea** begin to cultivate yams and taro roots and domesticate pigs and chickens. **ca 2700 Tea** is in use in China.	

SCIENCE & TECHNOLOGY	PEOPLE & SOCIETY

THE BIRTH OF WRITING

The Sumerians' greatest accomplishment was the invention of writing, beginning as early as 3300 B.C.E. Propelled by the need to record business transactions for stored or traded goods or to keep count of numbers of sheep, the Sumerians invented *bullae*—soft clay balls that were hollow inside. Buyers or sellers would press sharp tokens into the clay and place them inside. Deeper indentations meant larger quantities. In case of a dispute, the bulla could be opened and the tokens recounted. This record-keeping rapidly advanced to pictographs—simple representations of the object traded—incised on clay tablets. Merchants used cylindrical clay seals to roll on and impress their signature on a deal.

In time the Sumerians found ways to express more complex ideas by combining symbols, for example, using the pictographs for water and a mouth to express "to drink." Over the centuries the pictographs became ever more abstract and began to express syllables. Working with wedge-shaped reeds, the impressions became known as cuneiform, from the Latin word for wedge. This form of writing continued to develop and expand and eventually conveyed the first laws and literature.

---

ca 3000 Copper is mined in Cyprus and exported throughout the Mediterranean.

ca 2800 Stonehenge is built in Wiltshire, England, a circular earthwork 320 feet in diameter with 56 pits along the edge, known as the Aubrey holes. The site may have been used as an observatory, to follow the positions of the sun and the moon.

ca 3000 Craft specialization and gender division of labor develop in eastern Europe.

ca 3000 Chambered barrows, also known as passage graves, are built throughout England, Ireland, and northern France.

---

ca 3000 The Egyptians invent papyrus, a forerunner of paper, made from reeds.

ca 3000 The abacus—a calculator using rods and beads—is in use in the Middle East and adopted in the Mediterranean.

ca 3000 Bronze, made from copper and tin, is invented in the area of Mesopotamia.

2700 The Sumerians develop a calendar of 354 days.

2550 Soldiers in Ur, Sumeria, use shields.

ca 3000 The city of Kish and other northern Sumerian cities are largely inhabited by Semitic people—Akkadians—whereas the south is populated by Sumerians. Northern Mesopotamia is the land of the Hurrians, and southwest Iran is populated by Elamites.

2625 Pharaoh Sneferu builds three major and two minor pyramids, the largest surpassing in size the Djoser pyramid.

2550 Sneferu's son Khufu builds the Great Pyramid at Giza, which stands 481 feet tall.

---

ca 3000 The plow is first used in China. The abacus, in use in the Middle East, is also developed in China.

ca 3000 Cotton fabric is first woven by the Harappans of the Indus Valley.

2700 China begins to cast bronze objects and to weave silk.

Sumerian cuneiform tablet

ANCIENT SUMER

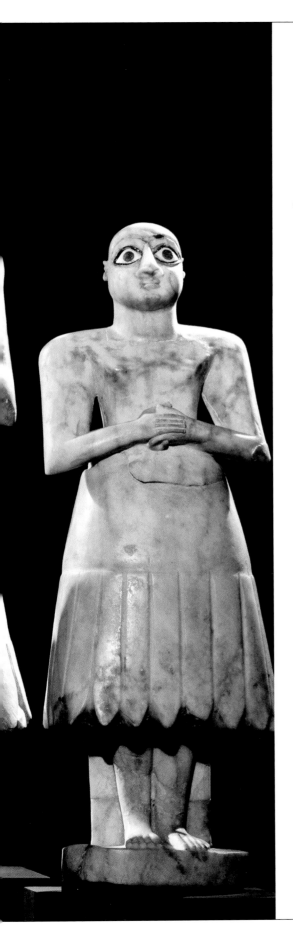

THE FERTILE LAND BETWEEN THE TIGRIS AND EUPHRATES RIVERS, CALLED SUMER in ancient times—or Mesopotamia by the Greeks later on—brought forth abundant crops to support tens of thousands of people. About 5,000 years ago the Sumerians organized life in large cities of mud-brick buildings, surrounded by lush fields and gardens with groves of figs and date palms. Early on they began to settle into an orderly society. As hallmarks of their civilization, they set up a division of labor, marshalled hundreds of laborers for public works, invented a written language, devised a system of laws, educated their young, and prayed to a pantheon of gods. The gods included An of the heavens, Enlil of the air, and Enki of the waters, as well as gods of other natural phenomena, and patron gods for every city.

The Sumerians erected massive temples, topped by a shrine and rising in tiers to 150 feet or more, the most ancient one, shown below, in the city of Ur. These so-called ziggurats were administered by priests, who served the gods and received offerings from the people. Priests also collected food in storerooms surrounding the base of the temple and redistributed the goods, kept tax records, and oversaw the construction of other large-scale works such as irrigation canals. In their appeals to the gods to prevent disasters—flood, fire, or pestilence—people used stand-in figurines in their likeness, shaped of clay or stone, to be placed in the temple to pray for help. The Sumerians also believed in an afterlife, burying their kings with treasures and retainers and everything necessary to carry on the life to which they had grown accustomed.

ABOVE: *The massive, stepped ziggurat of Ur reaches to the heavens to honor Nanna, the god of the moon.*
LEFT: *Hands folded in prayer, these statues appeal to the heavens as proxies for ancient Sumerians.*

POLITICS & POWER	GEOGRAPHY & ENVIRONMENT	CULTURE & RELIGION
THE AMERICAS		
ca 2500 Arctic people develop campsites from North America all the way to Greenland. **ca 2500 Hunter-gatherers** are settling in permanent communities from North America south to the Andean region of South America.	**ca 2500 Cotton** is cultivated in what is now Peru, as well as potatoes, squash, and other gourds.	**ca 2500 People in the Grand Canyon caves** of North America leave signs of hunting magic.
EUROPE		
ca 2500 The Beaker culture, named for its pottery, expands from the Low Countries to France. **ca 2500 Stone-tool-using cultures** develop in Scandinavia. **ca 2500 Along the Danube River** and its tributaries in central Europe, people begin to till the soil. When the soil loses its fertility, they move westward.	**ca 2500 People in central Europe** use slash-and-burn methods to clear the forests and make land arable. **ca 2500 Overland trade routes** develop from the Balkans to Spain. **ca 2500 In Scandinavia,** barley and wheat are grown and oxen, pigs, and sheep are raised.	**ca 2500 A rock carving** in Rody, Norway, shows the earliest skiers. **ca 2200 Round communal tombs** are built in the Mesara plain of Crete. The snake and the bull are religious symbols.

A Nubian archer in Egypt's army

POLITICS & POWER	GEOGRAPHY & ENVIRONMENT	CULTURE & RELIGION
MIDDLE EAST & AFRICA		
ca 2500 Semitic Canaanite tribes settle on the coast of Palestine. **2334-2279 King Sargon of Akkad** conquers Sumer, Syria, and Elam (southwest Iran), and establishes the first empire. **2193 The Akkadian Empire** collapses. **2180 The Old Kingdom** in Egypt ends in political and social chaos. **2112 Ur-Nammu** builds the Sumerian Empire in Mesopotamia, centered at Ur. **2080 Mentuhotep II of Egypt** reunites the country, beginning the Middle Kingdom.	**ca 2300 Sumerian merchants** travel across the Arabian Sea to trade with the Harappans of the Indus Valley, carrying sesame oil, woolen textiles, leather goods, and jewelry in exchange for copper, ivory, pearls, and semiprecious stones. In other trade they procure silver from Anatolia, cedars from Lebanon, copper from Arabia, gold from Africa, and tin from Iran. **2180 Drought** disrupts the seasonal flooding of the Nile, causing famine and anarchy.	**ca 2500 Sumerian royal tombs** at Ur hold treasures and human sacrifices. **ca 2500 Egyptians** begin to mummify their royal dead. **ca 2240 King Naram-Suen of Akkad** attempts to solidify his state by declaring himself a god. **ca 2100 Hebrew patriarch Abraham** leaves Ur in Sumer with his clan. **2090 King Shulki of Ur** issues laws.
ASIA & OCEANIA		
ca 2500 Harappan society in the Indus Valley becomes a full-fledged civilization, complete with civic organization, religion, public works, and a system of writing. **ca 2200 According to legend,** the Xia dynasty in China develops at this time along the Yellow River.	**ca 2500 The Harappans** domesticate chickens in the Indus Valley. **ca 2200 Legendary founder of the Xia dynasty, Yu,** tames the flooding of the Yellow River and brings order to human society in China.	**ca 2500 The Harappan writing system** consists of 400 characters, which are incised on clay seals and copper tablets. The Harappans venerate various gods and goddesses; some form of this early belief system may have become part of Hinduism. **ca 2200 The city of Erlitou** near Luoyang in China is possibly the capital of the Xia dynasty, with a large palacelike structure and many more-modest buildings and workshops.

SCIENCE & TECHNOLOGY	PEOPLE & SOCIETY

ca 2500 People in the Arctic region develop delicate chipped-flint tools, known as the Arctic Small Tool tradition.

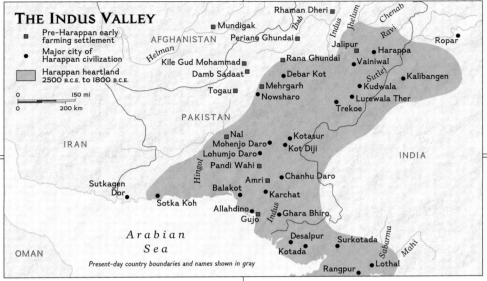

THE INDUS VALLEY

- Pre-Harappan early farming settlement
- Major city of Harappan civilization
- Harappan heartland 2500 B.C.E. to 1800 B.C.E.

0 — 150 mi
0 — 200 km

AFGHANISTAN
PAKISTAN
IRAN
INDIA
OMAN

Arabian Sea

Rhaman Dheri
Mundigak
Perian6 Ghundai
Jalipur
Harappa
Ropar
Kile Gud Mohammad
Rana Ghundai
Vainiwal
Damb Sadaat
Debar Kot
Kalibangen
Togau
Mehrgarh
Kudwala
Nowsharo
Lurewala Ther
Trekoe
Nal
Kotasur
Mohenjo Daro
Kot Diji
Lohumjo Daro
Pandi Wahi
Amri
Chanhu Daro
Sutkagen Dor
Balakot
Karchat
Sotka Koh
Allahdino
Ghara Bhiro
Gujo
Desalpur
Surkotada
Kotada
Rangpur
Lothal

Helman
Hingol
Indus
Zhab
Jhelum
Chenab
Ravi
Suttej
Saburma
Mahi

Present-day country boundaries and names shown in gray

The spread of Harappan civilization

ca 2500 Bronze technology acquired from the East begins to spread into Europe. Copper is mined in the Balkans, but stone remains the primary material for tools and weapons.

ca 2100 Sumerian healers prescribe beer and mustard poultices as cures for certain ailments.

ca 2100 Akkadian naval vessels conquer Persian Gulf islands.

ca 2050 Nubian bowmen support the Egyptian military, serving as scouts, interpreters, guards, and formidable archers.

ca 2500 Mesopotamian society is ruled by kings and nobles, who win distinction as successful warriors. Priests occupy the next stratum of society, entreating the gods to bring good fortune on their city-state. The priests are supported by offerings from the community; they have authority over large temple complexes and organize community life, agriculture, and the storage and redistribution of foodstuffs. The last rung of society consists largely of commoners, who till the fields, trade goods, and craft items for everyday life. About this time, writing is used for literary as well as economic purposes.

2500 Acupuncture is invented in China.

2296 The Chinese record the earliest sighting of a comet.

2200 A bronze foundry is established in Erlitou, China.

ca 2500 The Harappans of the Indus Valley build large, well-planned cities indicative of a highly organized government and develop a sophisticated culture, the roots of which can still be seen in Indian and Pakistani society today.

CIVILIZATION IN THE INDUS VALLEY

The Indus River Valley, located in modern-day Pakistan and western India, attracted herders and farmers as early as 6000 B.C.E. A fertile valley then, its people achieved a surplus in agriculture that gave rise to villages and cities. By 2500 B.C.E. the two largest cities, Mohenjo Daro on the lower end of the valley and Harappa on the upper end, represented the apogee of a highly developed civilization now referred to as Harappan.

The cities were built on a grid of straight, paved streets lined with mud-brick houses, shops, and communal baths that may have served ceremonial purposes. Houses for the elite were larger, often two stories high, built around a courtyard where meals were cooked and served. Each house was equipped with a bathroom, and wastewater flowed into street sewers. The invention of sewers served public hygiene well and allowed for increased population density, up to 40,000 people. The Harappans created a complex script that has not yet been deciphered and traded widely with Mesopotamia, Iran, and other distant lands. By about 1500 B.C.E. an influx of warriors from the north may have caused the Harappans to abandon the land.

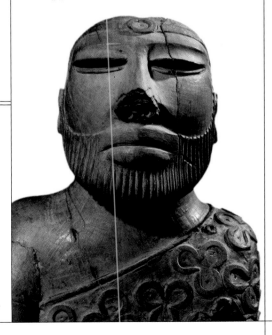

Indus Valley priest or ruler

POLITICS & POWER	GEOGRAPHY & ENVIRONMENT	CULTURE & RELIGION

THE AMERICAS

ca 2000 Hunter-gatherers populate North America.

ca 2000 Agricultural villages spread all over Mesoamerica and intensive farming begins.

1800 Andean people of South America build first ceremonial centers of pyramids and temples and shape distinctive pottery.

2000 Potatoes and quinoa become a major crop in the Andean highlands of South America.

EUROPE

2000 Minoan civilization emerges on Crete and nearby islands, with rulers organizing the building of palaces and cities.

2000 The Bell Beaker culture rises in England, so named for their bell-shaped pottery drinking vessels.

1800 Crete's central position in the Mediterranean extends Minoan influence as a trading hub to the south and east.

1800 Neolithic farmers settle the Orkney Islands off the coast of Scotland.

1600 The Mycenaean civilization arises in the south of Greece.

ca 2000 Aryan-speaking Indo-Europeans spread into Asia Minor, northern Greece, and Italy.

ca 2000 The Amber Trade Routes are established by the Etruscans and Greeks to transport amber and tin from northern Europe.

ca 1700 Aryan-speaking people from northern Turkey and the Ukraine move northwestward to Scandinavia.

ca 1700 A massive volcanic eruption on the island of Thera (Santorini) disrupts Minoan civilization.

ca 2000 The legend of the Minotaur, from which the Minoans obtain their name, tells of a time when gods begat kings, and a king's daughter begat a Minotaur: half human, half bull. The Minotaur lived in a maze on Crete and required an annual sacrifice of virgins until Theseus of Athens killed him.

ca 1800 More than 3,000 menhirs, or standing stones, are erected in Carnac, France.

1600 Stonehenge, the megalithic monument in England, is used as a religious center.

1600 The Minoans replace an earlier hieroglyphic script with an alphabetic script called Linear A.

MIDDLE EAST & AFRICA

2000 Sumer is overrun by the western Amorites and the eastern Elamites.

1960 Egypt invades Nubia, extending its borders to the second Nile cataract.

1800 Hebrew clans migrate to Egypt.

1792-1750 Hammurabi reunites and expands the Babylonian Empire.

1640 Egypt is defeated and ruled by nomadic Hyksos, marking the end of the Middle Kingdom. In 1550 Egypt's Theban kings rout the Hyksos and establish the New Kingdom.

1595 The Hittites sack Babylon.

WHAT LIFE WAS LIKE

Hammurabi's Code

Hammurabi's laws empowered men. As heads of households, they represented their families to the outside world. Men could sell their wives and children into slavery to pay for debts. Wives guilty of adultery were condemned to drowning, but men were allowed to engage in sexual relations with concubines, slaves, and prostitutes. A man could divorce his wife but had to return the dowry to her family, who had to take the woman back. Eventually, married women were required to cover their head outside the home.

ca 2000 The Epic of Gilgamesh is composed with king Gilgamesh as its hero. An earlier work of poetry is written by Enheduanna of Akkad.

1900 The Sumerians reduce cuneiform script to about 600 characters.

1792 Hammurabi compiles a collection of laws, known as the Code of Hammurabi. These laws rely heavily retaliation, as in "an eye for eye..."

1590 Pharaoh Tutmosis I begins tomb construction in the limestone cliffs west of Thebes.

ASIA & OCEANIA

ca 2000 The Harappans of the Indus Valley trade with neighboring Iran and engage in long-distance trade with Mesopotamia, exchanging copper, ivory, pearls and semiprecious stones for Sumerian wool, leather, and olive oil.

ca 2000 Austronesians reach Vanatu, and slowly move on to other islands, where they establish hierarchical chiefdoms.

ca 1750 The Shang dynasty establishes loose control over territory in the lower reaches of the Yellow River Valley and the north China plain.

ca 2000 Deforestation of the Indus Valley begins.

ca 2000 Traveling in outrigger boats, Austronesians settle various South Pacific islands, where they introduce yams, taro root, and breadfruit.

ca 1700 The Chinese of the Shang dynasty develop a writing system, used to record questions asked of the Shang kings' ancestors and the responses given. Known as oracle bone script—that is, cracks in burnt bones—these marks are the foundation of the Chinese written script.

SCIENCE & TECHNOLOGY	PEOPLE & SOCIETY
	ca 2000 Neolithic skills of weaving, basket-making, pottery making, building of shelter, and the formation of villages develop in the Americas.
ca 2000 Wheeled plows are used in some parts of Europe. **ca 2000 Large stone passage graves** are constructed in Scandinavia. **ca 1800 Bronze** is produced in the British Isles, probably brought in by the Bell Beaker people. **ca 1800 Bronze casting** begins in Scandinavia.	**1600-1150 The Mycenaeans,** an Indo-European people speaking an early form of Greek, move into mainland Greece and absorb the existing neolithic population. They establish cities on high ground, topped by a walled fortification. The Mycenaeans bring with them advanced knowledge of metallurgy, used in the production of tools, weapons, and armor. Skilled seafarers, they engage in maritime trade with nearby islands and the coast of the eastern Mediterranean and establish trading posts along the way. Mycenaean rulers are buried with treasures of gold and armor.
ca 2000 The shadoof, a device for lifting water with a bucket from a pole on a pivot and a counterweight, is invented in Egypt. **ca 1800 Assyrians** use a system of signal fires, a forerunner to the telegraph system. **ca 1650 Babylonians** record appearances of Venus. Later, Kassites relay an old text naming constellations and planets. **ca 1600 Egyptians** write a medical book showing accurate workings of the heart, stomach, bowels, and blood vessels. They also measure time of night by means of stars, now called the decans.	**2100-1570 Rulers at Kerma in the Sudan** become overlords of the lucrative Nile trade. **ca 1900-1700 Assyrians** set up a web of trading centers throughout the Near East. While husbands travel and sell merchandise, wives stay home, managing the business of importing, manufacturing, and exporting. **1738 Kim Suen II of Larsa** is the last Mesopotamian king to claim to be a god, until the arrival of the Greeks. **ca 1600 The Mitanni,** a small group speaking an Aryan language, rule northern Mesopotamia, populated mostly by Hurrians.
ca 1700 During the Shang era, the Chinese perfect the wheel, carve jade and ivory, and make ceremonial objects and weapons of bronze. The Shang rulers keep a tight monopoly on bronze production, thus limiting the manufacture of weapons for their own use.	**ca 1700 The kings of the Shang dynasty** are supported by aristocrats, who join them in warfare and royal hunts. The masses live in villages outside the royal cities and labor in the fields. The Shang build half-timbered houses over rammed-earth floors, with walls of wattle and daub and thatched roofs. Royal tombs are dug deep into the earth and equipped with splendid pottery and bronze objects, as well as sacrificial royal retainers, who accompany them into the afterlife. Family names carved into bone or brushed onto tortoise shells hint at future ancestor worship.

Minoan fresco

THE LOST WORLD OF THE MINOANS

An early civilization developed on the island of Crete in the eastern Mediterranean. The people were called Minoans, after the legendary King Minos. They fished and sailed and traded widely with Greece, Anatolia, Egypt, and Phoenicia.

About 2000 B.C.E. they built cities and a series of grand palaces on Crete and extended their influence to other islands. The palaces served as administrative centers and storehouses for foodstuffs and trade goods, such as grain, olive oil, wine, and finely crafted pottery. The Minoans also invented a script, called Linear A; although not yet deciphered, it seems to have served record-keeping in trade. About 1700 B.C.E. a series of earthquakes disrupted their mode of life, and a cataclysmic volcanic eruption on the nearby island of Thera rained volcanic ash on Crete and destroyed most of Thera.

Eventually the Minoans rebuilt their cities and palaces and added improvements such as indoor plumbing and sewer systems to their houses. But their wealth attracted invaders—most likely the warlike Mycenaeans—and by 1100 B.C.E. the island and their culture lay in ruins. Still, their legacy continued throughout the Mediterranean and among the inhabitants of Greece.

Hail to you, you august, great, and potent god.
Prince forever.
May you grant that I be among the living.

THE JOURNEY TO THE HEREAFTER

THE ANCIENT EGYPTIANS BELIEVED IN RESURRECTION AFTER DEATH, AS LONG AS the body was prepared properly. When a person of importance died, the embalmers went to work swiftly on the corpse, discarding the brain as useless and removing the internal organs to be placed in canopic jars. The organs would be reunited with the body upon resurrection. Once the organs were kept safe, the embalmers dried out the body with natron salt and stuffed it with straw or cotton, then coated it with fragrant balm and resin and wrapped it in hundreds of yards of linen strips. When all was wrapped and secured, a process accompanied by chanting of spells and charms, the mummy was placed in a coffin and buried in a well-equipped tomb, provided with all things necessary to start the journey through the underworld.

Beginning with the New Kingdom era, around 1550 B.C.E., royal tombs were cut into the rock of the Valley of the Kings. Consisting of long corridors and multiple chambers, the tombs held veritable treasuries of gifts. The rooms were painted extravagantly with prayers and spells for protection, repeating the person's name many times over in colorful cartouches and portraying the deceased as being received by all the important gods and goddesses. The example at left shows New Kingdom pharaoh Horemheb in his tomb, bearing offerings to Osiris, ruler of the underworld. Osiris is depicted with his royal crook and flail, wrapped tightly in linen, his face and hands the color of death.

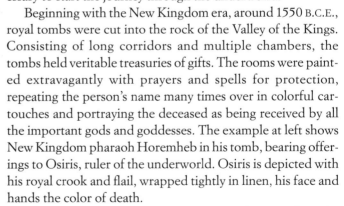

The underworld was thought to begin in the west where the sun set each evening, and tombs were usually placed on the west bank of the Nile. According to the *Book of the Dead*—sacred 13th-century-B.C.E. Egyptian texts—the body would travel by boat through the underworld to pass many tests of character. The heart of the deceased would be weighed against the feather of truth, and Osiris would judge whether the person was worthy of eternal life. If judged true, the deceased would be reborn, to rise gloriously the next morning with the sun god Re.

ABOVE: *In a tomb painting, New Kingdom Pharaoh Horemheb is received by Osiris to the underworld.*
OPPOSITE: *The mummy of Pharaoh Seti I lies well preserved in its tomb in the Valley of the Kings.*

	POLITICS & POWER	GEOGRAPHY & ENVIRONMENT	CULTURE & RELIGION
THE AMERICAS	**ca 1500 Olmec culture** develops in the region of the modern states of Veracruz and Tabasco in Mexico. **ca 1500 The nomadic Chichimeca people** expand in northern Mexico.	**ca 1500 Chiefdoms** in the lowlands of the Gulf of Mexico produce surplus crops of corn by achieving two crops a year. They also plant manioc.	
EUROPE	**1450 The Mycenaeans** expand their influence beyond mainland Greece, establishing settlements in Anatolia, Sicily, and southern Italy. They also take control of Crete, ending Minoan civilization.		**ca 1500 The Mycenaeans** are using a script called Linear B. Artisans make designs on bone, clay, and bronze with compasses. **ca 1500 Alpine copper** is used to make jewelry in England.
MIDDLE EAST & AFRICA	**1505 Queen Hatshepsut** takes over the rule of Egypt. She sends expeditions into Nubia and Somalia. **ca 1500 Kassites** assert a low-key rule over Babylon, adopting local customs. **ca 1500 Ugarit's ships** rule commerce in the eastern Mediterranean. The city houses as many as 8,000 people. **1490-1436 Tutmosis III of Egypt** leads successful campaigns into Palestine and Syria and presses deeper into Nubia, to Nile's fourth cataract.		**ca 1500 The cult of Amurra**, god of nomads, flourishes in Babylon. He is depicted wearing a long robe and hat, with a crook in his hand and a gazelle by his side. **ca 1500 Ugarit's cuneiform alphabet** is reduced from 600 signs to 30, although scribes retain the old version as well. **ca 1500 Urgaritic sailors** dedicate stone anchors to the god Baal in gratitude for a safe homecoming.
ASIA & OCEANIA	**ca 1500 Aryan-speaking Indo-Europeans** move into the Indus Valley from the north and take control of the region. Harappan civilization declines, perhaps because of drought, and its cities are abandoned. **ca 1500 The Jomon period** in Japan reaches its peak.	**ca 1500 The water buffalo** is domesticated in China. **ca 1500 Sorghum** is cultivated in India. **ca 1500 Austronesian mariners** establish settlements in the Fiji Islands. **ca 1500 Austronesian mariners** create the Lapita exchange network in the western Pacific islands.	**ca 1500 Japan's Jomon people** create human figurines of clay as fertility symbols.

WHAT LIFE WAS LIKE

Egypt's Female Pharaoh

Queen Hatshepsut, widow of Pharaoh Tutmosis II and daughter of Tutmosis I, seized the role of regent for her young stepson Tutmosis III. She was well suited to the role and took the title of pharaoh. To assure her subjects of her legitimacy, she claimed that the god Amun had fathered her and granted her the right to the title. She engaged in impressive building projects, with a mortuary temple near the Valley of the Kings and a sanctuary at Karnak temple for sacred boats. Instead of engaging in further conquests, she encouraged expeditions to foreign lands that expanded trade and brought new treasures into her realm.

SCIENCE & TECHNOLOGY

ca 1500 In an area virtually devoid of stone, Olmec move basalt boulders from the northern highlands to their homeland and work the stone without the use of metal tools.

ca 1500 Metalworking begins in Peru.

ca 1500 Unetice culture, near what is now Prague, mines, uses, and trades copper and tin.

ca 1500 Egyptians invent glassmaking.

ca 1500 Canaanite domestic architecture includes central or offset courtyards, a combination of large and small rooms, and stairways. Palaces are equipped with reception rooms and bathrooms.

ca 1500 Egyptian kings continue to construct elaborate tombs cut into the mountains west of Thebes—known as the Valley of the Kings—and build grandiose temples in their own name on the east bank of the Nile.

PEOPLE & SOCIETY

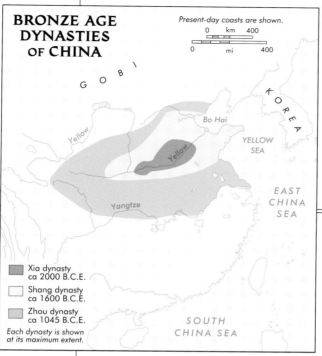

BRONZE AGE DYNASTIES OF CHINA

Present-day coasts are shown.

0 km 400
0 mi 400

GOBI

KOREA

Bo Hai

YELLOW SEA

Yellow

Yellow

Yangtze

EAST CHINA SEA

- Xia dynasty ca 2000 B.C.E.
- Shang dynasty ca 1600 B.C.E.
- Zhou dynasty ca 1045 B.C.E.

Each dynasty is shown at its maximum extent.

SOUTH CHINA SEA

Extent of the Xia, Shang, and Zhou dynasties in China

Bronze masks from the Shu culture in southwestern China, contemporary with the Shang

ca 1500 Aryan-speaking Indo-Europeans ride out of Central Asia into India as herders of sheep, goats, and cattle. They are famous for domesticating horses, which makes hem highly mobile, enabling them to cover long distances and to transport goods by hitching horses to carts and to use them as war machines.

CHINA'S ORIGINS UNEARTHED

In the past 50 years, the rapid pace of archaeological excavations in China has radically revised long-held ideas about the origins of Chinese civilization. Once thought to have begun in the Yellow River Valley, archaeologists have uncovered evidence of Neolithic cultures as early as the sixth millennium B.C.E. in sites from the southern coast to the far northeast. Thus the origins of Chinese civilization are much more varied—regionally, culturally, and ethnically—than previously thought.

According to traditional accounts, sage kings in antiquity like the Yellow Emperor taught the Chinese people the arts of agriculture, writing, and medicine, and early dynasties—Xia, Shang, and Zhou—were founded by virtuous rulers and ended by tyrannical ones. Modern scholarship now views these dynasties as not so much succeeding each other in ever larger geographical zones, but in part co-existing at the same time in different places. Rule in these dynasties evolved from a loose confederation under Shang kings to a decentralized territorial system under the Zhou. At times, archaeology has confirmed the written historical record. For example, the reign of Shang kings in traditional accounts has been verified by inscriptions on oracle bones and bronze vessels. Other bronze work has been discovered as far southwest as Sichuan province.

POLITICS & POWER	GEOGRAPHY & ENVIRONMENT	CULTURE & RELIGION
THE AMERICAS		
ca 1400 Olmec influence expands from the Gulf of Mexico to the Pacific Ocean.		
EUROPE		
ca 1400 People in settled communities all over Europe begin to accumulate material wealth and build fortified villages to defend their possessions.	**ca 1400 The eastern Alps** are mined for copper and salt. Salt is a precious commodity, and is exchanged for pottery, glass, and wine from the Mediterranean, tin from Britain, and gold from Bohemia.	**ca 1400 Cremation** rather than inhumation comes into practice, suggesting different ideas about the afterlife.
MIDDLE EAST & AFRICA		
ca 1400 The Phoenician cities Tyre, Sidon, and Byblos thrive as centers of trade, exporting purple cloth and cedars of Lebanon. **ca 1400 The city of Jericho**, destroyed by the Hyksos, is rebuilt and prospers. **ca 1350 Hittite king Suppiluliuma I** ends Mittani power and takes Syria. Ashurballit I regains Assyria's independence. **1335-1325 Tutankhamun** succeeds to the throne of Egypt as a boy of only 9 years old. He dies at 19.		**1353-1335 Pharaoh Akhenaten**, for a brief period, establishes a form of monotheism in Egypt. **1325 At the death of Tutankhamun**, his royal tomb in the Valley of the Kings is filled with food, drink, and splendid treasure to equip him for a luxurious afterlife: bejeweled ornaments; golden cases; furniture; a royal wardrobe, including armor; and even a boat.
ASIA & OCEANIA		
ca 1400 Aryans in India engage in frequent wars with the Dravidians and other early people settled there, eventually merging with them and establishing communities throughout the subcontinent. **ca 1400 Excavations** at the site of one of the Shang's several capitals—the city of Zhengzhou in Henan province—reveal city walls 33 feet high and 66 feet thick, surrounding a 32-square-foot area with a center platform of pounded earth 30 feet square.		**1400 India's Aryans** do not develop an organized political structure, but establish a firm social order. They develop a belief system that is the foundation of Hinduism. **ca 1400 Hindu sages** create the Vedas, a collection of hymns, prayers, and liturgy—the earliest Hindu sacred writings.

WHAT LIFE WAS LIKE

The Rebel Akhenaten

Pharaoh Akhenaten inherited the title from his father, Amenhotep III, whose temples and palaces epitomized Egyptian art and luxury. His son, however, eschewed such ostentation and denounced the powerful roles played by the priests. Akhenaten rejected all temple cults in favor of only one god, the sun god Aten. He moved the capital from Thebes to Amarna, where he built a new city with a sun-lit open temple, vastly different from the dark, mysterious older sanctuaries. Art styles changed during this period, too, portraying the king and his family with lifelike expressions. After his death, however, priests reinstated the old order.

SCIENCE & TECHNOLOGY

PEOPLE & SOCIETY

ca 1400 **The Olmec** are considered the "mother culture" of Mesoamerica because so many of the traits appearing there are repeated in subsequent civilizations.

ca 1400 **Farmers in central Europe** use some metals for making sickles and other tools, and probably rotate their crops.

ca 1400 **A shipwreck off the coast of Turkey** dating to this period, discovered in the 20th century C.E., is loaded with copper, tin, glass, terebinthine resin, ebony logs, ivory, ostrich eggshells, tortoise shells, murex shells, oripiment (yellow dye), figs, pomegranates, grapes, olives, safflower, and coriander.

Death mask of Tutankhamun

ca 1400 **The Chinese produce stoneware pottery** that is fired at high temperatures—the beginning of porcelain manufacture.

ca 1400 **The Shang dynasty** develops a calendar with a 366-day year of 12 lunar months.

THE TOMB OF TUTANKHAMUN

Although the boy king Tutankhamun had little opportunity to achieve greatness in his short life of 18 or 19 years, he is well known to posterity because of his tomb, which was discovered intact in 1922.

As was the custom for pharaohs in Egyptian society, Tutankhamun was buried in the Valley of the Kings. He was embalmed, mummified, and enshrined in a series of coffins, the innermost one of solid gold and an outer sarcophagus of granite. His death mask alone (left) was made of 22 1/2 pounds of gold. Some 50,000 other magnificent grave goods accompanied him to the afterlife, and the contents of the tomb, overflowing with bejeweled treasures, tell much about daily life among the elite in the 14th century B.C.E.

Tutankhamun was probably the son of Kiya, a minor queen, and Pharaoh Akhenaten, who had attempted to supplant the existing priesthood and gods with a single deity, the sun god Aten. After Akhenaten's death, when Tutankhamun was still a child and under the influence of advisers, the priests reinstated the old order along with a pantheon of gods, and moved the capital back to Thebes.

According to artifacts and paintings, Tutankhamun and his young wife, Ankhesenamun, lived a luxurious life and spent their time leisurely. He is shown driving a chariot, swimming and playing other sports, and sometimes hunting and fishing. Although murder was suspected, modern tests showed that he most likely died from a fracture in his left leg that became infected with gangrene.

You waken gladly every day,
all afflictions are expelled.
You traverse eternity in joy.

TOMB INSCRIPTION

POLITICS & POWER	GEOGRAPHY & ENVIRONMENT	CULTURE & RELIGION

THE AMERICAS

ca 1300 Olmec civilization continues to thrive, coalescing around San Lorenzo.

ca 1300 People at Poverty Point, in what is now Louisiana, import copper and flint, but do not develop agriculture.

ca 1300 Olmec practice ritual bloodletting and ball games, rites that will become characteristics of Mesoamerican civilization.

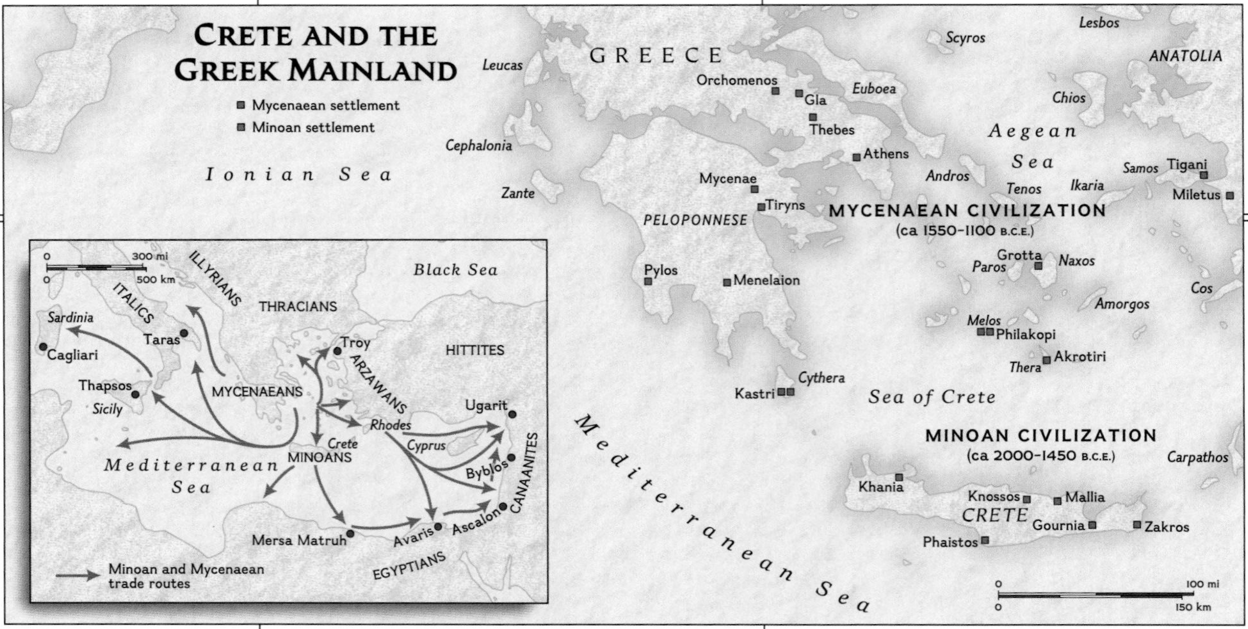

EUROPE

1300 The Mycenaeans of mainland Greece command Crete and numerous colonies along the eastern coast of the Mediterranean established through trade.

CRETE AND THE GREEK MAINLAND
- Mycenaean settlement
- Minoan settlement

MYCENAEAN CIVILIZATION (ca 1550-1100 B.C.E.)
MINOAN CIVILIZATION (ca 2000-1450 B.C.E.)
Minoan and Mycenaean trade routes

MIDDLE EAST & AFRICA

ca 1300 Led by Moses, the Hebrews leave Egypt for Palestine, where they establish Israel.

1298-1232 Egypt's Ramses II battles encroaching armies on all sides. He clashes with Hittite King Muwattalli II in the Battle of Kadesh, but preserves the empire.

1290 The city of Troy on the coast of modern-day Turkey is destroyed by the Mycenaeans.

ca 1285 Assyria's King Adadnirari I conquers the Mitanni and founds the Assyrian Empire across northern Mesopotamia.

ca 1250 Swarms of locusts destroy crops in the Nile Valley in Egypt.

ca 1250 An earthquake rocks Phoenician Nineveh and damages the temple of Ishtar.

ca 1300 Moses receives the Ten Commandments at Mount Sinai, in today's Egypt.

ca 1300 Assyrian kings are responsible to the national god, Ashur, for providing peace, prosperity, and justice to his people. If a king breaks his covenant with Ashur, the god will replace him with another.

1290 The story of the Trojan War—the battle of the Mycenaeans against Troy—is preserved by oral tradition for four centuries until retold in Homer's epic the *Iliad* in the mid-ninth century B.C.E.

ASIA & OCEANIA

1300 The Shang rulers of China move their capital to Anyang.

SCIENCE & TECHNOLOGY	PEOPLE & SOCIETY
ca 1300 People at Poverty Point construct a complex of earthworks around a plaza where traders and artisans work and ceremonies are held. The community of about 1,000 people is surrounded by smaller settlements.	**ca 1300 The Poverty Point society** demonstrates that settlements and the capacity to organize labor are not tied to agriculture. People in this community construct monumental projects, yet they are hunter-gatherers and rely on fishing and trade.
ca 1300 People of the Urnfield culture in central Europe use bronze to make weapons and jewelry. OPPOSITE: *Minoan civilization on Crete was eventually subsumed by the Mycenaeans, who came to control much of the Mediterranean.*	**ca 1300 Urnfield people cremate the dead** and bury their ashes in urns in cemeteries.
ca 1290 Centuries after the fall of Troy, Greek poet Aeschylus will report that Queen Clytemnestra of Greece was informed of the victory and the impending return of her husband, King Agamemnon, by a system of signal fires, a forerunner of the telegraph system.	**1298-1232 Long-lived Pharaoh Ramses II** of Egypt builds more monuments to himself than any other pharaoh: extensions at the temples of Karnak and Luxor; the Ramesseum on the west side of the Nile; and six temples in Nubia, the most splendid of which is at Abu Simbel. This warrior king fights many battles, but also negotiates for peace. Following the battle with the Hittites, he takes a Hittite princess as one of his many wives. After a reign of 67 years, Ramses dies and leaves 50 sons. The 13th one, Merenptah, becomes his successor.
1361 Chinese astronomers record an eclipse of the moon.	

Olmec athlete

THE OLMEC OF MESOAMERICA

As early as 2250 B.C.E., people of the lowlands along the Gulf of Mexico planted corn and other crops and exploited the sea for fish and shellfish. They organized into chiefdoms and lived in agricultural communities. By 1200 B.C.E. the Olmec—meaning rubber people, for the rubber trees growing in the region—had organized into Mesoamerica's first civilization.

An authoritarian society with a complex division of labor, the Olmec conscripted thousands of laborers to build elaborate ceremonial centers on earthen mounds with temples, walled plazas, and ball courts. Other workers mined and transported huge boulders of basalt from the mountains to be sculpted into colossal heads, which may have represented leaders or deities. These centers were reserved for the elite and priestly class; ordinary citizens attended only on special occasions. The first center was built at San Lorenzo, followed by a second one at La Venta in 800 B.C.E., and a third at Tres Zapotes in 400 B.C.E. Olmec influence reached far beyond Mexico, and much of their culture, including an early script and calendar, was adopted by later civilizations.

*Love thy neighbor as yourself,
I am your God.*

LEVITICUS 19:17-18

THE BIRTH OF MONOTHEISM

ACCORDING TO THE TORAH—THE JEWISH HOLY SCRIPTURES, WHICH ARE ALSO THE first five books of the Bible—life on earth began in the Garden of Eden, a spot from which four rivers sprang. Two of them, the Tigris and Euphrates, still flow today in Iraq. From this land, called Ur at the time, God commanded Abraham in about 2100 B.C.E. to "get thee out of thy country . . . unto the land that I will show thee . . . and I will make of thee a great nation."

As per the Torah, God led Abraham and his clan of nomadic herders to Canaan, the land between Egypt and Lebanon. From that time on, Abraham was connected to God in a personal relationship, following His commands and having his faith tested. He and his people had journeyed from a region where multiple gods were feared and had to be appeased, and yet he began to believe in a single, supreme God, transcendent in power.

Abraham's grandson Jacob had 12 sons, from whom the 12 tribes of Israel are said to be descended. To escape a famine, Jacob and his family migrated to Egypt where other Hebrews traveled regularly as traders and itinerant metalsmiths. Jacob died there, but the Israelites (so named because God called Jacob "Israel") were enslaved by the pharaoh, possibly Ramses II. Around 1300 B.C.E., Moses delivered them from bondage and led them safely out of Egypt.

At Mount Sinai, Moses received the words of the covenant, the Ten Commandments, written in stone. Stating above all, "You shall have no other gods before me," the Ten Commandments laid the foundation of moral law for Judaism, which eventually became the moral code for Christianity and Islam as well. According to the commandments, idolatry was forbidden; parents were to be honored; murder, adultery, theft, and lying should be punished; and the seventh day of the week should be reserved for rest—a time for prayer and reflection. Virtuous living would be rewarded and wickedness punished.

Returning to Canaan, the Hebrews established the kingdom of Israel. Their belief in a single God set them apart from their neighbors and placed on them a heavy burden, but their religion has survived endless trials to this day.

OPPOSITE: *In Rembrandt's 17th-century painting, Moses holds aloft the Ten Commandments.*
RIGHT: *The Torah holds the laws and history of ancient Israel, handwritten on a scroll of parchment.*

	POLITICS & POWER	GEOGRAPHY & ENVIRONMENT	CULTURE & RELIGION
THE AMERICAS	**ca 1200 The Sioux people** live a subsistence existence in the Canadian plains. **ca 1200-200 For a thousand years** people along the California coast sustain their communities through marine life. While men fish, women grind acorn flour. **1200 Olmec society** is at its peak with a monumental ceremonial complex of huge pyramids, temples, and palaces at San Lorenzo.	**ca 1200 Maize** is a staple crop in Mesoamerica.	**ca 1200 The Olmec sculpt colossal stone heads,** representing aspects of an awesome religion. Their pantheon includes jaguar deities and fertility goddesses. They are also noted for their elaborate serpentine mosaics, some as large as 15 by 20 feet.
EUROPE	**ca 1200 Proto-Celtic people** of Indo-European origin settle in central Europe. **ca 1200 Dorian-speaking Greeks** arrive on the Peloponnesus. **1150 The Mycenaean civilization** declines on mainland Greece.	**1226 An eruption of Mount Etna** in Sicily is recorded for the first time.	**ca 1200 Spiral decoration styles** spread from the Caucasus northward.
MIDDLE EAST & AFRICA	**ca 1200 Assyria's King Tukulti-Ninurta I** defeats Babylon. **1180 The Hittite homeland** in Anatolia is invaded, ending the empire. **1174 The 12 tribes of Israel,** ruled by judges, meet at the sanctuary of Shiloh to agree on a united front. **1173 The Elamites** sack Babylon. **1125 Israelites** fight the Canaanites in the Battle of Meggidoh. **1114 Assyria's King Tiglath-Pileser** extends his influence as far as Lebanon, before losing most of his empire to the Arameans.	*Mount Etna, Sicily* **ca 1150 An earthquake** hits Nineveh again, damaging the Ishtar temple. **1141 A plague** kills 50,000 people in Israel.	**ca 1200 Canaanites, Phoenicians, and Israelites** build pillared houses. **ca 1200 A Samarian hilltop shrine** features a circle of large stones with a standing stone on one side; a bronze figurine of a bull is found on the site.
ASIA & OCEANIA	**ca 1200 The Shang dynasty** in China is showing signs of turmoil.		

SCIENCE & TECHNOLOGY

ca 1200 The Olmec develop a lunar calendar.

ca 1200 Reed boats are in use in Ecuador and Peru.

PEOPLE & SOCIETY

ca 1200 Olmec society is well organized with the elite mobilizing large groups of people for the labor necessary to erect huge structures and monumental sculptures. They develop a far-ranging network of exchange, trading obsidian, jade, and cocoa beans.

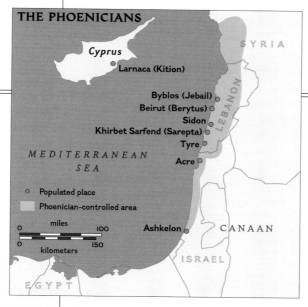

The Phoenician coast

THE PHOENICIANS

Cyprus

Larnaca (Kition)

Byblos (Jebail)
Beirut (Berytus)
Sidon
Khirbet Sarfend (Sarepta)
Tyre
Acre

MEDITERRANEAN SEA

○ Populated place

Phoenician-controlled area

miles
0   100
0   150
kilometers

Ashkelon   CANAAN

ISRAEL

EGYPT

SYRIA

LEBANON

ca 1200 Craftsmen in Mesopotamia perfect iron tools and weapons, although experimentation with iron begins at an earlier date.

1180 The empire of the Hittites—Indo-Europeans of mixed Anatolian, Babylonian, and Hurrian culture living in Anatolia since 1650—is destroyed by invaders. The empire was held together by elaborate treaties and powerful kings, among them Hattusili I, who abolished most death penalties; Mursili I, who conquered Aleppo and destroyed Hammurabi's Babylon; and Tudhaliya II, who reconquered most of Anatolia and challenged Egypt and the Mittanni in Syria. The Hittites fought Egypt's mighty Ramses II to a draw in the battle of Kadesh, which resulted in a Hittite princess joining Ramses' harem.

ca 1200 Fu Hao, chief consort of Shang King Wu Ding, is buried in a royal tomb with bronze, jade, and ivory artifacts that date back to pre-Shang times.

PHOENICIAN SEAFARERS

By the end of the third millennium, Semitic tribes had settled on the coast of present-day Lebanon and Syria. The Greeks later named them Phoenicians, from the word "phoinix," or purple, because of their purple cloaks.

The Phoenicians established the cities of Tyre, Sidon, and Byblos at the crossroads of trade and began sailing along the Mediterranean coast. By 1200 they were known as preeminent seafarers, navigating by the stars and trading their cedar wood and cloth dyed in a unique purple made from Murex snails. They established a trading network that reached from Spain and North Africa to Turkey and Greece and made the first recorded circumnavigation of Africa. To keep track of their far-flung networks, they devised an alphabetic, rather than a pictorial, system of writing, which they passed on to the Greeks and on which the Western alphabet is based.

Never a unified kingdom, Phoenicia consisted of a handful of independent city-states. As Assyrian and then Persian power rose in the east, Phoenician cities were invaded. In 334 B.C.E. Alexander the Great destroyed the last one.

Phoenician carved ivory

POLITICS & POWER	GEOGRAPHY & ENVIRONMENT	CULTURE & RELIGION

THE AMERICAS

ca 1100 The Chavín de Huántar people in the Andes in South America organize in a complex society around a religious cult and construct a large temple.

ca 1100 The Chavín culture is located at 9,000 feet in the Andes with a population of more than 3,000.

ca 1100 Andean society in South America is becoming ever more complex. Weavers begin to construct intricately patterned textiles and craftspeople work with gold, silver, and copper to make finely wrought jewelry and sturdy tools.

EUROPE

ca 1100 Indo-Europeans stream into Italy from the north, among them the Latin, the Sabine, and the Samnite tribes.

ca 1100 In northern Scandinavia, hunters carve images of hundreds of deer on rock cliffs, hoping for a good hunt.

CONNECTIONS

Indo-European Languages

The Indo-Europeans were herders and horse-breeders, a hard-charging group of people who exploded out of the Eurasian steppes on horseback and in battle chariots to conquer new lands. Organized into rival tribes, Indo-Europeans spoke a language that gradually branched into many related tongues as groups like the Hittites and the Aryans spread out across a vast area ranging from Asia Minor to India and Europe, losing contact with one another but forming new relationships. Among the linguistic innovations were Sanskrit, the classical language of India, as well as Persian, Greek, Latin, the Germanic and Slavic languages, and the so-called Romance languages, including French, Spanish, and Italian. Today the Indo-European language family is the largest in the world, with more speakers than any other.

MIDDLE EAST & AFRICA

ca 1100 Incursions by Aramaeans into Assyria and Babylon cause those countries to lapse into a dark age.

1075 Central rule is weakened in Egypt and local governments pursue their own interests. A chaotic era begins, spelling the end of the New Kingdom period.

1050 Samuel, the prophet and last of the judges, becomes ruler of Israel and defeats the Philistines.

1025 Saul, who has fought the Philistines under Samuel, is anointed king of Israel.

ca 1100 Hittite refugees and Arameans found many city-states in Syria, northern Mesopotamia, and southern Anatolia.

ca 1050 Saharan farmers and herders move southward as the region experiences significantly drier episodes.

ca 1100 Phoenicians standardize the first alphabet of 22 letters, simplifying writing and thus allowing more people to become literate. This alphabet is adapted by the Mycenaeans and is the basis for our modern alphabet.

ca 1100 The Tale of Wen-Amon tells of an Egyptian official, passing through Canaan on his way to buy cedars in Lebanon. He stays for a while with the Sea Peoples, who seem to control the coastal trade.

ASIA & OCEANIA

ca 1100 *Homo floresiensis*—the small people of Flores, Indonesia, descended from *Homo erectus*—probably die out at this time. Despite having only a small brain, this human species uses stone tools and fire.

1045 The Shang dynasty is toppled by a challenger from northwestern China, who founds the Zhou dynasty.

ca 1100 Austronesian people speak variations of Malayan, Indonesian, Filipino, Polynesian, and other Oceanic languages.

|

ca 1100 The Olmec manufacture rubber balls from the sap of rubber trees in the tropics to play the famous ball games of Mesoamerica.

KINGDOMS OF ISRAEL

Cyprus

Mediterranean Sea

PHOENICIA

SYRIAN DESERT

Sea of Galilee

Jordan R.

CANAAN

Nile Delta

Samaria AMMON

Jerusalem

PHILISTIA

Dead Sea

MOAB

Nile

EDOM

SINAI

Euphrates

Tigris

■ Kingdom of David and Solomon ca 1004-930 B.C.E.

□ Kingdom of Israel ca 929-721 B.C.E.

■ Kingdom of Judah ca 929-586 B.C.E.

MOAB Historical region

Each kingdom is shown at its maximum extent.

0 km 200

0 mi 200

Present-day boundaries and coasts are shown.

After the death of King Solomon, Israel split into the northern kingdom of Israel and the southern kingdom of Judah.

ca 1100 Amber from the Baltic Sea begins to be traded widely in Europe.

ca 1100 Esagilkinapli of Borsippa in Mesopotamia puts together a medical diagnostic textbook.

ca 1100 The library of Assyrian King Tiglath-Pileser includes manuals for horse training and glassmaking.

1025-1000 King Saul of Israel engages in many military campaigns. After success against the Philistines, he fights against Moab, Ammon, Edom, the kings of Zobah, and the Amalekites in the Negev desert. Renewed fighting with the Philistines brings him the victory at Socoh, where David fights Goliath. Saul makes David an officer in his army, but David, suddenly popular, fears Saul's jealousy and hides in the mountains. In renewed fighting, Saul succumbs to the Philistines.

ca 1045 The Zhou people, ethnically distinct from the rulers of the Shang dynasty, move into Shang territory from the northeast and establish their capital in the Wei River Valley near the modern city of Xi'an.

Beware, lest your heart be deceived, and you turn and serve other gods, and worship them.

DEUTERONOMY 11:16

THE KINGDOM OF ISRAEL

L ed from bondage by Moses, the Hebrews left Egypt around 1300 B.C.E. to settle in the "promised land," the uplands of Canaan. Philistines, Phoenicians, and other sea peoples already occupied the coastal area. The Hebrews formed a loose coalition of 12 tribes, ruled by judges. By 1025 B.C.E. fear of the warlike Philistines caused the Hebrews to unite into the kingdom of Israel. They chose Saul as their first king.

In 1000 B.C.E. David followed Saul and made Jerusalem the capital of his kingdom. David's son, Solomon, succeeded him in 960 B.C.E., and the kingdom thrived. Massive building projects were completed, most famously the magnificent Temple of Solomon. With Solomon's death in 925 B.C.E., a golden era ended. His sons split the kingdom into two feuding countries: Israel in the north and Judah in the south, a division that would prove fatal.

The Assyrians to the north had been a long-time threat and in 721, they conquered Israel's capital of Samaria. Thousands of survivors, now known as the ten lost tribes of Israel, were forced into exile, scattered in small populations all over the Middle East. The assaults continued in 701, when Judah's major city of Lachish fell, but the Assyrians could not capture the capital, Jerusalem.

Subjected to constant power struggles between Babylonians, Assyrians, and Egyptians, Judah's fortunes ebbed and surged. Once Assyria declined and fell to the might of Babylon, however, its king, Nebuchadrezzar, took new aim at Jerusalem. He first appointed Zedekia to be king of Judah and sent some 10,000 prominent Jews into exile in Babylon. Then, when Zedekia proved unreliable, Nebuchadrezzar laid siege to Jerusalem. In 597 B.C.E., Babylonian forces breached the city's defenses and destroyed the former capital, bringing an end to what was left of the once-united kingdom of Israel.

	POLITICS & POWER	GEOGRAPHY & ENVIRONMENT	CULTURE & RELIGION
THE AMERICAS	**ca 1000 In the Ohio River Valley**, the Adena people form an agricultural society. **ca 1000 The Cochise culture** dominates the area of modern-day New Mexico and Arizona.	**ca 1000 Inuits and Aleuts**, who have migrated across the sea by boat to the Arctic during the last 2,000 years, have successfully adapted to their polar environment.	**ca 1000 The Adena people** of North America carve stone tablets with bold reliefs of birds and geometric designs. **ca 1000 The Chavín temples in Peru** hold galleries for religious rites with statuary. The temples are also used for storing food supplies. The Chavín elite is buried with objects of precious metals and woven textiles.
EUROPE	**ca 1000 Proto-Etruscans** develop independent city-states between the Arno and Tiber Rivers in Italy. **ca 1000 Greeks** migrate across the Aegean Sea and colonize parts of Asia Minor.	**ca 1000 A mass migration** of Germanic peoples into central Europe begins. **ca 1000 Oats** are cultivated in Europe.	**ca 1000 Etruscans** cremate their dead and bury them in terracotta urns, sometimes shaped like a house.
MIDDLE EAST & AFRICA	**ca 1000 Phoenician city-states** continue to send out merchant fleets to establish trading posts in Cyprus, Sicily, Malta, and Spain. **1000 David** becomes king of Israel, uniting the states of Judah and Israel. **1000 Indo-European Medes and Persians** migrate from Central Asia to Iran. **960-925 Solomon** succeeds his father David as king of Israel. At his death, his sons split the kingdom in two: Jeroboam becomes king of Israel; Rehoboam king of Judah. **920 The Assyrians** begin to reconquer lost territories.	*King Solomon of Israel*	**1000 King David** brings the Ark of the Covenant, containing the Ten Commandments, to Jerusalem. **ca 950 Egyptians** simplify their writing style by using an alphabetic script, called demotic. **945 Israel** trades with the Queen of Sheba of South Arabia and Ethiopia, who sends camel trains bearing spices, gold, and precious stones. **ca 925 Solomon** builds a temple in Jerusalem, using Phoenician logs and craftsmen. Hebrew literature expands with the "Song of Deborah," later collected in Song of Songs.
ASIA & OCEANIA	**ca 1000 Aryans in India** settle into permanent communities between the Himalyan foothills and the Ganges River. Regional kingdoms form in northern India. **ca 1000 Zhou kings** rule the "central kingdom" and apportion rule of outlying territories to their kin, granting titles of nobility as they confer the right to rule.	**ca 1000 Variations in climate and food supply** affect the populations of Jomon Japan, scattered from the northernmost islands of Hokkaido to the southernmost island of Kyushu. **ca 1000 Austronesians** settle the islands of Tonga and Samoa.	**ca 1000 The Hindu caste system** in India is organized into four main varnas: Brahmins—priests Kshatriyas—warriors and aristocrats Vaishyas—farmers, craftsmen, merchants Shudras—landless peasants These were followed later by the untouchables—people who do unpleasant tasks, such as burying the dead.

SCIENCE & TECHNOLOGY

ca 1000 The Pinto Indians in California build housing of wood interwoven with reeds and covered with earth.

ca 1000 The use of iron begins in Greece.

ca 1000 Phoenicians dye fabrics purple with an extract from Murex snails.

ca 1000 Assyrians make effective use of horse-drawn chariots as mobile firing plaforms for archers. They devise many types of siege engines and battering rams.

ca 1000 Iron metallurgy becomes known in China, allowing for a more widespread production of tools, especially weapons. Local governments can arm themselves more cheaply and oppose central rule to follow their own pursuits.

PEOPLE & SOCIETY

ca 1000 People of the southwestern Cochise culture develop pit houses. They also produce pottery figurines.

ca 1000 The Olmec invent the tortilla, which includes *atole,* or corn gruel. This food is easily transported and does not perish rapidly; it is the original "fast food" of the Americas.

HINDUISM: AT ONE WITH THE UNIVERSE

Of the world's great religions, Hinduism may be the oldest, its roots going back to the Indus Valley civilization in Pakistan and western India and mixed with beliefs brought into India by Aryan-speaking Indo-Europeans. Their orally transmitted religious hymns, prayers, and rituals were written down in the Vedas between 1400 and 900 B.C.E.

As traditions developed further, they were again compiled in the Upanishads around 800 B.C.E. These sacred scriptures hold that everything is part of one cosmic spirit—infusing every living being—called Brahman.

Hinduism venerates thousands of different gods, ranging from household and village protectors to the great Vishnu and Shiva, who have many incarnations. Vishnu, the protector of the world, also appears as Krishna. Shiva—often shown with four arms, indicating his power, and encircled by flames—is the god who destroys ignorance.

The many different gods present different pathways by which a person can approach the divine. Depending on what kind of life a person has lived, he or she will be reincarnated into a better or meaner existence. The ultimate right way of living will lead to liberation from the cycle of birth, death, and reincarnation.

The third-largest religion in the world, with almost a billion followers, Hinduism is unique among world religions in having no single founder.

The Hindu god Shiva, shown in his incarnation as Nataraja, Lord of the Cosmic Dance, dances on a prostrate demon, surrounded by flames.

	POLITICS & POWER	GEOGRAPHY & ENVIRONMENT	CULTURE & RELIGION
THE AMERICAS	**ca 900 The Olmec capital** of San Lorenzo in Mexico is destroyed; a ceremonial complex at La Venta becomes the new focal point of Olmec civilization. **ca 900 People on the Paracas Peninsula** of Peru develop ceremonial centers.		**ca 900 A large pyramid** and several smaller ones mark the center of the Olmec La Venta complex. **ca 900 The Paracas people** mummify their dead, wrapping them in finely woven cotton fabrics. *Paracas cloth*
EUROPE	**ca 900 The Etruscans** develop a rich culture, spreading along present-day Tuscany, Latium, and Umbria in Italy. **ca 900 The Euboeans,** Greek traders, found colonies on the west coast of southern Italy. **ca 885 Lycurgus** creates the laws and institutions of Sparta in Greece.	**ca 900 Etruscan mariners** ply the waters of the Tyrrhenian Sea to the islands of Elba, Corsica, Sardinia, and Sicily.	**ca 900 The Etruscans** excel in fashioning artistic sculpture, ranging from alabaster and marble to bronze objects, and are renowned for their elegant marble sarcophagi with lifelike portraits of the deceased. They also develop a form of writing that has not yet been deciphered. **ca 885 Mandatory physical education** begins in Sparta.
MIDDLE EAST & AFRICA	**ca 900 The Nubian kingdom of Kush** establishes its capital at Napata. **883-859 Under king Ashurnasirpal II,** Assyria regains its lost land and again becomes a great power in Mesopotamia. **876-869 King Omri** rules in Samaria, Israel. **859-824 Assyrian king Shalmaneser III** invades Syria. He is stopped by a coalition including Ahab of Israel. **ca 850 The Urartian kingdom** is founded in eastern Anatolia by relations of the Hurrians. Citadels are built on mountain crags. The capital is Van.	**813 Carthage** is founded by the Phoenicians on the coast of North Africa.	**ca 860 Samaria** becomes a religious center in Israel. Ahab's queen, Jezebel of Sidon, introduces the worship of Baal. **ca 860 The prophets Elijah and Elisha** fight against the worship of Baal, resulting in the murder of the royal families of Israel, Judah, and Damascus and the slaughter of all whose form of worship does not meet Elijah's approval. **841 Jehu**, as part of Elisha's fundamentalist revolution, seizes the throne of Israel. The anti-Assyrian coalition collapses, and Jehu is forced to pay tribute to Shalmaneser III.
ASIA & OCEANIA	**ca 900-800 During the Zhou dynasty** craftsmen excel in producing artistic bronze wares, which are prized and traded beyond China's borders.		**ca 900 The Law Code of Manu** in India is a compilation of rules of proper moral behavior in Vedic society, including the treatment of women. Men are encouraged to treat women with respect, but women are subject to the men in their lives: first their fathers, then their husbands or brothers, then their sons. The code also advises: Wound not others, do no injury by thought or deed, utter no word to pain thy fellow creatures. He who habitually salutes and constantly pays reverence to the aged obtains an increase in four things: length of life, knowledge, fame, and strength.

SCIENCE & TECHNOLOGY	PEOPLE & SOCIETY
	ca 1000 The Olmec maintain trade relations as far south as El Salvador. They also trade for jade with the modern-day Mexican state of Guerrero and for obsidian from Oaxaca.
ca 900 The Etruscans exploit the mineral wealth of copper and tin in their region.	**ca 900 Scandinavians** build large burial mounds and sometimes include stone ships among the grave goods.
	ca 850 Homer writes the *Iliad* and the *Odyssey,* the epic poems recounting parts of the Trojan War and the journey home for Greek hero Odysseus. Though their authorship is often disputed, the two epics are thought to be the oldest literary documents in the Greek language and are considered prototypes for much of Western literature.
	ca 900 The Nok people of Nigeria fashion sculptures of fired clay.
	883-745 Assyrians bring conquered people to the Assyrian heartland and move Assyrians to the newly conquered territory. All are now considered equal Assyrian citizens. The royal road and postal system is extended throughout the empire.

CELTS: EUROPE'S METALSMITHS

The people known to the Greeks as Keltoi, or Celts, were settled about 800 B.C.E. in the salt mining region of Hallstatt, in today's Austria. They formed agricultural villages and mined and traded salt, a precious commodity at the time, especially prized for preserving meats. Instead of the draped garments known to the Mediterraneans, Celtic men wore trousers, which the toga wearers viewed as ridiculous.

Of Indo-European origin, the Celts' loose and shifting tribes, united only by language and religious beliefs, spread across central Europe. They brought with them a highly developed skill in bronze work for weapons and functional items. They had horses and four-wheeled wooden wagons, which later evolved into lighter, faster two-wheeled carts. They fortified their villages with huge earthen ramparts but never formed a unified nation. Burial mounds of chieftains held treasures of gold, amber, and other precious goods, indicating trade links to the Baltic and Mediterranean Seas.

With the advent of iron smelting in about 750 B.C.E., the Celts became experts in the technology Their highly skilled metalsmiths produced hoops for wagon wheels, agricultural tools, functional household items, and brooches and other jewelry, plus swords, lance heads, and shield bosses. Thus well-armed, the Celts swiftly dominated much of Europe. From Austria, they spread into Switzerland—La Tene—Germany, France, and Scandinavia. By 500 B.C.E. they had moved into Spain and Britain, where they thrived for centuries before falling to the Romans.

The whole [Celtic] race . . . is madly fond of war, high-spirited, quick to battle, . . . even if they have nothing on their side but their own strength and courage.

GREEK GEOGRAPHER STRABO

	POLITICS & POWER	GEOGRAPHY & ENVIRONMENT	CULTURE & RELIGION
THE AMERICAS	**ca 800 The Chavín culture of Peru** reaches a high point as a religious center and as market center in the long-distance-trade network developing in the Andes.	**ca 800-700 The people on the coast of the Bering Strait** shift their entire existence to the sea: whale, other mammals, and fish become their main source of food.	**ca 800 The temple at Chavín** is U-shaped and contains 1,600 feet of internal drainage and ventilation ducts. It faces the rising sun on the east.
EUROPE	**800 The Celts**, settled in central Europe, spread westward from the region near Hall-statt, Austria, and move into England. **800 Independent city-states** develop in Greece; foremost among them are Sparta and Athens. **753 The city of Rome** is founded by Romulus and Remus on seven hills in central Italy. **750 Scythian horsemen** sweep in from the east, moving into the Crimea and the Dnieper and Danube River regions.	**ca 800 The Greeks** found colonies around the Mediterranean and Aegean coast.	**ca 800 The Celts** worship at springs and under oak trees. Druid priests hold rites. **ca 800 The Scythians** lead only partially settled lives as herders, but amass vast riches as raiders. They fashion graceful gold objects and jewelry and bury their dead in *kurgans*—large mounds of earth. Kings' burials are accompanied by golden treasures, retainers, and horses to guide them into the next life. **ca 800 Apollo** is worshiped at Delphi in Greece. **776 The first Olympic Games** are recorded at Olympia.
MIDDLE EAST & AFRICA	**ca 800 The Assyrian Empire** encompasses Mesopotamia and conquers Syria and parts of Anatolia. **750 The Phoenician colony of Carthage** in North Africa develops into an independent hub of trade for the western Mediterranean. **750 The Nubian kingdom of Kush** conquers Egypt and rules for nearly 100 years. **721 After a siege of three years,** Israel falls to the Assyrians. Many Hebrews are resettled in other parts of the empire, replaced by ancestors of the Samaritans.	**745 Assyrian king Tiglath-Pileser III** begins the policy of exchanging part of the population of one newly annexed land for that of another. Agricultural development is a primary Assyrian aim. New unwalled farming settlements are founded all over the empire. **ca 740 Babylonians** begin recording celestial phenomena, river levels, commodity prices, and historical events.	**ca 800 At the Nubian capital of Napata,** a large temple complex is built in honor of Amun Re, the same god revered by the Egyptians. Other Nubian cities build pyramids and temples in Egyptian style. **ca 745 Assyrians** standardize Aramaic, written alphabetically with pen and ink, as the language of imperial administration. They also use Assyro-Babylonian, written in syllabic cuneiform on clay.
ASIA & OCEANIA	**771 Nomads attack the Zhou,** forcing them to move their capital east to Luoyang, and dividing China into Eastern Zhou and Western Zhou kingdoms.		**ca 800 Indian teachers** consolidate Aryan beliefs into scriptures called the Upanishads, which form the basis of Hinduism. **ca 800 Chinese poems** from this period are later compiled in the *Book of Songs*.

SCIENCE & TECHNOLOGY

ca 800-700 The coastal people of the Bering Strait develop the toggling harpoon to hunt marine life. They also invent kayaks and hide boats to enable them to harvest marine life.

ca 800 Artisans at Chavín combine llama and alpaca hair with cotton fibers to produce durable fabrics and weave them into special designs.

ca 800 The Celts of the Hallstatt region adopt iron metallurgy and help spread it throughout Europe. Weapons and agricultural tools, such as sickles and plows, hammers, anvils, roasting spits, and axes come in use.

ca 800 Nubians forge iron tools and weapons; the iron industry leads to deforestation.

ca 725 Assyrians begin to chart the heavens in a scientific way. By about 720 they invent the martingale and effective bow cavalry.

PEOPLE & SOCIETY

ca 800-700 The coastal people of the Bering Strait develop teamwork for communal whale hunts.

ca 800 The city of Sparta, situated on the Peloponnesus, extends its influence over the entire peninsula, obligating neighboring people to provide agricultural labor. To keep people subjugated, the Spartans develop a highly trained military force—prizing, above all, discipline and an austere lifestyle. Spartan boys enter a rigorous military school at age seven; at age 20, they begin active military service and remain in service until retirement.

Blue faience figurine of Nubian woman and child, from the third millennium B.C.E.

THE NUBIAN KINGDOM OF AFRICA

Ancient Nubia—the area between the first and fifth cataract of the Nile that is today part of Egypt and Sudan—has a history as long as ancient Egypt. Between 3000 B.C.E. and 500 C.E., Nubia was known variously under the names of Yam, Kush, Napata, Meroe, and Ethiopia. Prosperous as a result of agriculture and cattle herding, the Nubians were renowned for their archery skills and often served in the Egyptian armies as mercenaries. In trade they functioned as middlemen, distributing the riches of Africa as far north as Crete, offering much coveted African gold, ebony, ivory, exotic animals, and animal skins.

During Egypt's Middle Kingdom period, various pharaohs pushed into Lower Nubia to the second cataract. Around 1450 B.C.E. Egypt again invaded the kingdom of Kush up to the fourth cataract, and Nubian princes were sent to the court in Egypt, where they adopted Egyptian mores. In the eighth century B.C.E., with Egypt in the throes of anarchy, turnabout was fair play: The Kushite King Piye marched downriver and conquered Egypt. He established a dynasty that would rule Egypt for nearly a hundred years, and the combined kingdom became the largest country in Africa.

In 664 B.C.E. the Assyrians, then the Persians, and finally the Greeks of Alexander the Great and the Romans occupied Egypt. Independent Nubia continued on, building pyramids, smelting iron, and developing an alphabet that has not yet been deciphered.

Map showing the comparative extents of the Egyptian and Nubian kingdoms at their respective heights

POLITICS & POWER	GEOGRAPHY & ENVIRONMENT	CULTURE & RELIGION
THE AMERICAS		
ca 700 Reliefs at Monte Albán in Oaxaca, Mexico, show far-ranging Olmec influence.	**ca 700 Despite the thin, fertile layer of earth on top of limestone,** the Maya manage to develop settled agriculture in the Yucatán Peninsula.	**ca 700 Olmec reliefs** include short hiero-glyphs that show the presence of the earliest written language in Mesoamerica.
ca 700 Maya begin to organize into 50 sepa-rate religious-political entities in the diffuse civilizational network they are known for.		
EUROPE		
ca 700 Athens and other Greek city-states become centers of learning. Maritime trade brings riches to Athens.	**ca 700 Mediterranean wine,** and the equipment needed to serve and drink it, is imported into central Europe.	**ca 700 Greek epic poet Hesiod** writes about farm life in *Works and Days,* describing the planting of barley, wheat, legumes, grapes, olives, and figs and the raising of horses, cat-tle, goats, sheep, and pigs.
ca 700 Etruscans in northern Italy become prosperous because of their mineral wealth, trading with Egypt, Syria, Asia Minor, and Greece.		
616 The Etruscan Tarquinus Priscus becomes king of Rome.		
MIDDLE EAST & AFRICA		
ca 700 Mounted horsemen—Cimmerians and Scythians—sweep into the Middle East. Assyrian King Sargon II is killed in battle.	**ca 700 Bantu-speaking hunters, fishers, and farmers** expand from Cameroonian grasslands into equatorial forests and farther eastward.	**ca 620 Zarathustra**, of an aristocratic Persian family, leaves his home in search of a way to improve religious practices that are heavy on sacrifice and ritual. Inspired by visions, he synthesizes his message of one supreme god and six lesser ones and recommends moder-ation in all things and a moral way of life.
664 Assyrians drive the Nubians out of Egypt and install Necho I. Nubians move their capi-tal from Napata south to Meroe.		
647 Assyrian King Ashurbanipal vanquishes the Elamites in southwestern Iran.		**605 Babylonian god Marduk** absorbs the attributes of all the other gods; worship of Marduk alone begins, possibly because of the Jewish influence in Babylon. At the New Year priests slap Babylonian kings across the face to remind them of their place with respect to Marduk.
625-605 A new Babylonian empire—the Chal-daean empire—emerges under Nabopolasser.		
614-609 The Assyrian Empire is annihilated by the combined forces of King Nabopolasser of Babylon and King Cyaxetes of Media.		
ASIA & OCEANIA		
ca 700 With the decline of the Zhou dynasty, China is torn by a power struggle between rival semi-autonomous states in what becomes known as the Spring and Autumn states.		

SCIENCE & TECHNOLOGY	PEOPLE & SOCIETY

ca 700 The Chavín of Peru appear to be the first Americans to develop three-dimensional metal objects through the art of soldering.

ca 700 Timber-reinforced stone and earth ramparts are built around villages in ever increasing numbers.

ca 700 Iron slashing swords become more common.

ca 700 The use of iron in England is established.

ca 645 Assyrian king Sennacherib has hanging gardens built at Nineveh, river-sized aqueducts for agriculture constructed, and public parks created. Assyrians invent the so-called Archimedes screw for irrigation, introduce cotton from India, devise glazed brick and pottery, and invent the two-power magnifying glass.

ca 700 Assyria's king Sargon II is kept informed by a spy system, employing agents trained in foreign languages and also native informants.

668-625 Assyrian king Ashurbanipal, the first king to be taught to write, collects copies of all the known scientific, historical, religious, and literary works into a library of tens of thousands of tablets.

ETRUSCANS: LOVERS OF LIFE

Settled in hilltop agricultural villages between the Arno and Tiber Rivers of Italy, the Etruscans rose to swift prominence during the first millennium B.C.E. The mineral wealth of the area—copper, tin, and iron—allowed for lively trade with neighbors and the seafaring Phoenicians. By the eighth century B.C.E. the villages grew into city-states with a stratified society.

The Greeks established colonies near the Etruscan realm and heavily influenced Etruscan arts and culture. Trade brought in luxury goods from Egypt, Syria, Anatolia, and Greece, while Etruscan influence spread north and south. In 616 Lucius Tarquinius Priscus became ruler of Rome. He established a dynasty that transformed Rome into an urban center, constructing monumental buildings, paving the forum, and establishing a sewer system. In 509 B.C.E. the Romans deposed the last Etruscan ruler and formed a republic, and Etruria became part of Rome.

Etruscan sarcophagus

	POLITICS & POWER	GEOGRAPHY & ENVIRONMENT	CULTURE & RELIGION

THE AMERICAS

ca 600 The Arctic Dorset people construct housing of stone and driftwood and semi-subterranean sod shelters along the Hudson Strait of Canada.

600-500 Olmec culture declines.

600-500 Native people in Canada begin farming and form villages.

The hare, spiritual talisman of the Dorset Inuit

EUROPE

594 Aristocratic leader Solon of Athens, Greece, introduces reforms that allow all free citizens to participate in government. He is called "the father of democracy."

509 The Romans drive the Etruscans out of Rome and establish the Roman Republic. In a move to finish off Etruria, they conquer Etruscan cities one by one.

508 Cleisthenes of Athens invents gerrymandering.

ca 600 Herding is more important than farming among people in Ireland and northern Britain.

ca 600 People in Denmark cast bronze *lures,* six-foot-long instruments modeled on horns, which can play a range of notes.

ca 600 The Princess of Vix, a Celtic woman, is buried in France with a wagon, a huge Greek imported bronze drinking vessel, and gold jewelry.

525-456 Aeschylus writes the *Oresteia,* the earliest dramatic poems using a Greek chorus.

MIDDLE EAST & AFRICA

587 Nebuchadrezzar II sacks the kingdom of Judah. Many people are carried off to Babylon as captives.

558-529 Cyrus the Great rules Elam and Persia and conquers Media, Asia Minor, and Babylon. The Jews are permitted to return to Jerusalem; some do, but many remain in Babylon. Cyrus's son Cambyses gains Egypt.

545 Wealthy Croesus of Lydia in Anatolia loses his kingdom to the Persian army.

522 Darius I usurps rule in Persia.

ca 600 Phoenician sailors in the employ of Pharaoh Necho II circumnavigate Africa. They also found a Phoenician colony at Mogador/Essaouira, on the Atlantic coast of what is now Morocco.

ca 550 Cyrus the Great extends the Persian Royal Road and the courier system to Susa and Sardis, with lodging posts along the way for a relay of horses and riders. He founds Persepolis, a ceremonial center of palaces, monumental gateways, and colonnaded halls.

587 Solomon's temple in Jerusalem is destroyed by Nebechadrezzar II. In 520 the Jews rebuild the temple.

560 King Croesus of Lydia in Anatolia mints the first gold and silver coins from ores mined near the Pactolus River.

522 Darius I introduces Mazdaism to the Persian empire.

ASIA & OCEANIA

ca 600 In the wars of expansion on the Indian subcontinent, several small kingdoms vie for power, but none achieves domination over the others.

520 Parts of northwestern India are conquered by Persia.

ca 600 Chinese philosopher Lao Zi, the founder of Daoism, which encourages a simple life in tune with nature, is born.

560 Kong Fuzi, known in the West as Confucius, is born in the region of Shantong in northeastern China.

ca 560 Prince Siddhartha Gautama is born in the foothills of the Himalayas; he is later known as the Buddha and introduces Buddhism.

540-468 Mahavira, the founder of Jainism in India, lives a life of asceticism and teaches a doctrine of nonviolence toward other living beings and of detachment from the world.

SCIENCE & TECHNOLOGY	PEOPLE & SOCIETY

ca 600 The Dorset people invent a form of illumination by lighting moss wicks set in whale blubber.

Austronesian mariners established the Lapita exchange network, which spread culture and farming skills throughout the South Pacific.

EXPLORERS OF OCEANIA

Humans migrated to the land-mass of Australia and New Guinea and nearby islands around 60,000 B.C.E., arriving from Southeast Asia in simple boats outfitted

581-497 Pythagoras, Greek philosopher and mathematician, develops basic principles of mathematics and astronomy and formulates his theorem to calculate the area of a right triangle: The square of the length of the hypotenuse of a right triangle equals the sum of the squares of the length of the other two sides.

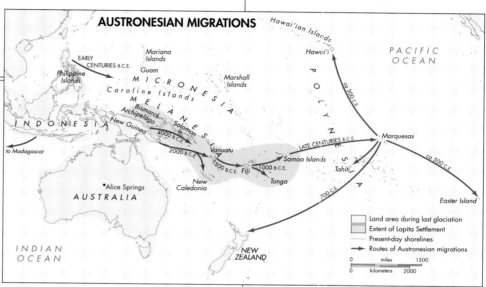

ca 600 The Persians develop an irrigation system of subterranean aqueducts called *qanats.* These channels carry water from the mountains to the desert with a minimum of evaporation.

587 Nebuchadrezzar II, who restores Babylon to greatness, is infamous for his conquest of Judah and the destruction of Jerusalem. He defeats the Assyrians and Egyptians at Carchemish and destroys the Phoenician city-states. After his victories, he sets to enlarge his city. He surrounds Babylon with fortified walls, rebuilds a temple to the god Marduk, and adds several hundred more temples and palaces. He may have constructed the famous hanging gardens of Babylon, considered one of the wonders of the ancient world, in imitation of the gardens in Nineveh.

with sails. Around 8000 B.C.E., rising seas caused by a warming climate separated Australia and New Guinea.

Shortly thereafter, Austronesian seafarers, speaking languages with roots in Malayan, Indonesian, Filipino, Polynesian, and Malagasy, began exploring and trading along the northern coast of New Guinea, introducing the farming of root crops such as yams and taro and the husbanding of pigs and chickens. They sailed the open ocean in outrigger canoes following slight cues such as wind direction, cloud formation, the stars, or the flight of a bird to find the next habitable island. In succeeding waves of discovery, they settled on the Solomon Islands by 4000 B.C.E., Vanuatu in 2000 B.C.E., Fiji in 1500 B.C.E., Tonga and Samoa before 1000 B.C.E., Hawaii about 300 C.E., and finally Easter Island in 500 C.E. and New Zealand in 700 C.E. Other groups of Austronesians explored Micronesia and Madagascar, introducing crops and farming at each new settlement.

There is no guilt greater than to sanction ambition, no calamity greater than to be discontented with one's lot, no fault greater than the wish to be getting.

LAO ZI

560-483 Buddha, the son of a princely family, leaves his wife and children to live as a hermit and to seek spiritual fulfillment. After wandering through the Ganges Valley, begging for food and living a life of extreme asceticism, he reaches enlightenment. He begins to preach the Four Noble Truths, explaining that life involves suffering; desire causes suffering; elimination of desire ends suffering; and a balanced, moral life eliminates desire. Meditation and disciplined self-control will eventually lead to personal salvation and end the cycle of reincarnation so that a person can reach nirvana. His message catches on among the common people but is also supported by kings, and it spreads rapidly.

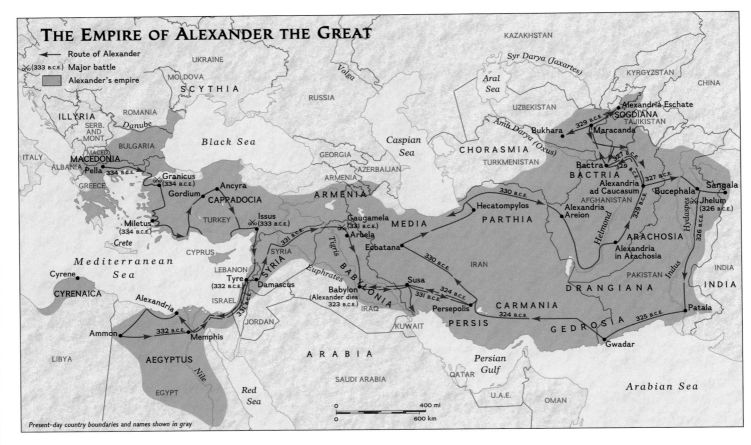

THE EMPIRE OF ALEXANDER THE GREAT

← Route of Alexander
✕ (333 B.C.E.) Major battle
▨ Alexander's empire

Present-day country boundaries and names shown in gray

BEGINNING AROUND 500 B.C.E., CIVILIZAtions arose that had such lasting power and influence they were recognized in later times as classical. Much as Greek and Roman civilization influenced later European cultures, classical civilizations in Persia, Africa, India, China, and Mesoamerica had an enduring cultural impact on those areas. Vast empires were forged by brilliant conquerors and held together by shrewd administrators. Travel and commerce increased greatly in scope as roads were built across continents and navigation improved. Merchants, missionaries, and philosophers spread goods and ideas that gave far-flung provinces a common culture. So durable and expansive were these classical societies that they fostered beliefs, customs, and laws that remain in force today.

Persian Precedents

The dawn of the classical age is often associated with the flowering of Greek civilization. But before Greeks won glory, they had to reckon with the Persians, who ruled the greatest empire the world had yet seen,

extending from the Indus River to the Nile and northward to the Black Sea. Much of that was conquered by Cyrus the Great, who took control of what is now Iran around 550 B.C.E. and led his rugged Persian troops against foreigners who could not match their skills on horseback. The Achaemenid Empire won by Cyrus and his son Cambyses was consolidated by Darius, who divided his realm into provinces, or satrapies, and appointed men he trusted to govern them. He set tax levies for each province and used the income to build a new capital at Persepolis and a royal road extending to Ephesus on the Aegean Sea, more than 1,500 miles away. That road facilitated trade and tax collection, as did coins Darius issued. Later emperors here and elsewhere would adopt similar measures to govern vast areas.

Around 500 B.C.E., Greeks living on the east coast of the Aegean rebelled against Darius and won support from Greeks elsewhere. Avid seafarers, the Greeks were divided politically into many city-states, including such powerhouses as Athens and Sparta on the Greek mainland and distant colonies around the Aegean, the Mediterranean, and the Black Sea. Greeks sometimes fought each other and vied commercially in marketplaces or athletically at festivals such as the Olympic Games. Thanks to their easily mastered phonetic alphabet, many Greeks were literate and shared the values extolled in epics attributed to Homer. The Homeric hero Odysseus was a cunning warrior guided safely home after the siege of Troy by the goddess Athena, who like other Greek deities shared human attributes and concerns.

Athena was the patron deity of Athens, which led the fight against Darius and repulsed Persian troops at the Battle of Marathon in 490 B.C.E. According to legend, a messenger ran 26 miles from Marathon to Athens to proclaim victory before dropping dead. Darius's son and heir, Xerxes, later renewed the conflict. The Greeks were badly outnumbered, but Persian commanders had trouble supplying and coordinating their diverse forces, which came from many countries. In 480 the Greeks shattered a huge but unwieldy Persian fleet at Salamis and went on to defeat the Persian army at Plataea a year later. This marked the end of Persian expansion and the dawn of a golden age for Greece.

Classical Greece

Greek civilization reached its height in Athens after the Persian Wars. "Athens is the school of Greece," boasted the Athenian leader Pericles. Among the geniuses who flourished there were the philosophers Socrates and Plato; the playwrights Sophocles, Aeschylus, and Euripides; the historian Thucydides; the physician Hippocrates; and the sculptor Phidias, whose work adorned the Parthenon, a temple overlooking the city. This burst of creativity coincided with the rise of democracy in Athens. Slaves had no rights, and female citizens were largely confined to separate women's quarters at home. But by allowing male citizens to elect their leaders, Athens set a democratic standard not soon surpassed.

Athenians had joined with Spartans to defeat the Persians, but afterward the two leading city-states in Greece became bitter rivals. In Sparta, all men lived and trained together until they were 30. That made them formidable foes of the Athenians in the Peloponnesian War, an epic conflict that left both the victorious Spartan alliance and their Athenian-led foes weaker. Around 340 B.C.E. Greece fell to King Philip

II of Macedon, who swept down from the north with a formidable army. Macedonians had long traded with the Greeks and had adopted their language and culture. Philip's son, Alexander, was schooled in Greek literature and claimed descent from Achilles, hero of Homer's Iliad. Having inherited his father's army, he set out to make the Persian Empire his own.

Alexander struck at the right time. Rebellions in Egypt and other provinces had weakened the Persians. They could still muster a huge army, but the Macedonians were better organized and more loyal to their leader, who entered battle with them and was wounded several times. Within a decade, Alexander had conquered the Persians and all they possessed, from Egypt to the Indus River. He died in 323 B.C.E. at 33, a legendary figure of Homeric proportions. Afterward, Alexander's empire was divided among his generals, who founded their own dynasties. Greece and Macedon were left to Antigonus; Egypt was left to Ptolemy; and the remainder was given to Seleucus, who became the new Persian emperor. Greeks spread throughout the lands conquered by Alexander, disseminating their language and culture. Ptolemy built a new capital in Egypt at Alexandria (one of many cities dedicated to Alexander). With its great library and museum, the city attracted scholars from various lands and embodied the cosmopolitan spirit of the larger Greek world.

Greek artists celebrated the human form in sculptures like this one portraying a discus thrower, whose skills were tested both in warfare and in athletic contests such as the Olympic Games.

Asian Empires

India was the one land Alexander tried and failed to conquer. After crossing the Indus River, he and his war-weary troops were bogged down by monsoon rains and turned back. But his campaign had a profound impact on India,

He who exercises government by means of his virtue may be compared to the north polar star, which keeps its place, while all the stars turn toward it.

CONFUCIUS

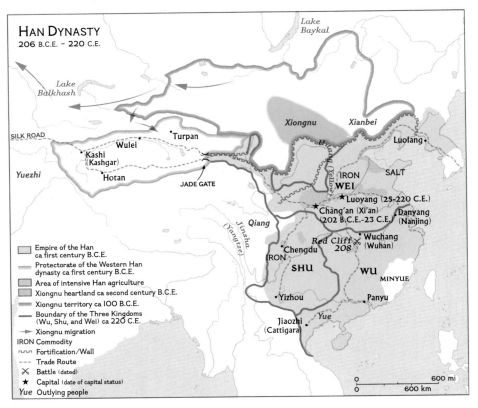

HAN DYNASTY
206 B.C.E. – 220 C.E.

Lake Baykal

Lake Balkhash

SILK ROAD

Kashi (Kashgar)

Wulei

Turpan

Hotan

JADE GATE

Yuezhi

Xiongnu

Xianbei

Luolang

IRON

SALT

WEI

Luoyang (25-220 C.E.)

Chang'an (Xi'an)
(202 B.C.E.-23 C.E.)

Danyang (Nanjing)

Qiang

Jinsha (Yangtze)

Red Cliff
208

Wuchang (Wuhan)

Chengdu

IRON

SHU

WU

MINYUE

Yizhou

Panyu

Jiaozhi (Cattigara)

Yue

Empire of the Han ca first century B.C.E.

Protectorate of the Western Han dynasty ca first century B.C.E.

Area of intensive Han agriculture

Xiongnu heartland ca second century B.C.E.

Xiongnu territory ca 100 B.C.E.

Boundary of the Three Kingdoms (Wu, Shu, and Wei) ca 220 C.E.

Xiongnu migration

IRON Commodity

Fortification/Wall

Trade Route

Battle (dated)

Capital (date of capital status)

Yue Outlying people

600 mi
600 km

Rulers of China's Han dynasty expanded their domain by seizing territory from the Xiongnu to their north and bringing other groups in Central Asia under their protection. In the first century C.E., the capital moved from Chang'an to Luoyang, where the Han remained in power with the help of officials guided by the teachings of the philosopher Confucius, opposite, until the empire fractured into competing kingdoms in the third century.

which was divided into many kingdoms. Before withdrawing, Alexander shattered kingdoms in the Indus Valley, creating a power vacuum that was filled by a conqueror named Chandragupta Maurya, who was from Maghada, along the Ganges River. By 300 B.C.E. he had forged an empire that reached from the Ganges to the Indus. The Mauryan dynasty he founded reached its peak under his grandson Ashoka, who conquered much of southern India. Ashoka then renounced warfare and worked to consolidate his realm by building roads that were used by officials and merchants.

Ashoka's most far-reaching act was to embrace Buddhism, a religious philosophy inspired by the Indian holy man Siddhartha Gautama, who died around 480 B.C.E. Known to followers as the Buddha, or Enlightened One, he renounced worldly desires, lived moderately, and meditated intently until he entered nirvana, a perfect state of enlightenment that released him spiritually from all striving and suffering. Buddhism taught that one's capacity to achieve enlightenment had nothing to do with one's place in society. For that reason, it won many adherents among Indian merchants, considered socially and spiritually inferior to the priests and warriors who had long dominated Aryan India. During and after Ashoka's reign, traveling Buddhist merchants served as missionaries and spread their faith from India to Tibet, Southeast Asia, and China.

The Mauryan Empire fractured into competing kingdoms soon after Ashoka's death in 232 B.C.E. Not until the fourth century C.E. did another ruler from Maghada, known as Chandra Gupta in honor of Chandragupta Maurya, begin reuniting India. The Gupta Empire that he and his successors forged was not as large and cohesive as the Mauryan Empire, but trade and crafts such as weaving flourished, as did science and the arts. By this time, India's dominant faith was Hinduism, whose followers honored many gods and goddesses and believed in reincarnation. Whether one's soul rose to a higher level in the next life or descended to a lower state depended on one's actions. A classic Hindu text called the *Bhagavad Gita* taught that people at all levels of society, from exalted princes and warriors to those of low caste, would be rewarded in the next life if they lived honorably and fulfilled the duties of their caste.

In China, Confucianism came to influence rulers and officials and provided a moral framework for society. The Chinese philosopher Kong Fuzi, or Confucius, who died in 479 B.C.E., had little impact in his own time. China was descending into a violent era called the period of Warring States, and a teacher who advised rulers to rely more on moral authority than on armed force seemed irrelevant. But his principles, set down in writing by his disciples, eventually became the dominant social and political philosophy in China

Roman soldiers like those portrayed below fought with great discipline and dedication, often defeating numerically superior opponents. The Roman Empire resulting from their conquests reached its greatest extent under the Emperor Trajan, stretching from Mesopotamia to Britain, on map opposite. As the empire expanded, ambitious generals such as Julius Caesar and his nephew Augustus Caesar assumed dictatorial powers and did away with the old Roman Republic and its defenders, including the orator Cicero, executed in 43 B.C.E.

and much of East Asia. Other Chinese thinkers responded to strife and disorder with competing philosophies. Daoists urged people to disengage from worldly ambitions and conflicts and seek harmony with nature. Legalists believed that order could be achieved only through strict laws and harsh punishments imposed by rulers whose authority was absolute. For Confucians, the family was the foundation of society, but for Legalists the state was all important.

Legalism guided the rulers of Qin, the strongest of the Warring States. In 221 B.C.E. China was unified by a conqueror from that state known as Qin Shihuang-di (First Emperor of Qin). As emperor, he was denounced by Confucians and Daoists for ruling with an iron hand, and he executed his critics. He made heavy demands on the populace, drafting millions of laborers for public projects, including work on the defensive barrier that became the Great Wall of China. But like Darius of Persia and other resourceful rulers of the classical age, he imposed order on his vast realm by building roads, standardizing laws,

coinage, weights, and measures, and instituting a common Chinese script that allowed people belonging to many different language groups within the empire to communicate in writing, which helped unify China culturally. At his death in 210, he was buried in an immense tomb surrounded by the bodies of slaves sacrificed for the occasion and thousands of lifelike soldiers, molded of clay with great artistry. Not long after he died, rebellions broke out among the populace, and the government collapsed.

The fall of the short-lived Qin dynasty served as a lesson for the Han dynasty that followed. Han emperors governed China with the help of Confucian officials who believed in leading by moral example. "Approach your duties with reverence and be trustworthy," Confucius advised rulers; "employ the labor of the common people only in the right seasons." Emperors did not always follow that advice. Many were actually Legalists but endorsed Confucian ideals to legitimize and prolong their rule. One such ideal was the mandate of heaven, the belief that rulers were blessed by heaven

Law stands mute in the midst of arms.
CICERO

so long as they governed wisely and justly. The dynasty's strongest emperor was Han Wudi, who reigned around 100 B.C.E. Under him, Han armies advanced deep into Central Asia, established outposts on the Korean Peninsula, and drove south into Vietnam. As a Legalist, he asserted his authority by conscripting huge numbers of troops and laborers to strengthen the empire, but he allowed Confucianism to prevail among officials educated in the imperial university he created.

The Han capital at Chang'an was the terminus of the Silk Road, which extended to the eastern Mediterranean. That road, which was actually a network of trade routes, brought Chinese silks and other goods to Roman markets and carried ideas and beliefs to and from China. Buddhism came to China as early as the first century C.E. and gained followers as the Han dynasty weakened and ultimately collapsed. One recurring problem Han rulers faced was social strife between wealthy landowners and poor farmers or peasants. Early in the 1st century C.E., a reformer named Wang Mang redistributed land from the wealthy to the poor, but he and the young emperor he advised were overthrown as a result, and later Han rulers had to contend with peasant rebellions.

In the early 3rd century C.E., the Han dynasty collapsed, and China once again fractured into rival kingdoms. Confucianism lost appeal, and many people turned to Buddhism or Daoism when China was assailed by epidemic diseases and invaders from central Asia. No walls could fend off such far-reaching agents of destruction and change. They affected Europe as well and contributed to the decline of the Roman Empire and the spread of Christianity.

The Roman World

Rome expanded from a small Italian city-state to a world power not just by conquering other societies but by assimilating them. Romans granted many of those they subdued citizenship and won their coopera-

THE ROMAN EMPIRE

Greatest extent at the time of Trajan, 117 C.E.

0   400 mi
0   400 km

tion and loyalty, freeing Roman troops to seize more territory or crush rebellions. Roman citizenship gave people legal protection, including the right to confront their accusers in court and maintain their innocence until proven guilty. But it did not give them democratic rights, for Rome was never a democracy. After throwing off Etruscan rule in 509 B.C.E., Romans organized themselves as a republic with a dominant Senate for patricians, or aristocrats, and a subordinate assembly for plebeians, or commoners. Reforms in this system increased the political power of plebeians, but social tensions persisted and gradually undermined the republic.

The political system functioned well enough while Roman power was confined to Italy but came under severe stress after Rome conquered Carthage, an expansive Phoenician city-state on the North African coast. After withstanding an invasion by the Carthaginian general Hannibal, Romans struck back and leveled Carthage in 146 B.C.E. Roman generals gained great power and prestige from such triumphs abroad and began intervening in domestic political disputes between wealthy landowners employing slaves seized in Roman conquests and dispossessed farmers who demanded land reform.

The most imposing of those generals was Julius Caesar, who conquered the Celts in Gaul, in what is now France, and returned to Rome to seize power in

49 B.C.E.. As dictator, he took land from the wealthy and gave it to veterans loyal to him. Senators angered by his policies and his refusal to yield power assassinated him, hoping to restore the republic. Instead, they unleashed a tumultuous civil war in which they were crushed by Caesar's nephew Octavian, who then clashed with his co-ruler, Mark Antony. By defeating Antony and his ally, Queen Cleopatra of Egypt, the last ruler of the Ptolemy dynasty, Octavian won firm control of the Mediterranean world. He took the title Augustus Caesar and reigned supreme as emperor.

Augustus and later Roman emperors were cult figures, worshiped at shrines. Most people under their authority recognized many gods and tolerated that imperial cult. Jews rejected other gods, however, and some hoped for a messiah, or savior, who would end Roman rule and restore the kingdom of Israel. Around 30 C.E., a Jewish visionary named Jesus who promised to restore God's kingdom on earth was condemned and crucified by Roman authorities who feared he might incite rebellion. His disciples called him Christ, meaning "anointed one," or messiah, and said that he rose from the grave and joined God in heaven. Christianity was inspired mainly by Jewish scriptures, which became part of the Christian Bible, but it was also influenced by Zoroastrianism, which originated in Persia and taught that righteous souls would avoid the torments of hell and enter paradise.

Christians faced persecution as Roman power expanded under such strong-willed emperors as Vespasian, who sacked Jerusalem in 70 C.E. to end a rebellion there; and Trajan, who challenged defiant Parthians in the east and extended the Roman Empire to Mesopotamia before he died in 117. Later emperors consolidated those gains by expanding the network of Roman roads; building defensive barriers such as Hadrian's Wall in Britain; and founding or expanding provincial cities like Lyon in Gaul, which grew to resemble Rome, with fountains and baths fed by aqueducts, and coliseums or circuses to entertain the masses. The poet Juvenal scoffed that Romans who once took an active part in government now cared only for "bread and circuses." But the attractions of urban life helped transform conquered people into grateful Roman citizens. In time, some leading provincial citizens like the North African Septimus Severus became Roman emperors.

During the third century, Roman power declined. Here as in China, epidemics introduced along trade routes ravaged the population and disrupted harvests and shipments of grain on which cities depended. As the empire weakened, Christianity grew stronger by offering those in distress charity and the promise of eternal life. In the early fourth century, the emperor Constantine embraced Christianity and moved his capital from Rome to Byzantium on the Bosporus Strait. Known as Constantinople, that new capital became the seat of the Byzantine Empire, which endured while the old Roman Empire to the west crumbled. In the fifth century, Huns advancing from Central Asia into eastern Europe displaced Vandals, Visigoths, and other nomadic peoples, who then overwhelmed Italy. Rome fell in 476, but the invaders absorbed and perpetuated many elements of Roman culture, including Christianity.

Global Advances

While empires rose and fell elsewhere, peoples of Oceania, sub-Saharan Africa, and the Americas formed durable and productive societies, laying the foundation for the emergence of strong states or kingdoms there during the classical or later eras. The most adventurous seafarers of classical times were Austronesians (ancestors of the Polynesians), who traveled eastward across the Pacific in outrigger canoes fitted with sails and colonized many Pacific islands, taking with them pigs and chickens and crops such as taro and breadfruit. In later times, their societies grew more complex, and chiefs arose who took control of entire islands or island chains.

Around the fourth century C.E., Malays from Indonesia sailed west across the Indian Ocean and colonized Madagascar, where they introduced bananas. From there, the cultivation of bananas spread to Africa and provided food surpluses that helped sustain populous societies in sub-Saharan Africa, some of which later developed into kingdoms. The societies that preceded those kingdoms were loosely knit politically and held together largely by kinship ties. But long before powerful states emerged in the region, cultures in areas rich in natural resources such as the Niger River Valley were growing more complex and accomplished. As early as 500 B.C.E., people of the Nok culture in what is now Nigeria were forging iron

The massive Pyramid of the Sun looms above the plaza at Teotihuacan, a great commercial and ceremonial center that dominated the Valley of Mexico and reached the height of its power around 500 C.E.

implements and sculpting highly expressive human and animal figures in clay. In North Africa, societies were absorbed by the Roman Empire and transformed by cultural forces such as Christianity that permeated the Roman world. By the fourth century C.E., Christianity was spreading southward from Roman-ruled Egypt to kingdoms in Nubia and Ethiopia.

In North America, the cultivation of corn spread northward from Mexico, allowing hunter-gatherers to begin settling down and building complex societies. In South America, the Moche of Peru carried out massive irrigation projects and disseminated their culture through warfare, trade, and artistry. In Mesoamerica, great cities arose such as Teotihuacan, located in the fertile Valley of Mexico not far from what is now Mexico City. Home to more than 150,000 people, this was one of the most impressive urban centers of classical times, with broad avenues, soaring temples, and bustling workshops.

Among those who traded with Teotihuacan were the Maya, who lived around the Yucatán Peninsula. They were divided like the Greeks into rival city-states such as Palenque and Tikal, which grew to a population of more than 50,000. Scribes recorded Maya history in writing, and astronomers charted the heavens and advised kings, who waged so-called star wars based on astrological readings of the planet Venus and other celestial bodies. The main purpose of Maya warfare was to seize captives, whose blood was then offered to the gods. Some captives were forced to compete in ball games, and the losers were beheaded. But the Maya were no more bloodthirsty than the Romans, who watched captives killed in arenas by gladiators or wild animals. People around the world believed that sacrifices were required if societies were to expand and prosper, and they expressed that belief in various religious and civic rituals, from the ball court in Tikal to the Colosseum in Rome. ■

THE WORLD AT A GLANCE

THE CLASSICAL AGE 500 B.C.E.-500 C.E

	500 B.C.E	400 B.C.E	300 B.C.E	200 B.C.E	100 B.C.E
THE AMERICAS	**ca 500** The Olmec of Mesoamerica move their capital to Tres Zapotes, on Mexico's Gulf Coast. **ca 500** The Paracas of coastal Peru refine traditions that continue in Andean regions for centuries. **ca 500** The Adena society constructs earthen burial mounds in portions of eastern North America.	**ca 400** Zapotec society develops, centered around the town of Monte Albán in the Oaxaca Valley in Mexico. **ca 400** Nascent agriculturalists settle the Valley of Mexico, from which will soon emerge the Teotihuacan culture. **ca 350** Origins of the Maya culture are evident in Nakbe, a town in modern-day Guatemala.	**ca 300** The Maya center of Tikal begins construction on a number of monumental pyramids. **ca 300** La Tolita culture of coastal Ecuador shows a skill in gold metallurgy unequalled elsewhere in the Americas. **ca 250** Moche society develops in northern coastal Peru at the same time as Nazca society develops in southern coastal Peru.	**ca 200** The Teotihuacan influence spreads to neighboring peoples. **ca 200** The Nazca lines begin to appear in the deserts of southern coastal Peru. **ca 200** Hohokam people of modern-day Arizona begin construction on a large system of canals. **ca 200** Hopewell society appears in river valleys of eastern North America.	**ca 100** Pyramid temples appear in the growing urban center of Teotihuacan as well as in other parts of Mesoamerica. **ca 100** Moche and Nazca cultures of coastal Peru begin building large ceremonial structures. **ca 100** The cocoa plant is cultivated in equatorial regions of South America.
EUROPE	**490** Greek forces halt a Persian incursion into the Greek peninsula. **ca 480** Celts of Europe begin migrating to Britain. **450** Rome's first standardized code of law is placed in the forum. **ca 440** Pericles presides over the Golden Age of Athens. **ca 430** Herodotus completes his *Histories*.	**ca 400** Hippocrates of Cos begins compiling the *Corpus Hippocraticum*. **ca 396** Rome draws Etruscan lands of northern Italy into its sphere. **ca 387** Plato founds the Academy, a school of philosophy in Athens. **338** Philip II of Macedon occupies all of Greece. **312** Rome builds its first major road, the Via Appia.	**ca 300** Rome is the dominant power on the Italian peninsula. **275** The Antigonid Empire rules Greece following Alexander the Great's death. **264** Rome holds its first gladiatorial games. **215** Rome wages both the Second Punic War and the First Macedonian War, after which it dominates the Mediterranean.	**ca 200** Romans invent concrete and go on to develop the first paved streets, as well as immense aqueducts and bridges. **146** Rome destroys Carthage and establishes the province of Africa. **133-123** The reforms of the Gracchus brothers are stifled by a corrupt Roman senate.	**88** The Social War in Italy ends with Sulla becoming dictator in Rome. **73** Spartacus leads an army of rebel slaves against Rome. **46** Having expanded Roman dominion into Gaul, Caesar becomes dictator-for-life of Rome. **27** Having defeated his rival, Marc Antony, Augustus becomes the first emperor of Rome.
MIDDLE EAST & AFRICA	**ca 500** Semitic people from Arabia migrate to Ethiopia and Eritrea and set up a trade network. **486** Achaemenid Emperor Darius I is succeeded by Xerxes, who prepares an invasion of Greece. **ca 450** Iron tool technology spreads across Africa. **445** Nehemiah rebuilds Jerusalem's walls and institutes social reforms.	**ca 400** The *qanat* system of underground canals is used to distribute water to arid regions of the Iranian plateau. **ca 350** Nok culture of Nigeria is among the earliest to refine the manufacture of iron in sub-Saharan Africa. **334** Alexander the Great invades Persia and carves out an empire stretching from Greece to northwestern India.	**ca 300** The Parthians of Central Asia turn increasingly to agriculture. **ca 300** Ptolemaic rule is established in Egypt; the Seleucid rule in the Middle East following Alexander's death. **280** The library of Alexandria is founded and draws scholars such as Euclid and Herophilus. **218** Hannibal marches against Rome.	**ca 171** Mithridates I takes the throne of the Parthian Empire and goes on to conquer much of the Seleucid Empire, including Mesopotamia. **ca 150** Ptolemaic mariners from Egypt learn from Indians and Arabs the art of sailing the Indian Ocean on its monsoon winds. **ca 150** Bactria imports a number of goods from southwest China.	**ca 100** The art of glassblowing is refined in Syria. **83** Rome incorporates Syria into its growing domain. **30** The Ptolemaic dynasty in Egypt ends with the suicide of Cleopatra and Marc Antony. **ca 10** The oldest extant Hebrew documents, the Dead Sea Scrolls, are produced in Judaea.
ASIA & OCEANIA	**ca 500** The northeastern Indian state of Maghada emerges as a regional power. **ca 500** Jainism and Buddhism begin their spread through northern India. **ca 450** Confucianism gains momentum in scholarly circles in China. **403** The dissolution of the Zhou dynasty in China brings about the period of Warring States.	**ca 390** Legalism, emphasizing the military and agriculture, appears in China. **ca 380** Walls are built by various states in northern China to repel nomadic tribes. **321** Chandragupta Maurya pushes the borders of his kingdom into northwestern India, following the invasions of Alexander the Great.	**ca 300** Wet rice cultivation begins in Japan. **260** Ashoka takes the reins of the Mauryan Empire in India, expanding its borders and sponsoring the spread of Buddhism. **221** King Zheng of the Qin state defeats rival states and becomes emperor of unified China. **206** The Han dynasty is established in China.	**ca 200** The Xiongnu people of Central Asia form a wide-ranging federation. **ca 185** The Mauryan Empire of India loses central authority. **ca 150** Austronesians arrive on Tahiti and the Marquesas Islands. **141** Han Wudi begins a 54-year-long reign in China, during which he expands Chinese influence abroad.	**ca 100** Buddhism spreads into Central Asia along the Silk Road. **ca 100** Historian Sima Qian writes *Records of the Historian,* a history of China. **ca 100** The use of negative numbers becomes standard for Chinese mathematicians. **ca 100** Ice is used in China for refrigeration.

1 C.E-100 C.E	100 C.E	200 C.E	300 C.E	400-500 C.E
ca 1 Inhabitants of the Amazon rain forest utilize a highly fertile soil called *terra preta* for farming. **ca 1** The use of houses and the domestication of certain vegetables spreads to southwestern North America. **ca 50** The population of Teotihuacan grows three times larger while that of the rest of Mexico decreases sharply.	**ca 100** Moche culture of coastal Peru extends influence over neighboring peoples, bringing advanced agricultural and metalworking techniques. **ca 100** Anasazi people settle into the four corners region of southwestern North America. **ca 100** The Adena of eastern North America dwindle, perhaps assimilating with contemporaneous Hopewell people.	**ca 200** Stone-walled compounds begin to replace mud-brick buildings of Teotihuacan. **ca 250** Maya societies of the Yucatán Peninsula enter into what is considered their Classic period, characterized by divine kings ruling over powerful city-states.	**ca 300** Maya societies formulate a system of writing, develop an incredibly accurate calendar based on movement of the celestial bodies, and make advancements in architecture and agriculture.	**ca 400** Hopewell culture of eastern North America gradually dissipates into a number of more loosely organized groups. **ca 450** Zapotec culture and Teotihuacan culture approach their zenith with a trade network extending throughout Mesoamerica. **ca 450** The Huaca del Sol, the largest adobe structure in the Americas, is built by the Moche.
ca 60 Roman forces defeat celtic Queen Boudicca, stripping women in this society of all political status. **69** The "year of the four emperors" ends with Vespasian establishing the Flavian dynasty. He begins construction on the Colosseum shortly afterwards. **79** Mount. Vesuvius erupts, burying Pompeii.	**ca 100** Slaves account for a third of the Roman Empire's population. **101** Trajan extends the boundaries of the Roman Empire into Dacia. **ca 150** Goths arrive on the Danubian frontier of the Roman Empire. **180** The population of the Roman Empire declines sharply after a long smallpox epidemic.	**235-284** Twenty-six claimants to the imperial throne of Rome successively attempt to seize power. **259** A first wave of barbarian incursions hits the Roman Empire. **286** Diocletian splits the Roman Empire into two administrative units, the eastern and western.	**303** Diocletian orders four edicts of nontoleration against Christianity. **312** Constantine I takes Rome from the last pagan emperor and grants toleration of all religions. **376** The Huns arrive on the Danubian frontier of the Roman Empire. **378** Roman forces are annihilated by Goths at the Battle of Adrianople.	**406** Vandals invade Gaul, then move on through Spain to North Africa. **410** Visigoth forces sack Rome, then move on to Spain. **441** Attila the Hun launches a massive attack on the deteriorating Roman Empire. **476** The final western Roman Emperor is deposed by German chieftain Odoacer.
ca 30 Jesus of Nazareth is crucified by Roman authorities suspicious of his "kingdom of God." **ca 50** The kingdom of Axum is founded in Ethiopia. **66** The Great Jewish Revolt against Roman control of Judaea ends with the destruction of the temple in Jerusalem. **ca 70** Work on the Gospels begins.	**ca 100** Heron of Alexandria devises a number of labor-saving devices. **ca 130** Roman Emperor Hadrian is hailed at Palmyra, Syria, as a god. **132** Bar Kochba leads a revolt against Roman dominion in Judaea. **152** Farmers in Egypt revolt, causing a grain shortage in Rome.	**ca 200** Bantu-speaking farmers migrate into much of southern Africa. **ca 200** The Ethiopian kingdom of Axum grows into the largest market for foreign goods in sub-Saharan Africa. **224** The Parthian Empire is brought down by the Sassanid Empire, which will rule much of the Middle East for the next 400 years.	**ca 350** The Ethiopian kingdom of Axum, recently converted to Christianity, invades and occupies the ancient kingdom of Meroe. **ca 350** The Hephthalites, or White Huns, take Bactria and prepare to invade India. **396** Augustine of Hippo becomes bishop of his diocese in modern-day Algeria.	**442** The Vandals establish a short-lived autonomous state in North Africa, from which they harass the deteriorating western Roman Empire. **451** The Council of Chalcedon formalizes Christian orthodoxy. **483** Nestorian Christians flourish in Persia, after being evicted as heretics from the eastern Roman Empire.
9 Wang Mang usurps the throne of the Han dynasty and establishes his own short-lived rule. **25** The Han dynasty is restored. **39** The Trung sisters lead a rebellion in Vietnam, establishing a short-lived autonomous state. **ca 50** Sanskrit becomes the standard mode of written communication in Southeast Asia.	**ca 100** Paper becomes the main medium of written communication in China. **ca 100** Funan emerges as a regional power in Southeast Asia. **184** The Yellow Turban uprising of peasants erupts in eastern China.	**ca 200** Silkworms from China are introduced into Korea and Japan. **220** The Han dynasty falls and the three kingdoms of Wei, Wu, and Shu emerge. **ca 250** Himiko, a shaman queen, reigns in Japan.	**ca 320** Chandra Gupta expands his kingdom into northern and central India and establishes the Gupta dynasty. **ca 350** A Buddhist monastery is founded at Nalanda, on the Ganges. **ca 350** Nomadic peoples from northern China migrate south, assimilating with existing cultures and bringing Buddhism with them.	**ca 400** Tomb culture flourishes in Japan **ca 400** The golden age of India is ushered in by Chandra Gupta II. **ca 400** Indian monk Rumarajiva oversees the translation of Buddhist texts into Chinese. **ca 300** Austronesians settle Hawaii.

POLITICS & POWER	GEOGRAPHY & ENVIRONMENT	CULTURE & RELIGION

THE AMERICAS

ca 500 Tres Zapotes, on Mexico's Gulf Coast, is the center of Olmec culture, following the abandonment and ritual destruction of La Venta.

ca 500 Monte Albán is established in the Valley of Oaxaca, Mexico, on a hill from which leaders can survey their lands.

ca 500 The Paracas culture of coastal Peru practices mummification and delivers their dead to sacred places in mountainous regions, a tradition which will continue to the time of the Incas.

400s The Olmec employ a kind of hieroglyphic writing that may be a very early precursor to Maya hieroglyphics. It has not yet been deciphered.

Fresco from the Tomb of the Diver in Peastum, Italy

EUROPE

490 Greek forces prevail at the Battle of Marathon, halting a Persian incursion into the Greek peninsula.

480 At King Xerxes' behest, Carthaginians attack Greek cities in Sicily where they are defeated at the Battle of Himera. Meanwhile, Persian forces are weakened by a small band of Spartans at the pass of Thermopylae.

446 Athenian statesman Pericles avoids a possible war with Sparta and afterwards becomes the leading political voice in Athens.

500 Greek traveler and writer Hecataeus of Miletus details the geography and ethnography of Europe, northern Africa, and Asia in his *Tour Around the World*—considered the first geography book.

ca 480 Celts of mainland Europe begin migrating to Britain in large numbers, greatly changing the makeup of its population.

464 A severe earthquake in Sparta kills tens of thousands of people. A serf revolt follows, throwing the city into disarray.

ca 500 Etruscan art flourishes, inspired by Greek influences to the south.

472 Greek dramatist Aeschylus wins the Athenian tragedy prize for his earliest extant play, *Persians*.

450 The first written code of law of Rome, the Twelve Tables, is placed in the Roman Forum.

447 Athenian statesman Pericles commissions the sculptor Phidias to be artistic director for the construction of the Parthenon. It is finished in ten years and houses the Athena Parthenos, a 38-foot-tall gold and ivory statue of the patron deity.

MIDDLE EAST & AFRICA

500 The cities of Ionia, ethnically Greek but located in Asia Minor, throw off their Persian governors to begin the Persian Wars between the Greek city-states and the Achaemenid Empire of Darius I of Persia.

483 Xerxes, son and successor of Darius I, prepares a huge incursion of perhaps 100,000 troops into the Greek mainland by constructing a floating bridge over the Hellespont, consisting of 676 ships lined up in two rows.

449 The Peace of Callias is struck between Persia and the Greek city-states. It will last for most of the next century.

490 Carthaginian navigator Hanno sets sail with 30,000 people on 60 boats with the intent of founding colonies on the Atlantic Coast of Africa. He reaches modern-day Gambia, Sierra Leone, and perhaps Cameroon, founding colonies the entire way.

ca 460 Herodotus embarks on his tour of the known world, traveling to spots as far-flung as Egypt, Aswan, Libya, Syria, Babylon, and Susa. Upon his return to Athens, he publicly recites his history of the war between the Greeks and Persians.

521-486 Darius I claims divine right to rule through Zoroastrianism, a belief system founded in the late sixth century by Iranian thinker Zarathustra. This new religion, popular among Persian aristocrats and elites, gains a sizeable priesthood and a considerable following in Persian lands.

445 Nehemiah returns to Jerusalem from captivity in Babylon. He becomes governor, rebuilds the city walls, and institutes social reforms. Together with Ezra, he oversees the signing of the Jewish covenant to obey the laws of Moses, avoid mixed marriages, and support the temple.

ASIA & OCEANIA

ca 500 Achaemenid rule in the northwestern Indian province of Gandhara introduces Persian techniques of imperial administration to autonomous rulers on the Indian sub-continent, and encourages commerce between the two areas.

ca 500 The Indian state of Maghada, near the mouth of the Ganges, emerges as a regional power. Over ensuing centuries, it will expand control over neighboring states.

ca 480 The Zhou dynasty collapses, bringing about the Warring States period in China, characterized by political disunity and philosophical inquiry.

ca 450 Sinhalese migrants from northern India settle in modern-day Sri Lanka and set up a capital at Anuradhapura, along the Aruvi Aru River.

400s Trade is conducted on a regular basis between Indian merchants and those of Indonesia and southeast Asia.

ca 500 Vardhamana Mahavira, the great teacher of Jainism, abandons all worldly goods to live as an ascetic and preach his doctrine of rigorous austerity to disciples throughout northern India. Jainism's guiding principle of *ahimsa* demands nonviolence toward all living things and their souls.

ca 500 Siddhartha Gautama, the historical Buddha, teaches disciples in northern India a philosophy of compassion and wisdom to transcend worldly suffering.

ca 500 Confucius teaches disciples in China the principles of propriety and filial devotion.

SCIENCE & TECHNOLOGY

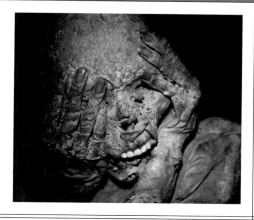

PEOPLE & SOCIETY

400s The cloaks that enshroud Paracas mummies are of a remarkable quality. Their intricate designs will have a strong influence on later Nazca art.

400s A common practice of the Paracas people of Peru is to bind the skulls of infants, resulting in a more elongated, peaked crown.

ca 500 Groups of people in modern-day Indiana, Kentucky, and West Virginia, known collectively as the Adena, live in circular houses with conical roofs. They construct earthen burial mounds, which influence the later Hopewell culture.

A remarkably preserved Paracas mummy

ca 500 Pythagoreans hypothesize from mathematical principles that the Earth is a sphere.

ca 500 The trireme is developed in Greece. It will become the essential warship for both Greeks and Romans.

ca 500 The catapult is developed in Italy.

ca 450 Mechanical starting gates for chariot and foot races are employed at the Olympic Games for the first time.

ca 450 Greek philosopher and astronomer Anaxagoras of Clazomenae is banished from Athens for his theory that the sun is a giant ball of molten iron.

ca 500 The use of coins expands throughout most of Greece—except in Sparta, where ownership of silver or gold is unlawful.

ca 500 The chariot is introduced in Britain.

445 The office of tribune is opened to plebeians in Rome. Also, the ban on marriage between a plebeian and a patrician is lifted.

400s Spartan society, characterized by military rigor and social austerity, dominates southern Greece. Neighboring people are relegated to the status of agricultural farmhands.

400s Pederasty between a young boy and his tutor is openly accepted in Greek society.

ca 500 Expansion continues on Persia's Royal Road, which stretches about 1,600 miles, from Sardis in western Anatolia to Susa in western Persia. It is set up with 111 staging posts.

480 During a siege of Athens, the Persian army uses arrows wrapped with fibers that have been soaked in oil—the first known projectile torches.

ca 450 Iron tool technology spreads across Africa, bringing with it an increase in agricultural surplus, trade, and population.

ca 500 Gimillu, a slave of a temple community in Mesopotamia, is involved in a number of legal cases involving fraud, bribery, and embezzlement. In each case he manages to avoid harsh punishment. His example shows that at this time, even slaves could form powerful, protective relationships.

ca 500 Semitic people from Arabia migrate to Eritrea and Ethiopia and set up a trade network of ivory, spices, and incense.

486 Darius I of Persia, having set up a system of administration that will last for centuries, dies at the age of 35. He is succeeded by his son Xerxes.

ca 500 Indian surgeon Susrata performs operations on cataracts as well as creating new noses from skin grafts.

ca 500 Horse-riding nomadic groups are firmly established on the Eurasian steppes. They live in tents that can be easily dismantled and transported.

ca 483 Siddhartha Gautama, called the Buddha, dies. His teachings, the core of which are known as the Four Noble Truths, go on to influence scores of adherents all over the world.

479 Chinese thinker and educator Confucius dies. Having unsuccessfully attempted to become a powerful administrator in his own day, his teachings compiled in the *Analects* will go on to profoundly influence subsequent political and cultural traditions in China.

ZOROASTRIANISM

Zarathustra, founder and prophet of ancient Iran's foremost state religion, Zoroastrianism, was born of Indo-European stock, of the same ancestry as polytheistic Etruscans to the west and Hindi to the south. Stories of Zarathustra's early life hold many parallels to familiar motifs. Like Muhammad, he is said to have shone with a radiating light while still in his mother's womb. Like Siddhartha Gautama, he was born into a position of considerable privilege, only to rebuke it all following a transcendent vision. And like Jesus, whose nativity was reputedly visited by three Zoroastrian clerics, the Magi, he tested his own faith before embarking on his ministry by wandering into the desert armed only with the word of Ahura Mazda, the "greatest God."

Elements of Zarathustra's moralistic teachings also resound through several religions that succeeded him, concepts like heaven and hell, judgment day, a holy path, and his timeless credo, "good thoughts, good words, good deeds." Greek and Roman philosophers as well held him in high esteem. Unlike many other prophets, however, Zarathustra was regarded as a great sage and his teachings were widely accepted in his own day. In 522 B.C.E., when Darius I of Persia took the reins of the Achaemenid Empire, the word of Ahura Mazda was spread all the way from the Indus River in the east to the Aegean Sea in the west. Zoroastrianism had become the state religion of the largest empire the world had yet known.

In the beginning, there were two primal spirits, twins spontaneously active; these are the good and the evil, in thought, and in word, and in deed: between these two, let the wise choose aright; Be good, not base.

ZARATHUSTRA

POLITICS & POWER	GEOGRAPHY & ENVIRONMENT	CULTURE & RELIGION

THE AMERICAS

ca 400 The Olmec cultural tradition and trade network in Mesoamerica is on the decline. Patterns the Olmec have established will continue through the Maya, Zapotec, and Teotihuacan cultures.

ca 400 The Chavín de Huántar culture maintains its position of prominence in northern Peru.

400s The domestication of beans spreads from Mexico into the North American Southwest. This enhances the diet of native peoples and helps nurture depleted soil. Together with squash and corn, beans become a staple food of North America.

Zapotec urn recovered from Oaxaca, Mexico

400s The Barrier Canyon rock-art style of the Colorado plateau is characterized by stylized, anthropomorphic figures.

ca 400 The burgeoning Zapotec culture of southern Mexico uses a calendar and a system of writing, possibly derived from the previous Olmec culture.

EUROPE

400s Rome consolidates its power in central Italy over Etruscans and neighboring peoples.

431 The Second Peloponnesian War breaks out in Greece between the two main powers of the Delian League, Athens and Sparta.

430 Athenian statesman Pericles exhorts his countrymen and infantry to remain within the walls of Athens to avoid a battle on land with Sparta. Plague sweeps through the city, decimating his forces and souring his people's loyalty. Pericles dies soon afterwards.

404 After 27 years of a pitched civil war, the city of Athens falls to Sparta and its allies. Athens loses its fleet and its territories.

436 A famine strikes Rome. It is so severe that thousands commit suicide by throwing themselves into the Tiber River.

ca 400 Celtic tribes known collectively by the Romans as Gauls move across Europe into northern Italy, France, and Germany.

ca 396 Once Rome draws the Etruscan lands of northern Italy into its sphere of influence, it gains access to the large-scale iron industry already in place there.

ca 430 Greek historian Herodotus completes his *Histories*, in which he details the interactions between the Greek world and Persia. Taking a wider view of history than its predecessors, this work garners its author the title "father of history."

415 Athenian dramatist Euripides writes *Trojan Women*. It is a harsh critique of the cruelty and misogyny of war.

396 The Olympic Games hold contests for trumpeters and heralds for the first time.

ca 387 Greek philosopher Plato founds the Academy, a school of philosophy in Athens.

MIDDLE EAST & AFRICA

424 In the year of the four emperors in Persia, King Ataxerxes I dies and is succeeded by his son Xerxes II. Xerxes II is murdered in his bed by his illegitimate brother Sogdianos, who is defeated and put to death by another illegitimate brother, who reigns as Darius II during a period of revolt. Darius II's successor, Ataxerxes II, rules for 46 years in constant conflict with the Greeks and, later on, with rebellious governors in Egypt and Anatolia.

399 Xenophon's *Anabasis* details all the stages of his retreat from Kounaxa, near Babylon, to Greece, crossing Mesopotamia and Asia Minor. He describes the 29 nations making up his army, the soldiers' weapons and dress, the terrain traversed, and all the events of the march.

390s The hanging gardens of Babylon are described by Greek writer Ctesias, who had served in Babylon as the queen's physician.

500-300 The development of Torah Judaism brings with it a detailed application of law to all aspects of Jewish life, sets Jews off from surrounding peoples, and preserves Jewish customs and rites.

430 The Hall of a Hundred Pillars in Persepolis is completed during the reign of King Ataxerxes I.

378 Nekhtenebef initiates Egypt's 30th dynasty and ushers in a period of prosperity and building, including the earliest temple on the island of Philae, which is now covered by the waters of the Aswan Dam.

ASIA & OCEANIA

400s Walls are built by various states in northern China to repel nomadic Xiongnu tribes to the North and as a defense against rival Chinese states. Many of these walls will later be consolidated into the Great Wall.

400s The northeastern Indian state of Maghada increasingly controls trade along the Ganges River and between India and Burma.

400s Jainism, which recognizes no hierarchical classes of human beings, draws many converts in northern India from members of lower castes, who do not derive much esteem from the traditional social order of Indian society. Its ascetic doctrine, though, is too demanding to appeal to the masses.

400s Buddhism spreads through northern India. Early monks, actively preaching and disseminating the teachings of the Buddha, use the vernacular language of the day, rather than Sanskrit, in order to reach a wider audience.

SCIENCE & TECHNOLOGY

ca 400 Trephination, a surgical procedure by which sections of the skull are excised with a sawlike implement, is developed in modern-day Peru. It is effectively used to treat head injuries, migraines, and seizures.

440 Greek mathematician Hippocrates of Chios writes what is considered the first mathematical textbook. It expounds on the proofs of geometry.

ca 400 Hippocrates of Cos begins compiling his *Corpus Hippocraticum*, consisting of around 70 works presumably by various authors. It initiates the science of medicine with subjects ranging from pharmaceutical mixtures to a rejection of superstition.

ca 400 The seminomadic Scythians of what is now Crimea in southern Russia develop saddles equipped with stirrups.

ca 375 The screw is invented in Italy.

ca 440 Democritus visits Babylon and brings its astronomy, but not its medicine, back to Greece.

400s The *qanat* system of underground canals to distribute water to arid regions for agriculture is expanded on the Iranian plateau. The product of an enormous amount of free and slave labor, many of these tunnels are still in use today.

437 The first known hospital is established in Ceylon, modern-day Sri Lanka.

ca 400 The Chinese begin using bitumen in lamps, the first known use of oil as a source of energy.

ca 400 The Chinese invent the iron for pressing garments. Live embers provide the necessary heat.

400s Iron replaces bronze as the dominant metal of warfare in China.

PEOPLE & SOCIETY

400s Benefitting from abundant marine and inland food sources, the population of modern-day coastal California becomes one of the largest concentrations of people in North America.

400s The origins of the Zapotec culture appear around the city of Monte Albán, in the Oaxaca Valley of Mexico, which is home to some 5,000 inhabitants.

ca 400 The Valley of Mexico is settled by nascent agriculturalists.

ca 440 At the height of his influence, Pericles broadens opportunities for participation in government, employs thousands in grand building projects, and strongly encourages the arts, sciences, and philosophy.

404 Athenian historian Thucydides dies. His work *History of the Peloponnesian War* appears soon afterwards.

399 Greek philosopher Socrates, having established the foundations of the Western philosophical tradition, is sentenced to death for impiety and corrupting the youth.

423-404 Parysatis, wife and half-sister of Darius II, is an able queen who owns land in many parts of the empire and is involved in politics. She is accused of imprisoning several of her husband's rivals.

401 Greek historian Xenophon joins the mercenary troops of Persian rebel Cyrus the younger. After Cyrus is killed near Babylon, Xenophon commands the rear guard for the long march back. He will write his history of the expedition soon afterwards.

ca 430 Chinese philosopher Mozi founds his school of Mohism, based on universal love, the virtues of egalitarianism, and a rejection of war and extravagance.

ca 400 The use of coins is spread to northern India from Greece via Persia.

ca 390 Legalism appears in China, a system of thought which seeks to strengthen and expand the state at all costs. It strongly emphasizes agriculture and the military over trade, art, and education and seeks to order society through a rigid set of severe laws.

The Parthenon atop Athens' acropolis

THE ROOTS OF DEMOCRACY

Though many regard fifth-century Athens as the birthplace of democracy, this system of governance likely existed in hunter-gatherer societies—well before static communities, which tended toward a more hierarchical social organization, became prevalent. At the very least, Athens reintroduced a primitive idea in an advanced form, coining the term we use today, democracy, Greek for "rule by the people."

Following a century of aristocratic power mongering, Athenian statesman Cleisthenes in 508 B.C.E. garnered popular support for a series of reforms that would strip hereditary claims of their political clout. He encouraged participation in government by extending the right to participate to all free adult males born into townships. Townships chose representatives by lot to present their constituents' vote at a weekly assembly that met near Athens' acropolis. Though Athens was not a true democracy—only about 15 percent of the populace were adult male citizens, with women, immigrants, and slaves given no voice—it was a step up from tyrannical rule by a small group of aristocrats. A form of democracy continued in Athens until 146 B.C.E., when conquering Romans annexed the city into their growing realm.

THE MIGHT OF PERSIA

W HAT WAS KNOWN AS PERSIA AT THE BEGINNING OF THE SIXTH CENTURY B.C.E. encompassed only the southwestern portion of modern-day Iran. In a matter of decades, a dynasty of rulers emerged, known as the Achaemenid dynasty, which would incorporate regions stretching from the Aegean Sea off the coast of Greece to the Indus River of northwestern India, essentially becoming the first of the ancient world's classical societies. Though its borders would expand and contract and its rulers would adopt varying policies, Persia maintained itself as a continual political entity for the entirety of the next millennium and, some would say, to this very day.

The founder and first great ruler of the Achaemenid Empire was Cyrus, whose kingdom could be said to have become an empire in 546 B.C.E., when he conquered the powerful Lydian kingdom in Anatolia. In 539, he seized Babylon and with it large areas of Syria and Palestine. A benevolent ruler, Cyrus allowed his conquered lands to retain their own religions and cultural mores, even releasing Jews captive in Babylon and allowing them to rebuild their temple in Jerusalem. Cyrus took cues from those he conquered, adopting the use of coins from the Lydians and administrative practices from the Babylonians. His empire was further extended by his son, Cambyses, who took Egypt in 525, and by his grandson, Darius I, whose rule reached into northwestern India to the east and into Thrace and Macedonia in the west—easily the largest empire the world had yet known. The forces of Darius's son and successor, Xerxes I, even took Athens for a short time before being turned back.

Though an able military leader, Darius's true greatness was as an administrator. He organized his empire into 20 provinces and fixed the annual tribute due from each; he standardized coinage, weights, and measures; he established Zoroastrianism as the state religion, providing a cohesive Persian identity to his far-flung empire; he built a grand capital of magnificent proportions at Persepolis; he built a system of underground canals to increase agriculture; he started construction on the 1,600-mile Royal Road and equipped it with 111 courier stations at equal intervals; and he kept sedition to a minimum through the use of imperial spies, the "eyes and ears of the king."

Through these measures and a policy of toleration for cultural traditions, Darius saw trade and productivity in his empire increase along with the standard of living, and the stage was set for a long history of Persian rule in the Near East.

A grand decorative stairway ascends to a banquet hall in Persepolis, constructed during the reign of Darius I of Persia to serve as the nerve center of the expanding Achaemenid Empire.

	POLITICS & POWER	GEOGRAPHY & ENVIRONMENT	CULTURE & RELIGION
THE AMERICAS	**ca 350 The Olmec city of La Venta**, located on an island surrounded by marshland, is completely abandoned and no longer serves as a political or cultural center.		**ca 350 Inhabitants of Nakbe**, in modern-day Guatemala, decorate a monumental platform with a large bust of a supernatural bird, evidence of the beginnings of the Maya cultural tradition.
EUROPE	**359 King Philip II** takes power in the northern Greek state of Macedon. He immediately begins assembling a hardy, well-trained army, equipping his infantry with the *sarissa,* a pike 13 to 21 feet long. **350 A plebeian** is elected censor in Rome for the first time. **338 Philip II of Macedon**, after two decades of extending his empire, subdues all of Greece and sets his sights on Persia. **336 Alexander the Great**, following the assassination of his father, Philip II, inherits his expanding empire at the age of 20.	**330s Alexander the Great** encourages the building of roads and cities throughout his empire, setting a pattern for the later Roman Empire. **300s Greek farmers** grow more barley than wheat, as the yield is greater on poor soil.	**ca 378 Greek philosopher Plato** composes his dialogue, *The Republic*, in which he elaborates his notion of the ideal state. **ca 350 The Apollo Belvedere, attributed to Greek sculptor Leochares**, is made. It is widely considered the ideal form of masculine beauty in the ancient Mediterranean world. **347 Coins are introduced into Rome**; soon afterwards, the stores of the Roman Forum are replaced by banks. **ca 318 Greek philosopher Aristoxenus of Tarentum**, living in southern Italy, composes his discourse on music entitled *Harmonics*.
MIDDLE EAST & AFRICA	**334 Alexander the Great, son of Philip II,** invades Persia with his small but extremely well trained army of Macedonian soldiers. **331 Alexander** destroys the Persian forces of the Achaemenid Empire at the Battle of Gaugamela. He then goes on to raze the grand imperial center, Persepolis. **312 Seleucus, Alexander's general and heir to his Asian Empire**, enters Babylon and ushers in the Seleucid era, regaining Bactria from Chandragupta Maurya in 306. **300s Carthage, a Phoenician colony** in modern-day Tunisia, dominates the politics and commerce of the western Mediterranean.	**ca 350 A new strain of wheat** is introduced into Egypt, from which bread can be easily produced. Combined with the Ptolemaic dynasty's support of agriculture, this development helps make Egypt the granary of Rome. **332 Alexander destroys Tyre** and builds Alexandria in Egypt to be the center of Hellenistic commerce. **329 Alexander** crosses Hindu Kush into Bactria to defeat its satrap Bessos, completing a 1,500-mile march through Northwest India. On his return to western Iran, he marries his troops to Iranian women in an attempt to meld Greeks and Persians into one people.	**356 The Temple of Artemis at Ephesus** is burned by Herostratus and rebuilt even more magnificently, demonstrating the wealth of the Greek cities of Asia Minor under Persian rule. **ca 332 As they campaign through the Achaemenid Empire, Alexander's forces** burn many Zoroastrian temples and kill many priests, or magi. Since doctrines of this faith are transmitted orally, many holy verses and hymns are lost to posterity, and the future of the religion is left uncertain. **324 3,000 musicians arrive from Greece** to northwestern Iran to perform at a feast for Alexander.
ASIA & OCEANIA	**ca 360 Shang Yang, Chinese Legalist and administrator of the state of Qin,** grants plots of land to peasants to boost agricultural production. Increased surplus creates enough economic growth to equip the army with iron weapons and to begin conquering rival states. In 338 he is executed, then mutilated, after the death of his patron. **327 Alexander the Great** takes his army across the Indus River into northwestern India, where he begins subjecting local rulers. He retreats only when his troops refuse to proceed any farther from home.	**327 Alexander the Great's** incursion into northwestern India and conquests throughout the Middle East connect the Indian subcontinent to the growing sphere of the Mediterranean basin. Trade will thus be facilitated for centuries to come.	**ca 330 Confucian thinker Mencius** travels extensively through China, extolling the virtue of government through benevolence and respectfulness. Critics deride his teachings as naively optimistic. **ca 320 The classic Daoist texts, the Daodejing and the Zhuangzi**, are compiled. They advocate following patterns and processes of nature as a guide to human life and social order. **ca 315 Mauryan court adviser Kautalya** composes his *Arthashastra*, which serves as a manual for imperial administration.

SCIENCE & TECHNOLOGY	PEOPLE & SOCIETY

300s **The Jama Coaque culture** of modern-day coastal Ecuador continues to produce a number of clay figurines often with very well-defined features and almost always adorned with headgear and jewelry.

Though God was indeed the common father of all mankind, still he made peculiarly his own the noblest and best of them.

ALEXANDER THE GREAT

THE NOK

The Nok culture of central Nigeria in the fourth century B.C.E. was at the cusp of a revolution in how West African society was organized— the move from the Neolithic to the Iron Age. The Nok were early producers of iron in sub-Saharan Africa, with furnaces dating back to the fifth century B.C.E. Produced by melting and separating the element from chunks of ore taken out of the Earth, iron was made into hoes and tools and put to use in clearing lands and growing crops such as yams. The surplus that was created spurred not only the growth of urban centers, but also the development of a sophisticated artistic style.

By firing clay in their furnaces, the Nok created domestic pottery, animal figurines, and stylized human sculptures, which sometimes were just heads. These human figurines show exaggerated facial features, elongated body parts, and abstract geometrical treatments. The Nok's unique style of art is exceptionally preserved and provides testimony to the independent mastery of pottery manufacture in sub-Saharan Africa.

ca 350 **People in the Spartan city of Lacedaemon** direct hot air through pipes underneath their floors—an early form of central heating.

350 **Aristotle** writes *Concerning the Sky* in which he correctly supports the theory that the earth is a sphere, and incorrectly supports the theory that the earth is the center of the universe.

312 **The first major Roman road, the Via Appia,** is commissioned by censor Appius Claudius Caecus. It extends 162 miles from Rome to Tarentum in southeastern Italy.

342 **Greek philosopher Aristotle,** a disciple of Plato whose writings encompass topics from metaphysics to politics to biology to literature, travels to Macedon to become the tutor of young Alexander the Great.

336 **King Philip II of Macedon** is assassinated at the wedding of his daughter. His plans for an invasion of Persia fall to his son Alexander.

323 **Alexander the Great,** strategist, leader, and conqueror of a vast empire stretching from mainland Greece to parts of India, falls ill at a feast and dies a week later at the age of 33. Theories of his cause of death range from poisoning to cirrhosis of the liver.

367 **Kidinna of Sippar** improves the astronomical calendar to a greater degree than even 19th-century astronomers could achieve with telescopes.

ca 366 **Greek mathematician and astronomer Eudoxus of Cnidus** establishes a school in Cyzicus, Asia Minor. Here he works to formulate a systematic explanation of the motion of the sun, stars, moon, and planets around the earth.

ca 350 **The Nok culture,** an agricultural community of West Africa, develops the manufacture of iron, yet continues the use of stone tools.

350 **The city of Ife-Ife** in present-day Nigeria is first occupied. Construction of city walls suggests that urbanism in West Africa accompanies advances in agriculture and iron technology, but predates the formation of major states.

338 **Persian eunuch and general Bagoas** poisons Ataxerxes III and in 336 Ataxerxes IV. He is then poisoned in turn by Darius III, but too late to save the Achaemenid Empire from dissolution at the hands of Alexander.

330 **Alexander the Great** proclaims himself emperor of Persia. Not long afterward, he begins donning Persian garb.

365 **Chinese astronomers** discover the existence of Jupiter's moons without the aid of a telescope.

352 **The earliest known record of a supernova** is made by Chinese astronomers.

ca 350 **The use of coins** appears in China.

ca 325 **Ambitious upstart Chandragupta Maurya** seizes control of the Indian state of Maghada, embarking on an imperial career that will establish the Mauryan dynasty in most of the Indian subcontinent.

321 **Chandragupta Maurya** pushes the borders of his kingdom into northwestern India, where Alexander's withdrawal has left a vacuum of power. In 320 he wrests control of Bactria, modern-day Afghanistan, from Alexander's successors.

Stylized head of a Nok terra-cotta figurine

POLITICS & POWER	GEOGRAPHY & ENVIRONMENT	CULTURE & RELIGION

THE AMERICAS

ca 300 Tikal, a center of Maya culture located in the lowland rain forest of modern-day Guatemala, moves from a small farming community to a populous ceremonial complex. Around this time, it begins construction on a number of monumental pyramids and temples.

ca 250 The Zapotec population of Monte Albán reaches 15,000 and is governed by an identifiable ruling elite.

ca 250 Construction begins at the site of Tiahuanaco (Tiwanaku) on the southern shore of Lake Titicaca in the Andes.

ca 300 The Anasazi of southwestern North America begin cultivating corn.

ca 250 The Palacio de Danzantes in Monte Albán demonstrates Olmec influence. Its friezes are believed to be a public declaration of the political and martial power of the city's elite. Many represent scenes of ritual bloodletting.

EUROPE

ca 300 Rome becomes the dominant power on the Italian peninsula. Through the establishment of military colonies and equitable treatment of vanquished states, it secures a wide base of political and military authority.

275 Following Alexander the Great's death, his chief generals carve up his new empire into three large realms: the Seleucid, including most of the former Achaemenid Empire in Persia; the Ptolemaic, including most of Egypt; and the Antigonid, including Greece, Macedon, and nearby islands.

241 The First Punic War ends with Rome wresting control of Sicily from Carthage.

ca 300 Greek navigator Pytheas is the first Greek to reach the British Isles and Scandinavia. In his book, *On the Ocean*, he describes tin mining in modern-day Cornwall. His description of a land where the sea is solid and the sun never sets in summer is ridiculed in his own day.

250 Romans begin utilizing systematic crop rotation on a two-year round.

280 The Colossus of Rhodes is constructed. This bronze statue of the sun god Helios stands 100 feet tall at the mouth of Rhodes's harbor as a symbol of freedom of trade.

200s Three schools of philosophical thought arise in Greece—Epicureanism, which views pleasure as the ultimate good; skepticism, which doubts the possibility of any certain knowledge; and Stoicism, which takes as its goal tranquillity of mind by means of a virtuously led life.

MIDDLE EAST & AFRICA

305 Seleucus takes the title of king, making Seleucid Asia independent of Greece. In 280, his son Antiochus I takes the titles "great king, king of the world, king of Babylon."

ca 300 Ptolemaic rule in Egypt fosters the widespread organization of agriculture and industry and establishes royal monopolies over the textile, salt-making, and beer-brewing industries.

247 The Parthian satrap in Iran stages a successful revolt against his Seleucid overlord, starting a hundred-year shift in the balance of power between these two forces in the Middle East.

ca 300 Aramaic and Greek are the common languages of newly founded Hellenistic cities in the Middle East.

280 The Alexandria Museum and Library are founded. These centers of classical learning will foster scientific and literary scholarship for centuries.

ca 275 The first five books of the Old Testament are translated from Hebrew to Greek by scholars in Alexandria.

200s The Egyptian cult of Osiris spreads across the Hellenistic world, with its message of eternal salvation.

WHAT LIFE WAS LIKE

The Parthians

Originally a group of nomads from the central Asian steppes, the Parthians gradually settled into an agricultural way of life in modern-day Iran. Without access to conventional feed grains such as those used in more advanced agricultural societies, the Parthians allowed their horses to graze in winter on alfalfa growing naturally on the nearby steppes, a practice which not only made their animals larger than average, but also made them strong enough to support warriors equipped with full metal armor. Already skilled in the art of horseback combat, the fully armored and well-trained Parthian cavalry was a formidable match to any rival, and was integral in establishing the Parthian Empire.

ASIA & OCEANIA

ca 300 The Mauryan Empire administers trade, agriculture, taxes, and foreign affairs across northern India from the Indus to the Ganges.

260 Mauryan Emperor Ashoka conquers the Indian state of Kalinga, killing an estimated 100,000 in the fighting and drawing all but the southern tip of India into his empire. Later, he becomes a devout Buddhist, gives up hunting, and founds hospitals and monasteries throughout his country.

ca 250 The Yayoi culture, characterized by advanced skills in metallurgy and wet rice cultivation, becomes dominant in Japan.

ca 305 Under the patronage of Emperor Chandragupta Maurya, the city of Taxila in northwestern India becomes a prominent center of learning and commerce.

ca 300 The cultivation of wet rice is introduced into Japan from China.

ca 268 Mauryan Emperor Ashoka of India establishes his capital at Pataliputra along the Ganges River. The city is fortified by a moat and a timber wall equipped with 570 towers and 64 gates. It also houses a central treasury system to oversee tax collection.

256 Mauryan emperor Ashoka founds hospitals in India, supplies them with medicines, and encourages the education of women.

ca 250 With the sponsorship of Mauryan Emperor Ashoka, Buddhism spreads throughout India and to Bactria and Ceylon, modern-day Sri Lanka. Mariner merchants take it along sea routes to Southeast Asia.

200s Trade along the Ganges River flourishes in the hands of private entrepreneurs. This new middle class does not fit readily into the caste system already in place in India, so guilds form that function as subcastes.

SCIENCE & TECHNOLOGY	PEOPLE & SOCIETY
200s Craftsmen of the La Tolita culture of modern-day coastal Ecuador continue to produce a multitude of finely wrought gold pieces that show a skill in casting and overlay unequalled elsewhere in the Americas.	**ca 250 The Moche culture** develops in northern coastal Peru at the same time as the Nazca culture develops in southern coastal Peru. Both are characterized by the high quality of their pottery and weaving. **ca 250 Lapis lazuli from the Chilean desert** appears in Chavín de Huántar sites of Peru—evidence of an extensive trade network among the Andeans.
ca 300 Babylonian astronomer Berosus, living on the Greek island of Cos, develops an early form of the sundial to tell time of day. **ca 280 Greek astronomer Aristarchus of Samos** writes *On the Size and Distances of the Sun and the Moon*, in which he employs Euclid's geometric method to estimate the distance of the sun and the moon from the earth. He also insists that the earth revolves annually around the sun and rotates daily about its own axis. **ca 250 Greek anatomist Erasistratus of Chios,** considered the father of physiology, explains the functions of the heart's valves.	**270 Apollonius of Rhodes** begins work on his epic *Jason and the Argonauts*. It will take him 25 years to complete. **264 Originating from an Etruscan funereal tradition, the first gladiatorial games** are held in Rome. Along with chariot races, wild animal hunts, and mock naval battles, they will become wildly popular in the Roman world for the next few centuries. **200s Cities on the Greek peninsula,** such as Athens and Corinth, benefit tremendously from the increased trade made possible through the expansion of Greek cultural ideas that characterize the Hellenistic era.
ca 300 Prominent mathematician Euclid, teaching in Alexandria, expounds on the laws of geometry in his *Elements*. **ca 300 Egyptians write** using hollow reeds filled with ink, an early form of the fountain pen. **297 The world's first lighthouse**, the Pharos of Alexandria, begins to be constructed. The light of a fire at its base is reflected out to sea by bronze mirrors. **ca 285 Herophilus**, working in Alexandria, practices human dissection, a research technique banned elsewhere. He recognizes the brain as the seat of intelligence.	**ca 300 Greek colonists** bring to the Middle East traditions and laws of the polis. Under Seleucid rule, lands are awarded to cities as well as to individuals; serfs already on the land become free taxpayers, while native city-dwellers become citizens. Seleucid rulers also introduce uniform coinage and calendar. **ca 300 Peaches, citrons, and cotton** move west from Iran, as does the water wheel. **ca 280 Alexandria** becomes the bureaucratic center of the Ptolemaic empire. Greeks, Macedonians, Phoenicians, Jews, Arabs, and Babylonians migrate through its harbor, which can hold up to 1,200 ships at a time.
ca 300 Indian merchants turn increasingly to sea routes to conduct trade, having mastered the art of sailing the Indian Ocean on its seasonal monsoon winds. **ca 255 The idea that feeling a person's pulse** is an important aspect of medical diagnosis gains ground in China. **ca 250 Mauryan Emperor Ashoka** expands on his grandfather's system of roads to encourage overland commerce and builds an extensive irrigation system to encourage agriculture. **240 The earliest known record of Halley's comet** is made by Chinese astronomers.	**ca 300 Chinese philosopher Zhuangzi** writes a compendium of Daoist views, extolling the virtues of nature and the oneness of all things. **ca 250 Confucian thinker Xunzi** advocates ritual propriety, a cornerstone of Confucian views on social order, as a means for the state to create order in human society. **ca 250 Chinese Legalist Han Feizi** formulates views on the state that will influence Chinese politics for centuries.

THE LIBRARY OF ALEXANDRIA

The Hellenistic Age was characterized by a confluence of ideas and a blending of traditions between the Greek West and the Persian East. Greek merchants poured into the cities recently founded by Alexander the Great, and a cultural interchange of unprecedented proportions ensued.

Nowhere was this more true than in Alexandria, Egypt, one of the most cosmopolitan cities of the ancient world, established by Alexander on the Nile delta in 332 B.C.E. After the partitioning of Alexander's empire following his premature death, Alexandria came under the domain of the Ptolemaic dynasty, which soon established a research library and attendant "museum"—in the original sense of the word, a temple to the muses—the likes of which the world had not yet seen.

Scholars converged from across the Mediterranean world on this burgeoning center of learning, which housed an estimated 400,000-700,000 scrolls, though some were acquired through questionable methods. Prominent geometrician Euclid came to work on his groundbreaking textbook, *Elements*. Physician and anatomist Herophilus came to research human physiology through dissection of cadavers, a practice usually banned elsewhere. Aristarchus of Samothrace set into collated form the various texts associated with Homer. Jewish scholars came to translate from Hebrew to Greek the Old Testament of the Bible.

Libraries subsequently were established throughout the Hellenistic world in emulation of Alexandria's center of scholarship, but until its destruction in the late fourth century C.E. by Christian Roman emperor Theophilus, who was attempting to do away with all remnants of paganism in his realm, few compared.

The unexamined life is not worth living.

SOCRATES

POLITICS & POWER	GEOGRAPHY & ENVIRONMENT	CULTURE & RELIGION

THE AMERICAS

ca 200 Teotihuacan, the "city of the gods," near modern-day Mexico City, begins extending its influence over nearby areas, most likely by means of military force.

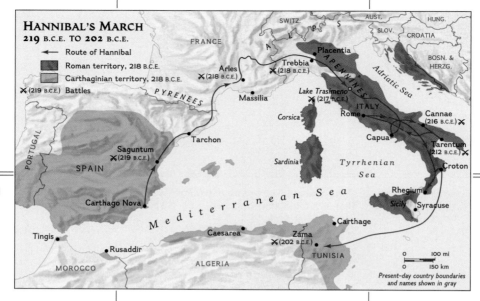

HANNIBAL'S MARCH
219 B.C.E. TO 202 B.C.E.
← Route of Hannibal
▨ Roman territory, 218 B.C.E.
▨ Carthaginian territory, 218 B.C.E.
✗ (219 B.C.E.) Battles

Map of Hannibal's invasion route from Spain to Italy

ca 200 The Nazca lines begin to appear in the arid deserts of southern coastal Peru. Giant ground markings created by removing dark, oxidized rocks from the desert surface, some are animal figures, others straight lines or trapezoids emanating from ray centers.

EUROPE

218 Carthaginian general Hannibal, at the outbreak of the Second Punic War, crosses the Alps into northern Italy with 40,000 men and 37 elephants. His successful invasion threatens Rome.

215 Resentful of Rome's interference with affairs in Illyria, on the eastern shores of the Adriatic, King Philip V of Macedon sends a war fleet to begin the First Macedonian War, thus occupying Rome on two fronts.

240 Greek scholar of natural history Eratosthenes of Cyrene maps the Nile River valley.

225 The Colossus of Rhodes, one of the seven wonders of the ancient world, is toppled by an earthquake.

ca 200 The Riace bronzes, incredibly realistic Greek sculptures, are lost to sea in the Strait of Messina. They will be recovered in 1972.

ca 195 Greek scholar Aristophanes of Byzantium introduces accent marks to Greek writing.

ca 193 The Aphrodite of Melos, better known to posterity as the *Venus de Milo,* is produced. Nothing is known of its sculptor.

MIDDLE EAST & AFRICA

212 With Rome's encouragement, Numidian chiefs declare war on Carthage, their neighbor to the west. The rebellion is quickly put down by Carthaginian general Hasdrubal.

202 Roman forces under General Scipio Africanus Major defeat the amassed Carthaginian forces under General Hannibal at Zama, in modern-day Tunisia. The peace agreement forces Carthage to cede to Rome most of its fleet as well as its holdings in Spain.

201 Masinissa is made ruler of the newly formed North African kingdom of Numidia.

189 Roman forces defeat Seleucid ruler Antiochus III and establish Roman Asia.

*Certain is death for the born
And certain is birth
for the dead;
Therefore over the inevitable
Thou should not grieve.*

BHAGAVAD GITA,
CHAPTER 2, VERSE 27

ca 230 The *Dying Gaul* is dedicated. This sculpture may commemorate a victory over the Galatians, a Celtic group pushing into Asia Minor. It represents a great advance in the artistic depiction of the anguish of war.

196 A description of the coronation of Egyptian Pharaoh Ptolemy V is inscribed three times on the Rosetta Stone, once in Greek, once in Egyptian hieroglyphs, and once in demotic script.

ASIA & OCEANIA

221 Having subdued rival warring states to his rule, the 13-year-old king of Qin proclaims himself the first emperor of a unified China. He takes on a new title, Qin Shihuangdi, which means first emperor of Qin.

207 Following the death of Emperor Qin Shihuangdi, civil insurrection breaks apart the Qin dynasty. Though the dynasty lasts only 14 years, the tradition of centralized imperial rule will last for centuries.

206 Methodical and determined military commander Liu Bang manages to restore order to China and positions himself at the head of the new Han dynasty.

ca 220 Chinese Emperor Qin Shihuangdi divides his kingdom into 36 administrative units, each governed by a civil administrator or a military commander, and each checked on by an imperial inspector.

ca 206 The Han dynasty sets up its capital in Chang'an, near modern-day Xi'an. This cosmopolitan city will serve as an important cultural center for much of Chinese history.

ca 185 The Mauryan Empire of India dissipates as its expenditures outweigh its revenues. Large regional kingdoms control India for the next five centuries.

ca 200 The *Classic of Filial Piety* is composed. It encourages obedience and respect for elders and authorities.

ca 200 The *Bhagavad Gita,* or *Song of God,* a sacred Hindu text, is further refined. It ruminates on the divine in the form of a dialogue between a warrior prince and his charioteer.

SCIENCE & TECHNOLOGY

ca 200 The Nazca people of southern coastal Peru begin constructing a huge network of underground irrigation channels, called *puquios,* many of which are still in working order. They enable the Nazca to make their desert environment arable and may have a connection with the Nazca lines.

ca 200 Inhabitants of modern-day Ecuador and Peru develop clay furnaces used to melt gold and silver.

ca 230 Greek mathematician and inventor Archimedes, working in Syracusa, Sicily, creates all manner of military instruments using levers and pulleys, comes to an approximation of pi, and finds the ratio between the volume of a cylinder to that of an inscribed sphere—the so-called golden ratio.

ca 200 The horseshoe is invented by nomads of the Eurasian steppes. This technology soon spreads to the Roman world.

ca 200 The Romans invent concrete.

ca 230 Mathematician Apollonius of Perga, an early contributor to the field of mathematical astronomy, introduces the terms parabola, ellipse, and hyperbola from his detailed study of the cross-sections of a cone. He works out of Alexandria, Egypt.

ca 200 The astrolabe is developed in Alexandria. It is used to chart the positions and altitudes of the stars.

ca 220 Chinese Emperor Qin Shihuangdi begins construction on a mausoleum spanning 20 square miles and adorned with a pearl-inlaid map of the sky, rivers of flowing mercury, and an army of terra-cotta soldiers.

ca 220 Emperor Qin uses a vast force of slave labor to build a system of roads, bridges, and canals across China. He also consolidates the Great Wall.

ca 200 The Chinese develop coal as a fuel.

ca 190 Chinese mathematicians begin expressing magnitude using powers of ten and early forms of scientific notation.

PEOPLE & SOCIETY

ca 200 Builders of the Zapotec city of Monte Albán create central plazas surrounded by public and religious structures.

226 A force of Gauls threatens Roman holdings in northern Italy. They are turned away decisively the following year at the Battle of Telamon.

ca 200 Lands conquered by Rome largely become property of the wealthy elite, who set up massive, slave-operated plantations known as latifundia. These plantations prosper at the expense of their smaller neighbors.

ca 195 Following military successes on both sides of the Mediterranean, Rome's attitude toward its Italian allies becomes harsher and the political sway of its aristocratic landowners becomes greater.

ca 200 Permanent settlement at Jenne-Jeno (modern-day Djénné) in the Niger Delta begins the gradual process of urbanism in West Africa. Rice cultivation, trade, and crafts contribute to this process.

182 Hannibal, in exile in Asia Minor, commits suicide rather than submit to the Romans.

ca 171 Soldier and conqueror Mithradates I assumes the throne of the Parthian Empire. He will soon rule over lands stretching from India to the Mediterranean.

210 Obsessed with immortality, Chinese Emperor Qin Shihuangdi dies while journeying in search of an elixir of life. His many reforms include standardizing laws, writing, currency, weights, measures, and even the width of roads.

206 First Han Emperor Liu Bang synthesizes the decentralization of the Zhou dynasty with the tight centralization of the Qin dynasty to create a system that will stay in place for the first 50 years of Han rule.

ca 200 The Xiongnu people of Central Asia form a wide-reaching federation under the ruler known as Maodun.

HANNIBAL

As a young man in Carthage, Hannibal once asked his father to take him along on a military campaign in Spain. It is said that his father agreed, on one condition: that Hannibal swear never to become an ally of Rome. Hannibal more than held up his end of the bargain, eventually using his military genius to challenge the power of Rome, and very nearly succeeding.

Commander in chief of his own army by age 26, Hannibal pushed Rome into the Second Punic War against Carthage. He then amassed a force of about 40,000 troops, as well as 37 African war elephants, and embarked on an invasion of northern Italy through the Alps that would become legendary. When told it was impossible to cross the Alps with elephants, Hannibal responded, "We will either find a way, or make one." They did, though the feat cost Hannibal half his army.

Hannibal's army crosses the Alps.

Hannibal went on to score victories throughout Italy and seriously threatened to conquer Rome. But after the death of his brother and a failed alliance with the Macedonians, Hannibal returned to Africa, where Roman forces were threatening his native city. Carthage was taken and Rome's hegemony in the Mediterranean was firmly established for the next 500 years.

THE TIGER OF QIN

THE FIRST EMPEROR OF A UNIFIED CHINA, QIN (PRONOUNCED CHIN) SHIHUANGDI did far more than lend his name to the modern-day country. Shortly after assuming the throne of the state of Qin in 246 B.C.E. at the age of 13, the young king led Qin armies to defeat all rival states and unify their territory into China's first empire. The ferocity with which he ate up his neighbors earned him the nickname "tiger of Qin." Shihuangdi then set to work reorganizing the political and social structure of the empire with himself at the center; organizing the army; codifying the law; establishing standards for weights, measures, axle lengths, coinage, and a writing system; building new roads, canals, and irrigation systems to crisscross his empire; and even consolidating and enlarging a series of walls built by northern states into what we now know as the Great Wall of China.

Obsessed with immortality, Shihuangdi began work on a mausoleum so elaborate, its construction would last 36 years and required a workforce of slave laborers equal to that used on the Great Wall. The entire complex covered 23 square miles, guarded by a full army of life-size terra-cotta soldiers (three of which are shown on pages 62-63). According to legend, the mausoleum is equipped with all the accoutrements an emperor might desire in the afterlife, including a scale model of the empire replete with flowing rivers of mercury and a map of the sky with constellations of pearls. So far, only legend qualifies these claims, as Chinese archaeologists hesitate to begin a full-scale excavation until they can be sure of not harming the structure. Through the use of remote sensing survey technology, one very important discovery has been made: the presence of unusual amounts of mercury, up to 100 times above normal.

Beginning with the succeeding Han dynasty, Qin rule was viewed as tyrannical despotism and rejected as the illegitimate wielding of unlimited autocratic power. A famous essay by the noted Han writer, Jia Yi (201-169 B.C.E.), "The Faults of Qin," elegantly describes the rise and fall of the Qin state, attributing its demise to the absence of Confucian values in its government. In order to justify their own rule, the founders of the Han dynasty carefully distanced themselves from the Qin and, even though they ruled through the centralized political institutions created by the Qin, they legitimized their power by appealing to Confucian ideals of good rulership.

As Confucian ideas became state orthodoxy during the Han, a bureaucracy of officials evolved who were modeled on Confucian notions of service to a ruler who held the Mandate of Heaven. Under the Han and later dynasties, the Mandate of Heaven became the key source of legitimacy for founders of new dynasties. Like Liu Bang, the founder of the Han dynasty, future dynastic founders also justified their conquest by claiming that heaven had bestowed its mandate on them because they had proven their virtue and ability. From this perspective, Qin Shihuangdi, the first emperor of China, neither sought nor claimed the Mandate of Heaven, ruling instead through the Legalist doctrines of "strict laws and harsh punishments," which served the Qin state so well in its centralization of power, rapid territorial expansion, and unification of the country.

The Great Wall of China was unified into a contiguous structure by Qin Shihuangdi in the 3rd century B.C.E., then reconstructed and refortified by the Ming dynasty in the 15th and 16th centuries C.E.

POLITICS & POWER	GEOGRAPHY & ENVIRONMENT	CULTURE & RELIGION

THE AMERICAS

100s The Street of the Dead, the main thoroughfare of Teotihuacan, is lined with about 100 palaces that house priests and dignitaries. The working populace lives outside of the city.

100s Wind instruments—such as flutes and panpipes made of bone, clay, or hollow cane—are used for ceremonial and entertainment purposes by cultures throughout the Andean regions of South America.

Roman aqueduct near Nîmes, France

EUROPE

146 Rome destroys Carthage and establishes the province of Africa. Rome is now the dominant political and economic force in the Mediterranean.

133 Roman tribune Tiberius Gracchus sponsors a law limiting the power and estates of large landowners. He is assassinated a year later.

123 Roman tribune Gaius Gracchus, Tiberius's brother, pushes for land reform and wider distribution of Roman citizenship. Pursued by political enemies, he commits suicide two years later.

122 Mount Etna on the island of Sicily erupts.

166 Latin comic playwright Terence produces his first play, *The Girl from Andros.*

100s Romans frequently pay professional sorcerers to write curse tablets calling for divine actions against their rivals in love or business.

MIDDLE EAST & AFRICA

161 Judah Maccabee establishes diplomatic relations with Rome after the Hasmonean Revolt, spurred by the Seleucids' dedication of the temple to Zeus.

150 The city of Carthage, following incursions by Numidian King Masinissa, violates the terms of peace of the Second Punic War and provides Rome an impetus to begin the Third Punic War in 146. Roman forces led by consul Scipio Aemilianus take the city, raze it, evict the inhabitants, and salt the surrounding earth to hinder agriculture.

141 Parthian ruler Mithradates I enters the royal city of Seleucia in Mesopotamia and is recognized as king.

ca 200-100 Dry episodes in the Sahel, a semi-arid region of West Africa, shift the climate as well as the people that inhabit the area.

129 Ctesiphon, on the Tigris River, is selected as the capital of the Parthian Empire.

125 A plague of locusts afflicts Roman areas in northern Africa, raising the price of grain.

164 Judah Maccabee reclaims the Jerusalem temple for Jewish worship, inaugurating the feast of Hanukkah.

ca 150 Jewish philosopher Aristobolus of Paneas derives Greek philosophy from the wisdom of Moses.

100s Parthians officially sanction worship of the god Mithra, after whom Mithradates I is named.

Mulberry silk moth caterpillars work at their variably colored cocoons.

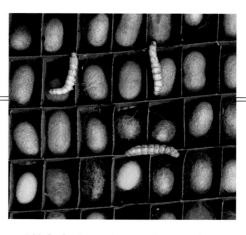

ASIA & OCEANIA

141 Han Wudi, the "martial emperor" of the Han dynasty in China, begins his 54-year-long reign. Through Legalist principles and an enormous bureaucracy, he seeks to augment the power and sway of the central government. He levies large taxes and establishes imperial monopolies on essential goods.

136 Chinese Emperor Han Wudi declares Confucianism the state ideology.

130s With the invasion by China into northern Vietnam and Korea comes the import of Confucianist principles and a Chinese form of government.

ca 140 Sericulture, the manufacture of silk, spreads from its point of origin in the Yellow River Valley to more southern portions of China and further west to India, where it becomes a highly prized commodity, as in Persia, Mesopotamia, and the Roman Empire.

124 Emperor Han Wudi establishes an imperial university to stock his bureaucracy with educated officeholders. Confucian classics are used as the basis of the curriculum, ensuring Confucianism's place in Chinese society.

113 Liu Sheng, a prince of the Han dynasty in China, dies. A member of the wealthiest class of society, he and his wife are buried in full jade suits threaded with two and a half pounds of gold wire.

ca 109 Chinese historian Sima Qian takes the reins from his father on a project to document the entire history of China. His *Records of the Historian* is a valuable resource to this day.

SCIENCE & TECHNOLOGY	PEOPLE & SOCIETY
100s Construction begins on the Pyramid of the Sun and the Pyramid of the Moon at the growing urban complex of Teotihuacan in the northeast portion of the Valley of Mexico.	
ca 170 The first paved streets in the world appear in Rome. **144 Rome's highest and longest aqueduct, the Aqua Marcia**, is built. **142 Rome's first stone bridge, the Pons Aemilius**, is completed. **129 Greek scientist and astronomer Hipparchus of Bithynia** creates the earliest known catalog of stars, using an early form of the astrolabe at his observatory on the Greek island of Rhodes. He documents the brightness and position of nearly 850 stars.	**152 Greek athlete Leonidas of Rhodes** wins three running events for the fourth straight time at the Olympic Games. **ca 115 Despite the efforts of the Gracchi brothers**, power and money in Rome remain centered in the hands of a small group of privileged elite. Small farmers continue to constitute the bulk of the Roman army. **107 Gaius Marius** is elected consul in Rome. In order to engage in the ongoing war with Numidian King Jugurtha, Marius recruits an army of landless farmers and urban workers.
ca 140 Greek philosopher Crates of Mallus, living and working in Asia Minor, develops the first known globe. **100s Ptolemaic mariners from Egypt** learn from Indian and Arab seamen the art of sailing the Indian Ocean utilizing its monsoon winds, thus enabling them to safely sail trade routes between India and the Mediterranean. The southwestern wind of summer is named Hippalus, after the merchant who successfully sailed it from the Gulf of Aden to the Indian peninsula.	**ca 104 John Hyrcanus, nephew of Judah Maccabee**, temporarily expands Judaea south to Negev and north to Galilee and becomes a Seleucid vassal. Popular appeals against his Hellenizing policies bring in the Romans, who annex the Judaean state in 63. **100s Women are employed by imperial and temple workshops** in urban centers throughout the Parthian Empire. They weave textiles in exchange for rations of grain, wine, or beer. **100s Bactria**, bordered to the east by India, imports Chinese goods such as textiles and bamboo by way of Bengal in southwest China—a precursor to the Silk Road.
ca 165 The earliest known record of sunspots is made by Chinese astronomers. **121 A Chinese inventor** develops the magic lantern, an early kind of image projector. **100s Iron tools**, such as shovels, picks, hoes, and sickles, enter into much more widespread use in China under the Han dynasty. The resulting agricultural surplus allows for the specialized manufacture of other crafts. **100s Suits of iron armor** are developed by Chinese craftsmen and employed with great success.	**ca 150 Seafaring Austronesians** arrive from Samoa to the Marquesas Islands and Tahiti. **139 Han Wudi sends his envoy Zhang Qian** on a 12-year expedition to explore the "far West." He engages in diplomatic and cultural exchange with the Xiongnu, Tibetan, and other Central Asian peoples. **106 Chinese historian and author Ban Zhao** composes her *Admonitions for Women*, claiming fidelity and devotion to husbands as the essential feminine virtue. It goes on to influence social mores in China for millennia.

THE BROTHERS GRACCHI

In the latter half of the Roman Republic, small landowners, the backbone of Rome's subsistence economy, suffered under a new rule that required every man of age to serve in the army for an entire campaign, regardless of duration. With Rome's manpower extended to its limit, the farms of peasants who were too far from home for too long fell into bankruptcy, only to be snatched up by wealthy aristocrats who were establishing large estates worked by slave labor. The gap between rich and poor was growing exponentially.

Tiberius Gracchus was born into this deteriorating situation. Well connected politically, he was elected in 133 B.C.E. to the tribunate of the plebs—representative of the lower classes of the Roman people—just like nearly every man in his family before him. He proposed a series of reforms to limit the power of large estate owners, which met with fierce opposition from senators with vested interests. Yet Gracchus was able not only to pass his bill, but also to fund it. In doing so, he gained fierce loyalty from masses of plebeians and fierce enmity from powerful patricians. He was clubbed to death in 132 in a riot initiated by the senator Scipio Nasica.

Ten years later another Gracchus, Tiberius's younger brother Gaius, was elected to the tribunate in 123. With the death of his brother, Gaius had inherited not only his family's holdings, but also its strong political views. Gaius turned his attention both to the problem of Rome's landless poor and the maltreatment by Rome of its Italian allies. His proposal to grant citizenship to all Latin-speaking allies led to Gaius's persecution and suicide in 122. A thousand men suspected to have been his supporters were killed soon afterwards at the hands of consul Lucius Opimius.

Latin-speaking allies were granted Roman citizenship only 33 years later, in the aftermath of a bloody and unnecessary civil war.

	POLITICS & POWER	GEOGRAPHY & ENVIRONMENT	CULTURE & RELIGION
THE AMERICAS	**ca 100 The population of Teotihuacan** reaches approximately 10,000.	**ca 100 The cocoa plant**, from which chocolate is made, is cultivated in equatorial regions of South America. **ca 50 A massive lava flow** covers the town of Cuicuilco and much of its surrounding farmland in the southwestern portion of the Mexican basin. Refugees flock to nearby Teotihuacan, increasing the extent of the city's regional influence.	**ca 100 The Moche culture** of northern coastal Peru begins constructing pyramid temples made of mud brick. **ca 100 Cahuachi, the major ceremonial center of the Nazca culture**, is constructed in southern Peru. With a very small permanent population, it most likely serves as a pilgrimage shrine to host large numbers only for ceremonial events.
EUROPE	**87 Gaius Marius**, in exile since his political rival, Lucius Cornelius Sulla, took power following the Social War, marches on Rome. He places the city under military occupation and begins a massacre of his political enemies. **83 Following Marius's death, Sulla** marches on Rome and begins his own purging of political enemies. In short time, he brings about the execution of nearly 10,000 Romans. **49 Political maneuvers in Rome** come to a head when Julius Caesar marches his troops across the Rubicon River into Italy. By 46 B.C.E., he is named dictator for life. By 44, he is assassinated by a group of senators.	**58 Gaius Julius Caesar** begins his conquests of Gaul, modern-day France. By the end of the decade, he brings a large number of these Celtic groups into the growing sphere of the Roman world. Through these victories and his subsequent writings, *On The Gallic War,* he also gains greater popular support in Rome.	**70s-40s The orations of Roman rhetorician Cicero**, lauded for his unique style, firmly establish Stoicism in the Roman psyche. **ca 60 Latin poet Catullus** composes his *Love Poems to Lesbia.* **42 Caesar** is recognized by the Roman state as a god, initiating the imperial cult that will characterize Roman society for centuries.
MIDDLE EAST & AFRICA	**83 The remainder of the deteriorating Seleucid Empire**, a holdover from the conquests of Alexander the Great, is conquered by Roman forces. This brings Syria and portions of Asia Minor into Rome's growing dominion. **53 The Battle of Carrhae**, during which the Parthian cavalry routs a Roman army in Mesopotamia, prevents the Romans from moving farther east. **51 Cleopatra** comes to the throne in Egypt. In 48 she meets Julius Caesar, marries him, and has his son; later she marries Marc Antony after having twins by him.		**ca 100 Bactrians** write the local Iranian language with Greek characters, mint gold coins, propagate Buddhism, and develop a syncretic style of art. **63 The Jewish state shrinks** when Roman general Pompey conquers Palestine and storms Jerusalem.
ASIA & OCEANIA	**81 "Debates on Salt and Iron"** are held at the Han capital of Chang'an. Confucian arguments to limit government intervention in the economy prevail.	**ca 100 Sugar cane** is developed and cultivated based on wild varieties found in the East Indies. **ca 100 Chinese Emperor Han Wudi** establishes agricultural communities in the Tarim Basin of Central Asia. Interaction with the Parthians and Bactrians farther to the west is facilitated, and the oasis city of Dunhuang becomes a major station along the Silk Road.	**ca 100 Towns along the Silk Road in Central Asia**, such as Merv, Bukhara, Samarkand, Kashgar, and others, which are economically dependent on trade, allow merchants to build Buddhist monasteries and invite monks into their midst. The populace of these towns is soon largely Buddhist. **ca 100 Hindu scholars** continue to revise and put into writing the two great epic oral poems of India, the *Mahabharata* and the *Ramayana*. They infuse these reworkings with Hindu theology and ethical teachings.

CONNECTIONS

Crossroads of East African Trade

The benefits of widespread trade between far-flung lands, made possible by the administrative policies of imperial states throughout the ancient world, was not lost on cities in sub-Saharan Africa. Mentioned in multiple Greek sources, the East African city of Rhapta came to prominence as a stopping-off point for Arab mariners who traded metal weapons and iron tools for quantities of ivory, coconut oil, tortoise shell, and rhinoceros horn. Greek and Roman coins unearthed in Tanzania suggest a Mediterranean presence, and a connection to Indonesian seamen has been theorized as well. Though extant until at least the sixth century C.E., no remains of this ancient marketplace have been found, keeping its exact location a matter of dispute.

ca 100 The Moche culture of northern coastal Peru uses bronze to make tools and weapons.

ca 50 The inhabitants of Cerros, on Chetumal Bay of the Yucatán Peninsula, raze portions of their village to the ground in order to build a civic center dominated by a small pyramid. It is decorated with immense countenances of the sun and Venus.

Bust of Caesar, crowned in laurel

ca 100 Syrian-born philosopher Poseidonius, working from Rhodes, discovers the correlation of tides to the lunar cycle.

ca 100 Following its refinement in Syria, glass is used in windows by wealthy Romans.

ca 90 Roman writer and scholar Marcus Terentius Varro proposes the idea that invisible particles which enter the body through the nose and mouth can cause illness and disease. This is the first known postulation of germ theory.

80 Philosopher Poseidonius estimates the circumference of the Earth to a high degree of accuracy.

ca 90 The earliest known British coins are used.

88 The Social War in Italy ends with Rome granting citizenship to allies on the peninsula.

73 Escaped slave Spartacus leads a rebel army in Italy that requires eight Roman legions to quell.

46 As dictator, Julius Caesar centralizes control of the Roman army, extends citizenship to the provinces, begins ambitious building projects to employ the urban poor, and reworks the Roman calendar.

JULIUS CAESAR

At the age of 30, Gaius Julius Caesar approached a statue of Alexander the Great in tears, weeping that "Alexander at my age had conquered so many nations, and I have all this time done nothing that is memorable." That would not be the case for long. In 59 B.C.E. Caesar was appointed proconsul of three Roman provinces. With legions of the Roman army at his command and considerable political clout in Rome, Caesar was set to pursue his long-held ambition to conquer the known world. Over the course of the next eight years, Caesar would not only extend Roman dominion as far north as Britain, but also pave the way for the transformation of Roman governance from a republic to a dictatorship to an empire.

In 59 B.C.E., Caesar took his troops into Gallia Comata, a vast stretch of land comprising modern-day France. Caesar forced the Celtic tribes there to succumb to Roman domination and sent hundreds of thousands of newly made slaves back to Rome. He then conquered much of Britain in one of the largest naval invasions in history. After subduing 800 cities and 300 tribes, causing the death of over a million Gauls and enslaving a million more, Caesar returned to Rome where he was heralded as a liberator, as dictator for life, and even as a god.

ca 100 The art of glassblowing is refined to a highly advanced level by Syrian craftsmen.

Lusterware glass of Syria

ca 100 The use of negative numbers becomes standard for Chinese mathematicians.

ca 100 Ice is used in China for refrigeration.

ca 100 In order to finance his military expeditions and other undertakings, Chinese Emperor Han Wudi raises taxes and confiscates property from wealthy landowners on oftentimes erroneous charges.

87 Emperor Han Wudi dies. Though his power is severely weakened by the end of his reign, at its height Han China reaches as far as modern-day Kyrgyzstan in the West and the Korean peninsula in the East.

POLITICS & POWER	GEOGRAPHY & ENVIRONMENT	CULTURE & RELIGION

THE AMERICAS

ca 1 C.E. Inhabitants of the Amazon rain forest of modern-day Brazil utilize a highly fertile soil, called *terra preta,* for their agriculture—which may be evidence of a complex society.

ca 25 C.E. The Tiahuanaco culture, centered at Lake Titicaca in modern-day Bolivia, begins constructing ceremonial centers, which the Inca will later copy.

EUROPE

40 B.C.E. Gaius Julius Caesar Octavianus, later known as Augustus, takes control of the Western Roman Empire after avenging his adoptive father's death. His temporary ally and Caesar's former lieutenant, Marc Antony, takes control of the East along with Queen Cleopatra of Egypt.

32 B.C.E. Octavianus declares war on Cleopatra in a bid for sole control of the Mediterranean. The following year, his trusted military commander Marcus Agrippa defeats Marc Antony's forces at the Battle of Actium, and Egypt is annexed to Rome.

ca 30 B.C.E. The population of Rome surges as the state employs hundreds of thousands of workers for numerous building projects of temples, baths, stadiums, and aqueducts.

12 B.C.E. Marcus Agrippa creates a map of the world based on surveys of the Roman road system.

ca 1 C.E. The Roman world has incorporated large parts of Spain, Gaul, Britain, and Germany, and the pace of life and the economy in these areas increases. Cities such as Toledo, Paris, Cologne, and London trace their origins to this period.

27 B.C.E. Latin poet Virgil begins composition of his *Aeneid,* an epic account of the legendary founding of Rome.

ca 23 B.C.E. Latin poet Horace composes his *Odes,* rustic vignettes of moral, philosophical, and amorous ruminations.

23 B.C.E. The cult of Rome and Augustus initiates the practice of worshipping living emperors as gods.

ca 20 C.E. Druidism, a Celtic religion based on nature worship and reincarnation, flourishes in Britain and Gaul. Attempts at suppression are made by Roman Emperor Tiberius.

MIDDLE EAST & AFRICA

40 B.C.E. Parthians briefly capture Syria and Asia Minor, ending myths of Roman invincibility.

6 C.E. On King Herod's death, revolts in Palestine lead to its incorporation as a Roman province.

ca 30 C.E. Jesus of Nazareth, preaching at a time of great tension between Roman overlords and Jewish subjects in Palestine, is crucified by Roman authorities suspicious of his message of an impending "kingdom of God."

ca 30 C.E. The kingdom of Axum is founded in northern Ethiopia.

19 C.E. An earthquake in Syria kills more than 100,000 people.

37-4 B.C.E. King Herod supports Hellenistic culture and begins a massive building program in Palestine.

ca 1 C.E. The Dead Sea Scrolls, the oldest extant Hebrew documents, are composed, expounding the belief system of the Essenes or another ascetic sect. Baptism in water is described as well as hope for deliverance from Roman rule.

ca 29 C.E. Jesus of Nazareth begins his ministry in Palestine and attracts devotees through his message of compassion and eternal salvation.

Fragments of one of the 800-900 Dead Sea Scrolls

ASIA & OCEANIA

9 C.E. Han minister Wang Mang, regent to the five-year-old emperor of China, claims the imperial throne as his own, ending the former Han dynasty. He then attempts a reform of land distribution that he is unable to enforce.

23 C.E. The revolt of the Red Eyebrows helps to bring down Wang Mang's rule and leads to the restoration of the Han dynasty in China.

ca 25 C.E. The capital of the Han dynasty in China is moved to Luoyang from Chang'an following a rash of damage inflicted upon Chang'an during the previous years of chaos and rebellion.

18 C.E. A severe drought strikes eastern China and continues for years. Flooding of the Yellow River in 25 C.E. compounds the impact of poor harvests due to drought.

ca 30 C.E. The practice of Buddhism undergoes changes that make it more accessible to the layman, facilitating a rapid spread throughout the Indian subcontinent. Termed Mahayana, this new form of Buddhism reveres the Buddha as divine, allows for the existence of Boddhisatvas (enlightened beings who delay their entry into nirvana to provide guidance to others), and regards acts of munificence as meritorious of salvation.

ANCIENT TECHNOLOGY

The sculpture Laocoön and His Sons, *depicting the Trojan priest's death in the* Iliad

25 B.C.E. Roman architect Vitruvius describes the first known elevator, a dumbwaiter operated by pulleys and cranks.

ca 1 C.E. Roman roads continue to be built, spanning the Roman world from Britain to Africa to Mesopotamia. Stations are set up at intervals for the Roman postal system.

In the Time of Jesus

Judea in the first century C.E. was a land rife with political and social tension between gentiles and Jews, between Roman overlords and subjects, and among various sects of Judaism itself. Any man capable of attracting crowds was viewed as politically dangerous by a number of interested parties, Roman governors and Jewish high priests alike, as there was no dearth of Jews ready at a moment's notice to begin a holy war against Rome. Jesus of Nazareth was never charged in his native region of Galilee with any serious legal offense, but when he entered Jerusalem to observe the Passover and was greeted by a mass of admirers, even his message of compassion became a portent of conflict.

ca 1 B.C.E. The Chinese invent the wheelbarrow.

PEOPLE & SOCIETY

ca 1 C.E. The building of houses made of wood and plaster begins in southwestern North America. The earliest examples of pottery in this area date to this period as well.

ca 1 C.E. Hopewell culture emerges in present-day southern Ohio and in the Illinois and Mississippi River Valleys.

30 B.C.E. Greek sculptors Agesander, Polydorus, and Athenodorus of Rhodes sculpt *Laocoön and His Sons,* depicting a scene from the *Iliad.* The work later influences Renaissance sculptors.

27 B.C.E. The Roman Senate grants Octavianus the unprecedented title of Augustus, meaning consecrated, beginning his 45 years of unopposed rule. He ushers in his so-called Pax Romana, an era characterized by increased law, trade, communication, and prosperity throughout the Roman world. He is widely considered the first Roman emperor.

30 B.C.E. Marc Antony and Cleopatra, on the verge of losing their political power in the eastern Mediterranean, commit suicide. The Ptolemaic dynasty of pharaohs ends and Egypt becomes a Roman province.

ca 20 C.E. Roman geographer Strabo describes the Arabian Peninsula as a land of fabulous wealth, a source of spices and frankincense, and a home to men who are free.

39 C.E. Sisters Trung Trac and Trung Nhi lead a rebellion against their Han overlords in what is now northern Vietnam. They briefly establish an autonomous state before being put down by Chinese forces in 43 C.E.

THE REBELLION OF THE TRUNG SISTERS

Women in ancient Vietnamese society were far from the idealized Confucian wife and mother described by Chinese historian and author Ban Zhao in her *Admonitions for Women.* In Vietnam, women were respected and played active roles in social and economic life. This cultural tradition came into conflict with that of Han China, which had invaded and occupied northern Vietnam in the second century B.C.E. Local resistance built up, and in 39 C.E., two sisters, Trung Trac and Trung Nhi, led a rebellion against Chinese occupation.

When Trung Trac's husband was assassinated for plotting against the Chinese, she took control of the operation. Along with her sister, mother, and members of the aristocracy, she raised a force of 80,000 men and women and marched on Lien Lau, forcing the Chinese general who had killed her husband to flee along with all his troops. Over the next three years, this force of untrained and under-supplied Vietnamese rebels wrested dozens of citadels in northern Vietnam from Chinese rule. In many cases, the leaders of the Vietnamese forces were women, including the Trung sisters' mother.

At Me Linh, on the Red River near modern-day Haiphong, the Trung sisters proclaimed themselves joint queens of an autonomous Vietnamese state extending from southern China to central Vietnam. But when Chinese General Ma Yuan arrived with his battle-hardy and well-trained troops in 43, the sisters and their forces were little match for them. With sure defeat at hand, the Trung sisters threw themselves into the Red River, and the Vietnamese people were once again brought under Chinese dominion. Though their efforts were short-lived, the Trung sisters are still celebrated as heroines and symbols of the first organized resistance against foreign occupation in Vietnam. Their rebellion was certainly not to be the last.

POLITICS & POWER	GEOGRAPHY & ENVIRONMENT	CULTURE & RELIGION

THE AMERICAS

ca 50 Hopewell peoples of eastern North America develop increasingly more sophisticated structures made of earth.

ca 50 The population of the Mexican Basin decreases significantly except in Teotihuacan, near modern-day Mexico City, which grows three times larger.

ca 50 The ceremonial center of Teotihuacan covers 12 square miles and contains 600 pyramid temples.

ca 50 Hopewell peoples of eastern North America hone their artistic style. As they expand their rituals associated with burial, many finely produced crafts go to the graves of important persons.

EUROPE

ca 60 Boudicca, queen of the Celtic Iceni tribe in Britain, is defeated by Roman forces. The Romans later reduce the political and legal status of Celtic women.

69 Following Emperor Nero's forced suicide and the end of the Julio-Claudian line of succession, generals across the Roman Empire vie for the imperial title. At the end of the "year of the four emperors," Vespasian, a commander fresh from his conquests in Judaea, establishes the Flavian dynasty.

64 Fire destroys half of Rome. Emperor Nero blames the Christian community; meanwhile, he undertakes an opulent imperial building project, his Golden House, on the ashes.

79 Mount Vesuvius erupts, burying the nearby cities of Pompeii, Herculaneum, and Stabiae under many feet of ash and pumice.

77 Roman jack-of-all-trades Pliny the Elder completes his *Natural History,* a compilation of writings and remarks that runs the gamut of observable phenomena.

92 Roman Emperor Domitian begins the widespread execution of Christians for not adhering to the imperial cult.

MIDDLE EAST & AFRICA

66 After Greeks in Jerusalem desecrate a synagogue as Roman troops look on, the first Jewish-Roman War begins, with the Jewish high priest leading a successful attack on the Roman garrison. In the end, the skirmish results in the destruction of Jerusalem and its temple by Roman troops under Vespasian.

72-73 Roman forces put an end to the Great Jewish Revolt in Judaea by sieging and overcoming the remaining holdouts of Jewish rebels, some of whom are in the hilltop fortress known as Masada.

Roman soldiers carry spoils home following the destruction of the temple in Jerusalem.

65 An earthquake destroys the Phrygian city of Laodicea in Asia Minor.

ca 50 Christian convert turned missionary Paul of Tarsus begins efforts to bring non-Jews into the Christian community. He travels throughout the eastern Roman Empire, corresponding with converts in epistles on matters of faith.

ca 70 Work on the Gospels, accounts of Jesus of Nazareth's life and teachings, is undertaken by members of the new Christian faith.

ca 85 Christians are expelled from the Jewish faith.

ASIA & OCEANIA

ca 60 Han forces under General Ban Chao reestablish Chinese control of Central Asia from the nomadic Xiongnu tribes, a pattern that is often repeated during the Han dynasty.

ca 50 A number of Roman trading posts are established along the Indian coast. From these settlements, Indian textiles are presumably prepared to Roman specifications for export.

92 A cycle of floods and droughts in China is worsened by plagues of locusts.

ca 50 Sanskrit becomes the mode of written communication in Southeast Asia, as rulers begin to lead based on an Indian model.

50 Christian apostle and missionary Thomas, after some initial success converting Indians to Christianity, is martyred for attempting to convert King Gondophernes of Gandhara in northwestern India.

58 Buddhism is introduced to China by Han Emperor Ming Ti. Initially, it garners only lukewarm interest there.

68 The White Horse Temple, one of the earliest Buddhist temples in China, is built just outside the new Han capital at Luoyang.

SCIENCE & TECHNOLOGY

ca 50 The Street of the Dead, Teotihuacan's major avenue, stretches two miles in length and 150 feet in width.

ca 50 The Pyramid of the Sun in Teotihuacan rises 215 feet tall and measures 500,000 square feet at its base. It is one of the largest structures of its type found in the Western Hemisphere.

ca 70 Roman Emperor Vespasian begins construction of the Flavian Amphitheater, better known as the Colosseum, over the top of Nero's former Golden House. With a 50,000-spectator capacity, it is equipped with underground passageways and trap doors. It can even be flooded to host mock naval battles.

ca 80 Greek physician Pedanios Dioscurides writes his *Medicinal Materials,* a catalog of over 600 plants and their medicinal effects.

ca 80 An astronomical calculator incorporating 31 interlocking wheels is produced on the Greek island of Antikythera.

46-47 The Mesopotamian calendar is readjusted, only a month off after 800 years.

ca 62 Mathematician and inventor Heron of Alexandria, stressing practicality over pure theory, describes mechanical labor-saving devices such as a steam engine, a water clock, a water fountain, and an odometer. A world highly dependent on slave labor pays him little heed.

90s Remarkably well-wrought tombs and temples are hewn directly into the sandstone cliffs near the city of Petra, the capital of the kingdom of Nabataea in modern-day Jordan, whose wealth derives from the spice trade.

PEOPLE & SOCIETY

ca 50 Most of Teotihuacan's inhabitants, about a third of whom do not farm, live near the ceremonial complex within structured residential grid patterns.

40s Roman Emperor Claudius creates an imperial bureaucracy of professional administrators, composed largely of former slaves.

80 An epidemic of anthrax runs through the Roman Empire, killing thousands of animals and people and reaching the western border of the Han empire in China.

ca 90 Stoic philosopher and former slave Epictetus studies and lectures among Rome's intellectual elite. His achievement demonstrates the social opportunities available to urban slaves of the Roman empire.

1st centuries c.e. The Silk Road from China passes through Parthian territory, enriching the treasury and bringing new prosperity to war-torn Mesopotamia.

ca 50 The Periplus of the Erythraean Sea, a Greek navigational document, describes trading in the Red Sea and along the East African coast to India.

ca 50 Romans displace Arabs in the rich spice trade of the Red Sea.

1st centuries c.e. Indian textiles, Chinese silk, Afghan turquoise, and southeast Asian spices are traded along the Silk Road for Roman gold and silver.

92 Ban Gu, author of the History of the Han, dies. His sister, Ban Zhao, completes the work.

MASADA

In 66 C.E. a group of Jewish rebels took a fortress in the Judaean Desert overlooking the Dead Sea. Known as Masada, from the Hebrew word for fortress, it had been built a hundred years earlier by the Roman-appointed King Herod. This act of rebellion was one of the first of the Great Jewish Revolt that lasted the next seven years and resulted in one of the diasporas that characterize much of Jewish history.

In 73, having already destroyed and looted Jerusalem itself, Roman forces approached Masada with the intention of putting down with finality this local nuisance. The story, as told by Jewish historian Flavius Josephus, is that after an unopposed siege of the fortress, Roman forces knocked through the walls only to find 1,000 dead bodies of men, women, and children, the result of a mass suicide. Archaeological remains tell a slightly different story. Twenty-five skeletons found in a nearby cave hint that some attempted escape. Others, greatly outnumbered, may have fought to the death. In any case, the story of Masada provides a vivid example of the ongoing human struggle for freedom.

Masada, a hilltop fortress in the Judaean Desert

FROZEN IN TIME: POMPEII 79 C.E.

O N THE EARLY AFTERNOON OF AUGUST 24, 79 C.E., the cone of Mount Vesuvius erupted 17 miles into the air, sending forth a column of dust, smoke, and pumice, the fallout of which covered a 25-mile span from Mount Vesuvius outward. It buried nearby towns such as Pompeii, Herculaneum, and Stabiae under many feet of ash and pumice, at the same time preserving certain delicacies of their construction, such as the fresco of a young Roman couple (left). Pliny the Elder—statesman, naturalist, and author of *Natural History*—was stationed at the time at the nearby port of Misenum. He ventured into the midst of the destruction out of academic interest and a heroic bent; he never made it out. His nephew, Pliny the Younger, who had stayed behind at Misenum, later wrote a description of the day's events to the historian Tacitus:

> A dense, black cloud was coming up behind us, spreading over the earth like a flood. . . . Darkness fell, not the dark of a moonless or cloudy night, but as if a lamp had been put out in a closed room. You could hear the shrieks of women, the wailing of infants, and the shouting of men; some were calling their parents, others their children or wives, trying to recognize them by their voices. People bewailed their own fate or that of their relatives, and there were some who prayed for death in their terror of dying. . . . I could boast that not a groan or cry of fear escaped me in these perils, but I admit that I derived some poor consolation in my mortal lot from the belief that the whole world was dying with me, and I with it.

In the days and weeks that followed the eruption, former residents along with teams of salvage workers sent from Rome by the Emperor Titus dug out what they could from the buried cities. Residents searched for family members or personal belongings left behind, salvage workers looked for statuary or marble to be shipped back to Rome, looters sought newly buried treasure. Within decades, though, Pompeii and other nearby cities had become the stuff of legend, disappearing completely from maps by the fourth century C.E.

Rediscovered in the late 1500s, the ruins of Pompeii have preserved a glimpse into the daily life of citizens of the Roman Empire that would otherwise be lost to history. The city center, its amphitheater, its shops and sidestreets, its domestic architecture and interior decoration, even the remains of Vesuvius's victims can still be seen as they were, frozen in time, August 24, 79 C.E.

ABOVE: *This fresco of a young Roman couple was kept in pristine condition for centuries by Vesuvius's eruption. Much of what is known about Roman wall painting derives from such Pompeiian examples.*
RIGHT: *Mount Vesuvius looms in the background over one of its victims. This graphic moment in time has been preserved by plaster poured into the cavity left by a man's decomposed body, a technique developed in 1864 by archaeologist Giuseppe Fiorelli.*

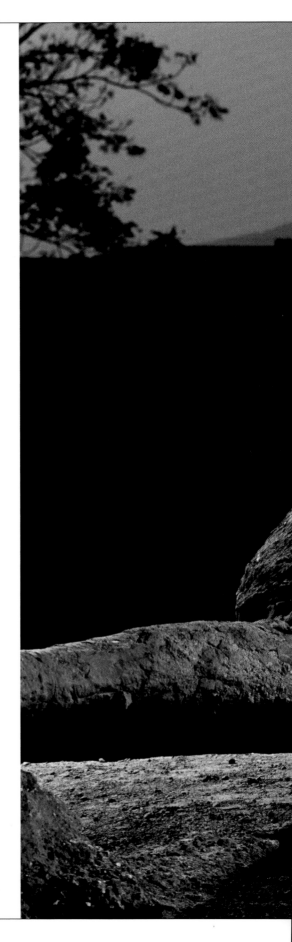

	POLITICS & POWER	GEOGRAPHY & ENVIRONMENT	CULTURE & RELIGION
THE AMERICAS	**ca 100 The Moche culture** of northern coastal Peru further extends its influence over neighboring peoples. It serves as the political nerve center of about 2,500 square miles of river valleys. **ca 100 Competition** among peoples in what is now California divides the region into distinct political territories, each with leaders who hold considerable sway over the social life of their communities, trade and diplomatic exchange, and matters of war.	**ca 100 Hopewell peoples** of eastern North America engage in trade that gathers materials from regions as distant as the Rocky Mountains, the Great Lakes, and the Appalachians.	**100s Moche artisans** continue to create a great variety of ornate ceramics, taking as their subjects the rulers of the day as well as mythological, floral, erotic, and everyday motifs. **ca 100 Moche culture** continues to be characterized not only by a high level of agricultural knowledge, but also by advanced metalworking. Artisans master the technique of inlaying turquoise designs on gold plaques.
EUROPE	**101 Roman Emperor Trajan** further extends the boundaries of the Roman Empire beyond the Danube River into Dacia. **161 Marcus Aurelius** becomes emperor of Rome following the death of his adoptive father Antoninus Pius. Though he espouses the Stoic philosophy throughout his emperorship, he is almost constantly at war.	 *Gladiators spar in this third century C.E. mosaic.*	**ca 100 Roman historian Tacitus** writes a history of Rome sharply critical of the emperors following Augustus. **ca 100 Eastern cults**, such as those of Mithra and Isis, spread in Rome. They become popular even though the authorities attempt to suppress them. **ca 150 Greek philosopher and theologian Justin Martyr** reconciles Platonic philosophy with Christian teachings and rejects Greek mythology.
MIDDLE EAST & AFRICA	**107 Petra**, in modern-day Jordan, is conquered and subsumed into the Roman Empire. **114 Roman Emperor Trajan** conquers Armenia and Mesopotamia. **162-66 Warfare** is renewed between Romans and Persians over control of Armenia. The result is Persian losses.	**151 Egyptian geographer Claudius Ptolemy** in his *Geography* sets out the whole of the world as it is known to the Romans. It stretches from modern-day Iceland to Sri Lanka, with broad swaths of unknown lands to the east and south.	**132-35 Bar Kochba** leads a revolt against Rome, the last of a series of uprisings that lead to the persecution and expulsion of Jews from Palestine. This also leads to the rise of rabbis—scholars who begin compilation of the Mishnah, a codification of traditional Jewish oral law. **ca 150 The rise of Gnostic sects** inspires the Christian community to push for the canonization of scriptures.
ASIA & OCEANIA	**100s Large landowners** gain an upper hand in the government of Han dynasty China. They evade taxes and burden peasants with the costs of governance, even raising private armies to enforce their interests.	**153 Powerful earthquakes and plagues of locusts** afflict areas of China.	**ca 100 Less expensive and easier to write on than silk, paper** becomes the main medium of written communication in China. The cost of education is dramatically lowered and a high level of cultural sophistication results. **147 A Parthian monk, An Shigao**, arrives in Luoyang and begins the first translations of Indian Buddhist texts into Chinese. He is instrumental in the establishment of Buddhism in China.

SCIENCE & TECHNOLOGY	PEOPLE & SOCIETY
ca 100 The Moche begin construction on Huaca Cao Viejo, a massive ceremonial complex consisting of a six-tiered pyramidal structure and a large plaza. It is adorned with ornately detailed and colorful friezes. **ca 100 The Moche** begin construction of the Huaca del Sol, or Pyramid of the Sun, which serves as either a palace or a mausoleum and is the largest structure of its day in the Americas.	**ca 100 Evidence of the Adena culture** of eastern North America gradually dwindles and vanishes, due to either their assimilation into the contemporaneous Hopewell culture or a mass migration. **ca 100 Early Anasazi people** settle into the four corners region of southwestern North America. They weave baskets and sandals for everyday use and supplement hunting and gathering with the cultivation of corn and pumpkins.
ca 100 Romans expand their system of roads so they can supply their border forts and move troops more quickly. **ca 100 Mines in Britain** supply the Roman Empire with lead and tin.	**ca 100 Slaves** account for as much as a third of the population of the Roman empire. **ca 100 Men from the provinces** join the Roman army in order to gain citizenship and learn a trade. **ca 100 Successful chariot drivers** become popular heroes in Rome. **ca 150 Goths** arrive on the Danubian frontier of the Roman Empire. Although they at first raid the empire heavily, forcing Roman forces to eventually abandon Dacia, they also adopt many Roman laws and customs.
ca 100 Heron of Alexandria sets up a series of gears to perform simple calculations—a kind of computer that is ages ahead of its time. **ca 100 Parthians** develop the *liwan*, a large central arch, and a dome supported on squinches, both of which become characteristic forms of Islamic architecture.	**152 Farmers in Egypt** revolt, affecting a grain shortage in Rome. **144-173 Under Kanishka, the Kushans of Central Asia** become middlemen in the silk trade. Kanishka, a convert to Buddhism, is instrumental in spreading Buddhism to the West as well as north into Central Asia. The Kushans develop Gandharan art, a merger of Greek and Indian styles that is sometimes called Greco-Buddhist.
105 Chinese court official Cai Lun describes the modern method of making paper from hemp, bark, or bamboo pulp. Some sources trace its invention back to 150 B.C.E. **132 The seismograph and armillary sphere** are developed by Zhang Heng, an astronomer of Han China.	**100s Malay people of Southeast Asia** participate in the widespread trade network made possible by classical empires. Due to their seafaring way of life, Malay culture expands throughout the Malay peninsula and neighboring islands.

ART OF THE MOCHE

How does an ancient culture preserve and pass along a history of its leaders, gods, mores, and daily life in the absence of a system of written communication? In the case of the Moche people of coastal Peru, it was through their art.

A people of extremes, the Moche were able to produce pieces breathtaking in their emotional expressiveness or shocking in their gruesome brutality. They used molds to create fired clay for ceramics but worked each piece in an individual way, leaving to posterity a great quantity of unique artifacts. Subjects of their ceramic vessels run the gamut, from portraitures of important people to scenes of mythology, sexuality, or everyday life.

Moche temple complexes were adorned with colorful murals, a common motif of which is a character named the Decapitator, who is often represented with a multitude of arms, always with a knife in one of them and a severed head gripped by the hair in another. Some scenes are so gruesome that scholars assumed them to be hyperbole until archaeological remains confirmed their place in Moche ritual. Through the abundance and remarkable clarity of these pieces of art, a glimpse into the workings of this lost society is made possible.

Victim of the Decapitator, a common Moche motif

POLITICS & POWER	GEOGRAPHY & ENVIRONMENT	CULTURE & RELIGION

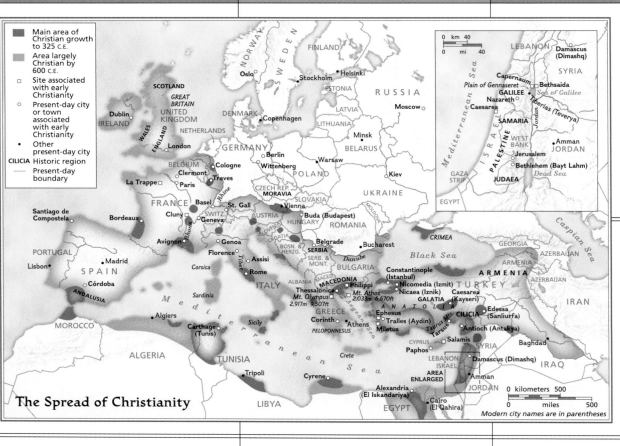

The Spread of Christianity

Legend:
- Main area of Christian growth to 325 C.E.
- Area largely Christian by 600 C.E.
- □ Site associated with early Christianity
- ○ Present-day city or town associated with early Christianity
- • Other present-day city
- CILICIA Historic region
- — Present-day boundary

Map showing the extent of the Christian religion by the seventh century C.E.

Modern city names are in parentheses

THE AMERICAS

ca 200 The monumental architecture of Teotihuacan includes the Temple of the Feathered Serpent, Quetzalcoatl. It is one of the architectural masterpieces of Mesoamerica.

EUROPE

203 Vibea Perpetua, a young Roman woman, writes an account of her imprisonment for being a Christian. She is later martyred.

MIDDLE EAST & AFRICA

ca 200 The Kingdom of Axum, centered in Ethiopia, grows into the largest market for foreign goods in sub-Saharan Africa. It dominates commerce on the African coast of the Red Sea and trades with Alexandria and beyond.

224 Already weakened by internal rebellion, the Parthian Empire is brought down by the Sassanids of Persia. They will rule Mesopotamia from their capital at Ctesiphon, on the Tigris River near modern-day Baghdad, for the next 400 years.

ca 200 Bantu-speaking farmers from West Africa migrate into much of southern Africa, bringing with them advanced agriculture, herding, and ironworking.

ca 185 The New Testament is canonized under the leadership of Irenaeus, and an early Christian creed, called the rule of faith, is promulgated. Tertullian of Africa writes an apologia for the faith; Clement and Origen, bishops of Alexandria, write theological works. "Acts of the martyrs" also proliferate.

226 The first king of the Sassanid Empire in Persia, King Ardashir I, makes Zoroastrianism the state religion. Zoroastrian priests, known as magi, begin to compile the remnants of their scriptures, previously transmitted only orally, into a single volume of five parts, the *Avesta*. New adherents flock to the religion.

ASIA & OCEANIA

184 The Yellow Turban uprising erupts in eastern China. Led by Daoist leader Zhang Jiao, this peasant rebellion contributes to the weakening state of the Later Han dynasty, requiring a huge army and great expense to suppress.

220 After the collapse of the Later Han dynasty, China is divided among three territorial states: Wei in the north, Wu in the southeast, and Shu in the southwest. This is known as the Three Kingdoms period.

ca 200 Silkworms from China are introduced into Korea and Japan, stimulating the textile industry in both of these countries.

ca 215 Trade between the Asian world and the Roman Empire is in severe decline.

175 Confucian classics are inscribed on stone stelae at the Imperial Academy in the Han capital of Luoyang.

ca 220 With the dissolution of the Han dynasty, interest in its state ideology, Confucianism, begins to wane.

SCIENCE & TECHNOLOGY	PEOPLE & SOCIETY
ca 200 Stone-walled compounds begin to replace the previous, less substantial mud-brick buildings of the city of Teotihuacan in the Mexican basin. **ca 200 The Hohokam people** develop dry farming techniques and build an extensive irrigation system to harvest squash, beans, and corn twice a year in the harsh, semiarid environment around the Phoenix basin, in today's Arizona.	**ca 200 The Maya city of Copán** is founded in Honduras. **ca 200 Peoples of coastal California** develop advanced fishing skills to extract food from the abundant marine supply. They also engage in long-distance trade that spreads seashells throughout the region.
ca 200 Cologne and Lyon become the most important glassmaking centers in the Roman Empire. **203 The Arch of Septimius Severus**, still standing at the east end of the Roman Forum, is dedicated. Its reliefs depict scenes from Severus's campaigns in Mesopotamia. **217 The immense baths of Caracalla** in Rome are completed. Equipped with an Olympic-sized swimming pool, a cold and hot pool room, and numerous exercise courts, it can accommodate up to 10,000 people at once.	**180 The population of the Roman Empire** declines significantly following a 15-year outbreak of smallpox that even claims Emperor Marcus Aurelius. This not only decreases trade, but also contracts the empire's economy into more regionalized markets. **201 Greek physician Galen** dies at the age of 71. In his lifetime he was a prolific thinker and writer, perhaps even developing an early form of brain surgery. **229 Historian Dio Cassius** retires from politics to finish his *History of Rome,* an effort comprising 80 books, many of which are still in existence.
ca 224 The cultivation of eastern crops such as rice, sugarcane, and eggplant is introduced into Iran by merchants of the newly formed Sassanid Empire, who trade extensively with peoples to both the East and West.	**ca 200 The Nok culture of West Africa,** modern-day Nigeria, fades from the historical record. The clay figures it produced are some of the earliest examples of stylized sculpture in sub-Saharan Africa.
	208 General Cao Cao, who has spent the past decade attempting to keep the Han dynasty from falling apart at the hands of imperial usurper Dong Zhuo, is appointed prime minister of the state of Wei in northern China. He will spend the remainder of his life consolidating power there. **220 Cao Pi, son of General Cao Cao,** is crowned the first emperor of the Wei dynasty in northern China.

THE RISE OF CHRISTIANITY

The Christian church began as a clandestine sect of Judaism that met in homes, as opposed to public centers of worship, and was deemed illegal by the Roman Empire. Around 45 C.E., the freshly converted Paul of Tarsus began a lifetime of missionary work that sought to spread Jesus's message to the non-Jewish world, at the expense of early Christianity's essentially Jewish character and to the dismay of many early Christian conservatives.

Paul traveled throughout the eastern Mediterranean, evangelizing and making converts with whom he corresponded by letter, a corpus of writing that now constitutes a portion of the New Testament. The production of the Gospels soon afterward paved the way for a more structured ministry, and persecution by the Roman Empire served only to strengthen the missionary zeal of the church's faithful. Sympathy for this salvation-based religion continued to increase, culminating in 313 C.E. when Emperor Constantine I extended toleration for Christians throughout the Roman Empire and subscribed to the religion himself.

A great influx of new converts who saw the advantages of adopting the emperor's faith ensued. Though this may have diluted the church's constituency, it did not slow its pace of expansion. Gregory the Illuminator was already converting the kingdom of Armenia, while Nestorian Christians pushed further into Central Asia, all the way to China. Ulfilas was soon preaching to the Goths and translating the Bible into their language; Martin of Tours found converts in Gaul, Patrick in Ireland, and Frumentius in Ethiopia. A Christian church, which was said to have been founded by the missionary apostle Thomas, was even known to exist in southern India. Indeed, by the close of the fifth century, barely a corner of the Western world was untouched by this religion of humble origins.

	POLITICS & POWER	GEOGRAPHY & ENVIRONMENT	CULTURE & RELIGION
THE AMERICAS	**ca 250 The Maya societies** in the southern lowlands of the Yucatán Peninsula enter into what is considered their Classic period, characterized by divine kings ruling over powerful city-states that conduct their own affairs and carry out their own trade.	**200s A series of droughts** afflicts coastal regions of modern-day California and continues for centuries. **200s Peoples of California** plant oak trees to produce acorn crops and ensure a stable supply of food. To protect their stands of oak, they use fire to remove competing plant life and harmful insects and parasites.	
EUROPE	**235-284 Twenty-six claimants to the imperial throne of Rome** successively seize power, hold it briefly, and then die violently either at the hands of rivals or their own troops. **286 Roman Emperor Diocletian** splits his empire into two administrative units. He rules the eastern half from Nicomedia in Asia MInor and appoints his soldier Maximian to rule as co-emperor from Milan in northern Italy. **293 Roman Emperor Diocletian** sets up the tetrarchy, a system of deputy emperorship with an Augustus ruling in either half of the Roman Empire and a Caesar assigned to him as collaborator and successor.	**ca 265 A five-year epidemic of plague**, likely transmitted via the Silk Road, afflicts Rome and much of its empire.	**275 Denis, patron saint of France and reputedly first bishop of Paris**, arrives in Gaul in an attempt to convert the region to Christianity. **303 Roman Emperor Diocletian** issues four edicts of nontoleration of Christianity. Thus begins the most severe period of Christian martyrdom.
MIDDLE EAST & AFRICA	**ca 260 The Sassanid Empire under Shapur I** defeats several Roman armies, ravages Syria, and captures Roman Emperor Valerian. **272 Romans capture Palmyra** in south-central Syria and its queen, Zenobia. **ca 299 A treaty is struck between Persia and Rome**, bringing peace to their frontier. Romans build forts and roads for the frontier defense system; Sassanians establish buffer states and turn their armies north to the Caucasus and Central Asia. Greek culture flourishes in Iran for the last time.	**256 An epidemic ravages Alexandria.** In its wake, many survivors are drawn into the Christian church. **ca 300 Despite intensive, yet sporadic, imperial persecutions**, Christian communities flourish in the Middle East and North Africa, as well as in even more distant locales.	**ca 230 Gregory the Wonderworker** makes many Christian converts in central Anatolia. **ca 250 The prophet Mani** preaches a new ascetic religion that blends elements of Zoroastrianism, Christianity, and Buddhism into a cosmopolitan message. **286 Christian monk Anthony of Egypt** wanders into the desert, where he remains for 20 years in solitude and austerity. He is widely considered the founder of Christian monasticism.
ASIA & OCEANIA	**ca 230 Chinese historical accounts** describe a female ruler named Himiko, or "sun princess," in Archaic Japan who wielded both political and religious authority, lending credence to the idea that early Japanese society may have been matriarchal. **243 An embassy from the Funan kingdom of Southeast Asia**, an important trading partner of the Chinese, arrives at the southern Chinese court in Nanjing.	**265 Chinese geographer Pei Xiu** produces a large and detailed map of China during the period of the Three Kingdoms. He is the first to use a system of north-south and east-west parallels.	**200s Shinto**, the name given to the indigenous religion of Japan, focuses on the worship of kami, deities of nature and anthropomorphic gods and goddesses. **200s Daoism** gains more adherents in China than ever before, thanks in part to less competition from Confucianism and an ideology that seeks inner peace in a confusing world. **200s Buddhism** spreads from towns along the Silk Road to the nomads of Central Asia.

Jaina figurine depicting a ballplayer

SCIENCE & TECHNOLOGY	PEOPLE & SOCIETY
ca 250 Mogollon farmers of southwestern North America and northern portions of Mexico adopt irrigation techniques of the deserts and grow *chapalote* corn, a strain that has greater volume than other varieties. **ca 300 The Maya** develop an architectural arch that employs levels of overlapping stones built into massive walls, instead of a single keystone, to provide the necessary support.	**ca 250 The inhabitants of Becan**, on the Yucatán Peninsula, build a defensive moat around their settlement, evidence of the large role warfare played in Maya civilization. **ca 300 A group of Maya people** settle Jaina, an island off the coast of the Yucatán Peninsula. This small but busy trading post will become well known for its immense cemetery and an estimated 20,000 burials. **ca 300 Anasazi patterns of life** become widespread in the San Juan Basin, on the Colorado Plateau, and in northern regions of modern-day New Mexico.
271 Construction of Emperor Aurelian's defensive wall is undertaken in Rome. This massive barricade, 12 miles long and 12 feet thick, is representative of the walls being built around cities throughout the Roman empire, a trend that continues well into the Middle Ages.	**259 A first wave of barbarian incursions** into the Roman Empire occurs as Germanic tribes such as the Burgundians and the Alemans sweep into the regions of Romanized Gaul. **274 Emperor Aurelian** reinstitutes paganism in Rome, building a temple to Helios, the unconquered Sun. **305 Following Diocletian's retirement** from politics and his own imperial post, the tetrarchy he established to govern the far-flung Roman Empire devolves into a number of factions vying for sole control, and civil war ensues.
200s The minting of coins is begun in the Ethiopian kingdom of Axum.	**ca 260 Roman soldiers captured in Antioch** by the Sassanid forces of Shapur I are moved to Iran, where their advanced technical skills are used to advantage in building the city of Gondeshapur and a dam at Shushtar, named the Dam of Caesar. Other captives start Christian communities in Iran. **270 Plotinus** dies, having founded the school of Neoplatonism, which dominates philosophical thinking for centuries and affects Christian and, to a lesser degree, Islamic theological thought.
269 A manual on astrology is composed by Indian scholar Sphujidhvaja. It is based on translations of Greek originals. **297 A Chinese military commander**, interred in a tomb of this date, wears to the afterlife a belt bedecked with ornaments of aluminum. This metal is not isolated from its natural compounds by Western scientists until 1825.	**ca 250 Chinese and Tibetan sources** make the first known references to the game of polo. **ca 300 The Tomb culture of Japan**, in which leaders are buried in elaborate sepulchres with clay figurines, flourishes. **ca 300 Austronesian mariners** establish colonies on the Hawaiian Islands.

THE NAZCA LINES

The Nazca lines, located in the arid deserts of southern coastal Peru, are a jigsaw puzzle that scholars and conspiracy theorists alike have been grappling with since their discovery by airline pilots in the 1920s. Visible only from the air, they consist of an immense number of geoglyphs, or markings made in the ground, in a variety of shapes and sizes. Some are strictly geometric—lines, triangles, trapezoids, and spirals—while others are more animated representations of flowers, trees, birds, other animals, and even one peculiar anthropomorphic figure who is referred to as the Owl Man.

The presence of these lines has elicited a number of explanations to justify their presence, some scientifically rigorous, others less so. Since the bulk of the lines were made over an 800-year period from about 200 B.C.E. to 600 C.E., it is reasonable to assume they may have served manifold functions largely associated with rituals, planting, and the extraction of water from a harsh desert environment. We know the Nazca were skilled in irrigation, constructing a network of channels that linked the Nazca River with underground water flowing from the Andes. Just how connected the lines may be to these irrigation channels or other subterranean water supplies remains unknown.

Two workers measure the lines of the Spider glyph.

	POLITICS & POWER	GEOGRAPHY & ENVIRONMENT	CULTURE & RELIGION
THE AMERICAS			**300s During the Classic period of Maya civilization**, many intellectual endeavors are pursued, including formulation of a system of writing and a standard calendar based on the movements of celestial bodies.
EUROPE	**312 Roman general Constantine I** marches on Rome and at the Battle of Milvian Bridge usurps the imperial title from the last fully pagan emperor, his brother-in-law Maxentius. **358 After continued raids and increasing pressure on its borders**, the Roman Empire is compelled to abandon the region of modern-day Belgium to the Franks.	**330 Constantine I** dedicates the ancient Greek city of Byzantium as his new capital. Fashioning it a "new Rome," he renames it Constantinople. It is located on the European side of the Sea of Marmora, the entrance to the Black Sea.	**313 The Edict of Milan** is issued by eastern Roman Emperors Constantine and Licinius, confirming official toleration by the Roman Empire of Christianity and all other religions. **ca 350 Following its imperial sanction, the Christian Church** organizes itself into a top-to-bottom hierarchy of ranking officials.
MIDDLE EAST & AFRICA	**300s The Hephthalites**, a nomadic people from northern China also known as the White Huns, take the state of Bactria, centered in modern-day Afghanistan, from which they prepare to mount an offensive into India. **ca 350 The Ethiopian kingdom of Axum** invades and brings about the fall of the kingdoms of Meroe in Sudan and Saba in the southwestern Arabian Peninsula.		
ASIA & OCEANIA	**300s Chandra Gupta and his son Samudra** expand dominion throughout most of India through alliances and military force. They create the first centrally administered empire in India since the Mauryan, yet allow local governments to remain intact. **313 The Chinese colony of Lo-lang** in the northwestern portion of the Korean peninsula is retaken by Korean forces. **316 The Xiongnu army** sacks Chang'an, bringing an end to the western Jin dynasty. **ca 350 From humble beginnings, the Yamato culture** extends its base of power throughout the Japanese archipelago and into Korea.	*Model showing the Colosseum's place amid the monuments of Rome at the time of Constantine I*	**300s Buddhism** gains a firm foothold in China due to efforts by Indian missionaries and an influx of Central Asian nomads. **310 Buddhist monk Fotudeng** arrives in Chang'an. **ca 360 A Buddhist monastery is founded at Nalanda** in the Ganges River Valley near the former Mauryan capital of Pataliputra, also renowned as an educational center. Pilgrims and students alike converge here to study Buddhist doctrine, as well as archaic Sanskrit texts, Hindu philosophy, logic, and medicine.

SCIENCE & TECHNOLOGY	PEOPLE & SOCIETY
300s At the edges of swamps and rivers, the Maya excavate thin channels between rectangular plots of raised soil. This keeps the plots well watered and impervious to flooding at the same time, enabling farmers to yield several crops a year. **300s Maya people** make sophisticated astronomical observances and develop a system of mathematics that incorporates the number zero.	
ca 313 Roman Emperor Constantine I undertakes construction on a number of impressively ornate basilicas in Rome, including the Basilica of St. Peter and of St. Paul. **361 The city of Constantinople** passes regulations requiring physicians to receive a license in order to practice.	**ca 320 The manufacture of textiles** is begun in Britain for export to the rest of the Roman Empire. **325 Roman Emperor Constantine I** embraces Christianity and institutionalizes the faith throughout the Roman Empire. To settle conflicts regarding church doctrine, he calls bishops to the first ecumenical council, located at Nicaea near Constantinople. At this council, the Nicene Creed is developed, specifying the doctrinal relationship of Jesus to God. **ca 365 Martin of Tours**, a former Roman soldier, founds the first monastery in Gaul, dedicated to spreading Christianity to rural areas.
300s The kingdom of Axum erects immense monolithic black granite obelisks, perhaps in memorial to deceased kings and queens. The largest one weighs approximately five tons and stands taller than even the largest Egyptian obelisk.	**331 Axumite King Ezana** is converted to Christianity by the Syrian monk Frumentius. During Ezana's reign, the Ethiopian kingdom of Axum reaches its height, extending its borders west into modern-day Sudan and east into the southern Arabian Peninsula.
ca 350 The Yamato culture of Japan spreads iron tool technology and advanced agricultural techniques across Japan and into Korea.	**300s Nomadic people from the north** pour into northern China following the dissolution of the Han dynasty. They establish large kingdoms there that will dominate the region for many successive centuries. They adopt many Chinese customs as well, gradually assimilating into the existing culture, with one distinct difference—a widespread acceptance of Buddhism. **300s Betrothal of girls eight or nine years old** to men in their twenties is a common practice of Gupta-era India. **365 Famous Chinese calligrapher Wang Xizhi** dies. Even in his own lifetime, his signature is said to be priceless.

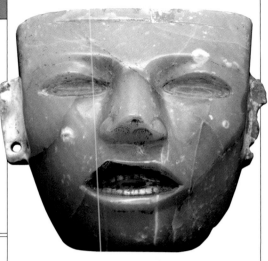

Stone mask unearthed at Teotihuacan

TEOTIHUACAN

Teotihuacan, located in the Valley of Mexico only 30 miles northeast of modern-day Mexico City, was one of the most vital cities of the classical age. At its height, around 400 C.E., it was not only the largest city in the Americas, but one of the largest in the world. Boasting a monumental center that stretched across 12 square miles, Teotihuacan housed an estimated 150,000 inhabitants or more—many times the population of London at the time.

Aside from being an important religious center, it was also a hub of manufacturing and economic development, anchoring a trade network that extended throughout Mesoamerica. Its specialty product was green obsidian, a glasslike volcanic stone that was hewn into knives, points, and scrapers; the city also produced a great number of ceramics and votive figurines for export.

Settled by farmers around 400 B.C.E., Teotihuacan began exerting its will over nearby areas around 200 B.C.E., most likely through military force. Its cultural and economic influence outmatched even the later Aztec Empire. Sacked and abandoned sometime in the seventh or eighth century, the city continued to be visited by pilgrims who gave the city the name known to posterity, Nahuatl, for "where men become gods."

	POLITICS & POWER	GEOGRAPHY & ENVIRONMENT	CULTURE & RELIGION
THE AMERICAS	**ca 400 The Hopewell culture** of eastern North America gradually dissipates into less sedentary, more loosely organized groups of people. Mound building declines along with the Hopewell's network of trade. **ca 400 Teotihuacan** approaches the height of its cultural sophistication. With perhaps over 150,000 inhabitants, it is one of the largest cities in the world. London by comparison has only a few tens of thousands of people.	**400s Scarcity of food** in the Great Basin region of western North America causes many inhabitants to pursue a migratory lifestyle. These people come to understand their environment intimately, so as to know when and where food will be available. Men bring down large game, while women pursue small game. To survive their harsh environment, both collect plants in wicker baskets.	**ca 400 The Maya ceremonial site of Cuajilote** on the Caribbean coast of Mexico in Veracruz is constructed, complete with a steam bath-house, presumably for communal bathing.
EUROPE	**378 Roman infantry forces led by Emperor Valens** are annihilated by Visigothic and Ostrogothic horsemen at the Battle of Adrianople in modern-day Turkey. **406 Groups of Vandals and other Germanic people, led by King Gunderic**, invade and devastate much of the Roman province of Gaul. **410 Visigothic forces led by Alaric** capture and sack Rome, having laid multiple sieges to it over the previous year. Though it has not been the capital of the empire for over a century, this represents the symbolic fall of the western Roman Empire. The invaders spare the churches of St. Peter and St. Paul.	**405 The Rhine River in central Europe** freezes over in the winter, facilitating the entry into the Roman Empire by a great number of Vandals, Alans, and other migratory groups. **407 Germanic tribes** moving into northwest Europe bring with them the manufacture of butter and the cultivation of crops such as rye, oats, and hops.	**380 Roman general turned emperor Theodosius I** makes Christianity the official religion of the Roman Empire. He then begins a purging of all things pagan, destroying libraries and temples and abolishing the Olympic games. **428 Greek theologian and bishop of Constantinople, Nestorius,** emphasizes Jesus' human as opposed to divine nature, sparking much conflict within the Catholic Church. **432 Patrick, a Christian bishop from Britain,** travels to Ireland as a missionary. He sets up his diocese at Armagh and begins trying to convert the island to Christianity.
MIDDLE EAST & AFRICA	**ca 390 Following Roman Emperor Theodosius I's outlawing of paganism**, crowds destroy the temple of Serapis in Alexandria and, along with it, Alexandria's great library. **429 The Vandals** invade Africa from Spain, capturing Carthage by 439.		**372 The Orthodox Christian church St. Mary of Zion** is built by Axumite King Ezana in Ethiopia. Probably the oldest Christian church in sub-Saharan Africa, it is said by some to house the remains of the original Ark of the Covenant. **396 Augustine of Hippo** becomes a bishop in modern-day Algeria. His writings, such as *Confessions* and *City of God,* synthesize Christian theology and Platonic logic and expound on topics such as the "just war" theory. **438 Jews** are barred from public office in the Roman Empire.
ASIA & OCEANIA	**375 Emperor Chandra Gupta II** assumes the throne of the Gupta dynasty in northern India. During his reign, the art, architecture, and sculpture of northern India reaches a new height. After extending his rule west and south from the Ganges, peace and prosperity are said to grace his lands. **ca 400-450 The Gupta Empire of India** repeatedly keeps the Hephthalites at bay in Bactria—at great expense to their treasury and to their central administration. **424 Luoyang falls to the northern Wei,** a regime established by Turkic people of northern China.	**ca 400 Chinese populations** decline significantly as diseases find their way along the Silk Road to new areas that have no inherited or built-up immunities.	**ca 400 Indian monk Kumarajiva** oversees Chinese translations of Buddhist texts in Chang'an. **ca 400 Sanskrit poet Kalidasa** is reputedly one of the nine gems of the court of Chandra Gupta II. He is widely considered one of the greatest of Sanskrit poets. **ca 400 The *Bhagavad Gita,*** a discourse on Hindu ethical teachings, takes on its final form after a number of revisions. **400s Under the patronage of the Gupta Empire, Hinduism** gradually replaces Buddhism as the dominant religious and cultural tradition of India.

CONNECTIONS

The Spread of Contagion

The vast network of land and sea routes, known collectively as the Silk Road, that connected distant empires into an integrated web of commerce across the Eurasian landmass, carried not only exotic goods and new ideas, but also infectious diseases hungry for fresh populations of immunity-free victims. In both the Roman and Han Empires, and most likely in the areas between, epidemics ravaged populations in the third, fourth, and fifth centuries C.E., decreasing these empires' ability to maintain their borders against invasions. As trade consequently declined, so did imperial economies, resulting in pockets of regionalized markets that would not again achieve a global level for centuries to come.

SCIENCE & TECHNOLOGY	PEOPLE & SOCIETY
ca 400 By this time, the peoples of Meso-america have developed the concept of the wheel, but have made no use of it outside of toys produced for children. In the absence of beasts of burden, wheeled vehicles may have served no use.	**ca 400 Teotihuacan** continues to participate in an intensive trade network that stretches throughout Mesoamerica. It exports ceramics, clay figurines, and its most distinctive wares—knives, points, and scrapers made of green obsidian. **ca 400 Fremont culture** develops in modern-day Utah, southern Idaho, and adjacent portions of Colorado and Nevada. Its sedentary communities survive on horticulture. **417 Hieroglyphs in a tomb on the Rio Azul** in modern-day Guatemala record this as the birth date of an important Maya ruler; the name is lost to history.
430s Roman Emperor Theodosius II expands the triple walls of Constantinople and builds huge cisterns for water, making the city almost impossible to conquer.	**376 The Huns, a nomadic group of people from eastern Asia**, arrive on the frontier of the Roman Empire after defeating Goths living on the Danube River. Over the course of the next seven decades, they will carve out an empire of their own in central Europe. **410 During Alaric's multiple sieges of Rome**, many Germanic slaves in the city join his side. In fact, Alaric's forces only enter Rome when a slave opens the gates for them. **415 The Visigoths** move out of Italy and into southern Gaul and Spain, where they remain with their capital at Toledo for the next three centuries.
431 Nestorian Christians, persecuted by the Orthodox Roman emperor Zeno, flee to Persia and India, bringing with them a number of Greek texts on medicine and astronomy.	**ca 400 Rev Ashi** is one of the prime movers in the compilation of the Babylonian Talmud, a commentary on the Mishnah. At the same time, rabbis in Palestine compile the Palestinian Talmud, completed around 425.
ca 400 A suspension bridge measuring 400 feet is constructed over the Sanchipan gorge in the Himalayas. **ca 400 Advances in astronomy and mathematics** are sponsored by the court of Chandra Gupta II in India. **ca 400 The composite recurved bow**, possessing so much tensile strength that its ends bend back upon themselves, is developed by nomads of northern and central Asia.	**ca 400 Emperor Chandra Gupta II** maintains free rest houses for visitors to his empire, as well as free hospitals for his infirm subjects. **414 Faxian, Chinese scholar and monk**, returns from India bringing Sanskrit texts that will become central to Chinese Buddhism. He writes a *Treatise on Buddhist Kingdoms*. **427 Tao Qian,** Chinese Daoist poet, dies.

Wall mural dated to the Gupta dynasty

India's Golden Age

Chandra Gupta II took the throne of the Gupta dynasty in 375 C.E. and proceeded to usher in an era of cultural and economic prosperity sometimes referred to as the golden age of India. Gupta reestablished traditional Indian mores and administrative practices following an era that had been dominated by Greek influences.

Through a combination of military and marital alliances, Gupta extended his empire from the Ganges to the Indus and north into modern-day Pakistan. This imperial expansion brought an influx of wealth that was lavished in part on science and the arts. Gupta established a circle of poets known as the nine gems of his court, which probably included Kalidasa, the chief figure in classical Sanskrit literature. Astronomy and mathematics also prospered in Gupta's court.

Chandra Gupta created free rest houses and hospitals, abolished capital punishment, and promulgated a single code of law. The Iron Pillar near Delhi, virtually uncorroded after 1,600 years, commemorates this benevolent ruler.

POLITICS & POWER	GEOGRAPHY & ENVIRONMENT	CULTURE & RELIGION
THE AMERICAS **ca 450 The Zapotec population of Monte Albán** (today's Oaxaca, Mexico) continues to grow. At its height, it may have had up to 30,000 inhabitants. **ca 490 The population of Teotihuacan** begins to decline due to internal divisions and strife. This disrupts the trade networks and affects Monte Albán and many other Mesoamerican cities, which also experience a decline in population. **ca 490 Leaders emerge** among people of the northwest coast of North America. Each one's importance is tied to his ability to control resources and mobilize labor.	**455 The Maya city of Chichén Itzá** is founded on the Yucatán Peninsula. Comprising six square miles, it will house numerous pyramid temples and an observatory.	**ca 450 An eighth stage of construction is completed on the Huaca del Sol**, or Pyramid of the Sun, a Moche complex located near the peak of Cerro Blanco near modern-day Trujillo, Peru. Over 100 million bricks are used in its construction, each one stamped with a maker's mark.
EUROPE **441 Under the command of King Attila,** the Huns launch a massive assault on the Roman Empire, invading first modern-day Hungary, then the Balkan region, then Gaul and northern Italy. Nearly unstoppable, they wreak havoc until Attila's death in 453. **455 Vandals. led by King Gaiseric**, invade Italy from North Africa, even taking Rome and plundering it of many works of art. **476 German chieftain Odoacer** deposes the final western Roman emperor, Romulus Augustulus, and proclaims himself king. Though a Roman system of administration persists for a time, the western half of the Roman Empire is extinguished.	**ca 476 Angle, Saxon, and Jute invasions** of England force many Celtic inhabitants to migrate across the English channel to Brittany, France. **480 An earthquake shakes Constantinople**, the capital of the eastern Roman Empire, for a reputed 40 straight days.	**ca 450 Followers of Christian ascetics** living in Egypt write down their words as the "Sayings of the Desert Fathers and Mothers." **451 The ecumenical Council of Chalcedon** institutionalizes the doctrines of Christianity as set out in the Nicene Creed. It brands the Nestorian and Monophysite branches of Christianity as heretical. **493 Clovis, King of the Franks**, is baptized a Christian at the urging of his wife, Clothilde. He goes on to expand his reign throughout Gaul and lays the foundations for the most powerful kingdom of early medieval western Europe.
MIDDLE EAST & AFRICA **442 The Vandals, a Germanic group of migratory people**, settle finally in North Africa with Carthage as their capital. The Western Roman Emperor Valentinian III recognizes their independence, yet Vandals continue to harass the crumbling Eastern Roman Empire. **484 Sassanid king Peroz I** loses his life fighting the Hephthalites. Nobles become the real power in the Sassanid Empire. **ca 490 The Soninke Empire** emerges as a commercial power in West Africa. It controls trade in salt, gold, and other goods, and in ensuing centuries will link trans-Saharan trade with Mediterranean economies demanding African gold.	**400s The deserts of Palestine and North Africa** become home to ascetic monks who live in solitary cells, in the open air, or on the tops of columns to separate themselves from the luxuries and temptations of the world. The best known of these if Simeon Stylites. **ca 450 The great dam of Marib** in Yemen, built in the seventh century B.C.E., is restored.	**483 Nestorian Christians** flourish in Persia after being evicted from the Eastern Roman Empire by orthodox Emperor Zeno. They will carry their mission to China centuries before Jesuit missionary Marco Polo. **ca 490 The Lydenburg heads**, pieces of life-size fired earthenware, are produced. The earliest known sculpture in southern Africa, they are perhaps used in the rituals of agricultural communities. **ca 496 The Mazdakite movement** in Iran, preaching communality of goods and social equality, is persecuted by authorities.
ASIA & OCEANIA **400s The Korean Peninsula** is divided into three kingdoms, the Koguryo in the north, and the Paekche and Silla in the south. **ca 450-500 The Hephthalites** wear down the defenses of the Gupta Empire in India, which splits readily along fault lines of regional districts that have maintained a noncentral form of government.	**485 The Wei State of northern China** implements a system of equal land distribution, in which it distinguishes between crop land and orchards.	**400s Buddhism continues to attract converts** in China, due largely to efforts of expatriot merchants from India, Parthia, and Central Asia. It will soon become the dominant faith throughout East Asia. **495 Work begins on the Buddhist cave temple** at Longmen, near Luoyang, the new capital of the Northern Wei.

SCIENCE & TECHNOLOGY	PEOPLE & SOCIETY

ca 490 Peoples of the Northern Plains of North America develop the atlatl dart point for use in hunting.

ca 490 Peoples of the northwest coast of North America begin to exploit rich schools of salmon and other fish life as a food source.

ca 450 Eastern invaders into Europe bring with them the idea of nailed horseshoes.

ca 455 After a number of attacks by germanic groups, much of northern Italy is devastated. Towns are walled in, farms are left vacant, and the population shrinks exponentially.

493 After assassinating Odoacer, Theodoric establishes an Ostrogothic kingdom in Italy with his capital at Ravenna.

Map showing the numerous attacks that led to the fall of the Western Roman Empire

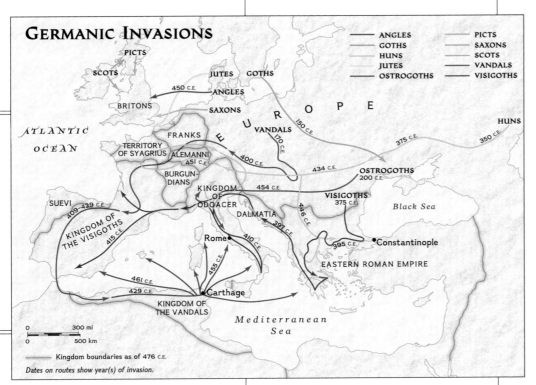

GERMANIC INVASIONS

ANGLES	PICTS
GOTHS	SAXONS
HUNS	SCOTS
JUTES	VANDALS
OSTROGOTHS	VISIGOTHS

Kingdom boundaries as of 476 C.E.

Dates on routes show year(s) of invasion.

477 The stirrup is described for the first time in a Chinese text.

444 Daoism becomes the official ideology of the Northern Wei kingdom in China.

THE FALL OF ROME

Though Germanic peoples had been pushing against the borders of the Roman Empire for centuries, they did not become an acute threat until the fourth century. Rome had been weakened by military usurpers and unqualified leaders for some time, causing emperor Diocletian to split the empire in 286 into two distinct units, eastern and western. Constantine I in 330 moved his capital to Constantinople, modern-day Istanbul, fashioning it a "new Rome"; it would become the center of the Byzantine world. Meanwhile, old Rome and the Western Empire were left in the hands of corrupt and inadequate administrators, managing undertrained and underpaid soldiers.

Around 370, a group of nomadic horsemen known as the Huns rode out of the east. They were skilled archers who could move in tandem in cavalry maneuvers for which the Romans were completely unprepared. From the north came the Vandals, who pushed into Gaul, disrupting Germanic groups that were already established there, namely the Franks, Alemanni, and Burgundians. The Vandals continued into North Africa, where they enjoyed short-lived autonomy and continued to harass the deteriorating Roman Empire. Goths pushed into the Balkans, and after a failed conciliation with Rome, they decimated Roman forces at the Battle of Adrianople in 378. The Goths proceeded into Italy and took the city of Rome by 410.

Meanwhile, Roman forces had abandoned Britain to invading Scots, Picts, Angles, and Jutes, while the Huns of Attila invaded Gaul and Italy, their assault halted only by Attila's death. Finally, in 476, the German chieftain Odoacer deposed the last Western Roman emperor and proclaimed himself king, finally extinguishing the last sign of life from a once-powerful empire.

CHAPTER 3

FAITH AND POWER

WITH THE RISE OF ISLAM IN THE seventh century and the spread of Christianity and other established religions, faith became a more powerful force than ever, inspiring rulers and setting armies in motion. Worldly ambitions combined with religious zeal propelled Arab conquerors across Africa and the Middle East and fueled the expansion of the Byzantine Empire around the Mediterranean and Christian kingdoms in western Europe. These devout societies sought imperial glory and learned lessons from old imperial cultures. Christians in Byzantium were inspired by Greek traditions, while those in western Europe built on Roman foundations, and Muslims inherited the cultural legacy of Persia.

Religion had a profound impact elsewhere as well. Muslims invaded northern India, setting that region apart from Hindu kingdoms to the south. Farther east, Buddhism expanded through the efforts of monks and nuns, much as Christianity did in Europe, and competed with the traditional beliefs of Confucianism and Shinto, the ancestral

PREVIOUS PAGE: *Hundreds of thousands of Muslims climax their pilgrimage to Mecca by bowing in prayer at the Great Mosque before the cube-shaped Kaaba, their holiest shrine.*

OPPOSITE: *Religious fervor and Greek artistic traditions inspired majestic Byzantine icons such as this mosaic of Christ, which survived when the Hagia Sophia in Constantinople (modern-day Istanbul) was transformed from a cathedral to a mosque.*

faith of Japan. In the Americas, rulers among the Maya and other cultures built soaring monuments to their gods and reached new heights of authority. Faith transformed societies, strengthening some and destroying others.

Byzantine Expansion

When the Roman emperor Constantine moved his capital to Byzantium, or Constantinople, in the fourth century, he laid the foundation for a Greek Empire in the east that outlasted the Roman Empire in the west. Greek later became the official language of Byzantium, and Byzantine scholars studied the works of Aristotle and other classical Greek authors.

The Byzantine Empire reached its height in the sixth century under Justinian, who raised a great cathedral called the Hagia Sophia and other monuments in Constantinople after much of the city was destroyed by rioters protesting high taxes and food shortages. Those protests nearly drove him from power, but his iron-willed wife, Empress Theodora, persuaded him to hold his ground, and troops crushed the uprising, killing tens of thousands of

This map shows the Byzantine Empire at its height during the reign of Justinian in the sixth century. Byzantines regarded Constantinople as the second Rome and carried on Roman imperial traditions by spreading their faith and culture to places as distant as Moscow, later hailed by Russians as the third Rome (inset).

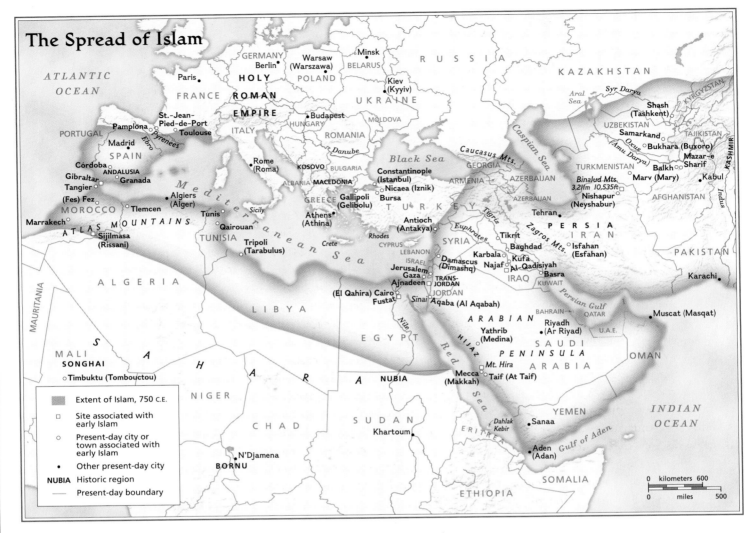

The Spread of Islam

ATLANTIC OCEAN

GERMANY
Berlin
Warsaw (Warszawa)
POLAND
BELARUS
Minsk
RUSSIA
KAZAKHSTAN

Paris
HOLY ROMAN EMPIRE
FRANCE
ITALY
Budapest
HUNGARY
ROMANIA
Kiev (Kyyiv)
UKRAINE
MOLDOVA

St.-Jean-Pied-de-Port
Pamplona
Pyrenees
Toulouse
Ebro
Madrid
SPAIN
PORTUGAL

Córdoba
Gibraltar
ANDALUSIA
Granada
Tangier
(Fes) Fez
Algiers (Alger)
MOROCCO
Tlemcen
Marrakech
ATLAS MOUNTAINS
Sijilmasa (Rissani)

Rome (Roma)
KOSOVO
BULGARIA
ALBANIA MACEDONIA
Sicily
Tunis
TUNISIA
Qairouan
Tripoli (Tarabulus)
Mediterranean Sea
Crete
Rhodes
CYPRUS

Black Sea
Constantinople (Istanbul)
Nicaea (Iznik)
Gallipoli (Gelibolu)
Bursa
GREECE
Athens (Athina)
TURKEY
Antioch (Antakya)
SYRIA
LEBANON
ISRAEL
Damascus (Dimashq)
Jerusalem
Gaza
TRANS-JORDAN
Ajnadeen
(El Qahira) Cairo
Fustat
Sinai
Aqaba (Al Aqabah)
JORDAN

Caucasus Mts.
GEORGIA
ARMENIA
AZERBAIJAN
AZERBAIJAN
Tehran
Caspian Sea

Tigris
Euphrates
Tikrit
Baghdad
Karbala
Kufa
Najaf
Al-Qadisiyah
IRAQ
Basra
KUWAIT

Aral Sea
Syr Darya
KYRGYZSTAN
Shash (Tashkent)
UZBEKISTAN
Samarkand
Bukhara (Buxoro)
Oxus (Amu Darya)
Balkh
Mazar-e Sharif
TURKMENISTAN
Marv (Mary)
Binalud Mts. 3,211m 10,535ft
Nishapur (Neyshabur)
PERSIA
IRAN
Isfahan (Esfahan)
Zagros Mts.
TAJIKISTAN
KASHMIR
Kabul
AFGHANISTAN
Indus
PAKISTAN
Karachi

MAURITANIA
ALGERIA
LIBYA
EGYPT
Nile
Red Sea

MALI
SONGHAI
Timbuktu (Tombouctou)
S A H A R A
NIGER
CHAD
N'Djamena
BORNU

SUDAN
Khartoum
NUBIA

Persian Gulf
BAHRAIN
QATAR
U.A.E.
Muscat (Masqat)
ARABIAN
Riyadh (Ar Riyad)
Yathrib (Medina)
SAUDI
PENINSULA
ARABIA
OMAN
Mt. Hira
Mecca (Makkah)
Taif (At Taif)
HIJAZ
Dahlak Kebir
YEMEN
Sanaa
ERITREA
Aden (Adan)
Gulf of Aden
SOMALIA
ETHIOPIA
INDIAN OCEAN

Legend:
- Extent of Islam, 750 C.E.
- □ Site associated with early Islam
- ○ Present-day city or town associated with early Islam
- • Other present-day city
- **NUBIA** Historic region
- — Present-day boundary

0 kilometers 600
0 miles 500

By 750, when the Abbasid dynasty took power in Persia, the Muslim Empire extended all the way from Spain to northern India.

people. Justinian's forces then embarked on foreign conquests, seizing Italy, northwestern Africa, and southern Spain. At his death in 565, his empire nearly encircled the Mediterranean.

The Byzantine Empire endured for many centuries, but it would never again be as strong as it was under Justinian. His successors lost control of Italy and other western lands, where Christians recognized the bishop of Rome rather than the Byzantine patriarch as their spiritual father, or pope. Within the Byzantine world, a bitter religious dispute arose over iconoclasm—an imperial effort to ban sacred images as idols. Wealthy landowners defied Byzantine emperors by raising their own troops and refusing to pay taxes. But nothing did more to weaken Byzantium than the spread of Islam by Muslim forces, who claimed Egypt, Palestine, and Syria and threatened Constantinople itself.

The Islamic World

Islam arose in Mecca, an oasis where Arabs gathered to trade and worship at shrines devoted to many gods. The prophet Muhammad was born there around 570 and traveled widely as a merchant, coming in contact with Jews, Christians, and people of other faiths. When he was around 40, he experienced a revelation in which he recognized Allah (God) as supreme and all-encompassing. Muhammad shared his revelation with others and promised salvation to those who embraced Islam, meaning submission to Allah. "There is no God but Allah," Muslims declared ever after, "and Muhammad is his prophet."

Muhammad's message angered those in Mecca who remained devoted to other gods. In 622 he fled Mecca and joined followers in the city they named Medina, where they gained strength. Their ancestors had long engaged in clan warfare, and they were prepared to fight for their beliefs. In 630 they conquered Mecca and made its holiest shrine, the Kaaba, the focal point for pilgrimages to Mecca by devout Muslims in years to come. Muhammad died in 632, but his teachings lived on in the Koran (Quran), inscribed in Arabic not long after his death. His leadership role fell to caliphs, or deputies, who united the Arabian Peninsula under Islam and embarked on far-ranging conquests. By 650 Muslim forces had seized a vast area extending from Egypt to Persia. Over the next century, they expanded southeastward to the Indus River and westward across North Africa, reaching as far as Spain.

During this expansive era, the Islamic world was ruled from Damascus by caliphs of the Umayyad dynasty. One Muslim sect known as the Shiite opposed them because they were not descendants of Muhammad. Other Muslims known as Sunnis accepted their legitimacy, but some Sunnis in conquered lands shared the resentments of Shiites and non-Muslims toward the caliphs. Rebels of various sects in Persia rallied around Abu al-Abbas, who ended Umayyad rule in 750. He and his Abbasid successors built a new capital at Baghdad, where scholars from many lands studied the Koran as well as classical works by Persian, Greek, and Indian sages, including treatises on medicine and mathematics. Arabic numerals and algebra were among the gifts Muslim scholars bequeathed to modern science.

Islamic culture and literature flourished in many cities besides Baghdad. Muslims learned through trade with China how to make paper and produced books in great numbers, kept in libraries like that in Córdoba, the elegant Spanish capital. They did not allow pictures or sculptures in mosques, but their artists were masters of abstract designs and calligraphy. Islamic authorities generally tolerated people of other faiths but required them to pay a special tax. Caliphs recognized leading Jewish rabbis in Persia as *geonim,* or excellencies, and allowed them to resolve all religious issues that arose in Jewish communities under Muslim rule by applying the Talmud, a compilation of Jewish laws and traditions completed in the sixth century. Muslim laws based on the Koran provided protection to women as well as servants and slaves. At the same time, they perpetuated ancient Middle Eastern customs by requiring women to wear veils in public and allowing men to have more than one wife.

Ferment in Africa

By the ninth century, Muslim traders from North Africa were crossing the Sahara by camel in caravans to seek wealth in West Africa, where prosperous societies had developed along the Senegal and Niger Rivers. Farmers there cultivated rice and other crops in fertile floodplains, providing food surpluses that supported potters, coppersmiths, ironworkers, and other artisans. Here as elsewhere in Africa, long-distance trade was well-established before Muslims arrived, fostering the growth of commercial centers such as Jenne-jeno, a town of more than 10,000 people near the confluence of the Niger and Bani Rivers (today's Djénné, Mali.)

To the west, between the Niger and Senegal Rivers, the kingdom of Ghana developed. Merchants there obtained gold from lands to their south, and that wealth attracted Muslim traders, who also sought ivory and slaves. (West Africa was just one source of slaves—a word derived from *Slavs;* many Slavs were seized in eastern Europe and enslaved.) The rulers of Ghana later converted to Islam but were slow to abandon such traditional religious practices as praying to images of their ancestral spirits or nature gods. Trade with the Islamic world brought Ghana wealth and power, and it grew from a kingdom into an empire.

In East Africa, Muslim merchants arriving by sea at busy ports like Mogadishu and Mombasa encountered people who spoke Bantu languages and had long been involved in maritime trade, plying the Indian Ocean and the Red Sea in ships. Referred to by Muslims as Swahilis, or coasters, they incorporated many Arabic words into their dialects and readily communicated with each other and with their Muslim trading partners, to whom they sold gold, ivory, and slaves from the interior. Here as in West Africa, rulers who profited from such trade embraced Islam and grew stronger politically. As East African ports grew into city-states adorned with mosques, Swahili society became part of dar al-Islam, or the Islamic world. With its far-flung trade networks and vibrant markets, this flourishing Islamic world was the envy of rulers in Constantinople and western Europe, where there were no Christian cities to compare with Córdoba or Baghdad.

A Divided West

The collapse of the Roman Empire left western Europe divided among various Germanic tribes.

Visigoths (western Goths) held Iberia until Muslim forces seized much of what is now Spain and Portugal in the eighth century. Ostrogoths (eastern Goths) dominated Italy until Byzantine forces intervened in the sixth century, followed by Lombards. Britain was occupied by Angles and Saxons from Denmark and northern Germany. But the strongest of the Germanic peoples in Europe were the Franks, whose kingdom expanded far beyond France under the dynamic ruler Charlemagne, who conquered much of Germany and northern Italy. In 800, Pope Leo III crowned him emperor in Rome, rivaling the Byzantine emperor in Constantinople.

Charlemagne's empire fractured not long after he died in 814. His successors could not withstand fierce pressure from invaders, including Magyars advancing from the east and Vikings pouring down from Scandinavia in longships. Vikings pillaged coastal ports and monasteries and surged inland to take control of large areas, including much of Britain, Normandy, Sicily, and parts of Russia, where missionaries from Byzantium later introduced Christianity. Other Vikings sailed westward across the Atlantic and colonized Iceland and Greenland before establishing a short-lived colony in Newfoundland around 1000.

Invasions by Vikings and other marauders left western Europe as divided as ever. In feudal society, serfs toiling on estates owed the lord of the manor rent and other obligations, including labor and military service. Those lords were in turn obligated as vassals to higher nobility and supported them in wars. In some places, kings arose such as Alfred of Wessex, who reclaimed part of Britain from the Vikings; and Otto I of Saxony, who defeated the Magyars and laid the foundation for the Holy Roman Empire. But much of Europe was controlled by nobles and their vassals, who oversaw manors. Those estates were largely self-sufficient, and few traders ventured far from home.

The one great unifying factor in western Europe was Roman Christianity, which was organized hierarchically like the old Roman Empire with local priests supervised by bishops under the supreme authority of the pope. Roman culture endured in churches of classical design called basilicas, in the colorful robes of Roman origin that priests and bishops wore, and in the Latin language, used by priests, teachers, and other literate people. Monks copied

OPPOSITE: Serpents coil around the neck of a sacred figure wearing an amulet and other tokens of magical power, found at Jenne-jeno in West Africa.

Bibles and other books in Latin and lavishly illustrated them. Nuns also copied manuscripts in convents and taught children to read and write. Through the influence of the church, Latin shaped western European culture and gave birth to Italian, Spanish, French, and other romance languages.

Diversity in the East
In contrast to Christian Europe, most Asian societies and their rulers allowed for religious diversity. King Harsha, who reunited much of northern India under his rule in the early seventh century after the collapse of the Gupta Empire, was a devout Buddhist, but he did not seek to impose his beliefs on Hindus or those of other faiths. Harsha's empire crumbled after his death, and Muslim forces came down from the north in 711 and conquered Sind, embracing the Indus River Valley. Distant caliphs had limited authority over Sind, and not many people in northern India converted to Islam before Muslim Turks invaded the region around 1000. To the south, Muslim merchants settled in coastal towns and attracted some converts, but most people remained Hindus. In the southern Indian kingdom of Chola, donations from Hindus who prospered as traders or manufacturers of trade goods such as cotton cloth supported temples that controlled large tracts of land, just as the well-endowed Christian monasteries in Europe did.

Muslim traders influenced the culture and beliefs of India, but Indian merchants had an even greater impact on countries in Southeast Asia that lay along maritime trade routes between India and China. Rulers of Funan, in southern Cambodia and Vietnam, called themselves rajas, like Indian kings; worshiped Hindu deities; and adopted Sanskrit as their official language. Funan collapsed in the sixth century, and Khmers took control of Cambodia. They too became Hindus but later adopted Buddhism, introduced to nearby Malaysia and Sumatra by Indian merchants.

In China, the Sui dynasty reunified the empire in the late sixth century, ending three centuries of turmoil following the collapse of the Han dynasty. Sui rulers constructed the Grand Canal linking the Yellow and Yangtze Rivers, a massive project that helped integrate China economically and culturally. Millions of Chinese were conscripted to labor on the canal or serve as soldiers in Korea, where Chinese

invasion forces suffered setbacks, triggering a revolt that brought an end to the Sui dynasty in 618 and ushered in the Tang dynasty.

Tang emperors endorsed Confucian ideals of benevolent leadership and claimed the mandate of heaven—a divine right to rule that belonged only to those who governed virtuously, according to Confucius. Office-seekers under the Tang had to demonstrate their knowledge of Confucian texts in civil service examinations. The Tang dynasty lasted for nearly three centuries, during which time their capital at Chang'an (Xi'an) grew to a population of nearly two million. Chinese inventors devised the magnetic compass, gunpowder, and porcelain, which became China's most prized export after the secrets of fine silk production reached Byzantium in the seventh century.

Official backing for Confucianism in China did not thwart the spread of other religions or philosophies. Buddhism also received support from Tang rulers and nobility, who sponsored Buddhist monasteries and temples. Chinese Buddhist pilgrims and missionaries

Founded by Siddhartha Gautama, who grew up in India in the sixth century B.C.E. amid the foothills of the Himalaya (inset) and became known as the Buddha, or Enlightened One, Buddhism achieved wide appeal in centuries to come, attracting followers in Tibet, China, Korea, Japan, and Southeast Asia.

journeyed to India to visit sacred sites and spread their faith to Japan and Korea, which reconciled with China after the kingdom of Silla united Koreans against Chinese invaders in the seventh century and induced the Tang emperor to withdraw his forces. In return, the Silla king agreed to acknowledge the emperor as his overlord, but Korea remained essentially independent.

Buddhism, Confucianism, and other cultural influences from China greatly affected the development of Japan, whose emperors claimed their own heavenly mandate by tracing their ancestry to the Shinto sun goddess, Amaterasu. By the ninth century, Japanese emperors were largely ceremonial figures, controlled by regents from the powerful Fujiwara family, which was linked by marriage to the imperial family. Literature and the arts flourished at the imperial court at Heian (Kyoto) under Fujiwara Michinaga, who became regent in 995. While men at court wrote in classical Chinese, women wrote in Japanese, using a new phonetic script. The pioneering novelist Murasaki

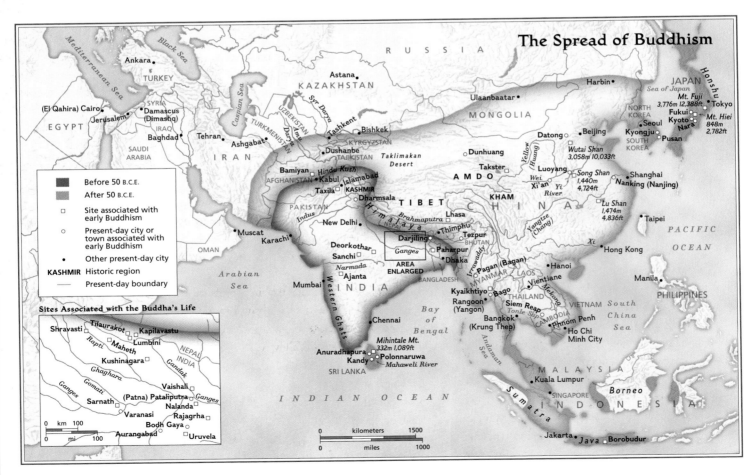

The Spread of Buddhism

Before 50 B.C.E.
After 50 B.C.E.
□ Site associated with early Buddhism
○ Present-day city or town associated with early Buddhism
• Other present-day city
KASHMIR Historic region
— Present-day boundary

Sites Associated with the Buddha's Life

Shikibu drew on her experiences at court to compose *The Tale of Genji,* portraying the life of a prince involved in romantic intrigue.

Few rulers around the world claimed direct descent from the gods like the emperors of Japan, but many were sacred figures before whom lesser mortals groveled or kowtowed, as visitors did before Chinese emperors. In Polynesian society, which expanded to New Zealand during this period, chiefs were so exalted that foods they ate and objects they touched were kapu (taboo), or forbidden to common people. Polynesian chiefs and priests made offerings to the gods at temples called *marae,* some of which were shaped like pyramids and rose up to 50 feet high.

In Mesoamerica, Maya rulers offered their own blood or that of captives to the gods at temples set atop pyramids. Soaring Maya pyramids at Copán and Palenque, where King Pacal was buried in splendor in 683 after reigning for 68 years, marked the high point of Maya civilization, which declined in the ninth century as city-states exhausted their resources. By 1000, most lay abandoned like once-mighty Teotihuacan, which suffered a ruinous assault a few centuries earlier. But the feats of those bygone pyramid builders inspired the Toltec—who rose to power in the Valley of Mexico in the tenth century and built an imposing capital at Tula—and they in turn would inspire the Aztec.

In North America, meanwhile, chiefs oversaw the construction of great earthen burial mounds, first in the Ohio Valley, center of the Hopewell culture, and later in the Mississippi Valley, where large towns such as Cahokia grew up around the mounds. Mississippian rulers were buried with offerings that sometimes included human sacrifices. Like other complex societies, these mound builders invested rulers with godlike authority, as long as they retained heaven's blessing and kept the land safe and prosperous. ■

Buddhist monasteries like this one, perched on a cliff side in Bhutan, between India and China, have long offered seclusion to those seeking release from worldly concerns through meditation.

FAITH AND POWER 500-1000

	500-549	550	600	650	700	
THE AMERICAS	**ca 500** Temple mound builders trade in the Mississippi Valley. **ca 500** Teotihuacan in central Mexico reaches the height of its influence. **ca 500** Maya civilization on the Yucatán Peninsula flourishes. **ca 500** Nazca and Moche people in Peru develop a rich artistic culture.	**550** Native people in southwest Colorado begin building pit houses. **562** The Maya city-state of Tikal, in present-day Guatemala, is defeated by rival Calakmul. **578** Buts'Chan, Smoke Serpent, the 11th ruler of Copán in Honduras, begins his 50-year-long reign.	**ca 600** The Hohokam culture is spreading in North America's Southwest. **ca 600** The Huari people rise in Peru. **ca 600** The Tiahuanaco Empire rises in southern Peru and Bolivia. **615** Maya ruler Pacal of Palenque, Mexico, begins to build a lavish palace, pyramid, and temple.	**683** Maya king Pacal, ruler of Palenque in Mexico, dies at 80. **694** The 13th Maya ruler of Copán, 18 Rabbit, begins his 44-year-long reign.	**ca 700** Pueblo people in the Southwest of North America live in houses above ground and embrace farming. **ca 700** The mound-building Caddo culture flourishes in Texas and Oklahoma. **ca 700** The Moche and the Nazca civilizations collapse.	
EUROPE	**500** Ostrogoth Theodoric becomes ruler of what remains of the Roman Empire in Italy. **500** Visigoths rule Spain from Toledo. **500** Angles and Saxons move into the British Isles. **511** Clovis of Gaul dies. **527-567** Under Justinian I, Byzantium regains lost territory of the once powerful Roman Empire.	**561** Civil war breaks out among the Merovingians in France. **568** Refugees from the Lombard invasions settle in the lagoons of Venice. **570** Byzantium and Persia establish a 50-year peace. **590** Gregory becomes pope in Rome.	**602** Vikings invade Ireland. **602** Flavius Phocas Augustus becomes emperor in Byzantium. **610** Heraclius of Carthage overthrows Augustus and regains Asia Minor, Syria, Jerusalem, and Egypt for the Byzantine Empire. **633** In England, the Mercians defeat the Northumbrians.	**668** Byzantine emperor Constans II is assassinated. His son, Constantine IV, begins his rule, battling Muslims and Slavs in succession. **675** Bulgars settle south of the Danube, establishing their first kingdom. **680-700** The French kings are known as "do-nothings." Power passes to the mayor, Pépin of Herstal in 687.	**ca 700** Vikings invade the British Isles. **711** Muslim armies invade southern Spain from North Africa. **717** Leo III becomes Byzantine Emperor and ends a period of instability. **732** Charles Martel, son of Pépin, halts the advance of a small group of Muslims from Spain at Tours, France.	
MIDDLE EAST & AFRICA	**ca 500** The empire of Ghana rises in importance in West Africa; it is a trading center for gold. **530** Gelimer becomes king of the Vandals in North Africa. **531** Sassanid King Khosrow I reunites Persia. **543** Nubian kingdoms in North Africa adopt Christianity.	**570** Muhammad, the Prophet and future messenger of Islam, is born in Mecca. **570** The Abyssinians of North Africa establish a protectorate over Yemen.	**610** Muhammad experiences a spiritual transformation and receives a message from God. **622** Muhammad and his followers flee to Medina. **630** Muhammad conquers Mecca. **632** Muhammad dies. His father-in-law, Abu Bakr, succeeds him and takes up the cause of conquest for Islam.	**651** The Muslims conquer Persia. **656** Ali, Muhammad's son-in-law, becomes the new leader of Islam. **661** Ali is assassinated in Iraq. Muawiyah becomes caliph and begins the rule of the Umayyad dynasty.	**ca 700** Arab traders begin settling along the coast of East Africa. **705-715** Under Umayyad al-Walid I, Muslim armies conquer Turkmenistan and Sind, pushing as far as the borders of China. In 711 Muslim armies also invade southern Spain from North Africa.	
ASIA & OCEANIA	**500** China is split into several warring kingdoms and suffers a period of great instability. **500** Northern Funan falls to the Khmer people of Cambodia. **ca 500** Easter Island is settled by Austronesian mariners. **535** India's Gupta Empire collapses. Rival states control parts of India.	**587** The powerful Soga clan champions Buddhism in Japan. **587** Japan's ruling Yamato court accepts Chinese ideas. **589** The Sui dynasty under Yang Jian reunites fragmented China and fosters an era of great culture and invention.	**604** Prince Shotoku issues principles for rule based on Buddhism, Shinto, and Confucianism. **618** Li Yuan, a Sui official, founds the Tang dynasty in China. **606-647** Harsha Vardhana reunites parts of northern India. **607** King Songstan Gampoh unifies Tibet.	**650-663** Under Tang Emperor Kao Trung, the Tang dynasty reaches its greatest extent. The civil service examination system is introduced. **660** Sogdiana—in today's Uzbekistan—becomes part of China. **668** The Silla kingdom unites the Korean Peninsula.	**ca 700** Austronesians settle Cook Island. **710** Nara becomes the capital of Japan. **712-756** Under emperor Xuanzong, the Tang dynasty reaches the height of its power.	

750	800	850	900	950–1000
750 Teotihuacan is sacked and burned by the invading Toltec. **750** The Zapotec city of Monte Albán in Mexico's central valley is abandoned. **763** Yax Pasah, the 16th Maya ruler of Copán, Honduras, assumes power.	**805** The last record of the Maya ruler of Copán, Honduras, appears on July 25. After Yax Pasah's death, the city is abandoned.	**ca 850** The Maya civilization is in full decline. **ca 850** The Anasazi in the Chaco Canyon of present-day New Mexico begin building a series of urban communities, sustained by corn agriculture.	**ca 900** Toltec from the north, led by Mixcoatl, conquer the central valley in Mexico. **918** Tolpiltzin, Mixcoatl's son, founds the city of Tula and conquers most of Mexico.	**978** Toltec merge with the Maya on the Yucatán Peninsula. **990** The Huari and Tiahuanaco Empires in Peru begin to decline.
751-768 Charles Martel's son, Pépin the Short, rules the Franks. **757-796** Offa, king of Mercia, rules parts of England. **768** Pépin's son, Charlemagne, ascends to the Frankish throne. After conquering the Lombards in Italy, in 774, Charlemagne is also crowned king of the Lombards.	**800** Pope Leo III crowns Charlemagne in Rome as Holy Roman Emperor. **814** After Charlemagne's death, his son, Louis the Pious, becomes emperor. **843** By the Treaty of Verdun, the Carolingian Empire is divided among Louis's three sons.	**860** Vikings attack Constantinople. **862** The Viking Rus tribe seizes control of northern Russia. **871** Alfred the Great becomes king of England. **874** Vikings settle Iceland. **882** Oleg of Russia founds Kiev as the capital.	**900** Upon King Alfred's death, his son Edward the Elder takes the throne of England. **907** Russian prince Oleg sails to Constantinople to arrange a treaty on trade with Byzantium. **936** Otto of Saxony is proclaimed king of Germany.	**954** Erik Bloodaxe, last Viking ruler of York, dies. **958** King Harold of Denmark accepts Christianity. **959-975** Edgar the Peaceful consolidates the English kingdom. **960** Mieczyslaw I is first ruler of Poland. **962** Otto I of Germany becomes Holy Roman Emperor.
750-754 Abu al-Abbas overthrows the Umayyads and takes up the Islamic leadership, founding the Abbasid dynasty. **750** Prince Abd al-Rahman I flees the massacre of the Umayyads and escapes to Spain. **786** Harun al-Rashid becomes caliph in Baghdad.	**ca 800** A city takes shape in the inland Niger Delta at Jenne-Jeno, becoming a bustling trade center of 10,000. **809** Harun al-Rashid dies. After internecine feuds, al-Ma'mun reigns in Baghdad from 813 to 823, enlarging the empire with Afghanistan and Turkmenistan.	**847-861** Al-Mutawakkil is the last great Abbasid caliph. **ca 870** Tegdaoust in Mauritania begins to flourish as the ancient city of Aoudaghost. **870** The Turkish army of mercenaries plays a heavy hand in choosing the next caliph, but al-Mu'tamid restores calm in the Muslim Empire.	**901** Muslims conquer Sicily. **907** The Fatimids—descendants of Muhammad's daughter Fatima and Ali—break away from the Abbasids and migrate to North Africa. **945** Abbasid power declines in Baghdad.	**950** Abbasid caliphs are mere figureheads as provincial governors act independently. The once mighty Muslim Empire is falling apart.
ca 750 In the search for a better form of landholding in Japan, shoen (estates) begin to rise. **751** Tang Chinese forces are defeated by Arabs and Turks at the Talas River in Central Asia. **755-763** The An Lushan rebellion in China weakens the Tang dynasty. **775** The Srivijaya kingdom extends from Sumatra and Java to Malaysia.	**ca 800** Jayavarman II consolidates small Khmer states into one kingdom in present-day Cambodia. **838** The last of the great Japanese missions leave for China's Tang court.	**850** The Chola kingdom of South India keeps to its Hindu roots, ruling the Coromandel coast. **ca 850** Maori sailors discover New Zealand. **877-889** Indravarman I of the Khmer in Cambodia unites his kingdom and builds a temple mountain (Bakong), a forerunner to Angkor Wat architecture. **879** Nepal gains independence from Tibet.	**907** The Tang dynasty in China collapses. **935** Silla rule of the Korean Peninsula is replaced by the state of Korea.	**960** The Song dynasty reunifies China and ushers in an intensive economic, social, and cultural change.

POLITICS & POWER	GEOGRAPHY & ENVIRONMENT	CULTURE & RELIGION

THE AMERICAS

ca 500 Temple mound builders trade in the Mississippi Valley.

ca 500 Maya civilization on the Yucatán Peninsula flourishes.

ca 500 Nazca and Moche people in Peru continue to develop a rich artistic culture along the northern Andean coast.

Moche pot with warrior's face

ca 500 The Thule, a coalition of various Bering Strait peoples who subsist largely on whale meat, begin to move into Alaska.

ca 500 In the midst of a prolonged draught, indigenous people in present-day California turn to game and fish for survival. They also subsist on acorns and other nuts.

ca 500 Moche society is stressed by decades of El Niño draughts and floods, beginning a long period of retrenchment.

ca 500 Maya hieroglyphs constitute one of the first written languages in the Americas. More than 80 large ceremonial centers develop in Tikal, Guatemala; Uxmal and Palenque in Mexico; and other sites in Mesoamerica.

ca 500 Teotihuacan, Mexico, is the largest city in the Americas.

ca 500 Moche people in Peru produce spectacular pottery. The pots are painted with intricate scenes of daily life or sculpted as portraits of warriors, kings, and animals.

EUROPE

500 Ostrogoth Theodoric becomes ruler of what remains of the Roman Empire in Italy.

500 Visigoths rule Spain from Toledo.

500 Angles and Saxons move into the British Isles.

511 Clovis, ruler of Gaul, dies. His kingdom is divided among his four sons.

527-567 Under Justinian, the Byzantine Empire begins to regain lost territory of the once powerful Roman Empire.

530 Frankish tribes overtake Germany and northern France.

ca 500 Eastern tribes spread across Central Europe.

ca 500 Slavs migrate to Eastern Europe and Russia.

ca 500 Ostrogoths range into Macedonia.

ca 510 Irish nuns under Bridget of Kildare teach, pray, and copy Christian manuscripts.

521 Roman scholar Boethius introduces Greek musical letter notation to the West.

529 St. Benedict establishes Monte Cassino Abbey in Italy. His rule for monastic life—with vows of obedience, chastity, and poverty—is adopted by other monasteries, including one run by his twin sister Scholastica.

529 Justinian's Code of Civil Law, the Codex Vetus, is issued. This codification of Roman law will influence all future European civil law codes.

MIDDLE EAST & AFRICA

ca 500 The Ghana Empire rises in importance as a trading center for West African gold.

ca 500 Yoruba-speaking people, southwest of Nigeria, establish large settlements.

525 King Kaleb of Aksum avenges massacre of Christians in the southern Arabian Peninsula. Leaving a garrison there, he returns to Africa.

530 Gelimer becomes king of the Vandals in North Africa, a realm reaching from Tangiers to Carthage, Corsica, Sardinia, and Sicily.

531 Sassanid king Khosrow I reunites Persia, holds Turkish incursions from the northeast at bay, and begins forays west into Byzantium.

ca 500 Sedentary Jewish tribes live in the regions of Mecca and Yemen on the Arabian Peninsula, engaged in farming and crafts.

526 An earthquake in Antioch, Turkey, devastates the area, killing some 250,000 people.

Ornately decorated Talmud

ca 500 Ethiopians adopt Christianity.

500 Jewish scholars compile the Talmud, a collection of scholarly tracts of the Bible, law, science, and parables. Talmudic scholars continue to interpret these texts of Jewish law and custom to this day.

ASIA & OCEANIA

500 China is split into several warring kingdoms and suffers a period of great instability.

500 Northern Funan falls to the Khmer people of Cambodia.

500 The Korean Peninsula is divided among three kingdoms: Silla, Paekche, and Koguryo.

500 The Yamato court consolidates its rule in Japan.

535 India's Gupta Empire, already weakened by nomadic attacks from the northwest, collapses and rival powers take control of different parts of India.

ca 500 Easter Island is settled by early inhabitants of Australia and New Guinea.

500 Trade on the Silk Road continues to connect Asia with Europe in a lively exchange of goods and culture. Two-humped Bactrian camels, uniquely adapted to the extreme cold of the mountains and the heat of Asia's deserts, carry much of the merchandise.

ca 500 The sweet potato is distributed to many Pacific islands through the voyages of Austronesian mariners.

ca 500 India's Gupta kings, followers of Hinduism, support the arts and poetry, science and mathematics. Striking murals in the Ajanta caves, depicting court life, musicians, and dancers adorned with pearls and jewels, speak of the wealth and elegance of the period.

528 The Bulguksa Buddha temple is built in the Silla (Korea) capital, Kyongju.

SCIENCE & TECHNOLOGY	PEOPLE & SOCIETY
ca 500 The Maya develop astronomical calendars; they include a 260-day sacred calendar and a 365-day solar calendar. Incised in stone, the calendar serves ritual purposes, to schedule events for favorable days, and to record history. **ca 500 The Kumeyaay people** of present-day California develop a keen understanding of botany, growing plants both for food and for medicinal properties.	**ca 500 Maya society** is organized into city-states covering parts of present-day Mexico, Guatemala, Belize, Honduras, and El Salvador. The city-states are ruled by kings, who are considered divine and serve as intermediaries between gods and the people. Architects build grand palaces, plazas, and terraced pyramids topped with sacred shrines. Priests perform rituals and sacrifices, maintain calendars for the planting seasons, and foretell fortuitous times for raids on other states. They grow corn, beans, pumpkin, chili, sweet potato, yucca, and jicama, and make land more arable by means of irrigation canals.
ca 500 The iron-tipped moldboard plow comes in common use in Germany, improving agriculture. **537 Hagia Sophia** in Constantinople is completed, the largest Christian church built at the time, with a dome spanning 100 feet. The construction of the dome alone is a technical feat; workers spend five years reconstructing the dome after it collapses in an earthquake in 557.	**ca 500 Legendary King Arthur**, as immortalized in Thomas Malory's *Morte Darthur,* leads the Britons against the Saxons in battles and carries the Christian cross against the heathen. Together with his Knights of the Round Table and their armies, he conquers Scotland, Ireland, Iceland, and Orkney. He is said to have fallen in the Battle of Camlan in 539.
530 The game of chess is introduced to Persia from India. **531 Chosroes I** of Persia builds a palace, topped with the largest iwans ever built. Iwans are high vaulted halls that serve as a great entrance. Similar portals become architectural features of future mosques.	**ca 500 Zarathustra**, prophet of the supreme god, Ahura Mazda, and six lesser deities, preached a theology in ancient Persia that is revived during the Sassanid Empire. Like other religions, Zarathustra's faith encourages high moral standards and promises rewards and punishments at life's end. In "The Divine Songs" he extols: "The worst existence shall be the lot of the followers of evil, and the good mind shall be the reward of the followers of good."
ca 500 Indian astronomers and mathematicians Varahamihira and Aryabhata discover that the earth turns on its axis. They introduce the concept of zero and deal with sophisticated concepts in mathematics.	**ca 500 Northern Funan** along the Mekong River is an independent kingdom, influenced by Indian mores and religion. By the end of the fifth century, Funan controls much of what is now southern Vietnam, Cambodia, central Thailand, northern Malaysia, and southern Myanmar (Burma). Civil wars and a steady influx of Khmer people lead to the kingdom's collapse.

Moai Statues

EASTER ISLAND

Many Pacific islands were settled by experienced seafarers from New Guinea and Australia who traveled far in the open ocean with their outrigger canoes. By about the year 500, Austronesians had reached what they called Rapa Nui, one of the most remote areas in their sphere.

As on other islands, they established an agricultural and fishing society, but sheer distance from other inhabited worlds—more than 2,500 miles to Chile, 2,000 miles to Tahiti—kept the islanders largely in isolation.

The Rapa Nui people developed a sophisticated culture, including the only written language in Oceania—the Rongorongo script—which has not yet been deciphered. Around 1100 they began erecting giant stone monoliths known as *moai* to represent sacred chiefs and gods. Carved from volcanic rock without the aid of metal tools, some were as high as 40 feet and weighed up to 80 tons.

Slash-and-burn agriculture eventually led to ecological disaster. The island could no longer support its inhabitants and civil wars brought its population to near extinction.

The island's discovery by Europeans on Easter Sunday, 1722, gave the land its current name.

POLITICS & POWER	GEOGRAPHY & ENVIRONMENT	CULTURE & RELIGION

THE AMERICAS

562 The Maya city-state of Tikal, in present-day Guatemala, is defeated by rival Calakmul, Mexico. The attackers are encouraged by a propitious alignment of the stars.

578 Buts'Chan, Smoke Serpent, the 11th ruler of Copán in Honduras, begins his 50-year-long reign.

ca 540 Hopewell Indians of North America spread through the eastern woodlands.

Hopewell Indian copper plaque

ca 540 An elite society in the city-state of Copán in the lowlands of Honduras fosters literature and architecture. Copán is one of the smaller Maya sites, but ranks among the most important ones because of its many hieroglyphic texts and chronologies.

EUROPE

546 Rome is destroyed by a new wave of Ostrogoths.

553 Byzantine Emperor Justinian sends an army into North Africa and reconquers lost Roman territory from the Vandals.

561 Civil war breaks out among the Merovingians in France, to last for 50 years.

568 Refugees from the Lombard invasion settle in the lagoons of Venice, Italy.

570 Byzantium and Persia establish a 50-year peace.

542-594 A series of plagues strikes Europe, halving its population.

558-559 The Huns invade Thrace, Macedonia, and Greece.

568 The Lombards, a Germanic tribe, invade northern Italy.

543 The Church of St. Germain-des-Pres is founded in Paris.

550 Church bells come in use in France.

ca 550 Justinian's missionaries are said to have smuggled the secrets of silk-spinning and silkworm culture from China. These first few silkworms signify the beginning of the European silk industry.

563 Christianity gains in Saxon England.

539-594 Bishop Gregory of Tours is influential in religious and political matters in the Merovingian kingdom and writes the history of France.

MIDDLE EAST & AFRICA

570 The Abyssinians of North Africa establish a protectorate over the southern Arabian Peninsula when Abraha, the Yemeni king, marches on Mecca with war elephants, which terrify the Meccans. The period is called the "year of the elephant," and many events are dated from this confrontation.

570 Muhammad, the Prophet and future messenger of Islam, is born.

575 The Persians overthrow the Abyssinians in Yemen.

551 Beirut is destroyed by an earthquake; 250,000 lives are lost.

570 Mecca is an important city on the Arabian Peninsula, lying halfway on the trade route along the Red Sea from the Mediterranean to Yemen in the south and at the crossroad to the Persian Gulf. Caravans carry spices, frankincense, myrrh, and other luxury goods.

ca 540 Kalila and Dimna, a book of political allegory, is translated into Persian from Sanskrit and later becomes a favorite in the Arab world.

543 The first Christian mission is established in Nubia. Scholars begin to translate the Bible into the local language.

ASIA & OCEANIA

542 Ly Bon leads the Vietnamese in a successful rebellion against China's occupation. Within six years China retakes the territory.

550-589 China's warring kingdoms begin to solidify into three dynasties: the Southern Chen (557-589), the Northern Zhou (557-581), and the Northern Qi (550-577).

574 Crown Prince Shotoku of the powerful Soga clan in Japan is born. He becomes regent for his aunt, Empress Suiko.

ca 540 Nomadic tribes from the north invade and attack land along China's border.

ca 540 Buddhism wanes in India, but continues to spread farther east.

552 Buddhism reaches Japan.

557 Luoyang becomes the capital of China and the center of Buddhism in eastern Asia, with more than a thousand temples and monasteries in the city alone.

SCIENCE & TECHNOLOGY

550 Native people in southwest Colorado begin building pit houses, roofed with mud and logs.

ca 550-570 Constantinople's sturdy triple walls and massive brick water cisterns, all kept in good repair, allow the city to repel the Huns, Slavs, Avars, and Persians.

ca 540 Iron smelting—allowing for better tools—aids the expansion of Bantu speakers into heavily forested regions of Africa between the Cameroon highlands and the eastern and southern African savannah.

549 The kite is invented in China. Although it may have been in use earlier, the year 549 is the first recorded mention of it.

Camel and rider, Northern Qi dynasty

PEOPLE & SOCIETY

553-578 Moon-Jaguar, the 10th Maya ruler of Copán, marks his reign by adding a terraced two-story temple, known as Rosalila, to the administrative complex, plazas, and ball-courts. His name is carved on its front stairway. The temple decorations—a true testament to Maya culture—honor the sacred maize plant.

548 St. Columba, a recluse from Dublin, Ireland, founds the monastery of Iona in Scotland and helps spread Celtic Christianity throughout Scotland and Northumbria. On subsequent missions, he establishes a monastery in Luxeuil, France, and one in Bobbio, Italy. His followers spread Christianity into continental Europe.

ca 540 The people of the Arabian Peninsula consist of loosely linked nomadic clans—the Bedouin—who herd goats, sheep, and camels in the desert, and settled tribes who are engaged in commerce and long-distance caravan trade.

502-549 Emperor Wu, founder of the Liang dynasty, reforms the nine-rank system of advancement in China's government so that only "those with talent may advance along the road to success." He becomes a devout Buddhist and sponsors construction of numerous temples. In 549 when his city of Jiankang is besieged, Wu orders a kite to be flown above the city to alert allies of his plight. His ploy is unsuccessful, and he and his kingdom fall to the Chen dynasty.

Seated Buddha, China.

BUDDHISM SPREADS EAST

Arising in India about 500 B.C.E., Buddhism slowly gained adherents along the Silk Road. As traders plodded along the trails, monks followed. By the third century C.E. they had founded monasteries at some of the caravan stops in the Kushan Empire of Afghanistan.

In China, Daoism and Confucianism prevailed. After the fall of the Han dynasty—when China split into several warring kingdoms—people may have longed for a religion that offered peaceful meditation and the prospect of personal salvation. Rulers began to support the construction of temples and monasteries, many in caves and on mountainsides. By about 550, China could boast of nearly 14,000 Buddhist temples. In Korea, Buddhism found the support of kings as well. In 552 the ruler of Paekche recommended Buddhism to the Yamato ruler in Japan, and the religion gradually developed adherents there, too.

This dharma . . . bestows endless and immeasurable blessings, even the attainment of supreme enlightenment.

PRINCE OF PAEKCHE TO EMPEROR KIMMEI

One more cup of wine
for our remaining happiness.
There will be chilling
parting dreams tonight.

A NINTH-CENTURY CHINESE POET

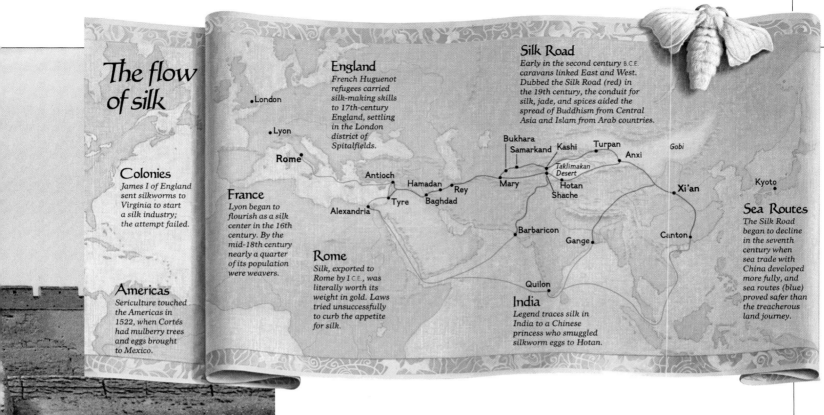

The flow of silk

England
French Huguenot refugees carried silk-making skills to 17th-century England, settling in the London district of Spitalfields.

Colonies
James I of England sent silkworms to Virginia to start a silk industry; the attempt failed.

Americas
Sericulture touched the Americas in 1522, when Cortés had mulberry trees and eggs brought to Mexico.

France
Lyon began to flourish as a silk center in the 16th century. By the mid-18th century nearly a quarter of its population were weavers.

Rome
Silk, exported to Rome by I C.E., was literally worth its weight in gold. Laws tried unsuccessfully to curb the appetite for silk.

Silk Road
Early in the second century B.C.E. caravans linked East and West. Dubbed the Silk Road (red) in the 19th century, the conduit for silk, jade, and spices aided the spread of Buddhism from Central Asia and Islam from Arab countries.

India
Legend traces silk in India to a Chinese princess who smuggled silkworm eggs to Hotan.

Sea Routes
The Silk Road began to decline in the seventh century when sea trade with China developed more fully, and sea routes (blue) proved safer than the treacherous land journey.

Map labels: London, Lyon, Rome, Alexandria, Tyre, Antioch, Hamadan, Rey, Baghdad, Mary, Bukhara, Samarkand, Kashi, Turpan, Anxi, Gobi, Taklimakan Desert, Hotan, Shache, Xi'an, Kyoto, Barbaricon, Gange, Quilon, Canton

THE SILK ROAD

THE FABLED SILK ROAD, A NETWORK OF FOOTPATHS AND CARAVAN trails across rugged mountains and barren lands, linked the Mediterranean to China as early as the second century B.C.E. Alexander the Great's army had blazed trails from Greece to the Indus River; Chinese emissaries had scouted the way from the Far East to Central Asia, where they traded for horses from Ferghana to defend against mounted raiders along their northern border.

The main route led from China's capital of Chang'an, modern-day Xi'an, west to the forbidding Taklimakan, or "desert of no return." There the road split into a northern and southern trail, each threading through scarce watering holes. Rejoined at Kashgar (Kashi), the road wound its way through the snow-capped mountains of the Pamirs and the Hindu Kush, skirted the southern coast of the Caspian Sea, and continued via Antioch to the Mediterranean. Most merchants trekked only a short section of the way. The journey took months and was perilous. Sandstorms and mountain passes, marauders and self-appointed taxing agents took their toll.

By the seventh century, though, trade flowed steadily in all directions. China's Tang dynasty expanded far into western lands, setting up protectorates in Sogdiana and Ferghana in Central Asia and eastern Persia. Chinese merchants traded exquisite silks and porcelain for Roman glass, Bactrian gold jewelry, Sassanian bronze and silver vessels, and Indian precious stones. Religion, science and technology, artistic styles, and foods also traveled along the road. Buddhism flowed east from India in the sixth century. A century later Islam began to spread through the Middle East, Central Asia, and far into western China.

This exchange continued well into the 14th century, contributing to a Eurasian culture that was vibrant, luxurious, and complex. Only when trade became more profitable via new sea routes did commerce along the ancient paths began to decline.

Having crossed the most inaccessible regions of the ancient Silk Road, a caravan reaches Jiayuguan fortress in China's Gansu Province. From here traders braved the unknown, conveying goods and ideas to the West.

POLITICS & POWER	GEOGRAPHY & ENVIRONMENT	CULTURE & RELIGION

THE AMERICAS

594 Lady Yohl Ik'nal, ruler of the Maya city-state of Palenque, suffers defeat by the rival state Calakmul in Mexico.

ca 600 The Athapaskan people arrive from Canada in the plains of North America.

ca 600 The Huari people rise in northern Peru.

ca 600 The Tiahuanacan Empire rises in southern Peru and Bolivia.

615 Maya ruler Pacal of Palenque begins to build a lavish palace, pyramid, and temple.

ca 595 The Joya de Ceren Maya site in El Salvador is buried under 12 to 19 feet of ash from the erupting Loma caldera volcano.

ca 600 Athapaskans from northwestern Canada and the northern United States decorate their shields with pictographs of warriors.

Maya maize god

EUROPE

589 Christianity is proclaimed the official religion in Spain after King Recared's conversion.

590 Gregory, abbot of St. Andrew's monastery in Rome, becomes Pope Gregory I and establishes the pope as de facto ruler of central Italy.

602 Flavius Phocas Augustus overthrows Byzantine Emperor Maurice. He suffers defeat from the Slavs and the Persians along the empire's eastern borders.

610 Heraclius of Carthage arrives in Constantinople and usurps the throne, beheading Augustus. In renewed battles, he regains Asia Minor, Syria, Jerusalem, and Egypt.

ca 600 The Byzantine Empire can no longer hold the vast territory of the Roman Empire together. Germanic tribes have settled large portions of the West. The Sassanids of Persia and Slavic tribes of the East are constantly trying the eastern borders of Byzantium and are gaining ground.

598 The first English school is founded in Canterbury, thought to have been introduced by St. Augustine, who was sent by Pope Gregory I to convert the Anglo-Saxons.

ca 600 A law is passed in Ireland forbidding women to go into battle.

ca 600 Gregorian chant is named for Pope Gregory.

612 The monasteries of St. Gall, Switzerland, and Bobbio, Italy, are founded.

MIDDLE EAST & AFRICA

589 Arabs, Khazars, and Turks invade Persia, but are repelled.

590-628 Chosroes II rules in Persia.

610 Muhammad experiences a spiritual transformation and begins to repeat a message received from God. When he proclaims in Mecca that there is only one God, he is reviled.

In the name of Allah, the Compassionate, the Merciful,
Praise be to Allah, the Lord of the Worlds,
The Compassionate, the Merciful,
Master of the Day of Judgment
Only You do we worship, and only You do we implore for help.
Lead us to the right path.

MUHAMMAD'S MESSAGE, KORAN, SURA I: 1-6

ASIA & OCEANIA

587 The Soga clan takes on political power at the Yamato court in Japan.

589 Yang Jian reunites a fragmented China and fosters an era of great culture and invention.

604-618 Emperor Yangdi continues the Sui rule in China.

604 Prince Shotoku issues principles for rule based on Buddhism, Shinto, and Confucianism.

607 King Songstan Gampo unifies Tibet. He introduces Buddhism and builds the Potola Palace and Jokhang Temple.

ca 600 Mon people from western China move into Thailand. Thai people from southern China begin to settle among the Mon and form small states.

ca 600 Early settlers from the Marquesas Islands build the Alekoko fishpond and taro fields on Hawaii.

ca 580 Buddhist missionaries introduce the art of flower arranging in Japan.

ca 600 Japanese scribes apply Chinese characters to write their own language and produce the first written constitution.

618-907 The Tang dynasty ushers in a golden age of poetry and culture in China.

SCIENCE & TECHNOLOGY	PEOPLE & SOCIETY
ca 600 The Maya develop bark paper. **ca 600 The Athapaskan people** hunt buffalo with bow and arrow, introducing a triangular arrowhead with serrated edges.	**ca 600-1000 The Huari Empire** (also spelled Wari), based in the central and northern highlands of the Andes, rules over most of Peru. Arising in the Ayacucho Valley, the Huari build elite cities, temples, and palaces and set up a major network of roads and communication that later serves as a model to the Incas. **ca 600 The Hohokam** culture is spreading in North America's Southwest.
ca 600 Byzantine soldiers and engineers improve earlier Roman siege machinery.	**540-604 As a young man, Gregory the Great** becomes prefect of the city of Rome, but he abandons that course to become a monk. He gives up his properties in Rome and Sicily and converts them into monasteries. In 578 the pope sends Gregory as emissary to Byzantium for help against the invading Lombards. Help is not forthcoming, and Gregory returns, convinced that Rome has to become independent of the Church of the East. In 590 he is elected pope and strengthens the papal primacy over the churches of the West.
620 Copper wire is in use in Dambwa, Zambia.	**ca 610 Bilal the Ethiopian,** a slave in Mecca, is one of the first people to accept Muhammad's message. Bilal's master tortures him for his beliefs, but Bilal does not renounce Islam. He soon joins Muhammad's forces on campaigns. When Muhammad looks for means to rally people, he turns to Bilal, who has a sonorous voice to call the Muslims to prayer, and thus he becomes the first muezzin.
593 Printing blocks are invented in China. **ca 600-618 During the Sui dynasty in China,** the emperors undertake construction of palaces and granaries, repair sections of the Great Wall, and build the Grand Canal. **607 Japan's Horyuji Temple** is completed, the oldest surviving wooden building in the world.	**590-647 Harsha Vardhana** becomes ruler of a small kingdom in the lower Ganges Valley of India at age 16, after the fall of the Gupta Empire. With youthful zeal, he leads his army through northern India and reunites a vast area of the country from Bengal to Gujarat. As a Buddhist, he is known for his piety and generosity and supports free medical care and hospitalization for his subjects. He holds his empire together until 647, when he is murdered, plunging his empire into anarchy.

The Grand Canal

CHINA'S GRAND CANAL

Though it took two thousand years for the Grand Canal to reach its full length of 1,000 miles, the largest parts were built during six years of furious building, between 605 and 611, under a mandate from Emperor Yangdi of the Sui dynasty.

Uncounted workers toiled and died undergoing this compulsory labor. They repaired and enlarged an older system of canals that had been started in the sixth century B.C.E. and blazed a new channel for hundreds of miles from Hangzhou to Yangzhou, creating a vital north-south link between the Yangtze and the Yellow Rivers. Kublai Khan later extended the canal to Beijing, and the Ming made further improvements.

This monumental feat of engineering—in use to this day—provided a much needed supply route to the agrarian south. Due to a new strain of rice that permitted two crops a year, the south had begun producing surplus yields that could now be easily distributed across the country.

Midnight, from out of the Han Shan Temple outside the city of Gu Su, I hear the sound of bells, as it reaches my lonely travelling boat . . .

ZHANG JI, TANG POET, ON THE GRAND CANAL

POLITICS & POWER	GEOGRAPHY & ENVIRONMENT	CULTURE & RELIGION

THE AMERICAS

628-695 Smoke Imix, the 12th ruler of Copán, Honduras, begins his long reign, wielding political control over a wide area of Maya countryside.

ca 650 The adoption of farming by the Mogollon ("mountain people") leads to permanent communities built along mountain streams in the Southwest of North America. They build semisubterranean pit houses and subsist by farming corn, beans, and squash.

ca 650 Hopewell people settle along the upper Mississippi River, making the river their highway for trade and expansion.

ca 650 Copán's architecture and cultural life reaches its apogee in Honduras. The city is crowned by an acropolis with ballcourts, plazas, temples, and magnificent sculptures.

650 Zapotec astronomers travel to Xochicalco, a Teotihuacan city, for a meeting of astronomers in which representatives of various Mesoamerican cultures synchronize their calendars.

EUROPE

620 Vikings invade Ireland.

630 Peace is announced between Byzantium and Persia.

633 In England, the Mercians defeat the Northumbrians.

641 Byzantine Emperor Heraclius dies. He is eventually succeeded by his grandson Constans II, who repels the Muslim onslaught on Constantinople and defeats the Slavs at the Danube River.

WHAT LIFE WAS LIKE

On a Viking Ship

Viking longships with double-ended hulls and pronounced keels—often sporting a carved dragon head—could carry as many as a hundred men across the sea. With a rectangular sail of woven wool, sometimes adorned with red stripes or a diamond design, the ships hugged coastlines, using familiar landmarks as guides. Equipped with only crude instruments, Vikings relied mainly on the position of the sun and the stars for navigation. A helmsman steered the ship with a side rudder and the crew controlled the sail with a network of rigging. Fearless sailors, Vikings raided, traded, and explored the unknown world.

626 The Abbey of St. Denis near Paris is founded.

632 Heraclius orders the forced conversion of Jews after accusing them of collaboration with Persian invaders.

635 Aidan, a monk of Iona, builds Lindisfarne Priory on an island off Scotland.

640 By decree of Emperor Heraclius I, the Greek language replaces Latin as the official language in Byzantium.

655 The Liber Judiciorum gives legal form to the Visigoths in Spain.

MIDDLE EAST & AFRICA

622 Muhammad and his followers flee to Medina. In 630 Muhammad returns and conquers Mecca.

632 Upon Muhammad's death, his father-in-law, Abu Bakr, succeeds him and brings Muhammad's message and Islam to Arabia, Syria, Palestine, and Iraq.

634-644 Umar—successor to Abu Bakr—takes up the sword for Islam and advances into Egypt and other Byzantine territories.

651 Muslims annex Persia.

656 Ali—Muhammad's son-in-law—becomes the new leader of Islam.

ca 630 With Muhammad's words to guide them, the once loosely allied Arabian tribes become a powerful nation, annexing within two decades much of the Middle East. A united Middle East revives trade across the region.

ca 650 Muslim camp towns spring up, such as Basra, Kufa, and Misr, where Muslim Arabs come into contact with the varied people of the Fertile Crescent in modern-day Iraq and begin to assimilate to sedentary lifestyles, farming, and trade.

624-627 Jews are evicted from Medina by Muhammad.

637 Jews are allowed to reside in Jerusalem after the Muslim conquest.

637-638 Non-Muslims obtain protected status (*dhimmi*) in the Muslim world.

644 Muhammad's message from God is written down to form the Koran.

656 The Battle of the Camel, over succession to the caliphate after the death of Uthman, is attended by Muhammad's widow Aishah on a camel. Her political participation is condemned and leads to the seclusion of women.

ASIA & OCEANIA

618 Li Yuan, a Sui official, founds the Tang dynasty and expands the Chinese Empire.

626-649 Tang emperor Taizong conquers Turkestan and Korea.

645 Following a coup against the Soga clan in Japan, the imperial court undertakes reforms modeled on the centralized imperial government of China's Tang dynasty.

647 Harsha Vardhana of India is murdered, and India falls into anarchy.

652 Afghanistan is conquered by Muslims.

ca 650 China stretches from Tibet to Korea and from Mongolia to the South China Sea.

ca 650 Srivijaya on the island of Sumatra establishes itself as a kingdom, a strategic landing point for ships sailing to or from China.

629-645 Chinese pilgrim Xuanzang travels to India and beyond to collect Buddhist teachings. He writes a lengthy account of his journey, entitled *Record of the Western Regions,* and thus ensures the survival of many Buddhist sacred texts when Buddhism fades in India. Among other things, he describes the giant Buddhas at Bamian, Afghanistan.

645 Buddhism reaches Tibet.

SCIENCE & TECHNOLOGY	PEOPLE & SOCIETY

THE RISE OF ISLAM

ca 650 The people of the North American Southwest—the Hohokam, Anasazi, and Mogollon—develop independently but share a harsh territory extending from northern Mexico to Arizona and New Mexico, southern Utah and Colorado, bounded by desert to the west and grassy plains to the east. They live as hunter-gatherers and begin a settled existence as they develop a tenuous agriculture. The development of pottery vessels to store and protect food from mold and pests is an important step in settling permanently and devising new kinds of shelter, be they rock caves, pit houses, or adobe homes.

ca 650 Lindisfarne Priory, like other monasteries in the north of England, is independent of Rome. Scottish kings variously adopt Celtic Christianity or become subject to Rome. At the priory, the monk Eadfrith copies and illuminates the four Gospels, which are later translated into a form of Old English, famously known as the Lindisfarne Gospels.

Heraclius battles the Muslims.

640 The Muslim government begins to mint its own coins from silver and gold, some of which is imported from East and West Africa.

ca 650 The realm of Islam becomes a new society. Disenfranchised people of the desert are given new hope with the words of the Prophet Muhammad:

Perform the prayer; give the alms-tax and bow down with those who bow down. . . . Seek assistance through patience and prayer. It is hard, except for the truly devout; who believe that they shall meet their Lord, and unto Him they shall return.

Koran, Sura II: 43-46

634 Chomsongdae Observatory is built in the Korean kingdom of Silla, the oldest known observatory in east Asia. Built as a round tower, its symbolic meaning signifies a connection from earth to heaven. The outer layer, constructed of 360 stones, denotes one calendar year.

645 Japan institutes the Taika reforms, establishing a new government and administrative system after the Chinese model. Land is bought by the state and redistributed among farmers to introduce a new tax system that is adopted from China.

In 610 Muhammad of Mecca had a revelation in the desert, when a voice commanded him to pay obedience to the one God, Allah. After further visions, he began to repeat the words revealed to him, later written down in the Koran (below).

His message to the powerful clans of the Arabian desert, bidding them to believe in only one God and to share with the poor, so enraged them that he and his followers were driven from Mecca. On his flight to the town of Medina—the Hegira—in 622, the tenets of his belief crystallized for him, and Muslims ever since have marked the calendar from this date as the year one.

In 630 Muhammad returned to Mecca with a force of men and defeated his opponents. He and his followers smashed the idols in the Kaaba—which had been a holy shrine since time immemorial—but preserved the sacred Black Stone inside. Muhammad spelled out the obligations of the faith by proclaiming the Five Pillars of Islam: belief in one God, prayer, almsgiving, fasting during

The Koran

the month of Ramadan, and performing the hajj (the pilgrimage to Mecca) once in a lifetime or more often if possible.

Muhammad died two years after taking Mecca, but his successors propagated the faith, seeking new converts by word and new territory by sword.

POLITICS & POWER	GEOGRAPHY & ENVIRONMENT	CULTURE & RELIGION
THE AMERICAS		
682 Maya ruler Ah Cacao becomes ruler of Tikal, Guatemala. Temple I on the Great Plaza is built as his funerary monument. **683 Maya king Pacal**, ruler of Palenque in Mexico, dies at age 80, after a long reign, and is buried in a pyramid. **694 The 13th Maya ruler of Copán**, 18 Rabbit, begins his 44-year-long reign in Honduras.	**697 The last major earthquake** to hit the Salt Lake City region in Utah occurs.	
EUROPE		
668 Byzantine Emperor Constans II is assassinated. His son Constantine IV begins his rule, battling Muslims and Slavs in succession. **680-700 The Frankish Merovingian kings** are known as "do-nothings." In 687 power passes to the mayor of the palace, Pépin of Herstal. **680-750 Arabic replaces Latin** as the primary learned language of Spain. **681 Bulgars** settle south of the Danube, establishing their first kingdom.	**650-850 Benedictine monks** clear forests, drain swamps, and experiment with crop rotation, becoming the most successful farmers in Europe and serving as models for their neighbors. **664 An unusually harsh winter** and deep snows leave animals and trees dead.	**ca 650 Christianity** is disseminated further in Europe. Bishops send missionaries into Celtic, Germanic, and Slavic areas. **664 At the Synod of Whitby,** the English church decides to follow Roman practices in Christianity instead of Celtic, linking the English church to Rome.
MIDDLE EAST & AFRICA		
661 Muhammad's fourth successor, Ali, is assassinated in Iraq. Muawiyah declares himself caliph of all Muslim lands and begins the rule of the Umayyad dynasty. He moves the Muslim capital from Iraq to Damascus, Syria. **685-705 Abd al-Malik,** fifth Umayyad caliph, has government records translated into Arabic and creates a new Islamic style coinage with religious quotations instead of pictures.	**661 Camel herds of the Sahara** support a nomadic way of life to people in one of the world's most inhospitable environments.	**ca 650 Copying the Koran** results in ever more artistic forms of calligraphy. Aspiring calligraphers study for years to achieve the perfectly rounded and proportioned letters. **ca 680 The Berber tribes,** who resist the Muslim conquest of North Africa, are led by a women named Cahina, thought to be Jewish. **691 The Dome of the Rock**, one of Islam's holiest shrines, is built in Jerusalem. The rock over which it is built is said to be the one from which Muhammad ascended to heaven. Judaism maintains that this is the same rock to which Abraham took his son Isaac to be sacrificed.
ASIA & OCEANIA		
650-683 Under Tang Emperor Kao Trung, the Chinese Empire reaches its greatest extent. **660 Sogdiana**—in today's Uzbekistan—becomes part of China. **661 China** goes to war against Korea, but is repelled. **668 The Silla kingdom** unites the Korean Peninsula. **690-705 Empress Wu** of China usurps the throne from her stepson Gaozong and establishes the short-lived Zhou dynasty.		**ca 660 Chinese royalty** adopts luxury drinking vessels and tableware of silver and gold from Central Asia and greater Iran. **670 The folding fan** is invented in Japan based on the structure of a bat wing. **685 A manual on calligraphy** summarizes the aesthetic ideals of Chinese script. **ca 700 Empress Wu** commissions construction of the Vairocana Buddha at the Buddhist cave temple at Longmen.

Empress Wu

SCIENCE & TECHNOLOGY	PEOPLE & SOCIETY
694-738 During the reign of Copán's 13th ruler, architectural and sculptural styles change from squared-off shapes to rounded monuments. The chamber of one temple holds an image of the night sky, with the Milky Way shown as an arching "cloud serpent."	
673 Byzantine warriors successfully use "Greek fire," an incendiary device, against Muslim attackers.	**660 Hilda of Whitby,** an English noblewoman, who governs a double monastery of monks and nuns, advises kings, encourages scholars, and hosts the Synod of Whitby. Women of the upper class often have positions as abbesses of monasteries, some of which house both women and men. **660 The Bulgars,** tribes from the East, are driven westward by the Khazars. In skirmishes with the Byzantine Empire, they win territory and settle south of the Danube in lands of ancient Thrace and Macedonia. Under Khan Asparukh, they establish their first kingdom in 681, which lasts until 1018.
Largest extent of the Tang dynasty	**680 Hussain,** the grandson of Muhammad and son of Ali, is killed in battle at Karbala, in a power struggle between Sunnis and Shiite. The Shiite continue to mourn his death on a holy day called Ashura.

THE SPLIT BETWEEN SUNNI AND SHIITE

When the prophet Muhammad died in 632, the Muslim leadership elected his father-in-law, Abu Bakr, to be the first caliph, or temporal leader of the Islamic state. The decision caused a permanent rift between the two major branches of Islam: the Shiite and the Sunni.

Shiites believed that only direct descendants of Muhammad were worthy of the caliphate. Sunnis supported Abu Bakr, as well as two subsequent caliphs who mobilized Arabia with the message of the Prophet and continued Islam's expansion, yet were still considered illegitimate by Shiites.

In 656 Muhammad's cousin and son-in-law, Ali, assumed succession as the fourth caliph—the first caliph recognized by Shiites. But plots against his life finally led to his murder in 661. His successor launched the Umayyad dynasty and moved the Islamic capital from Iraq to Damascus, Syria.

At this point the schism between the factions was complete. When Ali's last heir died, spiritual power according to the Shiite passed to the ulama, a council of 12 scholars who elected a supreme imam. The best known modern example of the Shiite supreme imam is the late Ayatollah Khomeini.

Shiite rituals differ slightly from those of the Sunni. Shiite believe that the imam's authority is infallible because it comes directly from God. Imams are often revered as saints, and people make pilgrimages to their tombs.

Sunnis believe that there is no need for a special class of spiritual leaders, nor do they believe that there should be appeals to saints for intercession. They have been willing to accept caliphs who are not of Muhammad's descent as rightful leaders.

Most people do not claim adherence to either group, but simply refer to themselves as Muslims.

TANG DYNASTY
618 - 907 C.E.

Lake Baykal

Western Turks
Aral Sea
Lake Balkhash
KUNLING
To China
Camels, jade, horses
751 Talas ✕ MENGCHI
SOGHDIANA
Kuqa
ANXI
Dunhuang
Anxi
TUKHARISTAN
TUFAN (TIBETAN KINGDOM)
To China Carpets, tapestries, jewelry
To China Camels, horses
To Central Asia Books
Tüpüt

Court of N. Turkish Khagan
NORTHERN TURKISH KHANATE
Khitan POHAI
Uygurs
To China Furs, hides, gold
Tianjin
SILLA
SILK SALT GRAND CANAL
Chang'an (Xi'an) ★
Luoyang
To Japan Books
TEA Hangzhou
PAPER
TEA
Chang Jiang (Yangtze)
Huang (Yellow)
PORCELAIN
To China Cotton textiles
SALT
COPPER ARTICLES
SILK
Guangzhou
Buddh Gaya (Birthplace of Buddhism ca 6th century B.C.E.)
NANZHAO
PYU
To China Gems, ivory, aromatics
CHAMPA
ZHENLA

Tang empire ca 700 C.E.
☐ China proper
— Greatest extent of Tang empire
▨ Limit of Muslim influence ca 661 C.E.
→ Commodities for trade
⤳ Spread of Mahayana Buddhism
◆ Major Buddhist site
⋯ Canal
TEA Commodity
⌒⌒⌒ Fortification/Wall
--- Trade route
✕ Battle (dated)
★ Capital
Tüpüt Outlying people

800 mi
800 km

POLITICS & POWER	GEOGRAPHY & ENVIRONMENT	CULTURE & RELIGION

THE AMERICAS

ca 700 The mound-building Caddo culture flourishes in Texas and Oklahoma.

ca 700 The Moche society in Peru collapses.

ca 700 The Nazca culture in Peru begins to fade.

721-764 Maya K'inich Ahkal Mo'Nob rules Palenque, Mexico.

Realm of the Maya

EUROPE

ca 700 Vikings invade the British Isles, raiding towns and villages.

704 King Aethelred of Mercia, England, gives up his kingdom to become a monk at Bardney in Lindsey. He is succeeded by Cenred, son of Wulhere. In 716 Aethelbald takes over.

711 Muslim armies invade southern Spain from North Africa.

717 Leo III becomes Byzantine emperor and ends a period of instability. He repels renewed attacks by the Arabs.

MIDDLE EAST & AFRICA

ca 700 Arab traders begin settling along the coast of East Africa. Trade centers become established at Mombassa, Malindi, and Manda Island.

705-715 Under Umayyad al Walid I, Muslim armies conquer Turkmenistan and Sind in India, pushing as far as the borders of China.

715 The Umayyad Empire reaches its greatest extent, reaching from Spain to Mongolia.

ca 700 The Umayyads develop desert agriculture in Syria, installing extensive irrigation works around their palaces at the desert's edge.

ca 700 Persians, Syrians, Copts, Berbers, and others under Muslim rule begin to adopt Arabic as their language.

711 Intolerance of Jews under Visigoths in Spain ends with Muslim conquest.

ASIA & OCEANIA

ca 700 Polynesians settle Cook Island.

710 Nara is built as the capital of Japan.

711 Sind in India is conquered by Umayyad forces.

712-756 Tang Emperor Xuanzong assumes his rule. He puts an end to Empress Wu and briefly installs his father to the throne. Under Xuanzong, Tang China reaches the height of its power.

710 Nara is the first urban center in Japan, rapidly gaining a population of 200,000.

ca 700 In Bhutan, the Buddhist Taktsang Monastery is founded.

712 Japan's history is recorded in the *Kojiki* (*Record of Ancient Matters*). A second chronicle, the *Nihon Shoki* (*Chronicles of Japan*) is compiled in 720.

SCIENCE & TECHNOLOGY	PEOPLE & SOCIETY
ca 700 An observatory at Tikal is sited so that the planets Venus and Jupiter align directly over the tip of the temple pyramid. **ca 700 The Caddo people** use a sophisticated technology in their use of clay, stone, bone, wood, shell, and other materials to make tools, clothing, ceramic vessels, basketry, and ornaments.	**ca 700 Pueblo people** in the Southwest of North America live in houses above ground and embrace farming.
ca 700 Infant mortality is roughly 50 percent in normal years. OPPOSITE: *Never a unified empire, the Maya city-states flourish across the Yucatán Peninsula as independent ceremonial centers between 600 B.C.E. and 900 C.E.*	**720 Byzantine Emperor Leo III** ignites the iconoclasm controversy with a decree outlawing the worship of icons. All western parts of the empire, including popes Gregory II and III, oppose the idea. A revolt in Greece is crushed and Leo transfers southern Italy and Greece from the papal diocese to that of the patriarch of Constantinople. An armed uprising in Ravenna severs that area from the Byzantine Empire for good.
ca 700 Villagers near modern-day Gatu, Kenya, produce a version of the world's oldest crucible steel.	
713-803 A 233-foot-tall Buddha is built in the Sichuan province in China.	**710-794 During the Nara period** in Japan, economic and administrative activity increases. Roads link Nara to provincial capitals, and government agents can collect taxes more efficiently and routinely. The government mints coins, although they are not widely used. In the provinces the authority of the imperial government gradually declines and landholding falls into private hands.

THE CADDO CONFEDERACY

In the eighth century, the Caddo Indians, who can be traced back to the Woodland period culture groups, settled in the Neches River Valley in eastern Texas. Able farmers, their skill with the land and a new development in maize production led to increased crops and rapidly caused a population growth. At their height, the Caddo numbered more than 200,000 people.

From Texas they slowly spread into Oklahoma, Arkansas, and Louisiana, where they knit together a loose federation of tribes, such as the Pawnee and the Wichita, united by custom and language. They lived in permanent village settlements dotted with distinctive beehive-shaped houses, made of layers of thatch attached to a framework of poles. These houses held multiple families, sometimes as many as 40 people.

The Caddo people developed a sophisticated rural hierarchy that incorporated a chief-priest who combined spectral and temporal authority. Chiefs led important ceremonies and councils for war expeditions and conducted the peace pipe ceremony with visitors to the community. They also provided sustenance and other essential revenue to the population to create loyal followers.

Like the Mississippians, the Caddo were mound builders, constructing civic ceremonial centers on high earthen mounds. Some served as burial grounds for the social and political elite. Others were topped by large temples lit with ceremonial fire. The Caddo were the most southwestern of the mound-building cultures.

Living where the woodlands met the Great Plains, the Caddo developed long-distance trade networks, marketing their surplus corn and other agricultural goods in exchange for buffalo hide and meat. Also in demand were their artistic and functional ceramic wares made for cooking and storage, for which the Caddo were renowned.

Maya Chronicles

I N THE ANCIENT NEW WORLD ONLY THE PEOPLE OF MESOAMERICA DEVELOPED A complete system of writing. Though the Olmecs and later the Zapotecs made simple inscriptions in stone, the Maya refined writing into a complex system of 800 pictorial and phonetic hieroglyphs. Inscribed on stelae, altars, and temples, the texts are lined up in a gridlike arrangement or by a linear set of square blocks to chronicle their history, describe the rule of kings, and date important battles. Genealogies and rituals were also recorded, on bark paper.

In addition, the Maya developed a numerical system expressed in dots and bars, known as the Long Count, to record dates. Bars had a value of five, and dots denoted one. The count was based on 20 rather than 10, as in our decimal system. In the relief shown at left, for example, the first glyph at top left expresses the exact date, October 28, 709.

Numbers were used to describe the passing of time in a calendar of interlocking cycles of time. The Maya counted a solar year of 365 days and a ceremonial calendar year of 260 days. A combination of the two cycles formed a larger span of time of 18,980 days, a 52-year cycle, and served as almanacs to farmers and priests. They also counted time back to the creation of the universe and arrived at the date of 3114 B.C.E.

Astronomers charted the movement of the planets and the stars from observatories such as the one at Tikal at right. Built on top of a pyramid, the observatory is sited so that Venus and Jupiter align directly overhead at times of conjunction.

The Maya city-states, each ruled by an independent king who served as an intermediary between gods and the people, created a sophisticated civilization. They played ritual ballgames, built pyramids topped with temples, engaged in elaborate rites to appease the gods, and waged war to obtain captives for human sacrifice. Ritual bloodletting was part of the religion; one method entailed the pulling of a thorn-studded rope through the tongue and catching the blood in a bowl, as shown in the relief at left. Bloodletting and sacrifice, whether among themselves or using prisoners, was thought to appease the gods, who had used their own blood to create the human race.

By the tenth century this high civilization mysteriously collapsed. People dispersed into the countryside and let the jungle overtake their splendid cities. The demise may have been brought on by a number of factors: endless wars, drought, deforestation, depletion of natural resources, and a reduction of the soil's productivity that could not provide for the increasing population.

BELOW: *A palace relief at Yaxchilán, Mexico, shows Lady Xoc, accompanied by her husband Shield Jaguar, pulling a rope barbed with thorns through her tongue, catching the blood in a bowl. Rulers engaged in such bloodletting rituals to repay the gods for the divine sacrifices that nurtured the human race. The hieroglyphs at bottom left state her name and the rite "she is letting blood."*

OPPOSITE: *The planets Venus and Jupiter align perfectly above the top of the observatory at Tikal in present-day Guatemala. The observatory was sited for such special conjunctions to help predict fortuitous events.*

	POLITICS & POWER	GEOGRAPHY & ENVIRONMENT	CULTURE & RELIGION
THE AMERICAS	**738 The 13th ruler**, 18 Rabbit, of the Maya city-state of Copán in Honduras is beheaded by chief Cauac Sky of the neighboring city Quiriguá. Copán does not recover its grandeur until the accession of its 15th ruler, Smoke Shell, in 749. **740 Maya Tah ak Chaun** begins a 50-year-rule in Cancuén, Guatemala. **ca 750 The city-state of Teotihuacan** in central Mexico is attacked and burned by the invading Toltec. The survivors disband into the countryside.	**ca 750 The city of Monte Albán** in Mexico is abandoned.	**757 Maya ruler Smoke Shell** indulges in a massive building program of temples and monuments in Copán.
EUROPE	**732 Charles Martel**, illegitimate son of Pépin of Herstal, halts the advance of a small group of Muslims from Spain at Tours in France. **751-768 Charles Martel's son**, Pépin the Short, rules the Franks. **756 Cuthred**, ruler of Wessex, England, dies, and Wessex falls under the control of Mercia. **757 Aethelbald**, king of Mercia, is murdered after ruling for 41 years as king. His death sparks a civil war in England.		**731 The Venerable Bede,** a monk and scholar at the monastery of Wearmouth in England, finishes his *Historia Ecclesiastica Gentis Anglorum,* the first English history, which introduces the term "anno Domini" (A.D.) into dating systems. He is also known for writing on natural history, poetry, Biblical translation, and exposition of the scriptures. **ca 700-850 The Old English poem** *Beowulf* is composed about this time, some hundred years or more before it is written down in the tenth century.
MIDDLE EAST & AFRICA	**750-754 Abu al-Abbas,** founder of the Abbasid dynasty, overthrows the Umayyads and takes up the leadership of the Muslim Empire, moving the administration from Damascus, Syria, back to Iraq. **750 Prince Abd al Rahman I** flees the massacre of the Umayyads and escapes to Spain, uniting his people there. He makes Córdoba the new capital of the Umayyads. **754 Al-Mansur** becomes second Abbasid caliph, after his brother's death, and founds Baghdad, Iraq, as his capital.	**749 An earthquake** near the Sea of Galilee causes massive damage. **750-760 African farmers and ironworkers** near the Great Lakes try to stem deforestation and soil erosion. Regional identities begin to form around the two food-producing systems of livestock-raising and mixed farming. **ca 750 Dessication** leads to the decline of Umayyad agriculture and shifts the economic hub of the empire to Mesopotamia, with its rich agriculture and trade routes along navigable rivers.	**ca 750 Flourishing since about the fourth century,** poetry called *qasidas,* or long odes, are sung at camp fires in the Arabian desert and at tribal gatherings. During the eighth century, these poems are collected under the title *Muallaqat,* meaning "suspended poems." The poems glorify the deeds of a noble warrior or lament the loss of a lover in elaborate meter and rhyme, expressing universal themes in a few words and setting poetic standards for centuries. **ca 750 Ja'far al-Sadiq,** the sixth Shiite imam, establishes a school of jurisprudence and supports the teaching of science.
ASIA & OCEANIA	**ca 750 In Japan** *shoen* (landed estates) become an important economic institution, as they offer a more manageable form of landholding. Public lands begin to revert to the shoen. **751 Tang Chinese** forces are defeated by a coalition of Arabs and Turks at the Talas River in present-day Kazakhstan and in the area of Turkestan. **755-763 An Lushan**, son of a Sogdian soldier and Turkic mother, leads a rebellion in Chang'an, modern-day Xi'an, in China and weakens the Tang dynasty.		**ca 730-846 During the Tang dynasty** the arts and literature flourish in unprecedented ways. Great poets such as Li Bai (701-762), Du Fu (712-770), and Bai Juyi (772-846) are especially celebrated. **ca 750 Pagodas** are introduced to Japan from China. **752 The statue of the Great Buddha** is erected at Nara, signaling Japan's prominence as a center of Buddhism in East Asia.

WHAT LIFE WAS LIKE

Maya Cenotes

The Maya of the Yucatán Peninsula believed that to receive the blessings of rain, they should propitiate Chac, the god who lived in the depths of sacred underground pools, called cenotes.

These freshwater pools were considered special gifts in an arid region and supplied water to the city-states. The cenotes were used for rites of passage and special ceremonies to benefit the gods. To propitiate the gods and ensure plentiful rain, priests and villagers dropped gifts of pottery—bowls, figurines, and incense holders—into the pools. Skeletal remains suggest possible human sacrifice, or they may indicate accidental drowning.

SCIENCE & TECHNOLOGY	PEOPLE & SOCIETY
	ca 750 An era ends for the Zapotecs of Oaxaca in Mexico. Beginning about 500 B.C.E., they developed a high culture and built important cities. A splendid ceremonial center at Monte Albán crowned a flattened mountaintop, complete with ball courts, patios, an observatory, palaces, and temple pyramids, similar to many ceremonial centers in Mesoamerica. They had their own form of picture writing and developed a numerical system and a calendar of 260 days. Mixtec incursions into the area may have been the cause of an abrupt and mysterious decline of Monte Albán.
ca 750 Handwritten herbals and medical books prescribe many treatments to get rid of lice and fleas, necessary advice because people rarely bathe.	**732 Charles Martel,** the mayor of the palace of the Frankish kingdom, achieves his renown for winning the Battle of Tours—also known as the Battle of Poitiers—in central France. This battle is memorialized as "the salvation of Europe from the Arab menace" by Christian historians, though Muslim historians see it as a minor skirmish. It marks the farthest Muslim advance into Europe and gives Charles's family great prestige. He reunifies the Franks and passes the kingdom on to his son, Pépin the Short.
ca 750 Ibrahim al-Fazari is the first Muslim to construct an astrolabe. **ca 760 Ya'qub ibn Tariq,** one of the great astronomers in Baghdad, brings Hindu mathematics to the court of al-Mansur.	**ca 750 African slave trade,** though in progress since antiquity, picks up momentum along with other trans-Saharan trade. Muslim merchants provide access for Indian, Persian, Southeast Asian, and Mediterranean customers. **ca 750 Ibn al-Muqaffa,** a Persian convert to Islam and secretary to early Abbasid rulers, translates much of Sassanian Persian literature into Arabic and writes advice for Muslim rulers.

An astrolabe

ARAB SEA TRADERS

By the middle of the eighth century, Arab seafarers had mastered the long ocean crossing from the Persian Gulf to the South China Sea. Equipped with compass and astrolabe, they could successfully calculate their route and navigate their sailing vessels across the open sea.

They traveled from ports of the Arabian Peninsula to Quilon in southern India; steered through the Strait of Malacca; called at Quang Ngai in Vietnam; and journeyed as far north as Canton, China. Muslim trading ships carried ivory, pearls, incense, and spices to China and returned with Chinese silk, paper, ink, tea, and porcelain.

The white porcelain from China, difficult to reproduce because the raw material—white kaolin clay—was not available elsewhere, led Arab potters to the invention of lusterware. This pottery was glazed with an opaque white slip and was decorated with designs of an iridescent metallic sheen, a process borrowed from the Islamic glass industry. This new technique traveled along the east coast of Africa and around the Mediterranean and was later adopted by Syria, Spain, and Italy, where it became known as majolica.

NIGHT THOUGHTS

Bright shines the moonlight at the foot of my bed,

Perhaps reflected from frost on the ground,

Lifting my head, I gaze at the bright moon,

Bowing my head, I think of my family home.

LI BAI

POLITICS & POWER	GEOGRAPHY & ENVIRONMENT	CULTURE & RELIGION

THE AMERICAS

763 Yax Pasah, the 16th Maya ruler of Copán in Honduras, assumes power.

776-795 Chaan Muan, Sky Screech-Owl, reigns over Bonampak in Mexico.

Mural at Bonampak depicting scenes of celebration, battle, and sacrifice

EUROPE

757-796 Offa, king of Mercia, rules parts of England, including Wessex, Sussex, Kent, and East Anglia.

768 Pépin's son Charlemagne ascends to the Frankish throne.

774 After conquering the Lombards in northern Italy, Charlemagne is also crowned king of the Lombards.

ca 760 Using irrigation techniques, which enriches the food supply, Muslims introduce cultivation of oranges, lemons, figs, dates, and eggplant in Spain.

786 Abd al-Rahman begins construction of the Great Mosque in Córdoba, Spain.

MIDDLE EAST & AFRICA

786 Harun al-Rashid of the Abbasids becomes caliph of the Muslim Empire in Baghdad, Iraq.

786 In Mecca, Arabia, an uprising by the Shiite results in the flight of many Shiites to the Maghreb (Libya), in North Africa.

762 Baghdad, Islam's new capital, is surrounded by a circular wall and becomes known as the Round City, the shape indicating a centralization of power.

ca 780 The Persian Sibawayh compiles the first grammar of written Arabic.

ca 790 Under Harun al-Rashid, Baghdad becomes a center of learning where Arab and Iranian cultures mingle to produce great philosophical, scientific, and literary works. During his rule the first two schools of Islamic law—the Hanafi and Maliki schools—are established.

ca 790 According to Yoruba mythology, the world was created at the sacred city of Ife in present-day Nigeria.

ASIA & OCEANIA

763 By the end of the An Lushan rebellion, the power of the Tang dynasty is weakened.

775 The Srivijaya kingdom extends its domain.

Borobudur Temple in Java

775 The Srivijaya kingdom encompasses Sumatra, Java, and the entire Malay Peninsula. A symbol of its importance is the Buddhist Borobudur Temple, built on Java, which requires two million feet of stone. It is decorated with 27,000 square feet of bas reliefs.

ca 780 Under the Fujiwara family, arts and culture flourish in Japan.

SCIENCE & TECHNOLOGY	PEOPLE & SOCIETY
	763-805 Yax Pasah, the last of the 16 rulers of Copán, builds onto the lavish temple compound and adds to the complex hieroglyphic chronicle. An altar at the site depicts a ceremony of animal sacrifice of 15 jaguars honoring his predecessors. In one image he receives a baton, referring to the transfer of power from the founder, K'inich Yak K'uk'Mo', who lived some 300 years earlier. Yax Pasah's own pyramid is the tallest one on the Acropolis.
784 King Offa has a dyke constructed running north-south, roughly along the border of England and Wales, between the Severn and Dee Rivers. It is the greatest building project of its kind in Europe and involves the deployment of thousands of laborers. A ditch on the Welsh side of the embankment serves both as a territorial boundary marker and a 70-mile-long defensive barrier.	**ca 780 Peasants in Europe** are generally free in early Germanic society. In the eighth century many begin surrendering their land and person to military leaders in return for protection. They become serfs, bound to the land and subject to the lord's control. By 800, about 60 percent of the peasants in western Europe are serfs.
762 Baghdad is beginning to rival Constantinople in size. By building dykes, canals, and reservoirs, the Abbasid administration is able to control the Tigris and Euphrates Rivers, resulting in surplus yields of grain for export.	**786 Caliph Harun al-Rashid,** who goes out at night in disguise to ensure that his people feel justly treated, figures in many tales of the *Arabian Nights*. He appoints able administrators to keep his vast empire at peace and collects tribute from vassal states. A poet himself, he invests much to further the arts while his wife, Zubeidah, is remembered for funding the construction of mosques, roads, and the drilling of wells. Still, toward the end of al-Rashid's reign, the empire stitched together of many factions begins to fray. Trouble in Syria makes him move his court to al-Ragga in the north of Syria, but revolts in other parts keep cropping up. He dies in 809.
	763 As the Tang dynasty begins to lose control, conflicts arise from across the borders. The Tibetans seize the Tarim Basin in 763 and even briefly conquer the capital of Chang'an, modern-day Xi'an. Although they are beaten back, the Tibetans conquer the province of Gansu in 791, establishing the kingdom of Xixia. Even so, the Tang dynasty continues on until 907, but the population begins to shift from the north to the more fertile south, where surplus crops of rice ensure a more comfortable existence.

MONASTIC LIFE IN EUROPE

By the end of the fifth century, raiding and conquering Germanic tribes had extinguished much of Roman civilization in Europe—a period often referred to as the Dark Ages.

After the founding of Monte Cassino Abbey by St. Benedict in Italy in 529, other monasteries developed elsewhere in Europe and began to fill a void. They took up the spread of Christianity and provided isolated centers of calm and learning that preserved Rome's legacy in books. Monks translated and illustrated the Bible (see below), as well as other ancient texts, and upheld moral values. St. Benedict established the Benedictine Rule, which required prayer and work, the two principles of monastic

A page from the Book of Kells

life. His twin sister Scholastica adapted the rule for nuns.

This rule was carried to England by St. Augustine and his fellow monks, and to the monasteries of the Franks and Lombards. In England, the Benedictine Rule was considered the only true type, whereas in Ireland the earlier Celtic monasticism was firmly established.

In the eighth century St. Boniface converted the pagan tribes in Germany and established the monastery at Fulda, which became the model of all future German monasteries.

POLITICS & POWER	GEOGRAPHY & ENVIRONMENT	CULTURE & RELIGION
THE AMERICAS		
ca 800 The Toltec begin to migrate into northern and central Mexico. **ca 800 Mixtec royal families** begin to intermarry with the old Zapotec elite, establishing the foundations for Mixtec rule. **805 The last record** of the Maya rulers of Copán in Honduras appears on July 25. After Yax Pasah's death, the city is abandoned.	**ca 800 Earth-lodge villagers** in the plains of North America cultivate maize, beans, and squash to supplement hunting. **ca 800 The increasingly warmer weather** and greater rainfall enable the Caddo people of Texas to develop a rich agriculture that incorporates corn, beans, squash, and pumpkin.	**ca 800 A rural hierarchy** led by chief-priests and ceremonial mounds distinguish Caddo communities.

POLITICS & POWER	GEOGRAPHY & ENVIRONMENT	CULTURE & RELIGION
EUROPE		
797-802 Irene, widow of Byzantine emperor Leo IV and mother of Constantine VI, has her son blinded and assumes the throne. When Harun al-Rashid's armies threaten Constantinople, she agrees to pay an annual tribute in gold to save the city. **800 Pope Leo III** crowns Charlemagne Emperor of Rome. **802-811 Nicephorus I** becomes Byzantine emperor. He refuses to pay tribute to the Abbasids and loses territory, but keeps the city of Constantinople safe. **814 Charlemagne** dies. His son, Louis the Pious, becomes emperor.	**ca 800-1000 The population of Europe** recovers from the plague and reaches 36 million. **ca 790-880 Raiding Vikings** attack Ireland, Scotland, and England, controlling most of the British Isles. **803-810 In a treaty** between Charlemagne and Nicephorus I, the borders of the Western and Eastern Roman empires are settled: Venice, Istria, the Dalmatian coast, and southern Italy are assigned to the East; Rome and Ravenna remain in the West.	**781 Alcuin of York** accepts an invitation from Charlemagne to head up a school. He develops a written Latin script that is later adapted to be used in the first printing press. **ca 800 The first castles** are built in western Europe.

POLITICS & POWER	GEOGRAPHY & ENVIRONMENT	CULTURE & RELIGION
MIDDLE EAST & AFRICA		
ca 800 A city takes shape in the inland Niger Delta at Jenne-Jeno at the junction of two distinct environmental zones—floodplain and hinterland. The mud-walled city represents a hub of crafts, fishing, farming, and commerce with an estimated population of 10,000. **801 Berber Kharijites** set up an independent Muslim state in North Africa. **809 Caliph Harun al-Rashid** dies. **813-823 After a battle** with his brother, which brings on a civil war, al-Ma'mun reigns in Baghdad, enlarging the Muslim Empire with Afghanistan and Turkmenistan.	**ca 800 An earthquake** in Egypt destroys the Nile port cities of Herakleion, Canopus, and Menouthis. **ca 800 Jewish immigrants** settle in North Africa and shift from farming to trade. Known as Rhadanites (multilingual Jewish traders), many settle in Timbuktu and ride with caravans, linking North Africa with Mesopotamia, the Caspian Sea region, and India.	**ca 800 The Judeo-Arabic** literary language emerges. **ca 800 The third school of Islamic law,** the Shafi'i school, is established. **802 Caliph Harun al-Rashid** sends an elephant, silks, perfume, and other luxuries to Charlemagne as a gift. **813-833 Caliph al-Ma'mun** founds a school in Baghdad where scholars translate Greek classics into Arabic. **815 Abu Nuwas,** Arab poet, dies. One of his verses extols liquor as "hot between the ribs as a firebrand."

POLITICS & POWER	GEOGRAPHY & ENVIRONMENT	CULTURE & RELIGION
ASIA & OCEANIA		
794 The Japanese capital is moved from Nara to Heian (Kyoto). **ca 800 Jayavarman II** consolidates small Khmer states into one kingdom in present-day Cambodia.		**ca 800 Kimonos** become fashionable in Japan. **ca 800 Shankara,** Indian Hindu philosopher, helps revive Hinduism with his writings on the study of the Vedas and combines the many strands into a consistent system of thought.

CONNECTIONS

South Asian Hub

India and the Srivijaya kingdom played a major role in keeping trade throughout the Indian Ocean supplied with exotic goods. One Greek sailor from Alexandria, Egypt, Cosmas Indicopleustes—his name means traveler to India—explored and later described the world as he saw it when he retired to the monastery of Raithu on the Sinai Peninsula as a Christian monk. In his book *Christian Topography* he writes of the ships that land in Ceylon, one of Srivijaya's islands. They come from Ethiopia, Persia, India, and China carrying silk, aloe, pepper, cloves, sandalwood, copper, musk, castor, and sesame logs and trade for emeralds, elephants, and horses. From Ceylon many of these goods are shipped to more remote ports in the Pacific.

SCIENCE & TECHNOLOGY	PEOPLE & SOCIETY
	ca 800 East of the Mississippi, the Woodlands people spread from north to south and begin to engage in large-scale agriculture. They live in settled communities, fenced in by wooden palisades. Men are in charge of hunting, fishing, and defense. Women take care of the fields.
ca 800 The technology for smelting iron improves and the Carolingian Empire begins to produce iron tools for agriculture, horseshoes, nails, and weapons.	**813 The hermit Pelayo** believes he has found the tomb of St. James in the region called Finistere—the end of the earth—in Spain. This discovery results in the annual pilgrimage to Santiago (St. James) de Compostela (field of stars) by thousands who come to worship at this place of sacred relics.
792 The first papermaking factory in the Muslim Empire is built in Baghdad. **ca 800 Arab mathematician and astronomer** Muhammad ibn Musa al-Khwarizmi furthers works on algebra. **815 Jabir bin Hunayn (Geber),** the first Arab alchemist, dies. **ca 820 Al-Ma'mun** builds observatories in Baghdad, Iraq, and Palmyra, Syria.	**800 Rabi'a the Mystic** dies. She is the first woman mystic, famous for writing: Oh God, if I worship you in fear of hell, burn me in hell; And if I worship you in hope of paradise, exclude me from paradise. But if I worship you for your own being, do not withhold from me your everlasting beauty.
ca 800 Refined rice paper is made in Japan.	

EMPEROR CHARLEMAGNE

On the death of Pépin the Short in 768, the Frankish kingdom was divided between Charlemagne and his brother Carloman. Carloman died three years later, leaving the kingdom to Charlemagne, whose rule would lay the groundwork for the Holy Roman Empire.

Charlemagne enlarged his holdings by beating back numerous Saxon raids from the east. When the Lombards began to invade Italy and threatened to assault Rome, Pope Hadrian II summoned Charlemagne for help. Charlemagne successfully restored the pope's control, and in 773 he claimed kingship over the Lombards.

In the year 800, at Mass on Christmas Day in Rome, Pope Leo III crowned Charlemagne Imperator Romanorum (Emperor of Rome). This title was intended to help make western Europe independent of Constantinople and to fix the Catholic Church's role in the secular affairs of Europe's monarchies. Charlemagne, however, did not use the title; he understood the ploy and feared it would create dependence on the pope. Instead he called himself Emperor ruling the Roman Empire.

Although Charlemagne was illiterate himself, he ardently supported scholarship, literature, the arts, and architecture. In fostering a renewal of learning, he called Alcuin of York to the court to establish a school that became the heart of the Carolingian Renaissance.

Most of the surviving works of classical Latin were copied and preserved by Carolingian scholars who came from all over Europe. This veritable united nations included Theodulf, a Visigoth; Paul the Deacon, a Lombard; and Angilbert and Einhard, both Franks. Alcuin also developed the written Latin script, which is known as the Carolingian minuscule script. The rounded letters were adapted for use in the first printing press and would later become the basis of our modern script.

	POLITICS & POWER	GEOGRAPHY & ENVIRONMENT	CULTURE & RELIGION
THE AMERICAS	**ca 820 The Maya** move about their land, abandon cities and reoccupy them, depending on the predominant military forces of the time.		
EUROPE	**814-840 Louis the Pious** inherits Charlemagne's empire, including the realm of the Franks, Saxons, and Lombards. **840-843 After Louis's death,** his three surviving sons fight for the throne of the Frankish kingdom. In 843 they agree to a partition in the Treaty of Verdun. **846 Muslim armies** sack Rome.	**843 With the Treaty of Verdun,** the Carolingian Empire is divided among the three sons of Louis: Charles the Bald inherits France; Louis the German inherits the East Frankish Empire, or Germany; and Lothair receives the Low Countries, Lorraine, Alsace, Burgundy, Provence, and most of Italy. This division, without regard to tribal or linguistic adherence, brings about a final separation between France and Germany.	**ca 825-827 Cyril and Methodius** are born in Thessaloniki, Greece. Working as missionaries, the brothers convert the Slavs to Christianity in 863. **842 Iconoclasm ends;** images of saints are permitted again in all Christian churches.
MIDDLE EAST & AFRICA	**833-849 Caliph al-Mutasim** reigns in Baghdad. He grants some independence to Tahir bin Hussain, the governor of Samarkand, Ferghana, and Herat, which eventually creates a rift in the empire. Other provinces vie for independence as well. **837 Al-Mutasim** conquers Byzantine Amorium in Anatolia, despite the ill omen of Halley's comet.		**833 Al-Mutasim** employs Turkish slaves as body guards. He encourages production from all parts of the empire: luscious brocade, damask, and satin fabrics, woven carpets, and perfumes. **ca 840 The fourth school of Islamic law,** the Hanbali school, is established.
ASIA & OCEANIA	**838 The last of the great Japanese missions** leaves for China's Tang court.	**ca 840 Whereas Asian trade routes** and networks connect the Philippines, Indonesia, and New Guinea and perhaps northern Australia, the people of the distant Pacific Islands build agricultural societies of their own and maintain trade networks that link many groups of islands.	**845 The Tang government** carries out a great proscription against Buddhism.

CONNECTIONS

Africa and China

A vibrant maritime trade connected the Afro-Asian worlds from about the year 800 on. Sailing vessels called dhows from the East African coast traveled across the Indian Ocean to China, carrying gold, ivory, iron, and exotic animals.

Chinese seafarers described Boboli, probably a town on the coast of Somalia or northern Kenya, where the inhabitants "stick a needle into the veins of cattle and drain blood, which they drink raw mixed with milk"—an accurate account of Masai practices to this day. African traders bartered mainly for cotton, silk, and porcelain objects from the Far East.

SCIENCE & TECHNOLOGY	PEOPLE & SOCIETY
	ca 800 **A division of labor** based on sex typifies Caddo society. Men assume the physically demanding tasks of turning the soil, while women handle planting and managing the crops. Women also assume control of the lodges that accommodate a number of families related by blood or marriage.
834 **The Utrecht (Holland) Psalter** mentions the use of the rotary grindstone to sharpen iron for the first time. Similar grindstones existed earlier in China. The European tool may be a copy or an independent invention.	**804-876** **Louis the German** rises from ruler of Bavaria, a southern state in Germany, to king of Germany, a country not fully unified and besieged on all sides by invaders. From the north the Danes press in, from the east the Wends and the Sorbs, and from the southeast the Bohemians, Moravians, and Magyars (Hungarians). Louis can barely keep them at bay nor contain grievances against his brothers.
ca 830 **Mathematican and astronomer al-Hajjaj ibn-Yusuf** translates Euclid's *Elements* into Arabic. **ca 830** **Philosopher al-Kindi** writes his work on science and philosophy *De aspectibus* and *De medicinarum,* which greatly influence the West. **ca 840** **Caliph al-Mutasim** encourages the building of factories in Baghdad and Basra for the manufacture of soap and glass.	**ca 840** **The wealth of the Muslim Empire** fuels urbanization and cultural development throughout the realm.
ca 850 **Chinese alchemists** discover that a mixture of sulfur and saltpeter, when combined with charcoal, creates an explosive product. Employed at first only for fireworks, the invention rapidly finds other uses, especially as gunpowder and eventually in bombs.	

Sts. Cyril and Methodius

THE CYRILLIC ALPHABET

The brothers Cyril and Methodius were born in Thessaloniki, Greece, and later served as priests in a monastery along the Bosporus. In 863, having worked as missionaries among the Khazars between the Black Sea and the Caspian Sea, the brothers were called by the patriarch in Constantinople to go to Moravia, beyond the Balkans, where they left a legacy in language.

Moravian Prince Rotislav sought missionaries to teach in the Slavonic, or Slavic, vernacular to forestall further German encroachment in his region. Cyril and Methodius achieved success but aroused hostilities among resentful visiting clergy. The brothers were recalled to Rome and questioned about their methods, but the pope could find no fault with them.

Cyril died in Rome, but Methodius was sent back as archbishop of Sirmium. He spent his remaining years translating the Bible and other important books into Slavonic, using a special alphabet which came to be known as Cyrillic, after Cyril. It was a version of Greek and Glagolitic, an ancient form of writing that could express Slavonic sounds. The brothers' influence reached into Bulgaria, Serbia, and Ukraine, where Slavonic is still the liturgical language.

	POLITICS & POWER	GEOGRAPHY & ENVIRONMENT	CULTURE & RELIGION
THE AMERICAS	**ca 850 Maya society** is in full decline as people abandon the cities of the Yucatán Peninsula. The cities revert to jungle and the people disperse into the countryside, though their descendants continue to live in the region to this day.	**ca 850 Living at the intersection of two ecologies**—the woodlands of the Southeast and the plains of the West—Caddo society develops thriving trading networks. They move farming products to the West in exchange for meat and hides from the buffalo. Caddo communities gather goods from areas as distant as the Florida Gulf region and the Great Lakes in the north.	
EUROPE	**860 Vikings** attack Constantinople. **862 The Viking Rus tribe**, led by Rurik, seizes control of northern Russia and establishes a capital at Novgorod. **870 Upon King Lothair's death,** his possessions of the Low Countries, Belgium, and Lorraine revert to France; Alsace goes to Germany. **871 Alfred the Great** becomes the first king of England. He defeats Viking invaders in 878 and pushes them to an area to the north and east called the Danelaw.	**850-950 Viking raids** stimulate agricultural production and horse breeding in France. **874 Vikings** settle Iceland.	**ca 850 Groups of Jews** settle in Germany and develop a new language—Yiddish. **863 The Cyrillic alphabet** is adopted in Eastern Europe. **865 Bulgaria accepts Christianity** and follows the Byzantine rites.
MIDDLE EAST & AFRICA	**847-861 Al-Mutawakkil,** the last great Abbasid caliph, relies on Turkish soldiers for control and is eventually murdered by one. **870 After al-Mutawakkil's assassination,** the Turkish army plays a heavy hand in choosing the next caliph, throwing the government into chaos. But with al Mu'tamid's ascension a period of calm is restored. **ca 870 Tegdaoust** in Mauritania begins to flourish as the ancient city of Aoudaghost. **874 Sassanids** in eastern Iran demonstrate new autonomy and reintroduce literature to Persia, but with Arabic script and vocabulary.	**856 An earthquake** devastates Damghan, Persia, killing more than 200,000. **872 Ibn Wahab,** a merchant-traveler of Basra, Iraq, describes a sea voyage to China's capital Chang'an. It takes him one year to cross the seas and another two months of travel overland from Canton to reach Chang'an. He describes Chang'an as "being divided in two by a wide road. East of the road were the palace of the emperor and residences of officers of government. The west side held the shops, other places of business, and the general population. The streets were traversed with channels of running water and bordered with trees."	**ca 850 The Egyptian Dhul-Nul** founds Sufism—Muslim mysticism. **850 A building boom** begins in Samarra, Iraq, the new capital of the Abbasids. With some 20 palaces and a huge mosque, it becomes one of the largest cities in the world. **850-880 Igbo Ukwu** in southeastern Nigeria produces intricately cast bronze objects. **865-870 Six canonical books of hadith**—sayings of the Prophet—are published in the Muslim Empire.
ASIA & OCEANIA	**ca 850 The Maori sailors**—probably hailing from Hawaii or Savaii, Samoa—discover New Zealand and establish a flourishing civilization. They drive the original inhabitants, the Moriori, to the South Island and Chatham Island. **850 The Chola kingdom** of southern India keeps to its Hindu roots, beginning a rule of the Coromandel coast that will continue for four centuries. **877-889 Indravarman I** of the Khmer in Cambodia unites his kingdom and builds a temple-mountain (Bakong), a forerunner to Angkor Wat architecture.	*O rain clouds* *seeming like dark clay outside* *liquid wax within* *rain down upon Venkatam* *where the handsome* *lord dwells.* NINTH-CENTURY POEM BY ANDAL, A FEMALE SAINT OF SOUTHERN INDIA	**868 The *Diamond Sutra*,** the earliest known complete woodblock-printed book with illustrations, is produced in China.

ca 850 The Caddo use osage orange wood, abundant in their homeland, to manufacture quality bows, which are in great demand by warrior societies and hunter communities.

King Alfred, the first king of England

ca 850 A medical school founded in Salerno, Italy, attracts Greek, Jewish, Italian, and Arabic teachers and students.

861 The Great Nilometer is built in Cairo by order of Caliph al-Mutawakkil to measure the annual flooding of the Nile.

VIKING RAIDERS

For three centuries, from about 800, Vikings––or Norsemen from Denmark, Norway, and Sweden— conducted lightening quick strikes on the coasts and rivers of Europe. These former traders found raiding more profitable thanks to formidable sailing vessels whose shallow draft allowed Vikings to beach easily and pillage surprised towns and villages in England, Scotland, Ireland, France, and Germany. They rounded Spain into the Mediterranean, followed the Russian Rivers into the Black Sea, and also ventured to new lands to the north and west, settling Shetland, the Faroe Islands, Iceland, and Greenland. They even made a short expedition to Newfoundland.

Eventually the Vikings settled much of the British Isles, clashing with the earlier Anglo-Saxons, and populated the coast of Normandy in France and the northern shores of Russia.

Like men
they traveled far for gold.

INSCRIPTION HONORING FALLEN VIKINGS

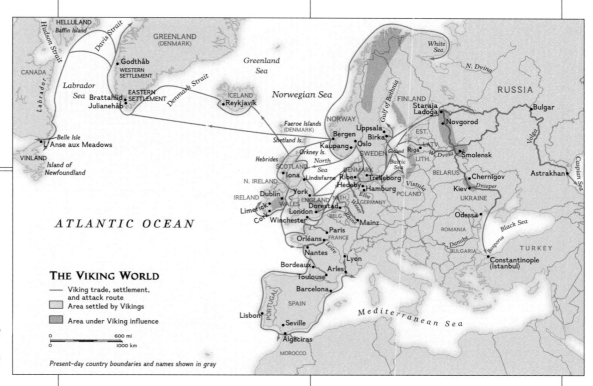

THE VIKING WORLD

— Viking trade, settlement, and attack route
☐ Area settled by Vikings
☐ Area under Viking influence

0 — 600 mi
0 — 1000 km

Present-day country boundaries and names shown in gray

Superb seamen, the Vikings used ocean and river routes to trade, raid, and colonize from the Caspian Sea to Newfoundland.

	POLITICS & POWER	GEOGRAPHY & ENVIRONMENT	CULTURE & RELIGION
THE AMERICAS	**ca 900 Toltec** from the north conquer the central valley in Mexico under Chichimeca leader Mixcoatl and provide a unified rule. **ca 900 The Anasazi** in the Chaco Canyon of present-day New Mexico begin building a series of urban communities, sustained by corn agriculture. They construct a sophisticated hydraulic system of dams, ditches, and canals to manage their water supply.	**ca 900 The Toltec** come from the arid land of northwestern Mexico and settle at Tula, near present-day Mexico City. They make the thin, dry soil productive by irrigating their crops of maize, beans, peppers, tomatoes, chilies, and cotton. **ca 900 Persistent rains** enable early Chaco society to thrive.	
EUROPE	**882 Oleg of Russia** seizes control of Slavic communities and founds Kiev. **885-887 Charles III,** son of Louis the German, briefly unites the West Frankish (France) and East Frankish (Germany) kingdoms. **887 Arnulf deposes Charles III** and is crowned emperor in 896. At his death in 899 the Carolingian Empire falls apart. **899 King Alfred** of England dies. His son Edward the Elder takes the throne and continues to battle invaders. **907 Oleg of Russia** sails to Constantinople to arrange a treaty on trade with Byzantium.	**889 Magyars** (Hungarians) invade Germany. **896 Seven Magyar tribes** and three Khazar tribes settle the Carpathian basin and form the kingdom of Hungary.	**906 Greek literature** is translated into Slavonic, or Slavic, in Bulgaria. **909 The Cluny monastery** in Burgundy is founded.
MIDDLE EAST & AFRICA	**901 Muslims** conquer Sicily. **909 Fatimids**—descendants of Muhammad's daughter Fatima and Ali, and thus Shiite—break away from the Sunni Abbasids and migrate to North Africa.	**883 The Zanj revolt of African slaves** who work on sugar plantations in Iraq is suppressed. In the process, dams are broken and marshlands of southern Iraq are flooded. **893 An earthquake** in Ardabil, Persia, causes 150,000 deaths. **ca 900 Africa's east coast** sees an influx of Arab, Persian, and Indian traders who mix with the native Bantu population. Locally, they describe themselves as Swahili, the Arab word for "people of the shore."	**881 Caliph al-Mutadim** moves the capital from Samarra back to Baghdad in Iraq. **882-942 Saadiah ben Joseph,** Jewish head of the Babylonian academy, institutes a calendar reform to decide the date of Passover and other holy days, and writes a treatise in Arabic on rational proof for the dogmas of the Torah.
ASIA & OCEANIA	**889 The Khmer** build a capital city at Angkor, Cambodia. **ca 900 The Chola kingdom** in South India expands in prosperity, building temples with massive, sculptural towers. **907 The Tang dynasty** in China disintegrates, and the era of Five Dynasties begins.	**ca 880 Nepal gains independence** from Tibet. Bhaktapur is founded under the Malla dynasty.	**ca 900 The Chola dynasty** produces some of the most spectacular bronze works of Indian sculptural art to be used in temple processions. As is characteristic of Indian art, the sculptures combine aspects of the sensuous with notions of the sacred. **ca 900 A phonetic syllabary** is developed to transcribe the Japanese language, allowing for the expression of native culture in contrast to that of imported Chinese literary forms.

SCIENCE & TECHNOLOGY	PEOPLE & SOCIETY

Anasazi bowl

ca 900 The Anasazi build a dense and sophisticated road system to integrate all towns in the Chaco Canyon region. They are noted for their pueblo-style homes.

ca 900 Indigenous people in the northeastern and Great Lakes region of North America are growing a variant corn, able to withstand the lower temperatures of this region and the lighter rainfall. This corn adapts to the limited growing season of a colder climate than that found farther south. Labeled "northern flint corn," it accelerates the spread of agriculture, which fuels centuries of rich agricultural growth.

ca 880 Stirrups come into use in France and elsewhere in Europe, an invention from China that took centuries to reach Europe. Stirrups provide an easy way to mount a horse and stay in the saddle, which is especially important to mounted cavalry.

882-911 Russia is united by Oleg, ruler of Novgorod. For centuries nomadic horsemen—Cimmerians, Scythians, Sarmatians, Huns, Avars, and Khazars—have ridden out of the steppes, often dominating the Slavs, a group of farmers and fur traders living in the forested areas around present-day Kiev, Novgorod, and Moscow. Using the inland waterways of the Volkhov and Dnieper Rivers, Oleg seizes Kiev in 882 and unites several Slavic tribes by delivering them from the Khazars. As leader of the Rus—a Slavic word for "red," for the red-haired Vikings—Oleg in 911 establishes lucrative trade agreements with the Byzantine Empire.

905 Persian astronomer al-Sufi describes the Andromeda galaxy as "little cloud."

ca 900-1200 A period called the golden age of North African science ensues, with scientists such as Tunisian Isaac ben Solomon writing treatises on medicine and philosophy and mathematician Dunash ibn Tamim. Hebrew philology is born in Fez, Morocco.

ca 900 Persian geographer Ibn Rustah sets out to describe the world, beginning with his native Isfahan. He travels with the Rus to Novgorod, observes the Slavs in the Balkans, and describes the British Isles. About Novgorod, he says: "As for the Rus, they live on an island . . . that takes three days to walk round and is covered with thick undergrowth and forests . . . They harry the Slavs, using ships to reach them; they carry them off as slaves and . . . sell them. They have no fields but simply live on what they get from the Slav's lands."

TREASURES OF THE DESERT

Since earliest times the people of America's Southwest have excelled in their arts and crafts. Paintings on rock walls, baskets woven with geometric designs, jewelry of turquoise, shell and jet beads, and blankets and shawls woven on belt looms attest to their skill.

The first potters learned to roll coils of clay into basketlike shapes and fire them to form crude vessels. By the tenth century these potters achieved a high level of artistry, moving from simple unadorned jugs to sophisticated polychrome designs and decorations. Each group of people developed its own distinctive shapes.

The Hohokam created pottery with broad-line designs. The Anasazi produced red clay vessels with multicolored geometric designs, embodying mythical concepts sacred to them. The Mimbre people, descendants of the Mogollon, covered their pottery with a white kaolin slip and painted the creatures of their Arizona environment—lizards, turtles, birds, and fish—in black outlines. They attached a particular burial rite to their pottery, ritually piercing bowls and placing them hatlike on the head of deceased family members in their burial pose.

POLITICS & POWER	GEOGRAPHY & ENVIRONMENT	CULTURE & RELIGION
THE AMERICAS		
ca 900 Hohokam culture flourishes in Arizona and New Mexico. **ca 900 Cahokia society** reaches its high point, building impressively high ceremonial mounds east of modern-day St. Louis. **ca 900 The Maya** abandon settlements in the lowlands. **918 Mixcoatl's son Topiltzin** of the Toltec nation founds the city of Tula and controls most of Mexico. By repeatedly invading neighboring lands, Toltec increase their holdings.	*Hohokam petroglyph at Saguaro National Park*	**ca 900 A militaristic tone** pervades Toltec cities; sculpted, massive stone warriors—complete with armor and feathered headdress—line temples and plazas.
EUROPE		
913 Simeon of Bulgaria lays siege to Constantinople and is given the title of emperor of Bulgaria. **924 Aethelstan** begins his rule of England and adds Wales and Cornwall to his kingdom. **925 Croatia** establishes its own kingdom. **929 Abd al-Rahman III** is caliph in Spain. **930 Iceland** forms Europe's first parliament. **936 Otto I of Saxony** becomes German king. **939-946 Edmund I** succeeds as English king and establishes friendly relations with Scotland and Ireland.	**ca 910 Transhumant grazing**—sheep grazing over long distances between summer and winter grazing grounds—expands in Spain with long-term ill effects on the environment. **930 Nomadic Lapps** begin to enter Norway above the Arctic Circle.	**930 Córdoba in Spain** is the largest city in western Europe with a population of 200,000. It is the seat of Arab learning and culture. **ca 930 Henry I of Bavaria,** Franconia, and Saxony—father of Otto I—is building fortified castles in Germany to guard against marauding Hungarians. These fortifications later become the cities of Goslar, Quedlinburg, Merseburg, and Nordhausen.
MIDDLE EAST & AFRICA		
939 Sayf al-Dawlah, a former commander of Hamdanid forces in Iraq, seizes Aleppo and most of Syria for himself and becomes emir of Aleppo. He conducts raids into Armenia, the region near Melitene, and Cappadocia, burning villages and the surrounding countryside and enslaving many prisoners.	**935 Algiers in North Africa** is founded by Arabs.	**917 A Byzantine embassy** sent by emperor Constantine VII to the court of Caliph al-Muqtadir in Baghdad reports on the splendors of 23 palaces there. They describe rooms decorated with rugs and precious armor, a silver tree with moving branches and gold and silver birds, royal stables, zoological gardens, orchards and gardens of palm trees with an artificial pond.
ASIA & OCEANIA		
ca 900 The Khmer rule an empire based in Cambodia that extends over much of present-day Thailand and Laos. **935 In southern Korea,** the last Silla king surrenders to form the state of Korea.		**ca 900 Korea's culture** begins an era of high artistic development.

SCIENCE & TECHNOLOGY	PEOPLE & SOCIETY
	ca 900 The Hohokam Indians, masters of irrigation, live in the Sonora Desert of Arizona in villages. The major settlement, Snaketown, centers on a large ball court for rituals. The ball court seems to indicate Mesoamerican contacts through trade or migration. The Hohokam are probably the ancestors of the modern Pima and Papago tribes.
ca 900 Hops are added to beer, giving it a slightly bitter taste. But the more important reason for this invention is that is stabilizes and preserves beer, allowing it to be kept longer and to travel.	**929 Wenceslas,** a Christian duke of Bohemia, is murdered by his pagan brother on his way to mass at the door of the church. Shortly thereafter miracles begin to occur at his grave, and he is ultimately canonized as the patron saint of Bohemia. The Christmas carol "Good King Wenceslas," based on the historic duke, is written much later, in 1849, by John Neale.
910 Arab physician al-Razi writes the first account of smallpox and theory of immunity, authoring more than 200 books on medical history.	

CAHOKIA MOUND BUILDERS

The Mississippian mound builders of North America traded along the waterways of the Mississippi and its tributaries, eventually reaching southeast to Georgia and Florida, north to Wisconsin, and west into Arkansas. They settled in thatch-roofed dwellings, developed a mixed farming and foraging lifestyle, and built earthen mounds for burial and worship.

By the tenth century hundreds of small towns dotted the river valleys, the largest among them Cahokia, near modern-day St. Louis. This early metropolis, surrounded by a stockade and watchtowers, held at least 100 mounds and supported a population of up to 15,000. Several earthen mounds were arranged around a central plaza, rising in steps to four broad terraces topped by ceremonial shrines or houses for chieftains. The largest structure, a pyramid of about 100 feet, covered an area of 23 acres.

At the death of a chieftain, the body, dressed in full regalia, would be carried up to a funerary temple, followed by family and attendants. The chieftain would be interred in the mound, at times accompanied by his attendants.

Cahokia bottle, modeled as a mother and child, left, and below, a reconstruction of Cahokia, which was the largest Mississippian town

	POLITICS & POWER	GEOGRAPHY & ENVIRONMENT	CULTURE & RELIGION
THE AMERICAS	**950 Toltec culture** is at its zenith. Its capital city, Tula, in the central valley of Mexico, supports a population of up to 60,000, with another 60,000 living nearby.		
EUROPE	**954 Erik Bloodaxe,** last Viking ruler of York, dies. **958 King Harold of Denmark**—also in control of Norway and Sweden—becomes a Christian. **959-975 Edgar the Peaceful** consolidates the English kingdom. **962 Otto I of Germany** establishes the Holy Roman Empire. **960 Mieczyslaw I,** first ruler of Poland, is baptized in 966.		**ca 950 Menahem ben Saruq** of Tortosa, Spain, composes the first Hebrew dictionary. **962 The Great Lavra Monastery** is founded on the Greek peninsula of Mount Athos.
MIDDLE EAST & AFRICA	**945 Abbasid power** declines in Baghdad. **962 Alptigin,** a Turkish slave, marches an army on Ghazna, Afghanistan, and sets up an Islamic state. He establishes the Ghaznavid dynasty that is to become the center of Islamic power. **969 The Fatimids** conquer Egypt and the coast of Syria and make Cairo their seat of government.	**ca 950 The Abbasid caliphs** are mere figureheads at this time, as provincial governors act independently. Persians take control of Baghdad, then Turks from Central Asia invade and convert to Islam. By absorbing many different races, the Muslim Empire is fundamentally changed.	**ca 940 Shanga residents** on the north Kenya coast build magnificent homes of coral and mud, on a site where a small mosque will be constructed later. **953 Buzurg ibn Shahriyar** writes the *Book of Wonders of India,* a collection of stories about travel and adventure. **953 The al-Azhar University** is founded in Cairo, becoming the premier Muslim university.
ASIA & OCEANIA	**950 King Gandaradiya** rules the Chola kingdom of India. **960 The Song dynasty** reunifies China and ushers in an era of intensive economic, social, political, and cultural change.		**ca 950 Sembiyan Madhavi,** wife of Chola king Gandaradiya, dedicates her life to building Hindu temples and monasteries. **ca 960 Landscape painting** begins to flourish during the Song dynasty in China.

CONNECTIONS

Salerno Medical School

The medical school in Salerno, Italy, was the first medical school of the Middle Ages and Europe's first university. Constantine the African, a monk and scholar from Tunisia, translated Arabic medical texts there into Latin, which profoundly influenced Western thought. Previously Greek, Salerno was under Norman rule at this time, and Constantine's excellent knowledge of Greek, Latin, Arabic, and several Oriental languages all came in good use in this southern location. The medical school became known for its physicians, who profited from a confluence of Arab, Greek, and Jewish medical thought from around the Mediterranean basin. It was a tolerant and progressive institution, teaching anatomy, dissections of the human body (previously prohibited by the Church), and admitting women as physicians.

SCIENCE & TECHNOLOGY	PEOPLE & SOCIETY
ca 950 The Toltec become skilled in irrigation, tapping the waters of the Tula River and raising crops of maize, beans, peppers, tomatoes, chilies, and cotton.	**ca 950 The Toltec** protect their empire from invading nomads with a large army and exact tribute from adjoining provinces. They maintain contact with the remaining Maya and the people of the Gulf Coast and import luxuries, such as jade, turquoise, and exotic bird feathers, from other parts of Mesoamerica. Their artisans excel in weaving, pottery making, and obsidian work.
ca 950 The horse collar comes in use, allowing horses and oxen to be harnessed for plowing. The collar probably originated in Bactria, where similar collars had been in use for camels since the sixth century.	**ca 950 As iron smelting** becomes more widespread in Europe, enabling better toolmaking and thus higher agricultural production, village life improves. Every village has a smithy and other workshops. The innovations soon give rise to cities, where craftsmanship develops further. **ca 950 Dublin develops** as an ironmaking center, linked to the rest of northern Europe by Viking traders.
ca 950 All new scientific discoveries are published in Arabic, making the language the international vehicle of scientific progress.	**915-965 Al-Mutanabbi,** regarded by many as the greatest Arab poet, is called the "wandering poet." Born in Iraq, he lives with the Bedouin for a time and later becomes part of the brilliant court of the Hamdanid ruler Sayf al-Dawlah in Aleppo, Syria, where he writes many of his elaborate orations.

THE HOLY ROMAN EMPIRE

With the partition of Charlemagne's empire among his grandsons, Germany developed into many small estates ruled by dukes and princes. These estates and their nobles were often in conflict with one another and with the pope in power struggles between church and state.

In 936 Otto of Saxony unified some of the northern regions and was pronounced king of Germany. He was victorious in many military campaigns against the Slavs and Magyars in the areas of present-day Poland, the Czech Republic, and Hungary, and expanded the boundaries of his realm farther to the east. Forays into Italy to keep encroaching tribes away made him the protector of the church.

To show his gratitude, Pope John XII crowned Otto Holy Roman Emperor in 962. The title included rule over the German principalities as well as Lorraine, northern Italy, and Burgundy, and the empire was meant as a Christian revival of the earlier mighty Roman Empire.

This was not to be. The French kings thwarted Otto's efforts to annex any part of France. Germany itself never achieved the political unity that France enjoyed and could not dominate Europe. Relations with the pope proved precarious as well. The pope's authority covered Italy and the church, and he tried to keep the emperor from enlarging his empire.

With mounting disagreements, Otto convoked a synod in Saint Peter's and had Pope John XII deposed and Leo VIII elected. Leo then confirmed Otto's right to a veto in papal elections, which the citizens of Rome had bestowed on him.

Upon Otto's death in 973, his title was transferred to his son Otto II, followed by his grandson. This largely German Empire endured for nearly a thousand years, until 1806, waxing and waning at times and ruled by both elected and hereditary emperors.

*I split through his shielding armor
with my solid lance . . .
and left him carrion
for the wild beasts to pounce on.*

ANONYMOUS

ISLAMIC ARTS AND SCIENCES

STRETCHING FROM SPAIN TO INDIA, THE MUSLIM EMPIRE WAS A RICH AMALGAM of cultures, held together by its religion and the Arabic language. Deeply influenced by Greek, Persian, and Indian traditions, Muslim scholars combined the latest insights in the arts and sciences and developed them further. Using Hindi numerals, which included the concept of zero—later adopted in Europe as Arabic numerals—they advanced mathematical thought to an understanding of algebra and trigonometry.

Relying again on Hindi and Persian advances in astronomy, they built observatories, computed the movement of the planets, measured the altitude of stars, discovered new stars, and theorized that the earth rotates on its axis. The use of the astrolabe and compass allowed for fearless navigation across the open sea and thus increased trade.

Arab literature, long honed by a tradition of storytellers, flourished with prose and poetry that rang with musical rhythm in ways no Western translation can do justice. Whether a fable ending in moral advice, an amusing story, or an adventure, the texts—full of puns, sly allusions, and clever metaphors—were meant to be recited. Foremost among the written words is the Koran, which renders the word of Allah in beautiful verse.

An unprecedented building boom—especially of palaces and mosques—occurred after each new conquest. Islamic architecture, sometimes called the architecture of the veil, concentrates its beauty on interior spaces, with courtyards, gardens, and fountains. Invoking Allah's infinite power, the mosques soar with large domes, minarets, and central prayer halls. The human form and even animals are rarely depicted, because Allah's work is said to be matchless. The decorations therefore consist of geometric patterns and arabesques or quotations from the Koran in calligraphy. Construction of the Great Mosque at Córdoba, left, began in 785 and marks the beginning of Islamic architecture in Spain and northern Africa. The mosque is noted for its striking interior, especially the dome, which is built over 850 columns and 19 aisles, and achieves its elegance through symmetry.

The ceiling of the great dome of Córdoba's mosque is testimony to the elegance of Muslim art and architecture, embellished solely with arabesques and geometric patterns.

POLITICS & POWER	GEOGRAPHY & ENVIRONMENT	CULTURE & RELIGION
THE AMERICAS		
ca 970 The Huari and Tiahuanacan Empires in Peru begin to break up and retrench. **987 The Toltec** merge with the Maya on the Yucatán Peninsula, Mexico.	**ca 970-1000 The climate change** that brings warm and wetter weather to the North American plains also allows the Cahokia people to accelerate the production of corn. With increased food supply, the population density grows as well. **ca 980-1000 Groups of indigenous people** have developed corn agriculture "west of the 100th meridian." This effort is the first to farm successfully in a dry climate of what will become the western regions of Nebraska and Kansas.	
EUROPE		
971 Byzantine Emperor John Tzimisces (John I) beats Russian forces in the Balkans and fixes the borders of the empire to the Danube. **973 German Emperor Otto II** succeeds his father, followed by Otto III in 983. **976 Byzantine Emperor Basil II** drives the Muslims back to the gates of Jerusalem. **983 The Wends**—Slavic tribes—sack eastern Germany as far west as Hamburg. **987 Hugh Capet** is elected king of France.	**974 The earliest documentation** of an earthquake in England is recorded.	**976 The Great Mosque** of Córdoba is completed, holding 70 libraries, the largest one with 500,000 books. About 70,000 books a year are copied by hand. **980 Vladimir,** Grand Prince of Kiev, adopts the Christian faith of the Byzantine Church and founds the Russian Orthodox Church. **980 Nikon** reconverts the people of Crete to Christianity after the Muslim conquest. **996 The Tithe Church** in Kiev, Russia, is built by Byzantine craftsmen.
MIDDLE EAST & AFRICA		
970-1000 Koumbi Saleh, ancient remains of a city of wide streets, stone architecture, and rich material culture, may have once been the capital of the empire of Ghana. Its origins predate the spread of Islam. **999 Turkic Ghaznavids** and Karakhanids conquer northern India and all of Central Asia, bringing them into the Islamic realm.		**ca 970 Islam** is the dominant religion along the coast of East Africa. **977 The Shrine of Iman Ali** is built in Najaf, Iraq, at the burial site of Ali, son-in-law of the Prophet Muhammad—a holy site for all Shiite Muslims.
ASIA & OCEANIA		
985 Under king Rajaraja I, Chola power reaches its zenith in South India. He conquers Kerala and occupies northern Sri Lanka. **995 The Japanese noble Fujiwara Michinaga** is one of the most powerful statesmen in the Heian period and exercises nearly complete control over the imperial court. **997 Afghan raiders** repeatedly attack northern India.	**994 The city of Delhi** is founded by the Tomaroes in India.	**977-983 About 1,000 volumes** of an encyclopedia are compiled during the Song dynasty in China. **ca 990 Kundavi,** a Chola queen and elder sister of Rajaraja I, has a Vishnu and a Shiva temple built at Dadapura and a Jain temple at Traumalai in southern India.

WHAT LIFE WAS LIKE

Women in China

During the Sui and Tang dynasties women in China moved about easily, even riding horses, elegantly dressed in silks and wearing a veil against the dust. Toward the end of the tenth century the status of women declined as they were more and more confined to the home. "A virtuous woman," it was said, "never takes more than three steps from the threshold." Around 950, during the Song dynasty, the custom of footbinding began, keeping feet exquisitely small. The painful procedure further restricted women's movements. Fashions changed as well, the slender look of earlier centuries giving way to more voluptuous lines, including blouses, long skirts, wraps, and shawls of patterned silks.

SCIENCE & TECHNOLOGY	PEOPLE & SOCIETY

ca 970-1000 The growing abundance of food in the Cahokia region escalates construction of a sophisticated urban place and specialized labor and socioeconomic groups. Cahokia also produces elites who bridge the gap between ordinary people and the gods they worship.

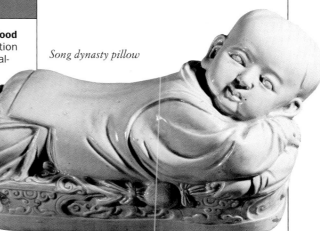

Song dynasty pillow

ca 970 Jewish physician Shabba thai Ben Abraham in Salerno, Italy, develops new pharmacological prescriptions.

ca 970 A monastic hospital in Constantinople divides patients into wards by type of illness. Male physicians specialize in surgery, hernias, and eye diseases; female specialists are on staff for women's illnesses.

970-1000 Hroswitha of Gandersheim, the abbess of a convent in Ottonian Germany, writes poems, a history of the reign of Otto I, and several plays, all in Latin, modeled on those by classical Roman authors. The plays focus on heroic Christian women, who maintain their virginity and unmarried state at all costs.

980 Avicenna, a Persian philosopher and physician, writes more than 450 books on medicine and is considered by many the forefather of modern medicine. Translations of his books exert great influence in Europe.

971-1030 Mahmud of Ghazni, Afghan ruler and Alptigin's grandson, leads numerous raids into Iran, Central Asia, and the Punjab of India, looting treasures and imposing Islam on the population. At Ghazna, his capital, he builds a magnificent mosque.

THE SONG DYNASTY

The collapse of the Tang dynasty brought on some 50 years of internecine warfare in China. Finally, in 960, a strong military leader, Zhao Kuangyin, founded the Song dynasty. He reimposed centralized imperial rule and vastly expanded the bureaucracy, though reducing the military. He placed emphasis on civil administration and education instead. With renewed order, Chinese culture underwent another remarkable flowering of the arts and literature, creating ever more artistic porcelains and delicate landscape paintings on paper and silk.

The Song dynasty also saw remarkable improvements in agriculture. A new fast-ripening rice produced two crops a year in the fertile south, which—thanks to the Grand Canal—could be easily distributed throughout the country. Vastly improved, the food supplies in turn supported the expansion of markets, commerce, and a money economy. Cities grew and flourished as both economic hubs and centers of urban and popular culture.

Their reduced military capacity ultimately proved to be the Song dynasty's downfall. Steppe horsemen from the north were a constant threat and demanded heavy tribute. In the early 12th century, the nomadic Jurchen conquered northern China, chasing the Song government to the south of China.

PREVIOUS PAGE: *Mongol invaders arriving by sea meet fierce resistance from Japanese warriors defending the island of Kyushu in 1281. Storm winds devastated the huge invasion fleet and helped the Japanese beat back the Mongols.*

RIGHT: *Beginning in 1095, Christians from many parts of Europe joined in Crusades aimed at defeating Muslim forces and capturing the Holy Land. Many crusaders marched overland, but some traveled by sea and disembarked at encampments along the eastern Mediterranean, opposite.*

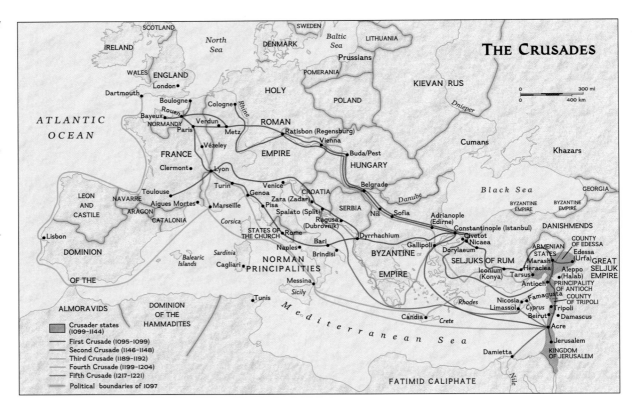

BETWEEN 1000 AND 1500, INVADERS, TRADERS, and explorers crossed continents and oceans and brought societies that were worlds apart into contact and conflict. Christian crusaders from western Europe traveled to Jerusalem to battle Muslims for control of the Holy Land. Turks and Mongols from Central Asia overran vast areas extending from China to eastern Europe. Traffic between Asia and Europe spread a ruinous plague—and sustained a lucrative trade in spices and other goods that spurred advances in navigation. In the late 1400s European mariners seeking new sources of wealth and new routes to Asia rounded Africa and crossed the Atlantic, inaugurating trade and colonization on a global scale. By 1500 few places on Earth were beyond the reach of intruders from distant lands and the unsettling changes they brought about.

Turmoil in the Middle East

By 1000 the Islamic world was no longer united. The once-mighty Abbasid caliphs in Baghdad had lost much of their authority, and the rival Fatimid dynasty controlled Egypt, Palestine, and Syria. Divisions within dar al-Islam—the house of Islam—allowed outsiders to lay claim to its wealth and holy places. Before the crusaders arrived, Seljuk Turks infiltrated the Middle East from Central Asia, where they had long lived as nomadic herders and clashed with rivals on horseback. They fought for Abbasid caliphs and converted to Islam but preserved their Turkish language and customs. In 1055, a Seljuk Turk named Tughril Beg became sultan (chieftain) in Baghdad. He and his successors left caliphs in place there as figureheads and embarked on conquests, capturing Syria and Palestine from the Fatimids and advancing into Anatolia, or what is now Turkey.

The Turkish advance posed a grave threat to the Byzantine Empire. Under Emperor Basil II, known as Basil the Bulgar Slayer, Byzantine troops had conquered Bulgaria earlier in the century and reached the fertile Danube River Valley. But that gain would be more than offset if Byzantium lost Anatolia, which provided Constantinople with food and trade goods and shielded it from invasion. In 1071 Byzantine forces were defeated in Anatolia by the Turks, who later split into rival camps after their sultan died. Hoping to beat them back, the Byzantine emperor sought help from western Europe, where Christians had their own reasons for opposing the Turks. The Eastern Orthodox Church had recently broken with the Roman Catholic Church, and Pope Urban II in Rome saw a chance to regain authority in the eastern Mediterranean by becoming the spiritual guardian of Jerusalem and other sites in the Holy Land sacred to Christians as well as Muslims. In 1095, he called for a crusade against the Turks to "expel that wicked race from our Christian lands."

The First Crusade, launched in response to the pope's appeal, began badly when a zealot named Peter the Hermit led a motley army to a disastrous defeat. Meanwhile, nobles in France were assembling a stronger fighting force, one that succeeded in capturing Jerusalem in 1099. Bands of crusaders then carved out states along the eastern Mediterranean. The capture of one such state by Turks prompted the Second Crusade in 1147, which ended in failure. In 1171 the Sultan Saladin wrested Egypt from the

Fatimids and went on to reclaim Jerusalem for Muslims in 1187. Later crusaders from Catholic Europe were unable to win the Holy Land back and turned against Orthodox Christians in Constantinople, sacking that city in 1204 and leaving the Byzantine Empire vulnerable to future assaults by Turks.

Europe Gains Power

Although the Crusades accomplished little of lasting value, they exposed Europeans to the larger world and encouraged them to unite under strong leaders. Crusader armies led by Kings Louis IX of France and Richard I of England—a successor to William the Conqueror, who had crossed over from Normandy and claimed England in 1066—demonstrated the growing might of European monarchs, whose claims of authority were resisted by some nobles. In Eng-

land, nobles forced King John I in 1215 to sign the Magna Carta, placing legal limits on royal power.

European noblemen were knights, who fought on horseback and were expected to honor the code of chivalry by serving God, obeying their overlords, and honoring and protecting women. Ladies promoted chivalry by patronizing troubadours, who celebrated love, honor, and courtesy in poetry and song. Much the same values prevailed in the courts of Muslim nobles in Spain, whose romantic verses inspired troubadours in France and other Christian countries.

Some knights formed religious orders that fought to spread their faith. Teutonic Knights from Germany invaded Prussia and other countries in the Baltic region and imposed Christianity there. Germany formed part of the Holy Roman Empire, which extended from the Baltic Sea to northern Italy. The first Holy Roman emperor was crowned by the pope in the 10th century, but his successors later clashed with Rome by claiming the right to appoint their own bishops.

Italy, meanwhile, remained divided into many political units, including city-states such as Venice and Genoa, which prospered through trade with the Islamic world. Italian merchants met Europe's demand for eastern goods such as sugar, spices, and silk that became more popular after crusaders encountered them. Marco Polo and other Italian merchants journeyed to China to promote trade. The city-state of Florence emerged

In the 13th century, descendants of Genghis Khan divided the vast area conquered by Mongol forces into four khanates, each with its own leader. Kublai Khan served as the supreme leader, or great khan, and held sway over the Mongolian homeland and China.

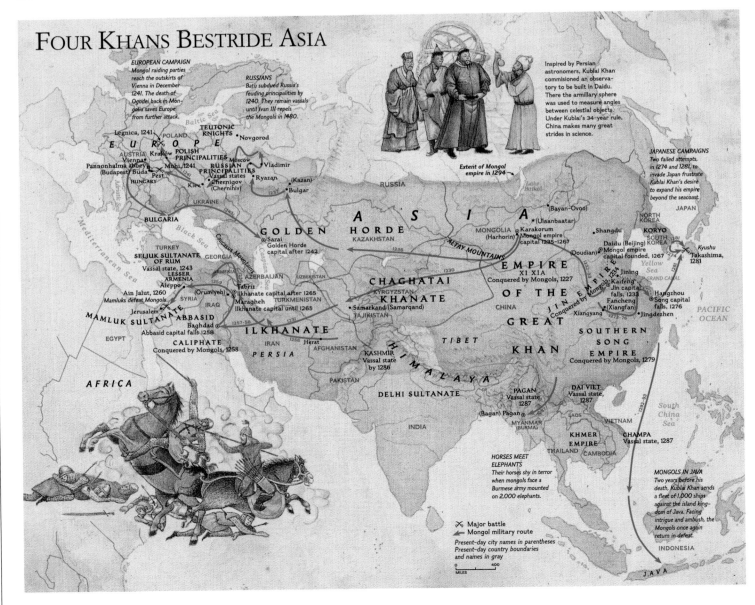

FOUR KHANS BESTRIDE ASIA

EUROPEAN CAMPAIGN
Mongol raiding parties reach the outskirts of Vienna in December 1241. The death of Ogodei back in Mongolia saves Europe from further attack.

RUSSIANS
Batu subdued Russia's feuding principalities by 1240. They remain vassals until Ivan III repels the Mongols in 1480.

Inspired by Persian astronomers, Kublai Khan commissioned an observatory to be built in Daidu. There the armillary sphere was used to measure angles between celestial objects. Under Kublai's 34-year rule, China makes many great strides in science.

JAPANESE CAMPAIGNS
Two failed attempts, in 1274 and 1281, to invade Japan frustrate Kublai Khan's desire to expand his empire beyond the seacoast.

Extent of Mongol empire in 1294

HORSES MEET ELEPHANTS
Their horses shy in terror when mongols face a Burmese army mounted on 2,000 elephants.

MONGOLS IN JAVA
Two years before his death, Kublai Khan sends a fleet of 1,000 ships against the island kingdom of Java. Facing intrigue and ambush, the Mongols once again return in defeat.

⚔ Major battle
← Mongol military route
Present-day city names in parentheses
Present-day country boundaries
and names in gray

0   400
MILES

around 1300 as a great cultural center, home to the poet Dante Alighieri, the painter Giotto di Bondone, and the scholar Petrarch. Their works drew on classical culture and served as a bridge between Europe's age of faith and the humanism of the Italian Renaissance.

Throughout Europe, the expansion of trade supported the growth of cities inhabited by prosperous merchants and skilled artisans, who organized guilds that controlled production and set prices. Booming cities such as Paris boasted towering cathedrals and cathedral schools that evolved into universities headed by scholars such as St. Thomas Aquinas, who drew on the works of Aristotle to give Catholicism a strong intellectual foundation. Europe benefited greatly from contacts with distant lands, but those contacts would soon expose it to severe trials.

Mongol warriors like the one portrayed here were expert cavalrymen who used stirrups to steady themselves and could fire arrows with deadly force in any direction.

The Mongol Invasions

By 1200 various Turkish dynasties ruled North Africa, the Middle East, and northern India. But the Turks would soon be surpassed as conquerors by the Mongols, who occupied what is now Mongolia. They were superb at mounted warfare but lacked political unity until a charismatic chieftain named Temujin created a powerful confederation. He was chosen khan (ruler) at a council of tribal leaders in 1206 and became known as Genghis Khan (Universal Ruler).

His first target as a conqueror was northern China, which had already slipped from the grasp of the Song dynasty. Under Song rule, China remained one of the most accomplished and inventive societies in the world. Printers there invented movable type, and shipbuilders devised rudders to make vessels more maneuverable—breakthroughs that spread to the West along with earlier Chinese inventions such as gunpowder. The printing of paper money stimulated China's economy, and its cities grew larger and wealthier. New techniques of irrigation and fertilization helped feed a population that soared from roughly 60 million in 1000 to nearly twice that two centuries later. Song rulers entrusted their armies to officials who knew little of military matters, however, and lost northern China to invaders called the Jurchens a century before Genghis Khan launched his offensive. The Jurchens put up fierce resistance, but most of northern China was in Mongol hands by 1220.

Heirs to Genghis Khan would later seize all of China, but he himself campaigned westward across Central Asia as far as the Caspian Sea, devastating all who defied him. After Genghis Khan died in 1227, his heirs continued to campaign and divided the vast Mongol Empire into khanates, each ruled by its own khan. Kublai Khan completed the conquest of China and launched large naval expeditions against Japan in 1274 and 1281, both of which were battered by typhoons. The Japanese thanked Shinto gods for sending the kamikaze, or divine wind, that saved them. Those Mongols who made it ashore were beaten back by samurai warriors, whose code required them to commit suicide if they failed to do their duty. Many lost faith in Japan's shogun, or military ruler, when he did not reward them as hoped and raised taxes to pay for the costly defensive preparations.

By 1300 the Mongol Empire extended from China to Russia. Princes in Moscow and other cities were forced to pay tribute to Mongols of the Golden Horde, who pushed eastward into Poland and Hungary. Western Europe escaped invasion, but many there fell prey to an epidemic that Mongols and traders who dealt with them helped convey. Around 1330 bubonic plague, known as the Black Death, erupted in China and devastated that country. Amid the chaos, the Mongols lost power, leading to the resumption of Chinese rule under the Ming dynasty. The plague, carried by fleas that infested rodents, spread from Asia along sea and land routes traveled by merchant ships, caravans, and armies. Most people who became infected died, and outbreaks caused hysteria. In some parts of Europe, Christians blamed Jews for the plague and massacred them.

By 1400 the Black Death had reduced the European population by nearly 25 percent. The devastation in the Middle East was even worse and caused turmoil in lands ruled by Mongols, allowing Turks to regain control. Forces led by the conqueror Tamerlane, or Timur, seized Mesopotamia, Persia, and northern India and were preparing to invade China when he died in 1405. His empire perished with him, leaving a void that was filled by other Turks, notably the Ottomans in Anatolia. They believed that a warrior who died fighting for Islam gained everlasting glory. "He lives in beatitude with Allah," one poet proclaimed; "he has eternal life." After invading the Balkans, Ottomans shocked Christian Europe by capturing Constantinople in 1453.

By this time western Europe had largely overcome the effects of the plague, and its monarchs were more powerful than ever. In the same year Constantinople fell, an epic struggle between England and France known as the Hundred Years' War came to an end. France succeeded in rebuffing English claims to French territory, but the royal families of both countries grew stronger during the war by raising armies and imposing taxes to finance their campaigns. In Spain the Christian kingdoms of Castile and Aragon, which had earlier reclaimed much of that country from Muslims, were united by marriage in 1469 and went on to conquer Granada, the last bastion of Islam in Spain. Portugal, for its part, became a maritime power under Prince Henry the Navigator, who promoted the study of navigation and sponsored expeditions that colonized the Azores and other islands, where slaves imported from West Africa worked sugar plantations.

Advances in navigation enabled Europeans to bypass Muslim traders and seek maritime routes to Asian markets. In the late 1400s, Portuguese navigators rounded Africa and reached India while the Italian mariner Christopher Columbus opened a transatlantic route for Spain to what he thought were the Indies but proved to be islands in the Caribbean. The stage was set for momentous European ventures that would impact Africa, the Americas, and other regions and disrupt or destroy powerful societies there.

Advances in Africa and the Americas

Before Columbus reached the New World or Portuguese traders visited the coast of West Africa, empires had arisen on those continents. The West African empire of Ghana collapsed in the early 1200s under pressure from nomads who swept down from the Sahara, lured by the gold that had long drawn Arab traders. That trade revived with the growth of the Mali Empire, which succeeded Ghana and embraced a wider area. The Mali emperor Mansa Musa dazzled the Islamic world by making a pilgrimage to Mecca in the early 1300s with thousands of followers and a fortune in gold. Most of Mali's population lived more modestly and adhered to ancestral beliefs. Great artistry and devotion went into crafting masks and other objects they used in rituals honoring their spirits.

On the East African coast, prosperous city-states developed where Swahili merchants imported prized items such as silk, cotton, and porcelain by sea from India and other countries. Inland, the kingdom of Zimbabwe flourished, with impressive stone architecture and an imposing capital that housed nearly 20,000 people. Like Mali and the Songhai Empire that succeeded it, Zimbabwe prospered by selling slaves as well as gold and ivory. But the slave trade did not become a consuming enterprise until Europeans began sending shiploads of black Africans to colonies across the Atlantic. By the late 1400s, Portuguese traders were exporting a few thousand slaves each year from Africa, and that was a mere trickle compared to the massive transshipments to come.

In the Americas, the period preceding the arrival of Europeans was marked by similar cultural advances. In North America, the mound-building societies of the Mississippi Valley and the Southeast declined in the 1200s as large towns exhausted their natural resources. But tribal societies made up of smaller villages linked by trade and diplomacy flourished throughout the eastern woodlands. In the Northeast, the five tribes of the Iroquois coalesced during the 15th century into a strong confederation that would play a major role in the colonial era to come. In the Southwest, the Anasazi culture reached its peak in the 12th century at Chaco Canyon, a political and ceremonial center linked by roads to outlying settlements. Severe drought later caused the Anasazi villagers to disperse. Some settled along the

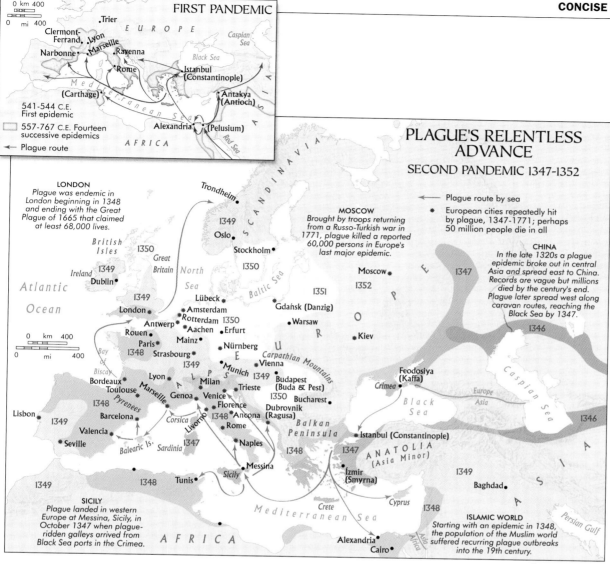

FIRST PANDEMIC

0 km 400
0 mi 400

541-544 C.E.
First epidemic

557-767 C.E. Fourteen
successive epidemics

← Plague route

EUROPE

Trier
Clermont-Ferrand
Lyon
Narbonne
Marseille
Ravenna
Rome
Istanbul (Constantinople)
(Carthage)
Antakya (Antioch)
Alexandria
(Pelusium)
AFRICA
Caspian Sea
Black Sea
Mediterranean Sea
Red Sea
ASIA

Bubonic plague, or the Black Death, first swept the Mediterranean world in the 6th century and returned with a vengeance in the 14th century, taking a terrible toll. Later outbreaks were less severe, but the disease remained a dreaded scourge in the 17th century, when a German artist portrayed a physician wearing a mask he hoped would ward off infection (below).

PLAGUE'S RELENTLESS ADVANCE
SECOND PANDEMIC 1347-1352

← Plague route by sea

• European cities repeatedly hit by plague, 1347-1771; perhaps 50 million people die in all

LONDON
Plague was endemic in London beginning in 1348 and ending with the Great Plague of 1665 that claimed at least 68,000 lives.

MOSCOW
Brought by troops returning from a Russo-Turkish war in 1771, plague killed a reported 60,000 persons in Europe's last major epidemic.

CHINA
In the late 1320s a plague epidemic broke out in central Asia and spread east to China. Records are vague but millions died by the century's end. Plague later spread west along caravan routes, reaching the Black Sea by 1347.

SICILY
Plague landed in western Europe at Messina, Sicily, in October 1347 when plague-ridden galleys arrived from Black Sea ports in the Crimea.

ISLAMIC WORLD
Starting with an epidemic in 1348, the population of the Muslim world suffered recurring plague outbreaks into the 19th century.

Trondheim
SCANDINAVIA
1349 Oslo
Stockholm 1350
British Isles
1350 Great Britain
North Sea
Ireland 1349 Dublin
Atlantic Ocean
1349 London
Amsterdam
Rotterdam 1350
Antwerp
Aachen Erfurt
Rouen
Paris
Mainz
1348 Strasbourg
Nürnberg
1349
Munich 1349
Vienna
Lyon
Milan Trieste
Bordeaux
Toulouse
Marseille
Genoa Venice
Florence
1348 Ancona
Livorno Rome
Dubrovnik (Ragusa)
Lisbon
1349 Barcelona
Corsica
Valencia
Seville
Balearic Is. Sardinia 1347
Naples
Messina
Sicily
1349 Tunis 1348
Mediterranean Sea
AFRICA
Lübeck
Gdańsk (Danzig)
Warsaw
Kiev
Budapest (Buda & Pest)
1350 Bucharest
Balkan Peninsula
1348
1347
Istanbul (Constantinople)
ANATOLIA (Asia Minor)
Izmir (Smyrna)
Crete
Cyprus 1348
Alexandria
Cairo
Moscow 1352
1351
EUROPE
1347
Black Sea
Feodosiya (Kaffa)
Crimea
Europe Asia
Caspian Sea
1346
1346
ASIA
1349 Baghdad
Persian Gulf
Asia Africa

0 km 400
0 mi 400

Rio Grande and inspired the Pueblo society that emerged there.

In South America, the traditions of earlier cultures such as the Moche were carried on by the Chimu, who extended their domain along the Peruvian coast for over 500 miles before they fell to the Inca. Originating in the Andean highlands, the Inca became a great power in the mid-1400s under a ruler who took the name Pachacuti (He Who Transforms the Earth). By 1500 their empire reached from what is now Ecuador to central Chile and included thousands of miles of paved highways, with inns at regular intervals to accommodate traders and officials, who lacked a written language but kept records by tying knots on strings.

In the Valley of Mexico, meanwhile, the Aztec, or Mexica, had forged their own empire centered at Tenochtitlan, a majestic capital built on an island. A plaza nearby housed one of the world's greatest markets, visited daily by tens of thousands of people and filled with alluring items such as jaguar pelts and macaw feathers as well as pottery, cotton fabric, and other crafted goods. Like the Maya, the Aztec had priests who served as astronomers, kept intricate calendars, and preserved their lore in writing. Aztec priests also conducted human sacrifices as offerings to their gods atop the Great Pyramid in Tenochtitlan and other sacred sites. Kings waged wars after their coronations and sacrificed captives by the thousands to seek divine blessings. Aztec demands for tribute from people they ruled caused further resentments that Spanish invaders later exploited to divide and conquer the Aztec Empire. ■

THE WORLD AT A GLANCE

	1000	1050	1100	1150	1200
THE AMERICAS	**ca 1000** Leif Eriksson is believed to have discovered America. **ca 1000** The "southern cult" of mound builders develops. **ca 1000** Iroquois peoples in northeastern North America live in communities and farm. **ca 1000** Agriculture is embraced by peoples in the eastern woodlands and in the Southwest.	**ca 1050** More than 5,000 Anasazi settlers inhabit Chaco Canyon in modern-day New Mexico. **ca 1050** Central Mexican groups such as the Chontal Maya, Putun, and Toltec invade Maya settlements and influence Maya culture. **ca 1085** Thule Eskimo culture spreads across the Arctic to Greenland and Siberia.	**ca 1100** The Anasazi Indian site at Pueblo Bonito reaches its height in New Mexico's Chaco Canyon. **ca 1100** The Third Pueblo Period occurs in southwestern North America. **1100** The Sinchi Roca civilization exists in Peru. **1125** Civil strife begins in Tula, the capital city of the Toltec.	**ca 1150** Cahokia and other mound-building cultures in the Mississippi region achieve prominence. **ca 1150** Chimu civilization expands from north to south, 625 miles along the coast, and signals the return of coastal Peruvian civilization after a hiatus of 500 years. **1151** The Toltec Empire in Mexico draws to an end.	**ca 1200** The city of Cuzco in Peru is founded by Inca leader Manco Capac. **ca 1200** Mixtecs, noted for their mosaic veneers, construct large and beautiful palace complexes at Mitla. **ca 1221** Warring factions of lowland Maya rulers compete for control of resources.
EUROPE	**ca 1000** Christianity reaches Greenland and Iceland. **1013** The Danes conquer England. **1040** King Duncan of Scotland is murdered by Macbeth, who then becomes king. **1045** El Cid (Rodrigo Díaz) is proclaimed a national hero in Spain.	**1054** The schism between Roman and Eastern Churches becomes permanent. **1066** William of Normandy (the Conqueror) defeats King Harold II at the Battle of Hastings, becoming king of England. **1096** The First Crusade begins. **1099** Crusaders take Jerusalem.	**ca 1100** Motte and bailey wooden castles are built by the Normans. **ca 1100** Middle English replaces Old English. **ca 1100** Annual trade fairs are held just outside town walls and last for days. **1125** Troubadour and trouvère music begins in France.	**1163** Work begins on Notre Dame Cathedral in Paris. **1170** Thomas à Becket is murdered at Canterbury Cathedral by Norman knights. **1194** *The Elder Edda,* a collection of Scandinavian mythology, is written. **1199** Richard the Lion-Hearted is killed at a siege in France and is succeeded by King John.	**ca 1200** The early Gothic period begins in England. **1209** Francis of Assisi relates the first rules of his brotherhood, the Franciscans. **1215** King John signs the Magna Carta put forth by English barons at Runnymede. **1230** The crusaders bring leprosy to Europe.
MIDDLE EAST & AFRICA	**1025** Byzantium begins to decline when Constantine VIII succeeds Basil II at his death. **1030** Masud seizes the Ghaznavid throne in Afghanistan, and his empire reaches from Persia to the valley of the Ganges. **1040** The Seljuk Turks defeat the Ghaznavids in Persia and move toward Baghdad.	**1071** Turks seize and occupy Jerusalem. **1071** The Byzantines are defeated by the Seljuks in Asia Minor. **1071** Constantine, the African, brings Greek medicine to the West. **1077** The Almoravids invade the kingdom of Ghana in Africa. **1092** An Islamic sect called the Assassins kill the Seljuk vizier.	**1104** Christians call for a crusade against Constantinople. **1118** The Order of the Knights Templar is created to protect the road to Jerusalem. **1123** The Egyptian fleet is defeated off Ascalon by the Venetian fleet. **1147** The Second Crusade fails when the crusaders perish in Asia Minor.	**1171** Saladin abolishes the Fatimid caliphate in Cairo, becomes the sovereign of Egypt, and re-establishes Sunnism. **1187** Saladin reconquers Jerusalem. **1191** Richard the Lion-Hearted seizes Cyprus. With Philip Augustus he takes Acre.	**ca 1200** In Egypt, Mamluk rule drives the Arab nomads south towards Nubia and sets in motion the Islamization of the Middle Nile. **1204** Crusaders seize Constantinople. **1235** The Berber kingdom of the Abd al-Wadids is founded at Tlemcen in the Maghreb in Africa.
ASIA & OCEANIA	**1000** An Indian mathematician recognizes the power of zero. **1010** Native Ly dynasty is founded in northern Vietnam. **1019** Armies of Ghazni occupy most of northern India. **1044** Government edict establishes schools throughout China to train students for the civil service exams.	**1050** The Japanese sculptor Jocho starts his school. **1086** The cloistered emperor system is introduced in Japan, which marks the decline of the powerful Fujiwara family. **1091** Building is under way for some 15,000 pagodas, temples, and palaces in Pagan, Burma (Myanmar), 5,000 of which still stand today.	**1100** Jayadeva writes *Gitagovinda,* an Indian love poem. **1108** Taira and Minamoto clans chastise the sobei, warrior monks of the Enryakuji temple, on Mount Hiei near Kyoto. **1115** The Jurchen from Manchuria, allied with the Song, overthrow the Khitan Liao and found the Jin dynasty in China.	**1151** The Chinese use explosives in warfare. **1156** Taira and Minamoto clans go to war in Japan. **1191** Tea arrives in Japan from China. **1192** Minamoto Yoritomo is awarded the title of military ruler of Japan.	**1200** The family of Hojo Masako assumes control of the Kamakura shogunate. **1206** Genghis Khan becomes leader of the Mongol confederation. **1227** Japanese monk Dogen introduces Zen Buddhism from China. **1234** Mongols seize Kaifeng in China, completing the destruction of the Jin Empire.

1250	1300	1350	1400	1450-1500
ca 1250 The Aztec, who call themselves Mexica, arrive in central Mexico. **ca 1250** Weaving by the Chimu is perfected to 200 waft per inch, whereas European cloth seldom surpasses 80 waft per inch. **ca 1275** A series of droughts hits the Mesa Verde pueblo in modern-day Colorado, driving the Anasazi away.	**ca 1300** The Toltec are no longer dominating Mesoamerica. **ca 1325** The Aztec found their capital, Tenochtitlan (modern-day Mexico City). **ca 1325** In modern-day Arizona, the Hohokam Indians begin building the largest structure south of the Gila River, a site later known as Casa Grande.	**ca 1350** The Aztec begin to extract tribute from numerous subject territories. **ca 1350** The Mapuche of Chile's southern coast gradually begin to develop into a military society that will be able to resist Inca imperialism for a long period. **ca 1350** Nahuatl becomes the dominant language of the Valley of Mexico.	**1410** Peruvian ruler Viracocha Inca expands his empire. **1428** Itzcoatl forms the Aztec Alliance with the Texcoco and Tlacopan, bringing the Aztec to the apex of their power. **1440** Moctezuma I becomes the ruler of the Aztec and begins conquering tribes outside the Valley of Mexico.	**1450** The Inca subdue the Chimu Indians in northern Peru. **1492** Christopher Columbus lands on the island in the Caribbean that he names Hispaniola (Santo Domingo). **1499** Italian navigator Amerigo Vespucci explores the northeast coastline of South America.
1263 The Venetians defeat the Genoese in a sea battle off Settepozzi. **1271** Venetian Marco Polo travels to China. **1294** Cities in the Hanseatic League recognize Lubeck as their leading member. **1297** William Wallace leads the Scots in a rebellion against the English, whom they defeat at Stirling Bridge.	**1337** The Hundred Years' War begins with Edward II of England getting allies among German princes to fight the French. **1347** The Black Death wreaks havoc in Europe. **1349** Jews are persecuted in Germany.	**1378** The Great Schism begins following the death of Gregory XI. **1381** Venice is victorious over Genoa at Chioggia, leading to a great flourishing of the arts, sciences, and commerce in that city. **1387** Geoffrey Chaucer writes *The Canterbury Tales*.	**1414** The Medicis in Florence become official bankers to the papacy. **1415** Henry V of England defeats the French at Agincourt. **1430** Middle English gives way to Modern English.	**1455** The Wars of the Roses begin in England between the Lancasters and the Yorks. **1468** Lorenzo (the Magnificent) and his brother, Giuliano, succeed their father as Medici rulers of Florence. **1478** The Spanish Inquisition begins.
1258 Mongols seize Baghdad and overthrow the caliphate there. **1261** Michael VIII Palaeologus regains Constantinople. **1270** Yekuno Amlak rules Ethiopia and founds the Solomonic dynasty. **1289** Qala'un, Sultan of Egypt, captures Tripoli, leaving Acre the only major Christian stronghold in the Near East.	**1301** Osman defeats the Byzantines at Baphaion. **1324** Mali ruler Mansa Musa makes his legendary pilgrimage to Mecca. **1338** Ottomans reach the Bosporus in Asia Minor. **1346** A strong earthquake hits Constantinople, causing the eastern arch of Hagia Sophia Cathedral to crumble.	**1352-53** Arab geographer Ibn Battuta explores sub-Saharan Africa. **1354** The Ottomans occupy Gallipoli. **1380** Tamerlane begins successful campaigns against Persia, Russia, Georgia, and Egypt. **1396** The Ottomans win a great victory over the crusaders at Nicopolis.	**ca 1400** Successful gold trade has been developed down the Zambezi Valley to the Sofala coast in southeast Africa. **1433** Tuaregs, desert camel riders from northern Africa, seize the city of Timbuktu. **1444** Ottomans defeat the Hungarians at Varna, a chief port for coffee export.	**1453** Ottoman Turks take Constantinople. **1471** The Ottomans now rule all lands from the Taurus Mountains to the Adriatic Sea. **1486** Kongo emissaries sail to Portugal, where they convert to Christianity. They return in five years with a fleet of three caravels carrying Portuguese priests, craftsmen, livestock, and a printing press.
1271 Venetian Marco Polo travels to China. **1279** Kublai Khan conquers the last Song resistance and reunites China under the Yuan dynasty. **1282** Nichiren, founder of a Japanese-centered Buddhist sect, dies. **1293** The Javanese defeat a Mongol expedition.	**ca 1300** Playwright Guan Hanqing writes popular dramas in Yian, China. **1318** The Delhi sultanate conquers the kingdom of Maharashtra. **1320** Gharzi Khan of the Tughlak dynasty becomes sultan of Delhi when Mubarak dies. **1333** The Ashikaga shogunate is established in Japan.	**1350** Noh theater begins in Japan. **1350** Li Xingdao writes *The Chalk Circle,* a Chinese play about justice and retribution adapted centuries later for the Western theatre. **1368** Zhu Yuanzhang founds the Ming dynasty. **1398** Tamerlane invades India and sacks Delhi.	**1405** Chinese admiral Zhen He leads first of maritime expeditions to the Indian Ocean. **1420** The Ming capital is moved to Beijing. **1434** The Khmer capital moves from Angkor to Phnom Penh. **1443** The Hangul Korean phonetic syllabary is created.	**1450** Defensive walls along the northern frontiers of China are rebuilt to create the Ming era Great Wall. **1483** Russians start exploring Siberia. **1492** The sultan of Delhi, Sikander II Lodi, annexes Bihar.

	POLITICS & POWER	GEOGRAPHY & ENVIRONMENT	CULTURE & RELIGION
THE AMERICAS	**ca 1000 The multiethnic city of Tula** in Mexico is at its height with some 30,000 people. **ca 1000 The Moundville settlement** of the Mississippian culture reaches its apogee in modern-day Alabama. **ca 1000 The Huari Empire** of the Highland Andes breaks up. The Chimu Empire is one of several empires that ascend. Its capital is at Chanchan.	**ca 1000 Leif Eriksson** is believed to have discovered America (Nova Scotia). **ca 1000 The Mandan, Hidatsa, and Arikara** peoples build communities along the Missouri River in the Northern Plains. Their communities depend on corn production for their food supply. They also use corn to trade for buffalo meat with plains hunters.	**ca 1000 The Maya world** is divided into three horizontal strata: the celestial world, the middle or earthly world, and the underworld, Xibalba. Only those dying in battle or giving birth or sacrifice are exempt from Xibalba. **ca 1000 The Mandan and Hidatsa** make corn central to their origins myth. The Mandan, in particular, trace their beginnings to the corn people in the distant past, who lived below the surface and were led above ground by their chief. He established the first Mandan communities based on corn production and distributed cornfields to Mandan families. He also gave corn seed to Mandan women, who planted and cared for the corn.
EUROPE	**1000 The Danegeld** is levied in England, a tax to protect against Danish invasion. **1004 Arabs** sack Pisa. **1013 The Danes** take England. **1016 The Danish king Canute** becomes undisputed king of England and unites England and Scandinavia in 1019. He names his mistress, Aelgifu, regent of Norway. **1018 Byzantine Emperor Basil II** completes his conquest of Bulgaria. **1025 Byzantium** begins to decline when Constantine VIII succeeds Basil II at his death.	**1000 Frisian dikes** are built against floods and invasions. **1000 Bohemia and Moravia** are united. **1000 Saxons** settle at Bristol. **1018 Southern and northern Scotland** are united.	**1000 Christianity** reaches Greenland and Iceland. **1000 The spiritual center of Judaism** moves to Spain from Mesopotamia. **1008 Berno, abbot of Reichenau,** writes books on music theory. **1015 Vladimir, Prince of Kiev,** dies after converting to Christianity upon his marriage to Anne, sister of Byzantine Emperor Basil II. His conversion opens Russia to Byzantine influences. **1026 Italian Guido d'Arezzo** introduces solmization in music.
MIDDLE EAST & AFRICA	**1009 Fatimid Caliph al-Hakim** destroys the Church of the Holy Sepulcher in Jerusalem. **1011 Caliph al-Hakim** protects Jerusalem from a mob riot (pogrom).		**1000 Al-Muqaddasi,** geographer and author of a physical and human geography of the known world, dies. **1010 Firdausi** writes the greatest work in Persian literature, the *Shahnama*. **1020 Fatimid Caliph al-Hakim** dies after claiming to be the Mahdi (messiah); his followers escape persecution in Egypt to start the Druze religious sect in the mountains of Lebanon. **1027 Samuel ibn Nagela** becomes the first nagid (head of the Jewish community) in Granada; Jewish communities organize across North Africa.
ASIA & OCEANIA	**1000 Seljuk Turks** occupy Transoxiana in Central Asia east of the Oxus River (Amu Darya). **1004 The Treaty of Shanyuan** between China and Khitan Liao is drawn up. **1008 Mahmud of Ghazni** defeats Hindus at Peshawar. **1018 The sacred city of Muttra** is sacked by Mahmud of Ghazni, who occupies most of northern India by 1019. **1021 Cholas** invade Bengal in India. **1023 Mahmud and Ghaznavids** turn north and occupy Transoxiana in Central Asia.	 *Carving of tattooed Maori leader in New Zealand*	**1019 Mahmud** founds the Great Mosque at Ghazni in Afghanistan. **1023 Amidism,** a movement dedicated to the worship of Amida Buddha, is born in Japan. **1025 Takayoshi** founds the school of Tosa painting in Japan.

SCIENCE & TECHNOLOGY

ca 1000 Maya and most Mesoamerican societies develop two calendar cycles, one of 260 days and another of 365 days, which coincide every two years.

ca 1000 The Toltec construct La Quemada, their fortress in the north, designed to protect their capital, Tula, from invasions by the Chichimec (Aztec), the northern barbarians.

ca 1000 Agriculture is embraced by peoples in the Eastern Woodlands and in the southwestern part of North America.

1000 Arabs and Jews become court physicians in Germany.

1018 Strasbourg Cathedral in France is begun.

1000-1040 Metallurgists at the West African urban centers of Ife and Benin cast intricate copper-alloy sculptures. Benin kingdom walls and earthworks display surveying and civil engineering skills.

1012 Mosque of al-Hakim is built in Cairo, Egypt.

1000 Gunpowder is perfected by the Chinese.

1000 An Indian mathematician recognizes the power of zero.

1023 The first paper money is printed in China.

PEOPLE & SOCIETY

ca 1000 The Southern Cult of mound builders develops in the lower Mississippi Valley.

ca 1000 Iroquois peoples in northeastern North America live in communities and cultivate beans and maize.

1000 Tiahuanaco society extends all over Peru; potatoes and corn are planted.

Portrait of Jewish rabbinic scholar, Moses Maimonides

ca 1000 Black pepper becomes a major Javanese export.

ca 1000 Pacific islands experience a rapid population growth.

1006 Muslims settle in northern India.

1006 Granaries for emergency famine relief are established throughout China.

JUDAISM MOVES WEST

After the arrival of Islam, Jews lived chiefly in lands that were ruled by Muhammad's followers. Centered in Mesopotamia, the geonim, or heads of the academies of learning, held forth as supreme judges of Talmudic law and were consulted on matters both religious and nonreligious by Jews around the world.

One such gaon was Hai ben Sherira of Pumbeditha Academy in Baghdad, considered the last great Babylonian gaon. Hai's reputation for wisdom was such that he received questions from as far away as Spain and Ethiopia. Upon his death in 1038 at the age of 99, the Pumbeditha Academy closed permanently, bringing to an end 600 years of flourishing Babylonian Jewry.

Though some Talmudic academies did remain open in Babylonia and Palestine, the main force of scholarship moved with the Jews, who were relocating to Egypt, North Africa, and western Europe, particularly Spain, where an age of acculturation was beginning because of Islam's toleration of Christians and Jews. Jewish doctors, poets, and scholars were welcomed by the Muslim caliphs into their courts to help spread knowledge. Jews became so influential that in some cases they were appointed viziers to the caliphs.

But this golden age began to crumble when Christians came to power and the Moorish provinces fell to them. Persecution followed persecution, and in 1492 Queen Isabella and King Ferdinand decreed that Jews must convert to Christianity within three months or leave Spain. This decree occurred the same year the Spanish royals financed Christopher Columbus's voyage to the New World, which was also designed to strengthen Christianity. Spanish rulers forbade Jews from going to the Americas, although these areas ultimately offered freedom for those persecuted in Europe and the Middle East.

	POLITICS & POWER	GEOGRAPHY & ENVIRONMENT	CULTURE & RELIGION
THE AMERICAS	**ca 1050 More than 5,000 Anasazi settlers** inhabit Chaco Canyon in modern-day New Mexico. **1050 Mixtec kings** intermarry with Zapotec monarchs to continue the accomplishments of Monte Albán IV.		**ca 1030 Mandan women** belong to the Goose Society and hold special religious prominence because of their role in maintaining the cornfields. Led by a corn priest, the women celebrate corn in religious rituals. The women make offerings to the geese, which fly to the Old Woman Who Never Dies. Only upon the return of the geese from their annual migration do the Mandan begin their planting cycles. **ca 1050 Toltec architecture** demonstrates a fearsome militant religion, with large snakes and warriors. Chacmools, large reclining human figures, hold sacrificial hearts.
EUROPE	**1031 Deposition of the last Umayyad caliph,** Hisham III, ends the caliphate of Córdoba. **1040 King Duncan of Scotland** is murdered by MacBeth, who becomes king. **1043 Norman brothers William (Iron Arm) and Drogo de Hauteville** come to power in Apulia, southern Italy. **1045 El Cid** (Rodrigo Díaz) is proclaimed a national hero in Spain. **1050 Normans** penetrate into England. **1053 Henry IV** is elected and crowned Holy Roman emperor after father, Henry III, dies.	**1033 Castile** becomes a separate kingdom. **1050 Geographer Adam of Bremen** believes Baltic Sea to be an ocean opening to the east.	**1050 The oldest Russian monasteries** are erected in Kiev. **1050 Musical notes** are given time values. **1052 Edward the Confessor** begins building Westminster Abbey in London. **1054 The schism** between Roman and Eastern churches becomes permanent. **1059 Pope Nicholas II** decrees that future popes must be elected by cardinals.
MIDDLE EAST & AFRICA	**1040 Seljuk Turks** defeat Ghaznavids in Persia, then move westward toward Baghdad. **1047 Abu Sa'd al-Tustail,** Jewish courtier and former master of the Sudanese slave girl who became regent of Egypt, is assassinated because of his relationship with her. **1052 Seljuks seize Isfahan** in Persia. **1055 The Seljuk Tughril-Beg** restores the Sunni branch of Islam over the Shiites and installs himself as temporal master of the caliph in Baghdad. **1056-1147 The Almoravid dynasty** in North Africa and Spain reestablishes Sunni orthodoxy.	**1033 A severe earthquake** occurs in Palestine. **1046 Nasir-i Khusraw,** Shiite author and traveler, visits Egypt. **ca 1050 Arab nomads** (Banu Hilal) move into the Sahara and North Africa in large numbers.	**ca 1050 Hilal al-Sabi** writes *Rules of the Caliphal Courts,* and al-Mawardi writes *The Ordinances of Government* to reassert the position of the caliph as the Bayids weaken. Al-Mawardi's work becomes the basis for all further discussion of the caliphate. **1057 Hananel be Hushiel of Tunisia,** who wrote the first Talmud commentary, dies. **1058 Abu al-Ala al-Ma'arri,** the last great poet of the classical Arab tradition, dies.
ASIA & OCEANIA	**1030 On the death of Mahmud,** son Masud blinds his brother Mohammed and seizes the throne in Afghanistan. His empire reaches from Persia to the valley of the Ganges. **1038 The Kingdom of Tangut** is founded in Xi Xia, China. **1040 Seljuk Turks** defeat the Ghaznavid ruler Masud, who returns to Ghazni and is murdered. His brother Mohammed succeeds him.	**ca 1000 Early-ripening rice** is introduced from the Hindu Kingdom of Champa in southeast Asia.	**1050 Japanese sculptor Jocho** starts his school.

WHAT LIFE WAS LIKE

At a Medieval Trade Fair

Once a year in medieval Europe an annual trade fair brought merchants together from far and near to buy and sell goods outside a town's walls. A festive atmosphere reigned as clowns, acrobats, jugglers, and musicians strolled among the throngs, performing their arts as fascinated children looked on. Parents were involved in bargaining for a variety of goods, ranging from local wares to exotic silks and spices brought all the way from China. In addition, one might find stalls full of Russian furs, Italian glass, French wines, or Bruges lace, each to be haggled over before a final price was agreed upon. Monarchs supported such occasions to profit from tolls levied on the products, as well as to foster trade and to raise money for the town's cathedral, which could take hundreds of years to build.

SCIENCE & TECHNOLOGY	PEOPLE & SOCIETY
ca 1050 As with the Teotihuacan, the Toltec use obsidian as an economic mainstay. It is used for knives, darts, clubs, and decorative votive objects.	**ca 1050 Central Mexican groups** such as the Chontal Maya, Putun, and Toltec invade Maya settlements and influence Maya culture.

1040 Petrocellus of Italy writes *Practica,* an important early medical work.

1050 The astrolabe arrives in Europe from eastern countries.

1050 The harp is brought to Europe.

1050 Building of Exeter and Winchester Cathedrals begins in England, and Hagia Sophia is under construction in Novgorod.

1058 Building of Parma Cathedral in Italy begins.

1059 Bonn Cathedral is begun.

1050 English monks excel in embroidery.

1054 Commercial relations between Italy and Egypt are expanded.

1037 Ibn Sina, medical scientist and philosopher, dies.

1039 Ibn al-Haytham, astronomer and optical scientist, dies.

1048 Al-Biruni, historian and mathematician, dies.

ca 1040 Bi Sheng invents movable type in China.

1050 Jain temples at Mount Abu, India, are built.

1053 The Phoenix Hall is built near Kyoto, Japan.

WHEN THE MOORS RULED SPAIN

L anding at Gibraltar in 711, nomadic Muslims from North Africa invaded the Iberian Peninsula and began their conquest of Spain. Chiefly of Arab and Berber stock, the Moors penetrated all the way to Poitiers, France, before being stopped by Charles Martel in 732. For more than 700 years they would rule Spain to varying degrees, leaving a permanent impression on Spanish culture.

The Moors, whose name probably derives from the Latin "Mauri," the old Roman word for the Berbers of Mauritania (present-day Morocco), made themselves at home in the warm Andalusian countryside, establishing Islamic caliphates throughout the region. Their artistic influence is evident in Spain's mosques and palaces with their bright colors and arabesques. Flamenco music, though considered Spanish, contains the rhythm of medieval Muslim minstrels. And it is said that Arabic poetry inspired European troubadours. By the 12th century, Moorish Spain was a great center of learning where Muslims, Christians, and Jews mingled in study, attracting students from all over Europe.

Little by little, though, Christians retook the region, beginning with Alfonso VIII of Castile, when he drove the Muslims from central Spain in 1212. In 1492 Ferdinand and Isabella finally crushed the Moors' last stronghold in Granada, entering perhaps the most beautiful Moorish edifice of all, the Alhambra, and proclaiming victory.

El Patio de los Arrayanes in the Moorish palace of the Alhambra in Granada, Spain

POLITICS & POWER	GEOGRAPHY & ENVIRONMENT	CULTURE & RELIGION

THE AMERICAS

ca 1097 The Mixtec king, lord of Tilantongo, conquers 75 cities, including Monte Albán, to establish Mixtec power.

EUROPE

1066 William of Normandy (the Conqueror) defeats King Harold II at the Battle of Hastings and becomes king of England. Harold is killed.

1071 Norman Robert Guiscard takes Bari at the end of a three-year siege, bringing Byzantine rule in southern Italy to an end after five centuries.

1094 El Cid takes Valencia from the Moors.

1096 The First Crusade begins, led by Godfrey of Bouillon, Duke of Lorraine, and Tancred, Robert Guiscard's nephew.

1097 Alfonso VI of Leon presents son-in-law Henry of Chalon the land between the Tagus and Minho Rivers as a hereditary county known as Portugal.

1060 The Byzantine mosaic *Christ As Ruler of the World* is completed at Daphni, Greece.

1065 Westminster Abbey is consecrated.

1066 Norman (Romanesque) architecture arrives.

1067 The Bayeux Tapestry is begun in France.

1094 The Basilica of St. Mark is consecrated in Venice.

WHAT LIFE WAS LIKE

Hunting Buffalo on Foot

Before the Europeans came to America and brought with them horses, buffalo hunting on the plains required ingenuity. In winter a man might stalk Buffalo wearing snow shoes, while in other seasons he would sometimes sneak up on them covered in a wolf skin. But the greatest yield occurred when a group of Indians caused a controlled stampede, whereby they channeled a herd toward a cliff, and the bison either died from the fall or were killed by waiting hunters. The Indians built lines of stone cairns that helped guide the bison toward a bottleneck, until at a precise moment people leapt out from their hiding places to begin the stampede. An ideal height for a cliff was one that was tall enough to cause damage to the beasts without crushing them to pieces. And the wind had to be blowing away from the hunters, as buffalo make up for their poor eyesight with a keen sense of smell.

MIDDLE EAST & AFRICA

1071 Byzantines are defeated by Seljuk Turks in Asia Minor at Manzikert.

1071 Turks take Jerusalem.

1075 Seljuks take Syria and Palestine.

1090 The Isma'ili Assassin stronghold is established in Alamut.

1092 The Islamic sect called Assassins kill Seljuk vizier Nizam al-Mulk. The Seljuk realm begins to divide.

1098 Byzantines reconquer Smyrna, Ephesus and Sardis.

1099 Crusaders take Jerusalem.

ca 1060 Seljuks restore irrigation works in Mesopotamia, only to see them destroyed again by the Mongol invasions.

1062 Marrakech is founded by Almoravids.

1069 Yusuf writes *Wisdom of Royal Glory* for Karakhanids. It is the first major literary work in Turkish.

1076 King Hummay of Kanem converts to Islam and promotes literacy and education. He later dies on a pilgrimage to Mecca.

ASIA & OCEANIA

ca 1070 Prime Minister Wan Anshi institutes new policies to control economy and government bureaucracy in Song China.

1085 Sima Guang presents to the throne his *Comprehensive Mirror for Aid in Government,* a history of China up to 959.

1086 The "cloistered emperor" system in Japan marks the decline of powerful Fujiwara family.

Ananda Pagoda in Pagan, Burma, built in 1091

SCIENCE & TECHNOLOGY	PEOPLE & SOCIETY
ca 1085 Thule Eskimo culture spreads across the North American Arctic to Greenland and Siberia. They develop basic technologies for making kayaks and whale boats that surpass those of existing Arctic peoples.	**1000s North American Plains Indians** use collapsible tepees and sleighlike travois to break camp easily and follow the buffalo.
	1000s Eastern North American Woodland Indians, who live by hunting, dwell in small camps of about 20 people, since wildlife in that area will not support great numbers of people.
	1000s North American Indian women do the heavy work while men rest between hunts. When they get too old to work, women go willingly alone into the woods to die.
	1073 Pueblo ruins at Mesa Verde exist in southwestern Colorado.
1063 Pisa Cathedral is begun.	**1000s Walled towns** are built with houses close together for defense purposes as well as to break the force of the wind.
1070 York Cathedral is begun.	
1072 St. Etienne and La Trinitei are built in Caen.	**1066 The prestige of the English language** is diminished by the Norman invasion.
1075 St. James Cathedral and Santiago de Compostela are completed.	**1086 Compilation of the *Domesday Book*** (a survey for tax assessment) is completed in England.
1078 The Tower of London is begun.	
1080 The Toledan table of the positions of stars is written.	**1094 The first gondolas** are recorded in Venice.
1098 Nicholas Prevost of Tours writes *Antidotarum,* a collection of 2,650 medical prescriptions from Salerno.	
1065 The Nizamiyah Madrash, first great school for Muslim *ulama* (learned men) is established.	**1090 The Assassins** are a secret order of the Isma'ili sect of Islam, who hold blind obedience to their spiritual leader and are known for their use of murder to eliminate foes. The Arab translation of "assassin" is "user of hashish," which they were given in their strongholds to spur them on to conquest.
1071 Constantine the African brings Greek medicine to Western world.	
	ca 1090 Nizam al-Mulk writes *Siyasdname (Book of Government),* the most famous work of the "mirror for princes" genre in Middle Eastern literature. The next most popular are the *Qabusname* by Kaika'as and the counsel for kings by al-Ghazali, written around the same time.
1086 Shen Gua, a Song Chinese polymath, completes *Dream Pool Essays,* a collection of scientific observations.	
1088 A mechanical celestial clock is constructed by Su Song at Kaifeng.	
1091 Building is underway for some 15,000 pagodas, temples, and palaces in Pagan, Burma, 5,000 of which still stand today.	

WILLIAM THE CONQUEROR

From humble beginnings in Falaise as the illegitimate son of Duke Robert I, William became duke of Normandy at age seven upon his father's death. Accustomed to the violence of the troubled times in which he developed into a tall, strong man, William quickly found success as a warrior and a baronial leader in France, and soon turned his attention toward tumultuous England.

When William visited Edward the Confessor's court, Edward supposedly named him as his heir. Upon the king's death, however, the Witan, or governing body of England, named Harold as successor, a decision they would soon regret. After building a fleet, assembling

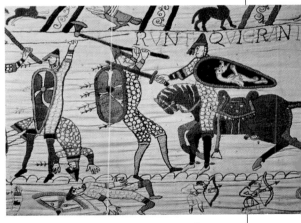

William the Conqueror (on horseback) killing King Harold during the Battle of Hastings in this detail from the Bayeux Tapestry

an army, and gaining the pope's permission to attack, William was ready to seize his inheritance. On October 14, 1066, William's troops met Harold's at Hastings near England's southern shore, defeating Harold's foot soldiers with a strong cavalry.

A victorious William rode to London, took the city, and had himself crowned King William I at Westminster Abbey on Christmas Day of 1066. He introduced Norman feudalism to the English, which enabled him to bring the country under his control via a monarchy that would last for centuries.

	POLITICS & POWER	GEOGRAPHY & ENVIRONMENT	CULTURE & RELIGION
THE AMERICAS	**ca 1100 The Anasazi** site at Pueblo Bonito reaches its height in the valley of modern-day New Mexico's Chaco Canyon. **ca 1100 The Cahokia Indian** settlement of the Mississippian culture is the leading metropolis north of Mexico, with some 10,000 people. **1125 Civil strife** begins in Tula, capital city of the Toltec.	**ca 1100 Cenotes,** deep sinkholes in lowland Yucatán, are used for sacrifices near monument sites.	**ca 1100 The Hohokam Indians** create decorative incised items from cockleshells imported from the California coast.
EUROPE	**1106 King Henry** of England defeats brother Robert at Tinchebrai and reunites England and Normandy, divided since the death of William I. **1126 Alfonso** of Aragon and Navarre raids as far as Granada in Spain. **1128 Geoffrey V** of Anjou, known as Plantagenet, marries Matilda, daughter of King Henry of England and widow of Emperor Henry V. **1128 Hungarian Magyars** are defeated by Byzantine Emperor John II on the Danube near Haram.		**1100** *Chanson de Roland* is written. **1100 Secular music** appears and the polyphonic style of music develops. **1110 The earliest record** of a miracle play appears at Dunstable, England. **1122 The Concordat of Worms** in Germany settles the question of investiture. **1123 First Lateran Council** suppresses simony and marriage for priests. **1125 Troubadour** and trouvère music begin in France.
MIDDLE EAST & AFRICA	**1100 The crusaders** massacre Jewish defenders of Haifa (Hefa). **1104 Turks** defeat crusaders at Harran. **1118 The Order of the Knights Templar** is created to protect the road to Jerusalem. **1123 An Egyptian fleet** is defeated off Ascalon by a Venetian crusader fleet. **1123-24 Byzantine Emperor John II** defeats the Serbs and the Hungarians. **1125 Almohads** seize Morocco after the death of Ibn Tumart, a preacher who was proclaimed the Mahdi (Messiah).		**ca 1100 More than 200 spas** dot the Seljuk Empire, where the faithful perform daily ritual ablutions and bathe weekly. **1111 Al-Ghazali,** scholar and mystic, dies. He reconciled mysticism with Islamic orthodoxy. **1122 Al-Hariri,** who perfected the prose form of the story in his *maqamat,* dies. **ca 1122 Omar Khayyam,** Persian poet and astronomer, dies. He is best known as a poet for his *Rubaiyat,* a collection of quatrains in which the first, second, and fourth lines rhyme. It is later famously translated into English by Edward FitzGerald.
ASIA & OCEANIA	**1108 Taira and Minamoto clans** chastise the *sobei,* warrior monks of the Enryakuji temple on Mount Hiei near Kyoto. **1115 The Jurchen** from Manchuria, allied with the Song, overthrow the Khitan Liao and found the Jin dynasty.	**ca 1100 Two-way voyaging** between Hawaii and Tahiti begins.	**1100 Jayadeva** writes *Gitagovinda,* an Indian love poem. **1100 Krishnamisra** writes *Prahodha-Chandrodaya,* an Indian allegorical play. **ca 1119 *Okagami,*** or *The Great Mirror,* a history of the Fujiwara family in power at the Heian court between 860 and 1025, is completed by unknown author.

CONNECTIONS

Spices and Spoilage

Because preservation of food in medieval Europe relied on nothing more than a larder, or storage bin, which usually served only to keep vermin away, herbs and spices were used to enhance or even hide the flavor of some foodstuffs. Meat, in particular, which was liable to rot before it could be eaten, improved with the addition of pepper, nutmeg, and other exotic spices imported from the East, some actually helping to preserve it. Other dishes benefited from local herbs, such as thyme and rosemary from the kitchen garden and plentiful supplies of garlic, salt, and mustard. Sugar, though, was scarce and kept locked up in cone form. Returning crusaders brought it back from the Middle East, along with lemons and melons. Fish was a popular dish, as it was often eaten in observance of church rules on various holy days and every Friday.

SCIENCE & TECHNOLOGY	PEOPLE & SOCIETY
	1100 The **Sinchi Roca culture** exists in Peru.
	1100 The **Third Pueblo Period** occurs in south-western North America.
	1116 The **Aztec,** according to legend, leave mythical Aztlan of northern Mexico and begin migrating toward central Mexico.
1100 Gothic architecture appears.	ca **1100 Motte and bailey wooden castles** are built by the Normans.
1100 St. Germain-des-Pres is built in Paris.	ca **1100 Bridges** are early centers of commerce.
1100 The baptistry at Florence is erected.	
1113 St. Nicholas of Novgorod is founded, one of earliest onion-domed churches.	**1100 The dialect** of the Île-de-France becomes the dominant idiom there.
1123 St. Bartholomew's Hospital is founded in London.	**1100 Middle English** supersedes Old English.
1125 Alexander Neckam of England writes *De utensilibus,* the earliest account of a mariner's compass.	**1124 The first Scottish coinage** is made.
1100 Islamic science begins to decline.	
ca **1110 Abraham ibn David** of Toledo writes on astronomy and the measurement of celestial bodies and translates books from Arabic into Latin in all scientific fields, including magic, astrology, philosophy, and medicine.	
ca **1100 Easter Island natives** begin building their massive stone monuments.	ca **1100 Hula dancing** and new deities are introduced from Tahiti to Hawaii.
ca **1125 The Rainbow Bridge** is portrayed in the Song Chinese painting, *Spring Festival Along the River.*	ca **1100 Cambodia's aristocracy** often travel by palanquin, carried by palace servants and protected from the sun by an ornate canopy.
	1100 New clans ruled by chiefs of royal birth are introduced from Tahiti to Hawaii.

THE AGE OF CHIVALRY

Though knights existed before the Crusades, these holy wars led to the founding of the first official orders of chivalry, the Hospitalers and the Templars, both pledged to support Christianity's efforts in the Middle East. In France knights were one of the Three Estates, dedicated to the protection of the church and the common man. For assuming the risks of chivalry, knights were rewarded with lordly status and land and the privilege they brought.

The concept of chivalry developed into a code of ideal behavior that offered a sense of certainty in a chaotic and violent period of history. Training for young men born into the class began early and was strenuous. One might be born for knighthood, but one still had to publicly prove one's skills before being anointed. This meant mastering such martial skills as hunting, sword fighting, jousting, wrestling, and falconry.

As a squire, or knight in waiting, a young man was taught to care for his own knight's weapons and spare horse, serve as his valet, help him on with his armor, and attend him at table. After the apprenticeship, the squire was presented with sword, spurs, helmet, and shield. He knelt before his sponsor, who tapped him on each shoulder with a sword, thereby bestowing upon him his well-earned knighthood.

The word *chivalry* itself conjures up mounted men-at-arms, knightly skills, and gallant gentlemen who valued such traits as honor, bravery, and mercy as part of their Christian code. In practice, the code was often neglected, and as the centuries passed, many of the knightly displays became largely ceremonial, another form of showy aristocracy.

What is the function of orderly knighthood? . . . If needs must, to lay down your life.

JOHN OF SALISBURY,
12TH-CENTURY PHILOSOPHER

	POLITICS & POWER	GEOGRAPHY & ENVIRONMENT	CULTURE & RELIGION
THE AMERICAS	**ca 1150 The Chimu Empire** in coastal Peru begins to expand and flourish. **1151 The Toltec Empire** in Mexico draws to an end.	**ca 1150 Chimu civilization** expands from north to south, 625 miles along the coast, and signals the return of coastal Peruvian civilization after a hiatus of 500 years. **ca 1150 A dry Peruvian coastal climate** requires elaborate irrigation systems to support Chimu civilization.	**ca 1150 The Mixtec** perfect the high style of pictographic writing. Many sacred books commemorate Mixtec rulers; eight of these books survive.
EUROPE	**1138 Conrad III** of Hohenstaufen succeeds Lothar III as Holy Roman Emperor. Civil war ensues when he seizes Saxony and Bavaria. **1145 The Second Crusade** begins. **1152 Frederick Barbarossa** (Red Beard) is chosen emperor upon his uncle Conrad III's death and unites the factions that emerged after the death of Henry V. **1152 Eleanor of Aquitaine** divorces King Louis of France and marries the much younger King Henry II of England. **1154 Thomas à Becket** becomes Henry II's chancellor.	 *A later, romanticized view of the monk Abelard reading to his lover, the nun Héloise*	**1136 Peter Abelard** writes *Historia calamitatum mearum,* a description of his love affair with Héloise. **1149 Oxford University** is founded. **1150 *The Black Book of Carmarthen,*** the oldest Welsh manuscript, is written. **1152 Anna Comnena** writes *Alexiad,* a history of Byzantium. **1155 The Carmelite Order** is founded **1157 Kurenberg** is the first famous German minnesinger.
MIDDLE EAST & AFRICA	**1132 Almoravid Abd al-Mu'min** is recognized as caliph in North Africa. **1144 Seljuk Turk Naral-Din Zangi** (Atabeg of Mosul) takes the city of Edessa and pursues jihad against crusaders with similar ideals. **1147 Marrakech,** capital of the Almoravid Empire, falls to Almohads under Abd al-Mu'min. **1147 The Second Crusade** fails when crusaders perish in Asia Minor. **1159 Arabs** retake lands in Tunisia conquered by Roger of Sicily.		**1139 Judah Halevy** publishes *The Kuzari.* **ca 1140 Almohads** institute forced conversions of Jews in North Africa. **1154 Mohammed al-Idrisi** publishes *Geography.*
ASIA & OCEANIA	**1150 The city of Ghazni** in Afghanistan is destroyed by the rulers of Ghur. **1151 The Golden Age of Buddhist art** arrives in Burma. **1152 Alauddin of Ghur** sacks Ghazni and expels the last Ghaznavid ruler, thus bringing that empire in Afghanistan to an end after little more than a century. **1156 Taira and Minamoto clans** go to war in Japan.		**1145** Confucian scholar Kim Pusik compiles *Samguk Sagi.* *Larger-than-life Buddha inside an ancient temple in Pagan, Burma*

SCIENCE & TECHNOLOGY	PEOPLE & SOCIETY
ca 1150 **Mixtecs** are among the first peoples in Mesoamerica to master the art of metallurgy, crafting excellent gold jewelry.	
1134 The western facade of Chartres Cathedral is built. **1146** *Antidotarium Niclai,* a treatise on drugs, is written. **1147 Lisbon Cathedral** is built. **1150 Medical faculty** starts teaching at Bologna University. **1150 Arabs in Spain** manufacture paper.	**1132 Henry I** of France grants charters for corporate towns protecting industry and commerce. **1133 St. Bartholomew's Fair** takes place at Smithfield, London. **1151 The first fire and plague insurance** is offered, in Iceland. **1151 The game of chess** comes to England. **1158 Munich** becomes center of salt trade.
1150 The temple of Angkor Wat in Cambodia is completed by Khmer king Suryavarman II as both a Hindu religious complex and his burial site. It is one of the largest religious complexes in the world and a premier example of ancient Khmer architecture. **1151 The Chinese** use explosives in warfare.	**1132 Li Qingzhao,** a female poet, writes a famous memoir of her married life.

THE INVENTION OF GUNPOWDER

Legend has it that a Chinese scientist accidentally invented gunpowder while trying to create a potion that would ensure immortality. True or not, this explosive mixture has achieved immortality in its own right. The first mention of a gunpowder formula citing proportions of ingredients is found in a Song dynasty military manual dating to 1044. Alchemists attempting to negate the activity of sulfur by mixing it with saltpeter and other ingredients containing carbon had discovered a new fire compound they called *huoyao.* The nature of the mixture was so violent that the Song manual cautioned against attempting to make it.

Little more than a hundred years later the Chinese were experimenting with gunpowder in warfare, and by 1232 they were using large gunpowder flamethrowers to fight the Mongols at the siege of Kaifeng. These lethal explosives dashed the legend that the Chinese used their new propellant only for fireworks. Later, rockets were launched from huge batteries of racks. But bombs and guns needed a higher nitrate mix, and the Chinese succeeded in perfecting the mix, now known as black powder, by reducing the proportion of saltpeter used in the formula.

The first record of a Chinese cannon dates from 1288, though a carving from a Sichuan cave temple built in 1128 appears to depict a cannon in action. The Chinese apparently had cannons as much as two centuries before Europeans, who probably learned of the new weapons from Muslim traders. Soon the ability to cast cannons in one-piece metal tubes made them strong enough to fire 800-pound balls, making them the main weapon of siege warfare throughout Europe by the 15th century.

Gunpowder remained the only explosive in wide use until the middle of the 19th century, when nitroglycerine-based explosives proved to be more efficiently destructive.

THE GLORY OF ANGKOR

LOCATED AT THE NORTHERN END OF THE GREAT LAKE, OR TONLE SAP, IN MODERN-day Cambodia, Angkor reigned as the chosen site of Khmer capitals from the ninth to the 15th century. The ancient city covered an estimated area of more than 300,000 miles, stretching across vast areas of forest and plain, and at its height was home to more than 750,000 people. Here Khmer kings erected some of the world's most spectacular temple complexes, some devoted to Hinduism, others reflecting the kingdom's conversion to Buddhism. The principal complex is Angkor Wat (City Temple), but more than 70 other temples also grace the area.

Angkor Wat was the vision of King Suryavarman II, who ruled in the early 12th century and wanted a glorious temple and administrative center for his empire. A full square mile in size, it is perhaps the largest religious structure in the world and is designed to represent the structure of the Hindu cosmos. The outer gate is protected by a moat, suggesting the oceans at the edge of the world. Inside, exquisitely carved bas-reliefs tell the stories of Krishna, Vishnu, and Rama, as well as stories of the Khmer kings. Visitors pass through a rising series of towered galleries and courtyards that lead to the main temple and its central tower, which is shaped like a lotus blossom. The difficulty in reaching this ultimate sanctuary reflects the difficulty in reaching the kingdom of the gods.

Despite this glorious dedication to the Hindu gods, Angkor was sacked by the rival Cham people in 1177, causing the next Khmer king, Jayavarman VII, to look elsewhere for divine protection. He dedicated his own temple complex, Angkor Thom, to Buddhism, and converted Angkor Wat to a Buddhist shrine, replacing many of the Hindu statues. The king's imprint is inescapable here: The central tower of Angkor Thom displays a giant image of Buddha; 50 smaller towers surrounding the complex, however, each feature multiple images of the king as a Buddhist god. As part of a massive building campaign, Jayavarman also built Ta Prohm (left) as a Buddhist monastery and university. Subsequent rulers continued to expand Ta Prohm through the 13th century. The site has become the most popular attraction for visitors because of its picturesque merging with surrounding forest.

Ultimately, Buddhism also couldn't protect Angkor, which was raided and sacked by the Siamese in the 15th century. The Khmer moved their capital to Phnom Penh, where it would remain. Most of Angkor was abandoned, left to be swallowed by the jungle, except for Angkor Wat, which was conserved as a Buddhist shrine by monks who trimmed the vegetation and made repairs. The French, upon colonizing Indochina in the 19th century, rediscovered the "lost city" of Angkor and began the effort to restore this marvelous legacy of the ancient Khmer.

The roots of a strangler fig tree creep over temple walls at Ta Prohm in Cambodia, one of the many magnificent temple complexes built throughout Angkor by Khmer kings.

	POLITICS & POWER	GEOGRAPHY & ENVIRONMENT	CULTURE & RELIGION
THE AMERICAS	**ca 1175 Toltec power** ends as Tula falls.	**ca 1175 Climatic change** leads to a crisis in the irrigation systems that had supported peoples in northern Mexico since the Classic Era. Power shifts south to the Valley of Mexico.	
EUROPE	**1170 Thomas à Becket** is murdered at Canterbury Cathedral by Norman knights. **1176 Emperor Frederick Barbarossa** is defeated by Italy's Lombard League. **1189 King Henry II** of England dies and is succeeded by Richard I (Coeur de Lion, or Lion-Hearted). **1191 Henry VI,** son of Frederick Barbarossa, is crowned emperor in Rome by Pope Celestine III. **1199 Richard I** is killed at a siege in France and succeeded by King John, the youngest son of Henry II and Eleanor of Aquitaine.	**ca 1160 English fens** are drained for farmland. **ca 1160 German peasants** migrate eastward and found new villages. **1177 Belfast, Ireland,** is founded.	**1160** Celtic epic *Tristan et Iseult* is written. **1170 Pope Alexander III** issues rules for the canonization of saints. **1170 Chrétien de Troyes** writes *Lancelot,* a romance of courtly love. **1176 Walter Map** compiles the Arthurian legends in their current form. **1182 Jews** are banished from France. **1194** *The Elder Edda,* a collection of Scandinavian mythology, is written.
MIDDLE EAST & AFRICA	**1169 Saladin** becomes vizier of the Fatimid caliphate of Cairo. He abolishes the caliphate and re-establishes Sunnism. **1183 Saladin** conquers Syria and becomes sultan. **1187 Saladin** reconquers Jerusalem, provoking the Third Crusade and setting up his battle with Richard I. **1191 Richard I** defeats Saladin's forces at Acre, but Saladin ultimately holds Jerusalem. **1193 Saladin's death** at Damascus sets off a civil war among his heirs.	**1194 The death of the last Seljuk ruler** of Iraq splinters the kingdom.	**ca 1160 Seljuk arts** emphasize the human form and use it to symbolize ideas and abstractions, rather than emotions; it is closely tied to poetry and poetic symbolism. **1166 Saladin** builds Cairo Cathedral. **1180 Moses Maimonides,** the foremost intellectual figure of medieval Judaism, completes Mishnah Torah, his great law code. **1190 Maimonides** completes *Guide of the Perplexed.* **1198 Jews in Yemen** are forced to convert to Islam.
ASIA & OCEANIA	**1185 The Punjab** in India is conquered by Mohammed of Ghur. **1185 Minamoto Yoritomo** annihilates the Tairas and sets up a military government at Kamakura in Japan. **1189 Minamoto no Yoshitsune** commits suicide, along with family and partisans, after being attacked by brother Yoritomo. **1192 Mohammed** of Ghur takes Delhi and installs Qutb-ud-Aybak as first Muslim ruler. **1192 Minamoto Yoritomo** is awarded the supreme title of *seitaishogun.*	**1177 King Jayavarman VII** relocates the Khmer capital from Angkor Wat to Angkor Thom after the Cham invasion. Unlike Angkor Wat, which was dedicated to the Hindu gods, the Angkor Thom complex reflects the king's conversion to Buddhism.	**1192 China's greatest segmental arch bridge** is built near Beijing and comes to be known as the Marco Polo Bridge because Polo writes about it during his travels in China.

Saladin, founder of the Ayyubid dynasty and Muslim hero

THE LION AND THE SULTAN

The Third Crusade brought into confrontation the two most legendary soldiers of these holy wars: England's Richard I (Richard the Lion-Hearted) and Saladin, founder of the Muslim Ayyubid dynasty. Saladin was a scourge to the crusaders, having vanquished them and captured Jerusalem in 1187, ending 88 years of Christian control. The goal of the Third Crusade, charged to Richard, was to win Jerusalem back.

Both men were born into families of power, well educated, and dedicated to spreading their respective faiths. Richard, who was the son of Henry II and Eleanor of Aquitaine, spent only six months of his reign in England. For most of his life he was defending his mother's territories in France, and he spoke French rather than English. Saladin, son of prominent Mesopotamian Kurds, rose to power in a Muslim world fractured by clannish dissension. Given the title of king but known as the sultan, he united Syria, Mesopotamia, Palestine, and Egypt into a spiritual and military force through a combination of diplomacy and military skill.

The talent marshaled by Christendom to recapture Jerusalem only enhanced Saladin's reputation. In addition to Richard, Phillip II of France and Holy Roman Emperor Frederick Barbarossa took part in the Third Crusade. But it was Richard's military genius that was the true threat. His crusaders defeated Saladin's forces on the Levantine coast, taking the city of Acre in 1191. From there he defeated Saladin at Arsuf, giving him control of Jaffa. But Saladin held onto Jerusalem, denying Richard the ultimate prize.

Although Richard and Saladin never actually met each other, each earned the other's admiration as soldiers of the first order. Saladin succumbed to illness in 1193 in Damascus; Richard died as a result of an arrow wound in 1199 while fighting in France.

ca 1160 **Hildegard of Bingen** writes *Causa et Curae,* a medical treatise.

1163 **Notre Dame Cathedral** in Paris is begun.

1174 **The Campanile** (Leaning Tower) of Pisa is constructed.

1194 **The present Chartres Cathedral** is erected.

1199 **Siena Cathedral** is begun.

1100s **Annual trade fairs** are held just outside town walls and last for days. Money is raised here to build cathedrals.

1100s **Wives and servants** often take food to be cooked at the baker's (for example), since most houses do not have ovens.

1100s **As a result of the Crusades,** Persian and Turkish rugs are seen in English homes.

1180 **Glass windows** appear in English private homes.

Richard the Lion-Hearted leads crusaders in a battle against Muslims at Arsuf.

1100s **Seljuk soldiers,** and later Mamluk soldiers, are expected to play polo weekly in order to keep themselves in shape.

1100s **Persian craftsmen** create hand-woven carpets designed with birds, flowers, beasts, trees, fountains, and watercourses, representing a Persian garden, which to their imagination is like a walled paradise on earth.

1198 **Ibn Rushd (Averroes)** dies. His commentary on Aristotle is esteemed throughout Europe and the Muslim world.

1100s **Samurai** begin to dominate Japanese society.

1100s **A large variety of porcelain wares** are being produced for functional as well as decorative purposes in China.

ANCIENT CITIES IN STONE

I N THE AMERICAN SOUTHWEST THERE EXISTS A SWEEPING PANORAMA THAT WAS ONCE home to a progressive group of Indian peoples who came to be called the Anasazi, or "ancient ones." Known as the Four Corners region—where Colorado, New Mexico, Utah, and Arizona meet—canyons, mesas, plateaus, cliffs, and desert create a dramatic landscape where winters are harsh and where summers offer both dusty drought and violent thunderstorm.

It was into this unfriendly yet beautiful natural environment that the Anasazi chose to settle at the beginning of the Common Era. Around 1050 they began gathering in large pueblos, or towns, first in a valley called Chaco Canyon (located in present-day New Mexico), and then on the tableland of Mesa Verde to the north, in what is now Colorado. At Mesa Verde they began building elevated shelters for themselves in the cliffs, most likely for protection from the growing threat of Navajo and Apache invasion. The Anasazi were expert masons, using hand-cut stone building blocks and adobe mortar of exceptional quality to build these terraced apartment-like cliff dwellings, which seem to defy gravity as they cling together in huge crooks and crannies of the canyon walls. Rising as high as five stories, the cliff houses could only be entered by ladders that could easily be pushed away in case of attack. Ground-floor rooms had no doors or windows and were accessible only from within. The largest of these distinctive pueblos, the monumental Cliff Palace, contained about 200 separate residences with rooms of about 200 square feet each.

The Anasazi of the Pueblo period evolved from earlier nomadic tribes of the Basket Maker culture. They turned from basketmaking to building as they began to master dry farming, which allowed them to cultivate maize, squash, beans, and cotton in this arid landscape, and thus settle permanently. In addition to sophisticated irrigation systems, they built subterranean round storage facilities to store grain. These circular pits, or kivas, eventually were adapted for shelters and then gathering places for important ceremonies or communal activities, for which they are still used today. Kivas became the heart of growing pueblo communities, both symbolically and architecturally. At the Chaco Canyon site known as Pueblo Bonito, two great kivas and 37 smaller ones occupy the central courtyard of an enclosed urban site. Perhaps the largest of all the settlements of this period, Pueblo Bonito housed around 800 separate residences.

By the late 13th century, periods of severe drought, and possible internal conflict in these increasingly crowded towns, forced the Anasazi to abandon their sandstone palaces. Their skill in agriculture, as well as cotton weaving and pottery making, have passed to the current generations of Pueblo people, who still conduct ceremonies in the ancient kivas and look with pride on a rich society that went the way of the winds.

Cliff Palace at Mesa Verde, Colorado, is the largest of the Anasazi cliff dwellings.

POLITICS & POWER	GEOGRAPHY & ENVIRONMENT	CULTURE & RELIGION

THE AMERICAS

ca 1200 The Tarascan, or Purepecha, state is well established in its capital of Tzintzuntzan in western Mexico. It is powerful enough to resist all other postclassic empires.

ca 1200 The Tiahuanaco civilization in the Andes collapses and the Inca begin to rise. They refer to their kingdom as Tawantinsuyu, *The Land of the Four Quarters.*

ca 1200 Chichen Itza's dominance ends and Mayapan, a less distinguished city-state, rises for 200 years.

ca 1200 The city of Cuzco in Peru is founded by Inca leader Manco Capac, 11,000 feet above sea level.

ca 1200 The Anasazi settle at Betatakin in modern-day northeastern Arizona, and in Bandelier, in present-day north-central New Mexico.

ca 1200 Mixtecs, noted for their mosaic veneers, construct large and beautiful palace complexes at Mitla.

ca 1200 The Maya Dresden Codex contains astronomical information about the cycles of the planet Venus.

EUROPE

1202 The Fourth Crusade is led by Boniface of Montferrat.

1209 King John of England invades Scotland and is excommunicated.

1215 After the sealing of the Magna Carta at Runnymede, King John of England asks the pope to annul it.

1217 Duke Leopold VI of Austria leads the Fifth Crusade.

1228 Holy Roman Emperor Frederick II leads the Sixth Crusade.

1228 James of Aragon launches a major offensive against Moslems in Majorca.

1200 Paris evolves into a modern capital.

1204 Amsterdam, Holland (the Netherlands), is founded.

1221 Vienna becomes a city.

1200 Cambridge University is founded.

1200 Jewish Kabalistic philosophy develops in southern Europe.

1203 Wolfram von Eschenbach writes *Parzival,* a German epic poem.

1209 Francis of Assisi relates first rules of his brotherhood, the Franciscans.

1215 Dominic founds the Dominican Order, whose mission will be to convert heretics.

1221 The sonnet form develops in Italy.

MIDDLE EAST & AFRICA

1200 Al-Malik al-Adil, who becomes sultan of Egypt when his brother Saladin dies, restores unity in the Ayyubids' lands and annexes Mesopotamia.

1204 Crusaders seize Constantinople and replace the Byzantine Empire with Eastern Latin Empire. Byzantines move their empire to Nicaea in Anatolia.

1217 The Crusade against the Egyptian sultanate fails.

1225 Ethiopian emperor Lalibela dies after moving his capital from Axum to Lasta and overseeing the building of rock-hewn churches there.

ca 1200 The kings of Kanem around Lake Chad (Sudan) have been Muslim for more than a century and have built a hostel for their subjects studying at the university mosque of al-Azhar in Cairo. Shari'a law is upheld and a literate class is emerging.

ca 1200 Konya flourishes; it is the capital of Anatolia and home to poets and authors from all over the Muslim world.

1203 Nizami, Persian poet of the *Hamsah,* five romantic epics, dies.

WHAT LIFE WAS LIKE

The Way of Tea

Originally imported from China in the 12th century, tea has been a significant aspect of Japanese culture ever since. Monks made it a part of Zen Buddhist religious ceremony, and merchants, shoguns, and samurai made a ritual of tea drinking as an escape from their busy lives. A formal etiquette of preparing, serving, and drinking tea was developed, based on the virtues of simplicity, gratitude, and solitude. The Way of Tea (Chado) became, as one monk stated, "a religion of the art of life." Tea masters purified their utensils and offered their bitter green tea with modesty and reverence as a way to cleanse one's own thoughts of ego and desire. A form of meditation, the tea ceremony satisfied both the physical and the spiritual thirst.

ASIA & OCEANIA

1206 Qutb ud-Din Aybak founds a Muslim dynasty, the Slaves, in India.

1206 Genghis Khan becomes chief prince of the Mongols and conquers Turkistan (1208), Peking (1214), and Persia (1218).

1219 Hojos assume the government of Kamakura in Japan after the death of Sanetomo, the third Minamoto shogun.

1223 Mongols invade Russia but are repulsed in India.

1227 Genghis Khan dies and his empire is divided among his three sons.

1220 The first Thai kingdom of Sukhothai is established.

ca 1200 Islam begins to replace Indian religions.

ca 1200 Shamanistic Mongols allow the practice of alien religions, such as Islam and Buddhism, in their conquered lands.

ca 1200 The monk Eisai returns from China, transmitting Zen Buddhism and tea drinking to Japan.

1227 Japanese monk Dogen also transmits Zen Buddhism after returning from China.

SCIENCE & TECHNOLOGY	PEOPLE & SOCIETY
ca 1200 The Anasazi sun calendar divides the year into four quarters by marking the first day of each season with a particular pattern of sunlight shining on spirals inscribed on the side of Fajada Butte.	**ca 1200 As the Inca expand,** they resettle conquered peoples to the far reaches of the empire. In order to maintain imperial control, they place *mitmaq,* or colonies of their own people, in the foreign communities.
ca 1200 Anasazi weave yucca plants into sturdy sandals.	

JAIN TEMPLES: SANCTUARIES FOR THE NONVIOLENT

Founded by Mahavira in the sixth century B.C.E., Jainism is the name of a religious movement in India founded on the principal of ascetic self-denial. Monks and nuns dedicated their lives to cleansing the soul and embarked on a mendicant's life. By sweeping all living things away before them as they walked, wearing masks over their faces, and blocking their ears, they avoided destroying the souls of all things living, including rocks and other inanimate objects.

SCIENCE & TECHNOLOGY	PEOPLE & SOCIETY
1200 Early Gothic architecture begins in England.	**1200 Engagement rings** become fashionable.
1200 Duke Leopold VI of Austria builds his burg (castle) in Vienna	**1202 The first court jesters** appear at European courts.
1201 The facade of Notre Dame Cathedral in Paris is built.	**1212 Wooden and thatched roofs** are replaced with tiles in London houses.
1202 Leonardo Pisano Fibonacci introduces Arabic numerals in Europe.	**1218 Denmark** adopts Danneborg, the oldest national flag in the world.
1210 The original Reims cathedral burns. Construction of its replacement begins the next year.	**1225 Cotton** is manufactured in Spain.

The Jain conception of karma, more extreme than what Hindus believe, considers suicide the ultimate sacrifice. Mahavira himself fasted to death at the age of 72, and following his death, the Jain sect grew along caravan routes to the west and south. In their original northern climate near Mount Abu in modern Rajasthan, beautifully carved temples (below) were built as a symbol of their devotion.

The movement today, though less widely practiced, includes prosperous city lawyers and scholars, as well as mendicants, but prohibits farming, as the nature of the occupation requires the killing of living objects.

SCIENCE & TECHNOLOGY	PEOPLE & SOCIETY
ca 1200 Paramount chiefs or kings emerge in complex farming and trading societies among the Teke and Kongo.	**1200 Sixty thousand Italian merchants** reside in Constantinople.
ca 1200 Abdallah al-Ruml writes the Arab geographical encyclopedia, "Mu'jam ul-Buldan."	**1207 Caliph al-Nasir** unites men's chivalric clubs to bring the Muslim world together for defense purposes. He converts the head of the Assassins to Sunni Islam.
1205 Al-Jarzari compiles a compendium of automata.	
1209 Al-Razi, author of a compendium of sciences, dies.	

1200 Early stages of the construction of a massive palace at Nan Madol on the Pacific island of Pohnpei are undertaken.

1225 An 1,100-foot-long megalithic beam bridge is built near Viamen in Southeast China.

1227 Japanese potter Toshiro returns home after traveling for four years in China and begins to manufacture porcelain.

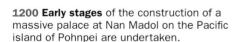
13th-century Jain Tejapala Temple at Mount Abu in Rajasthan, India

1230-1260

INVASIONS AND ADVANCES 1000-1500

	POLITICS & POWER	GEOGRAPHY & ENVIRONMENT	CULTURE & RELIGION
THE AMERICAS	ca **1250 Coastal Peru's civilization** revives in the Moche Valley. ca **1250 The Inca** settle into the small village of Cuzco in the southern Andes. ca **1250 The Aztec,** who call themselves Mexica, arrive in central Mexico.		
EUROPE	**1230 Ferdinand III** unites Castile and Leon. **1233 Pope Gregory IX** begins the Inquisition. **1237 Mongols** cross the Volga River, the boundary of Europe, eventually taking Moscow and conquering Russia. **1238 James of Aragon** reconquers Valencia from the Arabs. **1242 Batu,** grandson of Genghis Khan, establishes the Golden Horde at Sarai in Russia. **1248 Ferdinand III** takes Seville after a two-year siege, and most of its Muslim inhabitants flee to Granada.	**1230 Berlin** is founded on the site of former Slav settlements. **1240 The border** is established between England and Scotland. **1242 The town of Kiel** is founded in Germany. **1253 William of Rubruque** travels in Central Asia and reports adventures. **1255 Prague and Stockholm** are recognized as towns.	**1233 The Pope** entrusts the Dominicans with the Inquisition. **1240 Italian poet Guido Guinizelli** establishes a school of poetry called *dolce stil nuovo.* **1241 The Master of Naumburg** creates sculptures there and at Mainz and Meissen. **1250 The High Gothic period** in German art begins. **1252 The Inquisition** begins using torture instruments. **1255 Ulrich von Lichtenstein** writes *Frauendienst,* a poem about chivalry.
MIDDLE EAST & AFRICA	**1235 The Berber kingdom** of the Abd al-Wadids is founded at Tlemcen. **1230-1255 Sundiata Keita** seizes the major territories of the Sosso gold trade, including Ghana, and becomes the ruler of Mali. **1243 Mongols** conquer Seljuk Anatolia. **1250 Mamluks** take power in Egypt by assassinating the last Ayyubid caliph; Shajar al-Durr, slave concubine and ruler of Egypt, defeats Louis IX of France in the Fifth Crusade.	ca **1230 The Mongol rise** sets off migrations of Turks westward across Asia. ca **1250 The imperial expansion of Mali** produces a lucrative exchange of goods among three distinct ecological zones.	**1240 Ibn al-Arabi,** a Spanish Sufi mystic and cosmologist who believed in the "unity of being" and analyzed human nature as a microcosm of the natural and divine cosmos, dies. **1257 Sadi,** the Persian poet, writes *The Rose Garden.*
ASIA & OCEANIA	**1200s States** in the densely populated Pacific islands of Hawaii, Tahiti, and Tonga are formed. **1230 The Qutb Minar** is constructed in Delhi as a victory monument commemorating the Muslim conquest of northern India. **1234 Mongols** seize Kaifeng in China, completing the destruction of the Jin Empire.		**1250 Jain temple building** occurs at Mount Abu, India. **1250 Johannes Church** in Thorn (Torun) is built in northwest India.

CONNECTIONS

Chinese Living and Dead

Because the Chinese venerated their ancestors, each family had its own household religious hierarchy. The living needed the spiritual assistance of the dead so that they would be able to live a good life on earth; the dead required the devotion of their living descendants in order to nourish their souls in the afterlife. Death, therefore, signaled the start of a new kind of a relationship. Sons and daughters wore clothes made from uncomfortable sackcloth for 27 months after a parent's death. They were not allowed to use porcelain, have sexual relationships, eat meat, or shave. And every family breathed a sigh of relief when a son was born, since only individuals with sons could require devotion after their deaths.

SCIENCE & TECHNOLOGY	PEOPLE & SOCIETY
ca 1250 The Chimu perfect adobe construction of buildings. **ca 1250 Weaving** by the Chimu is perfected to 200 waft per inch, whereas European cloth seldom surpasses 80 waft per inch.	

Mask and horned helmet worn by elite Samurai—Osaka, Japan

1241 The Reims Cathedral's west facade is begun; it was finished around 1252. **1248 Cologne Cathedral** is begun. **1248 The Alhambra** in Granada is begun. **1250 A small portable organ** called a *portatio* is built. **1250 Jordanus Rufus** writes *De medicina equorum,* a veterinary manual. **1252 The Church of St. Francis of Assisi** is finished.	**1230 Leprosy** is brought to Europe by crusaders. **1233 Coal** is mined for the first time in Newcastle, England. **1250 An industrial and commercial boom** takes place in northern and central Italy. **1250 Hats** become fashionable. **1253 Linen** is first manufactured in England. **1258 The House of Commons** is established as part of the Provisions of Oxford.

THE WAY OF THE SAMURAI

By the 12th century an aristocratic class of warriors had begun to wield great power throughout Japan. For nearly 700 years samurai would continue to dominate Japanese society. Their original center, the military government of Minamoto Yoritomo, was located at the coastal town of Kamakura, near modern Tokyo. As power shifted from civil aristocracy to a new bureaucratic regime based on these provincial warriors, the samurai became famous for offering security through military prowess.

Somewhat like knights in medieval Europe, the samurai, who took orders from their lords, valued martial skills, with an emphasis on the ideals of bravery and austerity. In addition, they lived by a code that emphasized loyalty to their lords and honor in defeat. The honorable way to die was called seppuku, literally, "disembowelment," a ritual whereby the defeated warrior would commit suicide with his own sword.

These elite soldiers, wielding swords and wearing terrifying masks and horned helmets, won a number of battles through intimidation alone.

	ca 1250 The Mali Empire is taking tribute from its Mande core; the title of *mansa,* or king, is taken by the paramount ruler. **1256 Hulegu** founds the Mongol dynasty of Persia and in 1258 seizes Baghdad, overthrowing the caliphate.

The great path has no gates,

Thousands of roads enter it.

When one passes through this gateless gate

He walks freely between heaven and earth.

EKAI, CALLED MU-MON

	POLITICS & POWER	GEOGRAPHY & ENVIRONMENT	CULTURE & RELIGION
THE AMERICAS	**ca 1260 The Chimu civilization** reaches its height in coastal Peru's Moche Valley and expands up and down the coast. **ca 1260 The Aztec** live in the southwest quadrant of the Valley of Mexico, where they become over time valuable mercenaries for the city of Culhuacan, a city-state left over from the Toltec Empire. They are called "military maniacs" by the Culhua because of their ferocity in battle and the militaristic values of their culture.	**ca 1275 A series of droughts** hits the Mesa Verde pueblo in modern-day Colorado and lasts for 20 years, driving the Anasazi away.	
EUROPE	**1260 Florentine Ghibellines** defeat the Guelphs at Montaperti. **1271 Philip III,** King of France, unifies northern and southern France. **1283 The Teutonic Knights** finish conquering Prussia, which began in 1230. **1284 Genoans** destroy the Pisan navy at Meloria, becoming the rival of Venice. **1291 The Crusades** end. The Knights of St. John of Jerusalem settle in Cyprus. **1297 William Wallace** leads the Scots in a rebellion against the English.	**1295 Marco Polo** returns to Italy and begins to dictate his memoirs in a Genoese jail.	**1260 The first flagellant movements** appear in southern Germany and northern Italy. **1262 Adam de la Halle** writes *Le Jeu de la Feuillee,* the first French operetta. **1265 Franco of Cologne** and Pierre de la Croix develop the motet, a musical form. **1273 Thomas Aquinas** writes *Summa Theologica.* **1284 The Pied Piper of Hamelin** legend begins. **1295 Cimabue** creates *Madonna with St. Francis* at Assisi.
MIDDLE EAST & AFRICA	**1261 Michael VIII Palaeologus** regains Constantinople. **1262 The alliance** between Mamluks and Mongols of the Golden Horde is strengthened by cooperation of the Byzantines and Italian city-states. **1270 Yekuno Amlak** restores the Solomonic line and expands the Christian kingdom of Ethiopia against its Muslim neighbors. **1289 Qala'un,** Sultan of Egypt, captures Tripoli, leaving Acre the only major Christian stronghold remaining in the Near East. **1291 The Mamluks** seize Acre.		
ASIA & OCEANIA	**1279 Kublai Khan** overcomes the last Song resistance and reunites China under the Yuan dynasty. **1281 Mongols** try for a second time to invade Japan. **1287 Kublai Khan** sends expeditions to Burma. **1290 Kaikobad,** Sultan of Delhi, is murdered, then succeeded by Jala-ud-Din. **1296 Jala-ud-Din** of Delhi is murdered, then succeeded by Ala-ud-Din Khalji, who founds a dynasty and controls much of India.	*Worshippers at the rock-hewn church of San Giorgio in Lalibela, Ethiopia* **1271 Marco Polo** travels to China. In 1275 he is in the service of Kublai Kahn.	

SCIENCE & TECHNOLOGY	PEOPLE & SOCIETY
ca 1270 The Kayenta branch of the Anasazi build a 155-room dwelling named Kiet Sil in Tsegi Canyon, which is in modern-day northwestern Arizona.	**ca 1260 Hurons** develop trade relations with hunter-gatherers who live north of the Great Lake. They supply Hurons with meat and animal skins used for nutrition and clothing. **ca 1260 The Chimu** develop an intricate legal code.
1261 Thaddeus Florentinus teaches medicine at Bologna University. **1264 Roger Bacon** writes *De computo naturali.* **1266 Roger Bacon** writes *Opus maius.* **1275 William of Saliceto** writes *Chirurgia,* a record of early human dissection. **1296 Florence Cathedral** is begun.	**1200s Venice's Rialto bridge** is a bustling center of commerce. To forbid a merchant from trading there is sure bankruptcy for him. **1200s Jews,** known by their yellow hats, are prime moneylenders. **1200s The famous whores of Venice** are regulated by the state, which forbids them to have intercourse with Muslims and Jews. **1269 The first toll roads** are built in England. **1278 The first glass mirrors** are invented. **1290 Eyeglasses** are used in Europe.
1274 Al-Tusi, astronomer and ethical philosopher, dies; the Mongol observatory of Maragha was built for his observations. **ca 1280 Moses de Leon** composes the *Zohar,* the greatest work of Castilian Kabala. **1275-1450 At Zimbabwe** early stone walls are built without mortar to enclose ceremonial and administrative areas serving a population of up to 18,000.	**1200s Muslims** make inroads into the African interior by trade as much as by conquest, sometimes traveling 200 miles a week in camel caravans. **1290s Rashid al-Din** begins a history of Ghazan Khan, which he enlarges into a world history with books on the Chinese and the Franks. He founds the "Rashidian quarter" of Tabriz, with a hospital, orphanage, experimental gardens, and a manuscript workshop. Here Chinese and Middle Eastern artistic traditions are combined to create the Persian miniature, first seen in illustrations to his world history and Firdausi's *Shahnama.*
1266 Sanjusangendo Temple is built in Kyoto, Japan.	**1200s Mongols** build circular tents, or yurts, of light wicker frames, which are easy to dismantle when they are ready to move on. **1200s Horsemen** place meat under the saddles of their horses, and after a full day's riding, it is tenderized and eaten raw. **1200s Genghis Khan's** favorite sport is hunting, which he introduces to his people. **1200s Mongol soldiers** introduce stirrups and cruppers (leather straps to stabilize saddles). The added stability give them better aim when shooting with bows and arrows.

MARCO POLO

In 1271 as a boy of 17, Marco Polo set off on a travel adventure that would make his name legendary. Leaving Venice with his father, Niccolo, and his uncle, Maffeo, he finally reached Shangdu, China, the summer home of Mongol ruler Kublai Khan, after traveling four years and 7,500 miles.

When he got word via his pony express that Marco Polo was approaching, Kublai Khan sent escorts to guide him to the court of his shining palace. They became friends, and the Khan employed Polo on several diplomatic missions that added much rich material for the observant Italian's imagination.

When the Polos arrived back home 24 years later, according to legend, their relatives did not even recognize them, as they were dressed in rags and behaved in a foreign manner. Yet all of Venice, it was said, rushed to hear Marco's tales of wonder. His book, *The Description of the World,* relates many fantastic experiences, some so astonishing that they are almost certainly not true. Nonetheless he had made it possible for readers to travel by armchair to exotic places on the other side of the world.

Mosaic of Marco Polo in Genoa, Italy

POLITICS & POWER	GEOGRAPHY & ENVIRONMENT	CULTURE & RELIGION

THE AMERICAS

ca 1300 Anasazi refugees from Mesa Verde found the Acoma pueblo on top of a mesa in today's New Mexico.

ca 1300 The Highland Maya form a city-state under the Quiche at Utatlan.

ca 1300 The Toltec are no longer dominating Mesoamerica.

1325 The Aztec found their capital, Tenochtitlan (modern-day Mexico City), on an island in the middle of Lake Texcoco.

1300s Changing climate throughout the century rearranges populations in the Southwest. Diminishing rainfall and reduced agricultural yield weakens people in the region and also causes them to shift some of their production away from farming and into hunting game and collecting wild food. The population moves east as they disperse, encountering the Athapaskan, recently arrived at the end of their migration from northwestern Canada. The Athapaskan develop a modern relationship with the Southwest peoples, exchanging products harvested from buffalo herds for corn, turquoise, and other resources and participating in the Pueblo trade fairs.

1300s As drought menaces the population in the Southwest and these peoples disperse, a new reverence for kachina figures emerges. Kachinas are spirits who are believed to have power to control rain and to facilitate working relationships among the newly constituted villages of the dispersing population.

ca 1300 Significant evidence exists of central Mesoamerican culture penetrating the Highland Maya sites in this period. The latter enter a period of warfare and upheaval.

EUROPE

1302 Charles of Valois plots the return of the Guelfs, or "Blacks," and causes leading "Whites" to flee Florence.

1303 Byzantine Emperor Andronicus II employs mercenaries to defeat the Ottomans.

1306 Robert the Bruce is crowned king of the Scots and leads successful campaigns against the English.

1315 Robert the Bruce's brother, Edward, becomes king of Ireland.

1326 Isabella, wife of Edward II, and her lover, Roger Mortimer, invade England, capturing the king.

1312 Uninhabited Canary Islands in the North Atlantic are rediscovered.

ca 1315 A little ice age leads to poor harvests and famine across Europe.

1302 Dante is banished from Florence.

1303 The University of Rome is founded.

1305 Giotto, an Italian artist, paints frescoes in St. Maria dell' Arena, Padua.

1307 Dante writes *Divina commedia*.

1309 Clement V, a Frenchman, places the papal residence at Avignon, France. It is the beginning of the "Babylonian Captivity" during which Rome is not the papal seat.

1329 Philippe de Vitry calls the new, contrapuntal style of music ars nova.

MIDDLE EAST & AFRICA

1301 Osman, first ruler of the Ottomans, defeats Byzantines at Baphaion.

1312 Mansa Musa becomes ruler of Mali.

1314 Amda Siyon, powerful king of Christian Ethiopia, solidifies his territorial rule and incorporates Muslim merchants into his realm.

1326 The Ottoman Orhan captures Brusa from the Byzantines and makes it his capital.

WEST AFRICAN KINGDOMS
- Songhai 15th century
- Mali 14th century
- Kanem-Bornu 14th century
- Ghana 11th century
- Trade routes 1200-1450

Present-day country boundaries and names shown in gray

This map shows the boundaries of the major medieval kingdoms of West Africa and the trade routes that fueled their growth.

ca 1300 After the overthrow of the caliphate, Muslim theologians develop a justificaition for Islam's rule without caliphs.

ca 1320 Mansa Musa commissions the great Friday Mosque in Mali's capital, Timbuktu.

1324 Mansa Musa travels to Mecca.

ASIA & OCEANIA

1312 Ala-ud-Din Khalji conquers the Deccan.

1316 Ala-ud-Din Khalji is the last of the Khalji rulers of Delhi.

1318 The Delhi sultanate conquers the kingdom of Maharashtra.

1320 Gharzi Khan of the Tughlak dynasty becomes sultan of Delhi when Ala-ud-Din Khalji dies.

1300 Theatrical drama develops in China.

1307 The Archbishopric of Beijing is begun.

1350 Noh theater begins in Japan.

SCIENCE & TECHNOLOGY

ca 1325 In modern-day Arizona, the Hohokam Indians begin building the largest structure south of the Gila River, later known as Casa Grande.

Rose window at Notre Dame Cathedral in Paris

1300 Apothecaries become popular in German cities.

1300 The spinning wheel is invented.

1300 Examining urine as a means of diagnosis is used in medicine.

1325 Organ pedals come into use.

1328 The sawmill is invented.

ca 1300 Inhabitants of Hawaii begin the construction of massive fish ponds to ensure regular supply of favored fishes.

PEOPLE & SOCIETY

ca 1320 The Aztec develop chinampa gardens around the island in Tenochtitlan to feed their population.

1300 The European slave trade ends temporarily.

1300 Trade fairs take place at Bruges, Lyons, Antwerp, and Geneva.

1305 Edward I of England standardizes the yard and the acre.

1315 Italian immigrants develop the Lyons silk industry.

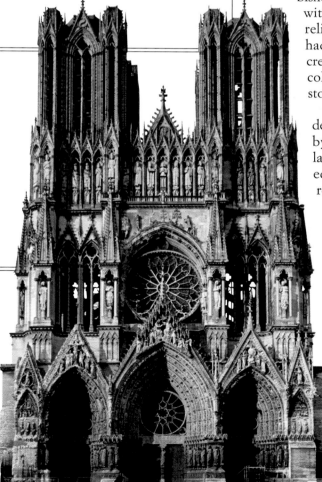

The Reims Cathedral, a masterpiece of Gothic architecture, was the coronation site for French kings after Louis VII.

GOTHIC CATHEDRALS

The 12th century in Europe saw the beginning of a soaring architectural style for churches that embodied the exalted place of religion in the Middle Ages. Later called "gothic" by Renaissance artists who viewed the style as barbaric, cathedrals were anything but crude.

Combining pointed arches, flying buttresses, and towering open spaces filled with shimmering light reflected through stained glass, these vaulted masterpieces conveyed a mystical sense of weightlessness, as if one might be able to take flight heavenward.

To Christians cathedrals were cities of God, and with great fervor and sacrifice they undertook the construction of such churches, which often took more than a century to complete. As the seats of bishops, cathedrals were filled with the finest sculp-tures, relics, and altarpieces to be had. Stained glass windows created atmosphere, and the colorful pictures told Bible stories to illiterate visitors.

A traveler could spot his destination from miles away by the sight of the town's largest and most magnificent edifice, with its towers reaching skyward and serving as a beacon to worshippers far and near. The wayward, lost, and lonely found solace within cathedral walls, as did the more fortunate, who arrived to give thanks. For both rich and poor, the cathedral was the abode on earth closest to Heaven.

MALI'S KINGDOM OF GOLD

THE RICH NATURAL RESOURCES OF WEST AFRICA GAVE RISE TO GREAT COMMERcial empires beginning in the eighth century and lasting until colonial times. Ghana was the first and Songhai the largest, but Mali achieved legendary status because of its flamboyant ruler, Mansa Musa. Under Musa, who ruled from 1312 to 1337, Mali became the largest empire of its day after the Mongol Empire—some "four months of travel long and four months wide," according to an Egyptian sheik. Its actual domain stretched west to east from the Atlantic Ocean to the boundaries of Nigeria, and from the edge of the rainforests in the south to the oasis markets of the central Sahara.

Mali's wealth and power was built largely on gold, for which it was one of the world's chief suppliers. Caravans of Arab merchants braved often dangerous trade routes into the region to acquire the precious mineral, bringing with them salt, luxury goods, and the Islamic faith. Mansa Musa embraced his kingdom's adopted religion, making a 1324 pilgrimage to Mecca that put Mali on the map. Accompanied by a retinue of 60,000 men and 500 slaves, each of whom carried a bar of gold weighing 500 *mitqals,* or four pounds, Musa made so many gifts of gold in Egypt along the way that the value of the local dinar was depressed for some 12 years in Cairo.

Mansa Musa made Mali an important center of Islamic scholarship, especially in his capital, Timbuktu. Literate in Arabic, he brought scholars and an Arabic library back from Mecca, and commissioned the famous Arab architect, al-Sahili, to build a palace and a mosque, which served as a university as well. Though the Muslim traveler Ibn Battuta, on a later visit to Mali, complained of the lack of Islamic custom, the durability of Islam here is evident in buildings like the great "mud mosque" in Djénné (above), built on the site of a previous Djénné (then Jenne-Jeno) mosque from the 13th century.

LEFT: *Camel caravans still transport goods in and out of West Africa.* ABOVE: *Mud mosque in Djénné, Mali*

	POLITICS & POWER	GEOGRAPHY & ENVIRONMENT	CULTURE & RELIGION
THE AMERICAS	**ca 1350 Aztec military elite** are at the top of a rigid social hierarchy. They begin to enjoy great wealth and privilege. **ca 1350 The Aztec** begin to extract tribute from numerous subject territories. **ca 1350 The Mapuche** of Chile's southern coast gradually begin to develop into a military society that will be able to resist Inca imperialism for a long period.	**ca 1350 Many Hohokam Indian villages** in present-day Arizona are abandoned. **ca 1350 The Amazon** discharges 15 times more volume of water than the Mississippi River and forms a tropical agricultural zone that supports six million people in the area covered by modern-day Brazil.	**ca 1350 Aztec priests** are among the elite, sometimes even becoming supreme rulers. **ca 1350 Nahuatl** becomes the dominant language of the Valley of Mexico.
EUROPE	**1330 Edward III** becomes king of England. **1333 Yusuf I,** caliph of Granada, marks the zenith of Arabic civilization there. **1337 Edward III,** claiming rights to the French throne, assumes the title King of France. The Hundred Years' War begins, with Edward III getting allies among German princes. **1347 The Black Death** begins spreading through Europe after arriving in Greece and southern Italy.		**1334 Giotto** begins building the campanile at Florence. **1341 Petrarch (Francesco Petrarca)** is crowned poet laureate at the Capitol in Rome. **1348 Giovanni Boccaccio** writes *The Decameron.* **1351 Tennis** becomes an open-air sport in England.
MIDDLE EAST & AFRICA	**1330-60 Islam** is seen by Ibn Battuta as only a veneer of the Mali Empire; the underlying substance of Mali culture is a belief in Mande superiority, the "ethnic core" holding disparate cultural groups together. **1335 Abu Said Khan's** death without children breaks up the Mongol Empire in the Middle East. **1338 Ottomans** reach the Bosporus in Asia Minor. **1354 Ottomans** occupy Gallipoli, having been brought in as mercenaries by the Byzantines.	**1331 The Arab traveler Ibn Battuta** visits the wealthy city-states of Africa's east coast. **1333 Ibn Battuta** visits Anatolia. **1346 A strong earthquake** hits Constantinople, causing the eastern arch of Hagia Sophia Cathedral to crumble. **1347 The Black Death** reaches Cairo, killing one-third of the population of Egypt. **1352-3 Ibn Battuta** explores the Sahara desert and then visits Mali.	**1332 African scholar Ibn Khaldun** is born in Tunis; he becomes a great philosopher and historian who argues that the spoken word conveys truth more directly than writing. **1344-1372 Zena Maryam,** an Ethiopian nun, is believed to have been blessed by God as a child for surviving a deadly plague that decimated her community near Lake Tana. **ca 1360 Ubayd-i Zakani's satires,** especially *The Ethics of the Aristocracy,* explain how the mighty redefine the virtues to suit their own convenience and for their own benefit.
ASIA & OCEANIA	**1331 A Japanese imperial succession dispute** leads to civil war against Hojo regents. **1333 Emperor Godaigo** overthrows the Hojo clan and captures Kamakura in Japan. **1336 The Ashikaga shogunate** is established in Japan. **1336 The Hindu kingdom of Vijayanagar** is founded in southern India. **1347 Bahman Shah** begins an independent sultanate in the Deccan. **1351 Firoz Shah** is sultan of Delhi.	**1330s Bubonic plague** (Black Death) originates in Asia.	**ca 1340 The Red Turbans and White Lotus Society,** popular religious movements, rebel in Yuan, China. **1350 Li Hsing Tao** writes *The Chalk Circle,* a famous Chinese play.

CONNECTIONS

Hanseatic League and Trade

Originating with a group of seafaring traders, German towns joined together in a commercial venture that boosted commerce throughout northern Europe beginning in the 13th century. Boycotts and sometimes force were used to control the markets that operated in Hanseatic towns, as well as in far-reaching areas in the North and Baltic Seas. Among the major members were Hamburg and Lubeck. The most important item of trade was textiles, followed by other such popular products as dried or salted fish, grain, beer, wax, and furs. The league reached as far as England before it began to decline in the 16th century, when Dutch sea power surpassed it. The fact remains, however, that the league had succeeded in taking the first step as the forerunner of what would later develop into Europe's Common Market.

SCIENCE & TECHNOLOGY	PEOPLE & SOCIETY
ca 1350 Aztec craftsmen begin to enjoy some prestige, while merchants supply exotic goods and military intelligence but are suspected as profiteers.	**ca 1350 Aztec slaves** work as domesticated servants, while cultivators work on *chinampas* (small plots of regained land) or on land owned by Aztec (Mexica) aristocrats. Both slaves and cultivators pay tribute and provide labor for public works.
ca 1334 The Alhambra palace in Granada is completed. **1337 William Merlee** of Oxford attempts the first weather forecasts. **1339 Construction starts on the Kremlin,** a grand ducal palace in Moscow. **1344 St. Vitus's Cathedral** is begun in Prague by Matthew of Arras. **1350 Edward III** begins to rebuild Windsor Castle. **1359 Work begins** on the nave of St. Stephen's Cathedral in Vienna.	**1332 The first record of English Parliament** being divided into two houses occurs. **1345 Two great banking houses** of Florence, Bardi and Peruzzi, go bankrupt. **1350s The Hanseatic League** continues to expand the trading interests of German towns throughout northern Europe, eventually securing a trade monopoly in Scandinavia. **1351 Between 1347 and 1351,** approximately 75 million people die of the Black Death.
ca 1350 The four-liwan architectural style is used to build mosques and schools. It consists of four large vaulted halls opening onto an open courtyard in the center.	**ca 1330 According to Islamic law,** Muslims cannot be enslaved. Thus, slaves are non-Muslim or born into slavery. They generally possess half the rights of free men, and Islamic law mandates that they should be treated with justice and kindness. It is a meritorious act to liberate them. The relationship of master and slave can be close, even after the slave is freed. He might conduct his master's business or marry the man's daughter. **1330 Inscriptions** are discovered in the citadel of Ankara, specifying tax rates, and cursing those who demand more.

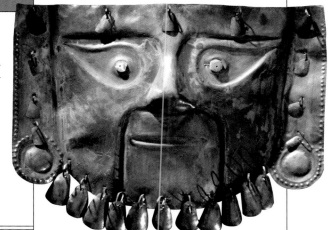

Chimu gold funerary mask

THE CHIMU SOCIETY OF PERU

Beginning in the 13th century, the Chimu state reigned as the largest and most influential political system in Peru. Its agricultural society thrived along the northern coastal desert, where people raised guinea pigs, llamas, squash, maize, sweet potatoes, cotton, and beans with the help of a sophisticated irrigation system, which also brought water via canals to Chanchan, their capital and the largest city in ancient Peru.

Chimu society was organized by the governing elite and hereditary rulers, whose burial grounds include 10 royal compounds, each about 20 acres in size. Cities were connected by roads to transport textiles and distinctive pottery made by artisans for a brisk trade industry. Superior metalworking in gold, silver, and bronze was also a feature of Chimu culture.

This high culture impressed the Inca, who conquered the Chimu around 1470 but adopted much of their political organization, irrigation systems, and engineering knowledge for their growing empire.

A great lord . . . sent him to govern this land . . . from across the sea.

EARLY SPANISH CHRONICLER, REFERRING TO
THE KINGDOM'S FOUNDER, TAYCANAMO

	POLITICS & POWER	GEOGRAPHY & ENVIRONMENT	CULTURE & RELIGION
THE AMERICAS	**1376 Acamapitchli** establishes the Aztec-Mexican dynasty by becoming the first *tlatoani* (He who speaks). This signals a political change from rule by a confederacy of clans to a monarchy. **ca 1390 The Chimu capital** of Chanchan occupies 24 square miles after two-and-a-half centuries of expansion.		
EUROPE	**1371 Ottoman Turks** defeat the Bulgarians and control all of Macedonia except Salonika. **1371 The death of David Bruce** in Scotland brings the Stewart dynasty to the throne. **1378 The Hundred Years' War** resumes after a period of truce. **1380 Dmitri IV** of Moscow defeats the Mongols at Kulikov. **1381 Venice** defeats rival republic Genoa. A flourishing of Venetian arts and sciences follows. **1381 English peasants** revolt.	**1361 The Black Death** reappears in England.	**1375 Robin Hood** appears in English literature. **1378 The Great Schism** begins following the death of Gregory XI, whereby two popes are elected, one at Rome and one at Avignon. **1382 John Wycliffe,** religious reformer, is expelled from Oxford for his doctrines. **1387 Geoffrey Chaucer** writes *The Canterbury Tales.* **1396 Manuel Chrysoloras** begins to revive Greek literature in Italy. **1398 Jan Hus,** Czech reformer, lectures on theology at Prague University.
MIDDLE EAST & AFRICA	**1375 The Mamluks** conquer Sis, ending Armenian independence. **1379 The Turk Tamerlane** (Timur) begins successful campaigns in Persia, Russia, Georgia, and Iraq. **1382 The Mamluk Burjite dynasty** replaces that of the Bahrites in Egypt. **1389 Yilderim Bayezid,** killed at Kosovo, succeeds his father, Murat, as sultan of the Ottomans. **1396 Bayezid** conquers the Christian army under Sigismund of Hungary at Nicopolis.		**1389 Hafiz,** the most important lyric poet in Persia, dies. His poems are still revered in Iran.
ASIA & OCEANIA	**1368 Zhu Yuanzhang** captures Dadu (Beijing) from the Mongols and estabishes the Ming dynasty, with its capital at Nanjing, China. **1392 The division** between northern and southern courts is dissolved in Japan; the Ashikagas become shoguns of Muromachi. **1395 Tamerlane** sacks Astrakhan. **1398 Tamerlane** invades India and sacks Delhi.		

WHAT LIFE WAS LIKE

Ibn Battuta Visits Mali

Moroccan Ibn Battuta traveled the world in his lifetime, recording his observations in his famous memoirs, *Rihla.* Battuta considered himself a citizen of the dar al-Islam, the entire "abode" of Islam, and in 1352 visited Mali, the African kingdom made legendary by Mansa Musa's 1324 trip to Mecca. Mali's great wealth was evident, but Battuta was shocked by the lack of Islamic custom. In Walata, the provincial governor offered him a meager calabash of millet, honey, and yogurt and spoke to him only through an interpreter. In Niani, the capital, partially clothed women, subjects who prostrated themselves before the mansa (king), and royal poets who danced in masks all violated orthodox Islam. Mali officially belonged to the Islamic world, which had greatly expanded its trading opportunities, but Battuta suspected the relationship was more a testament to commerce than to faith.

SCIENCE & TECHNOLOGY	PEOPLE & SOCIETY
	1360 The Aztec follow Mesoamerican tradition in dividing their capital city by the four cardinal directions.
14th-century knight aiming a crossbow	**ca 1390 The Aztec co-kingdom of Tlatelolco** draws 50,000 people to its island on major market days.
1363 Guy de Chauliac writes *Chirurgia magna,* a book on surgery in the Middle Ages.	**1300s Merchants** in many countries are required to wear long, dark robes to distinguish them from their aristocratic superiors.
1369 The Bastille in Paris is begun.	**1300s Five hundred cathedrals** are built.
1370 The steel crossbow is used as a weapon of war.	**1360 The first francs** are coined in France.
1388 Milan Cathedral is begun.	**1366 The Fuggers** arrive as weavers in Augsburg.
	1373 Merchants in England must use tunnage and poundage weights.
	1377 Playing cards replace dice in Germany.
	1392 Foreigners in England are forbidden to sell goods.
ca 1360 The Ottomans establish the timar system, which is a centralized method allocating land and revenue to military men and requiring regular government surveys of land, crops, productivity, and other revenue sources, such as beehives, fisheries, mills, industrial and commercial enterprises, and rates of trade.	**ca 1360 Janissaries** (new troops) are established as foot soldiers to supplement the Ottoman tribal cavalry. At first they are composed of prisoners of war. Later the troops are supplemented by youths recruited or levied from the Ottomans' Christian subjects in the Devshirme (forest); they are brought up by Turkish famlies and converted to Islam. After a while the best and brightest of the Devshirme boys enter the Palace School and are trained as administrators, reaching the highest positions in the empire, even that of grand vizier.
1377 Korean Buddhist text is printed for the first time with movable metal type.	
ca 1390 Samarkand in Central Asia is reconstructed as Tamerlane's capital. Its gorgeous buildings are tile covered and its gardens are irrigated.	

THE MERCHANTS OF VENICE

Favorably located on alluvial islets in a lagoon on the Adriatic, Venice is often referred to as the "bride of the sea." By the ninth century an independent republic was founded that during the next 600 years would become the European powerhouse of trade. Incessant fighting with Genoa, the republic's primary maritime rival, ended in 1380 when Venice was victorious in the sea battle of Chioggia.

The strength of Venice lay in her wealth of trade contacts worldwide. In the early years, trade with Constantinople was paramount; Italian merchants frequently moved there, until their population swelled to some 60,000. Eventually, though, Venice began importing the exotic luxuries of the East, such as silk, spices, and perfumes. When trade routes shifted south during the Pax Mongolica in the 13th century, Aleppo in Syria and Alexandria in Egypt became Venice's major trading partners.

This city of sailors also developed its own thriving shipbuilding industry, becoming world famous for its output of trading ships and launching a new galley every 200 days. Some of these same ships would become notorious in the middle of the 14th century for helping transport bubonic plague from Asia to Europe. Some accounts estimate that Venice lost two-thirds of her population to the Black Death.

During the Renaissance, Venice rivaled Florence and Rome in artistic glory, with giants such as Titian and Tintoretto calling the city home. The Turkish capture of Constantinople in 1453, which reduced trade between East and West, and the discovery of the Americas marked the beginning of Venice's decline as a trade power.

Merchandise passes through this noble city as water flows through fountains.

DECLARATION OF AN OBSERVER

POLITICS & POWER	GEOGRAPHY & ENVIRONMENT	CULTURE & RELIGION

THE AMERICAS

1410 Peruvian ruler Viracocha Inca expands his empire.

1418 Nezahualcoyotl, poet king of the Texcocan, begins his long rule.

1428 Itzcoatl defeats Atzcapotzalco and forms the Aztec Alliance with the Texcoco and Tlacopan.

ca 1400 The Aztec universe consists of three kinds of time: The transcendent time of the gods, the active time of the gods, and the time of humans.

1428 Itzcoatl's brother, a priest called Cihuacoatl, fuses Aztec theology, economics, and warfare to advance his empire.

Joan of Arc kissing the Sword of Deliverance—by Dante Gabriel Rossetti

EUROPE

1410 John XXIII is elected antipope, marking an important phase in the rise of the Medici family, who back him.

1411 Sigismund of Hungary is elected Holy Roman emperor.

1414 Henry V of England adopts the French claims of Edward II and assumes his right to the inheritance of the Plantagenets.

1415 Henry V defeats the French at Agincourt.

1428 Joan of Arc leads French armies against England.

1419 All of Normandy under the control of Henry V of England is united except Mont St. Michel.

1400 The first known literature in the Cornish tongue is written.

1408 Italian Donatello (Donato di Niccolo) sculpts *David* and *St. John*.

1411 St. Andrews University is founded in Edinburgh, Scotland.

1415 Jan Hus is burned at the stake in Constance, Germany.

1417 The election of Pope Martin V in Rome brings the Great Schism to an end.

1426 Holland becomes the center for European music.

MIDDLE EAST & AFRICA

1402 Tamerlane defeats Bayezid, the Ottoman sultan, and reaches the Bosporus.

1415 King John of Portugal seizes Ceuta in Morocco.

1421 Ottoman sultan Murat II resumes the policy of expansion after succeeding his father, Mehmed I, who had united the empire.

1427 Ethiopian Emperor Yeshaq dispatches envoys to Aragon in Spain to forge an alliance against Islam.

ca 1400 Successful gold trade has been developed down the Zambezi Valley to the Sofala coast in southeast Africa.

ca 1400 Islam reaches Malacca.

1405 Ibn Khaldun, historian and "father of sociology," dies. He analyzed the transition from nomadism to urbanism in his *Muqaddimah (Introduction to History)*.

1412 The Ottomans begin composing histories and administrative works in Turkish and translating Persian administrative literature, poetry, and histories written under the Mongols.

1417 The Disputation of Tortosa, which is a dispute over the anti-Christian statements in the Talmud, begins.

ASIA & OCEANIA

1402 After a long civil war, Zhu Di usurps the throne of the second Ming emperor, Jianwen, to reign as Emperor Yongle in China.

1404 Japan begins trading with Ming China.

1420 Emperor Yongle moves his main capital to Dadu, the former Yuan capital, and renames it Beijing (northern capital) to help defend the country against Mongols. The secondary capital is Nanjing.

1424 When Emperor Yongle dies, his reign is viewed as a "second founding" of the Ming dynasty.

ca 1405 Chinese eunuch admiral Zheng He leads seven massive maritime expeditions throughout the Indian Ocean basin.

1408 The multivolume encyclopedia *Yongle dadian* is completed under the patronage of Ming Emperor Yongle in China.

SCIENCE & TECHNOLOGY	PEOPLE & SOCIETY

ca 1400 The *quipu* is the numeric device used by the Inca for counting and a mnemonic device for recording oral histories. The Inca do not develop a scribal form.

1400 Middle and Upper Mississippi phases of mound builders develop in North America.

1400s The shortage of rain for the Caddo people reduces their corn harvest, making it difficult for them to maintain their large settlements. Forced to disperse into smaller communities, the Caddo's powerful ruling chiefdoms decline. The Caddo trade in buffalo meat with the Pueblo Indians in the Southwest and suffer a grievous blow when the Athapaskan arrive in their migration from Montana and Wyoming. They replace the Caddo as the main source of buffalo meat for the Pueblo.

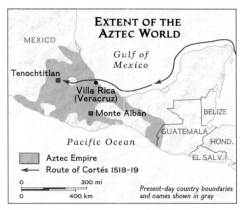

The Aztec Empire encountered by Cortés

1400 The dulcimer is first mentioned.

1402 Seville Cathedral is begun.

1405 The abbey in Bath, England, is erected.

1415 The longbow allows the outnumbered English to defeat the French at Agincourt.

1419 Brunelleschi designs the Foundling Hospital in Florence.

1420 Brunelleschi constructs the cupola (dome) of Florence Cathedral.

1407 Bethlehem Hospital in London becomes an institution for the insane.

1414 The Medicis in Florence become official bankers to the papacy.

1416 Dutch fishermen are the first to use drift nets.

1420 Cosimo (the Elder) becomes manager of the Medici bank in Florence.

1420 Prince Henry of Portugal (the Navigator) encourages settlement of Madeira and Porto Santo.

THE AZTEC EMPIRE

In the 13th century a people now commonly known as Aztec, but who called themselves Mexica, settled in the Valley of Mexico and quickly developed a reputation as fierce warriors. They provided mercenary services to the rival city-states that dominated the valley after the fall of the Toltec Empire.

In 1325 the Aztec founded their capital, Tenochtitlan, now Mexico City, on an island in the middle of Lake Texcoco, creating a strong defensible position that became the heart of an expanding empire. They erected a wondrous religious precinct of temples, pyramids, and palaces, supported by tribute paid by conquered foes.

The tribute system, however, left the Aztec vulnerable to potential enemies who could disrupt their tribute and thus, their livelihoods. As a result, the Aztec joined with the Texcoco and Tlacopan, two powerful potential foes, to form the Aztec Alliance, which, under Moctezuma I and II, began conquering tribes outside the valley, expanding the empire into Central America by the time the Spanish arrived in the early 16th century.

1405-1415 China's Grand Canal is reconstructed and improved.

1406 The mausoleum for Tamerlane is begun in Samarkand in Central Asia.

1420 Beijing is rebuilt as the Ming capital.

1428 Ulugh-Beg, Timurid ruler at Samarkand, builds an astronomical observatory there and both participates in and patronizes important astronomical observations, carrying on al-Tusi's work.

An Aztec priest cuts the heart from one sacrificial victim as another lies below. Human sacrifice atop the great temple was made to appease the tribal god, Huitzilopochtli, and to intimidate foes.

	POLITICS & POWER	GEOGRAPHY & ENVIRONMENT	CULTURE & RELIGION
THE AMERICAS	**1400s The Five Nations** of North American Iroquois Indians convene to frame their Great League of Peace, whereby the Iroquois, Mohawk, Oneida, Cayuga, Seneca, and Onondaga bands agree to live peacefully with each other. **1438 Pachacutec** founds Inca rule in Peru. **1440 Moctezuma I** becomes ruler of the Aztec and begins conquering tribes outside the Valley of Mexico. **1450 The Inca** subdue the Chimu in northern Peru.	**ca 1450 Droughts** and food shortages plague central Mexico.	**ca 1430 The Pawnee** develop a series of rituals to celebrate corn as their means of survival and even prosperity. Pawnee also honor white corn as sacred and distinct from red or black corn. The Pawnee reserve special fields for white corn in order to maintain its purity. **ca 1450 Virachoca** is the creator god of the Inca world. The sun god follows in importance. **ca 1450 The feather work** of the *quetzal,* a green Central American bird, signifies the Aztec high decorative art style.
EUROPE	**1431 Joan of Arc** is burned at the stake in Rouen. **1434 Cosimo de Medici** returns from exile and takes over Florence. **1444 Ottomans** conquer Hungarians at the Black Sea, opening their way to Constantinople. **1453 England** is defeated by France at Castillon, ending the Hundred Years' War. **1455 The Wars of the Roses** begin in England between the Lancasters and the Yorks.	**1434 Portuguese explorer João Diaz** rounds Cape Bojador.	**1431 Margery Kempe** dictates the first autobiography in English. **1431 Philip the Good,** Duke of Burgundy, founds the Order of the Golden Fleece, a chivalric order. **1440 The Platonic Academy** is founded in Florence. **1450 Florence** under the Medicis becomes the center of the Renaissance and humanism. **1455 Johannes Gutenberg,** inventor of modern printing, prints the 42-line (Mazarin) bible at Mainz.
MIDDLE EAST & AFRICA	**1433 Tuareg nomads** of the desert occupy the city of Timbuktu. **ca 1440 Mutota** controls the northeast Zimbabwe plateau and trade routes from gold mines to the Sofala coast through the Zambezi Valley. **1450 Mutota** is succeeded by his son, Matope, in southeast Africa. **1453 Ottoman Turks** under Mehmed II seize Constantinople, bringing an end to the Byzantine Empire and incorporating its last figures into the Ottoman elite.	**1436-1444 Portuguese navigators** explore the west coast of Africa, the Senegal River, and Cape Verde, and reactivate the African slave trade. **1442 Al-Maqrizi,** author of a detailed geography of Cairo, *Al-Khitat*—listing significant sites and local traditions—dies. **1455 Venetian navigator Cadamosto** explores the Senegal River in Africa.	**1430 Timurid illustrated manuscripts** of the life of Alexander the Great emphasize his travels in search of the Water of Life. **ca 1450 Mehmed II,** seeing himself as heir to both Roman and Islamic traditions, creates a cosmopolitan court culture that draws from East and West. Gentile Bellini, the Italian artist, visits his court. Timurid poets send poems in Persian, and Byzantine scholars and princes become Ottoman subjects and write histories of Mehmed's reign. **1453 Turks** convert Hagia Sophia Cathedral into a mosque, Aya Sofya (today a museum).
ASIA & OCEANIA	**1434 The capital of the Khmer kingdom** moves from Angkor to Phnom Penh after an invasion by the Siamese. **1447 Scanderbeg** defeats Murad II and gains independence for Persia, India, and Afghanistan.		**1438 The Jamma Musjid Mosque** of Husain is built in Jaunpur, India.

CONNECTIONS

Iroquois League and Peace

According to legend, two Indians—Deganawida and Hiawatha—went from village to village teaching the laws of peace to Iroquois people in the northeast region of North America. The Iroquois soon succeeded in persuading the chiefs of four other nations to join them: Cayuga, Oneida, Seneca, and Mohawk. At first a fifth nation, the Onondaga, resisted, but it was won over eventually. Now there were actually six different nations who worked together to prevent violent deeds in the case of grievances and other types of retribution against other members of the group. The founders of the confederacy, however, left a two-pronged legacy for future generations, one of inner peace and one of outward strife. Both Indian and non-Indian groups outside the league were considered enemies, and were thus repeatedly raided by these six Nations.

SCIENCE & TECHNOLOGY	PEOPLE & SOCIETY
1400s Huge stones are used in building Inca walls in Cuzco, Peru. They are close-fitted and mortarless, so that in case of an earthquake, the stones jump and settle back in their original formation. **ca 1450 The Inca** build 20,000 miles of road in the Andes by exploiting the communal labor system. Their language, Quechua, begins to spread and dominate the region.	**ca 1430 The Pawnee people** settle along the major rivers in Nebraska. Here they engage in farming corn and hunting. **ca 1430 Pawnee women** handle the corn planting, while the men see that the fields are cleared for planting. The Pawnee also rely on beans and squash. **ca 1430 Itzcoatl** uses *pochteca,* long-distance merchants, to improve both Aztec trade networks and imperial spy networks.
1430 The great cast-iron gun, "mad Marjorie," is introduced. **1444 Cosimo de Medici** founds the Biblioteca Medicea Laurenziana in Florence. **1450 The Vatican Library** is founded. **1455 Movable metal type** set in a permanent mold is used for printing. **1455 The Palazzo Venezia** is built in Rome.	**1430 Middle English** gives way to Modern English. **1433 The double eagle** becomes the symbol of the Holy Roman emperors. **1443 An order concerning quarantine** and cleansing is passed in England. **1445 Copenhagen** becomes the Danish capital. **1452 The first professional association** of midwives is formed in Germany.
ca 1430 Ottomans become expert cannon-makers, casting huge cannons on the battle-field and later employing mobile field cannons as well as galleys armed with cannons.	**1444 The sedentary Wolof** with their cavalry encounter the Portuguese at the Senegal River, where the Wolof exchange gold and slaves for the goods, horses, wheat, textiles, and silver of the Europeans. **1453 Istanbul's covered bazaar** supports the Aya Sofya mosque through its shop rents. There are 118 shops of valuable goods inside the market's Bedestan, where stone walls and iron doors resist fire and pillage; the 984 shops in the outer market sell imported silks and spices, as well as locally made textiles and crafts.
	1443 The Korean syllabary known as Hangul is created by order of King Sejong.

A Revolution in Publishing

Like so much else, printing with movable type can be traced to China, where Bi Sheng began using movable wood blocks to print around 1040. Koreans were using movable copper type to print as early as 1392. But the method developed by Johannes Gutenberg in Mainz, Germany, independent of his Asian predecessors, made printing truly practical and led to a revolution in mass communications. With refinements, Gutenberg's system remained the principle way to print until the late 20th century.

Wanting to mechanically reproduce illuminated manuscripts without losing their beauty, Gutenberg's key innovations involved the making of a punch-stamped mold that could cast large amounts of metal type with precision, a new type of press, and the use of oil-based ink. His masterpiece was the 42-line Bible, printed in Latin in an original edition of about 180 copies no later than 1455. This impressive work with its Gothic typeface represented a quantum advance over the handwritten Bible, which might take a monk 20 years to finish.

Gutenberg's new technology not only spread rapidly (by 1520 more than 200 printed editions of the Bible had been published), but many books were printed in the vernacular rather than in Latin. This made texts available to almost any literate person, not just scholars, which in turn resulted in more people becoming literate. News and ideas spread more quickly and widely, bringing the world closer together.

In his own time, Gutenberg reaped precious little from his invention. Not only did he have financial problems during development, but his backer, Johann Fust, became impatient and successfully sued him, forcing Gutenberg to relinquish all claims to the process. Fust went on to make a fortune with his Bible sales, while Gutenberg died in 1468 in relative obscurity.

	POLITICS & POWER	GEOGRAPHY & ENVIRONMENT	CULTURE & RELIGION
THE AMERICAS	**1470 Cuzco** defeats Chimu, ending the coastal empire's independence. **1471 Topa Inca** becomes emperor, assuming rule from Pachacutec. **1473 Aztec ruler Ayacatl** conquers the neighboring city of Tlatelolco. **1495 Christopher Columbus** orders Indians in Hispaniola more than 14 years old to pay tribute money in gold to the king of Spain every three years. He also starts a system of forced labor for Indians. **1499 Columbus** quells revolt by Spanish settlers and natives in Hispaniola.	**1492 Christopher Columbus,** sailing for Ferdinand and Isabella of Spain to discover a western route to the Indies, lands on Watling Island in the Bahamas on October 12, then goes on to Cuba and Hispaniola before returning to Spain to receive a hero's welcome. **1494 On his second voyage** to the Americas, Columbus lands in Jamaica. **1499 Italian navigator John Cabot** explores the North American coastline from Newfoundland to New England, but dies on the voyage. **1499 Italian navigator Amerigo Vespucci** explores the northeast coastline of South America.	**1400s In order to ensure the sun's daily rebirth,** Aztec priests sacrifice tens of thousands of people each year in Tenochtitlan temples. **1487 The temple of Huitzilopochtli,** the god of the Aztec, is dedicated. Up to 80,000 are sacrificed.
EUROPE	**1468 Lorenzo and Giuliano** become the Medici rulers of Florence. **1477 Maximilian** of Austria marries Mary of Burgundy, making the Habsburgs heirs to one of the most powerful states in Europe. **1478 The Spanish Inquisition** begins. **1480 Russian Tsar Ivan III** stops paying tribute money to the Mongols. **1485 The Tudor dynasty** is established in England when Henry VII defeats Richard III at Bosworth field, ending the Wars of the Roses. **1492 The Spanish** seize Granada, the last Muslim kingdom in Spain.	 Birth of Venus *by Sandro Botticelli*	**1465 The first printed music** appears. **1467 The first ballad** relating the story of Swiss national hero William Tell appears. **ca 1470 Sir Thomas Malory** completes *Morte Darthur*. **1474 William Caxton** prints the first book in English at Bruges. In 1477 he prints Chaucer's *Canterbury Tales*. **1483 Pope Sixtus IV** celebrates the first mass in the Sistine Chapel in Rome. **1484 Botticelli** paints *Birth of Venus*. **1490 Ballet** begins at Italian courts.
MIDDLE EAST & AFRICA	**1461 Ottoman Mehmed II** annexes Trebizond, the last outpost of Byzantine civilization. **1464 Sonni Ali Ber** leads the Songhai military cavalry to recapture Timbuktu. By 1473 he has besieged Jenne-Jeno with a fleet of 400 river boats on the Niger. **1471 Mehmed II** seizes Karamania, the last surviving Turkish emirate. The Ottomans now rule all lands from the Taurus Mountains to the Adriatic Sea. **1491 Mamluks and Ottomans** make peace in the Near East after six years of war.	**1468 Songhai King Sonni Ali** drives Tuaregs out of Timbuktu in West Africa. **1484 The Portuguese** land in Angola after discovering the mouth of the Congo River in Central Africa. Portuguese missionaries arrive the next year. **1488 Portuguese explorer Bartholomew Dias** rounds the Cape of Good Hope. **1497 Vasco da Gama,** on orders from King Manuel of Portugal, sails for India via the Cape of Good Hope at the tip of South Africa. He reaches Malindi (Kenya) in East Africa the next year.	**1490 Al-Nino de la Guardia** is involved in a trumped-up blood libel, where he gets converted Jews in trouble with the Inquisition; this event is used by Torquemada as an excuse for their expulsion.
ASIA & OCEANIA	**1488 Korean official Choe Pu** presents his diary of travels in China to the king. **1492 The sultan of Delhi,** Sikander II Lodi, annexes Bihar.	**1483 Russians** start exploring Siberia. **1495 The Yellow River** is diverted from its course north of the Shandong Peninsula to a new course south of the peninsula.	**1493 The Korean encyclopedia,** *Patterns of Musicology,* is published.

SCIENCE & TECHNOLOGY	PEOPLE & SOCIETY

1400s At the birth of a male Aztec child, his umbilical cord is buried with an arrow and shield, signifying his future life as a soldier.

1400s Known for their ornamental use of precious metal, the Inca call gold the "sweat of the sun" and silver the "tears of the moon."

1400s The Taino people of the Caribbean have trading contact with Mesoamerican civilizations.

View of the mountain-locked Inca citadel of Machu Picchu, Peru

1480 Leonardo da Vinci invents the parachute. In 1492 he draws a flying machine.

1484 The first European nautical almanac and manual of navigation are published. Now sailors can navigate by the sun as well as the stars.

1489 The symbols + (plus) and – (minus) begin to be used.

1492 Martin Behaim of Nuremberg constructs a terrestrial globe.

1494 Luca di Pacioli writes *Algebra*, which includes study of the problems of cubic equations.

1400s Europe's population has fallen to 60 million people, but fast growing towns everywhere are centers of trade and the arts.

1400s In Florence, artists have their own guilds and are mentored by wealthy patrons like the powerful Medici family.

1479 Brussels becomes the center of European tapestry making.

1492 The book publishing profession develops, made up of the three pursuits of type founder, printer, and bookseller.

ca 1463 Mehmed II builds a mosque in Istanbul and surrounds it with eight colleges, forming the pinnacle of the Ottoman Empire's educational system. The mosque, together with the Topkapi Palace at the heart of the city, overlooks both Europe and Asia, the Black Sea and the Mediterranean (white) Sea, symbolizing Mehmed's concept of his role.

1470s This decade marks a brilliant era in Ottoman mathematics under Ali Kusai and Mulla Lutf.

1463 Muhammed Rumfa, sarki of Kano, is the great mujaddid, defender of the faith, and converts the Hausa institution of kingship into a Muslim sultanate. By 1500 Kano is one of the major trade centers of West Africa.

1486 King Ozalua of Benin welcomes Portuguese traders to his kingdom and exchanges copper, brass, textiles, and glass beads for war captives and ivory.

1493 Askia Muhammed I usurps the throne of Songhai and conquers the territory that was formerly the Mali Empire. He creates the largest state in sub-Saharan Africa over the next three decades.

COLUMBUS DISCOVERS THE NEW WORLD

Toward the end of the 15th century, several elements contributed to the age of European exploration and discovery. Christians were anxious to spread their religion to stop the expansion of Islam. And overland trade routes had been cut off ever since Ottoman Turks has conquered Constantinople in 1453. In order to obtain the spices, silks, perfumes, and other exotic goods in great demand throughout Europe, it was necessary to discover a new way to the Orient.

Christopher Columbus, navigator and agent from Genoa, thought that sailing west across the Atlantic would lead to the East Indies. In 1492 King Ferdinand and Queen Isabella of Spain agreed to outfit him with three ships. From August 2 until October 12 Columbus and his crews were at sea, until with great relief they made landfall on an island in the Caribbean, where they met natives whom Columbus called Indians, because he believed he had reached India. Returning to Spain from his first voyage, he was received as a hero.

During the course of three more voyages, Columbus reached Central and South America. He died in 1506. His voyage remains one of the most important events in modern history, one that brought the Old and New Worlds together for better and for worse.

Reconstruction of Columbus's small sailing ships, the Niña, Pinta, and the Santa Maria

BEGINNING AROUND 1500, WESTERN EUROpeans greatly expanded their reach by establishing trading bases around the globe and colonizing the Americas. This process transformed both the Old World and the New World as people, plants, livestock, viruses and other pathogens crossed oceans and altered conditions on distant shores. The impact was greatest on the Americas, where native people were devastated by diseases communicated by Europeans. But the Old World also underwent profound changes as new crops and commodities arrived from the Americas, the slave trade destabilized Africa, and societies elsewhere reckoned with colonialism.

Reformation in Europe

Colonization of the Americas coincided with revolutionary developments in Europe. The Protestant Reformation began in Germany, where the printing press was devised and knowledge of scripture and other subjects, once confined to priests and scholars, became accessible to literate people. When the German monk Martin Luther launched

the Reformation in 1519, he insisted that the Bible, not the pope, was the ultimate religious authority. Luther's protests against controversial church practices such as the sale of indulgences, pardoning people for their sins, were set in print and reached a wide audience, as did his translation of the New Testament. Protestantism was strongest in urban areas in northern Europe, where many people were literate and began to question Catholic teachings. In response, Catholic leaders launched a Counter-Reformation, limiting the sale of indulgences and improving the education of priests, missionaries, and laypersons.

The struggle between Catholicism and Protestantism often involved political factors. In England, King Henry VIII broke with Catholicism in 1534 after the pope refused to allow him to divorce his wife, who had not provided him with a male heir. Henry then disbanded English monasteries and confiscated their wealth. A fierce rivalry ensued between Protestant England and Catholic Spain, where heretics were tried by the Spanish Inquisition. Henry's daughter Queen Elizabeth I survived a challenge from Spain's King Philip II in 1588 when her navy repulsed the Spanish Armada. Later, radical English Protestants called Puritans opposed their own king, Charles I, who was suspected of plotting to restore Catholicism and executed in 1649. King James II was overthrown in 1688 for similar reasons, and England emerged as a constitutional monarchy.

The Netherlands also emerged as a constitutional monarchy after fighting for political and religious independence from Spain, which tried to suppress Protestantism among the Dutch. In France, by contrast, a prominent Catholic, Cardinal Richelieu, helped King Louis XIII crush uprisings by nobles and their Protestant backers. Louis XIV—the so-called Sun King, who reigned in splendor at Versailles— later forced Protestants into exile and kept aristocrats loyal by entertaining them lavishly at court. In central Europe, Protestants rebelled in 1618 when the Habsburg dynasty that ruled both the Holy Roman Empire and Spain tried to enforce Catholicism, unleashing the brutal Thirty Years' War. The combined opposition of France, which aimed to weaken the Habsburgs, and Protestant countries such as Sweden and the Netherlands forced the Holy Roman Empire to

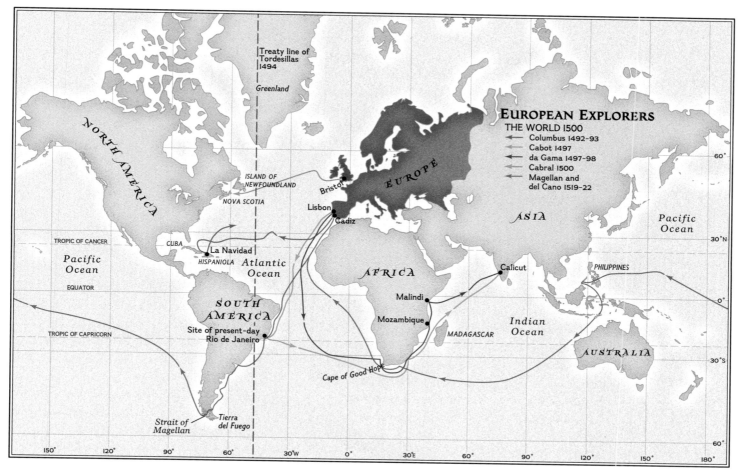

EUROPEAN EXPLORERS
THE WORLD 1500
← Columbus 1492-93
← Cabot 1497
← da Gama 1497-98
← Cabral 1500
← Magellan and del Cano 1519-22

grant sovereignty to Switzerland and freedom of worship to various Christian denominations in Germany.

In years to come, religious strife receded and Europe prospered. New crops from the Americas improved the diet of Europeans and raised life expectancies. Global trade fostered a wealthy merchant class that patronized musicians and painters such as the Dutch master Rembrandt van Rijn, who drew on the heritage of the Italian Renaissance and portrayed both religious and secular subjects. Scientific inquiry fostered a new view of the cosmos, put forward by astronomers such as Galileo Galilei and the physicist Isaac Newton, who explained gravity in mathematical terms. Advances in science and technology and the rise of corporate capitalism, which encouraged investment and economic risk taking, contributed to European expansion overseas.

Colonizing the Americas

Spanish colonization of the New World began in the Caribbean, where Columbus and others founded settlements on Hispaniola (the island shared today by Haiti and the Dominican Republic), Puerto Rico, Jamaica, and Cuba. Spanish settlers demanded labor and tribute from the native people they called Indians, who suffered severely from exploitation by colonists and diseases they introduced. As Indians died out in the Caribbean, Spaniards brought enslaved Africans to labor on plantations, and the population became largely African-American. A similar process occurred in Portuguese Brazil.

In 1519 the Spanish conquistador (conqueror) Hernán Cortés left Cuba with several hundred men to seek fortune in Mexico. Aided by a native woman called La Malinche who served as his interpreter and later bore his child, Cortés forged alliances with groups subject to the Aztec, who were devastated by smallpox and other Old World diseases. In 1521 Cortés and his forces razed the Aztec capital, Tenochtitlan, and founded Mexico City in its place. In South America, conquistador Francisco Pizarro used similar tactics to divide and conquer the Inca Empire.

This map charts the pioneering transatlantic voyage of Christopher Columbus, sailing for Spain, and subsequent voyages made by John Cabot for England; Vasco da Gama and Pedro Álvares Cabral for Portugal; and Ferdinand Magellan and Sebastián del Cano, who circumnavigated the globe for Spain.

Spain then took direct control of American colonies and appointed two viceroys, who ruled for the king at Mexico City and Lima, the Spanish capital of Peru. Missionaries introduced Catholicism and Spanish authorities abolished Indian slavery, but many Indians became peons, held in servitude by colonists to whom they owed debts. In the 1500s the Spanish Crown profited hugely from silver extracted from Mexico and Peru, but by the 1700s many Spanish-American colonies were a drain on the royal treasury. Spain regarded them strictly as sources of raw materials and discouraged colonists from manufacturing goods or entering into maritime trade.

By 1750 Spain had colonized a broad area north of Mexico, including Florida, Texas, and New Mexico, where colonists relied heavily on the labor of Pueblo Indians. Those frontier provinces were intended as buffers to shield Mexico from foreign intervention. Chief among the rivals to Spain in North America were the English, whose colonies along the Atlantic were prospering and expanding westward. The French also posed a threat to Spanish interests when they ventured south from Canada in the late 1600s and claimed Louisiana, a sprawling territory embracing the Mississippi River and its tributaries.

Blessed with fertile land, English colonies attracted far more settlers to the New World than French or Spanish colonies did. Some immigrants sought religious freedom, like the Puritans who settled Massachusetts and the Catholics who founded Maryland, only to become embroiled in further religious strife. Rhode Island, founded by religious dissidents from Massachusetts, became the first American colony to tolerate those of all faiths, including Jews.

Unlike Spanish or French colonists who intermarried with Indians and formed a mixed race known as mestizos or métis, most English colonists avoided contact with Indians except when trading with them for valued items like beaver pelts or negotiating for land. Colonists sometimes used liquor to extract treaty concessions from Indians and set one tribe against another when conflicts arose. The powerful Iroquois confederation was strained to the breaking point when its alliance with English colonists drew it into repeated battles with tribes loyal to the French. English planters who needed laborers relied not on Indians but on indentured servants from Europe,

In a romanticized 19th-century painting set in Tenochtitlan, the Aztec capital, King Moctezuma II stands beside the Great Pyramid and greets the Spanish conquistador Hernán Cortés, who posed as Moctezuma's friend before taking him hostage.

who worked under contract, or on slaves from Africa. By the 1700s ports such as Philadelphia and New York, founded by Dutch colonists but seized by English forces in 1664, had developed into thriving commercial centers, where colonists built ships, engaged in overseas trade, and met in assemblies that prepared them for self-government. Such advances came at a steep price, however, for native people in America, Africa, and other lands impacted by colonization.

Africa Besieged

Beginning in the late 1400s, Africa underwent wrenching changes as traders and troops from Europe and the Middle East intervened there. Ottoman Turks conquered much of North Africa in the 1500s but failed to take Morocco, which was bolstered by Muslims fleeing persecution in Spain. Moroccans and other North Africans crossed the Sahara in caravans to trade with the flourishing Songhai Empire in West Africa, whose Muslim rulers founded an Islamic university at Timbuktu. Their forces patrolled the Niger River in ships but lacked the firepower of Moroccans, who turned from trading to raiding and inflicted a crushing defeat on Songhai troops in 1591 that led to the empire's collapse. Afterward, power shifted to the coast, where African states like Oyo and Dahomey prospered by obtaining captives from the interior and selling them to Europeans along with gold and other items.

The Portuguese figured prominently in that coastal trade and sometimes used military force to secure their interests. The rulers of Kongo, a well-organized kingdom in the Congo River basin, at first welcomed Portuguese merchants and missionaries and embraced Christianity, only to lose faith in the foreigners when Portuguese slave traders made deals with their enemies. In the 1600s Portuguese troops overran Kongo and killed its king, leaving the country in disarray. The Portuguese also invaded Ndongo, or Angola, following the death of the defiant Queen Nzinga, who allied with Dutch merchants hostile to the Portuguese. The Dutch established a trading post at Cape Town in 1652 and later colonized South Africa, while the Portuguese occupied ports along the East African coast and drew profits and power away from Swahili merchants. By 1700 the Portuguese had been surpassed in the slave trade by the

As diagrammed here, slave traders crammed African captives into the holds of ships bound for the New World. Conditions on some ships were so terrible in the early years of the trade that more than half the slaves died before reaching their destination.

Store Room

Store Room

French and English, and they too had bases in Africa.

African kingdoms such as Dahomey (now Benin) acquired firearms from Europeans and expanded, selling captives into slavery as conquerors around the world had long been doing. Many African societies benefited from new crops imported from the Americas, including corn, peanuts, and cassava, which flourished in the tropics. But such gains were more than offset by the tragic impact of a slave trade that transported more than 15 million Africans to the Americas amid such dreadful conditions that many did not survive the journey. Millions more were sold into slavery in other parts of the world by Christian or Muslim dealers. Some who escaped enslavement were caught up in ruinous wars that were triggered or aggravated by the slave trade and left Africa vulnerable to deeper intrusions by Europeans in centuries to come.

Challenges in Asia

In Asia, societies responded in various ways to the challenges of a world in which traders and explorers often served as agents of imperial expansion, sometimes welcoming foreigners within prescribed limits and sometimes keeping them at a distance. China had the potential to dominate maritime trade in Asia, as shown by naval expeditions in the 15th century that involved hundreds of ships and projected Chinese power clear across the Indian Ocean. But emperors of the Ming dynasty grew increasingly concerned with fending off threats from Mongols and other foreigners and sought to restrict foreign trade instead of pursuing it as an instrument of state power, as Europeans did. Smugglers defied restrictions Ming rulers imposed, and pirates made incursions along China's southeast coast.

In the mid-1600s invaders from Manchuria called Manchus joined with Chinese rebels and toppled the Ming, installing their own Qing dynasty in Beijing and prohibiting maritime trade until they secured their hold on the country in the late 1600s. Overseas trade never stopped entirely, for there was strong demand in China for silver bullion, which fueled the economy and was obtained from Japan and Spanish America for Chinese products such as silk and porcelain. Foreigners purchased Chinese goods at the port of Guangzhou (Canton), where officials closely supervised trade, and at overseas ports such as Manila in the

Philippines, colonized by Spain and visited by galleons bearing silver from the New World. Chinese merchants had their own district there and were envied and resented for their success. Catholic missionaries brought knowledge of European culture and technology to the Chinese court and sought to ingratiate themselves with the emperor and high officials in order to spread their faith. They succeeded in winning some converts but were barred from proselytizing by the emperor after the pope ruled that Chinese converts must no longer venerate their ancestors.

Japan was less receptive to outsiders. The civil strife that wracked the country in the 1500s ended when shoguns of the Tokugawa family took control in the 1600s and pacified Japan's daimyo: lords who wielded great power over their domains and commanded the services of hard-fighting samurai. Tokugawa shoguns required those lords to spend every other year at court in Edo (Tokyo), and greatly restricted contact with foreigners to prevent them from supplying daimyo with firearms or otherwise destabilizing Japan. Christianity was banned, and missionaries and converts who violated the edict were executed. Some Dutch and Chinese ships were allowed to enter the port of Nagasaki and do business, but when Portuguese traders arrived there uninvited in 1640, most of them were killed and the rest deported. Like China, Japan prospered during this period. Merchants, long regarded as socially inferior to samurai and daimyo, gained wealth and influence but were not permitted to seek profit abroad.

In India, Turkish conquerors seized power in the 1500s and established the Mughal Empire. The Mughal emperor Akbar, who reigned for nearly half a century, defeated Hindus in southern India but did not force them to convert to Islam, his own faith and that of many people in northern India. Later emperors were less tolerant, leading Hindus to rebel. Mughal rulers were hard-pressed to finance campaigns in the south while maintaining a large bureaucracy and building costly monuments. Desperate for new sources of revenue, they allowed Europeans to establish fortified trading posts in Bombay, Calcutta, and other Indian ports. The British East India Company recruited its own troops and gained power in India as the Mughal Empire declined.

Even the Ottoman Turks, once so strong that

Christians feared they might overrun Europe, gradually lost power. They reached their peak in the mid-1500s with the conquests of Suleyman the Magnificent, who extended his realm from Baghdad to Budapest. By the 1600s, Ottoman rulers faced strong opposition both in Europe and in Persia, where Shah Abbas the Great mobilized Shiite Muslims against the Sunni Ottomans. By the 1700s, they confronted an even greater challenge from Russia, where Tsar Peter the Great westernized the economy and military, setting the stage for Russian advances into the Balkans and the Crimea. As the Ottoman Empire declined, fresh opportunities for European expansion emerged in the Middle East and North Africa. ■

Matteo Ricci, a Jesuit missionary from Italy, stands at left beside his Chinese convert and disciple, Xu Quangqi, who helped convert others in China to Catholicism in the early 1600s.

THE WORLD AT A GLANCE

CONVERGING WORLDS 1500-1750

	1500	1525	1550	1575	1600	
THE AMERICAS	**1500-1521** Spain explores and conquers vast areas of Latin America, including the Aztec Empire in Mexico. **1509** Slaves are first brought from Africa to the New World by the Spanish. **1519** Horses are brought to the New World by Hernán Cortés.	**1525** The Spanish expand Christian missionary activities in the Americas. **1532** Pizarro overthrows the Inca Empire in Peru. **1534** Cartier explores eastern Canada. **1541** Coronado's expedition searches the Southwest for gold. **1542** The New Laws of the Indies regulate life in the Spanish colonies.	**ca 1550** The Portuguese import slaves to Brazilian plantations. **ca 1550** Cattle are introduced on the South American pampas. **1553** The University of Mexico is founded. **1555** Many Mexican churches and monasteries are built by Indian converts. **1565** The Spanish explore and settle in Florida.	**1587** English colonists settle briefly at Roanoke Island. **1592** Juan de Fuca explores the northwestern American coast. **1595** Sir Walter Raleigh explores the Orinoco River, Venezuela. **1598** Spanish settlers in New Mexico introduce wheat, peaches, melons, and apricots.	**1600** Five Algonquin tribes unite to form the Powhatan Confederacy. **1607** The English establish a settlement on the James River. **1610-16** Hudson, Champlain, and Baffin explore Canadian waterways. **1612** Tobacco is first grown as a commercial crop. **1619** The first Virginia assembly meets.	
EUROPE	**1500-1520** Invasions and battles continue between France, Italy, the Holy Roman Empire, and Scandinavian countries. **1512** Copernicus postulates a sun-centered universe. **1517** Martin Luther instigates the Protestant Reformation. **1519-1522** Magellan circumnavigates the globe for Portugal.	**1525** The Peasants' War rages in Germany. **1528** Paracelsus writes a manual of surgery. **1530-1541** England, Scotland, and parts of Germany favor Protestantism. **1545** The Council of Trent meets to discuss the Catholic Counter-Reformation.	**1553** An English trading expedition reaches Russia. **1555** Europe imports tobacco. **1560s** The French continue religious wars. **1566-1571** The Ottomans threaten eastern Europe, then retreat after the Battle of Lepanto. **1572** The Dutch begin a battle for independence from Spain.	**1575-1582** Universities are founded in Leiden, Warsaw, and Edinburgh. **1577-1580** The English circumnavigate the globe. **1579** An English-Dutch alliance encourages Dutch independence. **1588** The Spanish Armada attempts to invade England, but is defeated. **1589-1591** Machinery is adapted to run knitting looms and saws.	**1600s** European powers expand their colonization efforts. **1610** Galileo discovers Jupiter's moons; Harriot discovers sunspots. **1614** Power struggles begin between the English king and Parliament. **1618** The Thirty Years' War begins in central Europe. **1619** Harvey describes circulation of the blood.	
MIDDLE EAST & AFRICA	**1500-1520** African-European trade expands in Africa. **1501** Ismail Sufan establishes Safavid Empire in Iran. **1506** King Afonso of Kongo introduces European customs. **1517** Ottoman Sultan Selim conquers the Arab world. His son Suleyman I expands the empire into the Balkans and Persia.	**1526** Ottomans overcome the Hungarians and continue to fight the Persians. **1530-1540** The Songhai Empire, with its capital at Timbuktu, dominates West Africa. Islamic studies flourish at the university and at many schools of the Koran in Timbuktu. **1540s** Ottoman urban and architectural achievements grow.	**1555** Ottomans and Safavids declare peace. **1556** Kongo wages war against Ndongo. **1560s** The slave trade increases in West Africa. **1568** Maize, manioc, and peanuts arrive in Africa. **1571** Ottomans suffer a naval defeat at Lepanto.	**1587** The Portuguese take control of the Cape Verde Islands. **1590** Shah Abbas of Persia settles his capital at Isfahan, which he rebuilds with magnificent mosques and markets. **1591** Morocco overthrows the Songhai Empire. **1593** Ottomans begin the Long War against Austria.	**1600-1620** Christian Ethiopia suffers attacks from Muslims. **ca 1600** European trade with Persia increases. **1616** Ethiopia attacks Jewish areas within their empire. **1620s** East African tribes move into the southern grasslands. **1623** Queen Nzinga drives the Portuguese from Ndongo.	
ASIA & OCEANIA	**1502-1510** The Portuguese establish colonies on the Indian coast at Cochin and Goa. **1514** The Chinese encounter Portuguese who sailed from India. **1520** The Chinese begin increasing their use of gunpowder weapons modeled on European designs. **1523** The Chinese expel the Portuguese.	**1526** Babur invades India from the north and founds the Mughal state. **1536** Emperor Akbar centralizes power in the Mughal territories. **1530** China expands the use of silver coinage. **1540-1550** The Japanese attack China's coasts; Mongols attack the interior. **1549** Jesuit missionaries enter Japan.	**1550s** Mughal Emperor Akbar of India reforms taxes and encourages religious toleration. **1550s** Japanese pirates continue attacks on the Chinese coast. **1550s** The Japanese merchant class grows; cities and leisure arts flourish. **1570** Japan opens the port of Nagasaki to Western traders.	**1577** Dalai Lama visits Mongolia, which adopts Tibetan Buddhism. **1581** Mughal Emperor Akbar of India conquers Afghanistan. **1581** Silver is used as the base for the monetary system of Ming China. **1592-96** The Japanese embark on attempts to conquer Korea; all fail.	**1600** Ieyasu begins the unification of Japan. **1604** Donglin Academy is founded in China. **1610** European powers skirmish over trade rights in India. **1611** The Spanish open trade with the Japanese. **1620s** The English and Dutch continue to expand trade in Asia.	

1625	1650	1675	1700	1725-1750
1625-29 Ironworks and printing begin in the English colonies. **1625-1643** The colonies of New Hampshire, Massachusetts, Rhode Island, Connecticut, Maryland, and New Sweden (Delaware) are established. **1630s** Southwestern Indians use horses. **1636** Harvard College is founded.	**1660s** Domestic stock and crops, not wild game, now provide most of the food in the English colonies. **1663-1670** Slave trade in Indian peoples begins in the Carolinas. **1664** The English take New Netherland and rename it New York. **1672** Marquette and Joliet explore the upper Mississippi River.	**1675** King Philip's War erupts in New England. **1676** Bacon's Rebellion terrorizes Virginians. **1680** The Pueblo Revolt drives Spaniards from New Mexico. **1678-1689** French explorers travel the Great Lakes, continuing west to the Great Salt Lake. **1680s** Rice is first planted in South Carolina.	**1700-1702** The French explore and trade along the Mississippi. **1700-1720** Industries develop further in North America, including distilling, ironworks, and gunsmithing. **1701** Yale University is founded. **1702-1715** Skirmishes are ongoing between English and French colonists and Indian allies.	**1730s** English colonies experience a religious revival: the Great Awakening. **1732** The colony of Georgia is chartered by King George II. **1744** Benjamin Franklin develops the Franklin stove. **1744-48** King George's War rages in New England.
1629 Branca invents a steam turbine. **1635** Postal service unites London and Edinburgh. **1642** Pascal invents an adding machine. **1642-49** The English civil wars pit king against Parliament. **1649** Ireland suffers an English invasion.	**1653-1660** England becomes a kingless Commonwealth, then restores the monarchy. **1654** Pascal and Fermat develop a theory of probability. **1656** Huygens discovers the rings of Saturn. **1666** Newton develops calculus; calculates the moon's orbit.	**1682-85** French religious conflict renews; Huguenots are persecuted and exiled. **1688** The English depose the king in the bloodless Glorious Revolution. **1697-98** Peter the Great travels and studies in western Europe. **1699** The English explore the South Seas and scout Australia.	**1700** Peter the Great begins a campaign of westernization in Russia. **1701** Tull invents a seed drill for efficient sowing. **1702-09** The English battle the French and Habsburg allies in the War of Spanish Succession. **1720s** English novelists, dramatists, and periodicals flourish.	**1727** English Quakers campaign against slavery. **1728** A treatise on dentistry appears in France. **1730-1743** Russia, the Holy Roman Empire, and Persia battle the Ottomans. **1740-48** The War of the Austrian Succession involves most of the European powers.
1626 The French establish settlements on the Senegal River. **1630-1660** Queen Nzinga continues fighting the Portuguese. **1631** The Gold Coast opens trade to the English. **1631** The Dutch and Portuguese battle for Gold Coast trade concessions. **1645** Ottomans invade Crete.	**1650** Muslims move into Fulani lands in West Africa. **1652** Arab traders in East Africa traffic in slaves and spices. **1657-59** The Dutch defeat Khoekhoen near the Cape of Good Hope and expand their holdings. **1670** Asante (Ashanti) clans begin to unify under Osei Tutu.	**1677** The Dutch continue expanding into South Africa. **1683** The Ottomans lose a last siege against Vienna and begin withdrawing from Europe. **1688** French Huguenots settle in South Africa. **1689** The Dutch colonize Natal. **1696** The Asante kingdom expands.	**1703** Islamic science is enriched by European instruments such as the telescope. **1713** Smallpox devastates South Africa, opening new land to settlement. **1720s** The Ottomans enter a decadent phase characterized by luxurious lifestyles and governmental corruption.	**1729-1742** The Ottomans relax laws against printing; publications on history, geography, and language appear in Turkish and Arabic. **1730** The Ottomans revolt against increasing taxes and western influences. **1750** The kingdom of Darfur expands in East Africa.
1620-1630 The Japanese expel foreign traders and repudiate foreign influences. **1644** Peasant revolts, bandit wars, and invasions plague the Ming rulers of China. **1644** Manchus from the north overthrow the Ming and establish the Qing dynasty.	**1651** The Qing control all of China except Taiwan and Yunnan. **1656** Pirates harry the Chinese coast; the Qing order evacuation. **1660** Mughal Emperor Aurangzeb battles insurgency from local states within India. **1668** The English East India Company controls Bombay.	**1679** Vietnam takes the Mekong delta from Cambodia. **1681** The Qing relax laws discriminating against the Han Chinese. **1681** The Chinese increase rice yields to three harvests per year. **1690s** The Mughal Empire fragments under pressure from European powers and Indian ethnic states.	**1700** Kabuki theater flourishes in Japan, enriched by samurai legends. **1707** Mount Fuji erupts. **1720** Tibet becomes a Chinese protectorate. **1722** The Dutch land on Easter Island.	**1736-1750** China reaches its greatest geographical extent. **1739** Persians attack the Punjab and loot Mughal cities. **1744** Jesuits reform the Chinese calendar; introduce western scientific instruments. **1750s** The Japanese merchant class stimulates theater, poetry, and Shinto scholarship.

	POLITICS & POWER	GEOGRAPHY & ENVIRONMENT	CULTURE & RELIGION
THE AMERICAS	**1500 Native American tribes** of the upper Midwest are unsettled; relations become uneasy between them. **1500s The Spanish Requermiento** demands that indigenous peoples met by the conquistadores submit to the Spanish monarch and to the pope. **1509-1511 The Spanish** invade and conquer Puerto Rico, Jamaica, and Cuba.	**1502 Christopher Columbus** makes his final voyage to the New World, visiting Panama and Honduras. **1502 Amerigo Vespucci** of Italy makes his second voyage to the New World. **1513 Vasco Nuñez de Balboa** crosses the Isthmus of Panama and sees the Pacific Ocean. **1513 Ponce de León** explores Florida.	**1508 Pope Julius II** grants Spain the right to control missionary efforts in the New World. **1511 Father Antonio Montesinos** condemns the Spanish settlers on Hispaniola for cruelty toward the Indians and questions Spanish right to rule the natives. *Leonardo da Vinci's* Mona Lisa *with her mysterious smile*
EUROPE	**1500 Invasions and battles** are ongoing between France, the Italian principalities, and parts of the Holy Roman Empire. Papal authority intervenes in many of the disputes. **1500 King Ferdinand of Spain** suppresses the Moors. **1508 Maximilian I** becomes Holy Roman Emperor; Pope Julius II rules that future German kings will be Holy Roman Emperors. **1509 Henry VIII** becomes king of England and marries Catherine of Aragon, his brother's widow.		**1500 Hieronymus Bosch** paints the allegorical *Ship of Fools*. **1500-1515 Active artists** include Botticelli, Cellini, Cranach, Dürer, Grünewald, Leonardo, Michelangelo, Palladio, and Raphael. **1501 Book burning** is authorized by papal bull. **1503 Leonardo da Vinci** paints *La Gioconda (Mona Lisa)*. **1508-1512 Michelangelo** paints the ceiling of the Sistene Chapel, Vatican Palace.
MIDDLE EAST & AFRICA	**1500 The population of the Ottoman Empire** is about nine million. The population of the Safavid Empire is about five million. The population of sub-Saharan Africa is about 34 million. **1500s The Ethiopian Empire** continues its expansion through conquest. **1500s The Songhai Empire** expands in North Africa. **1502-1509 The Portuguese** conquer East African coast peoples to gain control of trade. **1514 Ottomans** defeat Safavids at Chaldiran in northwest Persia.	**1500s Jews** move into Ottoman Empire from Europe. **1500s Tutsi herders** from the northwest drift into lands held by the Hutu. **1500s Somalis** settle in the area south and east of Ethiopia and convert to Islam. **1509 Constantinople** suffers a disastrous earthquake.	**1500 In many schools** in Timbuktu at this time, the Koran is studied. There is also an Islamic university there. **ca 1500 Neshri and Idris Bitlisi** write classical histories of the Ottoman Empire. **ca 1500 The first Ottoman miniatures** are painted. **1506 King Afonso I** of Kongo begins introducing European customs to the country. **1513 Piri Reis,** Ottoman geographer, draws a world map including the Americas.
ASIA & OCEANIA	**ca 1500 Japanese daimyo lords** struggle for control as the Ashikaga shogunate weakens. **1506 Zhengde** becomes emperor of China. **1510 The Portuguese** under Afonso de Albuquerque take over Goa. **1511 The Portuguese** capture Malacca in Malaysia.	**1502 Vasco Da Gama** establishes a Portuguese colony at Cochin. **1514 The Portuguese** reach China. **1514 Silver mines** open in western Yunnan, China.	**ca 1500 Landscape painter** Shen Zhou is active in China. **1506 Chinese fashion** favors military styles. Armor is worn over silk. **ca 1510 Zhon Chen,** a painter of street people, is active in China. OPPOSITE: *This map highlights the explorers and trade routes that made Portugal the first European country to establish an overseas empire.*

SCIENCE & TECHNOLOGY

1500 New World crops and planting methods begin to be exported to Europe: maize, tobacco, tomatoes, chocolate, potatoes, sweet potatoes, peppers, peanuts, manioc, squashes, pineapples, avocados, guavas, papayas, blueberries, vanilla, and maple syrup.

ca 1500 The English navy begins building ships with double gun decks, carrying up to 70 guns.

1500 The first successful caesarean birth from a living mother is recorded, in Switzerland.

1502 Peter Heinlein of Germany constructs the first working watch movement.

1505 Italian mathematician Scipione del Ferro solves cubic equations.

1512 Nicolas Copernicus first notes his belief that planets revolve around the sun.

PEOPLE & SOCIETY

1500s The encomienda system of land grants to individuals, including the right to command native labor, extends across Spanish possessions in the New World.

1500 The Inuit of Greenland encounter a Portuguese expedition under Gaspar Corte-Real.

1502 Moctezuma II becomes the ruler of the Aztec dominions.

1509 African slaves are brought to the New World in quantity for the first time. Bartolomé de Las Casas, planter in Hispaniola, encourages Spanish colonists to bring Africans to the Americas.

1500 Card games gain increasing popularity across Europe.

1500 Regular postal service is begun between Brussels and Venice; it is extended to other cities between 1504 and 1516.

1506 Niccolò Machiavelli organizes a militia in Florence, Italy.

1506 The first regular newspaper appears, published in Germany, called *Avisa Relation oder Zeitung.*

1513 Pope Leo X uses concave lenses to aid his vision while hunting.

PORTUGAL SETS SAIL

Determined to establish and control new trade routes, Portugal was exploring the Atlantic by 1420. Prince Henry the Navigator's center at Sagros collected information; supervised mapmaking; designed ships; and adapted the cross-staff, quadrant, and mathematical tables. By 1444 Portugal had reached West Africa. By 1482 they had a fort on the Gold Coast (Ghana) and commanded traffic in ivory, gold, pepper, and slaves.

From there, navigators such as Bartholomeu Dias and Vasco da Gama explored Africa's east coast, India, and southeast Asia, often impressing the locals by slaughtering them. Once new forts were established, priests followed to spread Catholicism.

Successful Portuguese and Spanish expansion in the 1500s signaled a new direction for European interests: outward into the Atlantic and the unknown. The colonial era was just beginning.

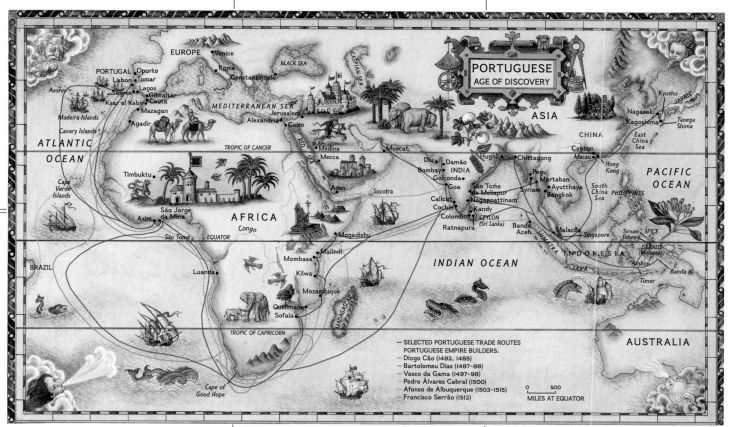

THE GENIUS OF THE RENAISSANCE

DURING THE RENAISSANCE THE CULTURAL ORIENTATION OF EUROPE CHANGED from a focus primarily on religious goals and values to one that blended Christianity with the classical past and direct observation of the world. Traditions of the Greco-Roman world were rediscovered as the works of authors like Plato, Pliny, and Cicero emerged from monastic libraries or were translated out of Arabic to circulate among the wealthy bankers and merchants of 15th-century Italy. The classics valued reason and visual evidence over belief and imagination as sources of truth. To understand the world as the ancients had, it was clearly necessary to look inward at oneself—inward examination set parameters for viewing from a verifiable, human vantage point. This new perspective was reflected throughout the arts, first in literature, then in painting and architecture.

In the 1400s Italian masters codified principles of representing three-dimensional objects on a flat surface by the use of perspective and foreshortening. In the 1500s Michelangelo, Mantegna, and Tintoretto used these techniques to produce emotional, convincingly realistic images. Leonardo noted that the far distance was bluer in color than the near; his manipulated tones and lines achieve panoramic landscapes such as appear behind *Mona Lisa.* As three-dimensional painting became more accomplished it introduced a new element: strong sensory appeal. By the later 1500s artists were working not merely to educate, but also to entertain. Contrasts and textures, shapes elongated and emphasized to create pleasing rhythms within compositions, studied repetitions of color that led the eye across an area—these became familiar components of successful paintings. In sculpture, artists made fresh use of exaggeration and a preference for dramatic moments. Both portraits and scenes abandoned the static; 16th-century figures seem arrested in the midst of vigorous action.

Interior decoration became popular, too. Following examples of excavated Roman rooms, the interior walls of palaces and public spaces were painted with lavish decorations ranging from charming domestic scenes to the sublime illusion of the ceiling of the Sistine Chapel at the Vatican.

Celebrated artists not only painted and carved, but also made dining vessels, jewelry, and other objects. Unlike medieval painters and sculptors, often identified only by the pieces they had painted or the churches they embellished, artists of the Renaissance were international stars—Michelangelo was known as Il Divino among contemporaries. In constant demand, engaged by emperors and popes, painters and sculptors documented themselves enthusiastically. Dürer painted himself repeatedly; Ghiberti and Michelangelo set their own recognizable features into their masterpieces. The printing press enabled important artworks to become popular: Paintings, statuary, and even architectural drawings, reproduced as wood blocks and engravings, spread Renaissance visions rapidly across the known world.

One of the masterpieces of Western art, Michelangelo's Sistine Chapel ceiling chronicles Biblical history, including the creation of Adam.

	POLITICS & POWER	GEOGRAPHY & ENVIRONMENT	CULTURE & RELIGION
THE AMERICAS	**1519 Hernán Cortés** lands on the coast of Yucatán and marches to the Aztec capital; Moctezuma is killed. **1520s The Spanish** take over Colombia, El Salvador, and Guatemala. **1521 Cortés** defeats the Aztec and claims Mexico for Spain. **1524 Spain** establishes the Council of the Indies for colonial affairs. Viceroys based in Mexico City and later in Lima, Peru, rule under the council. **1527 The Inca brothers** Huascar and Atahualpa begin a bloody civil war.	**1515 Spanish navigator** Juan Díaz de Solís reaches the mouth of the Rio de Plata on the Argentine coast. **1521 The Spanish** establish a colony in Venezuela. **1524 Italian Giovanni da Verrazano** explores the North American coast and discovers New York Bay. **1527 Cabeza de Vaca** and his companions, shipwrecked on the Texas coast, wander for nine years through the southwest before reaching Mexico.	**1524 Franciscan missionaries** arrive in Mexico from Spain. Franciscans are the main chaplains of the Spanish exploring North America. **1529 Bernardino de Sahagún,** Franciscan missionary, arrives in New Spain. In the later 1530s he begins recording oral histories of Aztec life and culture. Eventually his work appears as 12 volumes called *A General History of the Things of New Spain*.
EUROPE	**1515 Francis I** becomes king of France. **1516 Archduke Charles** becomes King Charles I of Spain. **1518 The Peace of London** is agreed to among England, France, Spain, the Holy Roman Emperor Maximilian I, and the pope. **1519 Maximilian I** dies and Charles I of Spain becomes Charles V, Holy Roman Emperor. The Habsburgs begin to consolidate power across Europe. **1520 Christian II,** king of Denmark and Norway, defeats the Swedes in battle and becomes king of Sweden as well.	**1519 Ferdinand Magellan,** Portuguese navigator, sets off with five Spanish ships to circumnavigate the globe. **1522 One ship of Magellan's expedition** arrives back in Europe. *Legend has it that Martin Luther nailed his 95 theses to a church door in Wittenberg.*	**1516 Sir Thomas More** writes *Utopia*. **1517 Martin Luther,** Augustinian monk, priest, and teacher at the University of Wittenberg, sends 95 theses questioning church doctrine to the Bishop of Mainz. **1519 Ulrich Zwingli** preaches reformation of the church in Switzerland. **1520 Pope Leo X** excommunicates Martin Luther. **1521 Luther** begins translating the Bible into German. It is completed in 1534. **1527 Protestantism** grows in Sweden. A Protestant university opens at Marburg.
MIDDLE EAST & AFRICA	**1515 The Songhai Empire** is at its height. Its capital is at Timbuktu. **1517 Ottoman Turks** defeat Mamluk forces in Egypt, take Cairo, and establish suzerainty over Egypt and the Hejaz (Arabian Peninsula). **1518 Khayr al-Din (Barbarossa),** a North African pirate, receives Ottoman aid against the Spanish. **1520 Suleyman I (the Magnificent)** assumes the throne of the Ottoman Empire. **1521-22 Suleyman's forces** capture Belgrade, then Rhodes. In 1526 he defeats the Hungarians at Mohacs.		**1515 Ottoman Sultan Selim I** declares Sunni Islam the state religion and begins persecuting Shiites in retaliation for Safavid persecution of Sunnis. Many Shiites join the mystical Sufi orders and masquerade as Sunnis. **1520 Henry,** son of King Afonso of Kongo, studies in Kongo, Lisbon, and Rome. He becomes the first sub-Saharan African to be consecrated a Catholic bishop. **1526 The Muslim state of Adal** declares a jihad on Christian Ethiopia. **ca 1530 Ibn Kemal** writes a multivolume history of the Ottomans and standard works on religious sciences.
ASIA & OCEANIA	**1523 The Chinese** expel the Portuguese. **1526 Babur,** a descendant of Genghis Khan in Central Asia, invades India, occupies Delhi and Agra, and founds the Mughal dynasty.	**1517 The Portuguese** establish a trade foothold in Colombo, Ceylon, and sail on to Canton, China.	**ca 1520 The neo-Confucian thinker** Wang Yongming is influential in Ming China.

SCIENCE & TECHNOLOGY	PEOPLE & SOCIETY
1517 The first coffee from the Americas is sent to Europe. **1519 Indians** encounter horses brought to the New World by Hernán Cortés. In time, using and riding horses will transform Indian economies, politics, and lifestyles. **1520 The first chocolate** from Mexico is sent to Europe. **1524 The first turkeys** from the Americas are sent to Europe.	**1515 Bartolomé de Las Casas,** now in holy orders as a Dominican friar, campaigns in Spain for freedom and better treatment for the indigenous peoples of the Americas. He proposes that Spanish farmers should come to colonize and work alongside the Indians. **1519 The indigenous population** of New Spain is estimated at 25 million. **1520 La Malinche,** a native woman, becomes the mistress and interpreter of Hernán Cortés.
1515 France opens the first national factories for production of weapons and textiles. **1518 Eyeglasses** to aid the shortsighted are made from ground lenses. **1518 Philippus Paracelsus,** Swiss physician, uses laudanum as a painkiller. **1522 Albrecht Dürer** designs a flying machine. **1528 Philippus Paracelsus** writes the first modern manual of surgery.	**1519 Vasco Nuñez de Balboa** is tried in Spain for desertion and treason. He is convicted and beheaded. **1519 Ferdinand Magellan** takes his expedition across the Atlantic, suppresses a mutiny, and navigates through a dangerous passage at the tip of South America into the Pacific Ocean. **1521 Magellan** is embroiled in a native dispute in the Philippines and killed. **1528 Henry VIII** of England seeks a divorce from Catherine of Aragon.
1511-1526 The Ottomans provide military aid in the form of cannon and harquebuses, shipbuilders, and captains to Egypt (1511), Mecca (1517), and Abyssinia (1526), and even send gunmakers to Babur in India (1526).	**1520 Under Suleyman the Magnificent,** the Ottoman Empire is at its height. Influence expands, programs of shipbuilding and construction fuel the economy, laws are reinterpreted and reformed, and art and literature flourish.
1520 The Chinese first use cannon bought from the Portuguese.	**1521 The people of Guam** encounter their first European visitor, Ferdinand Magellan.

CORTÉS THE CONQUEROR

Hernán Cortés was born in Spain in 1485, raised in a harsh region with a tradition of peasant hardiness and religious warfare. At the age of 19 he sailed for Hispaniola, where he became a farmer and town official before accompanying Diego Velásquez in the invasion of Cuba in 1511.

In 1518 Velásquez appointed Cortés to settle a colony on the American mainland, after previous efforts had failed. Cortés assembled a powerful invasion force and landed on the Yucatán with 11 ships, 600 armored men, cannon, and horses. He left no doubt as to his resolve by ordering his ships burned, committing his men to conquest with promises of gold and blessings from God.

Intimidating the Indians with his cannon and horses, Cortés assembled more than 200,000 allies against the Aztec and marched toward their capital of Tenochtitlan (Mexico City). He was aided by Aztec legends that foretold of a white conqueror and by the diplomacy of an Indian woman, La Malinche, who negotiated for him. Welcomed to the capital by its ruler, Moctezuma, who soon submitted to Cortés's authority, the Spanish were amazed by the splendor of the Aztec Empire, and they were eager to plunder it.

In 1520 Velásquez sent a force after Cortés, who sped to the coast and convinced his would-be arrestors to join him. But in his absence, the Aztec revolted. Moctezuma was killed, and ten months later, with a powerful army of Spanish and Indian allies, Cortés retook Tenochtitlan. He ordered the looting and wrecking of cities throughout the Aztec Empire, believing it was God's work to destroy this pagan culture.

This extraordinary conquistador had conquered an empire of 11 million people with just a few hundred men. But Cortés was beset by intrigue from jealous compatriots. He died in Spain at the age of 62, disillusioned and in embroiled in litigation.

POLITICS & POWER	GEOGRAPHY & ENVIRONMENT	CULTURE & RELIGION

THE AMERICAS

1530 The Spanish invade and conquer Ecuador, Paraguay, and part of Chile.

1532 Francisco Pizarro invades Peru and kills Inca ruler Atahualpa.

1535 The first viceroy of the New World arrives in Mexico City.

1536 Inca insurgents besiege Pizarro's forces in Cuzco, but are defeated.

1540 Francisco Vásquez de Coronado defeats Indians in an area north of Mexico.

1540s Native revolts against the Portuguese break out on the Brazilian coast.

1530 The Portuguese give individuals land grants in Brazil and extensive power to develop them.

1534 Jacques Cartier of France explores Labrador and the St. Lawrence River as far as the site of Quebec.

1536 Spain annexes Cuba.

1540 Spanish explorers discover the Grand Canyon of the Colorado.

1541 Francisco Vásquez de Coronado crosses southwestern North America in search of reputed cities of gold. He finds pueblos.

1530s Religion becomes a source of conflict. Many indigenous American religions are earth centered, in contrast to Spanish Christianity's focus on the afterlife.

1531 Indian convert Juan Diego has visions of the Virgin Mary at Guadalupe near Mexico City. A popular shrine develops at the site.

1542 Fra Bartolomé de Las Casas and Dr. Juan Ginés de Sepúlveda debate "the capacity of Indians to Christianize and westernize."

EUROPE

1530 Charles V, Holy Roman Emperor, is crowned king of Italy.

1530 German princes form the Schmalkaldic League to oppose Charles V and his threats to Lutheranism. Under the league's protection, the Reformation spreads through Germany.

1544 Swedish succession is attached to the hereditary male line.

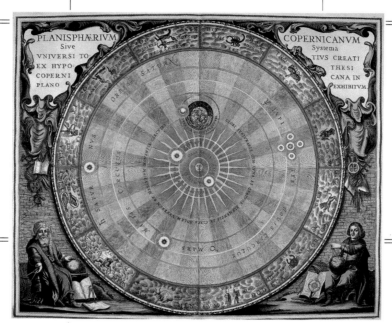

The Copernican world system challenged the traditional view of the solar system by placing the sun at the center; the earth and its moon, along with the planets, revolve around it.

1531 Henry VIII declares England free from the rules of the Catholic Church. He, as king, heads the English church.

1532 Francois Rabelais publishes the bawdy satire *Pantagruel.*

1534 Ignatius Loyola founds The Society of Jesus (Jesuits) in Spain.

1539 Angela Merici founds the Ursuline order.

1542 Pope Paul III begins the Inquisition in Rome.

MIDDLE EAST & AFRICA

1533 Khayr al-Din (Barbarossa) is made chief admiral of the powerful Ottoman fleet.

1533-34 The Ottomans wage war against Persia and take over Mesopotamia.

1538 Khayr al-Din defeats Charles V's fleet at Preveza. The Ottomans now rule the eastern Mediterranean region. Ottomans gain Basra.

1543 The Ottoman fleet winters in Toulon due to the Ottoman-French alliance against the Habsburgs.

1530s Fuzuli of Baghdad becomes the Ottoman court poet. His contemporary, Baki, who gains fame at 19 in 1545, becomes a close friend of Suleyman I.

ca 1535 Motrakci Nasru compiles a description of towns along the road from Istanbul to Baghdad after the Mesopotamian campaign, illustrated with miniatures of the major towns.

ASIA & OCEANIA

1533 North Vietnam splits into the kingdoms of Tonking and Annam.

1536 Akbar becomes emperor of India. He develops loyalty to his regime by giving local nobles government posts in his bureaucracy.

1543 The Portuguese reach Japan and introduce firearms there.

1542 Mughal Emperor Akbar's reforms unify Hindus and Muslims under his rule.

1543 The first *sowon,* or private academy, is founded by the Yi dynasty in Korea. It is patterned on the Chinese academies of earlier times that taught neo-Confucianism.

SCIENCE & TECHNOLOGY	PEOPLE & SOCIETY
1532 Sugar cane is first cultivated in Brazil.	**1534 Iroquois tribes** in the Northeast meet French explorer Jacques Cartier. **1535 Manco Inca** founds the state of Vilcam-bamba in the Peruvian highlands. It survives until 1572. Pizarro founds the capital of Spanish power at Lima on the coast. **1539 Hernando de Soto's** expedition commits rape and murder as the force travels through Indian lands in the American southeast. **1542 The New Laws of the Indies** regulate Spanish activities in the New World. They set limits on Indian tribute, restrict Indian enslavement, and prohibit forced labor, reducing the power of the encomiendas.
1530 The spinning wheel is now in general use in Europe, replacing the drop spindle. **1540 Michael Servetus** describes pulmonary circulation. **1543 Andreas Vesalius,** a Flemish professor at the University of Padua, publishes human anatomical studies based on dissections. **1543 Nicholas Copernicus** publishes his treatise on the heliocentric universe, *De Revolutionibus,* and dies shortly thereafter.	**1530 A criminal code** and rules to govern a police force are introduced in the Holy Roman Empire. **1536 John Calvin,** becoming an influential Protestant leader, writes *The Institutes of the Christian Religion.* He settles in Geneva.
1530s Major Ottoman works on logic, grammar, biography, and the religious sciences are written. **1530s African iron and steel** is exported to Portugal. **1543 Theorems in mathematical astronomy** and the description of the circulation of the blood, developed by Arab scientists and contained in Arabic and Byzantine manuscripts in European libraries, are employed by Copernicus.	**1539 Mimar Sinan,** the greatest Ottoman architect, designs his first nonmilitary structure. He will eventually create over 80 mosques, 34 palaces, 55 schools, and many other public buildings. His great ambition is to create a domed structure in which all the parts work together and which surpasses in size the dome of Aya Sofia. He finally achieves this in the Selimiye mosque in Edirne. **1540s Empress Sabla Wangel** of Ethiopia supervises the defense of her country against Arab attackers.
	1530 The Chinese extend the system of monetary taxation based on silver ingots (until 1581).

Torture on the fire wheel forced Inquisition victims to recant heresy.

THE SPANISH INQUISITION

Inquisition was a judicial process to investigate heresy, sorcery, or other deviations from the Catholic faith. Ferdinand and Isabella were granted an Inquisition in 1478 to quell civil conflicts between conversos (Jewish and Muslim converts) and Christian Spaniards. Eventually the Inquisition operated in Spanish colonies as well as Spain itself. The system relied on local courts and traveling inquisitors; a High Council of five members ruled over the local courts.

Individuals were accused, anonymously, of heretical behavior. Defendants had lawyers, and two impartial priests were present at examinations. But defendants were presumed guilty, and torture was sometimes used to extract confessions. If there was evidence of heresy, defendants were urged to recant or convert anew. Those who did so convincingly were freed. Civil authorities executed others, usually by burning at the stake.

During its 350-year history the Inquisition tortured and killed perhaps 5,000 people in Spain and the Americas, but damaged the lives of thousands more.

	POLITICS & POWER	GEOGRAPHY & ENVIRONMENT	CULTURE & RELIGION
THE AMERICAS	**1549 John III** of Portugal names a governor-general of Bahia, the most populous province in Brazil. **1555 France** establishes a settlement in Brazil at the site of Rio de Janeiro.	**1550s The Spanish** introduce European cattle to the pampas areas of Argentina.	**1549 Manoel da Nobrega** founds the first Jesuit mission in Brazil. **1553 The universities of Mexico** and Lima are founded. **1555 Indian converts** build churches and monasteries in Mexico using reliefs and shapes that imitate domestic forms like piles of dishes or the designs on pottery.
EUROPE	**1547 Ivan IV (the Terrible)** becomes tsar of Russia. **1547 Henry VIII** of England dies, succeeded by his 9-year-old son Edward VI. **1553 Edward VI** dies; his Catholic half-sister Mary becomes queen of England. **1555 The Peace of Augsburg** temporarily ends religious conflict in Germany. **1556 Charles V,** Holy Roman Emperor, abdicates in favor of his brother, Ferdinand I. His son becomes Philip II, King of Spain. **1558 Queen Mary** dies; Elizabeth I becomes queen of England.	**1555 Tobacco** is brought to Spain from the Americas.	**1545 Catholic clergy** convene at the Council of Trent to discuss strategies to counter the Reformation. **1548 Jesuit missionaries** arrive in Kongo at the invitation of the king. **1549 A new prayer book** is made official in England, solidifying Protestant practice. **1558 Gioseffo Zarlino** defines the modern major and minor musical scales. **1558 Pieter Breughel,** Flemish painter, begins his most productive ten-year period.
MIDDLE EAST & AFRICA	**1546 Songhai forces** overrun Mali. **1549 Askia David** becomes king of Songhai. **1550 The Wolof Empire** in West Africa dissolves. **1550s The Tutsi** establish the kingdom of Rwanda. **1550s The Ottomans** conquer Tripoli. **1555 Peace** reigns briefly between Ottomans and Safavids. **1556 War** breaks out between Kongo and Ndongo. The Portuguese lend support to Kongo.	**1550 The building of Great Zimbabwe** is completed. **ca 1550 Istanbul** attains a population of half a million. The total Ottoman population is 35 million. **ca 1550 Aqueducts** are built to bring water into Istanbul from hills and reservoirs near the Black Sea. The water flows through a network of pipes and fountains. **1554 Sidi Ali Reis,** Ottoman admiral, writes books on the Indian Ocean, his travels in the Ottoman Empire, astronomy, and mathematics.	**1543 Ethiopia** defeats Adal and remains Christian. **1545-1574 Abu al-Su'ud,** Ottoman chief religious authority, reconciles Islamic and Sultanic law codes, especially criminal and land law. **1548 Jesuit missionaries** arrive in Kongo. **1557 Architect Sinan** completes Suleyman I's mosque complex, including a university, religious school, hospital, and soup kitchen. The center gives a boost to mathematical and medical studies.
ASIA & OCEANIA	**1550 Mongol leader Altan Khan** attacks north China, and the Mongols besiege Beijing. **1550s Chronic warfare** rages among the Japanese daimyo lords, though commerce flourishes. **1550s Japanese pirates** launch repeated attacks on the Chinese coast.	**1555 A disastrous earthquake** in northwest China kills 830,000 people.	**1550s The growing export trade** in Japan creates a new merchant banker class. Cities grow, becoming centers of leisure arts, literature, and theaters.

CONNECTIONS

Riches of the North

The first treasure Europeans found in the American north was the North Atlantic codfish swimming in vast schools off Greenland and Newfoundland, where Basque whalers may have discovered them about 1400. The dried, salted cod they brought home became popular in Europe, but the Basques guarded its source. In 1497 John Cabot, exploring for England, reported that cod filled the northern waters. Jacques Cartier noted 1,000 Basque vessels there in 1535. English, French, and Portuguese fishermen began competing with the Basques and in the 1600s the powerful fleets of England and France claimed possession of the North Atlantic fishing grounds.

SCIENCE & TECHNOLOGY	PEOPLE & SOCIETY
1545-48 Silver mining begins in Potosí, Peru, and Zacatecas, Mexico.	**1550 An Indian fishing village** on the northwest American coast at Ozette is buried by a mud slide, preserving artifacts of a typical Makah settlement of this time.
1550s The Spanish discover gold in central Chile and Colombia.	
1556 A new process facilitating the separation of silver from raw ore boosts the New World mining industry.	**1550 Portuguese planters** begin importing large numbers of African slaves as laborers in the sugar fields.
1558 Silver mines are opened at Guanajuato, Mexico.	**1552 Bartolomé de Las Casas** writes *A Brief Account of the Destruction of the Indies*, describing the horrors of colonial oppression of native peoples.

1545 Italian mathematician Geronimo Cardano publishes solutions of cubic and quartic equations.	**1549 Ivan IV** calls together Russia's first national assembly.
1546 Flemish geographer Gerardus Mercator describes Earth's magnetic poles.	**1550 Cricket** is first described in England.
	1552 Mary, Queen of Scots, plays golf.
1550 German mathematician Georg Rheticus publishes trigonometric tables.	**1553 Richard Chancellor** leads an English expedition to find an overland route to China. He establishes trade relations between England and Russia.

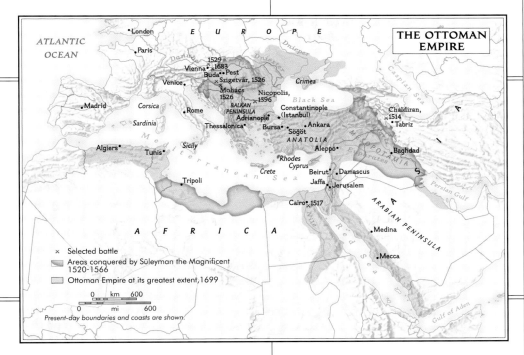

From its beginnings in Anatolia, the Ottoman Empire at its peak expanded until it reached from the Persian Gulf to almost Vienna.

1550 Tang Xi Anzu, Ming playwright and author of *The Peony Pavilion,* is born.

1556-1605 Akbar, Mughal ruler of India, conquers nearly the entire subcontinent, creates an integrated Muslim-Hindu society and culture, and encourages literature in Persian and a flourishing climate for art. He also reforms taxes and encourages religious toleration.

MINING THE NEW WORLD

Spanish conquerors in America produced immense wealth for the Spanish crown, who claimed rights to one-fifth (the Quinto Real) of all gold and silver mined from Mexico and Peru. Pirates preyed on the galleons that carried the precious metals back to Europe (a primary cause of the wars between England and Spain) and fueled the economy of northern ports with captured silver and gold. The flow of metals into Europe boosted supplies of coins, stimulated urban mercantile society, and made trade possible with India and China, who were not attracted by most European goods.

In 1540 the vast Andean silver deposits of Potosí were discovered; in 1548 Zacatecas, then Guanajuato, Mexico, opened up. To get workers for the mines, the Spanish adopted the mita, an Inca tax in the form of prescribed days of labor that took one worker from every family. Avoiding the mita, many fled from their homelands to distant areas, destroying village society.

The mines killed men quickly. Separated from their families, they suffered in the camps and boom towns from polluted water, inadequate shelter, and rampant disease. Narrow shafts pierced the great hill of Potosí; inside, the mines were stiflingly hot and subject to disastrous cave-ins. Miners crept along tunnels in almost total darkness before reaching the workable silver vein; many hours later they crawled out again, exhausted, carrying baskets of ore on their backs. By the mid-1600s mine operators were using mingas, paid laborers deployed in smaller mining camps that moved from place to place when lodes became depleted.

As New Spain developed a culture of its own, colonial governments retained silver to pay salaries, decorate churches, and defend borders. The flow of silver to Europe lessened as Spanish power in the Old World declined and the Americas established the beginnings of autonomy.

THE OTTOMAN EMPIRE

THE OTTOMAN EMPIRE WAS BORN AS MUSLIM HORSEMEN FROM ANATOLIA raided neighboring towns and brought them under their administration. A dynasty of leaders passed control to their sons, beginning with Osman I in the late 13th century. The empire developed siege craft that overcame fortified Byzantine cities, and it grew through both conquest and negotiation. The Ottomans crossed the Bosporus into the Balkans with mercenary troops and settlers in 1346 at the invitation of a rebel Byzantine claimant to the throne.

Bayezid I (1389-1402) expanded eastward into Anatolia, provoking an invasion by Tamerlane, who dismantled the administration of the Ottomans and restored the power of local rulers. Bayezid's son Mehmed I reestablished control and expanded the empire further. For years the Ottomans bypassed Constantinople, the great walled capital of Byzantium in the Bosporus that controlled Venetian trade to the Black Sea and overland to China. Mehmed II laid siege to it in 1453 with 300,000 men, a fleet of galleys, and one of the earliest and largest cannon ever used. Bringing ships overland to the Golden Horn and bombarding Constantinople on all sides, Mehmed took the city and renamed it Istanbul. It became his capital, and he refurbished it and encouraged industry, trade, and the mingling of people from across his domains. Selim I doubled the size of Ottoman territories, adding Syria and Egypt. Suleyman I (1520-1566) took Belgrade and won much of modern Hungary at the Battle of Mohacs in 1526.

The Ottomans were tolerant of different cultures and never imposed a single language or religion on their subjects. But the sultan's hold on power was absolute. The brothers of each new sultan were sometimes executed, along with their families, to avoid disputed successions. Boys were drafted from across the empire to serve in the sultan's *kapikulu,* or slave army. The sultan's slaves enjoyed prestige, however, and families competed to offer their sons. The best were educated with the princes in the palace school and became officials, administrators, and learned men.

Suleyman I, called the Magnificent, ruled Hungary, the Crimea, Iran, Arabia, Greece, and north Africa. But the empire felt increasing strain. European sea routes threatened trade, precious metals from America devalued coinage, and the empire failed to match Western Europe's military modernization, in part because the janissaries, elite corps of soldiers, stifled military innovation until their removal in 1826. The Ottomans were outmaneuvered on the sea at the Battle of Lepanto in 1571, marking a decline in their naval power. And their failed siege of Vienna in 1683 provoked further assaults by emboldened European armies, who drove the Ottomans out of Europe. Nevertheless, a smaller Ottoman Empire survived into the 20th century, when an alliance with the Central Powers in World War I led to final defeat. The sultanate was abolished in 1922, the republic was proclaimed, and the last Ottomans went into exile.

BELOW: *Sultan of sultans, conqueror on three continents, Suleyman I shook the world of the 16th century as he raised the Ottoman Empire to the height of its glory. Known to Europeans as the Magnificent and to his subjects as the Lawgiver, he was both brilliant strategist and equitable administrator.*

OPPOSITE: *A stylized painting depicts Suleyman I and his troops riding into the Battle of Mohacs on August 29, 1526.*

POLITICS & POWER	GEOGRAPHY & ENVIRONMENT	CULTURE & RELIGION

THE AMERICAS

1565 St. Augustine is founded as a refuge for shipwrecked sailors and a base for Spanish salvage operations, especially for the silver fleets that used Florida waters. The city strengthens Spanish claims to Florida against the rival French.

1569 Spanish Viceroy Francisco de Toledo arrives in Peru and stabilizes the government there.

ca 1570 The Spanish invade and take over Nicaragua.

1572 The Spanish capture and behead the last Inca leader, Tupac Amaru, who had ruled from Vilcabamba.

1562 John Hawkins sails from Guinea to the West Indies, carrying a cargo of slaves.

1567 Typhoid kills two million Indians.

1569 King Philip II establishes offices for the Inquisition in Mexico City and Lima, Peru.

1572 Jesuits arrive in New Spain to begin missionary activity. Franciscans forced out of Mexican missions move to the frontiers, where they are successful converting Indians in Florida and New Mexico.

1577 The Inquisition condemns Sahagún for recording pre-Columbian history and excommunicates him. To protect his manuscript, Sahagún sends it to Spain, but it disappears. It is later discovered in a library in Florence, where it becomes known as the Florentine Codex.

EUROPE

1560s France suffers periodic episodes of civil war over religion.

1562 Holy Roman Emperor Ferdinand I signs a truce with Ottoman Emperor Suleyman I.

1564 Ferdinand I dies; his son Maximilian II succeeds him as Holy Roman emperor.

1564 Ivan IV abandons Moscow during a power struggle with the boyars.

1566 The Ottomans and Hungarians renew war, disregarding the truce of 1562.

1572 The Dutch begin fighting for independence from Spain.

An illustration from the Florentine Codex documents an Aztec harvesting amaranth.

1564 The pope approves the publication of an Index of Prohibited Books.

1572 Two thousand French Huguenots are massacred on St. Bartholomew's Day.

1574 Richard Burbage obtains a license to open a theater in London.

1574 The University of Berlin is founded.

MIDDLE EAST & AFRICA

1560s Imbangala forces attack Kongo. King Alvaro I appeals to the Portuguese for arms and troops.

1568 The Portuguese influence pervades the affairs of Kongo and Ndongo (until 1622).

1571 The Ottoman fleet is destroyed by the Spanish at the Battle of Lepanto. A rebuilt fleet conquers Cyprus and Tunis but loses control of the area to pirates.

1573 Ottomans and Venetians sign the Peace of Constantinople.

1574 The Ottomans control much of North Africa, except for Morocco.

1560s New World crops, including manioc and peanuts, arrive in Africa.

1574 The Portuguese establish a colony in Ndongo (today's Angola), but fail to monopolize trade controlled by African merchants.

1560 The slave trade is well established in Central Africa.

1560 Shah Tahmasp of Persia sends Selim II, Ottoman emperor, an illustrated copy of the *Shahname* (Book of Kings), containing 258 miniatures, as a coronation gift. It is perhaps the most magnificent Islamic manuscript ever created.

ASIA & OCEANIA

1569 The Burmese conquer the Ayutthaya kingdom of the Thai peoples and rule until 1590.

1570 Japan opens the port of Nagasaki to Western traders.

1565 Spanish galleons begin annual voyages between Manila and Acapulco.

1567 Álvarode Mendaña de Neira, Spanish explorer sailing from Peru, discovers and names the Solomon Islands.

1573 The Chinese first plant New World crops: sweet potatoes, maize, and peanuts.

1570 The cult of tea reaches its peak of popularity in Japan.

1575 Japanese castle architecture and the related arts associated with powerful daimyo like Nobunaga and Hideyoshi reach the height of their development.

SCIENCE & TECHNOLOGY	PEOPLE & SOCIETY
ca 1560 Mercury is discovered at Huancavelica in Peru. It is used in a cheaper amalgamation process for refining silver ore. Spanish silver remittance begins a steady increase over the next 30 years.	**ca 1560 More than 40,000 Indians** are relocated into *aldeias,* reserved lands for pacified Brazilian Indians. In the 1560s and 1570s, Brazilians mount mass slaving raids against the Guaraní and Tupí peoples. **1570 Algonquin captive Opechancanough** accompanies a Jesuit mission to the Chesapeake, where he leads a band of natives to kill the Jesuits in 1571. In 1622-1632 he fights a losing war against the English in Virginia.
1561 Coins are first produced by a screw mechanism mill in England, in a process that is faster and more consistent than hammering coinage. **1569 Gerardus Mercator** makes a map using a cylindrical projection system to transcribe shapes from a globe to a flat surface. **1572 Danish astronomer** Tyco Brahe discovers a new star—a supernova in Cassiopeia. **1573 A sugar refinery** opens in Augsburg, Germany.	**1560 Catherine de Medici** becomes regent of France. The mother of three French kings, she controls France until 1574, attempting to control religious factions. **1564 Galileo Galilei,** Christopher Marlowe, and William Shakespeare are born. **1568 Bottled beer** is first produced in London.
1569 Ottomans attempt to dig a canal between the Don and Volga Rivers, which would create a passage from the Black Sea to the Caspian.	**ca 1560 Dona Gracia Nasi,** a wealthy Jewish businesswoman, moves to Istanbul with her nephew Don Joseph. She helps Jews settle in the Ottoman domains, vastly increasing the Jewish community there. She and Don Joseph become involved in state finances through their widespread family and economic connections. **1570s Major plague outbreaks** occur in Egypt; plague will recur there periodically until 1865.
1574 The Chinese publish *Taiping Guangzhi,* the first Chinese book printed with movable type.	**1570s Emperor Akbar** reorganizes Indian society, recognizing classes of nobles, zamindars (local agents), and farmers. **1570 New World silver** arrives in China.

GERM WARFARE

Early explorers from Columbus to John Smith reported thriving, populous societies in the Americas on their first visits. Just 20 years later the picture was very different: epidemic disease brought by Europeans devastated native civilizations. During the first 130 years after contact, diseases like smallpox, typhus, diphtheria, influenza, and measles wiped out perhaps 95 percent of the indigenous people.

The Arawaks of Hispaniola, severely afflicted by illness since 1495, were all dead by 1552. The loss of Indian workers encouraged the Spanish to import African slaves as replacements, establishing a new economy with far-reaching cultural consequences. In Peru, recurrent waves of smallpox quickly killed half the population, setting off a civil war among the rulers and enabling Pizarro's tiny force of 168 men to overthrow the vast Inca Empire.

The rich Indian settlements of New England lost 90 percent of their people between 1606 and 1620, probably due to viral hepatitis. The busy urban centers of the Caddo culture dwindled to widely scattered small villages by the mid-1600s as their populations dropped from 200,000 to 9,000.

Many factors contributed to the disaster. Above all, the pathogens were new to Native American immune systems; with no antibodies protecting any individuals, communities died en masse. Pigs introduced by De Soto in 1539 ran wild through the south from Florida to Texas and may have transmitted anthrax, trichinosis, and tuberculosis to wildlife through the food chain. Although Native Americans had many palliative medicines, few could combat the new European diseases.

Lands left empty or weakly defended made colonization easier. In 1763, Sir Jeffrey Amherst suggested giving Indians blankets infected with smallpox, a vicious policy that institutionalized what had begun as a tragic side effect of mingling people with diverse backgrounds and medical histories.

	POLITICS & POWER	GEOGRAPHY & ENVIRONMENT	CULTURE & RELIGION
THE AMERICAS	**1580s Spain** conquers Argentina. Buenos Aires, once abandoned, is now resettled. **1581 The Portuguese crown** is annexed to the Spanish crown in the reign of Philip II. Philip's political struggles against the Dutch in Europe lead to clashes between the Portuguese and Dutch in Brazil. **1584 Sir Walter Raleigh** sends an expedition to scout the North American Atlantic coastal area. They claim it for England and name it Virginia in honor of Queen Elizabeth I.	**1578 Sir Francis Drake** sails up the west coast of North America to the area of Vancouver. He claims the land for England. **1585 Sir Richard Grenville** plants 109 colonists at Roanoke Island, where they found the "city of Raleigh." Sir Francis Drake removes the colonists the next year. **1587 John White** brings 177 colonists, including women and children, to Roanoke Island. He returns to England for supplies.	**1580s The churches of New Spain** are adorned with magnificent altarpieces and paintings by Simón Perenyns and Baltasar de Echave Orio. **1580s The Spanish crown** depends on missionaries and the Catholic Church to bring the Indian peoples under Spanish control. Missionaries cost less than soldiers, and their impact is longer lasting. **1587 Manteo,** a Roanoke Indian, converts to Christianity.
EUROPE	**1575 Philip II** of Spain refuses to grant concessions to Dutch rebels. **1576 Rudolf II** becomes Holy Roman emperor. He will reign until 1612. **1579 The English and Dutch** sign a military alliance against Spain. **1579 The Union of Utrecht** allies seven northern provinces of the low countries against Spain. They later form the Netherlands. **1588 The Spanish Armada** battles the English and is defeated; Spanish power declines.	**1577-1580 Francis Drake** of England circumnavigates the globe.	**1575 The University of Leiden** is founded. **1576 The University of Warsaw** is founded. **1577 Ralph Holinshed** publishes the *Chronicles of England, Scotland and Ireland* in two volumes. **1577 El Greco** begins painting his most important works; this period continues until the 1590s. **1580 Edmund Campion** starts a Jesuit mission in England. He is quickly arrested, tried for treason, and executed. **1582 The University of Edinburgh** is founded.
MIDDLE EAST & AFRICA	**1576-1590 The Ottomans** take the Caucasus, Azerbaijan, and Tabriz in the Ottoman-Iranian war. **1578 Moroccan Sultan al-Malik** defeats the invading Portuguese forces of King Sebastian and deposed Sultan al-Mutawakkil in the Battle of the Three Kings. **1579 Ottomans** make their first trade agreement with England. **1588 Shah Abbas** becomes ruler of the Safavid Empire. He begins rebuilding and enlarging Isfahan and reforms the Persian military and government.	**1583 Traders** lead English expeditions to Mesopotamia, the Persian Gulf, and India.	**ca 1570 The kabalistic school** in Safed (Israel) under Joseph Cordovero and Isaac Luria is now at its height. **1582 The Surname,** or Book of Circumcision, is composed. Its miniatures record the many craft guilds active in the circumcision parade for Ottoman Murad III's sons. **1577-1580 The astronomer Takiyuddin** founds the Observatory of Galatu. Using advanced instruments, he corrects astronomical tables.
ASIA & OCEANIA	**1581 Emperor Akbar** of India conquers Afghanistan. **1581 Russians** complete their conquest of Siberia. **1581 The single-whip tax system** is established in Ming China; silver is used as a value base for monetary system. **1585 Hideyoshi** carries out a survey to establish control over the Japanese economy.	**1579 The Portuguese** establish a trading station in Bengal. **1584 The Dutch** establish a trading post in Arkangel'sk (Archangel), Russia.	**1578 A Chinese treatise on pharmacology,** *Bencao gangmu,* is published. **1580s Matteo Ricci** brings Jesuit missionaries to China. **1588 Under a reorganized Japanese society,** only samurai are privileged to carry weapons. **1584 The Chinese** define their tempered musical scale.

WHAT LIFE WAS LIKE

For Mary, Queen of Scots

Mary, Queen of Scots (1542-1587), only child of James V, was raised a Roman Catholic in France and returned to rule Scotland in 1561. An accomplished, educated woman, she nevertheless badly misjudged Scottish affairs and the power of the nobility. She made two unpopular marriages in succession, alienating powerful nobles and the Presbyterian populace and leading to a civil rebellion that left her faction defeated. Imprisoned in England for 18 years, Mary became the focus of several Catholic plots against Queen Elizabeth I, who finally had her tried for treason and beheaded in 1587. Mary's son, James, inherited the English throne upon Elizabeth's death.

SCIENCE & TECHNOLOGY

1575-1590 Silver production nearly doubles at the Potosí mine in Peru.

1580 Sugar dominates exports from Brazil.

1587 Spanish ships carry 100,000 hides from the cattle of New Spain back to Europe.

1581 Italian Galileo Galilei investigates the properties of the pendulum. In 1589 he is appointed to teach mathematics at the University of Pisa.

1582 Pope Gregory XIII adjusts the Julian Calendar to reflect a more correct year length. The Gregorian Calendar is quickly accepted in Catholic countries, but more gradually throughout Protestant Europe.

1589 William Lee invents the first English knitting machinery.

PEOPLE & SOCIETY

1575 Spanish America imports an average of 1,250 Africans as slaves yearly. Brazil brings in 1,000 Africans a year.

1584 Wanchese and Manteo, Indians from Roanoke Island, sail to England with Sir Richard Grenville.

1583 Life insurance policies are first issued in London.

1589 The French court begins using forks as eating implements.

ca 1575 Ottoman inflation leads to devaluation of silver coinage by 50 percent.

1589 The Ottoman janissaries mutiny over inadequate pay.

Emperor Akbar astride an elephant

THE ARMADA'S LAST STAND

By the late 1500s, Spain was facing a growing challenge to its trade routes with the New World. English merchantmen were making their own voyages to America, and Spanish sanctions provoked costly reprisals from the English corsair Francis Drake. King Philip II become exasperated with these provocations and with English anti-Catholic politics. Supported by the pope, he planned to defeat England using a fleet of 130 ships carrying 30,000 men against the English navy, adding an invasion army of 30,000 men under the Duke of Parma from across the Channel.

For her part, Queen Elizabeth of England authorized Drake to conduct a series of preemptive raids on the Spanish preparations. Philip's armada put to sea in May of 1588 and sailed into English waters in July. The English met them with a comparable number of warships and armed merchantmen commanded by Lord Howard. Winning engagements off Portsmouth, Plymouth, and the Isle of Wight, the English used superior maneuvering, gunnery, and fire ships to harry the Spanish along the length of the English Channel as they made for the French coast.

Parma's army never had to confront an invasion. Unfavorable winds and an English blockade at Calais forced the Spanish to retreat by sailing completely around the British Isles. Water and food supplies ran out and storms wrecked most of the remaining fleet. Survivors who struggled ashore were slaughtered.

The consequences were momentous. Although the Spanish mounted further attacks, their reputation of invincibility had been shattered while the English began their ascent as a major sea power. The outcome stimulated naval technology, secured the Protestant Reformation in England, and broke the Spanish and Portuguese monopoly on world trade. As Spanish power waned, the English, French, and Dutch advanced their own interests in the New World.

	POLITICS & POWER	GEOGRAPHY & ENVIRONMENT	CULTURE & RELIGION

THE AMERICAS

POLITICS & POWER

1598 Authorities in Mexico City send Juan de Oñate with 600 people to colonize the area north of El Paso.

1599 The Spanish enslave the Indians of the pueblos.

1600 Five Algonquin tribes join to form a confederacy under a single ruler, Wa-hun-sen-a-cawh, who is called the Powhatan.

1600s Europeans extend their interests in New World colonies.

GEOGRAPHY & ENVIRONMENT

1590 John White, returning to Roanoke Island with supplies, finds it deserted.

1592 Juan de Fuca, exploring for Spain, sails up the west coast of North America to Canada.

1595 Sir Walter Raleigh leads an expedition that penetrates 300 miles up the Orinoco River in Venezuela.

CULTURE & RELIGION

1595 The Inquisition condemns many conversos (converted Jews) to death at a public sentencing in Mexico City.

1600s Franciscan missionaries in Florida and New Mexico teach Catholic doctrine and liturgy to Indians, encouraging European culture in dress, food, and farming practices.

EUROPE

POLITICS & POWER

1590s The Spanish mount sporadic guerrilla actions against the English authorities in Ireland.

1598 The Edict of Nantes grants civil as well as religious liberties to French Protestants.

1600s Religious wars erupt across Europe.

1600s Power struggles afflict ruling monarchies; some new ruling houses are established.

CULTURE & RELIGION

1590 William Shakespeare's career as a London playwright begins; after 1593 he will produce a new work almost every year.

1593 Henry IV of France converts to Catholicism and reconciles his differences with the pope to end the French religious wars.

1594 Italian philosopher Giordano Bruno, supporter of Copernicus, is imprisoned by the Vatican. He is executed in 1600.

1599 The Globe Theatre is built in London.

A ceramic plate, created by a contemporary Mali artist, illustrates African myths preserved through a rich oral tradition.

MIDDLE EAST & AFRICA

POLITICS & POWER

1590s Kongo is invaded by neighboring states that are supported by Portuguese merchants.

1591 Moroccans conquer the Songhai kingdom. Songhai's subject states break away.

1598 Isfahan becomes the capital of the Safavid Empire in Persia.

1600s The Tutsis rule Urundi (Burundi).

1600s Muslim peoples from the Horn of Africa war against Christian Ethiopia. The Oromo of Ethiopia expand and raid southward.

GEOGRAPHY & ENVIRONMENT

1592 Portuguese traders settle in Mombasa.

1600s The Masai move south from the Rift Valley.

1600s Darfur is established in the Sudan.

CULTURE & RELIGION

1590s The Royal Mosque is constructed in Isfahan. It is a centerpiece of urban planning in the city's expansion. From the later 1500s into the 1600s Shiism assumes a more moderate tone in Persia. Religious and ethnic diversity is tolerated.

ASIA & OCEANIA

POLITICS & POWER

1591 Hideyoshi completes the unification of Japan and begins successive invasions of Korea.

1592 The Nguyen and Trinh lords begin rule in Vietnam; they will hold power until 1788.

1599 China invades Burma.

1600 Ieyasu, founder of the Tokugawa shogunate, defeats rival daimyo in the Battle of Sekigahara to become undisputed ruler of Japan.

1600 Edo (Tokyo) is made the capital of Japan. The emperor's court remains in Kyoto.

GEOGRAPHY & ENVIRONMENT

1592 Sir James Lancaster sails around the Malay peninsula in the Indian Ocean.

1597 The Dutch establish a colony, Batavia, on the island of Java.

1600 Unrestricted felling of trees denudes Easter Island.

1600s The Japanese sail to the East Indies, Malaysia, and Siam under government license.

1602 Spanish traders arrive in Japan.

1604 The Cossacks found a settlement at Tomsk in Siberia.

CULTURE & RELIGION

1592 The Chinese novel *Journey to the West* is published, describing the pilgrimage of a monk in search of Buddhist scriptures.

1600 Tung Ch'i-ch'ang, famous artist, critic and scholar, works in China.

1600s New worship patterns emerge for Hindus as Mughals practice religious tolerance. There are no programs of forced conversion to Islam.

1600s Statue building on Easter Island dies out. Incomplete statues are left in place.

1601 Matteo Ricci, Italian Jesuit missionary, settles in Beijing.

SCIENCE & TECHNOLOGY	PEOPLE & SOCIETY
1598 Spanish colonists introduce wheat, melons, peaches, and apricots to settlements north of El Paso.	**1600 The population of the Americas** begins to show evidence of a century of intermingled peoples. There are many children of mixed indigenous and European blood, especially in Latin America. **1600 Systemic plantation slavery** is well established in Brazil. Slaves learn to manage production of export sugar in factories. Runaway slaves begin to form *quilombos,* free communities in remote areas of Brazil. **1601 The harsh conditions** of life in New Mexico compel many Spanish colonists to abandon settlement.
1590 Galileo Galilei studies falling bodies. **1592 Saws** powered by windmills are used in Holland. **1592 Domenico Fontana** discovers the ruins of the Roman city of Pompeii. **1595 Gerardus Mercator's atlas** is published. **1596 Galileo** invents the thermometer. **1600 Tycho Brahe and Johannes Kepler** begin working together at Brahe's observatory near Prague.	**1597-98 The Elizabethan Poor Laws** are enacted, providing relief for indigent children and the elderly and employment for able-bodied people in parish workhouses. In effect, these laws set up an early social welfare system. **1603 Queen Elizabeth** of England dies, leaving her throne to James VI of Scotland, her nephew. He will reign as James I. **1603 James I** orders Sir Walter Raleigh, fashionable favorite of Queen Elizabeth I, arrested for treason and imprisoned in the Tower of London, signaling a new climate at the English court.
1600s Tobacco is introduced into the Ottoman Empire. **1600s Muslim Empires** import guns, powder, and swords from Europe, as these are of higher quality than those made in the Middle East.	**1600s The English East India Company,** the French East India Company, and the Dutch VOC all trade avidly with the Safavid Empire.

THE EMERGENCE OF RUSSIA

In 1480 Ivan III, Grand Duke of Moscow, freed Muscovy from the Golden Horde of Tartars that had defeated the city-states of Rus in the mid-1200s and exacted heavy tribute from Russian princes ever since. Ivan IV, called Ivan the Terrible, consolidated Ivan the Great's gains and formally took the title of tsar. Ruthless and unpredictable, he conquered even more land.

In the mid-1500s Russians started to move east. Cossacks sailed north-flowing rivers across the continent, attacking and spreading fear as they created settlements along the way, eventually reaching the Pacific Ocean.

Civil conflicts and foreign invasions, called "the time of troubles," followed until Romanov rule began in the early 17th century. Peter I (the Great) became tsar in 1682, reforming and reorganizing the government, adopting the Gregorian calendar, building bridges, roads, canals, and factories, and bringing European craftsman and doctors to Russia. Peter's reign linked Russia's future to the nations of Europe.

1590-1605 Mining fever grows in China, with new appetite for a coin economy.

1598 The Koreans invent an ironclad ship.

1602 Matteo Ricci publishes a Chinese atlas of the world.

This map documents the expansion of Russia from a small principality in 1462 to a major power in 1796.

POLITICS & POWER	GEOGRAPHY & ENVIRONMENT	CULTURE & RELIGION

THE AMERICAS

1607 Englishmen under the command of Captain John Smith build a small settlement on the James River in Virginia.

1608 Pocahontas, daughter of the Powhatan, intercedes in favor of John Smith, captured during a dispute.

1608 Frenchmen Samuel de Champlain establishes a trading fort that will become Quebec.

1616 Samuel de Champlain attacks the Oneida peoples of the Iroquois Confederacy.

1619 The first Virginia colonial assembly meets.

1610 Henry Hudson sails up the St. Lawrence River and discovers Hudson Strait and Hudson Bay.

1610 The city of Santa Fe is founded.

1616 William Baffin, searching for a north-west passage to China through Canada, discovers Baffin's Bay.

1616 Sir Walter Raleigh is released from prison to lead an expedition in search of El Dorado.

1612 Francisco de Parejo's Castilian-Timucuan catechism is published, a bilingual text that is one of the earliest to capture an indigenous language in print.

EUROPE

1605 English Catholic conspirators, including Guy Fawkes, set explosives in Westminster, but their Gunpowder Plot is discovered.

1608 An attempted Irish rebellion against the English authorities collapses.

1609 The northern Netherland provinces become independent of Spain.

1610 King James I discontinues a session of Parliament; disagreements between the kings and Parliament will continue for the next 50 years.

1613 Michael Romanov is chosen tsar of Russia. His family will rule until 1917.

1605-1612 Miguel de Cervantes Saavedra publishes *Don Quixote.*

1605-1612 Shakespeare writes his masterpieces *King Lear, Macbeth, The Winter's Tale,* and *The Tempest.*

1606-07 Italian opera is growing in popularity.

1610 Jeanne de Chantal and Francis de Sales found the Order of the Visitation.

1611 A new version of the Bible is published in English, authorized and patronized by King James I.

1612 Heretics are burned in England by the authorities for the last time.

William Shakespeare

MIDDLE EAST & AFRICA

1600s The Luba-Lunda peoples move into northern Zambia. Torwa and Mutapa grow as prominent Shona states on the Zimbabwe plateau.

1606 The Ottomans sign the Treaty of Tsitva Turok with the Habsburgs, acknowledging another ruler's equal status.

1606-08 A Kongolese embassy, led by Antonio Manuel Marchi, is sent to Brazil, Lisbon, and the Vatican.

1600s The timar system of landholders supplying military forces, especially cavalry, to the Ottomans declines. Tax farming, as practiced in France, eventually replaces it.

1609 The Blue Mosque, an enormous, elaborate shrine in Constantinople, is built under Sultan Ahmet I.

1616 The Falasha (Jews) are massacred by the forces of Ethiopian Emperor Sarsa Dengal.

ASIA & OCEANIA

1605 Emperor Jahangir becomes ruler of India. He will build a planned city at Shajahanabad (Agra), including the Red Fort. Intellectual and tolerant, he follows both the teachings of Muslim saints and those of the Hindu yogis.

1612 Safavids retake Azerbaijan and parts of the Caucasus. The border is restored to its 1555 position.

1615 Tokugawa Ieyasu issues Codes of the Military Houses to regulate lines of the samurai, or warrior class.

1611 Maize is mentioned as growing for the first time in the Balkans and Anatolia.

1617 Mughal Emperor Jahangir grants Sir Thomas Roe the right to maintain trade warehouses (factories) in port cities. This is the start of the English trading advantage in India.

1609 The illustrated encyclopedia *San-ts'ai t'u-hui* is published in China.

1615 Landscape painter Dong Qichang is active in Ming China.

1619 The Chinese printing trade flourishes.

SCIENCE & TECHNOLOGY

1607 The first American ship is built, in Sagadahoc, Maine.

1612 Virginia colonists first grow tobacco as a commercial crop.

1619 Virginia colonists attempt to build an ironworks, but the project is not finished.

1620 Hispanic Atlantic trade begins to decline in both volume and value.

1608 Galileo Galilei builds a telescope and in 1610 observes the satellites of Jupiter.

1609-1619 Johannes Kepler, German astronomer, describes the mathematics of celestial mechanics using elliptical orbits.

1610 Thomas Harriot discovers sunspots.

1614 Scottish mathematician John Napier publishes tables of logarithms, arithmetical functions he invented.

1619 English physician William Harvey describes the circulation of the blood.

1600s The increasing use of gunpowder weaponry by the Ottomans renders the cavalry obsolete.

1606 *Chi-yo yuan-pen*, a Chinese edition of Euclid's *Elements* (a compilation of geometrical knowledge) is published.

PEOPLE & SOCIETY

1605 The indigenous population of New Spain is estimated as one million.

1613-1620 Epidemics of smallpox and measles afflict the Indians from Florida northward.

1616 Pocahontas sails for England with her English husband, John Rolfe. In 1617 she dies at age 21.

1619 The first shipload of African slaves reaches the Virginia colony, where indentured servants provide much of the labor.

1620 People of mixed European, indigenous, and African ancestry begin to dominate the urban populations of Spanish America.

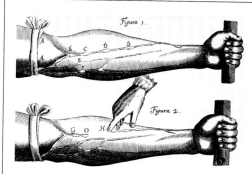

Engraving of a circulation experiment by William Harvey

1613 Khoekhoen tribesman Gorachouqua is kidnapped and taken to London. Learning English, he later becomes an agent for his people in dealing with the English. Gorachouqua is killed by Dutch sailors in 1626 for refusing to trade with them.

Thawing sea ice on Baffin Bay near Nunavut, Canada

THE NORTHWEST PASSAGE

When Europeans understood that Columbus had not reached Asia, efforts began to find a sea route through the American landmass to China. Magellan found a way to the Pacific, but only by sailing to the stormy southernmost tip of South America. Explorers hoped to find an easier route in the north.

As early as 1497, England's King Henry VII directed John Cabot to seek this Northwest Passage across the Arctic Ocean north of Canada. Many explorers would try and fail: Jacques Cartier, Francis Drake, Martin Frobisher, James Cook, and William Baffin. Humphrey Gilbert drowned in the attempt in 1583. Henry Hudson was set adrift by his mutinous crew in 1611 when they realized that Hudson Bay was an ice-bound trap. John Franklin and 129 men vanished on two ships in 1845. Robert McClure was locked in the ice for two winters, then sledged overland to complete the passage in 1854. These expeditions were not total losses—Europeans established trade with Indians and claimed the rich Mississippi River valley.

A passage did exist, threaded through the Arctic islands, but it was so challenging that it would be hundreds of years before it was transited. Thick pack ice chokes the sea throughout most of the year; the winds and water are lethally cold; visibility vanishes in whiteouts, fog, and arctic darkness; and a compass is useless so close to the magnetic pole.

The passage was finally negotiated in 1906 by Roald Amundsen, later the first person to reach the South Pole. More recently, the mammoth icebreaker *Manhattan* completed the trip in two weeks, smashing through 650 miles of pack ice in 1969.

	POLITICS & POWER	GEOGRAPHY & ENVIRONMENT	CULTURE & RELIGION
THE AMERICAS	**1620-1635 The French,** English, and Dutch seize Caribbean islands from Spain. **1621 The Dutch West India Company** is founded; later it will claim the North American coast from Virginia to Newfoundland. **1622 Indians** attack settlements around the Chesapeake Bay and Virginia; ten years of fighting begin. **1633-1654 The Dutch West India Company** rules northeastern Brazil.	**1624 The Dutch** barter for rights to Manhattan Island. **1630 A large group of English Puritans** sets up a colony at Massachusetts Bay. **1632 English King Charles I** issues a charter to Cecilius Calvert, Lord Baltimore, who founds a colony near Chesapeake Bay. It is later called Maryland in honor of Charles's consort, Queen Henrietta Maria. **1634 Jean Nicolet** of France explores Wisconsin and Green Bay.	**1630 John Winthrop,** leader of the Puritan colonists at Massachusetts Bay, inspires his people with a sermon on the purpose of their enterprise: to set an example of community to the world, to be "a city on a hill." **1630s French missionaries** begin work among the Huron tribes. **1630s The widespread Yaqui** of Sonora convert to Catholicism and settle in towns, a strategy for survival. **1632 John Eliot** begins establishing villages of Christian Indian converts in New England; he preaches in Algonquian.
EUROPE	**1622 James I** dissolves the English Parliament. **1624 Cardinal Richelieu** becomes First Minister in France; by 1626 he holds supreme power. **1625 James I** dies; his son Charles I becomes king of England. **1629 Charles I** dissolves the English Parliament. No Parliament will now be held in England until 1640. **1630s Sweden** becomes heavily involved in the Thirty Years' War.	**1621 Germans** plant their first New World crop, the potato.	**1625 Vincent de Paul** founds the religious Order of the Sisters of Mercy. **1627 Heinrich Schütz** writes the first German opera, *Dafne.* **1631 Dutch painter Rembrandt van Rijn** paints a portrait of his mother. He paints a masterpiece almost every year until the late 1640s. **1634-36 French dramatist Pierre Corneille** publishes popular comedy and tragedy.
MIDDLE EAST & AFRICA	**1622 Ottoman sultan Osman II** is deposed and assassinated. His successor, Murad IV (1623-1640), eliminates banditry, reforms morals, and issues the "justice edict." **1623 Nzinga Nbandi,** Queen of Ndongo, drives the Portuguese out of Ndongo, today's Angola. **1625 The kingdom of Dahomey** is established. **1631 English trading posts** are established on the Gold Coast (Ghana). The Dutch expel the Portuguese from the Gold Coast.	**1626 The French** establish settlements on the Senegal River.	**1623 Bandits** under Abaza Mehmed Pasha protest bureaucratic misrule. **1625 Inflation** reaches its high point in the Ottoman Empire. **1632-35 Murad IV's morality campaign** includes the execution of literary and cultural figures with unorthodox opinions. Coffeehouses are closed, and spies on the streets report deviant dress.
ASIA & OCEANIA	**ca 1620 Khmer king Chey Chetha** forges an alliance with the Vietnamese. **ca 1620 Donglin Academy** achieves its peak of influence in Ming politics. **1625 Eunuch grand secretary Wei Zhongxian** reaches his highest position at the Ming court. **1632 The English** drive the Portuguese out of Bengal.	**1624 The English** settle in eastern India. **1624 The Dutch** establish trading posts on the coast of Taiwan. **1626 A powerful earthquake** shakes Beijing. **1628 The Dutch** occupy Java and the Moluccan Islands. **1633 The English** establish a trading post in Bengal. **1634 The English** settle in Cochin and Malabar.	**1629 The Tokugawa shogunate** forbids women to perform in Kabuki theater because of its origins in prostitution.

WHAT LIFE WAS LIKE

In Fabulous Isfahan

When Shah Abbas (1587-1629) of Persia rebuilt Isfahan, south of Tehran in present-day Iran, he created one of the most beautiful cities of its time. At its center was a vast courtyard anchored by mosques and lofty ceremonial gates, and rimmed with two-story buildings ornamented by recessed arches. Wide, tree-shaded avenues featuring fountains and watercourses gave access to the city, which earned lavish praise from visitors. In the 1660s Isfahan boasted 162 mosques, 48 schools, 273 bath houses, and nearly 2,000 hostels. Much of the city was destroyed when Ghilzai Afghans invaded in 1722, and some 100,000 inhabitants perished.

SCIENCE & TECHNOLOGY	PEOPLE & SOCIETY

1620 Samoset, Tisqantum, and Massasoit meet Mayflower voyagers on the coast near Cape Cod.

1620s Horses become distributed throughout the southwestern Indian tribes.

1623 Miles Standish kills Massachusetts Indian leader Witawanet.

1629 Salem, Massachusetts, imports shipwrights to establish a shipbuilding center.

Horses were traded north across the plains to Canada by 1770, transforming native cultures by enlarging tribal ranges and increasing mobility.

1620 Cornelius Van Drebbel, a Dutchman living in England, invents a human-powered submarine. It travels 12 to 15 feet below the water, providing its sailors air through snorkel tubes.

1624 William Oughtred of England invents a slide rule for making calculations.

1629 Giovanni Branca invents a steam turbine.

1633 A wind-powered sawmill is built in London.

1622 Judith Leyster, Dutch painter, becomes the only female member of the Haarlem Painters' Guild.

1626 France institutes the death penalty for duelists who kill their opponents.

1630 Public advertising of goods is first used in France.

1633 Galileo Galilei is convicted of teaching the Copernican doctrine.

1631 Mir Damed, Iranian philosopher and metaphysician, dies, leaving work which later has implications for the field of psychology.

1630-1680s The influence of Kadizadelis, mosque preachers who encourage legalistic puritanism, grows. They oppose Sufi government clerics, coffeehouses, tobacco, and wine consumption. Ideological clashes between the Kadizadelis and Sufis peak in the 1680s when the Kadizadelis support the Ottoman war against Austria. After the Ottoman defeat at Vienna in 1683, the movement declines.

1621 A treatise on military arts, *Wubei Zhi,* is published in China.

1630 Shivagi Bonsle, a farmer's son in Maratha, India, becomes a guerrilla fighter. Opposing the rule of Emperor Aurangzeb, he is captured, then absorbed into the government system as a local ruler. He is acknowledged and crowned as king of the state of Maratha by Brahmans in 1679.

THE WARRIOR QUEEN OF NDONGO

Seeking mineral wealth, salt deposits, and slaves in the mid-1500s, the Portuguese moved into Ndongo, a federation of villages on the Lunda plateau of southwest Africa. The land was held by the Mbundu people under their ruler, known as the *ngola.* Dealings with the ngolas broke down over time under Portugal's increasing demand for slaves, and finally in 1621 the ngola sent his sister, Nzinga, to parlay on his behalf with the Portuguese.

A confident and clever woman, Nzinga entered the council chamber to find only one seat, which was occupied by the Portuguese governor. She motioned an attendant down on hands and knees, creating a living throne for herself, and proceeded to negotiate very favorable terms for the Mbundu. She forged a special connection to the Europeans by requesting Christian baptism, with the governor himself serving as her godfather.

By 1624 relations had once again deteriorated. Queen Nzinga organized an army, fought the Portuguese, and withdrew into the interior. She cast off Christianity to ally with the fierce Jaga raiders. A gifted guerrilla strategist, she took the hill country of Matamba as a Mbundu stronghold, welcomed runaway slaves to her ranks, and gave special inducements to recruit renegades from the Portuguese forces. She established a corps of *kilombo,* men who gave up ties to family and lived together in militia groups, totally dedicated to her army. Queen Nzinga led warriors herself until she was past 60, destroying the slave trade and diverting Portuguese energy into military forays that laid waste to the countryside. Only after her death in 1663 were the Portuguese finally able to penetrate the southwest interior, securing the country they called Angola until 1975.

1635-1650
CONVERGING WORLDS 1500-1750

POLITICS & POWER	GEOGRAPHY & ENVIRONMENT	CULTURE & RELIGION

THE AMERICAS

1639 The Fundamental Orders of Connecticut are written for settlers on the Connecticut River.

1640s The seigneural landholding system controls settlement in New France. Jesuit missionaries at Huronia extend the French influence throughout Indian tribes.

1641-1679 New Hampshire colony comes under the administration of Massachusetts

1643 New Sweden (Delaware) is established on the Delaware River.

Anne Hutchinson

1635 Roger Williams, expelled from Massachusetts Bay Colony for advocating religious freedom, founds a colony in Rhode Island.

1636 Harvard College is founded in Massachusetts

1638 Anne Hutchinson, believer in an individual's access to salvation, is banished from Massachusetts Bay and moves to Rhode Island.

1640 The Bay Psalm Book is the first book published in the English colonies.

EUROPE

1640 Frederick William, the Great Elector, becomes the elector of Brandenburg. He is influential in European politics until 1688.

1641 A Catholic rebellion breaks out in Ireland and Protestants are massacred in Ulster.

1642-49 Charles I of England is defeated by hostile Parliamentary forces led by Oliver Cromwell.

1648 The Peace of Westphalia concludes the Thirty Years' War. The period of the Frondes (rebellions against royal authority) begins in France and lasts until 1653.

1637 The introduction of a new prayer book in Scotland incites violence, precipitating the Covenanter rebellion against state authority.

1641 French philosopher René Descartes writes *Meditations Metaphysiques.*

1642 Puritan influence in England closes the theaters of London.

1642 Molière founds a theater group in Paris that eventually evolves into the Comedie Française.

1648 George Fox founds the Society of Friends (Quakers).

MIDDLE EAST & AFRICA

1640 A Fante state is founded in Ghana.

1640-48 Ottoman sultan Mad Ibrahim lines his palace walls with fur, while his mother Kosem and his tutor rule the empire.

1645-1669 The Ottomans conquer Crete.

1648 Ottoman Mehmed IV becomes sultan at the age of six; his mother Turhamn and grandmother Kosem struggle for power.

1630s African ironsmelting deforests vast regions; the climate becomes drier. More open landscape encourages the spreading use of cavalry in warfare.

1639 Evliya Chelebi, Ottoman administrator, begins his journeys, describing geography, buildings, people, and legends of the Ottoman Empire and beyond in *Travels.*

1640s The Ottoman fur trade with Russia increases.

1640s Ottoman domains are surveyed for extraordinary taxes, obtaining new population and revenue estimates.

1642-1666 Shah Abbas II reigns in Persia (Iran), the last great builder and arts patron of the Safavid dynasty. After his death, clerics gain importance in politics and culture.

ASIA & OCEANIA

1644 The Manchus invade from the north, overthrow the Ming ruler, and conquer China. They establish the Qing dynasty.

1645 The Manchus massacre the population in the Chinese city of Yangzhou.

1635 The Dutch settle in Ceylon.

1637 English traders set up a station in Canton.

1639 Cossacks advance to the Pacific coast.

1639 The English settle in Madras, India.

1642 Abel Tasman, Dutch navigator, sails along the coast of Australia, discovering Tasmania, New Zealand, New Guinea, and the Fiji Islands.

1644 The Dutch settle in Mauritius.

1637-38 The Shimabara Rebellion, fueled by Christian converts and socioeconomic ills, leads to the expulsion of the Portuguese and the banning of Christianity in Japan.

1645 The Qing government forces the Han Chinese to wear the queue—a shaved head with single braid behind.

SCIENCE & TECHNOLOGY

1639 The first printing press is set up in North America.

1644 An iron furnace is built at Braintree, Massachusetts.

1644 Ironworks are constructed throughout Massachusetts, Connecticut, and Rhode Island, utilizing bog iron near the coasts, then finding other ore deposits inland.

1637 René Descartes publishes a work on analytical geometry.

1639 Quinine, an Indian remedy derived from South American tree bark, is first used as a medication against fever in Europe.

1639 English astronomer Jeremiah Horrocks predicts and observes a transit of Venus.

1640 Coke, a fuel with high carbon content, is first produced from coal.

1641 England produces cotton cloth.

1642 Blaise Pascal, French philosopher, invents an adding machine.

1635 The Chinese publish *Ch'ung-chen Li-shu,* a collection of scientific works written with Jesuit collaboration.

1637 *Tiangong Kaiwu* is published, an encyclopedia of Chinese technology.

1644 The Jesuits reform the Chinese calendar, introduce Western maps, and use the telescope in Chinese observatories.

PEOPLE & SOCIETY

1637 The English begin restricting immigration to their colonies in the Americas.

1645-1654 Brazilians attack the Dutch settlers and finally force the Dutch from colonial Brazil.

1647 Massachusetts establishes the first public school system in America.

1650 The movement of Spanish soldiers, miners, and missionaries into Arizona and New Mexico precipitates outbreaks of disease that devastate indigenous populations.

1635 A postal service unites London and Edinburgh.

1636 Tea drinking is introduced in Paris.

1639 The Académie Française compiles a dictionary of French, beginning the movement to standardize language and spelling.

1644 René Descartes writes in *Principia Philosophiae,* "I think, therefore I am."

1648 The German population is now nine million less than it was in 1618 due to war, disease, and famine.

1638-1644 Kemankesh Kara Mustafa Pasha reforms the Ottoman budget, stemming inflation and improving the coinage.

1642-1674 Krotoa, or Eva, a Khoekhoen woman, translates for the Dutch. Her life shows the complexity of the emerging South African community.

Nurhachi, founder of the first Manchu state

IRELAND INVADED

The kings of Ireland were subdued by a Norman invasion in the 12th century. From then on, the incremental shift of land and power from the native Gaelic lords into the hands of foreign overlords fueled resistance that continues in Irish affairs today. To replace the ancient system of elected clan chiefs with hereditary barons answerable to the king, the Normans created earls who ruled Ireland throughout the Plantagenet era, separating the Gaelic population from political affairs. The Tudors later began the wholesale system of plantations—granting Irish land to English landholders to develop and administer in the English manner.

When the English church split from Rome, further divisions appeared. The Catholic Counter-Reformation encouraged Irish clergy to spread hostility against the English. In 1601 the pope supported a Spanish invasion of Ireland that England defeated at great cost. Royal favors to English landlords caused Catholics in the northern province of Ulster to emigrate; many Presbyterian Scots moved there as tenants. Local resentment boiled over in a bloody uprising in 1641 where thousands of colonists were killed.

Incursions of the Parliamentary and royalist forces during the English civil war traumatized Ireland. The victorious Cromwell's soldiers were granted land there and persecuted Catholics. After 1660 Catholics were forbidden to live in towns, all municipal power passed to Protestants, and Catholics claimed a mere 22 percent of Irish land.

By the early 1700s the Test Act prevented Catholics from holding office, the British House of Lords became the supreme court for Irish legal matters, and Irish Catholics owned only 14 percent of their homeland. This relentless genocide by bureaucracy, depriving the Irish of political and economic resources, ensured grievances that were soon emboldened by revolutionary examples in America and France.

	POLITICS & POWER	GEOGRAPHY & ENVIRONMENT	CULTURE & RELIGION
THE AMERICAS	**1650 The Dutch** incite Mohawks to attack the Swedish-allied Susquehannocks, disrupting Swedish settlers. **1656 The Virginia Assembly** endorses the death penalty for Indians found trespassing. **1663 Charles II** of England issues land grants for settlements in North Carolina. **1664 The English** annex New Netherland. The area is renamed New York.	**ca 1650 Indigo** becomes one of the most important exports of Mexico.	**1657 Jews** in New York are granted the rights of burghers (English citizens), but are not permitted to worship in public. **1660 The Inquisition** is used against the Pueblo; charges are brought against civilian officers who are critical of missionaries. **1661 John Eliot** translates the Bible into Algonquian. **1670s Missionaries** begin losing power over Pueblo peoples, unable to protect them from Apache raids, recurrent drought, or epidemic disease. Sexual exploitation of Pueblo women by missionaries also contributes to discontent.
EUROPE	**1653 Louis XIV**, now of age to rule in his own right, reasserts lawful royal government in France. **1653 The English and Dutch** begin sporadic fighting after the English Navigation Act (1651) restricts foreign trade. **1653 Oliver Cromwell** becomes the First Lord Protector of the English Commonwealth. He reorganizes England into districts ruled by military governors. **1660 Charles II** is proclaimed king of England as the Commonwealth dissolves.		**1651 Philosopher Thomas Hobbes** publishes *Leviathan,* a defense of monarchy and political absolutism. **1656 The first opera house** opens in London. **1660 The first female players** appear on stages in England and Germany. **1660 Samuel Pepys** of London begins writing his famous diary. **1661 The Edict of Orleans** attempts again to end persecution of Huguenots in France.
MIDDLE EAST & AFRICA	**1650 The Baganda** of Uganda mutiny against their leader, the kabaka. **1650 Venetians** blockade the Dardanelles. **1654 Mehmed Kopruli,** grand vizier, rebuilds the Ottoman fleet and breaks the Venetian blockade. **1656-1702 The Kopruli family** of grand viziers controls and reforms the Ottoman state. **1657-59 The Dutch** defeat the Khoekhoen in a fight over territory in southern Africa. **1665-1670 The Portuguese** invade and conquer Kongo.	**1652 Arab traders** from Oman begin to settle and control the East African coast. **1652 The Dutch East India Company** plants fortifications and gardens near the Cape of Good Hope. **1657 The Dutch** allow individual farmers to plant at the Cape of Good Hope. **1664 Swedish trading posts** on the Gold Coast of West Africa are sold to the Dutch.	**1650 Muslims** begin settling among the Fulani in West Africa. **1665 Nathan of Gaza** proclaims Chabbetai Tsevi the Jewish messiah, attracting many Jews, Christians, and Muslims as followers. Arrested for sedition, Tsevi converts to Islam, as do many of his disciples, forming the Donme sect in Turkey. **1670 The Fulani** mount jihads against their non-Muslim neighbors. By the 1680s West African states are practicing an orthodox form of Islam.
ASIA & OCEANIA	**1656 The Dutch** take Colombo (Ceylon) from the Portuguese. **1660 Mughal Emperor Aurangzeb** campaigns against other Muslim states. **1661 Kangxi** becomes emperor of China; his 60-year reign is one of prosperity and stability. **1662 The Qing** order an evacuation of the Chinese coast in response to pirate attacks. **1668 The English East India Company** controls Bombay.	**1660s The Mughal Empire** attains its widest extent in the Indian subcontinent.	**1650 The first Roman Catholic church** is established in Beijing. **1650 Japanese Noh drama** is performed regularly.

CONNECTIONS

The Jews

With the fall of the Roman Empire and the rise of Islam in the Middle East, the Jewish people dispersed: One group moved west into the Iberian Peninsula (the Sephardim); the other north into Germany and Eastern Europe (the Ashkenazi). During the Middle Ages, Jews retained a religious and cultural identity in spite of separation by studying the same teachings: the Torah (Hebrew scripture) and the Talmud—commentaries on the Torah. Expelled from Iberia in 1492, many Sephardim immigrated to England and Holland and formed the first Jewish communities in the Americas. Later, thousands of Ashkenazi joined them, fleeing recurrent waves of persecution in Eastern Europe.

SCIENCE & TECHNOLOGY	PEOPLE & SOCIETY
	1650 Portuguese Jesuit Antonio Vieira is renowned for his writings and sermons in Brazil.
	1655 Hopi Indian Juan Cura, accused of idolatry, is burned to death by a Spanish priest.
	1660s Meat from domestic livestock becomes more common in colonial diets than meat from wild game.
	1665 Caleb Cheeshatemauk attains a Bachelor of Arts degree at Harvard College. He is the first Indian college graduate.
	ca 1670 Baroque Mexican culture flourishes, with many literary and artistic works produced by Creoles and American-born Spaniards.
1651 Italian astronomer Giovanni Riccioli publishes a map of the moon.	**1650 The English** begin the habit of drinking tea; the leaves are imported from China.
1654 French scientists Blaise Pascal and Pierre de Fermat formulate a theory of probability.	**1660-1690 Public coffeehouses** are opened in France, England, and Germany.
1656 Dutch scientist Christian Huygens discovers the rings of Saturn.	**1662 Christopher Wren,** professor of astronomy at Oxford, designs his first building.
1660 King Charles II charters the Royal Society of London to promote the sciences.	**1666-67 Jean-Baptist Colbert,** finance minister for Louis XIV, reforms commerce in France.
1662 English chemist Robert Boyle publishes a description of the relationship between the pressure and volume of a gas; this is known as Boyle's law.	**1667 Margaret Cavendish** speaks to the Royal Society of London but the members trivialize her ideas. No other woman will be a member until the mid-20th century.
	1650s Slavery exists in the Dutch Cape colony. It will continue there until the 1830s. The Dutch obtain slaves from West Africa, then from Mozambique, Madagascar, Indonesia, and India.
	1652 Tarhonju Mahmed Pasha, Ottoman grand vizier, is the first to prepare a budget in advance of the fiscal year.
	1660 The English trade in indigo, saltpeter, pepper, and textiles from the East increases.
	1661 Qing Emperor Kangxi is interested in science, music, and poetry, and is a patron of Chinese scholarship. He reigns until 1722.
	1662 Koxinga (Zheng Chenggong), who rebelled against the Manchus and successfully fought against them in Taiwan, dies.

Early Noh mask

Isaac Newton discovered that white light is composed of every color of the spectrum.

SIR ISAAC NEWTON

Isaac Newton was born in 1642 to a humble Lincolnshire farming family. He was a sickly baby and not expected to live. As a child, he proved inept at farm chores. Raised by his grandmother and encouraged by a teacher and his uncle, he entered Cambridge a year later than most students. It was only when the university was closed in 1665 due to plague that Newton had his annus mirabilis. In the course of about one year, at the age of 23, he formulated principles that would change science forever.

Newton sought precise mathematical principles by which Nature functioned. He examined the reaction of bodies to forces and proposed the fundamental laws of motion that are the basis of mechanics. He not only formulated the law of gravitation, but also developed a new mathematical method known as calculus to compute his findings.

Newton's work was an astounding demonstration of precise physical laws governing universal phenomena and the power of mathematics to provide testable predictions. He established the scientific method and provided the intellectual impetus that has driven our scientific development ever since.

THE SPLENDOR OF THE MUGHALS

FROM THE EARLY 1500S TO THE MID-1700S, MUGHAL EMPERORS RULED AN AREA that expanded from Kabul, Afghanistan, to modern-day Pakistan and Bangladesh in the east, and down across the Deccan to Calicut on the west coast of India. Though they were aggressive in war, it was their talent for alliance with enemies that cemented their amazingly diverse empire.

The Mughal period in India is especially noted for flourishing arts, agriculture, economic development, and religious tolerance. The epitome of Mughal culture, wealth transmuted into beauty, is the glorious Taj Mahal, tomb of Shah Jahan's beloved wife. Constructed of marble that reflects changing tones of light throughout the day, the beauty and serenity of this monument are overwhelming. No one knows who designed the tomb, but it was completed between 1632 and 1643. The central dome with mausoleum beneath is 23 stories high, guarded at the corners by four minarets. Workmen from Persia and central Asia created its intricate flower inlays of semiprecious stone, religious inscriptions, and lavish gardens.

The Mughal Empire began with Babur, a Central Asian Muslim descended from both the Turk Tamerlane and the Mongol Genghis Khan. Hindustan, ruled by Muslim sultans since the 1200s, was rumored to be a land of gems and gold, but poorly defended. Babur marched down from Afghanistan and took Delhi with artillery in 1526. The personable leader quickly established a kingdom that expanded and prospered under seven generations of his heirs.

Babur's grandson, Akbar (1556-1605), ruled as a philosopher king. He founded cities across his land, attracting hundreds of architects, craftsmen, artists, poets, and merchants. In his new capital of Fatehpur Sikri near Agra, he built the Ibadakhana, or House of Worship, as a place for religious debate. Akbar himself often presided over the Hindus, Muslims, Sufis, Parsis, Jains, Jews, and Christians discussing their faiths there. To further intercultural understanding, he commissioned translations of Hindu epics into Persian. His personal library held 24,000 volumes, and classics of literature, philosophy, and history were read aloud to him throughout his day. Hired painters followed his campaigning armies, documenting the action. To gain the support of fierce Rajput warlords, Akbar married Rajput princesses, respected their Hindu faith, and installed their relatives in positions at court. He took Hindus into the civil service and abolished taxes levied on non-Muslims and pilgrims.

Akbar's son Jahangir's passion for art brought European and Chinese treasures into India. Jahangir (1605-1628) built the pleasure gardens of Shalimar and Nishat in Kashmir, where streams ripple across pierced marble screens to create tinkling water music. His son Shah Jahan secured his throne through a bitter rebellion and died a prisoner of his own son, Aurangzeb. Religious and ethnic divisions splintered the empire under Aurangzeb, a strict and doctrinaire Muslim. Persians invaded from the north, the Rajput alliance fractured, and by the mid-1700s European militaries were seizing power in India.

Light and shadow paint the Taj Mahal at sunrise in Agra, India.

POLITICS & POWER	GEOGRAPHY & ENVIRONMENT	CULTURE & RELIGION

THE AMERICAS

1675 King Philip's War (1675-76) begins when Metacomet, called King Philip by the English, attacks English settlers after the execution of a Wampanoag tribesman. King Philip is killed.

1677 The English sign a treaty guaranteeing autonomy to the Pamunkey and Mattaponi tribes of Virginia. This treaty is honored for the next 300 years.

1680 San Juan Pueblo tribesman Popé leads an uprising against the Spanish in the Southwest. The Pueblo Revolt drives the Spaniards out of their settlements and back into Mexico.

Taos Pueblo, center of a 1680 anti-Spanish revolt

1670s Jesuit artists Abbé Hugues Pommier, Père Claude Chauchetière, and Père Louis Nicolas flourish in Canada, creating views of Indian life, settlement, and portraits.

1675 The Spanish continue to punish Pueblo peoples for practicing their native religions.

1680s Jesuit missionaries arrive in the Southwest.

1688 Algonquin tribes ally with the French against the English and Iroquois in what is later called King William's war, an extension of wars of European alliances.

EUROPE

1674 Jan III becomes king of Poland after victorious military campaigns against the Turks and Cossacks.

1675-79 Frederick William, Elector of Brandenburg, fights the Swedish in Germany.

1682 Peter the Great becomes Russian tsar.

1685 Charles II of England dies, succeeded by James II, known for Catholic sympathies.

1688 James II is deposed in favor of his Protestant daughter Mary and her Dutch husband, Prince William of Orange, in the Glorious Revolution.

1680s Crop failures cause severe famines in many parts of Europe.

1683 William Dampier of England begins a circumnavigation of the globe.

1670s Christopher Wren begins his most active period as an architect. He designs more than 50 London churches and many other buildings, including St. Paul's, Christ Church, Trinity College, Cambridge, and Chelsea Hospital, London.

1670s Playwright Aphra Behn is the first Englishwoman to make her living by writing.

1678 John Bunyan writes *The Pilgrim's Progress*.

1685 Louis XIV revokes the Edict of Nantes; thousands of Huguenots leave France.

MIDDLE EAST & AFRICA

1670 The Alawids rule Morocco.

1670 Asante clans unify on the Gold Coast of West Africa.

1673-77 The Dutch and the Khoekhoen fight a second war. After a negotiated peace, the Khoekhoen cooperate with the Dutch.

1683 The Ottomans besiege Vienna fruitlessly for the last time. War with Austria (to 1699) loses much Ottoman European territory.

1680s Masai warriors expand southward in Africa with cattle to supply their diet of milk and blood.

1688 French Huguenots come to settle in Cape colony at the southern tip of Africa.

1689 Natal becomes a Dutch colony.

1680s Rapprochement draws Islamic orthodoxy and Sufi mysticism into closer agreement. More orthodox Sufis displace fringe movements that flouted Islamic custom. Sufi orders gain importance in education and social service.

1690s West African coastal merchants buy Eurasian cloth, unravel it, and reweave the threads into local patterns to sell to Africans.

ASIA & OCEANIA

1673 A rebellion arises against the Qing; southern Chinese provinces break away from Qing control, and China is engulfed in the War of the Three Feudatories.

1673 A French expedition attacks Ceylon.

1679 The Vietnamese and Cambodians go to war; Cambodia loses the Mekong delta.

1683 The Qing occupy Taiwan and consolidate their conquest of China.

1689 The Treaty of Nerchinsk defines the border and trading rights between Russia and Qing domains. It is the first diplomatic agreement between China and a European power.

1680 The French establish a trading station at Pondicherry, India.

1685 The Chinese open ports to European trade.

Hello! Light the fire!
I'll bring inside
a lovely bright
ball of snow!

HAIKU BY BASHO

SCIENCE & TECHNOLOGY

ca 1670 New Spain begins to take the lead from Peru in the production of silver.

1673 The Boston Post Road links settlements down the east coast of North America between Boston and Philadelphia.

ca 1680 Rice is first planted in coastal South Carolina.

1675 The Greenwich Observatory is established outside London.

1675 Leibniz describes integral and differential calculus.

1682 A weaving factory with 100 looms opens in Amsterdam, the Netherlands.

1687 Isaac Newton publishes *Philosophae naturalis principia mathematica,* an application of precise mathematical laws to describe the natural world, including the shape of the Earth, the tides, and the movement of heavenly bodies.

1681 The Jesuits introduce new western farming practices to China, including irrigation. They make three crops of rice per year possible, whereas only two were possible before.

PEOPLE & SOCIETY

1670s The native Chamorro population of Guam declines steeply after smallpox comes to the island.

1680s Sor Juana Inés de la Cruz of Mexico is at the height of her intellectual power. A prodigy of learning, she debates with university professors, writes poetry, composes music, and is sent to live in a convent for daring to challenge church authorities.

1680s Disease reduces the Pueblo population from 60,000 to 17,000.

1673 The Test Act bans Catholics from holding office in England.

1677 Benedicte de Spinoza, Dutch rationalist religious philosopher dies. His work, *Ethics,* is later published. Spinoza has a wide following among European intellectuals of the time.

1684 Parts of London are equipped with street lighting.

1687 A Turkish bombardment damages the Parthenon in Athens.

1670s Osei Tutu of the Asante battles his way to power. He is installed as the Asantehene and founds the Asante Empire.

Kente cloth from Ghana designed with traditional patterns, which have been woven in Africa for more than 2,000 years

1680 Basho, the Japanese master of haiku poetry, is at the height of his fame.

1682 Ihara Saikaku writes *The Life of an Amorous Man,* an example of the literature of "the floating world" of Osaka and other urban centers. In the 1680s the art of the woodblock print first shows "the floating world."

THE ASANTE UNITE

In the late 1600s Asante prince Osei Tutu escaped from service as shield-bearer (hostage) at the court of a powerful Denkyera overlord. He fled to Akwamu, a state on equal footing with the Denkyera confederacy. There he planned a union of the small Asante settlements, one that would be welded firmly enough to stand against Denkyera domination and could be defended by an effective army.

When Osei Tutu came home to his throne at Kumasi he brought Okumfo Anokye, an Akwamu adviser, with him. Anokye, who became high priest of the new king, received a miraculous gift—a Golden Stool, which he announced had descended from heaven in a cloud and come to rest on the knees of Osei Tutu, sanctifying his rule. Anokye interpreted the Golden Stool as more than a symbol of kingship: it was the embodiment of the spirit of all the Asante.

Osei Tutu and Anokye understood the use of such symbols, and they also comprehended the art of war. The Kumasi army made marching ants its model; savagery and surprise were its signature tactics. Osei Tutu purchased guns from European traders, and in the late 1670s his forces defeated the inexperienced new ruler of Denkyera. Osei Tutu's army gathered the prizes of war for 15 days, including an immense amount of gold.

Using gold-bought weaponry, the Asante took over West Africa's Gold Coast. Osei Tutu became Asantehene, the overall king, and produced a constitution for his union of peoples. The Asante consider him the legendary founder of the empire. When he was killed in an ambush by Akyem enemies, together with 300 followers and 60 of his wives, the Asante razed Akyem, slaughtering all the inhabitants. Today, the Golden Stool remains the symbol of the spirit of the Asante and is protected by the Asantehene in the modern nation of Ghana.

POLITICS & POWER	GEOGRAPHY & ENVIRONMENT	CULTURE & RELIGION

THE AMERICAS

1692 Periodic fighting breaks out between Spanish settlers and Pueblos until 1696.

1702 The English, French, and their respective Indian allies begin fighting Queen Anne's War. The conflict continues until 1713.

1704 French forces take Massachusetts settlers to Canada. They are ransomed and returned in the next few years.

1699 Frenchman Pierre Lemoyne establishes Fort Maurepas on the Gulf Coast of Mississippi. The next year, he brings settlers to the area, called Louisiana in honor of the King of France.

1700s A diverse and intermingled population grows in Spanish America, comprising Indians, Spanish, Africans, and people with mixed bloodlines.

1702 The French explore and settle in Alabama.

1692 Witch trials in Salem, Massachusetts, convict and execute 19 people accused of trafficking with Satan. In 1697 the trial findings are repudiated by one of the judges.

1695 A synagogue, Shearith Israel, is established in New York. It is the first in the English colonies.

1698 Mestizo style, characterized by dense, flat, floral and human relief forms, develops in Spanish American architecture.

1701 Yale University is founded in New Haven, Connecticut.

EUROPE

1690 William III of England invades Ireland to quell a rebellion by supporters of James II.

1700s European power struggles are reflected in wars in the New World colonies.

1701 Frederick III, Elector of Brandenburg, is crowned as King Frederick I of Prussia.

1707 Parliaments of England and Scotland unite to form Great Britain.

Halley's comet appears every 76 years.

1700 European merchants supply the Ottomans with coffee and sugar.

1699 Peter the Great decrees that Russia will recognize January 1, not September 1, as the beginning of the New Year. This is part of his program to westernize and modernize Russia.

1703 Peter the Great begins building a new city at St. Petersburg on the Neva River. St. Petersburg becomes the capital of Russia in 1712.

1704 Johann Sebastian Bach writes his first cantata. His composing career will last until the mid-1740s.

1709 An Italian harpsichord maker, Bartolomeo Cristofori, invents the pianoforte.

MIDDLE EAST & AFRICA

1696-1712 The Asante kingdom expands in West Africa.

1699 Oman controls much of the East African coast.

1700 The Ethiopian Empire divides into feudal states.

1700 The kabaka of Uganda concentrate their power, growing toward monarchy.

1700 Xhosa chiefs unite and grow more powerful in the Cape of Good Hope area, dominating the other tribal groups by midcentury.

1700 Dahomey and Oyo kingdoms flourish.

1699 The Treaty of Carlowitz removes Muslim-inhabited territory from Ottoman control, marking a decline in Ottoman fortunes.

1700 Sophisticated brass figurines, often called Benin bronzes, are produced in Dahomey (today's Benin).

1704 The Antonian movement in Kongo blends Christianity with African religious practice.

1706 The Portuguese arrest Doña Beatriz, leader of the Kongolese Antonians, on charges of heresy. She is convicted and burned to death.

ASIA & OCEANIA

1696 The Russians invade and conquer Kamchatka.

1700 Local lords called zamindars, increase their power in India.

1698-1700 William Dampier of England sails to northwest Australia and New Guinea.

1707 Mount Fuji, near Tokyo, Japan, erupts.

1700 The Genroku era of popular culture in Osaka and other urban centers reaches its height.

1700 Wang Yuanji, a painter, is named chief artistic adviser to Emperor Kangxi.

1700 An estimated 300,000 Christians populate China.

1703 The Treasury of Loyal Retainers, the Japanese story of the 47 ronin who avenged their lord, is performed as a Kabuki drama.

SCIENCE & TECHNOLOGY

1690 A paper mill is built in Pennsylvania.

1690s The scarcity of coins in the Americas encourages the North American colonies to print paper money and bills of credit. Strictly controlled, this currency holds its value well, and its use spreads.

1700 Liquor distilling becomes a more important part of the American economy, especially in New England.

1701 Englishman Jethro Tull invents a seed drill, which is much more effective than broadcast sowing of seeds. The new method increases farmers' yields, though it is adopted slowly because the drills are costly.

1704 Isaac Newton publishes *Opticks*.

1705 Edmund Halley, English astronomer, predicts that the comet of 1682 will return in 1758. He will not live to see his prediction confirmed, but the comet is named after him.

1707 French engineer Denis Papin invents a high-pressure steam boiler, forerunner of the steam engine.

1703 European scientific instruments such as the telescope come into use in Islamic observatories.

PEOPLE & SOCIETY

1700 Traditional Hopi massacre Hopi men for associating with Spanish priests, the only incidence of violence in Hopi history.

1700s Disease devastates Indians of the Carolinas; many survivors move West. When the elders die, people lose knowledge of important ceremonies, rituals, and traditions.

1704 Henriette Deering Johnson begins drawing pastel portraits of people and scenes in South Carolina.

1704 The *Boston News-Letter* begins publication, the first continuously published newspaper in America.

1691 A directory of street addresses is published in Paris.

1696 Isaac Newton is made director of the English mint. His reforms of the currency, not his scientific work, earn him a knighthood.

1697-98 Peter the Great travels through Prussia, the Netherlands, England, and Austria incognito, observing European life.

1700s Periodicals, both news and commentary, increase in popularity throughout Europe.

1702 Forms of street lighting appear in many German cities.

1700s The Trekboers expand the farms of European settlers into native territory in South Africa. Living in isolated frontier areas, these pioneers develop a different culture from the colonists on the coast, borrowing from and intermixing with the African societies and individuals.

Benin bronze plaque showing a warrior and two attendants

1703 Ottoman Ahmed III opens the empire to Western culture.

1700s Islamic poets with devoted followings in India include Bulhe Shah and Mir Taqi Mir.

1709 Russians are sent to Siberia as punishment for the first time.

THE SALEM WITCH TRIALS

By the late 1600s, as European witch trials were winding down, witch hunt fever was just beginning in the New World. Rumors of witchcraft in Puritan Massachusetts started in 1692 among the prosperous farmers of Salem, a village north of Boston. Quarrels over inheritances, lifestyles, and church affairs, anxiety over a frontier war just 70 miles away, and teenage boredom probably contributed to witchcraft hysteria.

In January, several young girls began jerking spasmodically in public, shrieking that they were being tortured by witches. They accused three women, including the minister's slave, Tituba. A court convened by local magistrates investigated, while the numbers of "possessed" girls increased and accusations multiplied. In May, Governor Phips appointed a new court to take over the cases, including famous witch hunters Samuel Stoughton and Cotton Mather.

The defendants had no legal counsel, and hearsay, gossip, and supposition were admitted as evidence. A skeptical tavern keeper, an elderly women who argued with neighbors, a former minister of Salem church, and a four-year-old child were among the hundreds accused of witchcraft. By October 1692, 19 people had been convicted and hanged, one had been pressed to death, and several had died in prison. Two dogs were executed as accomplices.

In 1693 the remaining defendants were pardoned. Judges regretted their parts in the trials; jurors admitted that they had made mistakes, and the minister of Salem preached repentance. In 1706 Ann Putnam, one of the afflicted girls, confessed that her accusations had in fact been false.

It was a great delusion of Satan that deceived me in that sad time.

ANN PUTNAM

	POLITICS & POWER	GEOGRAPHY & ENVIRONMENT	CULTURE & RELIGION
THE AMERICAS	**1710 English forces** invade Acadia in Canada and take Port Royal from the French. **1710 A group of Mohawk leaders** travels to England and asks Queen Anne to support them against their enemies. **1712 Settlers in North Carolina** attack the Tuscarora. Remnants of the tribe move north and join the Iroquois Confederacy. **1715 Yamasee Indians** of Georgia, resisting slavers, join Seminoles in impassible areas of Florida.	**1713 The Peace of Utrecht** cedes Acadia, Newfoundland, and other French colonial territory to Britain. Britain receives the exclusive right to bring African slaves to the Spanish colonies. **1720 The Spanish** occupy parts of Texas. **1723 The French** deliver Fort San Carlos at Pensacola Bay to the Spanish.	**1711 The Portuguese king** bans all religious orders from the gold fields of Minas Gerais, Brazil. **1716 The first theater** in the English colonies opens in Williamsburg, Virginia. It closes in 1723. **1724 The Convent of Corpus Christi,** first convent for indigenous women, opens in Mexico.
EUROPE	**1710 The South Sea Company,** a British colonial investment scheme, begins operations, but goes bust due to fraud in 1720, ruining investors. **1713 The Peace of Utrecht** between Britain and France ends the War of Spanish Succession and results in territories changing hands in Europe and the North American colonies. **1713 Philip V** becomes king of Spain. **1715 Louis XV** becomes king of France. **1715 James,** son of the deposed James II, enters Scotland in an attempt to regain the British throne, but his attempt fails.		**1710 Gottfried Wilhelm Leibniz,** German rationalist philosopher and developer of symbolic logic, publishes *Essais de Théodicée sur la Bonte de Dieu.* **1717 The English Grand Lodge of Freemasonry** is established in London. Masons begin to spread though Europe and North America. **1720s English writers** include Daniel Defoe, Jonathan Swift, and Henry Fielding. Richard Congreve, John Gay, and Richard Steele are active playwrights. **1728 The Spanish Inquisition** suppresses the Freemason's Lodge in Madrid.
MIDDLE EAST & AFRICA	**1711-18 The Ottomans** defeat Russian forces, regain Greece, but lose Bosnia. **1720 The Ottomans** begin sending ambassadors to represent them in European capitals and to learn about European culture. **1723 Afghan tribal conquerors** invade Iran, sack Isfahan, and put an end to the Safavid regime. **1727 Dahomey** expands to its greatest extent. **1729 Arab traders** drive the Portuguese out of Mombasa.		**1720s The "Tulip period"** occurs in the Ottoman Empire, when decorations, flower displays, and festivals distract the sultan and his people from vizier Ibrahim Pasha's power plays. **1729 The Ottomans** lift the ban on printing books in Turkish or Arabic. From 1729 to 1742 they print many volumes on history, geography, and language.
ASIA & OCEANIA	**1714 Burma** enters a period of growth and development that lasts until about 1733. **1720 Tibet** becomes a Chinese protectorate. **1720s Economic, social, and political reforms** are enacted under Shogun Yoshimune in Tokugawa Japan. **1723 Emperor Yung-cheng** tightens imperial control in China. He abolishes hereditary servitude and promotes education.	**1722 Dutchman Jakob Roggeveen** discovers Easter Island.	**1720s Jaipur City, India,** is planned out on a geometric grid. **1722 The Tokugawa shogunate** lifts the ban on foreign books; Dutch learning begins to enter Japan. **1724 Imperial edict** bans the teaching of Christianity in China. Christian missionaries are expelled from the country. **1725 Isida Baigan** founds Shingaku, a Japanese religion built on Shinto, Buddhism, and Confucianism. Many urban dwellers adopt it.

WHAT LIFE WAS LIKE

In 18th-Century Africa

At the height of the slave trade between Africa and the Americas, most people in Central and West Africa lived in small hamlets, often as extended family groups. Men typically led the family, though inheritance might depend on women. Slash-and-burn agriculture at the forest fringes supported millet, yams, and many cultivars of bananas; there was trade in iron, copper, salt, and shells. Disease was endemic and populations grew slowly. The removal of healthy men, women, and children by slavers crippled both the economy and social custom. Communities where only the sick and the old remained fell into disorder and never recovered.

SCIENCE & TECHNOLOGY	PEOPLE & SOCIETY
1715-16 Sybilla Masters of Pennsylvania invents a corn mill and a hat weaving process. King George II grants patents for them to Masters's husband, who gives her all the credit.	**1715 The gold fields** of Minas Gerais in Brazil are worked by 30,000 slaves.
1720s The Principio Company builds Accokeek Furnace in Virginia and exports iron to England.	**1718 Europeans** first describe the game of lacrosse as played by the Potawatomie of the Upper Midwest.
1724 The first levees are built along the banks of the Mississippi River in Louisiana to protect against damaging floods.	**1720s Epidemics** severely reduce the population of Peru.
1728 John Bartram opens a botanical garden in Philadelphia.	**1723 Indoor plumbing** is installed in a house in Newport, Rhode Island.
	1729 South Carolina slaves revolt.
1710 Jakob Christophe Le Blon, a German engraver, develops a three-color printing process.	**1719 Daniel Defoe** publishes his greatest novel, *Robinson Crusoe*. In 1722 *Moll Flanders* follows.
1717 Lady Mary Wortley Montague encourages inoculation against smallpox in Britain after observing its use in Turkey.	**1720s French philosopher Voltaire,** exiled in England, is influenced by English thought and scientific inquiry.
1725 Catherine I of Russia founds the St. Petersburg Academy of Science.	**1721 Bubonic plague** occurs for the last time in Europe.
1728 A treatise on dentistry is written in France.	**1721 Regular mail service** begins between London and New England.
	1727 The Society of Friends (Quakers) in England advocates the abolition of slavery.
1729 Printer Ibrahim Müteferrika publishes descriptions of European governments, military sciences, and geography. He also prints maps and mathematical tables.	**1713 A smallpox epidemic,** originating on a Dutch ship, sweeps through the Cape colony, killing both whites and Africans.
1729 *T'ushu ji cheng,* a 1,000-chapter encyclopedia printed in movable type, is published in China.	**1729 Emperor Yongzheng** prohibits opium smoking in China.

THE CASTE SYSTEM

Light-skinned Aryan invaders introduced castes to India in ancient times as a way of ordering society among the darker-skinned natives of the subcontinent. A form of the system survives today, with variations in Nepal, Sri Lanka, Pakistan, and Bangladesh. Caste is hereditary. One is born into a particular relationship with the rest of the world. Caste is related to religious purity as well: Priests are born into the highest caste. Although rooted in Hinduism, caste structure has also developed within Muslim, Sikh, Christian, and Buddhist traditions in Asia.

Caste rules social behavior. One must marry within one's caste, eat particular foods and only in allowable company, and assume specific obligations in business. The four original castes, called varnas,

Untouchables wash clothes at sunrise near Delhi

from a word meaning colors, are Brahmans, the priests; Kshatriyas, the kings, nobility, and warriors; Vaishyas, the merchants and farmers; and Sudras, or the peasants and laborers. Below all these are the people who perform the most menial and religiously impure duties, like garbage collection, sweeping, and cleaning latrines—the so-called untouchables. Within these groupings there are many special positions and levels, so that a person of a low caste may still be a person of great importance and influence locally, though he is deferential in his attitude to higher caste individuals.

1730-1750

CONVERGING WORLDS 1500-1750

	POLITICS & POWER	GEOGRAPHY & ENVIRONMENT	CULTURE & RELIGION

THE AMERICAS

POLITICS & POWER

1732 King George II grants James Oglethorpe a charter for a colony south of the Carolinas. Oglethorpe establishes Georgia, named for the king, as a refuge for poor and debtors.

1735 North and South Carolina agree on boundaries dividing them.

1737 The Walking Purchase claims Indian lands for Pennsylvanians under the terms of an old treaty. Thousands of Lenni Lenape are displaced.

1738 Britain sends troops to defend the Georgians against an attack from Spain.

GEOGRAPHY & ENVIRONMENT

1742-43 The French explore westward; passing through South Dakota, they continue on to the Rocky Mountains.

1743 Russians explore parts of mainland Alaska.

1749 Céleron de Blainville leads an expedition down the Ohio River to claim western lands for France. The Ohio Company is founded in London to block the French claims.

CULTURE & RELIGION

1730s The Great Awakening sweeps through the British colonies in North America. During this period of religious fervor, traveling preachers stress the individual's relation to God as being all-important, an idea that will weaken the colonists' respect for authority.

1730s Moravians establish settlements in Pennsylvania and later, in North Carolina.

1730s Portraiture flourishes with the work of John Smibert and Joh Hesselius.

1742 The Moravian College for Women is founded in Pennsylvania.

EUROPE

1730-1743 Russia, Persia, and the Holy Roman Empire engage in wars against the Ottoman Turks.

1740 Frederick William I of Prussia dies, succeeded by his son Frederick II (Frederick the Great).

1740 Holy Roman Emperor Charles V dies, succeeded by daughter Maria Theresa, who gains a respected reputation for diplomacy.

1745 Charles Stuart (Bonnie Prince Charlie), grandson of the deposed King James II, enters Scotland to regain the British throne but is defeated.

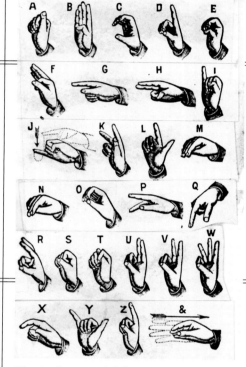

1730 John and Charles Wesley found the Methodist church at Oxford, England.

1730s François Boucher, Jean-Baptiste-Siméon Chardin, Jean-Honoré Fragonard, William Hogarth, and Canaletto (Antonio Canal) are all actively painting.

1734 George Sale translates the Koran into English.

1734 Emanuel Swedenbord, Swedish scientist, writes on the natural world and attains a great following as a philosopher and mystic.

1738 The pope publishes an edict against Freemasonry.

MIDDLE EAST & AFRICA

1730 The Patrona Halil revolt in the Ottoman Empire protests war taxes and elite dissipation.

1736-47 Nadir Shah reconquers Iran for a puppet Safavid ruler, invades India, and returns with the Mughals' Peacock Throne.

1739 The Ottomans defeat the Russians and Austrians, regaining Bosnia and the Crimea.

1750 The kingdom of Darfur expands in East Africa.

The sign language alphabet

1732 Istanbul's aqueduct system is rebuilt and expanded, bringing water to the European quarter of Beyoglu and creating the city center of Taksin.

1730s French Count Bonneral, a convert to Islam, brings European expertise to modernizing the Ottoman artillery corps and founding a military engineering school.

ASIA & OCEANIA

1739 The Persians sack Delhi. Nadir Shah attacks the Punjab and loots Mughal palaces.

1740s The Chinese civil service examination system comes under attack.

1744-48 Joseph-François Dupleix is governor general of French holdings in India, based at Pondicherry.

1746 Dupleix captures Madras in an action against the British during the War of the Austrian Succession.

1748-1750 The Afghans harry the Punjab.

1736-1750 China expands to its greatest geographical extent. By 1750 its population is close to 300 million.

1740s Bunraku puppet theater flourishes in Japan's urban centers.

1747 Jesuits design the Summer Palace at Beijing for Emperor Qianlong.

ca 1750 Wu Jingzi writes *The Scholars,* a novel satirizing the examination system in China.

ca 1750 Cao Xueqin writes *Dream of the Red Chamber,* a novel about a declining gentry family.

SCIENCE & TECHNOLOGY	PEOPLE & SOCIETY
1730 The first sugar refinery is built in New York.	**1730s Africans** begin to predominate over Indian slaves in southern colonies.
1738 Eliza Lucas Pinckney of South Carolina develops and markets indigo as a useful crop.	**1733 The first Masonic Lodge** in the British colonies is founded in Boston.
1739 Caspar Wistar opens a glassworks in New Jersey.	**1739 The people of Venezuela,** Colombia, and Equador come under the viceroyalty of New Granada.
1741 Savannah, Georgia, begins to produce porcelain.	**1740 Smallpox** decimates the Lakota of the northern plains.
1744 Benjamin Franklin develops the Franklin stove.	**1740s Coosaponakeesa** interprets for James Oglethorpe with the Creeks in Georgia.

1735 Swedish taxonomist Carolus Linnaeus publishes *Systema naturae,* describing a classification system for plants, animals, and minerals.	**1743 Russians** attack Jewish communities in pogroms.
1736 The first successful appendectomy is performed in France.	**1746 Celtic culture** in Scotland is suppressed after the rebellion of 1745 and the feudal clan system declines. Many Scots emigrate.
1736 Workshops on the island of Murano, near Venice, begin manufacturing glass.	**1749 Spaniard Giacobbo Rodrigues Periere** demonstrates a system of sign language he developed for those who can neither hear nor speak.
1736 Caoutchouc (rubber) is first imported to Britain from the West Indies.	
1738 Excavations begin at the Roman city of Herculaneum, buried by a volcanic eruption in 79 C.E.	

WHAT LIFE WAS LIKE

On the South African Frontier

In 1652 the Dutch built a fort and farms at the Cape of Good Hope to resupply ships of the Dutch East India Company. By 1700 Capetown had 3,000 settlers, and pastoral farmers called Trekboers were grazing sheep and cattle in outlying areas, carving out grants of 6,000 acres from lands of the indigenous African herders. After European disease devastated native peoples, Trekboers spread to the Orange River, 300 miles north of Capetown. The mixed race, multicultural society of this frontier adopted a rugged life of hunting, herding, and trading, hostile to government restraint. Eventually, patriarchal Dutch Calvinists claiming racial and religious superiority organized armed militias to defend their settlements from attack.

1740 Urban craftsmen in Istanbul, once supporters of Patrona Halil's revolt, support the sultan when trade improves with war and new contacts with the West. Military and religious leaders turn against the sultan in protests over Westernization.

1736 An independent merchant academy called the Kaitokudo is founded in Osaka.

1750s Wealthy Japanese merchants prosper, as do other urban dwellers; their lives are portrayed in Kabuki and puppet dramas.

INDIAN WARS

When Europeans and Indians shared a landscape, the first friendly contact and cooperation seemed inevitably followed by misunderstandings and conflict as cultures clashed. European technology enabled conquest everywhere, but land rights and the Indians' indifference to colonial law brewed perennial trouble. Disease weakened native groups and many fell prey to slave hunts in the south; the English sold Indian slaves throughout the colonies and down to the Caribbean plantations. As late as 1730 a quarter of the slaves in South Carolina were Indian.

As European demand for fur grew, planting and fishing were neglected by Indians, disease and alcoholism spread, and hostilities developed between native hunting groups. The Iroquois attacked the Hurons in 1649 to secure fur routes in the north and west. Recurrent warfare sparked by European trade favors displaced tribes and disrupted traditional ways throughout the colonial period.

By 1675 English encroachment on Indian lands had ruined the good relations Massachusetts settlers had established with the Wampanoags. Metacom, known to the English as King Philip, led attacks that spread across New England, burning 52 towns. 600 English and 3,000 Indians died before Philip was killed and his tribal alliance broken.

French, English, and Dutch authorities recruited Indian allies for colonial wars, too. Fur trade rights, land claims north and west of New England, and control of the West Indies trade were causes for King William's War (1689-1697), Queen Anne's War (1702-1713) and King George's War (1744-48). The Hurons and related tribes fought for the French; the Iroquois confederacy fought for the English, and frontier settlements suffered. In 1754 French, English, and Iroquois all laid claim to the riches of the Ohio country, precipitating the French and Indian War, a conflict that trained leaders like George Washington for the American Revolution.

Beginning in the late 1700s, political and technological advances gave highly industrialized countries a huge advantage over less-developed countries. The industrial revolution began in Great Britain and spread across western Europe along with nationalist fervor and demands for popular sovereignty, or government responsive to the will of the people. Revolutionary France abolished its monarchy, and some other European nations limited royal power by forming legislatures.

In the Americas, many countries rebelled against European rule and achieved political independence, but only the United States, Canada, and a few Latin American nations moved toward economic independence by industrializing. By the late 1800s, most countries in Latin America, Africa, Asia, and the Pacific had come under the economic influence or political domination of the world's major industrial powers, whose ranks grew to include the U.S., Japan, and Russia as well as Britain, France, Germany, and other western European nations. This new imperialism, based on industrial development, set the stage for worldwide convulsions in the 20th century as imperial powers battled for supremacy and developing countries struggled for independence.

American Revolutions

As of 1750, the New World remained divided into European colonies. Conflicts between colonial powers there proved costly for winners as well as losers. In 1763 France conceded defeat to Britain in the French and Indian War—linked to the Seven Years' War in Europe—and surrendered Canada. But Britain, in seeking to recover the costs of war, antagonized its American colonists by imposing new taxes on them without granting them representation in Parliament. In 1775 rebels in Massachusetts launched the Revolution by clashing with British troops. A year later, colonial delegates met in Philadelphia and declared independence. Thomas Jefferson of Virginia made popular sovereignty the cornerstone of the Declaration of Independence when he wrote that governments derived "their just powers from the consent of the governed" and should be altered or abolished if they denied people liberty and other "inalienable rights."

In 1781 the American Commander George Washington won a decisive victory over the British at Yorktown with help from French forces, who intervened to strike a blow against Britain. The British recognized American independence, and in 1789 Washington became the first president of the United States under a constitution that reserved many powers to the states. Most states originally restricted the right to vote to white male property owners, and slavery became entrenched in southern states and persisted until the early 1800s in some northern states.

Rebellions against colonial rule soon erupted in the Americas. In 1791 slaves and free blacks led by one of their own, Toussaint-Louverture, rose up against French rule in Haiti. In 1804 the French emperor Napoleon Bonaparte granted Haiti independence after selling the Louisiana Territory to the U.S. Napoleon's strategy was to concentrate his resources in Europe against rivals such as Britain and Spain. In 1808 he intervened in Spain and placed his brother on the throne there, triggering revolts in Latin America by colonists who saw Spanish authority eroding.

In 1810 a priest named Miguel Hidalgo y Costilla launched the Mexican war for independence by leading an uprising against Spanish authorities and landowners. Wealthy Mexicans turned against the rebels, and Hidalgo was executed, but the struggle continued. In 1821 a conservative general, Agustín de Iturbide, won independence for Mexico and became emperor. He soon fell from power, and Central American states broke away from Mexico, which reorganized as a republic in 1824.

In South America, Simón Bolívar of Venezuela led a rebellion against Spanish rule in 1810 and went on to become president of a state embracing Venezuela, Colombia, Panama, and Ecuador. Elsewhere, the Argentine rebel leader José de San Martín helped free his own country and neighboring Chile from Spain. He then led his forces into Peru, where he gave way to Bolívar, who took power in Lima. Bolívar went on to defeat Spanish royalists in the southern Peruvian interior, which became known as Bolivia in his honor. He hoped to hold the lands he liberated together as one nation, comparable in size to Brazil, which won independence from Portugal in 1822. But opponents assailed him as a dictator and pressured him into yielding power, and his confederation broke up into smaller, weaker states.

Unlike the U.S. and Canada, which as British col-

PREVIOUS PAGE:
A bare-headed Simón Bolívar battles on horseback against Spanish royalists in a modern depiction of the struggle for independence from Spain launched by Bolívar in South America in 1810.

OPPOSITE: *Welts cover the back of an African-American who fled brutal whippings as a slave and joined the Union Army during the American Civil War.*

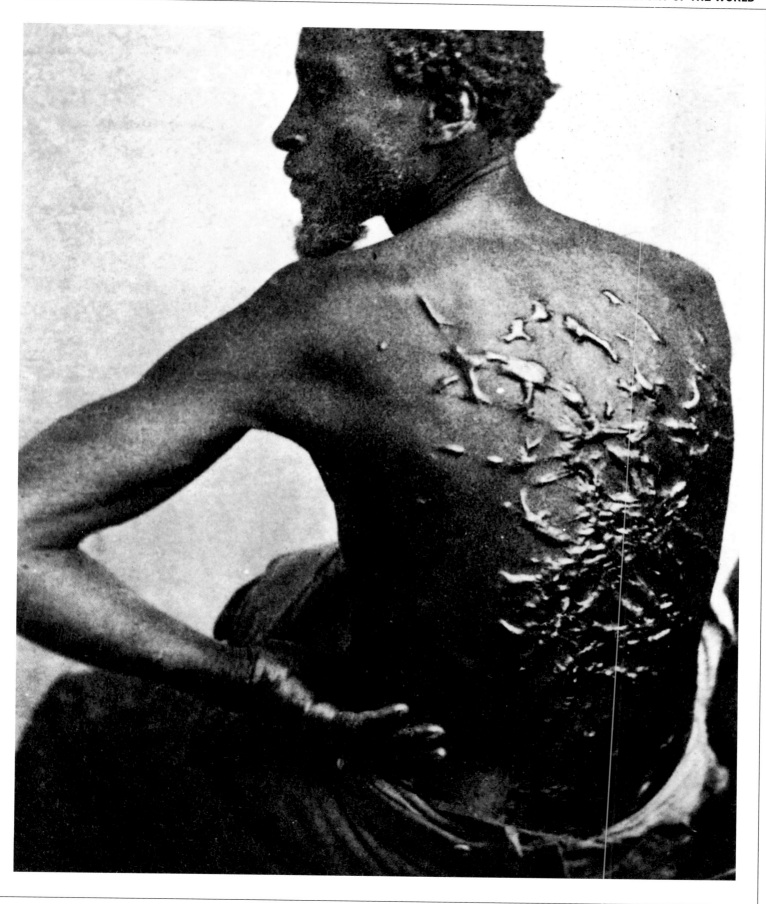

onies had formed their own assemblies and developed economically through trade, Latin America had no tradition of self-government and few sources of wealth other than agriculture and precious metals, much of which had been extracted in colonial times. Poor and politically unstable, many Latin American countries fell under the control of military rulers, or caudillos. One caudillo, Antonio López de Santa Anna of Mexico, was defeated by Anglo-American insurgents in Texas, who then declared independence. The annexation of Texas by the U.S. in 1845 led to war with Mexico, which lost New Mexico and California to the Americans.

Westward expansion caused bitter discord in the U.S. over the issue of slavery in western territories. After Abraham Lincoln, who opposed extending slavery, was elected president in 1860, Southern states seceded and formed the Confederacy. Lincoln gave the ensuing Civil War new meaning in 1862 by issuing the Emancipation Proclamation, which freed slaves in areas occupied by federal troops. This discouraged Britain, which had abolished slavery but still imported cotton from the slaveholding South, from aiding the Confederacy. The Union had a larger population and a stronger industrial base than the Confederacy and won the war in 1865. Reunited, the nation was ready for wholesale industrialization, a process that was well under way in Europe.

Europe's Industrial Powerhouses

In 1866 the first transatlantic telegraph cable was laid, allowing messages to be sent across the ocean in an instant. Much of the credit went to American financier Cyrus Field, but his Atlantic Telegraph Company was organized in Britain, where the industrial revolution had ignited a century earlier, yielding huge profits that were invested in new technologies in Britain, Canada, the U.S., and many other countries.

Several factors helped make Britain the birthplace of industrialism, including large deposits of coal and iron ore and a political system that encouraged private

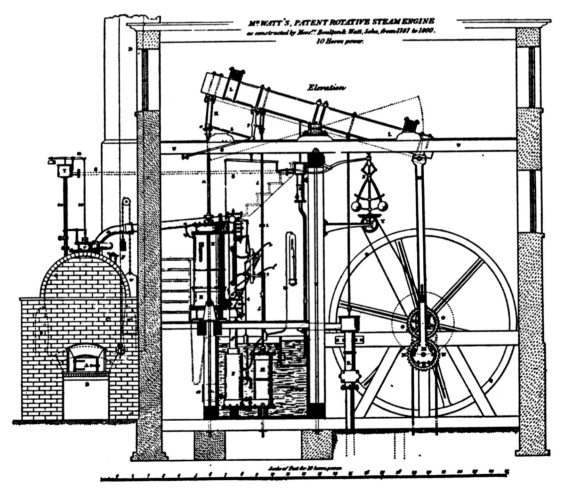

The industrial revolution in Britain received impetus from the steam engine, invented by James Watt, which used steam produced in a boiler to drive a piston and turn a wheel.

enterprise and investment. Britain already had a thriving cottage industry, involving workers who spun and wove wool and cotton by hand at home. When James Watt perfected the steam engine in 1765 and steam power was applied to spinning and weaving, the textile industry boomed. Cottages gave way to factories, and the productivity of workers soared, lowering the cost of their products. Steam-powered locomotives, introduced in the early 1800s, linked factories by rail to cities, ports, and coal mines. For laborers, the industrial regime was grueling, and protesters called Luddites sabotaged machinery. But working conditions slowly improved as trade unions gained bargaining power and Parliament enacted labor laws.

Other western European countries followed Britain's path toward industrial development by creating political conditions that favored capitalism, or control of the economy by private interests rather than the state. Prior to the French Revolution, economic policy was set by the king. As King Louis XIV had reportedly boasted, "L'état c'est moi" (I am the state). But he and his successors undermined their authority by spending heavily on wars and increasing tax burdens on peasants and the bourgeoisie, or middle class, who grew increasingly resentful of royalty and aristocracy. Unlike the American Revolution, the French Revolution that began in 1789 was a radical effort to transform society, inspired in part by ideas of equality and natural rights advanced by Jean-Jacques Rousseau and other Enlightenment philosophers. The execution of King Louis XVI and Queen Marie Antoinette in 1793 led Britain, Spain, and other countries to oppose the revolution, and France was in turmoil until Napoleon took power in 1799.

As emperor, Napoleon made French society more equitable and enterprising by reforming the tax system and legal code and by instituting public education, but he was a nationalist rather than a revolutionary. His troops were devoted to him, but they were even more devoted to France and demonstrated their patriotic fervor in one punishing campaign after another. Through conquest, Napoleon helped create a new Europe where patriotism, militarism, and capitalism combined to create nations of enormous power whose imperial ambitions were shared by many citizens who fought or worked for their homeland.

Napoleon met with defeat in 1812 when he invaded Russia and most of his army froze or starved to death. At the Congress of Vienna in 1815, the allied nations that opposed him tried to restore the old order in Europe by agreeing to put down uprisings that threatened established monarchies. But nationalist fervor could not be suppressed. Even conservatives were pleased when Greece rebelled against its Ottoman rulers and won independence, but when Belgium broke free of the Netherlands in 1830 defenders of the old order were appalled. Revolutionary passions overflowed in 1848 when demonstrators in Paris restored the French Republic while protesters in Vienna, Berlin, and other cities demanded constitutional government.

Some radicals were inspired by the Communist Manifesto, published in 1848 by the Germans Karl Marx and Friedrich Engels, but nationalism proved much stronger than communism. Germany was unified by the Prussian statesman Otto von Bismarck, who said that the fate of nations would be decided not by speeches or votes but by "blood and iron." True to his words, he drew on the industrial might of the Krupp family, producers of munitions, and launched wars of expansion that produced a second German reich, or empire, in 1871. (The first reich was the Holy Roman Empire.) Germany's emperor allowed for the establishment of a parliament, or Reichstag, as did the king of newly unified Italy. Reforms were introduced even in the Austro-Hungarian Empire, where the Habsburg dynasty endured, and in imperial Russia, where Tsarina Catherine the Great had ceased efforts to liberalize the political system in reaction to the French Revolution. Serfdom was abolished in Russia under Tsar Alexander II in 1861, and peasants there took part in local elections.

The population of Europe soared during the 1800s as industrial development and improvements in sanitation and public health raised standards of living. Tens of millions of Europeans immigrated to the U.S., Canada, and Latin American countries like Argentina. European investment helped build railroads across North America and provide electrical power to cities, and European immigration contributed to soaring agricultural and industrial productivity in the U.S., which emerged with the world's strongest economy. Canada became a British dominion in 1867, independent in all areas except foreign policy. But elsewhere, Britain and other industrialized nations tightened their grip on less-

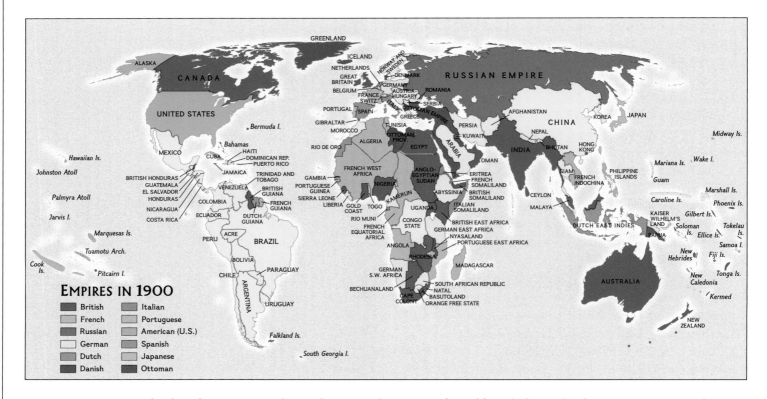

EMPIRES IN 1900

- British
- French
- Russian
- German
- Dutch
- Danish
- Italian
- Portuguese
- American (U.S.)
- Spanish
- Japanese
- Ottoman

By 1900 Britain, France, and other industrial powers dominated much of the world and had economic influence over China and Latin American countries that were not under their direct control. The once-mighty Spanish and Ottoman Empires had lost territory, while Germany, Japan, Russia, and the United States had recently gained ground.

developed countries as military advances such as steam-powered, steel-clad battleships allowed them to project power around the globe swiftly and surely.

Global Imperialism

British domination of India began in the mid-1700s when the East India Company established forts and trading posts there and recruited Indian troops called sepoys to bolster British forces. The Mughal Empire was fracturing, leaving local rulers to contend with the British. In 1757 the ruler of Bengal punished the British for violating trade restrictions by seizing their garrison in Calcutta and confining prisoners to the "black hole," where many died. In retaliation, British forces seized Bengal and replaced its defiant ruler with a compliant one, setting a precedent for the takeover of other Indian states. In 1857 the British Army took control of India following a mutiny by sepoys and imposed direct imperial rule. India became the jewel in Britain's crown, prized as a source of cotton and other raw materials and as a lucrative market for British manufactured goods such as cotton fabric, exported to India in such quantity that its native textile trade withered.

Among the items they exported from India was opium, which was sold illegally in China. When China tried to halt that trade in 1839, British forces intervened and forced China to legalize opium, open coastal ports to foreign trade, and grant Britain control of Hong Kong.

This was a humiliating blow for China's Manchu rulers. In the 1850s their Qing dynasty was nearly toppled by the Taiping Rebellion, an egalitarian movement inspired by Christianity that challenged China's social and political order by advocating that all property be held by the people in common. Government forces massacred the rebels in 1864, but calls for reform persisted. In 1898 reformers at court won support from the young Emperor Guangxu. His aunt, the Empress Dowager Cixi, soon usurped power and executed or exiled the reformers. She then encouraged the ongoing Boxer Rebellion, a popular uprising against foreigners and foreign influence. Foreign troops helped put down the uprising, and China was forced to pay an indemnity to nations that sustained losses. Afterward, many in China began to agitate for the overthrow of the Manchus.

With China debilitated, European powers were free to occupy Southeast Asia and exploit its resources. Britain took Burma and Malaysia, France claimed Indochina, and the Dutch extended their control over the East Indies. Japan escaped foreign domination by becoming an imperial power itself. Shocked when American warships entered Tokyo Bay in 1853 to demand trade rights with Japan, the Japanese overthrew the Tokugawa shogun and restored imperial rule under Emperor Meiji. He presided over a program of modernization in which Japan adopted a constitution, embraced foreign trade, industrialized, and built powerful armed forces that defeated China in 1894 and took control of Korea, Taiwan, and other territories.

In the Middle East, rulers of the Ottoman Empire made efforts at reform but failed to modernize sufficiently and lost much of their territory in the Balkans and North Africa to stronger powers. France first sent troops to Algeria in 1830 and went on to claim most of northwest Africa. In 1859 Britain began construction of the Suez Canal to secure a shorter maritime route to India and later seized control of Egypt and Sudan to protect that investment.

By 1880 many imperial powers were caught up in a scramble for Africa, where the ruinous transatlantic slave trade had come to an end only to be replaced by new forms of exploitation. Some of the worst abuses of African laborers occurred in the Belgian Congo, but conditions were little better in colonies ruled by other countries. Meeting in Berlin in 1884, delegates from more than a dozen nations, including the U.S., an emerging world power, drew up boundaries for existing colonies and rules for claiming new ones. That did not prevent Europeans from fighting over Africa. Conflict persisted in South Africa between British occupiers and Dutch colonists of longer standing called Boers (farmers). Advances inland by Boers in the 1830s had triggered the first Anglo-Boer War, which was in fact a three-way struggle between Boers, British forces, and Zulus, who fought mightily against both European factions. The last Anglo-Boer War broke out in 1899 and ended in 1902 with an agreement that confirmed British rule but made some territorial concessions to the Boers. When South Africa later became a self-governing British dominion, the white minority there took control and instituted the policy of apartheid, or strict racial segregation and discrimination.

The imperial land grab that convulsed Africa extended even to remote Pacific islands such as Tahiti, where Polynesians had welcomed Europeans in the 1700s. Most of those islands were too small for major colonization efforts such as Britain undertook in Australia, settled as a penal colony in 1788. But they were coveted by various nations as naval bases and as sites for plantations and proselytizing. American missionaries

Take up the White Man's burden
The savage wars of peace
Fill full the mouth of famine
And bid the sickness cease.

RUDYARD KIPLING

and sugar planters established a strong presence in Hawaii, where U.S. Marines came ashore in 1893 and deposed Queen Liliuokalani after she vowed to resist foreign domination. The annexation of Hawaii five years later coincided with the Spanish-American War, during which American forces seized Cuba and the Philippines. When the U.S. entered the imperial contest, it came full circle. A nation that began by throwing off colonial rule was now acquiring colonies of its own. ■

Queen Victoria sits for a portrait on her ivory throne upon being named empress of India on January 1, 1877. The title was intended to give notice that the British were in India to stay—a commitment imperialists regarded as in the best interests of Indians and Britons.

THE WORLD AT A GLANCE

EMPIRES AND REVOLUTIONS 1750-1900

	1750	1765	1780	1795	1810	
THE AMERICAS	**1752** Benjamin Franklin invents the lightning conductor. **1754** The French and Indian War breaks out between Britain and France. **1763** Chief Pontiac leads a Native American rebellion against British settlers.	**1765** The Spanish begin a policy of "comercio libre," loosening restrictions on American trade. **1775** Fighting at Lexington and Concord, Massachusetts, begins the American Revolution. **1776** The Declaration of Independence is adopted. **1778** France enters the American Revolution as an American ally.	**1783** By the Treaty of Paris, Britain accepts American independence. **1789** George Washington becomes the first president of the United States. **1794** Eli Whitney patents the cotton gin.	**1801** Former slave Toussaint-Louverture declares the island of Haiti independent. **1803** The Louisiana Purchase nearly doubles the land area of the United States. **1805** *El Diario de México*, the first Mexican daily newspaper, is published. **1807** Robert Fulton develops the first practical steamboat.	**1810** Miguel Hidalgo y Costilla begins the Mexican independence movement. **1812-15** The War of 1812 between the U.S. and Great Britain occurs. **1820s** José de San Martín and Simón Bolívar lead South American struggles for independence from Spanish rule. **1822** Brazil achieves its freedom from Portugal.	
EUROPE	**1755** A Lisbon earthquake kills more than 60,000 people. **1756** The Seven Years' War between Britain and France begins. **1762** Rousseau publishes *The Social Contract*. **1762** Catherine the Great becomes empress of all the Russias.	**1767** Catherine the Great commissions a new code of laws for Russia. **1768** War breaks out between Russia and the Ottoman Turks. **1769** James Watt patents the modern steam engine. **1772** The first partition of Poland by Russia, Prussia, and Austria is enacted.	**1783** Russia annexes the Crimea. **1789** The fall of the Bastille marks the beginning of the French Revolution. **ca 1790** The great age of European orchestral music occurs. **1792** Mary Wollstonecraft publishes *Vindication of the Rights of Woman*.	**1796** Edward Jenner discovers a smallpox vaccine. **1804** Napoleon's civil code is completed. **1805** Britain's Lord Nelson defeats the Franco-Spanish fleets at the Battle of Trafalgar. **1805** Napoleon defeats Russians and Austrians at the Battle of Austerlitz.	**1812** Napoleon invades Russia. **1812** The Brothers Grimm publish their volumes of fairy tales. **1814** George Stephenson invents the first practical steam locomotive. **1815** Britain's Duke of Wellington defeats Napoleon at the Battle of Waterloo. **1815** Napoleon goes into exile on St. Helena.	
MIDDLE EAST & AFRICA	**1752** The sultanate of Darfur dominates Sahel. **1757** Muhammad III becomes sultan of Morocco. **1758** The British capture Senegal in West Africa from the French. **1760** Boers cross the Orange River and begin settling the interior of southern Africa.	**1768-1774** The Russo-Ottoman war ends with major Ottoman losses. **1769** Egypt revolts against Ottoman rule. **1772** Scottish explorer James Bruce encounters the source of the Blue Nile. **1776** Abdelkader leads Muslims in a holy war along the Senegal River in West Africa.	**1781** Boer settlers massacre the Xhosa. **1786** Morocco agrees to cease raiding U.S. ships in the Mediterranean. **1787** The first freed slaves from Britain settle at Freetown in Sierra Leone. **1790s** Islamic proselytizing in West Africa reaches its zenith with the great Holy Wars.	**1798** Napoleon invades Egypt. **1799** The Rosetta stone is discovered in Egypt. **1800** Slave rebels deported from Jamaica settle in Sierra Leone. **1806** The British gain control of Cape Colony in southern Africa. **1807** The slave trade is abolished within the British Empire.	**1810** Mauritius and Seychelles are annexed by Britain. **1816** Shaka becomes ruler of the Zulu kingdom. **1821** Egyptians invade the Sudan. **1822** American abolitionists found Monrovia, the future capital of Liberia.	
ASIA & OCEANIA	**1750s** Dutch learning spreads Western knowledge in Japan. **1752** Ahmad Shah Durrani of Afghanistan invades India. **1755** Alaungpaya reunites Burma. **1760** Canton becomes the only Chinese port authorized for foreign trade.	**1768** Britain's Captain James Cook begins exploring the Pacific. **1771** The 30-year-long Tay Son Rebellion in Vietnam begins. **1776** Siam (Thailand) gains independence from Burma.	**1782** Rama I becomes king of Thailand and drives out Burmese invaders. **1788** A penal colony is set up at Botany Bay, Australia.	**1796** The British conquer Ceylon. **1796-1804** The White Lotus Rebellion occurs in China. **1798** Ranjit Singh, the Lion of the Punjab, founds the Sikh kingdom in India. **1802** Emperor Gia Long suppresses the Tay Son Rebellion and unifies Vietnam.	**1815** The Sumbawa volcano kills more than 50,000 in Indonesia. **1818** The Maratha are defeated by the British, who become in effect the rulers of India. **1820** Vietnamese emperor Minh Mang transforms his capital, Hué, into a Chinese-style imperial city and models his rule on Chinese laws and institutions.	

	1825	1840	1855	1870	1885-1900

1825 The Erie Canal is opened.

1830 The first wagon trains to cross the Rockies arrive in California.

1836 The Battle of the Alamo occurs.

1837 Samuel Morse sends the first message by electric telegraph.

1838-39 The Cherokee Trail of Tears takes place.

1846 The Mexican War begins between the U.S. and Mexico.

1846 The first professional baseball game is played, in Hoboken, New Jersey.

1849 The California gold rush begins.

1849 Harriet Tubman escapes from slavery and begins the Underground Railroad.

1850s Slavery is abolished in all Spanish-speaking republics of South America.

1861-65 The American Civil War occurs.

1867 The U.S. buys Alaska from Russia for $7.2 million—or two cents an acre.

1869 The U.S. transcontinental railroad is completed.

1876 Alexander Graham Bell patents the telephone.

1878 Thomas Edison invents the incandescent light bulb.

1883 Bolivia loses its entire coastline after the so-called saltpeter war with Chile.

1883 The Brooklyn Bridge is completed.

1835 The Statue of Liberty arrives in New York from France.

1885 The world's first skyscraper is built, in Chicago.

1897 People rush to the gold fields of the Klondike.

1898 The United States wins the Spanish-American War.

1825 The first passenger steam railway, between Stockton and Darlington, England, opens.

1829 Greece wins its independence from the Turks.

1830 Revolutions erupt in France, Germany, Poland, and Italy.

1832 In Paris, Louis Braille invents a reading system for the blind.

1845 The Irish potato famine begins.

1848 Karl Marx publishes *The Communist Manifesto;* revolutions occur across much of Europe.

1851 The Great Exhibition, the world's first industrial fair, opens in London.

1854-56 Russia is defeated by Britain and France in the Crimean War.

1860 Italian patriot Giuseppe Garibaldi leads a rebellion in southern Italy; unification of the country begins.

1861 Louis Pasteur develops the germ theory of disease.

1861 The emancipation of Russian serfs occurs.

1869 Leo Tolstoy publishes *War and Peace.*

1870s The Impressionist school of painting emerges.

1870-71 The Franco-Prussian War leads to the formation of the German Empire.

1878 Romania, Montenegro, and Serbia win independence from Turkey.

1882 Germany, Austria-Hungary, and Italy form the Triple Alliance.

1894 Nicholas II, last of the Russian tsars, ascends the throne.

1895 Guglielmo Marconi invents radio telegraphy.

1896 The first modern Olympic Games are held in Athens, Greece.

1898 Marie and Pierre Curie discover radium and polonium, in France.

1825 The powerful Zulu king Shaka is assassinated by his half-brother.

1830 The French begin their conquest of Algeria, still nominally part of the Ottoman Empire.

1830 Britain establishes a protectorate over the Gold Coast.

1835 The Great Trek of Boer colonists from the cape begins.

1839 The Ottoman Empire's First Reform Edict establishes civil rights.

1842 Boers found the Orange Free State.

1847 Liberia is formed as a home for released American slaves.

1851 Gold is discovered in southern Africa, bringing a flood of immigrants to the continent.

1855 Emperor Theodorus begins partial reconstruction of the Christian empire of Ethiopia.

1856 David Livingstone completes his crossing of Africa from the west.

1866 Diamonds are discovered in southern Africa.

1869 The Suez Canal opens, linking Egypt's Port Said to the Red Sea.

1870 The transatlantic slave trade between Africa and the Americas comes to an end.

1874 Henry Stanley discovers the source of the White Nile in Burundi.

1879 The French complete their conquest of Algeria.

1884 The Berlin Conference divides Africa among European powers.

1886 Gold is found in the Transvaal.

1890s The Arab slave trade on the east coast of Africa is stamped out.

1896 Ethiopia's Emperor Menelik II defeats the Italians at the Battle of Adowa.

1899 The Boer War breaks out between Afrikaners and the British.

1825-1830 Indonesians revolt against Dutch rule.

1833 Poor harvests bring famine to Japan; riots break out.

1839-1842 The Opium War between Britain and China occurs. China is forced to open ports to British trade and cedes Hong Kong.

1845-49 Britain conquers the Punjab and Kashmir.

1850 Australian colonies receive self-government from Britain.

1850 The Taiping Rebellion breaks out in China.

1853 India's first railroad and telegraph lines open.

1853 Commodore Matthew Perry sails into Japan's Edo Bay.

1856-1860 The Second Opium War between Britain and China leads to further incursions on Chinese sovereignty.

1857 The Indian Mutiny breaks out in opposition to British rule.

1863 France begins to establish protectorates in Indochina.

1868 The Meiji Restoration occurs in Japan.

1871-73 Japan sends the Iwakura Mission to the West.

1872 Universal military conscription is introduced in Japan.

1876 The Treaty of Kanghwa between Korea and Japan recognizes Korean independence.

1877 Disaffected samurai rebel against the Meiji government.

1887 The French establish the Indochinese Union.

1891 Construction of the Trans-Siberian Railroad begins.

1893 New Zealand becomes the first country to allow women to vote.

1895 The treaty ending the Sino-Japanese War gives Japan dominance over Korea and Taiwan.

	POLITICS & POWER	GEOGRAPHY & ENVIRONMENT	CULTURE & RELIGION
THE AMERICAS	**1750 French agents and traders** establish control over trade in the Mississippi Valley. **1754 The French and Indian War** breaks out on the North American continent between the European powers Britain and France. **1759 The British capture Quebec** from the French.	**1750 The Ohio Valley** has become home to numerous Indian peoples, such as the Shawnee, Delaware, Wyandot, and Miami, who seek escape from European pressures. **1751 Mason and Dixon** begin to accurately establish American territorial frontiers; the Mason-Dixon Line will ultimately mark the boundary between the American North and the American South.	**1750s African Americans** become a central part of the Great Awakening as it sweeps through the Chesapeake region. They see conversion as a means to "spiritual equality" and as an opportunity to voice their notions of a religious community. **1759 Jesuits are expelled** from Brazil because of their work on behalf of political rights for Indians.
EUROPE	**1750 Marqués de Pombal** becomes minister of Portugal and implements reforms. He is instrumental in helping Lisbon recover from the 1755 earthquake that destroys the city. **1756 The Seven Years' War** between Great Britain, France, Prussia, and Russia begins. It is related to the French and Indian War in North America. **1759 Charles III** becomes king of Spain and begins Bourbon reforms. **1760 King George III** ascends the English throne.	**1750 Half of English farmland** is enclosed by this date. **1755 More than 60,000 people** die in a huge earthquake in Lisbon, Portugal, estimated to be a magnitude 9.0 on the Richter scale.	**1751 France begins publication** of the *Encyclopédie*, a leading volume of the Enlightenment; the public eagerly buys all copies printed of the book, despite a ban by the authorities. **1753 Thomas Chippendale** begins making furniture in his workshop in London, England. **1754 The Royal and Ancient Golf Club** of St. Andrews is formed by a group of 22 Scottish golfers. **1755 The University of Moscow,** Russia's first university, is founded. **1759 Voltaire** publishes *Candide*.
MIDDLE EAST & AFRICA	**1752 The sultanate of Darfur** dominates Sahel, extending from Bornu in the west to the Nile Valley in the east. **1756 Tunisia** is occupied by the bey of Algiers. **1757 Muhammad III** becomes sultan of Morocco. **1757-1774 The reign of Mustafa III** maintains peace in the Ottoman Empire until 1768. **1758 The British capture Senegal** in West Africa from the French.	**ca 1750 Zahn al-Umar** begins planting and exporting cotton from Palestine. **1760 Boers cross the Orange River** and begin settling the interior of southern Africa. Descendants of the Dutch at the cape, they push the frontier of African-European interaction northward.	**1751-1779 Karim Khan Zand** institutes a reign of justice in Iran after the tyranny of Nadi Shah, but his descendants cannot sustain it. **1754-1793 The golden age of Tripoli** occurs in Libya; piracy is the main economic activity. **ca 1757 Mehmed Ragib Pasha,** Ottoman grand vizier, encourages diplomacy with Europe, issues orders of justice, balances the budget, and reorganizes the naval arsenal.
ASIA & OCEANIA	**1752 Ahmad Shah Durrani,** unifier of Afghanistan, invades India. **1755 Alaungpaya** founds Rangoon and reunites Burma. **1757 Robert Clive** defeats the French at the Battle of Plassey, laying the foundation for the British Empire in India. **1760 Canton** becomes the only Chinese port authorized to trade with other countries.	**ca 1750 China's population** reaches close to 200 million.	**1750s Dutch scholars** spread Western ideas in Japan. **ca 1750 *The Scholars*** is published, a satire of the Chinese civil service examination system. OPPOSITE: *In the mid-18th century, European claims in North America ranged from the French in Canada, the British along the eastern seaboard, and the Spanish in the Southwest. Russian fur traders had recently colonized coastal Alaska.*

SCIENCE & TECHNOLOGY

1752 The lightning conductor is invented by Benjamin Franklin, whose experiments with lightning include flying a kite in a thunderstorm.

ca 1754 The outbreak of the French and Indian War results in many Indian peoples becoming even more reliant on the French and British for vital supplies. Once the war ends these resources vanish, with calamitous results for the Indians.

ca 1755 In the aftermath of its devastating earthquake, Lisbon builds Europe's first quake-proof buildings.

1759 The British Museum opens in London.

1759 Marquise de Châtelet's French translation of Newton's *Principia* is published.

PEOPLE & SOCIETY

1754 21-year-old George Washington, commanding British troops, wipes out a French scouting party near Fort Necessity in Pennsylvania during the French and Indian War.

1755 Edward Braddock is mortally wounded leading British troops and Virginia militia during an attack on the French at Fort Duquesne.

1760 Quilombos (colonies of runaway slaves in remote areas of Brazil) still concern colonial administrators, who stage raids and suppression expeditions.

1750s Europe's population reaches about 140 million.

1755 Pasquale Paoli leads a nationalist revolt against Genoese rule in Corsica.

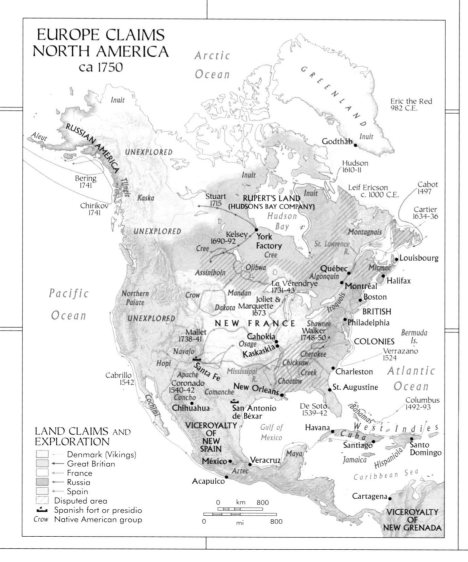

EUROPE CLAIMS NORTH AMERICA ca 1750

LAND CLAIMS AND EXPLORATION
- Denmark (Vikings)
- Great Britian
- France
- Russia
- Spain
- Disputed area
- Spanish fort or presidio
- *Crow* Native American group

THE AGE OF REASON

By the mid-18th century, writers and scholars all across Europe and even in the Americas were challenging traditional certainties about the authority of kings, the structure of the universe, and the temporal power of organized religion. Unquestioning obedience to religious, political, and social authority began to be supplanted by the scrutiny of ideas under the penetrating light of reason. If there were natural laws that governed the physical world, might there also be natural laws that applied to the social world—to the world of human activity and government? For many, the answer was a resounding yes.

This period in history became known as the Age of Reason. It has also been called the Enlightenment, because so many thinkers believed that reason could illuminate truth. Nowhere was this spirit of enlightenment more evident than in France, the most powerful country in Europe. The French leaders of this movement, the philosophes, came from a variety of backgrounds and traditions. They included Jean-Jacques Rousseau, a watchmaker's son; Montesquieu, a nobleman and magistrate; and Voltaire, who emerged from the ranks of the wealthy bourgeoisie.

Knowledge, the philosophes said, was the path to happiness. And in 1751 one of their number, the writer Denis Diderot, published the first installment of a 35-volume compendium that contained entries on everything from mathematics, politics, and music to ropemaking, tennis, and horsemanship. For the compendium had a simple, if perhaps unattainable, goal: to impart all knowledge. The work was referred to as the *Encyclopédie*.

Diderot published 27 more volumes over the next 20 years. The *Encyclopédie* caused an immediate stir. France's religious and political leaders condemned it, and the police banned it. But the public loved the *Encyclopédie* and bought every one of the 4,000 sets printed.

POLITICS & POWER	GEOGRAPHY & ENVIRONMENT	CULTURE & RELIGION

THE AMERICAS

1762 The Spanish temporarily lose control of Havana to the British in the Seven Years' War. The experience encourages them to rebuild defenses in the Caribbean.

1763 Chief Pontiac leads a Native American rebellion against British settlers in and around Detroit.

1763 The seat of Brazilian colonial government is shifted south to Rio de Janeiro.

1763 The Treaty of Paris ending the French and Indian War cedes to Britain all of Canada and the land east of the Mississippi.

1760s The introduction of rice cultivation fuels the economic growth from colonial North Carolina to Florida.

1769 Spanish begin to settle in southern California; the San Diego mission is founded, one of a string of missions throughout New Spain.

1770 Monterey becomes the capital of New California.

1763 Touro synagogue opens in Newport, Rhode Island, the first major Jewish center in North America.

1767 The Spanish government expels Jesuits from New Spain.

1768 Wesley Chapel, the first Methodist center in the North American colonies, opens in New York.

EUROPE

1762 Catherine the Great becomes empress of all the Russias after death of her husband.

1768 War breaks out between Russia and the Ottoman Turks, imperial rivals for dominance of the Balkans and the Black Sea region.

1760s Turnips, potatoes, and clover are increasingly planted and improve crop yields.

1763 Frederick the Great promotes agricultural reconstruction in Prussia after the Seven Years' War.

1762 Jean Jacques Rousseau publishes *The Social Contract*, an early work of the European Enlightenment.

1762 Sandwiches are invented in England and named after the Earl of Sandwich.

1770 Ludwig van Beethoven, a chief composer of the Romantic Age in European music, is born.

MIDDLE EAST & AFRICA

1768 The Russo-Turkish War begins; the Ottoman army is destroyed two years later.

1769 Local troops take control of Egypt away from the Ottoman governor.

1760-66 Two famous encyclopedias are written in Iran covering history, geography, science, and earthly and heavenly beings.

ca 1760 The "valley lords" rise in Anatolia, the Arab lands, and the Balkans. These are notable families who make themselves rulers on the local level, not to overturn the Ottomans but to elbow their way into the ranks of the elite.

ASIA & OCEANIA

1760s The Pomare dynasty is established in Tahiti.

1761 With the capture of Pondicherry, the British destroy French power in India.

1761 The Tay Son Rebellion begins in Vietnam.

1764 The Wang Lun Rebellion against the Qing occurs in China.

1765 Manchu Chinese invade Burma.

1768 Britain's Captain James Cook begins exploring the Pacific, putting ashore at such places as New Zealand and Australia.

1763 Cao Xueqin, author of the Chinese novel *Dream of the Red Chamber,* about an aristocratic family in decline, dies.

WHAT LIFE WAS LIKE

Captain Cook Visits New Zealand

Before Captain James Cook, few outsiders had ever seen the Maori islands of New Zealand. According to oral history, the Maoris had arrived in what they called the Land of the Long White Cloud some time around 1000 C.E., making the long voyage from other parts of Polynesia in just seven canoes. They adorned themselves with distinctive facial tattoos and clothed themselves in cloaks of woven flax and the feathers of native birds. Excellent hunters and fishermen, the Maoris carved wood, bone, and jade for tools and for weapons of war. Neighboring Maori tribes fought each other over territory or for revenge, with the losers ending up as slaves or, worse, as food.

SCIENCE & TE[CHNOLOGY]

1760s Rice planters in the American south introduce threshing machines to facilitate rice production.

1766 Bifocal spectacles are invented by Benjamin Franklin.

Benjamin Franklin

1762 John Harrison invents a marine chronometer for determining longitude at sea.

1769 James Watt patents the modern steam engine, which finds wide use in manufacturing. It is an early milestone of the Industrial Revolution.

1769 Richard Arkwright invents a waterpowered spinning frame, the first machine capable of producing cotton thread of the firmness and hardness required in the warp.

1767 Hungarian officer Baron de Tott is put in charge of the Ottoman Army. He introduces a rapid-fire artillery corps, and builds a modern cannon foundry and a new military engineering school.

PEOPLE & SOCIETY

1760s Slaves of the rice plantations in the American South begin to have children in sufficient numbers to replace themselves. The demographic revolution reduces the need for slave imports.

1764 The Sugar Act imposes a tax on molasses brought from non-British colonies; James Otis condemns Britain's "taxation without representation."

1765 Charles III allows commerce and trade to flow more freely between Spanish ports and the colonies.

1760s-1770s Jewish scholar Moses Mendelssohn urges that Jews be given civil rights.

1762 The French government opens manufacturing to rural areas.

1767 Catherine the Great commissions a new code of laws for Russia. Although Catherine sees herself as a monarch of the Enlightenment, serfdom increases in severity in Russia during her reign.

1760s Caty Loette, one of the wealthiest of West African signares (African women traders), owns 68 slaves.

1763 The Ottoman ambassador visits Frederick the Great in Berlin. After his return to Istanbul (Constantinople), he recommends important changes in the military and relations with Europe.

ca 1770 The European slave trade with Africa reaches its peak, transporting nearly 80,000 enslaved Africans across the Atlantic annually.

CHIEF PONTIAC'S REBELLION

Following the British capture of Detroit at the end of the French and Indian War, local Native Americans demanded that the British lower prices on their trade goods and provide the Indians with ammunition. When the British refused to meet these demands, an Ottawa Indian chief named Pontiac led an attack on Detroit in 1762, his warriors reinforced by the Wyandot, Potawatomi, and Ojibwa. When the raid failed, the Indians settled down to a siege of the fort, while news of the attack sparked similar raids throughout the region. Within weeks, every British post west of Niagara was destroyed and the borders of Pennsylvania, Maryland, and Virginia were in a state of terror, but still Detroit held out.

British reinforcements came to the relief of the beleaguered forts, while Pontiac hoped the French would come to his aid. But when it became clear this was not going to happen, he and his warriors withdrew off to the west, where he

Chief Pontiac stands amid warriors of the Ottawa, Wyandot, and Potawatomi tribes at the April 1763 council he called to gain support for his rebellion.

vainly tried to persuade tribes there to join the rebellion. A final peace agreement in 1766 marked the end of the rebellion; Pontiac was pardoned by the British, to whom the chief subsequently remained loyal. He is said to have been murdered by a Kaskaia Indian in 1769.

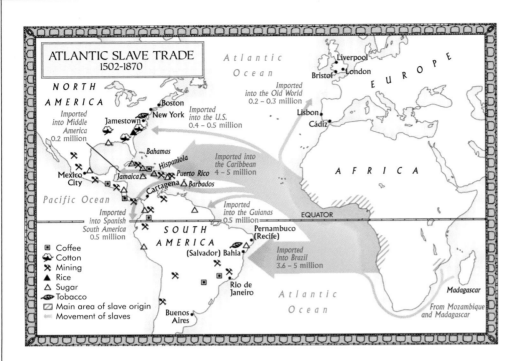

ATLANTIC SLAVE TRADE
1502-1870

THE TRADE IN HUMAN FLESH

BY THE 18TH CENTURY, SLAVERY HAD EXISTED IN AFRICA FOR MANY HUNDREDS OF years. Captives taken in war were often enslaved, as were those kidnapped from neighboring villages. Some enslaved Africans were kept locally; some were sent to Muslim lands to the east; and increasingly, some were lashed together by ropes, marched to the Atlantic coast, and inhumanely packed into ships bound for the West Indies or the Americas.

The transatlantic slave trade had begun with the Portuguese and the Spanish, who brought Africans to work on the sugar plantations of Brazil and the Caribbean as well as in the gold and silver mines of Mexico and Peru. But as other Europeans powers, such as the British, the French, and the Dutch, claimed colonies in the Americas, they too joined this terrible and increasingly global human commerce.

In the second half of the 18th century, when the transatlantic slave trade reached its peak, Great Britain ruled the seas and British merchants transported more slaves than any other European nation. Most slaves were taken to Britain's sugar plantations in the Caribbean. The rest traveled on to the British colonies in North America. By the middle of the 19th century, one-third of the New World's slaves lived in the United States.

Slaves sent to the Caribbean and to South America often did not live long. A harsh climate, disease, poor nutrition, and the brutality of slave owners led to a high mortality rate. Many Africans resisted their captivity, though, and runaway freedom fighters called maroons helped fuel resistance and sometimes succeeded in establishing their own communities. Despite the odds, some Africans did survive, transmitting their cultural values to new generations of African Americans.

The triangular trade between Europe, Africa, and the Americas (shown on the map above) enriched European industrialists and American plantation owners at the expense of African slaves like these.

	POLITICS & POWER	GEOGRAPHY & ENVIRONMENT	CULTURE & RELIGION
THE AMERICAS	**1775 Fighting at Lexington and Concord,** Massachusetts, begins the American Revolution. **1775 The Continental Congress** appoints George Washington head of the Continental Army. **1776 The Continental Congress** adopts the Declaration of Independence. **1776 Viceroyalty of La Plata** in Argentina is established. **1778 France** enters the American Revolution as an American ally.	**1770s The Indian population** of California goes into steep decline after encounters with Europeans. **1770 Coffee** grown in Venezuela and Cuba becomes one of the major export crops of the Caribbean along with sugar and cacao. **1776 The British** take hold of the Malvinas, held by the Spanish, and rename them the Falkland Islands. **1780 Spain** captures western Florida from Britain.	**1770s-1780s The Catholic Church** has its most powerful influence in colonial society through its monopoly of the education system. Power rests more with middle class Creoles than with the mestizo and indigenous population. **1776 Franciscan missionaries** who followed the Spanish into New California baptize thousands of Indians. **1779 The first school of arts** is established in the New World, in Mexico City.
EUROPE	**1772 The first partition of Poland** by Russia, Prussia, and Austria is enacted. (The second and third partitions were 1793 and 1795.) **1773 The Pugachev Rebellion** of serfs in Russia occurs.	**1770s Farmers** in England, France, and the Netherlands experiment with new crop rotation patterns.	**1770 Christian evangelist George Whitefield** dies. He is credited with inspiring the foundation of 50 colleges and universities in the United States. **1771 *Encyclopedia Britannica*** is first published. **1772 Pope Clement XIV** suppresses the Jesuit order. **1774 Maria Theresa** establishes compulsory elementary education in Austria. **1776 Adam Smith** publishes *The Wealth of Nations,* which lays the foundation for free-market capitalism.
MIDDLE EAST & AFRICA	**1771 Ali Bey of Egypt,** in alliance with the Russians, revolts against Ottoman rule; the revolt is suppressed in 1773. **1774 The Russo-Turkish War ends;** Ottomans lose Crimea, Moldavia, and lands around the Black Sea where Muslims live. **1779 Karim Khan,** who had managed to unite Persia under his rule, dies. The country disintegrates into anarchy again after his death.	**1772 Scottish explorer James Bruce** encounters the source of the Blue Nile. **1775 By this year,** five and a half million African slaves have been shipped to America.	**1772 Sidi Muhammad III,** ruler of Morocco, employs Jews as officials and ambassadors to European states, and favors Jewish merchants. **1776 Abdelkader** leads Muslims in a holy war along the Senegal River in West Africa.
ASIA & OCEANIA	**1776 Siam** (Thailand) gains independence from Burma. **1779 Captain James Cook** dies during a skirmish in Hawaii.		**1773 The Qianlong emperor** launches the *Complete Library of the Treasuries* project to compile the entire literary heritage of China into one massive collection. **1780 Japanese sumo wrestling** begins to be performed in public.

SCIENCE & TECHNOLOGY	PEOPLE & SOCIETY
1773 The Colombian botanist Mutis is charged with heresy for giving lectures on Copernican theory in Bogotá.	**1770s-1780s Labor struggles** break out in Mexican mines over working conditions. **1774 Ann Lee,** known as Mother Ann, founds the American Shakers. **1775 Benjamin Franklin and Benjamin Rush** form an antislavery group in Philadelphia. **1776 Nathan Hale** is caught spying on the British on Long Island and hanged, supposedly saying on the gallows, "I only regret that I have but one life to lose for my country." **1780 Benedict Arnold** betrays West Point to the British.
1770s William and Caroline Herschel begin sightings of comets and nebulae, and build telescopes. **1771 Joseph Priestly** discovers that plants release oxygen.	

THE AMERICAN REVOLUTION

For a decade, tension had been increasing between Great Britain and the American colonies over British control of colonial governments and over taxation of colonists without their consent. In 1775, Britain's Parliament declared Massachusetts, the center of most of the protests, to be in rebellion. And on April 19 of that year, the American War for Independence began with the battles of Lexington and Concord.

The Continental Congress appointed George Washington commander in chief of the Continental Army and, on July 4, 1776, adopted the Declaration of Independence. Great Britain, with its huge army and navy, launched a land and sea effort to crush the revolution. But the British had to transport and supply their army across the Atlantic. The British won many battles during the war but gained little from their victories, while the Americans, despite hardships that led to frequent desertion, always managed to form new forces and continue the fight.

Washington, with the help of French allies, scored a decisive victory at Yorktown, Virginia, and in 1783 the Treaty of Paris forced Great Britain to recognize the independence of the 13 colonies. The birth of a new and united nation would soon follow.

Almost every one has heard of the soldiers of the Revolution being tracked by the blood of their feet on the frozen ground. This is literally true, and the thousandth part of their sufferings has not, nor ever will be told.

PRIVATE JOSEPH PLUMB MARTIN, REVOLUTIONARY ARMY

General Washington (on right) and Lafayette confer at Valley Forge, the main camp of the Continental Army from December 1777 to June 1778. The harsh winter there severely depleted the morale and the number of troops.

1780-1790

POLITICS & POWER	GEOGRAPHY & ENVIRONMENT	CULTURE & RELIGION
THE AMERICAS		
1780-81 Guerrilla bands led by "Swamp Fox" Francis Marion and Thomas Sumter oppose Cornwallis in the South and force him into Virginia. **1781 American and French forces** bottle up Lord Cornwallis's army of 8,000 Redcoats at Yorktown, Virginia; Cornwallis surrenders. **1783 By the Treaty of Paris,** Britain accepts American independence. **1789 The U.S. adopts a constitution** giving greater power to the federal government. **1789 George Washington** becomes the first president of the United States of America.	**1780s Desperate to increase the population,** Spanish officials in Louisiana and Florida entice Americans with offers of land. **1783 The Treaty of Versailles** recognizes the Great Lakes in the north and the Mississippi River in the west as frontiers of the newly born United States.	**1780-81 Jesuit Francisco Clavigero** writes his *History of Ancient Mexico* from exile. **1789 Former slave Olaudah Equiano** publishes his memoirs, and he travels in Britain lecturing against slavery.
EUROPE		
1781 Joseph II abolishes serfdom in Austria and grants civil rights to Protestants and Jews. **1783 Russia** annexes the Crimea, a strategic peninsula in the Black Sea. **1789 The fall of the Bastille** marks the beginning of the French Revolution.	**1789 Chrysanthemums** from the Orient are first introduced to Britain. **1790 Europe's population** reaches about 190 million.	**1788 Charles Wesley** dies, author of several thousand hymns, including "Hark, the Herald Angels Sing" and "Jesu, Lover of My Soul." **1789 The Declaration of the Rights of Man and the Citizen** is issued in France. **ca 1790 The great age of European orchestral music** begins, featuring the works of Mozart, Haydn, Beethoven. **1790 Ninety percent of males** in Scotland can read.
MIDDLE EAST & AFRICA		
1780s An Asante blockade prevents guns from reaching the interior of the Gold Coast (West Africa) and remains in effect during the 19th century. **1786 Morocco** agrees to cease raiding U.S. ships in the Mediterranean in return for $10,000. **1787-1792 The Ottoman war** with Russia and Austria is financially devastating, though territorial losses are few.	**1780s Droughts in West Central Africa** accompany increased slave exports of more than 40,000 per year. **1787 The first freed slaves** from Britain settle at Freetown, Sierra Leone.	**1782 London** develops a band to play janissary music in imitation of those already established in Poland, Russia, and Austria. This so-called Turkish music becomes the rage in Europe, and Ottoman coffeehouses, slippers, dress, and carpets also become popular. **1790 Jews are persecuted in Morocco** as a reaction against the policies of the former king, who had favored them.
ASIA & OCEANIA		
1782 Rama I becomes king of Thailand, with his capital at Bangkok. He drives out Burmese invaders and restores the nation to a position of power and prestige. **1787 Rioting by townspeople** in the Tokugawa capital, Edo, breaks out in protest of economic exploitation.	**1789 Mutineers from the *Bounty*** settle on Pitcairn Island. **1793 The first free settlers** arrive in Australia from Europe.	

SCIENCE & TECHNOLOGY

The Montgolfiers' first balloon takes to the air near Paris.

1783 The first manned flight in a hot air balloon is made by the Montgolfier brothers.

1784 Edmund Cartwright invents a steam-powered loom that revolutionizes the production of textiles and helps the growth of the factory system.

PEOPLE & SOCIETY

1781 Tupac Amaru II leads an indigenous revolt across the southern Andes; the Comuneros revolt in New Granada.

1780s Growth of the cottage industry, an early form of sweat-shops, encourages earlier marriage.

1786 Frederick the Great, king of Prussia, dies. He was a military genius as well as a social reformer.

1781 The Xhosa are massacred by Boer settlers.

1789-1807 Ottoman Sultan Selim III introduces New Order Reforms, including the trimming and reorganization of existing military units and the creation of European-style new order troops.

1788 A penal colony is set up at Botany Bay, Australia; it is the beginning of the displacement of aboriginal peoples.

1789 Smallpox ravages aborigines of coastal New South Wales in Australia.

REVOLUTION IN THE ARTS

In late 18th-century Europe, a revolution began to sweep the arts that gave birth to what is now known as the Romantic Era.

The word romantic harks back to medieval tales of adventure, fantasy, and high emotion. These attributes gained a renewed importance in literature, painting, and music, eclipsing earlier classical concerns with balance and restraint. During the Romantic Era, expression became everything.

Romanticism stressed the importance of nature and reacted against the Enlightenment and 18th-century rationalism. It emphasized the individual, the subjective, the imaginative, the personal, and the spontaneous.

In music, Romanticism led to looser and more extended musical forms, with melody its dominant feature. No one exemplified these characteristics more than Ludwig van Beethoven, who pub-

Ludwig van Beethoven

lished his first works in 1783. Although his earliest compositions were very much in the classical tradition, he soon began to write more daring and expressive compositions. The first composer to earn his living directly from his work without patronage, Beethoven was free to give vent to his extreme individualism and challenged the public to follow him.

	POLITICS & POWER	GEOGRAPHY & ENVIRONMENT	CULTURE & RELIGION
THE AMERICAS	**1793 In accordance with the U.S. Constitution,** a Federal Fugitives Slave Law prevails, and the number of African Americans fleeing their masters begins a steady drop. **1800 Washington, D.C.,** becomes the home of U.S. government.	**1790s Yankee ships** increase trade between the newly formed United States and Latin America, especially with the Caribbean. **1790s The embrace of sugar and cotton** in the lower Mississippi moves the region from a marginal place in the production of staples to the very heart of the "plantation world." **1790s U.S. population** reaches about four million, 20 percent of it black. **1793 Alexander Mackenzie** completes the first east-west crossing of Canada.	**1790s-1800s The Virgin of Guadalupe cult** in Mexico is transformed from a movement encouraged by the Catholic Church to induce piety in lower classes of the Mexico City region to a symbol of Creole nationalism. **1790s The Methodist and Baptist congregations** in the Chesapeake who had once embraced black members disavow their commitment to abolition and equality. **1793 Former slave Katy Ferguson** opens an integrated school for poor children in New York.
EUROPE	**1790s Charles IV** of Spain increasingly comes under the influence of his inept minister and adviser, Manuel de Godoy. **1792 The French Republic** is proclaimed. **1793 King Louis XVI** of France is executed. **1793 Maximilien Robespierre** launches France's Reign of Terror in an effort to rid France of all "enemies of the Revolution." **1799 Napoleon Bonaparte** becomes First Consul and seizes power in France.	**1791 Russia** gains the Black Sea steppes from the Turks.	**1791 Wolfe Tone** forms the nationalist Society of United Irishmen, which appeals to both Presbyterians and Catholics to rid themselves of English rule. **1792 Mary Wollstonecraft** publishes *Vindication of the Rights of Woman.* **1793 France** introduces the decimal system. **1798 Thomas Malthus** publishes *Essay on the Principle of Population,* arguing that population will always grow faster than the food supply.
MIDDLE EAST & AFRICA	**1793 Rihadh falls to Wahhabi forces** in the Arabian Peninsula; Wahhabi clerics fill judicial and teaching posts. **1797-1834 The second Qajar shah of Iran,** Fath Ali, establishes dynastic legitimacy, makes Tehran the new capital, and patronizes poets and artists. **1798 Napoleon invades Egypt** and defeats Egyptians at the Battle of the Pyramids. He is soon forced to abandon his army and return to France with few gains to show .	**1796 Scottish explorer Mungo Park** travels up the Niger River. **1800 Slave rebels** deported from Jamaica settle in Sierra Leone. **ca 1800 The Ottoman population** is about 25-32 million.	**1790s Islamic proselytizing** in West Africa reaches its zenith with the great Holy Wars. **1793 The first permanent Ottoman embassies** are founded in London, Paris, Vienna, and Berlin. **1799 The Rosetta stone** is discovered in Egypt, allowing historians to translate ancient Egyptian hieroglyphs.
ASIA & OCEANIA	**1795 King Kamehameha I** unites the Hawaiian islands and establishes the Kamehameha dynasty. **1796 The British** conquer Ceylon, now known as Sri Lanka. **1796-1804 The White Lotus Rebellion,** an uprising against the Qing dynasty, occurs in China. **1798 Ranjit Singh,** the Lion of the Punjab, founds the Sikh kingdom in India alongside Hindu and Muslim neighbors.		**1797 The first Christian missionaries** reach Tahiti and Tonga. *Ranjit Singh employed European officers and introduced strict military discipline in his Punjabi army.*

SCIENCE & TECHNOLOGY

1794 Eli Whitney patents the cotton gin; cotton becomes the chief crop of the American South.

1800 William Young makes shoes specifically designed for the right and left feet.

1790s William Tuke opens the first humane sanatorium for the mentally ill in London.

1796 Edward Jenner develops a smallpox vaccine using cowpox.

1800 Alessandro Volta invents the battery.

ca 1800 West Africans are manufacturing their own gunpowder and expertly repairing imported European weapons.

The Rosetta Stone shows text in three versions: hieroglyphic, demotic, and Greek, enabling J. F. Champollion and Thomas Young to decipher the riddle of Egyptian hieroglyphics.

1793 Lord McCartney's mission to China fails to impress the court of Emperor Qianlong. McCartney had brought British goods such as clocks and Wedgwood porcelains, not realizing that "we possess all things," according to the emperor, "and have no use for your country's manufactures."

PEOPLE & SOCIETY

1790s Resentments of Creoles against *peninsulares* (Spanish-born Spaniards) increases under the restrictions of the Charles IV regime.

1792 The dollar is introduced as the currency of the U.S.

1791 John Wesley, founder of Methodism and 18th-century Protestant revivalism, dies.

1800 The population of China reaches 300 million.

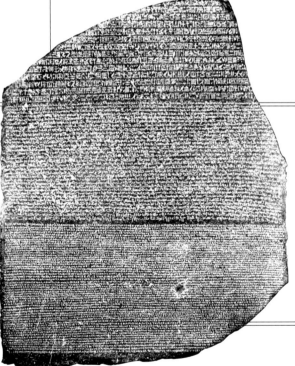

Execution of King Louis XVI

THE FRENCH REVOLUTION

After years of dissatisfaction with royal and aristocratic rule, the people of France took their first tentative steps toward self-government on June 17, 1789, with the formation of a National Assembly. Civil unrest soon followed, and less than a month later, a crowd stormed the Bastille prison in Paris, whose fall marked the beginning of the French Revolution.

After two years of detention, King Louis XVI attempted to flee France but was captured and returned to the capital. The king agreed to a constitution, but as the Revolution faced defeat at the hands of foreign armies, extremists pushed to rid the country of all opponents, and this included the monarchy. The Reign of Terror was unleashed, and in 1792 the French Republic was created. The following year, both the king and his wife, Queen Marie-Antoinette, were guillotined.

Maximilien Robespierre and his Jacobin allies in the Committee of Public Safety plunged France into even more bloodshed. Thousands of people were denounced as antirevolutionary traitors; more than 40,000 may have died during the Terror. Robespierre was eventually overthrown and then executed in the Coup de Thermidor in 1794.

POLITICS & POWER	...HY & ENVIRONMENT	CULTURE & RELIGION

THE AMERICAS

1801 Former slave Toussaint-Louverture declares the island of Haiti independent, with himself as ruler.

1807 The Portuguese royal family flees to Brazil for safety during the Napoleonic War.

1810 Colombia becomes the first European colony in South America to win independence.

Haiti's Toussaint-Louverture

1803 For $15 million, Napoleon sells all the prairie lands between the Mississippi River and the Rocky Mountains to the U.S.; The Louisiana Purchase nearly doubles the nation's land area.

1804 Meriwether Lewis and William Clark begin their exploration of the Louisiana Territory.

1804 Trying to reduce the church's influence, the Spanish government requires church institutions to call in all their loans. The near bankruptcy of many businessmen forces reconsideration of the policy.

1805 *El Diario de México,* the first Mexican daily newspaper, is published.

1806 Noah Webster publishes the first American dictionary.

1809 Edgar Allan Poe, creator of the American Gothic tale, is born.

EUROPE

1805 Napoleon defeats Russians and Austrians at the Battle of Austerlitz; the French ruler stands poised to dominate Europe.

1805 Britain's Lord Nelson defeats the Franco-Spanish fleets at the Battle of Trafalgar. Lord Nelson is killed, but his victory ends Napoleon's power at sea and makes a French invasion of Britain impossible.

1807 Serfdom is abolished in Prussia.

1808 Napoleon installs his brother as king of Spain.

1807 The slave trade is abolished within the British Empire.

1809 Sweden cedes Finland to Russia.

1804 Napoleon's civil code confirms the legal equality and property rights for men that emerged from the French Revolution; the code is adopted in many countries around the world.

MIDDLE EAST & AFRICA

1804 Serbians revolt against rebellious janissaries who kill the governor and ravage the province; rebels ally with Russia and declare independence, but Russia deserts them and Ottomans reoccupy the province.

1807 Selim III is overthrown by a janissary revolt in Istanbul, but rebels in turn are overthrown by provincial notables who put Selim's son Mahmud on the throne in 1808.

1806 The British gain control of Cape Colony in southern Africa.

1808 Sierra Leone becomes a British colony.

ca 1800 Al-Jabarti begins his perceptive chronicle of the French invasion of Egypt, the last great Egyptian chronicle in the old style.

1804 Uthman dan Fodio, a Fulani religious leader from western Sudan, is proclaimed Commander of the Faithful and declares a jihad, or holy war, against nonbelievers.

ASIA & OCEANIA

1802 The Nguyen dynasty is established by Emperor Gia Long in Vietnam after suppressing the Tay Son Rebellion.

ca 1800 Nguyen Pu writes *The Tale of Kien,* a long poem narrating the struggle of women to overcome adversity and remain moral and pure.

1807 Robert Morrison of the London Missionary Society arrives in Canton to being Protestant missionary work.

SCIENCE & TECHNOLOGY	PEOPLE & SOCIETY

1800-1803 Naturalist Alexander von Humboldt visits Mexico and writes influential accounts of his observations.

1807 Robert Fulton develops the first practical steamboat, the *Clermont*, which sails from New York City to Albany and back.

1801 Joseph Lalande, a French astronomer, publishes a catalog listing 47,390 stars.

Napoleon Bonaparte is shown crossing the Alps in Jacques-Louis David's famous portrait.

1807 Africans have at least 20 million guns, which they've been buying since 1750, fueling endemic warfare and the slave trade in some places.

1805 Muhammad Ali comes to power in Egypt and loosens Ottoman rule in the country. In 1811, he massacres the Mamluks and establishes central control, modernizing the administration.

1805 Japanese doctor Seishu Hanaoka uses general anesthesia for the first time.

1804 The sandalwood trade begins in the Pacific islands.

THE CONQUESTS OF NAPOLEON

After the execution of its king and the beginning of the Reign of Terror, revolutionary France found itself at war with its neighbors—Austria, Prussia, Spain, and Britain. A young artillery officer named Napoleon Bonaparte rose quickly through the ranks, capturing the hearts of his countrymen as completely as he overwhelmed his enemies on the field of battle. Napoleon was quick to capitalize on his popularity.

In 1804, in a grand ceremony in Paris's Notre Dame cathedral, he was crowned emperor of the French. During the coronation, just as the pope was about to place the crown on Napoleon's head, Napoleon took the crown out of the pontiff's hands and placed it on his head himself.

No longer at war to defend the Revolution, imperial France now went on the offensive. Napoleon scored a succession of impressive victories, among the greatest the Battle of Austerlitz in 1805, after which much of Europe lay at his feet. However, two countries continued to resist him: the island kingdom of Great Britain and the huge nation of Russia.

To invade Britain, Napoleon needed command of the seas. But the Royal Navy's victory at Trafalgar robbed him of that, and so disappeared any hope of crossing the Channel to England. Instead, Napoleon marched his Grand Army all the way across Europe to invade Russia. This fateful decision would lead to the emperor's downfall and the defeat of France. For although the French managed to fight their way deep into Russia and capture Moscow, they were unable to remain there during the winter of 1812. The army had no choice but to trek back to the west, through freezing temperatures and Cossack attacks. Of the 600,000 who invaded, only 40,000 returned to France.

Napoleon's hopes for a comeback were crushed in the Waterloo campaign, and he spent his last years in exile.

POLITICS & POWER	GEOGRAPHY & ENVIRONMENT	CULTURE & RELIGION

THE AMERICAS

1810 Miguel Hidalgo de Costilla proclaims September 16 the day of Mexican independence.

1811 Simón Bolívar, who was known as El Libertador, declares Venezuela an independent nation.

1811 Paraguay proclaims its independence from Spain.

1812-15 The War of 1812 between the United States and Great Britain is fought.

1814 The British army burns down the White House in Washington, D.C.

1812 Russians build settlements as far south as Fort Ross in California.

1814 The defeat of the Creeks by Andrew Jackson begins the departure of Indian peoples from the South.

1819 The U.S. purchases Florida from Spain.

1810-1820 The liberals and separatists in the Mexican independence movement raise the standard of the Virgin of Guadalupe at the head of their armies; they proclaim her the patron saint of independent Mexico and the oppressed.

1818 Professional horse racing begins in the United States.

EUROPE

1812 Napoleon invades Russia; he captures Moscow, but unable to spend the winter there when the city catches fire, he marches his army back to France.

1815 An allied army led by Britain's Duke of Wellington defeats Napoleon at the Battle of Waterloo.

1815 The Congress of Vienna restores the monarchical system of prerevolutionary Europe.

1812 The Brothers Grimm publish their volumes of *Fairy Tales*.

1813 English novelist Jane Austen publishes *Pride and Prejudice*.

1813 The waltz becomes a popular dance.

Title page to the Grimm fairy tale of Snow White

MIDDLE EAST & AFRICA

1810 Mauritius and Seychelles are annexed by Britain.

1811 Muhammad Ali's massacre of the Mamluks of Cairo permits a recentralization of state finances in Egypt.

1812 Egyptians revolt against military conscription.

1813 Egyptian forces retake Mecca from the Wahhabis.

1813 The governor of Aleppo massacres the janissaries, who control northern Syria.

1813-14 The first Egyptian agricultural survey is conducted under Muhammad Ali.

ASIA & OCEANIA

1811 The British conquer Java in the East Indies.

1818 The Maratha are defeated by the British, who become in effect the rulers of India.

1819 The British found Singapore as a free-trade port, permanently breaking the Dutch trading monopoly in the region.

1820 Vietnamese emperor Minh Mang transforms his capital, Hué, into a Chinese-style imperial city and models his rule on Chinese laws and institutions.

1815 Sumbawa volcano erupts in Indonesia, killing more than 50,000 people.

1812 King Pomare II of Tahiti converts to Christianity.

1814 The first British Protestant missionaries arrive in New Zealand to bring the Gospel to the Maoris.

1820 The first Christian missionaries arrive in the Hawaiian Islands.

SCIENCE & TECHNOLOGY	PEOPLE & SOCIETY
1819 The *Savannah* becomes the first steamship to cross the Atlantic.	**1810s Porteños,** citizens of Buenos Aires, the colonial capital, develop a political culture separate from the rural population living in the rest of Argentina. **1815 The market economy** begins to transform United States society in the years after the War of 1812. **1820 The Missouri Compromise** seeks to end the crisis concerning the extension of slavery in the U.S. Maine enters the Union as a free state, Missouri as a slave state.
1812 The cylinder printing press is invented; it is adopted by *The Times* of London. **1814 George Stephenson** invents the first practical steam locomotive, *Stephenson's Rocket*.	**1811-12 A Russian census** estimates the empire's population to be over 42 million. **1815 After his defeat at Waterloo,** Napoleon goes into exile on St. Helena.
1816 Wool mills, sugar refineries, glassworks, and other industries are established in Egypt.	**1816 Shaka** becomes ruler of the Zulu kingdom; his disciplined and mobile army conquers many peoples of southeastern Africa.
1819 The whaling industry begins in the Pacific islands.	

RISE OF THE ZULUS

Shaka Zulu is probably the most famous southern African leader in history. A fierce and militaristic king, Shaka took a then-insignificant Zulu clan and transformed it into a powerful nation with an army of 50,000 men.

An accomplished fighter at an early age, Shaka defeated his brother to gain control over the Zulu chieftaincy upon the death of their father. With great energy, he started to build a mighty army of Zulu warriors. He is credited with teaching his men to use the shield as an offensive weapon, hooking the enemy's shield to the side to expose his ribs. He also introduced a shorter version of the spear, which they brandished as a stabbing weapon. Scorning European firearms because they took so long to reload, he believed that man was the ultimate weapon. From each of his fighters he demanded total loyalty and obedience, punishing with death those who hesitated to follow his commands. But Shaka shared his army's hardships, drilling with his men and forsaking the comforts of a Zulu king.

Dressing in a fearsome battle costume of blue monkey fur and genet tails, Shaka scored victory after victory against neighboring people. Under his rule, Zulu territory expanded rapidly. By 1820 he had won control of most of southeast Africa and Natal. Zulu empire building, however, devastated huge areas and depopulated many regions as tribes migrated away from Zulu war bands. The period of turmoil came to be known as the *mfecane* or *difaqane*—the time of troubles.

Shaka's rule came to an end in 1828 when he was assassinated by his two half-brothers, who stabbed him to death with their spears and threw his body in an empty grain pot that was then filled with stones.

Shaka Zulu with his weapons of choice— the shield and the spear

	POLITICS & POWER	GEOGRAPHY & ENVIRONMENT	CULTURE & RELIGION
THE AMERICAS	**1821 Peru** declares independence from Spain. **1822 Dom Pedro in Brazil** achieves freedom from Portugal. **1824 Mexico** becomes a republic, three years after declaring independence from Spain. **1824 After San Martín's departure** from Peru, Simón Bolívar leads a rebel force into the Andes and conquers the last Spanish stronghold. **1828 Uruguay** becomes an independent state.	**1828 Cherokee Indians** cede to the U.S. their homelands in Arkansas and agree to migrate to lands west of the Mississippi River. **1830 The first wagon trains** to cross the Rocky Mountains arrive in California.	**1820s Because of Catholic Church support** for royalists in many independence movements, liberals develop a distrust of institutional religion.
EUROPE	**1829 Greece** wins its independence from the Turks. **1830 Revolutions erupt** in France, Germany, Poland, and Italy.		**1820s Romanticism** in European literature and art features the works of Byron, Chateaubriand, Heine, Turner, and Delacroix.
MIDDLE EAST & AFRICA	**1821 Egyptians** invade the Sudan. **1830 The French** begin their conquest of Algeria, still nominally part of the Ottoman Empire. **1830 The British** establish a protectorate over the Gold Coast.	**1824-25 Floods** devastate Egypt.	**1820 American Protestant missionaries** arrive in Lebanon to face strong Maronite resistance. **1828 The first Arabic newspaper** is published in Egypt. **1829 An Ottoman clothing law** outlaws turbans and substitutes the fez.
ASIA & OCEANIA	**1824 The British** begin their conquest of Burma and Assam in southeast Asia **1825-1830 In the Java War,** Indonesians revolt against Dutch rule.	**1820s Australian wool exports** replace earlier, less successful trade commodities, such as sealskins, seal oil, and sandalwood.	**1825 Queen Kaahumanu of Hawaii** converts to Christianity. **1828 The Brahmo-Samaj** Hindu revivalist movement is founded in India. **1829 Sati,** the practice of self-immolation by Hindu widows, is abolished in British India.

WHAT LIFE WAS LIKE

Crossing the Rocky Mountains in a Covered Wagon

In the early 19th century, families who wanted to move from the eastern United States to the Oregon Territory had only one way to go—by covered wagon. Family members traveled aboard a wagon topped with a white canvas that was stretched over big wooden hoops and rubbed with oil to make it waterproof. They closed both ends of the canvas to keep out the rain and the wind, or when it grew hot they rolled it up to get the benefit of the breeze. Adults and kids sat up front on a wooden board. From hooks inside the wagon hung such things as milk cans, bonnets, spoons, dolls, and jackets. Guns were also requisite supplies in case the family encountered hostile Indians.

SCIENCE & TECHNOLOGY	PEOPLE & SOCIETY
1820s U.S. manufacturers develop interchangeable parts, which are originally used to produce weapons for the U.S. Army.	**1820s In the aftermath** of successful independence revolts, most Latin American countries drift into rule by caudillos (military strongmen), rather than rule by republic.
1825 The Erie Canal opens, allowing boats to travel from the Great Lakes to the Atlantic Ocean.	**1826 Dom Pedro of Brazil** signs a treaty with the British that obliges Brazil to end the slave trade by 1851.
1828 Work begins on the first steam-powered railroad in the U.S., the Baltimore & Ohio.	**1830 The U.S. Congress** passes the Indian Removal Act.
1829 The typewriter is invented.	

1821 Michael Faraday invents the electric motor and generator.	**1824 The repeal of Combinations Law** allows British workers to form unions.
1825 The first passenger steam railway opens, between Stockton and Darlington, England.	**1829 Sir Robert Peel** founds a new British police force in London.
1826 Joseph-Nicéphore Niepce produces the first photographic image.	
1829 Louis Braille of Paris invents a reading system for the blind.	

1820s Zulu king Shaka, founder of a powerful and feared military in southern Africa, ridicules European firearms, favoring instead the assegai (short-handled spear).	**1822 American abolitionists** found Monrovia, future capital of Liberia.
	1825 Zulu king Shaka is assassinated by his half-brothers.

1830s Sugar cultivation begins in Hawaii.

Map showing the dates at which South American colonies won their independence from their respective colonial masters

INDEPENDENCE IN SOUTH AMERICA

FORMER COLONIES
- British, Dutch, French
- Portuguese
- Spanish

(1822) Year of independence

FREEDOM FOR SOUTH AMERICA

The fight for South American independence from Spain was led by Simón Bolívar, a wealthy Creole born in Venezuela but educated in Spain. It was in Europe that Bolívar came under the influence of Enlightenment ideas. Revolutions in France and North America at the end of the 18th century showed him that the people of South America could also take control of their own destinies. He was soon calling for independence for the continent of his birth. "I will not rest, not in body or soul," declared Bolívar, "till I have broken the chains of Spain."

At one time, Spain's control of its colonies was total, in both political and mercantile terms. But when Napoleon's armies invaded the Iberian Peninsula, Spain's colonial grip loosened, and revolutionary juntas began to set themselves up in South America. Bolívar led the revolutionary forces in his native Venezuela. In 1819, the rebels gained power in the country, then turned toward Colombia and Ecuador.

Meanwhile, in the south of the continent, José de San Martin rallied revolutionary elements in Argentina. After freeing that country, he led 5,000 men across the Andes to Chile, where they charged down upon panicked Spanish defenders. San Martin and Bolívar eventually met in Peru, the bastion of Spanish South America. Peru gained its independence in 1824, and San Martin acted as protector for more than a year, abolishing slavery and improving conditions for the Indian peoples. (Brazil had peacefully gained its freedom from Portugal two years earlier.)

Bolívar had hoped to unite all South Americans into a single nation. In this he was unsuccessful. Nevertheless, for all of his achievements throughout the continent, he is known as El Libertador—the Liberator.

	POLITICS & POWER	GEOGRAPHY & ENVIRONMENT	CULTURE & RELIGION
THE AMERICAS	**1830s General Antonio Lopez de Santa Anna** effectively rules Mexico through a series of dictatorial regimes. **1831 Juan Manuel Rosas,** the caudillo-dictator of Argentina, comes to power. **1836 Texans are defeated** by the Mexican army at the Alamo; Texas gains independence later that same year after winning the Battle of San Jacinto.	**1838-39 The Five Civilized Tribes**—Cherokee, Chickasaw, Choctaw, Creek, and Seminole—are forced west on the Trail of Tears.	**1836 The Academy of Letrán** is founded in Mexico City, which spreads Mexican poetry in the 19th century. **1837 Christian evangelist Dwight L. Moody** is born in Northfield, Massachusetts.
EUROPE	**1831 Giuseppe Mazzini** founds Young Italy, an organization dedicated to the creation of an Italian Republic. **1833 The Zollverein** is formed, a German customs union under the leadership of Prussia.		**1831 Football,** said to have existed in England since the 12th century, is revived at Eton and other British schools; the game becomes popular all over the world.
MIDDLE EAST & AFRICA	**1830 The French** invade Algeria. **1831-39 Muhammad Ali's son,** Ibrahim Pasha, conquers Syria and threatens to overthrow Ottoman centralized power. His introduction of equal taxation and conscription provokes revolts in Syria and Lebanon by people of all religions. **1832-1847 Muslim leader Abdelkader** resists the French invasion of Algeria. **1835 Ottomans** reassert control over Tripoli and Benghazi in North Africa.	**1830s The shifting ecology of West Africa** brings drier conditions and leads to widespread drought and dislocation. **1835 The Great Trek** of white trekboers, colonists from the Cape, pushes the Zulu north of the Limpopo River.	**1835 Synagogues in Jerusalem** are rebuilt under Egyptian governor Ibrahim Pasha. **1839 The Ottoman reform period** begins under Mahmud II, who grants increased rights to his subjects. The reform effort will be in vain. **ca 1840 The Omani dynasty** establishes Arab-Swahili settlements on the coast of East Africa.
ASIA & OCEANIA	**1839-1842 The Opium War** between Britain and China occurs. China is forced to open ports to Western trade and cede Hong Kong to Great Britain. **1840 In New Zealand,** the Treaty of Waitangi between the Maoris and Britain guarantees Maori lands and grants the Maori British citizenship.	**1833 Poor harvests** bring famine to Japan; riots break out in several towns.	**1830s Opium imports** outstrip Chinese exports of tea and silk. **1831 King George Tupou I of Tonga** converts to Christianity.

CONNECTIONS

British Opium and the Chinese

In the 1830s, British traders shipped tons of Indian-grown opium to Canton, where it was traded for silk, spices, porcelain, and tea. The trade produced serious social and economic problems because of drug addiction. In an effort to stem the tragedy, the Chinese imperial government made opium illegal in 1836 and began to close down the opium dens. But when Chinese junks attempted to turn back English merchant vessels in 1839, war erupted. Chinese old-style weaponry was no match for the British gunships, which prowled the coast, or the firepower of British land forces. In 1842, the Chinese were forced to accept the Treaty of Nanjing, which opened coastal treaty ports to foreign trade and ceded the island of Hong Kong to Britain.

SCIENCE & TECHNOLOGY

1834 Charles Babbage invents the "analytical machine," forerunner of the modern computer.

1834 The first mechanical reaper is patented.

1837 Samuel F. B. Morse sends his first message by electric telegraph—"What hath God wrought!"—on an experimental line between Washington, D.C., and Baltimore, Maryland.

1830s Belgium begins building state-owned railroads.

1836 The needle-gun is invented in Prussia, making breech-loading possible.

1840 The first postage stamp, called the "penny black" and bearing the image of Queen Victoria, is issued in England.

1830 Ishaq Efendi, a converted Greek Jew, becomes chief instructor in the military engineering college and translates European scientific works into Turkish.

PEOPLE & SOCIETY

1830s New dictatorships and occasional republics in South America leave indigenous people in exploitative relationships with Creole elites.

1830s Female textile workers in New England begin to take labor actions over wages, working conditions, and hours.

1833 Mexico suffers from a cholera epidemic.

1836 Davy Crockett and 182 others die fighting for Texas's independence from Mexico at the Alamo.

1832 German poet Johann Wolfgang von Goethe dies.

1832 A cholera epidemic kills 31,000 people in Britain.

1833 The Factory Act of 1833 limits the workday of children in Britain to 8 hours, adolescents to 12 hours.

ca 1840 Zanzibar becomes the commercial center of east Africa, exporting cloves and other spices across the Indian Ocean.

THE TRAIL OF TEARS

When the U.S. Congress passed the Indian Removal Act, the Cherokee nation attempted to fight the law's constitutionality in the Supreme Court. The effort failed, and in 1838 the federal government began the removal of Native Americans from east of the Mississippi River. In exchange, they were given land in the Indian Territory, in what is present-day Oklahoma, as well as the promise of money, livestock, and various provisions and tools.

Under orders from the President, Andrew Jackson, General Winfield Scott and 7,000 of his troops were given the task of removing the Indians. Thus began one of the saddest episodes in American history. Some Cherokees ran off and took refuge in the mountains, the swamps, and other places too inhospitable for whites. Others agreed to accept United States citizenship and were allowed to remain. But in the winter of 1838-39, some 15,000 Indians were marched more than a thousand miles through Tennessee, Kentucky, Illinois, Missouri, and Arkansas into the forbidding Indian Territory.

Many Indians walked the entire distance without footwear and barely clothed. Human losses were extremely high—about 4,000 died, from hunger, disease, exposure, and exhaustion. The Indians' forced journey westward became known as the Trail of Tears or, as a more direct translation from the Cherokee puts it, the "Trail Where They Cried."

Map depicting the routes of the Five Civilized Tribes from east of the Mississippi River into Indian Territory on the Trail of Tears

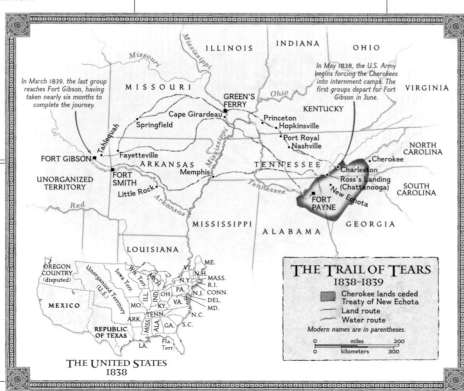

In March 1839, the last group reaches Fort Gibson, having taken nearly six months to complete the journey.

In May 1838, the U.S. Army begins forcing the Cherokees into internment camps. The first groups depart for Fort Gibson in June.

THE TRAIL OF TEARS
1838-1839
Cherokee lands ceded Treaty of New Echota
Land route
Water route
Modern names are in parentheses.

THE UNITED STATES 1838

POLITICS & POWER	GEOGRAPHY & ENVIRONMENT	CULTURE & RELIGION
1844 Santo Domingo proclaims its independence from the state of Haiti and becomes the Dominican Republic. **1845 Texas is annexed** by the United States. **1846-48 The Mexican War** between the U.S. and Mexico results in the U.S. possession of California and much of the Southwest, which had been Mexican territory. **1849 Abraham Lincoln,** Whig congressman from Illinois and critic of the Mexican War, retires from politics after one term in office to practice law. He reemerges the following decade as a moderate opponent of slavery in the new Republican Party.	**1846 The Oregon Treaty** delineates the U.S.-Canadian boundary. **1849 The California gold rush** begins; more than 100,000 people rush to California to make their fortunes after gold is found there in 1848.	**1845 Domingo Sarmiento** publishes the *Life of Juan Facundo Quiroga: Civilization and Barbarianism,* a critique of the cowboy, gaucho culture and its bargain with the Rosas dictatorship. **1846 The first professional baseball game** is played, in Hoboken, New Jersey. **1847 The first U.S. postage stamps** are issued.
1841 To stunt Russian imperial ambitions in the eastern Mediterranean, an international Straits Convention closes the Bosporus to Russian warships. **1846 Britain** repeals the Corn Laws that had supported the price of grain and moves toward complete free trade. **1848 Revolution breaks out** across much of Europe; the Second Republic is proclaimed in France.	**1845 The Irish potato famine** begins, one of the century's worst natural disasters. A million citizens starve to death, and a million others immigrate, mostly to the U.S.	 *Karl Marx, founder of communism*
1840-42 The Lebanese rebel against Egyptian occupation. **1847 Liberia** is formed as a home for released American slaves. **1848 Algeria** is declared a part of France.	**1849 Scottish missionary** and explorer David Livingstone reaches Lake Ngami in the African interior.	**1840 Bosnian rabbi Judah Alkalai** proposes Zionism, the idea of a Jewish homeland.
1840 The Treaty of Waitangi makes New Zealand a British protectorate. **1842 The Treaty of Nanjing** ends the Opium War between Britain and China. **1843-49 The British** conquer Sind, in northwest India; the Punjab; and Kashmir. **1850-1864 Millions of people die** in the Taiping Rebellion, China's—and the world's—bloodiest civil war.	**1840s The French** acquire various islands in the Pacific, among them Tahiti.	**1844 In China,** an imperial edict relaxes a ban on the Catholic Church. **ca 1850 Painter and printmaker Hiroshige** flourishes, known for his prints of the *53 Stations of the Tokaido.*

THE AMERICAS

EUROPE

MIDDLE EAST & AFRICA

ASIA & OCEANIA

SCIENCE & TECHNOLOGY	PEOPLE & SOCIETY

1848 Popular revolt breaks out in Pernambuco, Brazil, against powerful agrarian elites.

1849 Harriet Tubman escapes from slavery and goes on to lead more than 300 slaves to freedom on the Underground Railroad.

Harriet Tubman (extreme left, holding a pan) photographed with a group of slaves whose escape she assisted via the Underground Railroad.

1850 In Germany, Krupp metalworks produces the first all-steel guns; in 1867 Alfred Krupp presents the king of Prussia with a 50-ton steel cannon.

1842 After investigations into working conditions, women are forbidden to work underground in British mines.

1848 Karl Marx publishes *The Communist Manifesto,* which asserts that revolution by the working classes will ultimately destroy capitalism.

1849 A deadly cholera epidemic kills about 16,000 in London, England.

1849 Construction of the Suez Canal proceeds after the death of Egyptian leader Muhammad Ali, who had refused to sanction it.

1841 An Ottoman postal service is established.

1847 The Istanbul slave market is abolished.

1850 Arab traders cross Lake Tanganyika to collect ivory and slaves.

1848 The Great Mahele permits division and sale of land as private property in Hawaii.

1850 Australian colonies receive self-government from Britain.

1850 The Chinese population reaches 420 million; Manchu China is the world's most populous empire.

THE IRISH POTATO FAMINE

During the summer of 1845, a "blight of unusual character" devastated Ireland's potato crop. Grown for more than 200 years in Ireland, the potato was the basic staple in the people's diet. Most Irish peasants rented small plots of land from absentee British landlords, and because a single acre of potatoes could support a family for a year, the Irish came to depend on the potato as their chief source of food. Potatoes were nutritious and easy to grow, requiring a minimum of labor, training, and equipment; a spade was the only tool needed. But when the blight struck, the potatoes began to turn slimy, black, and rotten just days after they were dug from the earth.

Theories abounded about the cause of the blight. Some investigators said it was the result of "static electricity" or the smoke that billowed from railroad locomotives. Or even the "mortiferous vapours" rising from underground volcanoes. The actual cause was a fungus—*Phytophthora infestans*—that had traveled from North America to Ireland.

"Famine fever"—cholera, dysentery, scurvy, typhus, and infestations of lice—soon spread through the Irish countryside. Observers reported seeing children crying with pain and looking "like skeletons, their features sharpened with hunger and their limbs wasted, so that there was little left but bones." Masses of bodies were buried without coffins, a few inches below the soil.

The government did little to help the people, merely forcing hundreds of thousands into workhouses. Over the next 10 years, more than 750,000 Irish died and another two million left their homeland for Great Britain, Canada, and the United States. Within five years, the Irish Potato Famine, also known as the Great Hunger, had reduced the Irish population by a quarter. The blight also struck other northern European countries, such as Norway, leading to famine and increased immigration there as well.

1850-1860
EMPIRES AND REVOLUTIONS 1750-1900

POLITICS & POWER	GEOGRAPHY & ENVIRONMENT	CULTURE & RELIGION

THE AMERICAS

1855 Ottawa becomes Canada's capital by royal decree.

1855 Liberals take over the Mexican government and exile Santa Anna. Benito Juárez rises to leadership of the Mexican liberal cause.

1857 The Dred Scott decision makes the Missouri Compromise unconstitutional and increases tension between North and South over slavery in the U.S.

1857-1860 Conservatives and liberals struggle for power in Mexico in the Three Years' War.

1850s Because the Brazilians refuse to end slavery, the Royal Navy begins to blockade Brazilian ports and search Brazilian slave ships.

1852 Harriet Beecher Stowe publishes her antislavery novel *Uncle Tom's Cabin.*

1856 Ley Lerdo redistributes uncultivated church land in Mexico.

Demonstration of an early elevator model by Elisha Graves Otis in New York City

EUROPE

1852 The French Republic falls; Louis Napoleon (Napoleon III) is crowned emperor.

1853 Russians invade Turkey's Danubian provinces and, by sinking the Turkish fleet, gain control of the Black Sea.

1854-56 Russia is defeated by Britain and France in the Crimean War.

1856 Russia accepts humiliating terms of the Peace of Paris, undertaking to keep no navy on the Black Sea and to maintain no bases on its shores.

1857-1864 A series of mountain campaigns completes Russian control of the Caucasus; the armies thus set free are then used to subdue central Asia.

1850s Romantic music, featuring the works of Berlioz, Liszt, Wagner, Brahms, and Verdi, reaches it apogee.

1853 Baron Haussmann begins rebuilding Paris, which comes to be characterized by broad boulevards.

ca 1860 The great age of the European novel produces works of Dickens, Dumas, Flaubert, Turgenev, Dostoyevsky, and Tolstoy.

MIDDLE EAST & AFRICA

1850s Ethiopia, which had been divided into numerous small states since 1706, is unified by a chieftain named Kassa, who has himself crowned king of kings.

1858-1860 The first Lebanese Civil War occurs, leading to massacre of Christians in 1860.

1860 The French expand in West Africa by advancing up the Senegal River.

1860 The Spanish invade Morocco, just across the Strait of Gibraltar.

1851 Gold is discovered in southern Africa, bringing a flood of immigrants to the continent.

1854-56 Scottish missionary and explorer David Livingstone crosses Africa from the west coast to the east coast.

1857 Iran recognizes Afghan independence.

ASIA & OCEANIA

1855 The Kurile Islands are partitioned between Japan and Russia.

1856 New Zealand and Tasmania win self-government from Britain.

1856-1860 The Second Opium War between Britain and China leads to further incursions on Chinese sovereignty.

1857 The Indian Mutiny breaks out in opposition to British rule.

1858 The French occupy Saigon in Indochina.

1851 Gold is discovered in New South Wales and Victoria, accelerating immigration to Australia.

1858-1860 The Treaties of Aigun and Beijing bring the Russian frontier south to the Amur River and south of Vladivostok.

1860 Robert O'Hare Burke and William John Wills complete the first overland crossing of Australia; both die on the return journey.

CONNECTIONS

Commodore Perry and Japanese Expansion

When Commodore Matthew Perry sailed into Edo Bay in 1853, he found a mysterious island kingdom that had been closed to all but a few Dutch and Chinese merchants. To the shocked onlookers, the modern American ships were like "giant dragons puffing smoke." The Japanese realized how technologically far behind their country had fallen. On March 31, 1854, they signed a historic treaty agreeing to trade with the United States. The barrier between Japan and the rest of the world started to come down; the country began to industrialize and modernize rapidly. In less than a century, Japan would transform itself from a feudal nation to an international power ready to challenge the United States for dominance in the Pacific.

SCIENCE & TECHNOLOGY	PEOPLE & SOCIETY
1851 Isaac Singer patents the continuous-stitch sewing machine.	**1850s Slavery is abolished** in all Spanish-speaking republics of South America.
1852 The brown paper bag is created.	**1855 In Mexico, Benito Juárez** and the liberals head a legislative movement called La Reforma, designed to relieve social exploitation and modernize society.
1852 The elevator is invented, facilitating the future development of skyscrapers.	
1852 The first telegraph lines are laid in Brazil.	**1858 Abraham Lincoln,** running for the U.S. senate, declares "A house divided against itself cannot stand." He loses the race to Stephen Douglas, but his performance in their now-legendary debates leads to his Republican nomination for president in 1860.
1853 Potato chips are invented.	
1858 President Buchanan of the U.S. sends a message to England's Queen Victoria over the first transatlantic cable.	
	1860 The Pony Express begins cross-country mail delivery.
1851 The Great Exhibition, the world's first industrial fair opens in London. More than 100,000 exhibits are housed in the Crystal Palace.	**1855-1881 Alexander II,** the Tsar-Liberator, tries to remedy the backwardness of Russia in the wake of its defeat in the Crimean War.
	1860 Italian patriot Giuseppe Garibaldi leads a rebellion in southern Italy; unification of the country begins.
1857 The railway between Cairo and Alexandria in Egypt is inaugurated.	**1850s Khedive Ismail,** grandson of Muhammad Ali, consolidates Egyptian control over the Red Sea littoral and the Horn of Africa.
1859 James Beale "Africanus" Horton of Sierra Leone becomes the first African graduate of Edinburgh University, where he earns a medical degree. He writes a dissertation entitled "On the Medical Topography of the West Coast of Africa."	**1855 Emperor Theodorus** begins partial reconstruction of the Christian empire of Ethiopia.
	1857 The African slave trade is prohibited in the Ottoman Empire.
	1858 Ottoman and Egyptian land codes introduce private property; land is supposed to belong to peasant cultivators but often goes to local notables.
1853 The first railroad and telegraph lines are laid in India.	**1853 Commodore Matthew Perry** sails into Japan's Edo Bay with four modern, steam-powered warships, urging Japan to open trade policies with the U.S.
1860 The Japanese build a Western-style ship, which crosses the Pacific with a Japanese crew.	**1854 The first Chinese student** to graduate from an American university is Yung Wing, a graduate of Yale.

THE TAIPING REBELLION

During the mid-19th century, China was rocked by a series of natural calamities of unprecedented proportions, including droughts, famines, and floods. The ruling Manchu dynasty did little to relieve the widespread misery caused by these events, which inflamed popular resentment against the government into the largest uprising in modern Chinese history, and the bloodiest civil war the world has known—the Taiping Rebellion.

The Taiping rebels were led by Hong Xiuquan, a failed civil service examination candidate who claimed he was the younger brother of Jesus Christ. In 1851 Hong launched an uprising in the Guizhou province in southern China, where he proclaimed the Heavenly Kingdom of Great Peace (or Taiping) with himself as king. Two years later the rebels captured the old imperial capital of Nanjing.

Hong's new order was founded on a mixture of some Christian beliefs along with a utopian tradition drawn from Chinese sources in which the peasantry owned and tilled the land in common. This vision won Hong many supporters among China's poorest classes.

The revolt held sway across a large swath of southern and central China. Soon, however, the movement's leaders found themselves in a net of internal feuds, defections, and corruption. British and French forces came to the assistance of the Manchu government once they realized that the rebellion might affect foreign trade, but the suppression of the Taipings ultimately depended on the Chinese provincial officials, whose armies rallied to the government's aid.

Well over 20 million people were reportedly killed as a result of the Taiping Rebellion. Like the savagely suppressed revolutions of 1848 that had recently swept across the continent of Europe, the Taiping Rebellion resulted in a surge of immigration to the United States.

1860-1870
EMPIRES AND REVOLUTIONS 1750-1900

	POLITICS & POWER	GEOGRAPHY & ENVIRONMENT	CULTURE & RELIGION
THE AMERICAS	**1861-65 The American Civil War** begins when the Confederates fire on Fort Sumter, South Carolina, and ends when General Lee surrenders to General Grant at Appomattox Courthouse, Virginia. **1862-67 The French** attempt to erect a puppet empire in Mexico. **1864 Paraguay** goes to war against Argentina, Brazil, and Uruguay. **1867 The dominion of Canada** is established.	**1867 The U.S. buys Alaska** from Russia for $7.2 million—or two cents an acre. **1869 Railroad** cuts in two the buffalo herd of the plains, breaking the economic base of Native Americans.	**1868 Louisa May Alcott** publishes *Little Women*. **1868 Domingo Faustino Sarmiento,** the great intellectual, educator, and liberal leader, becomes president of Argentina. **ca 1870 Paiute prophet Wodziwob** develops the Ghost Dance.
EUROPE	**1862 Otto von Bismarck** is appointed prime minister of Prussia. **1866 Prussia** defeats Austria at the Battle of Königgrätz. **1867 The dual monarchy** of Austria-Hungary is formed. **1870-71 The Franco-Prussian War** leads to the formation of the German Empire.	 *Map showing the location and dates of major United States Civil War battles*	**1867 Johann Strauss's** *The Blue Danube* is first performed. **1869 Leo Tolstoy** publishes *War and Peace*. **1870 The Roman Catholic Church** proclaims the dogma of the infallibility of the pope.
MIDDLE EAST & AFRICA	**1861 The British** acquire Lagos in West Africa. **1864 European financial machinations** in Tunisia lead to increased taxes and the revolt of tribal and urban people. **1867 The British** conduct military campaigns against Emperor Theodorus of Ethiopia.	**1860-61 Famine** leads to bread riots in Iran; women lead popular protests. **1863 Cotton cultivation** booms in Egypt during the American Civil War. **1863 The Beirut-Damascus road** opens the interior of Syria to the West. **1866 Diamonds** are discovered in southern Africa.	**1865 An Arabic translation of the Bible** is published. **1866 American University** is founded in Beirut by Protestant missionaries; it contributes to the Arabic literary revival among Syrian Christians.
ASIA & OCEANIA	**1860s Land wars in New Zealand** enable British settlers to seize the islands' best lands. **1862 A Muslim revolt** breaks out in China's northwest. **1863 France** establishes a protectorate over Cambodia; other protectorates follow for Cochin China, Annam, Tonkin, and Laos. **1868 The Meiji Restoration** in Japan overthrows the Tokugawa Shogunate and lays the foundations of Japan's modern nation state.	**1860s Sugar cultivation** begins in Fiji. **1869 Japan** colonizes Hokkaido as part of its new nation state.	**1870 Anti-missionary sentiments** lead to the Tianjin massacre in China.

SCIENCE & TECHNOLOGY

1869 The transcontinental railroad is completed in the U.S.; Canada and the U.S. now possess about 56,000 miles of railroad.

1861 Louis Pasteur evolves the germ theory of disease, its first formulation since ancient times.

1863 The first underground railway is built, in London.

1870 Europe possesses some 64,000 miles of railroads.

1869 The Suez Canal opens, linking Egypt's Port Said on the Mediterranean coast to the Red Sea. At 101 miles long, it reduces the voyage from Britain to India by 4,000 miles.

1870 The Suez Canal carries some 437,000 tons of cargo.

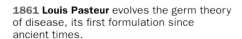

PEOPLE & SOCIETY

1865 Slavery is abolished in the U.S. at the end of the Civil War.

1865 John Wilkes Booth assassinates President Abraham Lincoln.

1869 Brazilians agitate for an end to slavery in Brazil.

1871 The Rio Branco Law in Brazil frees all newborn and aged slaves. Reformers denounce the law as a sham.

Completion of the transcontinental railroad

1861 Russian serfs are emancipated.

1863-1874 Britain and other European nations adopt a gold standard for their currencies.

1863 Charles Darwin's notoriety builds following 1859 publication of *The Origin of Species* after his travels to the Galapagos Islands.

1864 Henri Dunant founds the Red Cross, in Switzerland.

1865 The Young Ottoman Society is founded to popularize liberalism, constitutionalism, Ottoman patriotism, and Islamic modernism.

1870 The transatlantic slave trade between Africa and the Americas comes to an end.

1868 Emperor Mutsuhito comes to power in Japan; he calls his reign the Meiji (Enlightened Government).

1869 Mohandas Gandhi, hero of India's independence struggle is born.

Japan's Emperor Mutsuhito

DARWINISM

In the early 1830s Charles Darwin had served as a naturalist aboard the H.M.S. *Beagle* on a round-the-world science expedition. In South America, he found fossils of extinct animals that were similar to modern species. And on the Galapagos Islands in the Pacific Ocean, he noticed many variations among plants and animals of the same general type as those on the South American mainland. Darwin observed that isolated populations adapt and evolve in diverse ways. For example, several species of finch had evolved on the various islands, each with a beak adapted to a different way of feeding. Unless each tiny species was the product of a miracle, populations separated by isolation on the islands had each evolved in their own way.

Drawing on the work of earlier scholars, Darwin eventually developed the theory of natural selection. The theory held that the survival or extinction of an organism was determined by that organism's ability to adapt to its environment. Successful adaptation was based on randomly occurring variations within species that proved useful in their struggle for survival and thus increased the likelihood of reproduction. Favorable variations would then be transmitted to subsequent generations of offspring. (Darwin never actually used the expression "survival of the fittest," which was coined by a contemporary admirer of Darwin, the philosopher and sociologist Herbert Spencer).

Darwin set these theories forth in his book *On the Origin of Species by Means of Natural Selection, or the Preservation of Favoured Races in the Struggle for Life.* It is known better by its shorter title, *The Origin of Species.* Darwin's writings had a tremendous impact on society and religion during the 1860s. The theory of evolution challenged contemporary beliefs about the creation of life on earth and set off heated debates about the theory's implications—discussions that continue to this day.

BROTHER AGAINST BROTHER

WHEN ABRAHAM LINCOLN—THE MAN WHO HAD CALLED SLAVERY "A moral, social, and political evil"—was elected president of the United States in 1860, alarmed Southern states, one by one, began to secede from the Union. The breakaway states, citing their right to self rule, decided to form a new country, the Confederate States of America, and chose as its leader Jefferson Davis. President Lincoln declared the secession a rebellion, and on April 12, 1861, when Confederate troops fired on Fort Sumter, a federal post in Charleston, South Carolina, war between the Union and the Confederacy began.

Both sides in this "war between brothers" believed the conflict would be a short one. The North had more than five times as many factories as the South; it had more money, and and it had over 22 million people. The South had only nine million people, and three and a half million of them were slaves. Yet the Confederacy felt confident. Confederate soldiers would be fighting on familiar ground. And the South had many fine generals, including Robert E. Lee, the brilliant commander who took charge of Confederate forces. In July 1861, when a Union army marched on the Confederate capital of Richmond, Virginia, Southern troops sent them scampering back toward Washington. It would be four long years before the war was over.

In the end, the North's superior numbers were decisive. Eventually, too, the Union found a general the match of Lee—Ulysses S. Grant. After a daring Confederate invasion of U.S. territory was repulsed at Gettysburg, Pennsylvania, the Confederate armies were driven deep into Virginia. Grant pursued Lee relentlessly, finally forcing his surrender at Appomattox Courthouse on April 9, 1865. The American Civil War was over.

Early works of photojournalism drove home the savagery of war, as at right, the dead at Gettysburg, and captured moments in history, as above, Lincoln meeting his generals after the Battle of Antietam.

Tell my father I died with my face to the enemy.

COLONEL ISAAC E. AVERY, GETTYSBURG, JULY 2, 1863

	POLITICS & POWER	GEOGRAPHY & ENVIRONMENT	CULTURE & RELIGION
THE AMERICAS	**1876 Lieutenant Colonel George A. Custer** and his men are killed by the Sioux at the Battle of Little Bighorn. **1876 Dictator Porfirio Diaz** gains control of Mexico; he presides over spectacular economic progress, though most of the people remain in abject poverty. **1879-1883 The War of the Pacific** between Chile, Peru, and Bolivia breaks out over control of important Atacama nitrate deposits; Chile's victory in 1883 makes it the major Pacific power.	**1870-1900 More than 11 million immigrants** arrive in the United States. **1871 The Chicago Fire** results in 250 deaths and millions in property damage. **1879-1880 The Argentine government** begins the conquest of the desert. Indigenous peoples are driven out of the Pampas, which are converted into grazing lands for cattle.	**1870s Positivism** supports intellectual movements toward dictatorship across Latin America. **1873 Military dictator García Moreno** dedicates Ecuador to the Sacred Heart. **1876 Mark Twain** publishes *Tom Sawyer.*
EUROPE	**1877 Russians invade the Balkans** after the Turks repress revolts by its Slav peoples. **1878 The Treaty of Berlin** grants independence from Turkey to Romania, Montenegro, and Serbia. **1879 Germany and Austria-Hungary** form the Dual Alliance to protect against attack by other countries.	**1870s Cities** improve their water and sewer systems for better public health.	**1870s Labor and socialist parties** grow in Germany, Belgium, Holland, and Russia. **1874 The Impressionist school of painting** emerges, featuring works by Monet, Renoir, and Degas. **1878 The Salvation Army** is founded by a former Methodist minister, William Booth.
MIDDLE EAST & AFRICA	**1870s Samuri Ture,** a Mandingo Muslim leader, carves out an empire south of the Niger River. **1870s Illegal slaving** comes to an end in the states of Oyo and Benin, in modern-day Nigeria. **1879 Zulu warriors** defeat the British at the Battle of Isandhlwana in southern Africa. **1879 The French** complete their conquest of Algeria. **1880 The Indonesian-speaking Hova kingdom** expands to conquer most of Madagascar.	**1871 Henry Morton Stanley** finds David Livingstone in Africa, greeting the Scotsman with the famous words, "Dr. Livingstone, I presume."	**1870s Emperor Johannes** continues efforts to reconstruct the Christian empire of Ethiopia. **1870 Algerian Jews** gain French nationality. **1875 The *al-Ahram* newspaper** is founded, which is still published in Egypt today.
ASIA & OCEANIA	**1872 Japan** claims the nearby islands of the Ryuku archipelago, despite Chinese protests. **1876 The Treaty of Kanghwa** between Japan and Korea recognizes Korea as an independent state. **1877 Queen Victoria** is proclaimed empress of India. **1879 The Second Afghan War** gives Britain control of Afghanistan.	**1874 Fiji** becomes a British colony.	**1871-73 Japan** sends the Iwakura Mission to the West to study Western ideas and institutions.

SCIENCE & TECHNOLOGY

1874 The first electric tram operates in New York.

1876 Alexander Graham Bell patents the telephone.

1876 The first shipload of chilled carcasses arrives in France from Buenos Aires, introducing the great increase in demand for Argentine beef in Europe.

1878 Thomas Edison invents the incandescent light bulb.

1871 The *Oceanic*, a 3,800-ton transatlantic liner, is launched.

1878 The first electric street lighting appears, in London.

1878 The world's first oil tanker is launched, in the Caspian Sea; it plies the waters between Baku and Astrakhan.

PEOPLE & SOCIETY

1871 After a long struggle between conservatives and liberals, the liberals triumph in Chile under the rule of Manuel Montt. The Chilean Creole elite will become a powerful social model for the rest of Latin America, though less will be said of the Indians and poor masses.

1873 Spain decrees the end of slavery in Cuba, still a Spanish colony.

1879 F. W. Woolworth opens his first "5 and 10 cent store."

1880 About 4.9 million Jews live in the Pale of Settlement in the Russian Empire.

Map showing the routes of the major European explorers of Africa during the 19th century

THE SCRAMBLE FOR AFRICA

For much of the 19th century, European involvement in Africa centered on the continent's periphery—the Cape Colony to the south and the Mediterranean coast in the north. However, popular interest in the interior of the continent was sparked by a host of European explorers who trekked across Africa and left behind a trail of myths and misunderstandings.

The most famous of these was the Scottish missionary David Livingstone, who became the first white man to travel the width of the continent, from coast to coast, and the British-American journalist Henry M. Stanley, whose revelations of commercial possibilities in the Congo led to increased atrocities and ruthless exploitation.

Where missionaries and explorers led, the colonial powers followed. In 1876, King Leopold II of Belgium created the International Association for the Exploration and Civilization of Central Africa and engaged Henry Stanley to establish Belgian settlements in the Congo. Alarmed by Leopold's actions, the French moved into the territory north of the Congo River. And so the race to claim Africa began.

Englishman Cecil Rhodes conquered a vast region to the south and dreamed of a British Empire that sprawled from South Africa all the way to Egypt, or as he put it, "from the Cape to Cairo." To the east, the Portuguese carved out a colony along the coast. German traders were busy in East Africa and in the coastal territory bordering the northwest Cape. And the French completed their conquest of Algeria in 1879.

In the end, colonial borders were formally established among the European powers at the Berlin Conference of 1884. By the end of the century, the scramble for Africa was over. The European powers had carved up nearly the entire continent, and only Liberia in the west and Ethiopia in the east remained nominally free of their control.

EXPLORATION OF AFRICA

EXPEDITIONS

James Bruce	1769–1772
Mungo Park	1795–1797
	1805–1806
Denham-Clapperton-Oudney	1822–1825
Gordon Laing	1825–1826
Clapperton-Lander	1825–1827
René Caillié	1827–1828
Lander Brothers	1830
Heinrich Barth	1850–1855
David Livingstone	1852–1856
	1858–1863
	1866–1871
	1872–1873
Burton-Speke	1857–1859
Speke-Grant	1860–1863
Samuel Baker	1863–1865
Henry Stanley	1871
	1874–1877
Livingstone-Stanley	1871

Give me your tired, your poor,
Your huddled masses
yearning to breathe free . . .

EMMA LAZARUS, "THE NEW COLOSSUS"

MANHATTAN MELTING POT

AMERICAN CITIES GREW QUICKLY IN THE YEARS AFTER THE CIVIL WAR, AS RAPID industrial development fueled the dreams of those in search of better pay and a better life. So great was the movement of people to urban areas that the newspaper editor Horace Greeley declared, "We cannot all live in cities, yet nearly all seem determined to do so." Bold and dynamic, the greatest of these expanding American cities was New York.

During the 19th century, New York's expanding industries attracted job seekers from the surrounding countryside, just as had happened in London, Berlin, and other great cities of Europe. But New York was also swollen by another population source—the tide of European immigrants that was then flooding into the United States. Some of these new arrivals pressed farther afield after arriving in America. But many remained in the chief port of entry, New York City.

By the 1890s, immigrants and their children made up 80 percent or more of the city's population. New York had more Italians than the Italian cities of Florence, Genoa, and Venice put together. It was home to more Irish than Dublin, Ireland, and to more Germans than Hamburg, Germany. The city became famous for its ethnic diversity, with communities like Little Italy and Chinatown dating from this period. But providing adequate accommodation for all of these newcomers became a major problem.

People poured into New York faster than proper housing could be built for them. The population of New York and its suburbs grew from one million in 1860 to almost three and a half million in 1900. The poorest residents lived in tenements, rundown buildings in which several families rented rooms. New York's distinct neighborhoods soon included such notorious slums as Hell's Kitchen, Five Points, and the Bowery.

As these millions of people huddled in its tenements, New York's population density climbed to amazing levels. An average of 143 people per acre lived in the city, making it more crowded than the densest urban areas of Europe. Berlin, for example, had 101 inhabitants per acre. Population density in New York reached its highest level in a small area near the tip of Manhattan, where there were as many as 700 people per acre. New Yorkers were, literally, living on top of each other.

Immigrants like these on Mulberry Street on Manhattan's Lower East Side came to America for economic opportunity and a chance at the American dream.

1880-1890

EMPIRES AND REVOLUTIONS 1750-1900

POLITICS & POWER	GEOGRAPHY & ENVIRONMENT	CULTURE & RELIGION

THE AMERICAS

1885 The Statue of Liberty arrives in New York from France.

1886 Geronimo, Apache war chief, surrenders to the U.S. Army after years as a fugitive. Upon his release from prison, he becomes a farmer and, eventually, a national celebrity.

1887 The U.S. acquires Pearl Harbor, Hawaii, as a coaling station and future naval base.

1889 A military revolt under Benjamin Constant effectively ends the Brazilian monarchy.

1890 The U.S. Army massacres 200 Indians at Wounded Knee in South Dakota, ending the Indian wars of resistance.

1883 Bolivia loses its entire coastline after the so-called Saltpeter War with Chile.

1889 Thousands die in floods at Johnstown, Pennsylvania.

I never do wrong without a cause.

GERONIMO, 1886

EUROPE

1882 Germany, Austria-Hungary, and Italy form the Triple Alliance, pledging to aid each other in case of war.

1890 Otto von Bismarck is dismissed as German chancellor.

ca 1890 Realistic drama features works by Ibsen, Strindberg, Chekhov, and Shaw.

The Apache warrior Geronimo

MIDDLE EAST & AFRICA

1881 The Mahdi, an Islamic religious leader in the Sudan, launches a rebellion against Egyptian rule.

1882 King Leopold II of Belgium acquires the Congo, which he turns into his own personal colony.

1882 Revolt in Egypt leads to British occupation and the governorship of Lord Cromer.

1884 The Berlin Conference leads to the partitioning of Africa into European-controlled colonies.

1887 The French occupy Tunisia.

1884 Egypt controls the Nile Valley south to Lake Albert.

1886 Gold is found in the Transvaal; gold fields employ 100,000 workers by 1900.

1881-82 The Urabi revolt, aiming to Egyptianize Egypt's army and finances and to install a constitutional monarchy, fails because of British intervention.

ASIA & OCEANIA

1880s King Rama V implements reforms to modernize Siam and resist European imperialism.

1884-85 The French and the Chinese go to war over Vietnam.

1884 German colonial expansion begins in the Pacific islands.

1885 Japanese colonial expansion begins in the Pacific islands.

1887 The French establish the Indochinese Union.

1884 Xinjiang (Chinese Turkestan) is incorporated as province of the Manchu Qing Empire.

1886 The British annex Upper Burma in southeast Asia.

1882 Japan begins to introduce legal codes, largely based on French and German models.

1883 The Indian National Congress Party is formed, which pursues a moderate policy of constitutional reform.

SCIENCE & TECHNOLOGY

1882 The first hydro-electric plant opens, in Wisconsin.

1883 The Brooklyn Bridge is completed, at that time the world's largest bridge.

1885 The world's first skyscraper, the Home Insurance Company Building, is erected in Chicago.

1890 The U.S. becomes the world's leading industrial power, having tripled factory output over the previous quarter century.

1883 German engineer Gottlieb Daimler creates a portable engine that leads to the age of the automobile.

1888 John Boyd Dunlop invents the pneumatic tire.

Gottlieb Daimler rides in the back of his first automobile.

1880s West African Islamic reformer Samuri Ture employs large numbers of blacksmiths to manufacture breech-loading guns.

1888 Germans get concessions to build the Baghdad railroad.

1880s The textile industry begins in Japan.

1880s Chinese translations of Western works on science and other subjects are widely available.

PEOPLE & SOCIETY

1880 Porfirio Diaz of Mexico grants lucrative contracts to foreign railroads to develop a railroad system in Mexico.

1881 Clara Barton founds the American Red Cross.

1888 Slavery is abolished in Brazil; blacks and mixed-race peoples remain at the foot of the economic ladder.

1890 The superintendent of the U.S. census observes that for the first time a single frontier line no longer exists.

1881 The first migration of European Jews to Palestine occurs.

1888 46,531 sailing ships and 1,548 steam ships call at the port of Istanbul.

1889 Students in the Istanbul military college found the Young Turk revolutionary organization.

BUILDING THE BROOKLYN BRIDGE

In 1869, with the approval of President Ulysses S. Grant and the U.S. Congress, work on the construction of the Brooklyn Bridge began. The project was plagued with problems, though, and it would take 14 years to complete.

The driving force behind the project, John Roebling, died from tetanus during the construction. His son, Washington Roebling, took over, but he developed a crippling illness called caisson's disease, now known as the bends. Bedridden but determined to stay in charge, Roebling used a telescope to keep watch over the bridge's progress from his apartment. He dictated instructions to his wife, Emily, who passed them on to the workers, thereby guiding the completion of the bridge. Roebling was on his death bed during the inauguration on May 24, 1883, during which some 150,000 people crossed the bridge at a charge of one cent apiece. The bridge opened to vehicles later that day, and 1,800 made the crossing at five cents a vehicle.

The Brooklyn Bridge ranks as one of the greatest engineering feats of the 19th century and remains among New York's most popular and well-known landmarks. At the time it was built, the 3,460-foot span was also declared the longest suspension bridge in the world.

The Brooklyn Bridge, which connected Manhattan with the borough of Brooklyn

1890-1900

EMPIRES AND REVOLUTIONS 1750-1900

POLITICS & POWER	GEOGRAPHY & ENVIRONMENT	CULTURE & RELIGION

THE AMERICAS

1891 The constitution of the new republic of Brazil is passed.

1896 *Plessy* v. *Ferguson* declares legalized segregation in the U.S. (in particular, the South's Jim Crow laws) constitutional.

1898 The United States invades Cuba and defeats Spain in the Spanish-American War; as a consequence, the U.S. conquers Puerto Rico and the Philippines and annexes Hawaii.

1897 The gold rush to the Klondike begins.

1900 The population of Brazil reaches 17 million and of Argentina 4.7 million, boosted by massive immigration from Europe.

1890s Pasadas draws his famous Calaveras cartoons, mocking the elite Mexican classes.

1891 The first basketball game is played, in Springfield, Massachusetts.

1896 The first Sunday newspaper comics appear.

1896-98 Newspaper magnates Joseph Pulitzer and William Randolph Hearst engage in a bitter circulation war; their sensationalized news accounts became known as yellow journalism.

Prospectors in the Klondike

EUROPE

1894 Nicholas II, last of the Russian tsars, ascends the throne; France and Russia form the Dual Alliance.

1896 The first modern Olympic Games are held in Athens, Greece.

1898 Christian apologist and scholar C. S. Lewis is born in Belfast, Ireland.

1900 Freud's *Interpretation of Dreams* marks the beginnings of psychoanalysis.

MIDDLE EAST & AFRICA

1891 Sayyid Muhammed, "the Mad Mullah," leads Somali resistance to the British and the Italians.

1896 Ethiopia's Emperor Menelik II defeats the Italians at the Battle of Adowa, discouraging further European moves into his country for nearly 40 years.

1898 French and British troops face each other at Fashoda on the White Nile, narrowly averting war.

1899 The Boer War breaks out between Afrikaners and the British in southern Africa.

1890s Cecil Rhodes hopes to form a continuous belt of British territory "from the Cape to Cairo."

1893 The French conquer the ancient kingdom of Dahomey in West Africa.

1900 Copper deposits in Katanga in central Africa are reached by Europeans.

1891 Servet i Funum, an Ottoman scientific and literary journal, is founded.

ASIA & OCEANIA

1893 American planters and businessmen depose Queen Liliukalani of Hawaii.

1895 The Sino-Japanese War ends and Japan gains dominance over Korea and Taiwan.

1898 The United States annexes Hawaii as a territory.

1899 The United States and Germany divide Samoa.

1898 China leases Port Arthur in the Yellow Sea to Russia, providing it a warm-water port unimpeded by winter ice.

1898-1900 The Boxer Rebellion erupts in China, a popular uprising against the Qing emperor and foreign influence in Chinese affairs. The rebellion is put down by an eight-nation alliance and imperial troops.

SCIENCE & TECHNOLOGY

1891 America's first gas-powered automobile, the Lambert (invented by John W. Lambert), is built.

1894 Thomas Edison introduces the first motion pictures.

1895 John Harvey Kellogg invents cornflakes in Battle Creek, Michigan.

1897 America's first subway opens, in Boston.

1895 Guglielmo Marconi invents radio telegraphy.

1895 Wilhelm Conrad Röntgen discovers X-rays.

1895 A motion picture is first shown in public, in France.

1898 Marie and Pierre Curie discover radium and polonium, in France.

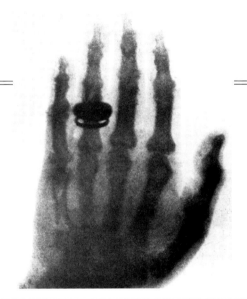

1891 Construction of the Trans-Siberian Railroad begins.

1895 Heavy industry begins to develop in Japan on a considerable scale.

PEOPLE & SOCIETY

1890s Buenos Aires experiences a massive immigration of Europeans into the city. Brazil and Uruguay also experience large immigrations.

1892 The Amalgamated Association of Iron and Steelworkers engages in a field battle with Carnegie Steel over wage cuts.

1898 Teddy Roosevelt sails to Cuba with his Rough Riders, a collection of cowboys, land speculators, Native Americans, African Americans, and Ivy League athletes.

1891 Thousands of Jews are forced into Russian ghettos.

1896 Hungarian Jew Theodor Herzl, convinced Jews cannot assimilate in Europe, publishes *The Jewish State*, a call for a Jewish homeland. He becomes the father of Zionism.

1896 Alfred Nobel's will establishes annual prizes for peace, science, and literature.

1900 The Labour Party is formed in Britain.

1890s Arab slave trade on the east coast of Africa is at last stamped out

1897 The Egyptian National Party is formed by Mustafa Kamil to rid country of the British.

1897 Zionist activity begins in the Middle East, under the World Zionist Congress called by Theodor Herzl.

One of the first X-ray photographs, taken by Roentgen, shows his wife's hand.

1890s Japanese foreign trade rises sharply; cotton textiles to China and silk to the United States are primary exports.

1892 Two female Chinese mission-school graduates sail to the U.S. and earn medical degrees at the University of Wisconsin.

1893 New Zealand becomes the first country to allow women to vote.

1895 Sun Yat-sen leads the Canton uprising, a failed rebellion against the Qing dynasty. He will later lead a successful rebellion and be elected president of the first Chinese republic.

THE PERSECUTION OF RUSSIA'S JEWS

Ever since the early Middle Ages, Jewish merchants had traveled through the Russian lands on their way to India and China. And later, as Jews began to face expulsion from the countries of Western Europe, they began to move east—into Poland, Lithuania, Ukraine, and other regions that eventually came under the control of the expanding Russian Empire.

In the 1790s, Catherine the Great established a Pale of Settlement, border regions of the empire where Jews were required to remain unless they had special permission to move to other parts of Russia. During the next century, restrictions on where Jews could live, work, and be educated were alternately eased and tightened. However, after the assassination of Tsar Alexander II—which some blamed on the Jews—these restrictions were reimposed, and in 1891 any Jews living in Moscow were systematically expelled and forced into ghettos. About 20,000 had to give up their homes and livelihoods and move to the already overcrowded Pale of Settlement.

During this period, Jews were beaten and killed and their property destroyed in a wave of government-tolerated (if not government-sponsored) pogroms, a Russian term originally meaning "riot" but which soon came to refer to violent attacks on Jews in Russia. Some in the government even tried to blame the pogroms on the Jews themselves, while the media engaged in unbridled anti-Semitic propaganda.

Despite these repressive conditions and high levels of immigration to the United States, the Jewish population in Russia continued to grow rapidly in the 19th century; by the beginning of World War I, there were an estimated 5.2 million Jews living in Russia. Only in 1917, after the outbreak of the Bolshevik Revolution, were the laws against Russia's Jews overturned, though persecution would continue during the Soviet regime.

CHAPTER 7

GLOBAL CONFLICT

BY THE EARLY 20TH CENTURY, COUNTRIES around the globe were closely linked by recent advances such as radio and diesel-powered ships. With the introduction of aircraft, armored vehicles, and guided missiles, the world became an even smaller place, where hostile nations could swiftly project power far beyond their borders and wreak havoc. But not until humanity suffered through two world wars would pressure build for international organizations strong enough to prevent crises from developing into catastrophes. And even then, the possibility of a third world war involving nuclear weapons threatened humans with an apocalypse of their own making and clouded the future of this uniquely inventive and destructive species.

A Gathering Storm

In the early 1900s rivalries between imperial powers resulted in regional struggles that foreshadowed larger conflicts to come. In Asia, Russia and Japan clashed over Manchuria, once firmly in China's grasp but now up for grabs. The Russian Empire had expanded southward in the 1800s to embrace places such as Chechnya in the Caucasus and the strategic port of Vladivostok on the Pacific. Now Tsar Nicholas II sought fresh conquests to distract Russia's disaffected populace. "What we need to stem the revolutionary tide," said the minister of the interior, "is a small, victorious war." What the tsar got instead was a crushing defeat by the Japanese, who challenged the Russians in 1904 and destroyed their navy. Russians rebelled in 1905, and Nicholas responded by establishing a parliament called the Duma. That failed to appease radicals, who formed workers' councils called soviets and seized power in some areas, keeping up their struggle until troops put down the uprising in 1907.

Japan, emboldened by victory, continued its imperial expansion, colonizing Korea and stationing troops in Manchuria. The presence of Japanese forces in the ancestral home of China's Manchu rulers further embarrassed the beleaguered Qing dynasty. In 1912 revolutionaries led by Sun Yatsen forced the boy emperor Puyi to abdicate and established the Chinese Republic, which was plagued by dissension and lost control of much of the country to warlords.

Two other troubled imperial powers—the Ottoman Turks and the Habsburg dynasty that ruled Austria-Hungary—figured prominently in events leading to world war. In 1908 liberals called Young Turks forced Sultan Abd al-Hamid to restore a constitution drawn up in 1876 and recall parliament. Those reforms gave Turks a stronger national identity but did not appease other groups under Turkish rule striving for independence. Turks maintained their grip on the Middle East but lost control of the Balkans, where Macedonia and Albania joined Greece, Romania, and Serbia as independent states.

In 1908 Austria-Hungary annexed Bosnia, which had broken away from the Ottoman Empire and was torn by strife between Serbs, Croats, and other ethnic groups. Bosnian Serbs resented Austro-Hungarian domination and were incited to rebel by neighboring Serbia and its ally Russia, which had designs on the Balkans. In June 1914 Archduke Franz Ferdinand, heir to the Austro-Hungarian throne, was assassinated by a Serbian nationalist while visiting the Bosnian capital of Sarajevo. Austria-Hungary blamed Serbia, and Russia pledged to defend Serbia.

War between Russia and Austria-Hungary would have been bad enough, but entangling alliances on both sides made things far worse. Austria-Hungary and Germany had joined with Italy to form the Triple Alliance—a partnership strained recently when Italy sided with Balkan states against the Turks while Germany and Austria-Hungary encouraged Ottoman rulers to join them in opposing Russia. Allied with Russia in a pact called the Triple Entente were France and Great Britain. Thus a seemingly minor flare-up in the Balkans threatened to engulf all the major imperial powers in Europe and their far-flung colonies. Diplomats had little time to avert disaster, for German generals hoped to avoid war on two fronts by delivering a knockout blow to France as soon as Russia mobilized for war. In late July of 1914, Austria-Hungary declared war on Serbia, and Russia mobilized to defend Serbia. In early August, German troops invaded Belgium on their way to France, and a catastrophic conflict was under way.

The Great War

Many Europeans who enlisted in the struggle they called the Great War assumed it would be swift and decisive. German hopes for a quick victory were

PREVIOUS PAGE: *A crewman aboard the American aircraft carrier* Enterprise *directs a fighter pilot in the Pacific during World War II, the first major conflict in which air power played a commanding role.*

OPPOSITE: *American troops in France during World War I wear gas masks before going into action against German forces, who introduced the use of poisonous gas to the battlefield in 1915.*

WORLD WAR I
1914-1918

Allied nations
Central Powers
Neutral nations

Farthest advance by Central Powers
Trench lines
Armistice lines
Major battles

0   400 mi
0   600 km

During World War I, France, the United Kingdom of Great Britain and Ireland, Russia, Italy, and other Allied nations opposed the Central Powers of Germany, Austria-Hungary, and the Ottoman Empire. The Central Powers advanced on the Eastern Front and forced Russia out of the conflict but lost the war on the Western Front (inset), where the entry of the U.S. on the Allied side in 1917 helped break the deadlock.

dashed, however, when they encountered strong resistance along the Marne River in northern France. The opposing armies entrenched along lines that moved little for years to come. Both sides tried to break the stalemate by launching offensives, but attackers suffered terrible losses struggling through minefields and barbed wire under murderous machine-gun fire. German and Austro-Hungarian forces fared better against the Russians to the east and pushed them back, but only by forcing Russia out of the war could they hope to alter the balance on the western front and achieve victory.

By 1915 it was clear this would be a long and exhausting struggle, a total war that would strain the military and economic resources of both sides. Italy abandoned the Triple Alliance and cast its lot with the Allies, led by Britain, France, and Russia. The Ottoman Empire joined with Germany and Austria-Hungary to form the Central Powers. Turks repulsed Allied invasion forces, many of them from the British dominions of Australia and New Zealand, at Gallipoli in 1915 and captured a British army from India in Mesopotamia in 1916. But the Allies later made headway in the Middle East by enlisting Arabs, who were

promised independence, to help drive the Turks out of the Arabian Peninsula and Palestine. Some Armenians opposed to Turkish rule joined the Russians to fight against the Turks, who retaliated by rounding up Armenians and deporting them to Syria and Mesopotamia. More than a half million Armenians starved to death in transit or were killed by Turkish guards, setting a grim precedent for ethnic cleansing in later times.

French and British colonial forces played a significant role in the Great War, invading German colonies in Africa and serving in other theaters as well. Blacks from South Africa, for example, fought for the British in German East Africa and in France. The British Indian Army contributed more than 300,000 soldiers to the Allied cause in 1914, and many in India expected to be rewarded afterward with independence or dominion status. Japan joined the Allies to pursue its own imperial aims, seizing the Marshall Islands and other German possessions in the Pacific. Only in the Americas did the war have little immediate impact. Mexico was caught up in a tumultuous revolution and remained neutral, as did many other Latin American countries. In the United States, isolationism gave way to support for the Allies as German U-boats attacked ships supplying Britain and France, claiming American lives in the process.

In April 1917 the U.S. entered the war, boosting Allied strength at a critical time. With the Russian army near collapse, the tsar abdicated. In late 1917 Bolsheviks espousing communism seized power in Moscow and withdrew from the war. Russia's capitulation came too late to save the exhausted Central Powers. Fresh American forces—and tanks impervious to machine-gun fire—helped the Allies thwart a final German offensive in 1918 and turn the tide. On November 11, Germany and its partners yielded and signed an armistice.

This ruinous conflict, which cost the lives of nearly 15 million soldiers and civilians, was not the war to end all wars, as some hoped. Instead, it set the stage for an even deadlier war a generation later, despite efforts by delegates to the Versailles Peace Conference in 1919 to impose order and stability. The defeated powers lost their imperial possessions and became the nations of Germany, Austria, Hungary, and Turkey (the core of the former Ottoman Empire). From old imperial domains came new nations such as Yugoslavia and Czechoslovakia and rehabilitated nations such as Poland. But many of them were prey to ethnic rivalries and were politically weak, making them tempting targets for future aggressors.

To discourage aggression, diplomats at Versailles created the League of Nations, but it lacked enforcement powers and lost crucial support when the U.S. Senate voted against joining the organization. Imperial ambitions that set the war in motion endured. Britain and France were drained by the carnage but retained their colonies and acquired new mandates, or dependencies, in the Middle East, which served to strengthen the determination of rival nations to build or restore their own empires.

An Uneasy Peace

Despite the persistence of old international tensions, the postwar world differed dramatically from what came before. Women had contributed greatly to war efforts and won the right to vote in many nations. Radio broadcasts, phonographs, and films proliferated and created an international popular culture that drew much of its energy from the U.S. Jazz music of African-American origin gained such wide appeal that some referred to the postwar era as the Jazz Age.

Hopes for the future faded when an economic panic hit the U.S. in late 1929 and spread quickly to Europe—where many nations relied on American investments—and to other regions dependent on trade with Europe and the U.S. American President Franklin Roosevelt responded to the Great Depression by working within the democratic system to implement his New Deal, which greatly increased federal aid to the poor and unemployed. In Germany, by contrast, the economic crisis destabilized the democratic Weimar Republic and helped bring Adolf Hitler to power. Hitler drew lessons from the fascist dictatorship of Italy's Benito Mussolini—who invaded Ethiopia in 1935—and sought to revive national pride and prosperity through rearmament and plans for a new German empire he called the Third Reich. France and Britain, fearful of renewed hostilities, allowed Hitler to defy the Versailles Treaty in 1936 and reoccupy the demilitarized Rhineland, bordering France. Hitler and his Nazi party practiced aggression both at home and abroad by persecuting Jews and terrorizing political opponents.

Another menacing dictatorship took hold in Moscow, where Bolshevik leader Vladimir Lenin had crushed resistance and preserved much of the old Russian Empire under a new title, the Soviet Union. Lenin's successor, Joseph Stalin, silenced dissent in the 1930s by carrying out purges in which millions were executed or sent to labor camps. Intent on collectivizing agriculture and making the Soviet Union an industrial power, Stalin imposed Five-Year Plans that caused turmoil and suffering but increased the war-making capacity of the Soviet economy.

In Asia, Japan remained committed to imperial expansion and sent more troops to Manchuria, taking control there in the early 1930s. That brought Japan into conflict with China, where Chiang Kai-shek, who had succeeded Sun Yatsen as leader of the Guomindang, or Nationalist People's Party, was vying with warlords and with communist insurgents led by Mao Zedong. Communists and Nationalists briefly set aside their differences in order to oppose Japanese forces who invaded China in 1937 and launched devastating air raids on Shanghai and other cities. An even worse fate befell the Nationalist capital of Nanjing, where Japanese troops raped and slaughtered civilians on a massive scale. By 1938 Japan controlled much of eastern China.

In Europe, meanwhile, Italy and Germany became Axis partners and intervened militarily in the Spanish Civil War to help General Francisco Franco defeat forces loyal to the republican government, backed by the Soviet Union. That conflict demonstrated the might of Germany's Luftwaffe, or air force, and left Britain and France with a dilemma—to challenge Hitler and risk a war for which they were ill-prepared or to appease him diplomatically. They chose appeasement and allowed Germany to annex Austria in 1938 and seize the Sudetenland, an ethnically German area within Czechoslovakia. When Hitler went on to occupy most of Czechoslovakia, Britain and France drew the line and backed Poland against German aggression. The pattern of alliances in Europe was similar to the alliances before the First World War with one crucial exception: The Allied powers of Britain and France could not count on Russian support. In 1939 Hitler signed a nonaggression pact with Stalin and sent his troops into Poland on September 1.

The Second World War

The conquest of Poland took less than a month, proving the efficiency of the German blitzkrieg, or lightning war, which combined air strikes with rapid advances by armored divisions. The same tactics allowed German forces to overrun Belgium and the Netherlands and defeat France in less than six weeks in the spring of 1940. Hitler expected Britain to come to terms, but newly appointed Prime Minister Winston Churchill vowed never to surrender. Aided by radar, British pilots countered onslaughts by the numerically superior Luftwaffe and forced Hitler to scrub a planned invasion that fall. Britain remained subject to air raids and devastating attacks on its maritime supply lines by German U-boats, which might have won the pivotal Battle of the Atlantic had not cryptanalysts broken German codes that revealed their location to Allied destroyers.

Events in 1941 greatly broadened the scope of the war. German forces invaded North Africa, the Balkans, and the Soviet Union as Hitler broke his pact with Stalin and pursued conquests of Napoleonic proportions. Unlike Napoleon, however, Hitler was not content to defeat opposing armies and targeted entire populations. His fateful thrust into Russia, launched in June, led to murderous attacks on Jews, Roma (Gypsies), and Slavs, groups Nazis considered less than human. Nazi officials went on to impose their "final solution" by forcing Jews into murderous prison camps where nearly six million died by war's end.

In December 1941 Soviet forces counterattacked the Germans, whose advance toward Moscow had stalled as winter closed in. Among the forces assailing the Germans were Siberian troops who had been guarding against a Japanese invasion. They were redeployed when Stalin learned that Japan—which was not obliged to join its Axis partners Germany and Italy in offensive operations—would instead attack American

In the opening phase of World War II, between 1939 and 1941, Germany occupied much of Europe and North Africa with little help from its Axis partner Italy but failed to conquer Britain and Russia, which joined with the U.S. as Allied powers. Allied forces prevailed in North Africa in late 1942, invaded Italy in 1943, ousted Axis troops from France and eastern Europe in 1944, and defeated Germany in 1945.

and Allied bases in Southeast Asia and the Pacific. Japanese leaders settled on that course in response to an American oil embargo that forced them to choose between making peace or widening their offensive to include American targets. On December 7, Japan attacked the U.S. Pacific Fleet at Pearl Harbor in Honolulu and went on to seize the Philippines from the Americans; Indonesia from the Dutch; and Burma, Singapore, Malaya, and other colonies from the British.

The German and Japanese offensives of 1941 brought the Soviet Union and the U.S., two nations with huge populations and industrial potential, into the conflict on the side of the beleaguered Allies. This proved decisive when Germany and Japan failed to win quick victories as planned and faced prolonged struggles against foes with far greater military and economic reserves. The Allies drew support in the form of troops or raw materials from colonies in Africa and Asia and from Latin America, where many countries were economically reliant on the U.S. and followed its lead in declaring war on the Axis.

Allied triumphs in 1942 at Midway in the Pacific, El Alamein in North Africa, and Stalingrad in the Soviet Union left the Axis on the defensive and gave Americans and Soviets time to bring their full might to bear. In 1943 the Soviets won an epic tank battle at Kursk and forced the Germans back toward their border, while Americans advanced on two fronts by seizing Pacific islands from the Japanese and joining with British forces in North Africa to invade Italy, where Mussolini fell from power.

Germany's fate was sealed in 1944 when Allied forces landed at Normandy on the French coast on D Day, June 6, punched through enemy lines during the summer to liberate Paris, and repulsed a German counterattack in December. By early 1945, American and British forces were pouring into Germany from the west as Soviet troops advanced from the east. Berlin fell to the Soviets on April 30, and Hitler committed suicide, leading to Germany's unconditional surrender on May 7. The war continued in the Pacific until August when American pilots obliterated the

German troops evict Jews from Warsaw, Poland, in 1943 after a fiery uprising in which occupants of the Jewish ghetto resisted removal. Many Jews here and elsewhere were sent to death camps, where they were murdered in gas chambers after a few months. Others were killed or died of mistreatment in concentration camps after toiling as slaves for years.

Japanese cities of Hiroshima and Nagasaki by dropping a single atomic bomb on each target. The 200,000 Japanese victims there were among the last of some 60 million civilians and soldiers who perished worldwide in the most destructive war ever waged.

From Hot War to Cold War

Meeting at Yalta in early 1945, Allied leaders set up postwar occupation zones that gave the Soviets control of East Germany but divided Berlin, within that zone, between the Allied powers. After the fighting ended, the Soviets imposed communist regimes in East Germany, Poland, and other eastern European nations they had occupied. Churchill, who had long feared Soviet expansion, declared in 1946 that an "iron curtain has descended across the continent," words that helped define the emerging struggle called the Cold War.

Like the hot war that preceded it, the Cold War between communism and its foes engulfed much of the world. Mao Zedong, whose communists defeated Chiang Kai-shek's Nationalists in 1949 and took power in China, signed a pact with the Soviet Union and joined with the Soviets in backing a communist regime in North Korea, partitioned from South Korea in 1945. The Soviets and Chinese also aided communist forces in Vietnam led by Ho Chi Minh, who had resisted Japanese occupation during the Second World War and opposed French efforts to recolonize Vietnam afterward. The United Nations, formed in 1945, excluded China under Mao and instead recognized Chiang Kai-shek's Nationalist government, which fled to Taiwan.

The leader of the independence movement in India, Mohandas Gandhi, stood apart from the bloody power struggles of the 20th century by advocating nonviolence and a free India unbeholden to any imperial power. In 1947 Britain yielded and dropped its longstanding opposition to Indian independence. Clashes between Hindus and Muslims then forced the partition of India from Pakistan.

The end of British imperial rule also caused unrest in the Middle East. Since taking charge of Palestine in

1919, the British had allowed Jews dedicated to Zionism, or a Jewish homeland in the Biblical kingdom of Israel, to settle there. After World War II, many Jewish refugees arrived in Palestine. In 1948 Jews declared an independent state of Israel, leading to fighting between Jews and Arabs and a new Arab refugee problem. Afterward, Israel remained at odds with Arab states and drew support from the U.S.

The U.S. also offered aid to Greece and Turkey in the late 1940s to fight communism there after President Harry Truman pledged to support nations "resisting attempted subjugation by armed minorities or by outside pressures." As the Cold War intensified, however, both the U.S. and the Soviet Union would pressure and subvert unfriendly governments. Tensions rose after the Soviets used nuclear secrets stolen from the U.S. to accelerate their weapons program and detonate an atom bomb in 1949. Something people had hoped for in vain earlier in the century now seemed a terrifying possibility—a war to end all wars. ■

Japan, which occupied Manchuria and large parts of China before its Axis partner Germany opened hostilities in Europe, broadened the scope of World War II in December 1941 by seizing colonies in Asia and the Pacific from Britain, the Netherlands, and the U.S. Beginning in 1942, Allied forces pushed the Japanese back in brutal fighting, in map above, epitomized by the battle for Iwo Jima, where U.S. Marines in early 1945 blasted Japanese troops, who refused to surrender and died in their bunkers, opposite.

THE WORLD AT A GLANCE

GLOBAL CONFLICT 1900-1950

	1900	1905	1910	1915	1920
THE AMERICAS	**1901** The century of electricity begins, following the century of steam. **1903** The Alaskan frontier is settled. **1903** Orville and Wilbur Wright fly a powered airplane at Kitty Hawk, North Carolina. **1904** Much of Chichén Itzá is discovered, in Mexico. **1904** Work begins on the Panama Canal.	**1906** Typhoid Mary (Mary Mallon) is identified and incarcerated in New York City. **1909** Civil War breaks out in Honduras. **1909** Commander Robert E. Peary and Matthew Henson reach the North Pole. **1909** W.E.B DuBois founds the National Association for the Advancement of Colored People.	**1910-11** The Mexican Revolution occurs. **1910s** African Americans migrate from the rural South to the industrial North. **1910** Thomas Edison demonstrates talking motion pictures. **1913** The 16th Amendment enacts a U.S. Federal Income Tax. **1914** The Panama Canal is opened to traffic.	**1915** Alexander Graham Bell places the first transcontinental telephone call. **1916** Margaret Sanger helps open the first birth control clinic in the U.S. **1917** The U.S. enters World War I; an armistice with Germany ends the war in 1918. **1918** A worldwide influenza epidemic strikes; by 1920 millions are dead.	**1920** Pancho Villa surrenders to the Mexican government. **1920** The U.S. Senate votes against joining the League of Nations. **1920** The 19th Amendment gives U.S. women the vote. **1924** The Pan-American Treaty is signed to prevent conflicts between nations.
EUROPE	**1900** Sir Arthur Evans starts excavating at Knossus, Crete, leading to the discovery of the lost Minoan civilization. **1901** Guglielmo Marconi transmits the first transatlantic radio signal. **1901** The Social Revolutionary Party is founded in Russia. **1902** The Triple Alliance between Germany, Austria-Hungary, and Italy renews.	**1905** The Treaty of Portsmouth ends the Russo-Japanese War. **1905** Tsar Nicholas II establishes reforms with his October Manifesto, hoping to quiet mounting unrest. **1905** Albert Einstein formulates the special theory of relativity. **1905** The Greeks in Crete revolt against the Turks.	**1912** The Titanic sinks on her maiden voyage from England to the U.S. after colliding with an iceberg in the North Atlantic. **1913** Niels Bohr formulates the theory of atomic structure. **1914** World War I begins after Archduke Francis Ferdinand, heir to the Austrian throne, and his wife are assassinated in Sarajevo on June 28.	**1916** The Sinn Fein Easter Rebellion occurs in Dublin. **1917** Russian Tsar Nicholas II abdicates; Petrograd suffers the October Revolution. **1918** The Armistice is signed between the Allies and Germany, ending World War I. **1919** The peace conference opens at Versailles.	**1920** The League of Nations is formed in Paris. It opens in Geneva. **1920** The Hague becomes the seat of an International Court of Justice. **1920** The Russian Civil War ends. **1922** Mussolini marches on Rome, then forms a Fascist government. **1923** Hitler's coup d'etat in Munich fails.
MIDDLE EAST & AFRICA	**1900** In the Boer War the British annex the Orange Free State and Transvaal, and take Pretoria and Johannesburg. **1903** Following the fall of Kano, West African Frontier Force troops take Sokota in Nigeria. **1904** Herero and other Africans revolt against German rule in southwest Africa.	**1905** The Iranian Constitutional Revolution begins with massive popular protests. **1907** Britain and Russia partition Iran into spheres of interest. **1908** The Young Turk revolution restores the constitution and parliamentary government in the Ottoman Empire. **1908** The Union of South Africa is established.	**1910** Louis Botha and James Hertzog found the South African Party. **1912** Montenegrans begin the first Balkan War; Serbs finish it. **1913** Albanians begin the second Balkan War; Bulgars finish it. **1914** Northern and Southern Nigeria are united. **1914** Ottomans close the Dardanelles.	**1915** Allied forces lose the Gallipoli campaign of World War I. **1916** Hussein is proclaimed king of the Arabs. **1917** The British defeat the Ottomans near Gaza and capture Jaffa; Turks surrender Jerusalem. **1918** Turkish resistance collapses in Palestine; the Ottomans surrender to the Allies.	**1920** The Red Army encroaches on Persia. **1922** Egypt declares independence under King Fuad. **1922** Mustapha Kemal declares Turkey a republic and is elected president the following year. **1922** Pharaoh Tutankamun's tomb near Luxor is discovered by Howard Carter and the Earl of Carnarvan.
ASIA & OCEANIA	**1900** The Boxer Rebellion ends. **1900** Russia annexes Manchuria. **1900** The Commonwealth of Australia is created. **1904** The Russo-Japanese War begins. **1904** The Dalai Lama flees to Urgu after the arrival of British in Lhasa, Tibet.	**1905** Sun Yatsen founds the Revolutionary Alliance in Tokyo, dedicated to expelling the Manchus and foreigners and creating the Chinese Republic. **1905** Abolition of the 1,300-year-old civil service exam system signals the demise of traditional Chinese scholarly class. **1906** The All-India Moslem League is founded by Aga Khan.	**1910** Japan annexes Korea. **1911** Sun Yatsen is elected president of the Chinese Republic and appoints Chiang Kai-shek as his military adviser. **1912** The Republic of China is established, and Sun Yatsen founds Guomindang (Nationalist People's Party). **1913** China grants Mongolia independence.	**1915** Japan makes 21 demands, which threaten Chinese sovereignty. **1916** China's New Culture movement begins; western-educated Chinese scholars argue for modernization. **1917** Sun Yatsen starts a military government in Guangzhou, opposing the Beijing government. **1917** China declares war on Germany and Austria.	**1920** Mohandas Gandhi becomes India's nonviolent leader in its struggle for independence. **1921** Sun Yatsen is elected president of China. **1921** Mongolia declares itself a people's republic, becoming the world's second communist state. **1921** Britain recognizes Afghanistan's independence.

1925	1930	1935	1940	1945-1950
1927 Charles A. Lindbergh flies the *Spirit of St. Louis* nonstop from New York to Paris.	**1930** Revolutions in Argentina and Brazil bring José Uriburu and Getulio Vargas to power.	**1935** President Roosevelt signs the U.S. Social Security Act.	**1940** Congress passes the Selective Service Act to mobilize the U.S. military.	**1945** World War II ends on September 14 after the Japanese surrender.
1929 The Partido Revolutionario Institucional (PRI) begins one-party rule and controls Mexican politics until the late 1990s.	**1930** The Empire State Building opens.	**1936** Paraguay installs the first Fascist regime in the Americas.	**1941** The Japanese bomb the American base at Pearl Harbor on December 7; the following day the U.S. joins the Allies in World War II.	**1945** The United Nations is established.
1929 The Wall Street stock market crash signals the beginning of worldwide economic hardship.	**1931** Martial law is declared in Cuba by President Machado to stop a rebellion.	**1938** Roosevelt recalls the American ambassador to Germany.	**1944** Allies land on Normandy beaches for the D-Day invasion, June 6.	**1948** The Marshall Plan, a huge economic aid package for Europe, goes into effect.
	1931 Chicago gangster Alphonse (Scarface) Capone is jailed for income tax evasion.	**1939** Roosevelt declares U.S. neutrality in World War II after Germany invades Poland.		**1949** NATO is founded in the U.S. as a regional military alliance against Soviet aggression.
1925 Hitler reorganizes the Nazi Party and publishes Volume 1 of *Mein Kampf.*	**1930** The last Allied troops leave the Rhineland and the Saar.	**1935** Nazis repudiate the Versailles Treaty and reintroduce compulsory military service.	**1940** Hitler's blitz on London begins.	**1945** Hitler shoots himself.
1925 The Art Deco movement's popularity is reflected in the Exposition des Arts Decoratifs in Paris.	**1930** France starts building the Maginot Line of defenses along its German border.	**1936** Germans occupy the Rhineland and start building the Seigfried Line of defenses.	**1942** The RAF (Royal Air Force) begins a round-the-clock offensive on German munitions factories.	**1945** V-E Day (Victory in Europe Day) is celebrated May 8 by all of the Allies.
1926 Mussolini takes total control in Italy.	**1932** Famine spreads in the U.S.S.R., reaching disastrous proportions.	**1936** The Spanish Civil War begins.	**1943** Germany loses the mightiest tank battle in history to the Soviets near Kursk.	**1946** An airlift is begun by the Allies in Berlin to beat the Soviet blockade.
1929 Joseph Stalin's first Five-Year Plan begins in the U.S.S.R.	**1933** Adolf Hitler is appointed German chancellor.	**1939** Germany invades Poland; Britain and France declare war on Germany.	**1944** Britain becomes a huge armed camp as the Allies prepare for the D-Day invasion.	**1949** The Federal Republic is established in West Germany and the Democratic Republic is formed in East Germany.
1925 Blacks, Indians, and peoples of mixed races are barred from skilled jobs in South Africa.	**1930** South African microbiologist Max Theiler develops a yellow fever vaccine.	**1936** The Native Representation Act keeps blacks out of office in South Africa.	**1941** Reza Shah of Iran is overthrown.	**1945** The Arab League is founded to oppose the creation of a Jewish state.
1925 Islam is abolished In Turkey as the state religion; modernization begins.	**1930** Ras Tafari becomes Emperor Haile Selassie in Ethiopia.	**1936** Addis Ababa, capital of Ethiopia, is seized by Italians.	**1942** British general Bernard Montgomery wins victory at El Alamein against Rommel.	**1946** The kingdom of Jordan is created.
1927 Saudi Arabia becomes independent.	**1933** Britain recognizes Iraqi independence.	**1937** The Royal Commission on Palestine recommends the formation of Arab and Jewish states.	**1943** Roosevelt and Churchill meet in Casablanca to orchestrate a strategy to win World War II.	**1948** The new state of Israel is created.
1928 King Fuad makes himself dictator of Egypt after dismissing the prime minister.	**1933** King Ghazi is crowned in Baghdad.	**1939** Palestinians revolt against Jewish settlement.	**1944** Lebanon gains independence.	**1948** South Africa gains independence.
	1934 Women get the vote in Turkey.			**1949** Apartheid goes into effect in South Africa.
1926 Nationalists on Java start a rebellion against Dutch rule.	**1931** Mao Zedong is named chairman of the central executive committee of the Chinese Soviet Republic.	**1936** Chiang Kai-shek declares war on Japan.	**1941** Japanese troops move into Cambodia, Thailand, and Vietnam.	**1945** The U.S. drops atomic bombs on Hiroshima and Nagasaki.
1926 Hirohito takes over the Japanese throne upon the death of his father, Hoshihito.	**1931** Japan invades Manchuria.	**1937** Under the Government of India Act, the Indian constitution is drawn up.	**1942** The British present a plan for Indian independence after the war's end.	**1945** Korea is divided.
1928 Japan breaks off relations with China.	**1933** Japan withdraws from the League of Nations.	**1937** Japanese seize Peking, Tientsin, Nanjing, Shanghai, and Hangchow.	**1942** Japanese occupy Bataan in the Philippines. They force-march American and Philippine prisoners to a POW camp.	**1948** India becomes a republic.
1929 Chiang Kai-shek drives communists into the rural areas of China.	**1934** The Red Army begins the Long March, their strategic retreat to China's northwest.	**1939** The Japanese occupy Hainan and blockade the British concession at Tientsin.	**1944** U.S. planes bomb the Japanese mainland.	**1948** China becomes the communist People's Republic under Mao.
				1948 Chinese nationalists form a government-in-exile in Formosa (Taiwan).

1900-1905
GLOBAL CONFLICT 1900-1950

	POLITICS & POWER	GEOGRAPHY & ENVIRONMENT	CULTURE & RELIGION
THE AMERICAS	**1901 The Bureau of Reclamation** in the U.S. becomes a large and powerful bureaucracy that controls Western development by uncovering widespread corruption. **1901 U.S. President William McKinley** is assassinated by an anarchist; he is succeeded by Teddy Roosevelt. **1903 The War of the Thousand Days** in Latin America between liberals and conservatives ends in conservative victory. **1903 A bill** is passed in the U.S. limiting immigration and banning undesirables. **1904 America** ends its occupation of Cuba.	**1901 The Cuba Convention** makes Cuba a U.S. protectorate. **1902 Martinique volcanic fire** devastates the town of St. Pierre. **1903 The Alaskan frontier** is settled. **1903 The Public Land Commission** establishes that public ownership of public lands is the only way to manage its resources. This idea becomes the basis for conservation. **1904 Much of Chichén Itzá** is discovered in Mexico.	**1900 Theodore Dreiser** publishes *Sister Carrie.* **1901 Ragtime jazz** develops in the U.S., led by Scott Joplin. **1903 Henry James** publishes *The Ambassadors.* **1904 The film "The Great Train Robbery"** is the longest film to date at 12 minutes. **1904 Oscar Hammerstein** builds the Manhattan Opera House in New York. **1904 Muckraking U.S. journalist** Lincoln Steffens publishes *The Shame of the Cities.*
EUROPE	**1901 Queen Victoria** dies and is succeeded by her son, Edward VII. **1901 The Social Revolutionary Party** is founded in Russia. **1902 An Anglo-Japanese treaty** recognizes the independence of China and Korea. **1902 The Triple Alliance** between Germany, Austria-Hungary, and Italy is renewed. **1903 Socialists** gain power in Reichstag elections in Germany. **1903 The Russian Social Democratic Party** splits into Mensheviks and Bolsheviks.	**1900 Archaeologist Sir Arthur Evans** starts excavating at Knossus, Crete, leading to the discovery of the lost Minoan civilization.	**1900 Giacomo Puccini's opera,** *Tosca,* is first performed. **1901 Rudyard Kipling** publishes *Kim.* **1901 Pablo Picasso** is in his "blue period." **1903 Anti-Jewish pogroms** are carried out in Russia. **1904 Anton Chekhov** publishes *The Cherry Orchard.* **1904 The Church and State are separated** in France. **1904 Beatrix Potter** publishes *Peter Rabbit.*
MIDDLE EAST & AFRICA	**1900 Revolutionary organizations** begin terrorist campaigns in Macedonia, creating thousands of refugees to join the million-plus refugees of prior Balkan wars. **1901 Boers** start organized guerrilla warfare, invading Cape Colony and coming within 50 miles of Cape Town. **1903 Following the fall of Kano,** West African Frontier Force troops take Sokoto in Nigeria. The sultan flees as a result. **1904 Herero** and other Africans revolt against German rule in southwest Africa.	**1900 In the Boer War** the British annex the Orange Free State and Transvaal and take Pretoria and Johannesburg. **1901 Britain** annexes the Asante kingdom as part of the Gold Coast (Ghana). **1902 The Treaty of Vereeniging** ends the Boer War. Orange Free State becomes British Crown Colony. **1904 Morocco is divided** by the French, British, and Spanish, inciting the Gilali rebellion.	**1900 Ottoman University** is reopened with 400 students plus schools of Law and Medicine. **1903 A pogrom in Russia** sends waves of Jews to Palestine. **1903 The Uganda scheme** proposes a Jewish homeland in East Africa. **1904 Ota Benga**, a young Mbuti man from the Belgian Congo, is exhibited at the St. Louis World's Fair and with the primates at the Bronx Zoo.
ASIA & OCEANIA	**1900 The Boxer Rebellion** ends in China. **1902 The Philippine Government Act,** under which the nation will be controlled by the U.S., is passed. **1903 The Coronation Durbar** is held for Edward VII, English King-Emperor, at Delhi. **1904 The Russo-Japanese War** begins. Japanese besiege Port Arthur in Manchuria, occupy Seoul, and defeat the Russians at Liaoyang, China, and at Telissa. **1904 Trench warfare** begins with the Russo-Japanese War.	**1900 Famine** and the bubonic plague in India abate. **1900 Russia** annexes Manchuria. **1900 The Commonwealth of Australia** is created. Edmund Barton is inaugurated as first prime minister the following year.	**1904 The Dalai Lama** flees to Urgu after the arrival of British in Lhasa, Tibet. Shortly thereafter the British sign a treaty with Tibet agreeing not to cede their territory to any foreign power.

SCIENCE & TECHNOLOGY

1900 R. A. Fessenden transmits human speech via radio waves.

1900 The Brownie camera becomes widely available throughout the U.S.

1901 The century of electricity begins, following the century of steam.

1901 The hormone adrenaline is isolated.

1902 The Yellow Fever commission reports that the disease is carried by mosquitoes.

1903 Orville and Wilbur Wright fly a powered airplane at Kitty Hawk, North Carolina.

1904 Work begins on the Panama Canal.

1901 Guglielmo Marconi transmits the first transatlantic radio signal, from Cornwall, England, to Newfoundland.

1901 The Metro subway opens in Paris.

1901 The Trans-Siberian Railroad reaches Port Arthur.

1901 The first British submarine is launched.

1902 The subway opens in Berlin.

1904 Sir John Fleming uses a thermionic tube to generate radio waves.

1901 The Mombassa to Lake Victoria railroad is completed in East Africa.

1901 Britain begins oil drilling in Persia.

1902 The first Aswan Dam is completed in Egypt.

PEOPLE & SOCIETY

1901 In Nova Scotia, New Brunswick, and Prince Edward Island, Canada, 421 strikes occur and continue throughout 1914.

1901 J. P. Morgan organizes the U.S. Steel Corporation.

1901 The Cadillac car company is founded in the U.S.

1903 Richard Steiff designs the first teddy bears, named after President Teddy Roosevelt.

1904 Helen Keller, who is deaf and blind, graduates from Radcliffe College.

1901 The Fifth Zionist Congress begins the Jewish National Fund.

1903 Emmeline Pankhurst founds National Women's Social and Political Union.

1903 The first motor taxis appear in London.

1904 The 10-hour workday is established in France.

1904 Drink licensing laws are enacted in Britain.

1904 Steerage rates for immigrants to the U.S. are cut to ten dollars by foreign lines.

1904 Rolls-Royce is founded in Britain.

1902 Casualties in the Boer War: 14,154 Africans, 5,774 British, and 4,000 Boers.

Orville Wright takes off at Kill Devil Hill, North Carolina, as brother Wilbur looks on, December 17, 1903.

A NEW WORLD OF FLIGHT

On December 17, 1903, when Orville and Wilbur Wright successfully flew their motorized airplane near Kitty Hawk, North Carolina, they opened up a whole new world for flyers who had thus far succeeded in becoming airborne only in dirigibles, hot air balloons, and glider planes. By demonstrating their theory of correcting the aircraft's position with movable portions of the wing, rather than shifts in body weight, the Wright brothers made a vast leap forward in aircraft design. In addition they created useful tables of wind pressure and drift.

Becoming fascinated with aviation in the 1890s by studying the German engineer Otto Lilienthal's work with glider flights, Orville and Wilbur put their expertise as mechanics to work in their bicycle repair shop. After successfully testing their theories with glider planes, which they took to the windy beaches of Kitty Hawk every autumn, they focused next on the engine. Not able to find one that was light and powerful enough, Orville designed an engine, which the brothers built and attached to their improved glider.

On the day that changed aviation history, the brothers went up four times—Orville stayed aloft in the first flight for all of 12 seconds, and by the fourth attempt, Wilbur was able to fly 852 feet in 59 seconds. Continuing their experiments, by 1909 they had become world famous and had added a more powerful engine, a passenger seat, and more intricate controls. Now the Wright brothers could utilize their invention commercially, for governments realized how useful their planes could be in combat, and began to order them in quantity.

My brother Orville and myself lived together, played together, worked together, and in fact thought together.

WILBUR WRIGHT

	POLITICS & POWER	GEOGRAPHY & ENVIRONMENT	CULTURE & RELIGION
THE AMERICAS	**1905 William Haywood** and others found the Industrial Workers of the World (Wobblies). **1906 After reconciliation** following the liberal revolt fails, U.S. troops occupy Cuba. **1907 The panic of 1907** causes a bank run, which is stopped by J. P. Morgan's importation of $100 million in gold from Europe. **1909 W.E.B. DuBois** founds the National Association for the Advancement of Colored People (NAACP) in the U.S. **1909 Teddy Roosevelt** undertakes the first inventories of public lands and their resources.	**1905 The National Forest Service** is established in the U.S. by Gifford Pinchot. **1906 A San Francisco earthquake** kills 700 people, with $400 million in property loss. **1909 U.S. explorer Commander Robert E. Peary**, accompanied by Matthew Henson, is the first person to reach the North Pole.	**1905 The Social Gospel Movement** in the U.S. embodies Christian progressive ideas about ameliorating the harshness of individual capitalism. **1906 Ruth St. Denis** introduces modern dance. **1906 Upton Sinclair** publishes *The Jungle*. **1908 Isadora Duncan** becomes a popular interpreter of dance. **1908 The "ashcan" school of painting**, portraying common life, is established by Robert Henri, George Luks, John Sloan, George Bellow, Williams Glackens, and Everett Shinn.
EUROPE	**1905 Tsar Nicholas II** establishes reforms with his October Manifesto, hoping to quiet mounting unrest in Russia. **1905 The Greeks** in Crete revolt against the Turks. **1907 Britain and France** agree on Siamese independence.	**1905 The most severe famine** in Russia since 1891 is reported. By 1908, 20 million are starving. **1906 Norwegian explorer Roald Amundsen** crosses the Northwest Passage on a two-and-a-half-year journey and determines the position of the magnetic North Pole. **1906 Vesuvius erupts**, devastating the town of Ottaiano, Italy. **1908 An earthquake** in southern Calabria and Sicily kills 150,000. It is the most violent ever recorded in Europe.	**1905 Pablo Picasso** arrives in Paris to begin his "pink period." **1905 Franz Lehar** presents *The Merry Widow*, an operetta, in Vienna. **1907 Henri Matisse** coins the term "cubism." The first cubist exhibition opens in Paris. **1907 E. M. Forster** publishes *A Room with a View*. **1907 Kenneth Grahame** publishes *The Wind in the Willows*. **1907 Bela Bartok** composes *String Quartet No. 1*.
MIDDLE EAST & AFRICA	**1905 Louis Botha** and his Het Volk Party ask for responsible government in the Transvaal. **1905 The Iranian constitutional revolution** begins, spurring massive demonstrations, but is hijacked by conservatives. **1906 Self-government** is granted to the Transvaal and Orange River colonies, along with white suffrage. **1908 The Young Turk revolution** restores the constitution and parliamentary government in the Ottoman Empire.	**1907 Nairobi** becomes the capital of British East Africa (Kenya), because it is located on the Mombasa-Uganda railroad. **1907 Belgian King Leopold II** makes the kingdom of the Congo part of the state. **1908 Four thousand die** during famine in the Usoga region of Africa. **1908 The Union of South Africa** is born. **1909 Tel Aviv**, the first Jewish town in modern Palestine, is founded.	**1907 The Second Young Turk Congress** meets in Paris. It includes Armenians, who suggest armed resistance to the Ottomans.
ASIA & OCEANIA	**1905 Japanese** sink the Russian fleet in the straits of Tsushima. **1905 Port Arthur** surrenders to the Japanese in the Russo-Japanese War. The Treaty of Portsmouth ends the war. **1905 The Anglo-Japanese Alliance** is renewed for 10 years. **1905 Sun Yatsen** founds the revolutionary alliance in Tokyo, dedicated to expelling the Manchus and foreigners and creating the Chinese Republic. **1906 Australia** takes control of Papua, New Guinea.	**1905 An earthquake** in Lahore, Pakistan, kills some 10,000 people. **1906 A typhoon** kills some 10,000 people in India. **1907 The Dutch** complete the occupation of Sumatra with the defeat of the Achinese tribe. **1907 New Zealand** becomes a dominion within the British Empire.	**1906 An All-India Moslem League** is founded by Aga Khan. **1908 Muslims and Hindus** riot in Calcutta, India.

SCIENCE & TECHNOLOGY	PEOPLE & SOCIETY
1905 The eugenics movement in the U.S. advocates that certain groups such as the mentally handicapped or criminals be stopped from having children.	**1905 The first neon signs** appear.
	1906 Night shift work for women is internationally forbidden.
1906 The New York State Meteorological Office reports that weather forecasting is within their grasp.	**1906 Typhoid Mary** (Mary Mallon) is found and incarcerated for being a carrier of typhoid in New York City.
1906 The U.S. Pure Food and Drugs Act is passed.	**1908 Jack Johnson** becomes the first black world heavyweight boxing champion.
1906 The first U.S. radio program of voice and music is broadcast by R. A. Fessenden.	**1908 General Motors Corporation** is formed.
1909 The plastic age begins with the first commercial manufacture of Bakelite.	**1908 The Ford Motor Company** produces the first Model T. Fifteen million are eventually sold.

Pablo Picasso's Les Demoiselles d'Avignon

1905 An obscure Swiss patent clerk, Albert Einstein, formulates the special theory of relativity and ushers in the atomic age.	**1905 The first buses** operate in London.
	1906 The French Grand Prix car race is run for the first time.
1906 Clemens von Pirquet introduces the term "allergy" to medicine.	**1907 Universal suffrage** is instituted in Austria.
1907 Pavlov studies conditioned reflexes.	
1907 Louis Lumière develops a process for color photography using a three-color screen.	**1907 Robert Baden-Powell** founds the Boy Scout movement, in Britain.
1909 Paul Ehrlich develops the Salvarsan medicine for syphilis and other diseases.	**1909 Men and women older than 70** receive their first old age pensions in London.
1909 T. H. Morgan begins research in genetics.	

THE BEGINNINGS OF MODERN ART

When 26-year-old Spanish artist Pablo Picasso painted *Les Demoiselles d'Avignon* in 1907, he did not know that he would help revolutionize the art world. Picasso, in fact, was so unsure of the work's significance that he showed it only to close friends for years, and he did not exhibit it publicly until 1916.

Its subject—five nudes in various poses, plus a still life—is aggressive and somewhat savage, unlike anything the art world had ever seen. The three angular figures on the left are distortions of classical ones, but the dislocated and fractured features and bodies of the two figures on the right draw inspiration from African sculpture. Organic integrity, proportions, and continuity of the human body are all ignored.

This iconic work embodied the new abstract approach to art and also signaled the birth of cubism, which represented its own world, akin to nature but constructed with different principles. Critics saw only sharp edges and angles, whereas Picasso actually combined voids and solids, giving his figures a three-dimensional quality. By the end of his long life in 1973, Picasso's numerous and varied works had made him the most revered artist of the 20th century.

$$E = mc^2$$

ALBERT EINSTEIN
THEORY OF RELATIVITY

Albert Einstein

1906 The *Satsuma*, the world's largest battleship, is launched in Japan.

1906 China and Britain agree to reduce opium production.

1907 France and Japan agree on an "open door" for China.

1908 Mohandas "Mahatma" Gandhi, leader of the Indian protest movement against laws requiring Asians to register in the Transvaal, is released from jail.

POLITICS & POWER	GEOGRAPHY & ENVIRONMENT	CULTURE & RELIGION

THE AMERICAS

1910-11 The Mexican Revolution occurs, with bandit and cavalry leader Pancho Villa helping defeat Porfirio Diaz.

1911 The U.S.Supreme Court orders the breakup of the Standard Oil Company.

1911 The Winnipeg Trades and Urban Council leads workers out on general strike in the metal and building industries.

1913 The Federal Income Tax is introduced in the U.S. with the 16th Amendment.

1910 The U.S. Congress establishes Glacier National Park.

Pancho Villa and Emiliano Zapata with Mexican Revolutionaries

1912 Textile workers strike in Lawrence, Massachusetts, showing the power of the Wobblies.

1913 The Armory Show introduces postimpressionism and cubism to New York.

1914 The American Society of Composers, Authors, and Publishers (ASCAP) is founded.

EUROPE

1910 Montenegro is proclaimed a kingdom under Nicholas I.

1910 Revolution occurs in Portugal.

1911 Winston Churchill is appointed First Lord of the Admiralty.

1912 The alliance of Germany, Austria-Hungary, and Italy is renewed.

1914 World War I begins after Archduke Francis Ferdinand, heir to the Austrian throne, and his wife are assassinated in Sarajevo, Bosnia, on June 28 by a Serbian nationalist. Austria-Hungary declares war on Serbia.

1911 Roald Amundsen of Norway becomes the first person to reach the South Pole.

1910 The South American tango becomes wildly popular in Europe and the U.S.

1912 Carl Jung publishes *The Theory of Psychoanalysis.*

1912 The S.S. *Titanic* sinks on her maiden voyage from England to the U.S. after colliding with an iceberg in the North Atlantic.

1913 D. H. Lawrence publishes *Sons and Lovers*.

1913 Thomas Mann publishes *Death in Venice*.

MIDDLE EAST & AFRICA

1910 Russia and Britain intervene as political unrest sweeps Persia.

1910 The Ottoman sultan declares a jihad; Ottoman forces attack Russian ports.

1910 Louis Botha and James Hertzog found the South African Party.

1912 The Allied Balkan armies advance on Turkey.

1912 The African National Congress is created.

1913 The Ottomans sign a peace treaty with the Balkan League.

1910 France renames the French Congo French Equatorial Africa.

1910 The Union of South Africa becomes a dominion within the British Empire.

1911 Italians occupy Libya.

1911 Refugees from the Balkan wars resettle outside Istanbul.

1912 Morocco becomes a French protectorate.

1914 Northern and Southern Nigeria are united.

1914 Ottomans close the Dardanelles.

1911 The first B'nai B'rith lodges appear in Istanbul.

1912 Ottoman minorities reject multinational Ottomanism, giving rise to Turkish nationalism. Ziya Gokalp stresses Turkish language and culture, raises the position of women, and promises a rational approach to religion.

1913 Hebrew becomes the dominant language of Jews in Palestine.

ASIA & OCEANIA

1911 A Republican Revolution brings an end to the Manchus in China.

1912 The Republic of China is officially proclaimed with Sun Yatsen as president. He appoints Chiang Kai-shek as his military adviser.

1912 Sun Yatsen founds the Guomindang (Nationalist People's Party).

1913 Mohandas Gandhi, leader of the Indian Passive Resistance Movement, is arrested.

1914 New Zealand occupies Western Samoa.

1914 Japan occupies northern Marianas.

1910 Japan annexes Korea.

1911 Flooding on the Yangtze River kills 100,000 people in China.

1913 China grants Mongolia independence.

1912 Rabindranath Tagore translates Gitanjali into English.

1913 Rabindranath Tagore receives the Nobel Prize in literature.

1915 The journal *New Youth* is published in China, a sign of the new cultural movement.

SCIENCE & TECHNOLOGY

1910 Thomas Edison demonstrates talking motion pictures.

1910 Halley's comet is observed.

1911 Charles F. Kettering develops the first practical electric self-starter for cars.

1913 H. N. Russell formulates the theory of stellar evolution.

1914 Robert H. Goddard starts his rocketry experiments.

1914 The Panama Canal is opened to traffic.

1911 Ernest Rutherford develops his theory of atomic structure.

1912 Edwin Bradenberger invents a process for manufacturing cellophane.

1913 The diphtheria immunity test is discovered by Bela Schick.

1913 Hans Geiger introduces the first successful electrical device capable of counting individual alpha rays.

1913 Niels Bohr formulates the theory of atomic structure.

1911 Istanbul tramways are electrified and public steamship service is started.

1914 A 900-mile railroad opens from Lake Tanganyika to Dar-es-Salaam.

PEOPLE & SOCIETY

1910s African Americans migrate in great numbers from the rural South to the industrial North for better jobs and to escape discrimination.

1912 Jim Thorpe is the outstanding sportsman at the Stockholm Olympic Games.

1913 Grand Central Station, the world's largest railroad station, opens in New York.

1914 The U.S. Federal Trade Commission is established to police interstate commerce.

1914 Some 10.5 million immigrants enter the U.S. from southern and eastern Europe between 1905-1914.

1912 A coal strike, London dock strikes, and a transport workers strike occur in Britain.

1912 The Royal Flying Corps is established in Britain (later becomes the Royal Air Force, or RAF).

1912 The International Lawn Tennis Federation is formed.

1913 German medical missionary Albert Schweitzer opens his hospital in Lambarene, French Congo.

1913 Zippers become popular.

1913 The first English female magistrate is sworn in.

CONNECTIONS

The Colonial World at War

The two world wars saw tens of thousands of colonists take up arms for the countries that had subjugated them. Many were conscripted, but many volunteered, believing their mother countries would reward them with independence. A total of 83,000 Africans fought with the Allies in the First World War. In World War II, South Africa sent 200,000 volunteers to fight the Germans, a third of them black. The British, Belgians, and French mined troops from sub-Saharan Africa, while the Dutch used Asian colonists to fight the Japanese. India, denied self-government after uniting behind the British in World War I, splintered. Some fought for the Allies, but an Indian "national army" fought in Burma in support of the Japanese, a symptom of the nationalistic fervor brewing under Hindu leaders Gandhi and Nehru and Muslim League leader Muhammad Ali Jinnah.

BUILDING THE PANAMA CANAL

Americans had long had their mind's eye on a proposed passageway through the narrowest part of Central America. Such a corridor would connect the region's east and west coasts and eliminate the 7,000 additional miles needed to sail around the southern tip of South America. When large numbers of pioneers began settling in Oregon and California, the desire for this seafaring shortcut intensified, which resulted in President Teddy Roosevelt's use of aggressive tactics to make construction of the Panama Canal possible.

It was not the first time such an ambitious attempt had been made. Led by Ferdinand de Lesseps, a French company had obtained a concession to construct a sea level canal across Panama in 1878. But because of disease, poor planning, and lack of funds, the project was eventually abandoned.

In 1901 the British agreed to allow the U.S. to build and fortify a canal, and the United States' choice was to cut across Nicaragua. A volcanic eruption at the site, however, made building through that country impossible, so Roosevelt turned his attention to Panama, which was a province of Colombia. After petitioning Bogota and being rebuffed, Roosevelt encouraged a group of Colombians to start their own country. Before trouble had time to erupt, he accepted a sea-to-sea right-of-way in perpetuity from the new Republic of Panama, and after several years of developing construction facilities, disease control, and surveys, construction got under way. In 1906 Roosevelt himself visited the site, becoming the first sitting president to travel outside the U.S.

In August of 1914 the Panama Canal was informally opened to traffic. Some 5,600 lives had been lost, mostly to tropical diseases. At 40 miles long, 500 feet wide, and 40 feet deep, the channel was the most ambitious construction project undertaken in modern times and would bring the world closer together.

DEATH IN THE TRENCHES

THE FIRST WORLD WAR SHOCKED MANY with its brutality and unprecedented loss of life. Mechanized weaponry, such as the magazine rifle, the machine gun, and quick-firing artillery, had enhanced every soldier's killing power, especially at a distance, compelling European armies to literally dig in to protect themselves on the open battlefield. Called trench warfare, it was first seen in the Russo-Japanese War but was elevated to a way of life here.

By the spring of 1915, with the Allies and the Central Powers stalemated, both sides began constructing more and more elaborate trench systems. Trench linings consisted of whatever material might be available, and included wattle, planking, and sandbags. The German trenches, often going quite deep, were superior to those of the British and French. The British system contained three lines of trenches: the front, which was composed of command-and-fire trenches; the support; and the reserve, behind which the artillery was positioned. Communication trenches ran at right angles, connecting the lines. No Man's Land, with barbed-wire entanglements running the length between opposing lines, could be as short as 50 yards or as much as half a mile wide. Wired telephone lines, semaphores, dogs, and pigeons were all used to transmit messages.

Trench warfare created a battlefield situation almost like siege warfare. Armies could not withdraw or pause. Soldiers lived in the fortified ditches. An individual's most essential weapons were his shovel and his machine gun. Grenades also came in handy in answer to machine gun fire. Bayonets proved unsatisfactory, so most infantrymen had a fighting knife and a homemade trench club used for raiding. Gas masks and breathing apparatuses for tunneling were also supplied. Periscopes were useful for keeping watch, and wire cutters were vital when parties were sent out under cover of darkness to cut the barbed wire before an attack.

Life in the trenches took a severe toll. Rain could turn ditches into a sea of mud up to one's waist, and many men, standing in freezing water for days at a time, developed trench foot. Lack of sleep and proper nourishment, exhaustion, and shell shock—not to mention lack of sanitation—were common problems. Lice thrived everywhere, spreading trench fever, and huge rats, some as big as cats from feeding on corpses, would brazenly gnaw a hole in a man's haversack pocket to obtain a morsel of food. Often to break the boredom of "wait and see," soldiers would shoot rats as target practice. After a few months of this life, a man was beyond his prime as an efficient soldier. The initial horror gave way to indifference, his main defense against insanity.

ABOVE: *The skeleton of a German soldier left in the trenches at Beaumont Hamel north of the River Somme in late 1916.* RIGHT: *An officer of the Ninth Battalion (Scottish Rifles) leads a raid in 1917.*

*You might be talking to a man one minute,
the next minute he was dead at your feet.*

An Allied sergeant, 1916

1915-1920

GLOBAL CONFLICT 1900-1950

POLITICS & POWER	GEOGRAPHY & ENVIRONMENT	CULTURE & RELIGION

THE AMERICAS

1917 The Mexican Constitution calls for land reform and national rights to minerals and oil.

1916 Mexican General Pancho Villa is routed by John Pershing's U.S. troops after killing 18 Americans in New Mexico. Villa had been angered by U.S. President Wilson's support for his rival, Carranza, who had driven Villa and Zapata out of Mexico City.

1917 The U.S. enters World War I; General Pershing goes to Paris to lead American forces.

1918 U.S. President Woodrow Wilson states his Fourteen Points for Peace.

1916 The U.S. agrees to purchase the Danish West Indies (Virgin Islands) for $25 million.

1917 Congress makes Puerto Rico a U.S. Territory.

1917 Stephen Mather organizes and directs the National Park Service. As a Sierra Club member, he advocates preservation and economic use of lands.

1918 Vilhjalmur Stefansson, Canadian explorer, returns from a five-year voyage north of the Arctic Circle.

1919 Immigration is curtailed in the U.S.

1915 Edgar Lee Masters publishes *A Spoon River Anthology*.

1916 Mariano Azueka publishes *The Underdogs*.

1916 John Dewey publishes *Democracy and Education*.

1916 Jazz sweeps the U.S.

1917 George M. Cohan composes the American war song "Over There."

1919 Henry Adams wins the Pulitzer Prize for *The Education of Henry Adams*.

EUROPE

1916 The Sinn Fein Easter Rebellion occurs in Dublin.

1917 The October Revolution occurs in Russia, followed by the Russian Civil War.

1918 World War I: The Allied offensive on the Western Front begins; the Armistice ending the war is signed between the Allies and Germany on November 11.

1919 Benito Mussolini founds the Fasci del Combattimento.

1919 Lady Astor becomes the first female Member of Parliament in England.

1918 Leonard Woolley begins Babylonian excavations.

1919 Ernest Shackleton publishes *South,* an account of his 1914-17 expedition to the Antarctic.

1915 Marcel Duchamp paints the first Dada-style works.

1917 Amedeo Modigliani paints *Crouching Female Nude.*

1917 Christian pilgrims visit Fatima, Portugal, where visions of the Virgin Mary have been seen.

1918 Controversies occur over the new psychology of Sigmund Freud and Carl Jung.

1918 Juan Miro first exhibits his works.

1919 The Bauhaus movement is founded by Walter Gropius in Germany.

MIDDLE EAST & AFRICA

1915 Compulsory military service in African colonies forces thousands of African males to join World War I.

1915 Mustafa Kemal commands Ottoman troops at Gallipoli, brilliantly resisting the Allied invasion.

1916 Russians launch an offensive against the Ottomans; Hussein is proclaimed king of the Arabs; the British defeat the Ottomans in a naval battle off Port Said; Persia makes an alliance with Russia and Britain.

1918 Turkish resistance collapses in Palestine; Ottomans surrender to Allies.

1917 The Balfour Declaration on Palestine occurs, pledging British support to the creation of a Jewish homeland, provided the rights of non-Jewish Palestinians are respected.

WHAT LIFE WAS LIKE

The 1918 Influenza Pandemic

Toward the end of World War I, a highly contagious virus swept the world. Often called the Spanish flu, as it was incorrectly thought to have begun in that country, the pestilence spread like wildfire among the troops as they moved about, and quickly became a pandemic. Doctors and nurses were short in number, hospitals overflowed, businesses closed down, and people were afraid to emerge from their homes. Laws were passed to prevent spitting and sneezing in public places, and many people donned face masks to try and protect themselves from the airborne germ, which was so virulent it could bring people down in an instant with a sudden fever, followed by respiratory ills. If they were lucky, the illness would eventually subside, but if not, pneumonia, "the captain of the men of death," set in and survival was less likely. Not since the bubonic, or black plague, swept Europe and Asia in the 14th century had so many victims been claimed by a single disease. Like the plague, as quickly as it came the influenza virus of 1918 disappeared, leaving millions dead.

ASIA & OCEANIA

1915 Japan makes "21 demands," which threaten Chinese sovereignty.

1917 China declares war on Germany and Austria.

1917 Sun Yatsen starts the Republic of China military government in Guangzhou, opposing the Beijing government.

1919 Amanullah becomes amir of Afghanistan.

1919 The Chinese demonstrate against the signing of the Versailles Treaty. It is part of the New Cultural Movement, combining Western ideas with Chinese national identity.

1916 The New Culture Movement gets under way in China, while Western-educated Chinese scholars argue the need for modernizing reform.

SCIENCE & TECHNOLOGY	PEOPLE & SOCIETY
1915 **The first transcontinental telephone call** is placed by Alexander Graham Bell in New York to Dr. Thomas A. Watson in San Francisco.	**1915** **Henry Ford** produces his one-millionth car.
1915 **Wireless service** begins between the U.S. and Japan.	**1916** **Margaret Sanger** helps open the first birth control clinic in the U.S.
1916 **Blood for transfusions** is refrigerated.	**1917** **Wartime fuel and food controls** are enacted in the U.S.
1917 **The 1,800-foot-long Quebec Railroad Bridge** is completed.	**1918** **Daylight saving time** is introduced in the U.S.
1918 **Harlow Shapley** discovers the true dimensions of the Milky Way.	**1918** **A worldwide influenza epidemic** strikes; by 1920 many millions are dead.
	1918 **The first airmail postage** is created in the U.S.

1915 **Albert Einstein** postulates his general theory of relativity.	**1915** **Tetanus epidemics** break out in the trenches of World War I.
1915 **British chemist James Kendall** isolates the dysentery bacillus.	**1916** **The British Military Service Act** is put in force.
1915 **Hugo Junkers** builds the first all-metal fighter plane.	**1916** **Food** is rationed in Germany.
1917 **Sigmund Freud** publishes *Introduction to Psychoanalysis.*	**1916** **Daylight saving time** is introduced in Britain.
1917 **The Trans-Siberian Railroad** is completed.	**1918** **Women older than 30 years of age** get the vote in Britain.
1918 **Max Planck** receives the Nobel Prize in physics for introducing the quantum theory.	**1918** **The food shortage in Britain** leads to the establishment of national food kitchens and rationing of butter and meat in London.

1915 **Cotton prices** lead to a soaring economic boom in Egypt as resources are devoted to war. Light industry expands and an Egyptian business class develops.

Survivors are fired on by machine gunners fleeing along the Nevsky Prospekt in Petrograd, or St. Petersburg, as the Bolshevik takeover falters briefly in mid-July of 1917.

THE RUSSIAN REVOLUTION

Tsar Nicholas, with his aristocratic heritage, had not realized the extent of the crisis that his country was undergoing. As early as 1905 in the Bloody Sunday uprising against his tsarist government, the proletariat, starving and desperate, rose up in anger against the current regime. Nicholas's inability to deal with the crisis facing his country inflamed the peasants to the extent that he was forced to abdicate on March 15, 1917.

A provisional government was organized in April of 1917, which quickly initiated such reforms as universal suffrage and other liberal innovations. By October of 1917, Lenin and his Bolshevik followers had mushroomed into a force powerful enough to take over the government. Lenin immediately abolished private property, granting land to the peasants, reallocating church lands to village soviets, and nationalizing industry and finance. Resistance from anti-Bolsheviks, however, led to a civil war that would cause another two years of strife and great loss of life.

In the meantime, the imperial Romanov family of Tsar Nicholas, who had surrendered to the Bolsheviks, was imprisoned on an estate in the Ural mountains, where they were shot, bayoneted, doused with acid, and tossed into an unmarked grave that would go undiscovered until 1991, when nine of the 11 bodies were found.

We must not be deceived by the present grave-like stillness in Europe. . . . Europe is pregnant with revolution.

VLADIMIR LENIN

POLITICS & POWER	GEOGRAPHY & ENVIRONMENT	CULTURE & RELIGION
THE AMERICAS		
1920 The U.S. Senate votes against joining the League of Nations.	**1920 The U.S. Congress** passes the Mineral Land Leasing Act.	**1920 Diego Rivera,** David Alfaro Siguieros, and Jose Clemente Orozco lead the politico-social school of painting, perfecting the form of Mexican muralism through the 1930s.
1920 The 18th Amendment goes into effect, enacting Prohibition, and the 19th Amendment gives American women the vote.	**1922 Aniakchak,** one of the world's greatest volcanoes, is discovered on the Alaskan coast.	**1920 The *indigenismo,*** a philosophy in literature and art, highlights the importance of indigenous culture in the formation of nation states.
1923 The Teapot Dome scandal rocks the Harding administration. Harding dies shortly after, making Calvin Coolidge U.S. president.	**1923 Argentinian Enrique Tiriboschi** is the first person to swim the English Channel from France to England.	**1920 Edith Wharton** publishes *The Age of Innocence;* Sinclair Lewis publishes *Main Street.*
1924 The U.S. grants Cuba independence.	**1924 Insecticides** are used for the first time.	**1921 Rudolf Valentino** stars in *Sheik,* establishing himself as the first Latin lover in silent films.
1924 The Pan-American Treaty is signed to prevent conflicts between nations.	**1924 A U.S. bill** limits immigration and excludes all Japanese.	
EUROPE		
1920 The League of Nations is formed in Paris and opens in Geneva.	**1921 C. K. Howard-Bury** and his British team explore the northern approaches of Mount Everest.	**1920 The first ecumenical council** convenes, bringing European, U.S., and Eastern churches together.
1920 The Hague is chosen as the seat of the International Court of Justice.	**1922 The Irish Free State** is officially proclaimed.	**1922 James Joyce** publishes *Ulysses* and T. S. Eliot publishes "The Waste Land," two significant works in the new literary movement called modernism.
1920 The Russian Civil War ends in victory for the Bolsheviks.	**1922 Soviet Russia** is renamed the Union of Soviet Socialist Republics (U.S.S.R.).	**1922 A. E. Housman** publishes *Last Poems.*
1920 English "Black and Tan" arrive in Ireland to put down republican revolt.	**1924 Danish polar explorer Knud Rasmussen** finishes the longest dog sledge journey ever undertaken across the North American Arctic.	**1923 P. G. Wodehouse** publishes *The Inimitable Jeeves.*
1922 Benito Mussolini marches on Rome, then forms a fascist government.		**1923 Vassily Kandinsky** paints *Circles in the Circle.*
1923 Adolf Hitler's coup d'etat (the Beer Hall Putsch) in Munich fails. Hitler is imprisoned for eight months.		**1924 Picasso** begins his abstract period.
MIDDLE EAST & AFRICA		
1922 Egypt declares independence under King Fuad. Wafd becomes the main nationalist political party.	**1922 Pharaoh Tutankhamun's tomb** near Luxor is discovered by Britain's Howard Carter and the Earl of Carnarvan.	**1924 A monument is erected** to West African soldiers who died by the thousands defending Reims, France, against the Germans.
1922 The League of Nations Council approves mandates for Palestine and Egypt.	**1923 Transjordan** becomes independent under Amir Abdullah.	
1922 After defeating a Greek invasion, Mustapha Kemal declares Turkey a republic. Kemal is elected president in 1923.	**1923 Rhodesia (Zimbabwe)** becomes a self-governing British colony.	
1924 The shah of Persia, Ahmed, is dethroned, and Reza Khan is appointed regent, then shah.	**1923 Ankara replaces Istanbul** as the capital of Turkey, and Turkey reorganizes around the Anatolian peasants and their culture.	
ASIA & OCEANIA		
1921 The first Indian Parliament meets.	**1920 An earthquake** in Gansu province, China, kills 200,000 people.	**1920 Mohandas Gandhi** becomes India's leader in its struggle for independence. His approach is one of nonviolent noncooperation with the Indian government.
1921 Takashi Hara, premier of Japan, is assassinated.	**1921 Britain** signs a treaty recognizing Afghanistan's independence.	**1922 Gandhi** is sentenced to six years' imprisonment for civil disobedience.
1921 The first congress of the Chinese Communist Party takes place in Shanghai.	**1923 The centers of Tokyo and Yokohama** are destroyed by an earthquake, leaving 120,00 people dead.	**1923 Lu Hsun** publishes *Na-Han,* a powerful collection of short stories that call his countrymen to unite and save China.
1921 Crown Prince Hirohito becomes regent of Japan, with Takashi Hara Kei head of the first parliamentary government.	**1924 A plague epidemic** kills 25,000 people in India.	**1924 Tsukiji Little Theatre** opens in Tokyo, signaling the start of the modern theatre.
1921 Mongolia declares independence as a people's republic, becoming the world's second communist state.	**1924 R. C. Andrews** discovers skeletons and skulls of Mesozoic dinosaurs in the Gobi Desert.	**1924 Gandhi** fasts for 21 days to protest feuds between Hindus and Muslims in India.
1923 A united front between Chinese nationalists and communists is announced.		

SCIENCE & TECHNOLOGY

1920 Dr. Harvey Cushing develops new techniques for brain surgery.

1920 John T. Thompson patents his submachine gun, nicknamed the "Tommy gun."

1921 Biologist Thomas Hunt Morgan postulates the chromosome theory of heredity.

1922 The first insulin to be administered to diabetic patients is prepared by Canadian physicians Banting, Best, and Macleod.

1922 Zoologist T. H. Morgan experiments with the heredity mechanisms of fruit flies.

1920 Herman Rorschach develops the inkblot test to diagnose mental disorders.

1921 Albert Calmette and Camille Guerin develop the B-C-G tuberculosis vaccine.

1921 Felix d'Herelle discovers bacteriophages.

1923 The U.S.S.R. opens its first polar station.

1924 The Central Office for the Examination of Rocket Problems is founded in Moscow.

PEOPLE & SOCIETY

1920s The Harlem Renaissance sees a flourishing of social thought and artistic achievement in dance, music, literature, and theater among African Americans in this "mecca of the new Negro."

1920 California passes a local law that blocks land ownership for noncitizens, aimed at the Japanese.

1921 The Unknown Soldier is interred at Arlington National Cemetery.

1923 Mexican bandit Pancho Villa is killed by gunmen, ending his long career as a revolutionary and adversary of both the Mexican and U.S. governments.

1920s Gertrude Stein coins the term "lost generation" to describe American expatriots Hemingway, Fitzgerald, Sherwood Anderson, and others living in Paris after World War I. The group was generally disillusioned by the war and disdainful of Victorian morality.

1920 Oxford enrolls its first female students.

1921 Marie Stopes opens Britain's first birth control clinic in London.

1921 The British Broadcasting Company is founded.

1921 Lenin's New Economic Policy goes into effect in the Soviet Union.

1923-1945 Throughout the Middle East, the economy keeps up with population growth, and living standards remain the same, with a dip during the Depression.

THE JAZZ AGE

Also known as the roaring twenties, the era of wonderful nonsense, and the flapper era, the 1920s was a decade of indulgence in the United States, as a booming postwar economy led to greater prosperity and a general increase in the pursuit of happiness. Exciting new consumer products like cars and radios, flashy new styles of clothing, and crazy dances like the Charleston held great attraction for those with a flare for individualism and improvisation, as epitomized in the hot new music of the day.

Developing from music brought by African slaves to the New World, jazz traveled up the Mississippi River from New Orleans to Memphis, Kansas City, Chicago, and New York. Louis Armstrong, or "Satchmo," his very name synonymous with jazz, mesmerized audiences with trumpet improvisations that connected the blues and ragtime to swing. Nightclubs such as the Cotton Club attracted white New Yorkers to Harlem in droves to see Armstrong and other all-black acts while drinking high-priced illegal liquor.

Prohibition, enacted in 1920, defined this era as much as the new music. Delivering a password to be admitted to an illegal speakeasy where you could drink bootleg liquor became a craze for those who could afford it. Adding to the excitement was the likelihood that the liquor had been provided by some big business mobster like Chicago's Al Capone. Despite attempts by the federal government to stem the flow of John Barleycorn, "bathtub gin" flowed freely.

As with F. Scott Fitzgerald's Jay Gatsby, the epitome of the jazz age playboy, the good times couldn't last. The stock market crash of 1929 ushered out the roaring twenties and brought on the Great Depression.

A kneeling Louis Armstrong plays the slide trumpet in Joe "King" Oliver's Creole Jazz Band, with Lil Hardin on piano, 1923.

POLITICS & POWER	GEOGRAPHY & ENVIRONMENT	CULTURE & RELIGION

THE AMERICAS

1927 Liberal Augusto César Sandino and his guerrillas begin a fight in Nicaragua against conservatives. He is assassinated in 1934 and is the inspiration for the modern term Sandanista, meaning a modern revolutionary movement.

1927 Canada is voted into the League of Nations Council.

1929 Albert B. Fall, secretary of the Interior under former president Harding, is convicted for his role in the Teapot Dome scandal.

1929 The Partido Revolutionario Institutional (PRI) begins one-party rule and controls Mexican politics until the late 1990s.

1925 An international group of flyers make the first successful crossing over the North Pole in an airship.

1925 A solar eclipse in New York is the first in 30 years.

1925 A tornado in the south-central U.S. kills 689 people.

1929 U.S. aviator Richard E. Byrd and three companions fly over the South Pole.

1925 F. Scott Fitzgerald publishes *The Great Gatsby*.

1926 Argentinian Ricardo Guiraldes publishes *Don Segundo Sombra,* the best of the "gaucho novels."

1929 William Faulkner publishes *The Sound and the Fury*.

1929 Ernest Hemingway publishes *A Farewell to Arms*.

1929 Georgia O'Keefe paints *Black Flower and Blue Larkspur*.

1929 The Museum of Modern Art (MOMA) opens in New York.

EUROPE

1925 Hitler reorganizes the Nazi Party and publishes Volume 1 of *Mein Kampf*.

1925 British troops pull out of the Rhineland after a seven-year occupation.

1926 Mussolini takes total control in Italy, banning all opposition.

1927 An economic conference in Geneva is attended by 52 nations.

1929 Joseph Stalin's first Five-Year Plan begins in the U.S.S.R.

1929 Trotsky is expelled from the U.S.S.R.

1925 Norway's capital, Christiana, is renamed Oslo.

1926 Norwegian explorer Roald Amundsen dies while attempting to rescue Italian explorer Nobile, whose airship had crashed in the Arctic.

1926 The republic of Lebanon is proclaimed.

1929 The Vatican State is born.

1925 The increasing popularity of art deco is reflected in the Exposition des Arts Decoratifs in Paris.

1925 Franz Kafka's *The Trial* is published posthumously.

1925 The first surrealist exhibition opens in Paris.

1926 T. E. Lawrence publishes *The Seven Pillars of Wisdom*.

1926 A. A. Milne publishes *Winnie the Pooh*.

1927 Virginia Woolf publishes *To the Lighthouse*.

MIDDLE EAST & AFRICA

1925 Ibn Saud of Najd conquers Hijaz and forms Saudi Arabia.

1928 Italy signs a 20-years treaty of friendship with Ethiopia.

1928 Britain recognizes Transjordan's independence.

1928 Wahabi tribesmen from Saudi Arabia launch attacks aimed at Kuwait and the Iraqi frontier, and are strafed by British planes.

1928 King Fuad makes himself dictator of Egypt after dismissing the prime minister.

1929 The Ibo Women's War mobilizes resistance to British colonial rule.

1925 Marshes around Haifa, Israel, begin to be drained in the fight against malaria.

1928 The Muslim Brotherhood is founded.

ASIA & OCEANIA

1926 A northern expedition is begun by nationalists in an effort to reunify China.

1926 Nationalists on Java start a rebellion against Dutch rule.

1926 Hirohito takes over the Japanese throne upon the death of his father, Hoshihito.

1927 Mao Zedong's autumn harvest uprising is defeated, but Mao begins to see potential for peasant revolution in China.

1928 Nationalists take Beijing, having set up a government in Nanjing.

1929 The All-India Congress claims independence.

Official portrait of Emperor Hirohito in his kimono coronation robe

SCIENCE & TECHNOLOGY	PEOPLE & SOCIETY
1926 Electrola, a new electric recording process, is developed.	**1925 The first motel** in the U.S. opens its doors in San Luis Obispo, California.
1927 The Iron Lung is developed by P. Drinker and L.A. Shaw.	**1927 Charles A. Lindbergh** flies the Spirit of St. Louis nonstop from New York to Paris.
1928 The first color motion pictures are exhibited by George Eastman in Rochester, New York.	**1928 Brazil's economy** collapses due to over-production of coffee.
1929 The "talkies" kill silent films.	**1929 Black Tuesday** in New York signals the beginning of a worldwide economic crisis and the beginning of the Great Depression, when the U.S. Stock Exchange collapses, losing $26 billion in value.
1929 Construction starts on the Empire State Building in New York City.	**1929 Frida Kahlo** of Mexico turns to painting after a crippling car accident.
1925 The Pasteur Institute in Paris announces the discovery of an anti-tetanus serum.	**1926 Lufthansa Airline** is founded.
1925 Rome's first subway opens.	**1927 The economic system of Germany** collapses on Black Friday. By 1929 three million Germans are out of work.
1927 I. P. Pavlov publishes *Conditioned Reflexes*.	**1927 Marcel Proust's** *In Search of Lost Time* is published posthumously.
1928 Hans Geiger and Walther Mueller construct the improved Geiger counter.	**1928 Women's voting age in Britain** is reduced from 30 to 21.
1928 Alexander Fleming discovers penicillin.	**1929 Aletta Jacobs**, a Dutch suffragist leader, is the first woman physician to practice in Holland.
1929 The Graf Zeppelin airship circumnavigates the world in 20 days, 4 hours, 14 minutes.	**1929 The Jewish Agency** becomes representative of all Zionist and non-Zionist Jews.
1925 Power plants are constructed in Palestine; a hydroelectric station is built on the Jordan River; telephone and electric lines are installed.	**1925 Afrikaans** becomes the official language of the Union of South Africa. A new law further excludes peoples of mixed race, Blacks, and Indians from skilled jobs.
1926 The North-African star movement organizes North African workers in France to participate in French industrial expansion.	**1925-26 Attaturk** secularizes the Turkish State. Reforms include the abolition of polygamy, prohibition of the fez, modernization of female attire, and the adoption of the Latin alphabet.
	1927 Iraq's first oil strike occurs at Kirkuk.
	1929 As a result of continued fighting among Arabs and Jews, the British declare martial law in Jerusalem.
1926 The first flight from London to Delhi takes place.	**1925 Japan** introduces general suffrage for men.
	1926 Indian women are allowed to run for public office.
	1926 Hindu-Muslim riots break out in Calcutta.
	1927 The Shanghai Massacre occurs when nationalist troops betray their communist Allies and slaughter them.

BLACK TUESDAY ON WALL STREET

Wall Street big shots were reveling in the glory of a surging bull market. As stock prices climbed higher and higher in 1927 and 1928, investors bought wildly, many using borrowed money. By September 1929 the world of finance had lent 8.5 billion dollars for such margin trades. Warning signs were overlooked, such as falling car sales and layoffs in automobile plants. Peaking in early September, the market bubble finally burst October 24, on what became known as Black Thursday, the first of several consecutive black days on Wall Street.

Although prices rallied briefly, by October 25, aka Black Friday, people had heard the bad news and started to panic. On Monday prices went into a free fall, and on Black Tuesday, a record number of shares were sold. In less than a week stocks lost a quarter of their value. Numerous margin buyers went bust, as their shares of stock were no longer valuable enough to allow them to repay the money they had borrowed to buy them.

Some who were completely ruined jumped from office windows to their deaths or otherwise committed suicide. Not just stockholders, but the entire American economy felt the force of the crash. Soon, the whole country entered the Great Depression, a period of severe economic hardship that was to last throughout the 1930s, with repercussions felt worldwide.

For the next decade Americans suffered massive unemployment, food shortages for millions, and numerous business foreclosures. President Franklin Roosevelt's New Deal enterprises such as the Works Progress Administration (WPA) and the Civilian Conservation Corps (CCC) provided jobs, but it was not until the early 1940s, when the government began to spend heavily on defense, that the Depression finally come to an end.

POLITICS & POWER	GEOGRAPHY & ENVIRONMENT	CULTURE & RELIGION

THE AMERICAS

1930 Revolutions in Argentina and Brazil bring José Uriburu and Getulio Vargas to power.

1930 The Smoot-Hawley Tariff Act is signed by U.S. President Hoover. It is blamed for worsening the Depression.

1933 Fulgencio Batista y Zaldívar begins a dictatorship in Cuba.

1933 Franklin Delano Roosevelt announces his Good Neighbor Policy to keep private U.S. companies from intervening in Central America and the Caribbean.

Construction workers relax on a steel beam 800 feet above ground at the building site of the RCA Building in Rockefeller Center. This was one of many skyscrapers being built in New York City at this time.

1930 Dashiell Hammett publishes *The Maltese Falcon*.

1930 Carlos Gardel becomes a popular Latin American musician, creating a love of tango.

1930 Grant Wood paints *American Gothic*.

1931 The Jehovah's Witnesses are formed.

1932 Alexander Calder exhibits "stabiles" and "mobiles," sculptures moved by air currents.

EUROPE

1930 The last Allied troops leave the Rhineland.

1930 The Nazis gain 107 seats from the center parties in the German elections.

1930 France starts building the Maginot Line of defenses along its border with Germany.

1932 The second Five-Year Plan starts in the U.S.S.R.

1933 Adolf Hitler is appointed German Chancellor; later the same year he is granted dictatorial powers.

1934 Hitler and Mussolini meet in Venice.

1931 The northern face of the Matterhorn in Switzerland is climbed for the first time by Toni and Franz Schmid.

1932 Famine spreads in the U.S.S.R., reaching disastrous proportions.

1931 Salvador Dalí paints *Persistence of Memory*.

1932 Aldous Huxley publishes *Brave New World*.

1933 All books written by non-Nazi and Jewish authors are burned in Germany.

1933 Carl Jung publishes *Psychology and Religion*.

1933 Leon Trotsky publishes *History of the Russian Revolution*.

1933 In Germany, modernism in art is suppressed in favor of superficial realism.

MIDDLE EAST & AFRICA

1930 British battleships head toward Egypt to quell anti-British and nationalist riots.

1930 Ras Tafari becomes Emperor Haile Selassie in Ethiopia.

1933 After the death of his father, King Faisal, Ghazi I becomes king of Iraq.

1933 Britain recognizes Iraqi independence.

1934 Saudi Arabia signs a truce with Yemen.

1936 The Egyptian constitution is restored; Egypt signs the Anglo-Egyptian treaty granting 20-year military alliance.

1930 A palace dating from 550 B.C.E. is discovered at the site of the city of Ur in ancient Sumer.

1934 The imam of North Yemen accepts the southern boundary with Aden, and thus the division of Yemen.

1930 The number of schools in Turkey doubles and the literacy rate more than doubles.

1931 Farhat Abbas publishes a program for full assimilation of Algerian Muslims with conversion. The Arabization movement begins.

1931 Taha Hussain, a radical Egyptian thinker, loses his university position.

1933 Ottoman University becomes Istanbul University and gains an influx of German refugee professors.

1933 Assyrian Christians are massacred in Iraq.

ASIA & OCEANIA

1930 Japanese Premier Hamaguchi is assassinated.

1931 Mao Zedong is named chairman of the central executive committee of the new Chinese Soviet Republic.

1931 Japan invades Manchuria.

1932 The Siamese army takes power in a coup against the monarchy.

1933 Zahir Shah becomes king of Afghanistan after his father's assassination.

1934 The Red Army begins the Long March, their strategic retreat to China's northwest.

1931 Australian explorer G. H. Wilkins captains the *Nautilus* submarine, taking it under the Arctic Ocean.

1934 The first Pakistani Nanga Parbat expedition fails to reach the summit.

1934 A dam bursts on the Yangtze River during a typhoon, killing hundreds of people in China.

1932 The Poona Pact is signed, giving the untouchables voting rights in India.

1934 Hu Shih publishes *Chinese Renaissance*.

SCIENCE & TECHNOLOGY	PEOPLE & SOCIETY
1930 The planet Pluto is discovered by astronomer Clyde Tombaugh.	**1930 Some 30,000 Filipinos** join California's workforce.
1930 Herbert Hoover opens the 1,245-foot, 120-floor Empire State Building.	**1930 The first World Cup Tournament** of the national soccer federations is played in Uruguay.
1931 Julius A. Nieuwland discovers a process for producing neoprene, a synthetic rubber.	**1931 Chicago gangster Al Capone** is jailed for income tax evasion.
1932 The balloon tire is first produced for farm tractors.	**1932 Roosevelt** uses the expression "New Deal" for the first time in a speech accepting the Democratic nomination for president.
1932 Work begins on the San Francisco-Oakland Bay Bridge (Golden Gate Bridge).	**1933 Prohibition** is repealed in the U.S.
1933 A refrigeration process for meat cargoes is used.	**1934 Canada** establishes a Central Bank.
1930 Walter Reppe makes artificial fabrics from an acetylene base.	**1931 All German banks** close when the German Danatbank goes bankrupt.
1932 The Nobel Prize for Physics goes to Werner Heisenberg for the creation of the matrix theory of quantum mechanics.	**1933 Boycotts of Jews** start in Germany.
1932 The Zuider Zee drainage project, begun in 1906, is completed in Holland.	**1933 Approximately 60,000 people in the arts** emigrate from Germany between now and 1939.
1933 New Nazi regulations hamper German scientific research.	**1933 The first concentration camps** are erected by the Nazis in Germany.
1934 Enrico Fermi proposes that neutrons and protons are the same fundamental particles in two different quantum states.	**1934 Hitler promotes a blood bath** in Germany by purging the Fascist party in the "night of the long knives."
1930 South African microbiologist Max Theiler develops a yellow fever vaccine.	**1933 Turkey's first Five-Year Plan** aims at developing chemical and textile industries and banks.
1930 Iranian tribes are pacified and a road network is extended. The Trans-Iranian railroad is built uniting northern and southern Iran.	**1934 Turkish women** get the vote.
1931 Benguella-Katanga, the first trans-African railroad line, is completed.	
1930 The Nobel Prize goes to Indian Sir C. Raman for his work on light diffusion.	**1930 Gandhi** demands Indian independence.
1930 Two halves of the new Sydney Harbor bridge are joined in Australia.	**1932 Japan** begins its conquest of world markets by undercutting prices.

Adolf Hitler raises a defiant, clenched fist during one of his haranguing speeches.

HITLER'S RISE TO POWER

Adolf Hitler's rise from undistinguished World War I veteran to chancellor and president of the German Nazi Party was unlikely indeed. Fanatical in his views concerning Jews and Marxists, he succeeded by 1921 in becoming chairman of the National Socialist German Workers', or Nazi Party, molding the group into a paramilitary group of storm troopers with the support of powerful men like Field Marshal Ludendorff.

Hitler's 1923 coup attempt, the Beer Hall Putsch, failed, but it made him famous throughout Germany. His brief imprisonment also gave him time to write *Mein Kampf*, which in time became the Nazi bible. With the backing of Paul Goebbels and Hermann Goering, the Nazis began to grow. Delivering frenzied hours-long harangues to large crowds, Hitler promised the economically depressed that he would despoil "Jew financiers" and restore security.

In 1933, after the Nazis became the largest party in the Reichstag, Hitler took advantage of government upheaval to make his move. Paul von Hindenburg appointed Hitler as chancellor, and by that summer, his takeover was complete.

POLITICS & POWER	GEOGRAPHY & ENVIRONMENT	CULTURE & RELIGION

THE AMERICAS

1935 President Roosevelt signs the U.S. Social Security Act.

1936 Paraguay installs the Americas' first fascist regime.

1938 Mexican President Lazaro Cardenes nationalizes private oil company properties of British and U.S. businessmen.

1939 Roosevelt demands assurance from Mussolini and Hitler that they will not attack 31 named states.

1939 Roosevelt announces the Neutrality Bill, which will permit Britain and France to purchase arms from the U.S.

1935 A series of dust storms roars over the U.S. plains. The most severe occurs on April 14, dumping tons of dust on each acre in western Kansas.

1936 Floods wash through Johnstown, Pennsylvania.

1936 Lake Mead, the largest reservoir in the world, is created by the completion of Boulder (Hoover) Dam.

1935 George Gershwin presents *Porgy and Bess*, an opera, in New York.

1936 Dale Carnegie publishes *How to Win Friends and Influence People*.

1936 Margaret Mitchell publishes *Gone with the Wind*.

1936 The Baseball Hall of Fame is founded at Cooperstown, New York.

1939 John Steinbeck publishes *The Grapes of Wrath*.

1939 Grandma Moses (Anna M. Robertson) is a popular artist in the U.S.

EUROPE

1936 German troops occupy the Rhineland in defiance of the treaties of Locarno and Versailles.

1936-39 The Spanish Civil War is fought.

1938 British Prime Minister Chamberlain signs the Munich Pact, allowing Germany to occupy the Czech Sudetenland, and announces that he has secured "peace in our time."

1939 Germany invades Poland on September 1; Britain and France declare war on Germany on September 3. Soviet troops invade Poland.

1936 Germany starts building the Siegfried Line.

A squadron of German dive-bombing Stukas heads over Poland in tight formation.

1936 BBC London inaugurates television service.

1937 Pablo Picasso paints *Guernica*, a mural for the Paris World Exhibition.

1938 *Kristallnacht* (night of broken glass) occurs in Germany. Nazis vandalize Jewish homes, synagogues, and stores, breaking many windows. Jews are arrested and beaten; 35 are killed.

1939 Adolf Hitler's *Mein Kampf* is translated into English.

MIDDLE EAST & AFRICA

1936 The Great Revolt of the Palestinians begins against Zionist settlement.

1936 The Native Representation Act keeps blacks out of office in South Africa.

1936 Addis Ababa, capital of Ethiopia, is seized by Italians.

1936 Upon King Fuad's death, 16-year-old Prince Farouk takes over Egypt.

1937 Iraq's dictator, General Bakr Sidki Pasha, is assassinated.

1935 Persia changes its name to Iran.

1939 An earthquake in Turkey kills 45,000.

1936 An Arab High Committee is formed to fight Jewish claims.

1936 Jews in Palestine begin inventing "overnight settlements" to evade restrictions on building.

1939 Algerian Muslims are denied French citizenship.

1937 The Royal Commission on Palestine recommends the establishment of Arab and Jewish states.

ASIA & OCEANIA

1935 Manuel Quezon becomes president of the Philippines.

1936 Chiang Kai-shek declares war on Japan.

1937 The Japanese seize Peking, Tientsin, Nanjing, Shanghai, and Hargchow.

1937 Under the Government of India Act, the Indian constitution is drawn up, and the All-India Congress Party wins elections.

1938 The Japanese enter Tsingtao, install a Chinese puppet government in Nanjing, withdraw from the League of Nations, and take Canton and Hankow.

1935 The Red Army ends the strategic Long March in Yanan, their wartime capital in the northwest.

1937 The Guomindang (Nationalist People's Party) government in Nanjing flees to its wartime capital of Chongqing, deep in southwestern China.

1935 An Anglo-Indian Trade Pact is signed.

1936 Shu She-yu writes *Lo-t'o Hsiang-tzu*, published in an unauthorized English translation in 1945 under the title *Rickshaw Boy*, which becomes a bestseller.

1937-38 Invading Japanese slaughter more than 300,000 Chinese civilians and POWs and rape an estimated 80,000 women during their occupation of Nanjing.

SCIENCE & TECHNOLOGY	PEOPLE & SOCIETY
1936 The Hoover Dam is completed.	**1935 Alcoholics Anonymous** is founded in New York City.
1937 Wallace H. Carothers patents nylon for the Du Pont Company in Delaware.	**1936 Jesse Owens** wins four gold medals at the Berlin Olympics.
1937 Frank Whittle builds the first jet engine.	**1937 Amelia Earhart** is lost on her Pacific flight.
1938 Albert Einstein and Leopold Infeld publish *The Evolution of Physics.*	**1938 The 40-hour workweek** is established in the U.S.
1939 Igor Sikorsky builds the first helicopter.	**1939 The U.S. economy** begins to recover after the recession of 1938 and profits from European countries' demand for war equipment and arms.
1939 Philip Levine and Rufus Stetson discover the Rh factor in human blood.	
1939 Nylon stockings first appear in the U.S.	
1935 Robert Watson-Watt of Scotland builds radar equipment to detect aircraft. In 1939 radar stations begin helping Britain detect the German Luftwaffe.	**1935 The Nazis** repudiate the Versailles Treaty and reintroduce compulsory military service.
1935 The Moscow subway is opened.	**1935 The Nuremberg Laws** go into effect, restricting Jewish rights in Germany.
1937 The dirigible *Hindenburg* bursts into flames while trying to dock at Lakehurst, New Jersey, after a much-anticipated transatlantic flight by one of the largest aircraft ever built.	**1936 German Max Schmeling** upsets American Joe Louis for the heavyweight boxing title.
1939 Frederic and Irene Joliot-Curie demonstrate the possibility of splitting the atom.	**1937 Albert Speer** becomes Hitler's chief architect.
1939 Balloons are utilized as barriers against air attacks in Britain.	**1937 The Duke of Windsor** marries Mrs. Wallis Simpson, an American socialite.
	1936 Palestine is the third largest exporter of citrus fruit in the world.

THE SINO-JAPANESE WAR

When the Treaty of Versailles in 1919 granted Germany's possessions in the Shandong Province to Japan, many Chinese felt this was the final blow to their wounded pride. Student protests roared through the cities, ending in a strike at Shanghai. Known as the May Fourth Movement, it marked a true cultural revolution inspired by nationalism and the desire to create a more modern society.

Following the Manchurian Incident of 1931, the Japanese Kwantung army occupied Manchuria and established the puppet state of Manchukuo, home to the last of the Chinese warlords. In 1936 Chiang Kai-shek, Nationalist leader of China, was kidnapped by the warlord, Zhang Xueliang, and pressed to agree to a united anti-Japanese front with the Communists. In 1937, after Chiang's release, the Japanese used a confrontation at the Marco Polo Bridge to occupy Beijing and Tianjin.

Japanese troops eventually moved on the Nationalist capital of Nanjing. On December 13, 1937, they launched a horrific rampage that has come to be known as the Rape of Nanjing. Chiang Kai-shek's army, plus millions of peasants trekked westward in an epic retreat that would go down as one of history's most torturous experiences.

For the next seven years fighting continued, further weakening the Nationalist army. After Pearl Harbor, the Sino-Japanese War became a part of World War II. China declared war on Japan, Germany, and Italy, and warred on against the Japanese. The Japanese surrender in 1945 was bittersweet for the battered Nationalists. A growing Communist Party would soon have complete control of the mainland, and Chiang Kai-shek would set up a Nationalist government-in-exile on the island of Taiwan.

An injured baby squalls amid the wreckage of Shanghai's South Station after a Japanese bombing attack.

	POLITICS & POWER	GEOGRAPHY & ENVIRONMENT	CULTURE & RELIGION
THE AMERICAS	**Trotsky** is assassinated in Mexico on Stalin's orders. **Congress** passes the Selective Service Act to mobilize U.S. military. **The Lend-Lease Act** goes into effect in the U.S., which offers aid to "any country whose defense the president deems vital to the defense of the United States." **President Franklin D. Roosevelt** is elected to an unprecedented third term. **Canada** institutes a National Unemployment Insurance Program, to which employees and workers contribute.	**"Galloping Gertie,"** a suspension bridge over the narrows of Puget Sound in Tacoma, Washington, breaks up in the wind and drops almost 200 feet.	**Ernest Hemingway** publishes *For Whom the Bell Tolls*. **Raymond Chandler** publishes *Farewell, My Lovely*. **Thomas Wolfe** writes *You Can't Go Home Again*, which is published posthumously. **Carl Sandburg** publishes *Abraham Lincoln: The War Years*. **Edmund Wilson** publishes *To the Finland Station*.
EUROPE	**April 9 Germans** begin a full-scale invasion of Norway; Denmark has already been overrun. **May 26 The Battle of Dunkirk** takes place; Hitler fails to halt the evacuation of Allied forces from the French port. **June 10 Italy** declares war on Britain and France. **June 14 German troops** enter Paris. **July 21 German-occupied Lithuania,** Latvia, and Estonia vote to become part of the U.S.S.R. **September 7 Hitler's blitz** of London begins.	**The Lascaux caves** are discovered in France. On their walls are prehistoric paintings dating to approximately 20,000 B.C.E.	**November 15 In Warsaw, Poland, 350,000 Jews** are confined to a ghetto. **J. M. Keynes** publishes *How to Pay for the War*. **Carl Jung** publishes *The Interpretation of Personality*. **Wassily Kandinsky** paints *Sky Blue*. **Arthur Koestler** publishes *Darkness at Noon*.
MIDDLE EAST & AFRICA	**July 3 The Royal Navy** destroys much of the French fleet off Algeria to prevent its falling into German hands. **December 9 British troops** launch an attack on Italians in the Western Desert. **The British Eighth Army** under Wavell opens an offensive in North Africa. **The Royal Navy** wrecks most of the French fleet at Algeria to keep it out of German control. **Syria** becomes part of Vichy France. **Italians** bomb Palestine.		**The Nationalist Islamic Party** is founded in Egypt. *German infantry dash through a Norwegian town in the spring of 1940.*
ASIA & OCEANIA	**Japan, Germany, and Italy** sign a military and economic pact. **The new five-year-old Dalai Lama** is enthroned in Tibet.	**Britain** reopens the Burma Road.	

SCIENCE & TECHNOLOGY

A huge cyclotron is built at the University of California to produce neutrons from atomic nuclei.

The first electron microscope is demonstrated by the Radio Corporation of America (RCA) in Camden, New Jersey.

The first successful helicopter flight is made in the U.S. by the Vought-Sikorsky Corporation.

Edward McMillan and Philip Abelson discover neptunium, the first transuranic element.

The British Scientific Advisory Committee is appointed.

Howard Florey develops penicillin for clinical use.

PEOPLE & SOCIETY

Edward R. Murrow broadcasts from London during the German blitz. He reports to Americans how much suffering the German bombings are inflicting on the British people.

March 27 Heinrich Himmler starts construction of a concentration camp at Auschwitz, near Krakow, Poland.

December 29 The *Luftwaffe* razes a third of London in the biggest air raid of the war.

Coventry Cathedral in England is devastated during the worst air raid of the war and becomes a symbol for all the British sacrifices in World War Two.

Winston Churchill visits Coventry Cathedral after the blitz in 1940.

THE BATTLE OF BRITAIN

By the summer of 1940, after Hitler's success on the Continent, he turned his attention to his biggest enemy, Great Britain. As a prelude to a planned invasion, the Nazi leader turned to one of his major assets—the mighty Luftwaffe. Knowing that the Royal Air Force (RAF) was much smaller, Hitler was confident his bombers could overwhelm the British with brute force, knocking out coastal defenses and shipping and eventually giving the Germans air control over the whole of southern England.

When this initial mission failed to destroy the RAF, the Nazis launched a nighttime bombing campaign, or blitz, of London. From September 7 through October of 1940, the Germans raided English cities as well as coastal installations. But the British, united under new Prime Minister Winston Churchill to defend their country at all costs, refused to cave, even as their cities continued to be pounded into the winter. Radar systems, in use for the first time, helped the British prepare for attacks, and the outmanned RAF fought bravely against Hitler's air force.

Gradually, realizing that their efforts to quash the RAF were in vain, the Germans gave up any hopes of invading the country. The Battle of Britain, as the various air battles were called, was the first major failure of the war for Germany. They lost about 2,300 aircraft, while the British lost some 900. And although thousands of civilians were killed, the British would fight on, determined that there would be many more losses to come for the dictator who had severely underestimated their resolve.

We will fight on the beaches, we will fight on the landing grounds, we shall fight in the fields and in the streets, we shall fight in the hills; we shall never surrender.

WINSTON CHURCHILL

POLITICS & POWER	GEOGRAPHY & ENVIRONMENT	CULTURE & RELIGION

THE AMERICAS

December 7 The Japanese bomb the American base at Pearl Harbor in Hawaii.

December 8 The U.S. declares war on Japan. Representative Jeannette Rankin casts the only dissenting vote in Congress to the declaration.

The Office of the Coordinator of Information opens, shortly to be renamed the Office of Strategic Services (OSS).

The U.S. government pours money into the West to build defense installations. Industrial plants begin to dot the Western landscape.

Edward Hopper paints *Nighthawks*.

Among the leading films are Orson Welles's *Citizen Kane* and John Ford's *How Green Was My Valley*.

Popular songs include "Bewitched, Bothered, and Bewildered" and "Chattanooga Choo-Choo."

EUROPE

April 13 Joseph Stalin signs a neutrality pact with Japan.

April 26 The Germans march into Athens.

June 22 Germany invades the U.S.S.R.

July 13 Britain and the U.S.S.R. agree to a mutual assistance pact.

October 2 The Soviet army starts a counterattack in Leningrad as winter begins.

December 8 Britain declares war on Finland, Hungary and Rumania.

December 11 Hitler and Mussolini declare war on the U.S.

Noel Coward writes *Blithe Spirit*.

William L. Shirer publishes *Berlin Diary*.

John Masefield publishes *The Nine Days Wonder* (about the Battle of Dunkirk).

Reinhold Niebuhr publishes *The Nature and Destiny of Man*.

Dmitri Shostakovich composes Symphony No. 7, during the siege of Leningrad.

MIDDLE EAST & AFRICA

February 14 Erwin Rommel's Afrika Korps arrives in Tripoli, North Africa.

March 6 Haile Selassie's troops capture the Italian stronghold of Burye, Ethiopia.

May 20 Italian East Africa surrenders to the British at Addis Ababa.

June 21 British imperial forces take Damascus.

September 19 British and Soviet troops enter Tehran, Iran.

Rommel retreats in North Africa.

Serbian victims in the Backa region of Yugoslavia, having been hanged by Hungarians

Turkey closes straits to ships of all nations.

June A pro-German coup in Iraq leads to massacres of Jews after the British-Jewish attack on Baghdad.

ASIA & OCEANIA

July 27 Japanese troops move into Cambodia and Thailand; Saigon falls in Vietnam.

October 17 Fumimaro Konoye, the Japanese prime minister, and his cabinet resign; General Tojo, a pro-Axis war minister, is appointed.

December 7 The Japanese launch an attack on the American base at Pearl Harbor in Hawaii.

December 25 Hong Kong surrenders to Japan.

SCIENCE & TECHNOLOGY

Whitfield and Dickson invent Dacron.

Donald Bailey invents the portable military bridge.

Atomic research begins on the Manhattan Project.

The Grand Coulee Dam in Washington State begins operation.

The Rainbow Bridge over Niagara Falls, New York, opens.

Edward McMillan and Glenn T. Seaborg discover plutonium.

Han Haas starts underwater photography.

Ferry command aircraft crosses the Atlantic from the West in eight hours and 23 minutes.

German Rudolf Hess lands in Scotland in an unsuccessful attempt to negotiate peace.

By year's end 951 U.S.-made tanks have been shipped to England; food shipment reaches one million tons.

British heroine Amy Johnson dies when her plane ditches in the Thames estuary.

PEOPLE & SOCIETY

The U.S. joins others using the letter "V" to signify support of allied efforts. Pins, buttons, clothing, hand signaling and music, to name a few, incorporate this victory symbol.

The Air Training Corps is established in Britain.

The fighter aircraft are in use.

The Shetland Bus, under the guise of Britain's Special Operations Executive (SOE), begins covertly shipping agents and weapons from the Scottish Island to resistance fighters in Norway.

The view from Hickam Field as the Japanese bomb Pearl Harbor

PEARL HARBOR

Sunday, December 7, 1941, an unforgettable date in the memory of U.S. citizens, began as a glorious morning, a supposed day of rest and relaxation for Naval personnel. Based on Oahu, the Pacific Fleet was unaware of what was soon to befall them. At 7:55 a.m. local time, Japanese carrier planes zoomed in without warning and attacked the bulk of the U.S. Pacific fleet, moored helplessly in the harbor. Nineteen naval vessels, including eight battleships, were sunk or damaged; 188 U.S. aircraft were destroyed. Military casualties mounted to 2,280 killed and 1,109 wounded. Sixty-eight civilians also lost their lives.

President Franklin Delano Roosevelt, after hearing the news, said to a shocked country that it would be "a day which will live in infamy." Ironically, at the time of the bombing, Japanese diplomats were meeting in Washington to negotiate. Americans watched through locked gates at the Japanese Embassy as officials burned piles of U.S. papers describing the attack.

The next day the United States declared war on Japan, and Americans rallied whole-heartedly behind the cause. The Pacific Fleet quickly regrouped, aided by aircraft carriers that were at sea when the attack occurred, and the distressed country joined the rest of the world in World War II.

*My spine tingled when I saw billowing black smoke. . . .
I looked way up and saw the formations of silver bombers riding in. Something detached itself from an airplane and came glistening down. My eyes followed it down, down and even with knowledge pounding in my mind, my heart turned convulsively when the bomb exploded in the middle of the harbor.*

CORNELIA CLARK FORT, FLIGHT INSTRUCTOR FLYING NEAR PEARL HARBOR, DECEMBER 7, 1941

POLITICS & POWER	GEOGRAPHY & ENVIRONMENT	CULTURE & RELIGION

THE AMERICAS

June 1 Mexico declares war on the Axis powers.

June 25 Major General Dwight Eisenhower receives command of all U.S. forces in Europe.

August 22 Brazil declares war on Germany and Italy.

Military bases are set up throughout the U.S. Some 60,000 civilian workers are recruited.

More than 100,000 Japanese Americans are transferred from the West Coast to inland camps.

WHAT LIFE WAS LIKE

Japanese Internment in the U.S.

On February 19, 1942, with fear and suspicion of the Japanese growing since the attack on Pearl Harbor, President Roosevelt ordered the forced evacuation of 120,000 people of Japanese descent, 77,000 of whom were U.S. citizens. Given just days to dispose of their homes, possessions, and businesses, they were transported under military guard by train to internment camps, often remote desert camps enclosed with barbed wire. Families lived in a small room furnished only with cots and a pot-bellied stove. In 1943 the U.S. Army began to accept Japanese-American recruits, even while maintaining the internment camps. The internees were finally released in 1944, and in 1990 the U.S. government began paying $1.25 billion in reparations for this shameful incarceration.

Thornton Wilder publishes *The Skin of Our Teeth*.

Among leading films are Disney's *Bambi* and *Holiday Inn*, starring Bing Crosby.

Navajo Indian soldiers use their language to code talk to one another in the Pacific, to ensure that the Japanese do not intercept important messages.

Langston Hughes, a central figure in the former Harlem renaissance, publishes *Shakespeare in Harlem*.

EUROPE

February 1 Vidkun Quisling is appointed puppet prime minister in Norway by the Germans.

March 28 The RAF begins a round-the-clock offensive on German munitions factories.

May 31 Czech partisans assassinate Gestapo leader Reinhard Heydrich.

June 29 Germans launch an offensive at Kursk, then advance on Stalingrad.

November 11 The Axis invade Vichy France.

November 26 Soviet troops break through German lines in Stalingrad.

The Mildenhall Treasure, a hoard of Roman silverware, is discovered in Suffolk, England.

Jean-Paul Sartre publishes *Les Mouches*.

Albert Camus publishes *L'Étranger*.

T. S. Eliot publishes *Four Quartets*.

G. M. Trevelyan publishes *English Social History*.

Pierre Bonnard paints *L'Oiseau Bleu*.

Benjamin Britten composes *Sinfonia da Requiem*.

Richard Strauss presents *Capriccio*, an opera, in Munich.

MIDDLE EAST & AFRICA

May 27 Rommel's panzer divisions launch an offensive in the Libyan Desert. Tobruk falls and 25,000 Allied soldiers become POWs.

August 30 Rommel starts a new offensive in Egypt.

October 30 British General Bernard Montgomery wins a key victory at El Alamein.

November 7 Allied troops land in Vichy-French North Africa. Rommel retreats into Libya.

Four hundred thousand American troops land in French North Africa.

Field Marshal Erwin Rommel, the "Desert Fox," commander of German forces in North Africa

ASIA & OCEANIA

January 2 Japanese troops take Manila in the Philippines.

April 18 U.S. planes bomb Tokyo, led by Major General Jimmy Doolittle.

June 7 The Japanese withdraw after heavy fighting around Midway Island.

August 7 U.S. Marines land in the Solomon Islands.

September 27 The Japanese pull back in New Guinea in the face of advancing Allies.

Americans win the Battle of the Coral Sea.

SCIENCE & TECHNOLOGY	PEOPLE & SOCIETY
Enrico Fermi splits the atom.	**U.S. automakers** are ordered to stop production, and tire and gas rationing are introduced.
Bell Aircraft tests the first U.S. jet airplane.	
The first electronic brain (automatic computer) is developed in the U.S.	**Five Sullivan brothers** serving in the U.S. Navy on the U.S.S. *Juneau* are killed when their ship is sunk. Their remaining sibling joins the WAVES after getting the news.
Industrialist Henry J. Kaiser develops techniques for building a 10,000-ton Liberty Ship in four days.	**More than 13,000 volunteers** sign up for the U.S. Women's Army Auxiliary Corps. (WAACS) on May 27. By year's end more than 300,000 women will serve in all arms of the military.
Max Muller of Junkers develops a successful turbo-prop engine.	**January 20 Reinhard Heydrich** reveals to German top officials his "final solution" to exterminate the 11 million Jews in Europe.
Cryptanalysts at Bletchley Park, the British government code and cypher school, number some 7,000 people.	**March 26 Nazis** start the deportation of Jews to the Auschwitz concentration camp.
	September 2 German SS troops "clean" the Jewish ghetto of 50,000 people.
	Gilbert Murray founds Oxfam.
	The wartime National Loaf is introduced in Britain, bread made with more grain to compensate for sugar rationing.
Robertsfield Airport is built in Liberia for refueling B-47 bombers; it remains the longest runway in Africa.	**African troops** from the Gold Coast and Kenya fight in Burma against the Japanese.
	Jewish women in Palestine join the Territorial Defense Service.
	January 15 Gandhi appoints Jawaharlal Nehru as his successor.
	March 29 The British present a plan for Indian independence after the war's end.
	August 9 Gandhi and other All-India Congress Party leaders are arrested.
	The Bataan Death March takes place in the Philippines after the Japanese occupy Bataan and force-march American and Philippine prisoners to a POW camp. Many die.

THE SIEGE OF STALINGRAD

Hitler's plan for the summer of 1942 was to capture Sevastapol on the Black Sea and press southward through the Caucasus to meet up with Field Marshal Erwin Rommel, who was advancing across North Africa toward Egypt with the intention of subduing the Middle East, granting Hitler control of its oil supplies. Almost as a second thought Hitler decided that the heavily defended city of Stalingrad might need to be subdued, in order to preempt a Soviet counterattack.

German forces took Savastapol but were stalled by rough terrain and fuel shortages in the Caucasus when Hitler's fateful Stalingrad notion took hold. He ordered Friedrich Paulus's Sixth Army to attack, and the siege of Stalingrad was on, with German troops ordered to hold their ground even as their losses mounted and their position weakened.

In November the Soviets counterattacked, encircling more than 250,000 German troops. The man-to-man fighting was vicious. By January the starving survivors were ready to surrender, and Hitler knew that he had sacrificed an entire army to the Allies. Some 300,000 Germans died in the fighting. Of the almost 100,000 Germans taken prisoner, only 5,000 returned home.

Here I am still in one piece, with a fairly normal pulse, a dozen cigarettes. Had soup day before yesterday, liberated a canned ham today from a supply canister. Am squatting in a cellar burning up furniture, twenty-six years old and otherwise no fool, one of those who was mighty keen on getting his bars and yelling, 'Heil Hitler' with the rest of you, and now it's either die like a dog or off to Siberia.

GERMAN SOLDIER'S LETTER HOME
TOWARD THE END OF THE SIEGE

POLITICS & POWER	GEOGRAPHY & ENVIRONMENT	CULTURE & RELIGION

THE AMERICAS

June 5 A military junta in Argentina is formed under President Arturo Rawson after he overthrows President Ramón Castillo. The new labor minister is Juan Perón.

The U.S. recaptures the Aleutian Islands.

The Quebec Conference takes place with British Prime Minister Winston Churchill, U.S. President Franklin Roosevelt, and Canadian Prime Minister Mackenzie King.

A pay-as-you-go income tax system is instituted in the U.S.

More than 20 million victory gardens are producing 40 percent of all vegetables in U.S.

Betty Smith publishes *A Tree Grows in Brooklyn*.

Ted Lawson publishes *Thirty Seconds Over Tokyo*.

The first All-American Girl's Professional Baseball League begins.

Jackson Pollock has his first one-man show.

Rodgers and Hammerstein present the musical *Oklahoma!* in New York.

WHAT LIFE WAS LIKE

The Warsaw Ghetto Uprising

From the time Germans invaded and occupied Poland at the beginning of the war, Jews were herded into ghettos in Warsaw, Krakow, Lodz, and Lvov and subjected to systematic humiliation and death. After thousands had starved, the half-million Jews left in the Warsaw ghetto mounted a heroic uprising in February of 1943. Germans killed some 7,000 Jews during the fighting, which continued street by street for several months. At the end about 70 Jewish fighters had escaped through the sewers. But more than 50,000 others were transported to work camps, or even worse, to the death camps at Treblinka or Majdanek. By the time of the Allied liberation there were scarcely 200 Jews left in the entire Warsaw ghetto.

EUROPE

January 18 The Soviets break the 16-month siege of Leningrad.

January 31 The Germans surrender Stalingrad.

July 13 Germany loses the mightiest tank battle in history to the Russians near Kursk.

July 25 Mussolini falls from power.

August 17 Sicily is under Allied control.

October 13 Italy declares war on Germany.

June 19 Joseph Goebbels declares Berlin "free of Jews."

The Keynes Plan for postwar economic recovery is published.

Piet Mondrian paints *Broadway Boogie-Woogie*.

Marc Chagall paints *The Juggler*.

Francis Poulenc composes *Les Animaux Modeles*, a ballet.

Arnold Schoenberg composes *Ode to Napoleon*.

MIDDLE EAST & AFRICA

January 14 Roosevelt and Churchill meet in Casablanca to orchestrate a strategy for ending the war.

January 23 The Allies seize Tripoli, Italy's last stronghold in North Africa.

April 14 Rommel evacuates his troops from Tunis. The Allies enter soon after.

November 21 The French free the Lebanese government in Beirut and reinstate the president.

November 22 Chiang Kai-shek meets with Roosevelt in Cairo and agrees to liberate Korea when the Japanese are defeated.

ASIA & OCEANIA

January 16 The Xinjiang province is reincorporated in China.

February 2 The Japanese begin a final effort to regain control of the Solomon Islands.

February 9 The U.S. navy secretary reports that Japanese resistance on Guadalcanal in the Solomon Islands has ended.

A 22-ship Japanese convoy is sunk in the Battle of the Bismarck Sea by U.S. planes.

The U.S. forces land in New Guinea.

Famine spreads throughout Bengal in India.

SCIENCE & TECHNOLOGY	PEOPLE & SOCIETY
Waksman and Schatz discover streptomycin, an antibiotic used to treat infection.	**An infantile paralysis epidemic** kills almost 1,200 in U.S. and cripples thousands more.
Penicillin is successfully used in the treatment of chronic diseases.	**Shoe rationing** begins in the U.S., followed by rationing of meat, cheese, fats, and all canned food.
A 1,300-mile-long oil pipeline from Texas to Pennsylvania starts operating.	**California whites** attack Hispanic communities.
Otto Stern wins the Nobel Prize for his discoveries in molecular beam theory and proton movement.	**California shipyards** rely on 280,000 workers to meet the huge federal orders for ships.
	Aircraft manufacturers in southern California recruit 243,000 workers to build planes for the war.

Polish concentration camp inmates are being used for medical experiments.	**January 28 Hitler** orders the mobilization of the entire population from ages 16 to 65.
Henrik Dam (Denmark) and E. A. Doisy (U.S.) win the Nobel Prize for the discovery and analysis of vitamin K.	**April 26 The unearthing of a mass grave** of 4,000 Polish officers in the Katyn forest of Poland causes diplomatic friction. Germany accuses Russia of the murders.
	June 1 French resistance fighter Jean Moulin is arrested by Gestapo Chief Klaus Barbie.
Lieutenant Walter Chewning climbs to the cockpit of an F6F Hellcat that has crash landed on the flight deck of the U.S.S. Enterprise *in November of 1943. The pilot, Ensign Byron Johnson, escaped with minor injuries.*	**The German government** calls up three million women between the ages of 17 and 45 for factory work.

THE ITALIAN CAMPAIGN

In July of 1943, with airborne troops preceding them by three hours, 3,000 Allied ships transporting 80,000 troops from North Africa landed on the beaches of Sicily in the first step of a major offensive to wrest Italy from the hands of Mussolini. Planning the campaign had not been easy. U.S. Army Chief George Marshall had wanted to ignore Italy and focus on the quickest route to Germany via France. Churchill, however, had convinced Roosevelt that more planning time was needed for such a huge conquest. If all went well in Sicily, the Allies there could then create a major diversion on the mainland, drawing German troops away from France to defend Italy.

Sicily's hilly and rugged terrain made hard fighting against the Germans, which was relieved somewhat by the war weary Italian soldiers' lack of heart in battle. When Palermo fell to George Patton's Seventh Army on July 23, Mussolini was deposed and his successor surrendered to the Allies, which left Hitler on his own to defend Italy. In September, Allied forces landed at Naples, where they faced a grueling battle up the backbone of Italy. The Germans set up two lines of defense—the Gothic Line in the north and the Winter Line at Monte Cassino, just south of Rome. They also blew up communications and anything else the Allies might find usable.

Finally, in 1944, the Allies broke through the Winter Line and took Rome, shortly before D Day on June 6. The "major diversion" had succeeded, though at a terrific loss of life and limb in some of the bloodiest fighting of the war.

With railroads wrecked, bridges destroyed, and many sections of roads blown out, the advance was difficult enough even without opposition from the enemy.

GENERAL DWIGHT D. EISENHOWER

POLITICS & POWER	GEOGRAPHY & ENVIRONMENT	CULTURE & RELIGION

THE AMERICAS

The Dumbarton Oaks Conference takes place in Washington, D.C., to draft proposals for what will become the United Nations.

Franklin Roosevelt and Winston Churchill meet in Quebec.

William J.Donovan heads 13,000 employees at the Office of Strategic Services (OSS), which later becomes the Central Intelligence Agency (CIA).

Canada institutes the Family Allowance Plan, which marks arrival of the welfare state.

John Hersey publishes *A Bell for Adano.*

Tennessee Williams writes *The Glass Menagerie.*

Jose Luis Borges of Argentina publishes *Ficciones.*

Aaron Copland composes *Appalachian Spring.*

More than 165 people are killed and 175 injured as a result of a fire at a Ringling Brothers and Barnum & Bailey Circus in Hartford, Connecticut.

Tuskegee Airmen of the 332 Fighter Group huddle near a P-51 Mustang on their base at Rametelli, Italy, to discuss their mission.

EUROPE

January 19 The Soviets crush the German siege of Leningrad.

June 6 D Day: Allies forces start landing in Normandy, beginning the invasion of Europe.

July 3 Minsk, the last large German base on Soviet soil, falls to the Russians.

July 31 The Allies drive the Germans from Normandy.

September 11 General Omar Bradley leads the Allies onto German soil.

December 16 The Battle of the Bulge begins in Belgium, Germany's final counterattack.

April 5 Germans begin deporting Jews.

April Britain becomes a huge armed camp as Eisenhower oversees Allied preparations for the D-Day invasion of Europe.

Albert Camus publishes *Caligula.*

Jean Giraudoux publishes *The Mad Woman of Chaillot.*

Stefan Zweig's *The World of Yesterday,* his autobiography, is published posthumously.

Henri Matisse paints *The White Dress.*

Sergei Prokofiev presents the opera *War and Peace* in Moscow.

MIDDLE EAST & AFRICA

Half a million African troops fight for the French and British in World War II.

Global war efforts rely on African rubber and minerals.

The Jewish Brigade Group is formed, which serves in Egypt and Europe under British auspices.

The Irgun under Menachem Begin proclaims a revolt against British rule in order to carry out the Biltmore Program of establishing a Jewish State in Palestine.

WHAT LIFE WAS LIKE

On the Homefront

The Second World War engulfed civilian and soldier alike as men, women, and even children were called upon to contribute to or make sacrifices for the war effort. In both Allied and Axis countries, food and critical supplies were rationed, curfews were enforced, and women were suddenly deemed worthy of "men's work" in factories. Japan had a long-term strategy for replenishing their forces, asking women to help create future "cannon fodder," while in Germany, the Nazis were trying to rid themselves of an entire segment of the population, the Jews. Propaganda was a major occupation on the homefronts as well, as art and media were used to encourage loyalty or to pump up flagging morale, such as the Westinghouse "We Can Do It!" poster featuring the woman who came to be called Rosie the Riveter.

ASIA & OCEANIA

February 3 U.S. warships shell the Japanese home island of Paramishu.

February 29 American troops land at Los Negros on the Admiralty Island in a new offensive on Japanese territory.

March 19 Allied troops are landed by glider 200 miles behind Japanese lines.

April 24 The Japanese evacuate New Guinea as U.S. troops land there.

June 15 U.S. planes bomb the Japanese mainland.

October 20 General MacArthur lands on the Philippine island of Leyte.

December 22 Vo Nguyen Giap institutes the Vietnamese People's Army.

SCIENCE & TECHNOLOGY	PEOPLE & SOCIETY

January 29 The world's largest warship, the U.S.S. *Missouri,* is launched.

A uranium pile is built at Clinton, Tennessee.

DNA is discovered by Oswald Avery in New York City.

Quinine is synthesized.

The U.S. cost of living rises almost 30 percent.

Chicago children collect 18,000 tons of newspaper in five month's time for the war effort.

School sales of U.S. War Bonds and stamps purchase 11,700 parachutes, 2,900 planes, and more than 44,000 jeeps.

The U.S. Army recruits Japanese Americans.

The U.S. Supreme Court declares internment of Japanese-Americans unconstitutional.

Some 17,000 U.S. citizens of Mexican descent work in Los Angeles.

January 4 Hitler orders the mobilization of all children over the age of ten.

Blackout restrictions are relaxed in Britain.

Glenn Miller's orchestra is performing in Britain, making up to 17 broadcasts a week over the Armed Forces Network.

U.S. tank and infantrymen on the attack in the jungle of Bougainville, the largest of the Solomon Islands, in March of 1944

ISLAND FIGHTING

On August 7, 1942, U.S. Marines attacking Guadalcanal and Tulagi in the Solomon Islands caught the Japanese completely by surprise. Encountering little resistance, by the next day they had seized the airfield on Guadalcanal. But the Japanese quickly regrouped, and ultimate victory by the Allies in the Pacific would only be won at a terrible cost.

After weathering the initial attacks, the Japanese on Tulagi held out for 31 hours of hard fighting before most were killed or committed suicide. And it was not until February 1943 that the Marines could claim a victory on Guadalcanal, having learned the indelible lesson that Japanese soldiers preferred a valiant death to living with the eternal dishonor of defeat.

On Papua New Guinea, the Japanese stronghold at Buna finally fell, along with the entire island, to the forces of General Douglas MacArthur, clearing the way for an Allied invasion of the Philippines. With the retaking of the Philippines in October 1944, followed by the November capture of Guam and Saipan in the Mariana Islands, the war in the Pacific was reaching its final phase.

On February 19, 1945, the Marines attacked the Japanese island of Iwo Jima, site of a key air base. Though Marines famously raised the American flag there, the victory was costly, and a hint of what was to come at Okinawa. Landing there on April 1, army and marine forces encountered Japanese soldiers fortified in the hills, while kamikaze pilots inflicted heavy damage on the ships offshore charged with supporting the landing. Not until late June was Okinawa won, after more than 12,000 Americans and 100,000 Japanese had been killed. At last, though, the landing strips that prepared the way for American bombers to island-hop to Japan were secured.

*S*ome were hit in the water and wounded.
Some drowned then and there. . . .
Those who survived kept moving forward with the tide.

OFFICIAL REPORT OF COMPANY A,
116TH REGIMENT, AT OMAHA BEACH

D-DAY

DWIGHT D. EISENHOWER, THE ALLIED SUPREME COMMANDER, BEGAN PLANNING Operation Overlord on May 8, almost a month before his proposed D-Day, or launch date, of June 5. Wary of loose lips and German code breakers, Eisenhower kept the plan shrouded in intense secrecy; as a result, the Germans knew little of the Allied plan to break through a portion of the 2,400-mile-long Atlantic Wall along the coast of France.

Weather, though, proved to be a formidable foe. The worst front the area had experienced in 40 years threatened to scuttle the whole operation, but Eisenhower, after postponing the invasion for a day, decided to take advantage of a small opening June 6. Even when the first airborne troops parachuted down, the Germans did not believe a major invasion was underway. The night before, Field Marshal von Rundstadt failed to pass on a warning to the sleeping Hitler, believing that bad weather would make an attack impossible. As a result, Erwin Rommel, in charge of Nazi troops, had no idea the Allied invasion was imminent. This mistake made all the difference.

The first Allied troops came ashore at Normandy. The Americans landed at Omaha and Utah beaches and the British and Canadians at Gold, Juno, and Sword Beaches. The worst of the fighting was at Omaha Beach, where 2,000 Americans lost their lives before securing the beachhead. The Germans, still thinking the invasion was a diversion and that the real assault would come at Calais, did not yet send reinforcements. In spite of heavy casualties, the Allies continued to receive reinforcements while destroyers pummeled the heavy German guns on shore beyond the sea walls.

For the Allies, the day would end with a huge victory. They had breached the Atlantic Wall and secured ground beyond it. While the battle for Caen, heavily defended by the Germans, would continue until July, the Germans had already begun their retreat to the Fatherland. Allied airborne troops, who had either parachuted inland or landed in an amazing fleet of glider planes, held their ground, backing up the land troops.

On D-Day plus one, and for a number of days following, the battle inward would continue with further loss of life. In the meantime, U.S. and British forces expanded their beachheads, connecting them, allowing them to funnel in more troops and material. A pair of artificial harbors were built in order to dock and unload ships, while sailors disgorged cargo directly onto the beaches from their large landing craft. Three weeks after D-Day, one million Allies, 500,000 tons of supplies, and 175,000 vehicles had come ashore to lend support to the D-Day invaders.

The only question now was how long it would take to reach Berlin.

American GIs wade toward Omaha Beach on D-Day, as Germans on the bluffs beyond hit them with heavy machine-gun and mortar fire. Omaha Beach saw the most casualties in the Normandy invasion.

POLITICS & POWER	GEOGRAPHY & ENVIRONMENT	CULTURE & RELIGION

THE AMERICAS

April 12 Franklin Delano Roosevelt dies; Harry S. Truman is sworn in as U.S. president.

July 28 The Empire State Building is accidentally hit at the 78-79 floors by a B-25 bomber.

The United Nations is established to keep world peace.

William L. Sperry publishes *Religion in America.*

Frank Lloyd Wright designs the Guggenheim Museum in New York.

Among leading films is Billy Wilder's *The Lost Weekend.*

Chilean poet Gabriela Mistral wins the Nobel Prize in literature.

U.S. war correspondent Ernie Pyle wins a Pulitzer Prize, then is killed in the Pacific three weeks after shipping out.

EUROPE

February 4-11 The Big Three Conference of Franklin Roosevelt, Winston Churchill, and Joseph Stalin takes place at Yalta.

May 2 All one million German troops in Italy and Austria surrender.

May 8 Victory in Europe Day (V-E Day) is celebrated as Field-Marshal Keitel signs Germany's final act of capitulation.

July/August The Potsdam Conference, led by Roosevelt, Churchill, and Stalin, determines the intended administration of Germany.

The three Allied giants, Churchill, Roosevelt, and Stalin, meet at Yalta.

April Allied troops liberate the concentration camps at Bergen-Belsen, Buchenwald, and Dachau.

George Orwell publishes *Animal Farm.*

Evelyn Waugh publishes *Brideshead Revisited.*

Sergei Prokofiev presents the ballet *Cinderella* in Moscow.

Women's suffrage becomes legal in France.

MIDDLE EAST & AFRICA

January 12 Turkey opens its straits to Allied shipping, declares war on Germany the following month.

February 24 Prime Minister Ahmed Maher Pasha is shot dead after reading Egypt's declaration of war on Germany and Japan.

The Arab League is founded to oppose the creation of a Jewish state.

Leopold Senghor is elected to represent Senegal in what will later become the French National Assembly.

WHAT LIFE WAS LIKE

Above Hiroshima

A column of smoke rising fast. It has a fiery red core. A bubbling mass, purple-gray in color, with that red core. It's all turbulent. Fires are springing up everywhere, like flames shooting out of a huge bed of coals ... Here it comes, the mushroom shape that Captain Parsons spoke about. It's like a mass of bubbling molasses ... It's nearly level with us and climbing. ...

SERGEANT GEORGE CARON,
TAIL GUNNER ON THE *ENOLA GAY*

April The Jewish flag is officially raised by the Jewish Brigade.

August Illegal immigration of Jews to Palestine is renewed. The Unified Jewish Movement begins large scale attacks on the British.

A general strike in Nigeria reveals postwar discontent.

ASIA & OCEANIA

August 6 & 9 The U.S. bombers drop atomic bombs on Hiroshima and Nagasaki. Japan surrenders August 14.

August 19 The Soviets occupy Harbin and Mudken in Manchuria; 100,000 Japanese surrender.

September 14 Victory in Japan Day (V-J Day) is celebrated as General MacArthur formally accepts the Japanese surrender on the aircraft carrier U.S.S. *Missouri.*

September 21 The Indian Congress Party calls for the freedom of India, Burma, Indochina, and Malaya from colonial rule.

September 8 The U.S. and the U.S.S.R. divide Korea.

November 17 The republic of Indonesia is declared.

More than 300 U.S. B-29s firebomb Tokyo, turning the city into an inferno where some 100,000 people perish. Before war's end, U.S. bombers destroy more than 60 cities in Japan.

August 28 Mao Zedong and Zhou Enlai discuss democracy, peace, and unity with Chiang Kai-shek.

SCIENCE & TECHNOLOGY	PEOPLE & SOCIETY
July 16 The first atomic bomb is detonated near Alamogordo, New Mexico.	**The war stimulates tremendous growth** in California, which overwhelms the infrastructure of its cities. **By war's end** U.S. citizens have purchased some 36 billion dollars' worth of war bonds. **The Seventh War Loan Drive** is kicked off in Washington, D.C. **The company of Brown and Root** buys pipelines financed at 147 million dollars by the U.S. government during the war. The company becomes Texas Eastern, a Fortune 500 firm.
The Nobel Prize is won by Fleming, Florey, and Chain for the discovery of penicillin. **The Atomic Research Center** is established at Harwell, England.	**April 28 & 30 Mussolini** is executed by Italians; Hitler shoots himself after the Allies reach Berlin. **Black markets** for food, clothing, and cigarettes occur throughout Europe. **Anne Frank** dies of typhoid in a German concentration camp.

ATOMIC BOMBS FALL ON JAPAN

Harry S. Truman first learned of his nation's big secret after becoming president, upon the death of Franklin D. Roosevelt on April 12, 1945, barely a month before V-E Day was announced with the fall of Germany. The United States, he was informed, had succeeded in building an atomic bomb, which was capable of wrecking a vast, but yet unknown havoc upon the enemy.

Japan, in spite of its losses and its starving population, had thus far shown no inclination to surrender to the Allies. The next step had to be a massive invasion of Japan, with at least 500,000 troops. Weighing the death toll of such a large operation against a bombing which all hoped would cause Japan to capitulate, Truman decided on the latter.

The Allies gave Emperor Hirohito another chance to surrender, which he refused. On August 6, the first bomb, Little Boy, was dropped from the *Enola Gay* on Hiroshima, followed by *Bockscar*'s Fat Man, detonated at Nagasaki three days later. The damage was horrendous —some 78,000 died at Hiroshima and some 25,000 died at Nagasaki, though the exact count will never be certain. Massive numbers of people died years afterward from radiation poisoning.

Emperor Hirohito, who was warned after the first bomb that more would fall if he didn't surrender, buckled after the destruction of Nagasaki. On September 2, General Douglas MacArthur formally accepted Hirohito's signed surrender papers aboard the battleship U.S.S. *Missouri*. But the world had changed forever with the invention and deployment of the atomic bomb. Nuclear winters would be an ever-present threat of the developing Cold War.

A mushroom cloud rises 20,000 feet above Nagasaki, Japan, on August 9, 1945, following a second nuclear attack by the U.S.

You are only numbers.
A shot, and the number is gone....
Don't try to escape; the only way to get out of here
is by the chimney.

AUSCHWITZ GUARD TO NEW ARRIVALS AND OTHER GUARDS

THE HOLOCAUST

THE NAZIS BEGAN TO PERSECUTE GERMAN JEWS IN 1933 when Adolf Hitler rose to power. In April they issued a decree that ordered compulsory retirement of all "non-Aryans"—meaning Jews—from the civil service.

Little by little Jews suffered more indignities—the removal of telephone service or the compulsory wearing of a yellow Star of David in public. But the intent to humiliate soon became an attempt to destroy. Jews were beaten and killed in the streets, women were assaulted, store windows were smashed, and property was confiscated. Some Jews left their homeland for safe havens, but most stayed, hoping and praying the Nazi terror would soon be over.

Hitler and his leaders considered the idea of deporting Jews to Africa or Madagascar, but quickly realized it would be impossible to accomplish such a feat involving so many individuals. In January 1942, Nazi officials convened at the Wannsee Conference to coordinate the so-called final solution: extermination of the entire Jewish population of Europe. In addition to Jews, captured Slavs, Gypsies, the mentally ill, and the deformed—in other words, all human beings considered inferior to the Aryan ideal—were included in this horrific undertaking.

The ghettos, where Jews had originally been confined, were sealed off in Warsaw, Lvov, Lodz, and Krakow. Those who had survived starvation, cruel punishment, or burning were packed into boxcars and sent to concentration camps, where many were worked to death after a few months, or to death camps, where Jews were herded into "showers" and gassed. Others were randomly gathered up, shot, and pushed into mass graves, which they sometimes had been forced to dig themselves. Early on the mentally ill and deformed had been subjected to medical experimentation. In the camps Jews became guinea pigs, too.

In 1945, when the concentration camps were finally liberated, German citizens and Allies alike saw the emaciated survivors and the dead bodies piled up for the crematoriums—a glimpse of the savagery that had been taking place. In the end, more than six million Jews had died. But ever resilient, the Jewish population, many of them Holocaust survivors, carried on in America, in other parts of Europe, and in their newly formed postwar state of Israel, rebuilding, but never forgetting their past.

ABOVE: *Bodies are removed from Gusen concentration camp, near Austria, by German civilians on May 12, 1945, for a decent burial.* RIGHT: *Survivors at the Buchenwald concentration camp peer through a barbed wire fence at their American liberators in April of 1945.*

POLITICS & POWER	GEOGRAPHY & ENVIRONMENT	CULTURE & RELIGION

THE AMERICAS

1946 Juan Perón is elected president of Argentina.

1947 The Taft-Hartley Act is passed, restricting the rights of U.S. labor unions, over President Truman's veto.

1947 The Truman Doctrine draws battle lines in the Cold War.

1948 The Marshall Plan goes into effect, providing more than $13 billion in aid to reconstruct Western Europe.

1949 The North Atlantic Treaty Organization (NATO) is founded to counter the threat of Soviet aggression.

1946 R. E. Byrd leads an expedition to the South Pole.

1946 Guatemalan Miguel A. Asturias publishes *Men of Maze*.

1947 Tennessee Williams writes *A Streetcar Named Desire*.

1947 The House Un-American Activities Committee holds hearings to determine if communist propaganda is infiltrating U.S. movies.

1948 Norman Mailer publishes *The Naked and the Dead*.

1948 Jackson Pollock paints *Composition No. 1*.

1949 Arthur Miller writes *Death of a Salesman*.

EUROPE

1946 A republic is proclaimed in Italy.

1946 An airlift is begun by the Western Allies in Berlin to beat the Soviet blockade.

1946 Winston Churchill warns of an "iron curtain" separating communist and noncommunist Europe.

1949 Germany is divided into the Federal Republic (West Germany) and the Democratic Republic (East Germany).

1949 The Soviet Union establishes the Council for Mutual Economic Assistance (COMECON) as an alternative to the Marshall Plan.

1947 The UN votes to partition Palestine.

1949 The republic of Ireland is created.

1946 Pablo Picasso starts the pottery at Vallauris.

1947 *The Diary of Anne Frank* is published.

1947 H. R. Trevor-Roper publishes *The Last Days of Hitler*.

1948 Winston Churchill publishes *The Gathering Storm*.

1948 The World Council of Churches is founded in Amsterdam.

1949 George Orwell publishes *Nineteen Eighty-Four*.

MIDDLE EAST & AFRICA

1946 The kingdom of Jordan is created.

1948 South Africa gains independence and the National Party comes to power, advocating further legal separation of the races.

1948 The state of Israel is born. Fighting ensues with Arab Palestinians.

1949 The war between Israel and the Arab League ends with a truce.

1949 Apartheid goes into effect in South Africa, officially codifying the long-standing practice of legal segregation.

CONNECTIONS

The Birth of Israel

The state of Israel was formed on May 14, 1948, after 60 years of Zionism on the part of the Jewish people. Their longtime leader, David Ben-Gurion, announced that "by virtue of the national and historic right of the Jewish people and the resolution of the United Nations: [We] hereby proclaim the establishment of the Jewish State in Palestine—to be called Israel." After World War I, Great Britain had received Palestine from the League of Nations as a mandate. Jews in Palestine, however, had been struggling for a Jewish state there since the late 19th century. The Arabs, long settled there, opposed such a state, and the British were unable to negotiate a settlement, so they turned their mandate over to the United Nations, which partitioned Palestine. Fighting ensued, with Israel increasing its land holdings and sending some 600,000 Palestinian Arabs into refugee camps in Lebanon, Gaza, Jordan, and Syria.

1946 The Baath Party is constituted in Iraq as nationalist and socialist in philosophy.

1947 The Dead Sea Scrolls, the oldest extant Hebrew documents, are discovered in Wadi Qumran. They date from around 1 C.E.

1947 "Exodus 1947" turns world public opinion toward establishment of a Jewish National Home in Palestine. The British turn over their mandate to the UN, which partitions Palestine.

1948 Mohandas Gandhi is assassinated.

ASIA & OCEANIA

1946 The Philippines gain independence.

1948 South Korea proclaims itself a republic; North Korea proclaims itself an independent communist republic.

1948 Chinese nationalists form a government-in-exile in Formosa (Taiwan).

1949 Mao Zedong defeats the Guomindang with his peasant army in a civil war and reunifies mainland China. He declares his country the People's Republic of China, creating a communist bloc to rival American power.

1946 The communist republic of Vietnam is recognized by France.

1946 India and Pakistan become separate British dominions. Both become independent the following year.

1947 The United Nations establishes several Trust Territories in the Pacific Islands.

1948 The Union of Burma becomes an independent republic.

SCIENCE & TECHNOLOGY	PEOPLE & SOCIETY
1947 The Bell X-1, piloted by Chuck Yeager, breaks the sound barrier.	**1946 Housing shortages in U.S**. are a problem for returning soldiers.
1947 Bell Laboratories scientists invent the transistor.	**1946 A record 3.8 million babies** are born in the U.S., launching the baby boom.
1948 Alfred C. Kinsey publishes *Sexual Behavior in the Human Male*.	**1946 Jackie Robinson** becomes the first African American to sign a contract with a major baseball club, the Dodgers.
1949 A U.S. guided missile is launched 250 miles, the highest altitude ever reached.	**1946 More than one million war veterans** enroll in U.S. colleges under the G.I. Bill of Rights.
	1947 Almost two million working women lose wartime jobs as men return from overseas.

GANDHI

As a young lawyer in South Africa in the late 1890s, British-educated Mohandas Gandhi got his first taste of the fight for independence, involving himself in efforts to end discrimination against Indians. He also began to develop a new philosophy that eschewed Western materialism in favor of Hindu ascetic ideals. He held his first *satyagraha* (holding to the truth), a non-violent approach to civil disobedience in reaction to unjust laws. The South African government responded by alleviating anti-Indian discrimination, and Gandhi used this approach throughout the rest of his life.

1946 Buckminster Fuller designs the Dymaxion House.	**1946 Women** get the vote in Italy.
1947 The British start operations at their first atomic pile at Harwell.	**1948 The first World Health Assembly** convenes in Geneva.
1948 The first port radar system starts operation in Liverpool, England.	**1948-49 Bread and clothes rationing** in Britain ends.
1949 Soviet physicists under Stalin create their own atom bomb, ending the American monopoly.	**1948 The National Health Service** is organized in Britain.
	1949 The British Gas Industry is nationalized.
	1949 Nineteen out of 22 Nazis on trial in Nuremberg for crimes against humanity are found guilty, and 12 are sentenced to death by hanging.

Returning to his native land, Gandhi pushed for India's freedom from Britain, supporting them in World War I in hopes that Britain would reward India with independence. He also led labor and agrarian reform demonstrations in support of the poor, worked to eliminate the caste designation "untouchables," and pressed to develop cottage industries. After a bloody British massacre at Amritsar, Gandhi led several campaigns, becoming so well known and revered that the title Mahatma (great soul) was given to him.

	1947 Kenyan women lead a revolt against forced labor in the British colony.
	1949 David Ben-Gurion becomes prime minister of the new state of Israel. Head of the Labor Party, he encourages Jewish immigration through the Jewish Agency, which helped administer Palestine under the British mandate.

In 1930 Gandhi led a 200-mile march to the sea to protest the British salt tax. He and other Indian National Congress leaders were jailed, but upon his release less than a year later Gandhi continued his fasts and nonviolent protests. At last, in 1947, he became a major figure in negotiations with British Lord Mountbatten and Muslim League leader Muhammad Ali Jinnah, which brought about Indian's independence and the separate Muslim state of Pakistan.

On January 30, 1948, while leading a prayer meeting in New Delhi, Gandhi was assassinated by a Hindu fanatic, who believed Gandhi had been too considerate to the Muslims. Thus came a violent end to the peaceful man cherished by Indians as the father of their country.

1946 The first U.S. atomic test is carried out over the Bikini atoll in the Pacific.

Mohandas Gandhi reads at home next to his spinning wheel, a symbol of his non-violent approach to India's struggle for independence.

FOLLOWING THE SECOND WORLD WAR, the global economy and population boomed. Human numbers climbed from 2.5 billion in 1950 to more than 7 billion by 2013, a biological success unprecedented in the history of humanity and probably in the history of large mammals. Meanwhile, the size of the world economy grew by about 18-fold. On average, people were richer than ever before by the 21st century, but the average concealed vast and growing inequalities. Rapid shifts in the global balance of power ensued, ultimately resulting from the different pace of economic growth in different countries. After 1950, less and less of the world's economic production took place in Europe, and more and more in the United States and eventually in China.

The United States and the Soviet Union emerged from the 1940s as nuclear superpowers and led opposing blocs of nations in a global power struggle that became known as the Cold War. Soviet leaders blamed the upheavals of the 20th century on capitalist imperialism, and promised that the spread of communism would bring peace and justice. American leaders argued that democracy and free enterprise would achieve the same goals, and blamed communist oppression for strife in the world.

These ideological differences helped make the Cold War a hot conflict in several places, such as Korea, Vietnam, Angola, and Mozambique. The U.S. and the U.S.S.R. avoided a direct clash. The balance of power seemed to swing in the direction of Moscow in 1949, when the Soviets tested their first nuclear weapon and the Chinese Revolution under Mao Zedong brought China into the Soviet bloc. But in the long run China and the U.S.S.R. could not stay together, and by the 1980s, the Soviet economy could no longer keep pace. The Soviets gave up trying to keep their restive bloc intact, and in short order even the Soviet Union itself ceased to exist.

The end of the Cold War did not bring peace and tranquillity. International politics had become more complex in the 1950s and 1960s with the wave of decolonization that swept through Africa and Asia. More than 100 new countries came into existence between 1956 and 1991, and a few more in the 1990s with the collapse of Yugoslavia. Many of these nations were born in wars fought against European militaries.

Independence sometimes brought peace, but often new rounds of warfare fueled by ethnic or religious grievance or the ambitions of a single leader, such as Saddam Hussein in Iraq.

Ethnic nationalisms and religious politics loomed ever larger on the world stage. A conspicuous demonstration came in 2001 with deadly attacks on the U.S. perpetrated by al Qaeda, a terrorist group led by Osama bin Laden and devoted to eccentric interpretations of Islam. The U.S. response came in the form of wars launched in Afghanistan and Iraq.

By the early 21st century, the strongest trend in world politics was the rise of China. Mao's 1949 revolution had unified the country, but his economic policies brought massive famine in 1958-1960, and his political policy known as the Cultural Revolution (1966-1976) yielded economic chaos. Soon after his death in 1976, however, China's leaders abandoned most of Mao's economic doctrines and permitted a measure of private property and capitalism, unleashing the economic ambitions of a large part of a very large population. They also permitted economic links, both investment and trade, with the capitalist world, and by the late 1980s presided over one of the world's fastest-growing economies. For a quarter century thereafter, China's growth was the world's most notable economic miracle. Like every booming economy before it, China set about translating economic strength into political and military power, which by the early 21st century alarmed its East Asian neighbors and provoked anxieties farther afield.

The heady economic and demographic growth of the decades after 1950 brought deepening environmental problems around the world. By the late 20th century, the one that seemed potentially the most dangerous, rapidly changing climate, proved resistant to political action. Leaders preferred to devote their efforts to issues with more immediate time horizons, such as national security and short-term economic growth.

Following a stock market crash in 2008, the world sank into a serious economic recession, the worst since the Great Depression of the 1930s. Many analysts believe that the origins of the recession lay in the American housing crisis of 2004, during which lenders gave loans to borrowers who should not have qualified for home mortgages, a practice called "subprime lending." The crisis and slow recovery revealed

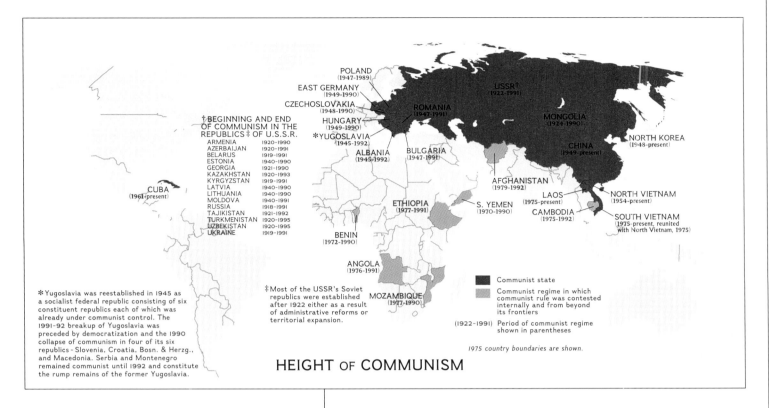

POLAND
(1947-1989)

EAST GERMANY
(1949-1990)

CZECHOSLOVAKIA
(1948-1990)

†BEGINNING AND END
OF COMMUNISM IN THE
REPUBLICS‡ OF U.S.S.R.

HUNGARY
(1949-1990)

✱YUGOSLAVIA
(1945-1992)

ARMENIA	1920-1990
AZERBAIJAN	1920-1991
BELARUS	1919-1991
ESTONIA	1940-1990
GEORGIA	1921-1990
KAZAKHSTAN	1920-1993
KYRGYZSTAN	1919-1991
LATVIA	1940-1990
LITHUANIA	1940-1990
MOLDOVA	1940-1991
RUSSIA	1918-1991
TAJIKISTAN	1921-1992
TURKMENISTAN	1920-1995
UZBEKISTAN	1920-1995
UKRAINE	1919-1991

ROMANIA
(1947-1991)

USSR†
(1922-1991)

MONGOLIA
(1924-1990)

NORTH KOREA
(1948-present)

CHINA
(1949-present)

ALBANIA
(1945-1992)

BULGARIA
(1947-1991)

CUBA
(1961-present)

AFGHANISTAN
(1979-1992)

LAOS
(1975-present)

NORTH VIETNAM
(1954-present)

ETHIOPIA
(1977-1991)

S. YEMEN
(1970-1990)

CAMBODIA
(1975-1992)

SOUTH VIETNAM
(1975-present, reunited
with North Vietnam, 1975)

BENIN
(1972-1990)

ANGOLA
(1976-1991)

MOZAMBIQUE
(1977-1990)

✱ Yugoslavia was reestablished in 1945 as
a socialist federal republic consisting of six
constituent republics each of which was
already under communist control. The
1991-92 breakup of Yugoslavia was
preceded by democratization and the 1990
collapse of communism in four of its six
republics – Slovenia, Croatia, Bosn. & Herzg.,
and Macedonia. Serbia and Montenegro
remained communist until 1992 and constitute
the rump remains of the former Yugoslavia.

‡ Most of the USSR's Soviet
republics were established
after 1922 either as a result
of administrative reforms or
territorial expansion.

▮ Communist state

▮ Communist regime in which
communist rule was contested
internally and from beyond
its frontiers

(1922-1991) Period of communist regime
shown in parentheses

1975 country boundaries are shown.

HEIGHT OF COMMUNISM

the degree to which national economies have become increasingly dependent on one another.

Beginning in December 2010, a series of popular revolts swept through the Middle East promising social and political change. First, riots rocked Tunisia's capital when a street vendor set himself on fire in protest against government corruption. Soon Zine Ben Ali, president since 1987, fled the country, and rebels set up a new government. Encouraged by Tunisian success, Egyptians, Yemenis, Jordanians, and Algerians instigated protests in early 2011. Among their complaints were huge wealth inequalities, high unemployment, government corruption, police brutality, and authoritarian rule. Dominoes continued to fall as disturbances broke out in more than a dozen other countries including Syria, Libya, Iraq, Saudi Arabia, and Oman. Some uprisings were successful, others not. By mid-2012, four countries had undergone regime changes, including Egypt, with the overthrow of dictator Hosni Mubarak, who had presided over a ruthless and repressive police state since 1981. Meanwhile, rebels in Libya overthrew and killed the tyrant Muammar Qaddafi, in power since 1969.

Similar events spelled trouble in Syria, where the government of Bashir al-Assad, whose father had seized

We will bury you.
NIKITA KHRUSHCHEV

During the fighting in Vietnam, a U.S. Marine with a head wound reaches out to a fallen comrade. The U.S. withdrew its remaining troops from Vietnam in 1975 and failed to prevent the unification of the country under communist leadership.

power in 1970, refused to step down. Syrians soon found themselves locked in a devastating civil war.

These revolutions, collectively termed the "Arab Spring," saw the uprooting of authoritarian regimes throughout the Middle East, with hope for lasting change for the region's people. For all the dangers the world faced in the early years of the 21st century, its leaders' capacity to communicate and to contain conflict had never been greater. International organizations devoted to every conceivable pursuit, interlinked economies, and even personal acquaintanceship gave them both means and motives to pursue peace and stability.

Showdown in Korea

In June 1950 North Korea, backed by the Soviet Union and China, launched an invasion of South Korea, seeking to unify the country under communist leadership. The U.S. responded by obtaining a UN resolution approving the use of force against North Korea. The Soviet Union would have vetoed that resolution but was boycotting the UN for not admitting China. Officially, U.S. troops fought as part of a UN force, but Americans called the shots and approached this conflict as they had World War II, seeking not simply to repel the aggressors and restore the status quo but to defeat them. When hundreds of thousands of Chinese troops entered the contest to prevent American-led forces from conquering North Korea, President Truman placed limits on the war effort to avoid a wider conflict with China. A cease-fire

arranged in 1953 fulfilled the U.S. goal of containing communism by restoring the prewar boundary between North and South Korea but fell short of the outright victory Americans had hoped for.

The Korean War provided an economic boost to Japan, where the American occupation that began in 1945 ended in 1951. Japan regained sovereignty but still housed American bases and produced more than three billion dollars worth of supplies for American and allied troops in Korea. Those orders helped revive struggling Japanese firms such as Toyota and set the stage for an industrial boom in later years that made Japan economically competitive with the U.S. Like Japan, the Philippines accepted the presence of American military bases in exchange for independence, granted in 1946. The U.S. continued to influence the Philippines by opposing communist insurgents there and backing pro-American politicians. Filipinos came to regard U.S. bases on their soil as infringing on their independence and secured their removal after the Cold War ended.

Decolonization was more traumatic for countries such as Vietnam where colonial powers fought to retain or regain control. The French kept up their battle for Vietnam until 1954, when they were defeated at Dien Bien Phu by forces loyal to Ho Chi Minh, a communist who led the fight for independence with Soviet and Chinese aid. At peace talks, Vietnam was partitioned between the communist north and noncommunist south, pending elections intended to unite the country under one leader. That partition became permanent when South Vietnam, fearing a victory for Ho Chi Minh, canceled the vote with American approval. In years to come, the U.S. grew increasingly committed to preventing communists from gaining control of South Vietnam.

In much of Africa, the end of colonial rule came slowly and painfully. Ethiopia and Libya gained independence quickly because they had been occupied by a defeated power, Italy, but other European nations were reluctant to part with African colonies, particularly those with large numbers of white settlers. In Kenya, British settlers had confiscated much of the best land from native Kenyans and now faced retribution by the Mau Mau, a secret society whose attacks led the British to crack down there in 1952. Among those jailed were foes of colonial rule who had nothing to do with the attacks, including Jomo Kenyatta, who later led the movement that won independence for Kenya in 1963. Other African nationalists who faced jail terms before achieving their goals included Kwame Nkrumah of Ghana, which gained independence from Britain in 1957; and Nelson Mandela of South Africa, sentenced to life in prison for armed resistance to the white government, which withdrew from the British Commonwealth in 1961 and continued its racist policy of apartheid. One of the fiercest anticolonial struggles took place in Algeria, where guerrillas clashed with French troops and settlers for eight years before winning independence in 1962.

In the Middle East, nationalism collided with the economic interests of western Europe and the U.S., which were increasingly dependent on Middle Eastern oil. In 1953 British and American agents engineered a coup against Iranian premier Mohammad Mosaddeq—who had been instrumental in nationalizing the Anglo-Iranian Oil Company—and restored to power Shah Mohammed Reza Pahlavi. The shah rewarded the U.S. and Britain by protecting their oil interests and opposing communism, but his efforts to westernize Iran and crush dissent made him increasingly unpopular and led to a revolution in 1979.

Economic interests also contributed to a crisis in Egypt in 1956 when President Gamal Abdel Nasser nationalized the Suez Canal, a vital conduit for oil shipments from the Persian Gulf. Britain and France then asked Israel to ignite hostilities with Egypt, which gave them a pretext for seizing the canal. The U.S. condemned their intervention, and it collapsed. Afterward, Nasser moved closer to the Soviets, and the U.S. moved closer to Israel. The deepening Arab-Israeli dispute threatened to bring the superpowers into direct conflict.

Efforts to subvert popular foreign leaders and thwart independence movements ran counter to the claims of the western powers that they were fighting for a free world. At the same time, however, Soviet domination of eastern Europe served as a warning to developing nations that communist imperialism could be worse than capitalist imperialism. Nikita Khrushchev, who became Soviet premier after Joseph Stalin's death in 1953, encouraged reform by disclosing details of Stalin's murderous purges and releasing political prisoners from dreaded Soviet gulags, or labor camps. Yet Khrushchev responded in Stalinist fashion

when Hungary was swept by anti-Soviet demonstrations in 1956 and pulled out of the Warsaw Pact, which bound eastern European countries to Moscow. Soviet tanks rolled into Budapest, and many dissidents were executed. The assault reinforced the view that eastern Europe was trapped behind an Iron Curtain, and the Soviets only strengthened that impression by erecting the Berlin Wall in 1961 to stop East Germans from fleeing to the west.

In the U.S., the Cold War shattered the sense of security people had long enjoyed knowing they were oceans away from hostile powers. In 1957 the Soviet Union launched the satellite Sputnik I into orbit. The feat demonstrated technology that could be used not only to explore outer space—leading to a space race that climaxed when the U.S. landed astronauts on the moon in 1969—but also to hit distant targets with missiles carrying nuclear warheads. A ballistic missile fired at short range left commanders so little time to respond that the superpowers considered missile bases near their borders grave threats to their security. The installation of U.S. missiles in Turkey came as an affront to Khrushchev, and he responded in 1962 by shipping Soviet missiles to Cuba, where the revolutionary leader Fidel Castro had seized power three years earlier by toppling a regime friendly to the U.S. and its powerful economic interests in Cuba.

Since taking control, Castro had antagonized Washington by railing against Yankee imperialism, seizing American-owned companies, canceling elections, and executing or imprisoning thousands of political opponents. A failed U.S.-backed invasion by anti-Castro exiles in 1961 drove him closer to Khrushchev and set the stage for the Cuban Missile Crisis a year later. When spy planes detected the missiles, President John F. Kennedy demanded their removal and blockaded Cuba. After nearly two weeks of agonizing suspense, Khrushchev ended the nuclear confrontation by agreeing to remove the missiles in exchange for private assurances that the U.S. would withdraw its missiles from Turkey and cease efforts to overthrow Castro.

A Balance of Terror
At the time of the Cuban Missile Crisis, the United States had a greater nuclear deterrent than the Soviet Union, but the gap narrowed in years to come. Many believed that a balance of power—or a balance

of terror—reduced the likelihood of nuclear war between the superpowers because both sides faced certain annihilation. Mutually assured destruction (MAD) did not apply to conventional conflicts pitting one superpower against forces backed by the other, and it was in such struggles that the Cold War took its heaviest toll. In the mid-1960s the U.S. sent hundreds of thousands of troops to defend an unstable regime in South Vietnam against communist insurgents, who regarded the Americans in much the same light as their former French colonizers. As casualties mounted on both sides, the war drew strong protests in the U.S. and around the world.

The American antiwar movement coincided with other social reform movements, including women's liberation, which called for equal rights for women in the home and in society at large; and the civil rights movement, which ended segregation in the South and secured voting rights for African Americans. The assassination in 1968 of civil rights leader Martin Luther King, who was inspired by Mahatma Gandhi's nonviolent resistance movement in India, caused rioting that devastated urban areas, raising fears that the U.S. faced revolutionary upheaval. Here as in other democratic countries, however, the political system proved flexible enough to respond constructively to dissent rather than stifle it, as often happened under communist regimes. Among the many uprisings that took place around the world in 1968 was a bold effort in Czechoslovakia to reform communism and promote freedom of expression. The Soviets brought that promising Prague Spring to a bitter end by sending in tanks and toppling reform leader Alexander Dubček.

In China as in other communist countries, poor people whose plight had long been ignored benefited from public education and health care, and women gained new rights and opportunities. But such gains were offset by ruinous social experiments such as the Great Leap Forward, an effort to ratchet up steel production and refashion agriculture in accordance with Mao Zedong's pet theories. A famine that claimed more than 30 million Chinese lives between 1958 and 1961 resulted. In the Cultural Revolution, launched by Mao in 1966, fervent young communists called Red Guards to question their elders and challenge teachers, intellectuals, and others in authority. Many suspected counter-revolutionaries were placed on trial, forced to recant, and sentenced to "reeducation," which often meant hard labor. Mao's lasting bequest to China was not communism but nationalism and self-determination. Born in 1893 when China was a decrepit empire dominated by foreign powers, he left it a strong and independent nation in 1976, no longer beholden to the Soviet Union and free to negotiate and trade with the U.S., which entered into diplomatic relations with China.

That realignment transformed the Cold War by ending fears of a monolithic communist bloc and deflating the domino theory, or the idea that if one small country such as Vietnam fell to communism, many others would follow around the world. In fact, communist victories in Vietnam and neighboring Laos and Cambodia in the 1970s had little impact beyond Indochina other than producing widespread revulsion for the mass murder of civilians by Cambodia's regime. After leaving Vietnam, the U.S. used its ample defense budget to rebuild its military and pursue an arms race the Soviet Union could ill afford. Despite promising results from Strategic Arms Limitation Talks (SALT) in the 1970s, the superpowers continued to spend huge sums developing and deploying nuclear weapons. The longer that continued, the greater the strain on the Soviet economy, which was plagued by inefficiencies and was far less productive than the American economy.

Upheaval in the Third World

Détente in the form of summits and SALT accords did not stop the United States and Soviet Union from intervening in the Third World or in developing regions subject to the economic and political influence of the superpowers. Cuba, now heavily dependent on Soviet aid, sent troops to Angola in 1976 to help communists there defeat opponents backed by South Africa. Soviet aid also fueled insurgencies in nearby Namibia, which resisted incorporation by South Africa, and in Ethiopia.

Zimbabwe won independence in 1980, overthrowing a white minority state called Rhodesia, itself recently independent from the British Empire. Most whites fled Zimbabwe, fearful of their future there, as elsewhere in Africa in the wake of independence struggles that left bitter resentments against white settlers and former colonial masters. One exception was South Africa, where Nelson Mandela, released from

prison in 1990, went on to become the country's first black president and upheld his long-standing commitment to a democratic multiracial society.

Like Africa, Latin America underwent great upheaval in the late 20th century for reasons that had only partly to do with the Cold War. Efforts by Latin American nations to industrialize faltered in many cases, and grinding poverty persisted in rural areas and in shantytowns surrounding cities, where migrants pouring in from the countryside found little economic relief. Even in Argentina, one of the region's most advanced countries, glaring disparities between rich and poor caused political instability and brought to power army officers prepared to use force to impose order. Some of those strong men were elected leaders like Juan Perón, a charismatic colonel who governed Argentina after the Second World War with the help of his immensely popular and politically astute wife, Eva Perón, and returned to power in the 1970s. Others were military dictators who formed juntas like the one that led Argentina to defeat

in a war with Britain for control of the Falkland Islands, or the Malvinas, in 1982.

Latin American leaders who responded to economic ills by advocating socialism or communism risked opposition from the U.S., which was determined to keep other nations in the hemisphere from following Cuba's path. The U.S. backed a coup by officers in Chile in 1973 who overthrew President Salvador Allende, an avowed Marxist, and crushed political dissent. In the 1980s the U.S. aided right-wing forces called Contras seeking to overthrow the left-wing government of Nicaragua. Aid to the Contras was forbidden by Congress but was obtained covertly through the sale of weapons to Iran, where American diplomats had been held hostage after the shah was overthrown in 1979 and where the Islamic government that succeeded him was suspected of supporting terrorism.

The Soviets had long exploited anti-American sentiments within the Islamic world, but they lost that advantage in 1979 when they invaded Afghanistan

South African police use a dog and a whip against a black man who has stepped out of line. Scenes like this one, photographed in 1967, remained all too common in South Africa until apartheid finally ended there in the 1990s.

to defend a puppet regime against Muslim fundamentalists. The U.S. as well as Iran and other Islamic countries funneled weapons to *mujahidin* (Muslim warriors), who waged a successful guerrilla war against Soviet troops, forcing them out of Afghanistan in 1989. By then, the Soviet Union was near collapse. Mikhail Gorbachev, the last Soviet premier, recognized the signs of economic and social decay and promoted perestroika (restructuring) and glasnost (openness). Like others who had tried to reform communism, he failed, but by permitting Warsaw Pact nations to cast off Soviet restraints without retribution, he helped transform what could have been bloody uprisings into jubilant coming-out parties for the new democracies of Eastern Europe.

Some in Moscow were appalled when Solidarity leader Lech Walesa won a free election in 1989 and became president of Poland, and when East Germans joined with West Germans to demolish the Berlin Wall that November. Blaming Gorbachev for failing to stem the tide, communist hard-liners staged a coup in 1991, but their bid collapsed when Gorbachev's aide Boris Yeltsin dissuaded troops from backing the conspirators. Under Yeltsin's leadership, the Soviet Union ceased to exist and a new Russia emerged where the seeds of democracy and free enterprise were planted in an environment long hostile to them. But before long, an authoritarian and fiercely nationalist state, headed by former Soviet intelligence agent Vladimir Putin, disappointed those hoping to see Russia harmoniously integrated into European society.

The world's tallest bridge, the Millau Viaduct, rises above clouds covering the Tarn River in France. Completed in 2004, the bridge is one of several recent technological feats, including the world's largest commercial aircraft, produced by Europeans of various nations that are unifying their economies to compete with the American economy.

Nation Building and Globalization

After the Cold War, the world's wealthiest countries promoted globalization by establishing economic and political relationships that transcended national boundaries, while developing countries struggled to assert their national identity. Many of the world's trouble spots in the 1990s were nations created in the 20th century with little regard for ethnic or religious barriers to national unity. Ethnically divided Yugoslavia, forged in 1919 at the Versailles Peace Conference, was held together after the Second World War by Marshal Tito, a communist who resisted Soviet control and managed to keep Serbia, the nation's largest state, in line with his native Croatia and other smaller Yugoslav states. In 1990 Yugoslavia broke up, and Serbian troops entered Croatia and Bosnia to support Serbian minorities there. UN troops sent as peacekeepers were unable to prevent ethnic cleansing by Serbian forces, who murdered thousands of people and drove many others from their homes.

Massacres on a larger scale occurred in 1994 in the young African nation of Rwanda, where militants belonging to the Hutu majority lashed out at the once-dominant Tutsi. Although a minority, the Tutsi had been favored under German and Belgian colonial rule. Nearly one million Tutsi and moderate Hutu were killed in the assaults.

The legacy of colonialism also contributed to strife in the Middle East, where Iraqi dictator Saddam Hussein used deadly force at home and abroad to hold together that fragile country, formed after British troops seized Baghdad from the Ottomans during the First World War. The Sunni Muslim minority to which Hussein belonged emerged from colonial rule as Iraq's dominant faction. However, the Sunnis came under pressure after Shiites took power in Iran and encouraged opposition to Hussein and his Baath party among the Shiite majority in Iraq and Kurds seeking independence.

After waging a long and indecisive war against Iran, during which he used chemical weapons against Iranian troops and Kurdish civilians, Hussein invaded oil-rich Kuwait in 1989. The U.S. responded by leading an international coalition that ousted Iraqi forces from Kuwait in 1990. Saddam Hussein survived the defeat but later fell from power when American and British troops returned in 2003 and occupied Iraq.

After Saddam was deposed, tried, and executed, Iraqis tried to form a stable and representative government, but factional strife among Sunni and Shiite Muslims, together with ethnic frictions between Arabs and Kurds, undermined all quests for stability.

The U.S. invasion of Iraq unfolded against the backdrop of startling terrorist attacks on September 11, 2001, that leveled the World Trade Center in New York City, damaged the Pentagon in Washington, and killed nearly 3,000 people. In response, President George W. Bush sent American troops into Afghanistan—which had served as a sanctuary for those organizing the attacks—and proclaimed a global war on terrorism that extended to regimes that were thought capable of supplying terrorists with weapons of mass destruction.

President Bush's subsequent decision to invade Iraq in 2003 proved highly controversial, especially after it became clear that Iraq did not have weapons of mass destruction, the main justification the President had offered for the war. The war, like the one in Afghanistan, dragged on for more than a decade, growing less popular with each passing year, which prompted President Barack Obama to withdraw most American forces. Both countries remained wracked by civil unrest and violence, but at least Iraq had a more representative government after the ouster of its longtime dictator, Saddam Hussein.

Whether globalization will solve the world's problems or compound them remains unclear. Strict enforcement of international limits on carbon dioxide emissions might remedy global warming, but it might also provoke defiance by nations unwilling to make the economic sacrifices required. International health workers have eliminated dreaded scourges such as smallpox, but acquired immune deficiency syndrome (AIDS) remains a ruinous plague in some African countries and international travel by millions of people each day increases the risk that a deadly new disease might spread beyond control. The lowering of trade barriers has given China and other rising industrial powers with cheap labor a huge boost and provided consumers around the world with inexpensive products, but wealthier nations might retaliate economically if their trade deficits continue to rise.

New technologies such as television and the internet have helped create an international mass culture, but those same technologies can be used to

Egyptian protesters fight police near Tahrir Square, as part of the greater Arab Spring that swept across the Middle East beginning in 2011.

fight globalization or set one culture against another. Televised images of civilians being executed by terrorists—or prisoners of war being abused by occupation forces—can divide viewers within the so-called global village created by television into hostile camps. The World Trade Center was targeted as a towering symbol of globalization, and engineers responsible for producing massive structures must now take extra precautions to ensure that their architectural Goliaths will withstand assault by small but determined groups opposed to the political, economic, and technological forces they blame for homogenizing the world's cultures and threatening their beliefs and traditions.

An economic downside of globalization revealed itself in 2008 when a financial collapse in the U.S. quickly rippled throughout the globe. Investment, trade, and employment nosedived in the U.S., Europe, Japan, and elsewhere, shrinking the world economy in 2009. The lingering recession was the world's worst since the 1930s, although some countries—China and Canada, for example—fared much better than most.

The world may never be fully at peace, but international laws and agencies designed to avoid a repetition of past horrors may help restrain those who make war in the future. The presumed right of conquerors to kill or enslave entire populations exercised by despots from ancient times well into the 20th century is now recognized as a crime against humanity, punishable by international tribunals. That alone is a significant step toward a new world order. ∎

	1950	1956	1962	1968	1974
THE AMERICAS	**1952** Jonas Salk discovers the polio vaccine. **1954** *Brown* v. *Board of Education* makes segregation in U.S. public schools unconstitutional. **1954** RCA introduces the first color TVs. **1955** Rosa Parks's arrest in Montgomery, Alabama, sets the American civil rights movement in motion.	**1956** Elvis Presley releases his first hit. **1956** Sixteen-year-old Pelé joins Brazil's Santos soccer team. **1957** The American baby boom peaks. **1959** Alaska and Hawaii become the 49th and 50th U.S. states. **1959** Cuba's Fidel Castro installs the first communist regime in the West.	**1962** The Cuban Missile Crisis occurs. **1963** U.S. President Kennedy is assassinated in Dallas, Texas. **1963** Martin Luther King, Jr., delivers his "I Have a Dream" speech in Washington, D.C. **1967** Che Guevera is killed by government troops in Bolivia.	**1968** Martin Luther King, Jr., is assassinated in Memphis, Tenn. **1969** More than 300,000 rock-n-roll fans attend Woodstock. **1969** Apollo 11 lands men on the moon. **1970** Pelé leads Brazil to their third World Cup. **1973** *Roe* v. *Wade* makes abortion a U.S. constitutional right.	**1974** Watergate forces Nixon to resign. **1974** Henry Aaron breaks Babe Ruth's all-time home run record. **1976-1983** Thousands disappear in Argentina's "dirty war." **1977** The Alaska pipeline opens. **1977** The U.S. returns the Panama Canal to Panama.
EUROPE	**1952** Elizabeth II becomes queen of England. **1953** Nikita Khrushchev succeeds Joseph Stalin as head of the Soviet Communist Party. **1953** Watson and Crick unveil their double-helix model of DNA. **1954** British runner Roger Bannister breaks the four-minute-mile barrier.	**1957** The Soviet Union launches Sputnik I, setting off a space race with America. **1958** The European Economic Community comes into being. **1960** The Irish Republican Army begins guerrilla fighting against the British. **1961** Yuri Gagarin of the Soviet Union becomes the first man in space.	**1962** The Second Vatican Council begins wide-ranging reforms of Roman Catholic practices. **1963** The Beatles release their first album. **1964** Nikita Khrushchev is forced to resign after the Cuban Missile Crisis. **1966** The Soviet Union lands the unmanned Luna 9 on the moon.	**1968** The Soviet Union invades Czechoslovakia during the Prague Spring. **1971** 73 British scientists develop the CT scan and MRI. **1972** Arab terrorists kill 11 Israeli athletes at the Olympics in Munich. **1972** Fourteen unarmed Catholic protesters are gunned down by British police on Bloody Sunday.	**1975** Soyuz 19 meets with Apollo ASTP in the first Soviet-U.S. space linkup. **1976** Nadia Comaneci wins three gold medals at the Montreal Olympics, with seven perfect scores. **1978** Cardinal Karol Wojtyla becomes Pope John Paul II. **1978** The first "test-tube baby" is born in England.
MIDDLE EAST & AFRICA	**1950** Apartheid is extended in South Africa. **1952** The Mau Mau rebellion begins in Kenya. **1953** The CIA helps restore the shah of Iran to power. **1954** Colonel Gamal Abdel Nasser seizes power in Egypt. **1954** A rebellion against French rule in Algeria begins.	**1956** The Suez crisis occurs. **1957** Kwame Nkrumah leads Ghana to independence, the first for a sub-Saharan African nation. **1958** Egypt and Syria join forces to create the United Arab Republic. **1960** OPEC is founded. **1960** The Year of Africa: 16 former European colonies become independent.	**1962** The French colonial empire is virtually nonexistent. **1964** The Palestine Liberation Organization is established, with Yasser Arafat as head. **1967** The Arab-Israeli Six Day War occurs. **1967** Dr. Christiaan N. Barnard of South Africa performs the world's first human heart transplant operation.	**1968-1974** Drought in the Sahel region of northern Africa kills 500,000. **1970** Anwar Sadat becomes president of Egypt. **1973** The Yom Kippur War occurs between Egypt and Israel. **1973** OPEC embargoes oil supplies, causing a worldwide energy crisis.	**1974** A drought-induced famine threatens millions in Africa. **1975** Civil war erupts in Lebanon between Muslim rebels and the Christian government. **1978** Egypt and Israel sign the Camp David Accords. **1979** Ayatollah Khomeini takes control in Iran; his followers seize the U.S. Embassy.
ASIA & OCEANIA	**1950** North Korea invades South Korea, initiating the Korean War. **1950** The Sino-Soviet Treaty of Alliance and Friendship is signed. **1952** Mother Teresa opens the Home for Dying Destitutes in Calcutta, India. **1953** Sir Edmund Hillary and Tenzing Norgay reach Mount Everest's summit.	**1956** Sony exports its first products, to Canada. **1958** China begins the Great Leap Forward, a disastrous, planned move toward rapid industrialization. **1960** Tibetans revolt against Chinese control. **1960** The Sino-Soviet split occurs. **1961** The Trans-Siberian Railroad is electrified.	**1964** The Gulf of Tonkin incident intensifies U.S. military involvement in Vietnam. **1965** Singapore declares full independence. **1966** Chairman Mao launches China's Cultural Revolution and begins purging intellectuals. **1966** Indira Gandhi, daughter of Nehru, becomes prime minister of India.	**1968** North Vietnam and Viet Cong troops launch the Tet Offensive. **1968** U.S. troops massacre men, women, and children in My Lai. **1970** Cyclones and floods kill 500,000 in East Pakistan (later Bangladesh). **1973** The U.S. and South Vietnam sign a cease-fire agreement with North Vietnam.	**1975** Pol Pot's Khmer Rouge takes control of Cambodia. **1975** Junko Tabei of Japan becomes the first woman to climb Mount Everest. **1976** North and South Vietnam are reunited. **1978** Japanese models account for half of the U.S. import car market. **1979** The Soviets invade Afghanistan.

1980	1986	1992	1998	2002-Present
1980 Smallpox is eradicated. **1980** CNN becomes the first 24-hour news station. **1980** Mount St. Helens volcano erupts. **1981** Scientists identify the AIDS virus. **1981** IBM introduces the first personal computer. **1983** Barney Clark receives the first artificial heart, the Jarvik-7.	**1986** GM overtakes Exxon as the largest company in the U.S. **1986** Oprah Winfrey's Chicago daytime talk show debuts nationally. **1988** Crack cocaine use grows. **1988** Prozac hits the U.S. market. **1990** The Hubble Space Telescope is put into operation.	**1993** A terrorist bomb explodes inside the World Trade Center in New York. **1993** The first graphical Web browser, Mosaic, is developed. **1994** The Americas are free of polio. **1995** A bomb explodes in a federal office building in Oklahoma City, Oklahoma.	**1998** Viagra becomes the fastest-selling drug in U.S. history. **2000** Scores of dot-com businesses go belly up. **2001** Planes hijacked by al-Qaeda terrorists crash into New York City's World Trade Center towers and the Pentagon in Washington, D.C., killing nearly 3,000.	**2002** Revelations of child molestation by priests embroil the Catholic Church in scandal. **2008** Barack Obama is elected the first black U.S. President. **2008** A financial collapse triggers worldwide recession.
1980 Lech Walesa becomes chairman of a new independent trade union (Solidarity) in Poland. **1980** Researchers find the Titanic in the North Atlantic. **1985** The U.K. begins screening blood donations for the AIDS virus. **1985** British scientist Alec Jeffreys announces genetic fingerprinting.	**1987** Earth's population hits five billion. **1989** The Berlin Wall is demolished. **1990** Lech Walesa is elected president of Poland. **1991** The U.S.S.R. officially ceases to exist on December 9. **1991** Tim Berners-Lee puts the World Wide Web online.	**1994** The Channel tunnel opens between England and France. **1995** The World Trade Organization is created to promote economic development worldwide. **1995** Great Britain establishes the world's first DNA-based crime database. **1997** British geneticists clone an adult sheep named Dolly.	**1990-2010** Millions of refugees struggle to relocate after the collapse of communism and ethnic splintering in Eastern Europe. **2000** Yugoslavian president Slobodan Milosevic is driven from office. **2000** Vladimir Putin is elected president of Russia.	**2002** Euros, the currency of the new European Union, begin circulating. **2003** The Concorde makes its final flight, ending the era of supersonic commercial flight. **2005** Angela Merkel becomes the first female chancellor of Germany. **2013** Pope Benedict XVI resigns, the first pope to do so in more than 500 years.
1980 Iraq invades Iran, beginning a decade-long war. **1981** Egyptian President Anwar Sadat is assassinated. **1982** Israel invades Lebanon in an attempt to drive out Palestine Liberation Organization (PLO) terrorists. **1983** The second Sudanese civil war begins between Muslims and non-Muslims.	**1987** The Palestinian *intifada* begins, an organized uprising against Israel led by children. **1991** Apartheid is dismantled; in 1994 Nelson Mandela becomes the first black president of South Africa. **1991** A U.S.-led coalition liberates Kuwait from Iraqi occupation in the Gulf War.	**1993** Israel and the PLO negotiate the Oslo Accords. **1994** Civil war erupts in Rwanda when Hutu gangs kills more than 500,000 Tutsi. **1995** Israel's Yitzhak Rabin is assassinated by a Jewish law student. **1995** Zaire suffers an outbreak of the Ebola virus, which is more lethal than AIDS.	**1998** Iraq prevents UN weapons inspectors from conducting a search. **2000s** AIDS becomes an epidemic in Africa, where in some countries almost 40 percent of the population is HIV-positive. **2001** Ariel Sharon becomes prime minister of Israel as violence with Palestinians worsens. Israel invades the Gaza Strip and West Bank in 2002.	**2003** The U.S. invades Iraq. **2003** Ethnic and religious conflicts boil over in Sudan's Darfur region. **2005** Mahmoud Abbas succeeds Yasser Arafat as president of the Palestinian Authority. **2011** Uprisings in Egypt climax the Arab Spring.
1980s Concern over the loss of rain forests in Asia and Brazil grows, becoming a major environmental issue. **1980** Japan surpasses the U.S. as the world's largest automaker. **1983** The population of China reaches one billion. **1984** Sony and Philips introduce the first commercial CD players.	**1987** Soviet troops begin withdrawing from Afghanistan. **1988** Benazir Bhutto of Pakistan becomes the first female head of an Islamic nation. **1989** Britain repatriates the Vietnam boat people from Hong Kong. **1989** Thousands of students occupy Tiananmen Square in Beijing, China, protesting for democracy.	**1992** Australia's high court legally recognizes the presence of Aboriginal peoples before European settlement. **1996** The Taliban takes over Afghanistan and imposes Islamic law. **1996** Osama bin Laden moves to Afghanistan after being expelled by Sudan. **1997** Hong Kong reverts to Chinese control.	**1998** An economic crisis known as the "Asian flu" hits Southeast Asia. **1998** India and Pakistan begin testing nuclear weapons. **1998** The world's largest suspension bridge opens in Japan. **2001** The United States topples Afghanistan's Taliban government.	**2003** The SARS virus spreads from China. **2004** An undersea earthquake triggers a tsunami that kills almost 300,000 in Indonesia and South Asia. **2011** U.S. Navy Seals kill Osama bin Laden in Pakistan. **2011** The Tohoku earthquake and tsunami cause the Fukushima nuclear disaster.

	POLITICS & POWER	GEOGRAPHY & ENVIRONMENT	CULTURE & RELIGION
THE AMERICAS	**1950 U.S. Senator Joseph McCarthy** of Wisconsin tells President Truman that the State Department is infiltrated with communists and communist sympathizers. **1950-51 Responding to the Soviet threat,** Canada significantly increases troop strength and defense spending. **1951 The 22nd Amendment** to the U.S. Constitution is passed, limiting the president to a maximum of two terms in office. **1952 Dwight D. Eisenhower** is elected president of the U.S., the first Republican president in 20 years.	**1951 Flooding** of the Kansas River in Missouri and Kansas causes the first $1 billion natural disaster in U.S. history.	**1950s The postwar baby boom** dramatically increases birthrates in North America. As the population grows, families in both the U.S. and Canada increasingly move to the suburbs. **1950 Fallout shelters** grow in popularity in the U.S. amid fears of nuclear war. **1950 The Diner's Club card** is introduced, the first "credit card" accepted at multiple retail establishments. **1951 Fifteen million televisions** are in use in the U.S., up from 1.5 million the previous year. By 1960 Americans own 85 million sets.
EUROPE	**1950s Konrad Adenauer** leads Christian Democrats as the majority party in Germany. **1952 King George VI** of England dies, succeeded by his daughter, Queen Elizabeth II.		**1950 Pope Pius XII** proclaims the dogma of the bodily assumption of the Virgin Mary. **1950s The postwar baby boom** dramatically increases birthrates in western Europe. *Marilyn Monroe, America's ultimate sex symbol, entertains U.S. troops.*
MIDDLE EAST & AFRICA	**1950 The Population Registration Act** in South Africa creates racial categories for all persons and extends apartheid to all aspects of social and political life. **1951 King Abdullah** of Jordan is assassinated in Jerusalem. **1952 Kenya** declares a state of emergency after an uprising by the Mau Mau, a native group opposed to British rule. **1952 Turkey and Greece** join NATO. **1952 Egyptian army officers** revolt against the monarchy and British occupation and establish a republic in 1953.	**1950 Israel's new "law of return"** grants automatic citizenship to any immigrant Jews. **1950 Iraq** founds a Development Board to provide flood control and infrastructure development. **1950-51 Iraq's Jewish community** migrates to Israel. **1951 Libya** becomes independent from Italy. **1952 The first Egyptian Land Reform Act** is introduced.	**1950s Beirut,** the "jewel of the Mediterranean," becomes the Middle East's banking and nightclub capital and bridge to the West. **1952 Israel and Germany** agree on restitution for damages done to Jews by Nazis. **1952-53 The Mau Mau uprising** in Kenya consists of a core of oath-taking guerrilla warriors based on the model of the Kikuyu secret society. The movement responds to British imperialism, including the brutal detention of more than one million Kikuyu in concentration camps after WW II.
ASIA & OCEANIA	**1950 The Soviet Union** and China sign the Treaty of Alliance and Friendship. **1950 China** sends forces to occupy Tibet. **1950 North Korea** invades South Korea and captures Seoul, initiating the Korean Conflict. U.S. General Douglas MacArthur is given command of United Nations forces. **1951 General MacArthur** is relieved of his Far East command for criticizing President Truman's policy of limiting the war to the Korean Peninsula. A stalemate begins to take shape. **1952 The U.S.-Japan Security Treaty** takes effect, bringing Japan into the U.S. camp.	**1950 The Republic of South Korea** is established after attempts to reunify with North Korea fail. The boundary between North and South is drawn along the 38th parallel. **1950 Drought** followed by flooding kills 10 million people in northern China. **1952 Japan** regains official independence as Allied occupation ends.	**1950s The postwar baby boom** dramatically increases birthrates in Australasia.

SCIENCE & TECHNOLOGY	PEOPLE & SOCIETY
1950 CBS broadcasts the first TV program in color. **1951 UNIVAC**, the first commercial computer, is introduced by Remington Rand. **1951 Electric power** is produced from atomic energy for the first time in Arcon, Idaho. **1952 Traffic lights** appear for the first time in New York City.	**1950 Former U.S. State Department official Alger Hiss** is convicted of perjury and sentenced to five years in prison. **1951 Julius and Ethel Rosenberg** are sentenced to death for espionage against the U.S. for selling classified information to the Soviet Union. They are executed in 1953. **1951 Cleveland disc jockey Alan Freed** coins the term "rock-and-roll." **1952 Jonas Salk** discovers the polio vaccine, which, after testing in 1953-54, is approved for widespread use in 1955.
1950 The Soviet Union puts ballistic missiles aboard submarines. **1952 The British-made Havilland Comet** becomes the first turbojet passenger plane in regular service.	**1952 Albert Schweitzer** wins the Nobel Peace Prize. **1950s-1960s Josip Tito** develops an independent communist state in Yugoslavia. He will remain president of the country until his death in 1980.
1950s Turkey constructs highway networks, dams, and irrigation canals and extends commercial agriculture.	**1950 The Arab League** institutes an economic boycott of Israel. **1950 The UN Relief and Works Agency** is founded to oversee Palestinian refugee camps with an annual budget of $27 per person. **1952 Egyptian president Gamal Abdel Nasser** pledges to control his country's annual flooding with a giant new dam across the Nile River. The Aswan High Dam will be completed in 1970 at a cost of $1 billion.
1950-53 The Korean War is the first war to feature extensive aerial combat by jet fighters, combat use of helicopters (tactical and logistical), and synthetic bullet-proof vests for infantry. **1950s The U.S.** tests nuclear weapons, including the first hydrogen bomb, at Bikini and Enewetok atolls in the Marshall Islands.	**1950 Chiang Kai-shek** establishes the anticommunist government of Nationalist China on the island of Taiwan (Formosa). **1952 Mother Teresa** opens the Nirmal Hriday (Immaculate Heart) Home for Dying Destitutes in Calcutta, India, after the Order of the Missionaries of Charity is formally established in 1950.

THE KOREAN WAR

The first major conflict of the Cold War played out on the tiny Korean Peninsula, where Soviet and U.S. forces had been occupying either side of the 38th parallel since the end of World War II. The establishment of rival governments in 1948 lit a fuse that finally exploded when communist North Korea invaded noncommunist South Korea on June 25, 1950.

President Harry Truman committed the U.S. military to Korea and returned a familiar face to Pacific combat—Gen. Douglas MacArthur, who was made supreme commander of a coalition force of United Nations members. North Korean forces had overwhelmed the South with their initial invasion, capturing the capital, Seoul. But MacArthur staged a daring amphibious landing at Inchon, cutting off North Korean supply lines and allowing UN forces to mount a counteroffensive. By the end of 1950 UN forces had driven their opponents all the way to the border of communist China.

The tide turned when 300,000 Chinese troops poured across the Yalu River to join the North Koreans. MacArthur wanted to take the war to China and even use nuclear weapons, but Truman believed this would only provoke the Soviets. Unable to resolve their differences, Truman relieved MacArthur of his command in 1951. The war became what one general called a "meat grinder"—with brutal infantry battles with names like Heartbreak Ridge and Pork Chop Hill that accomplished little more than a stalemate.

When new U.S. president Dwight Eisenhower finally wrangled an armistice in 1953, after 54,000 U.S. casualties and at least half a million Chinese and Korean casualties, the boundaries and governments of the North and South remained unchanged. Denied the outright victory they dearly wanted, the U.S. had to console itself with the fact that, for the time being anyway, they had kept communism contained.

POLITICS & POWER	GEOGRAPHY & ENVIRONMENT	CULTURE & RELIGION

THE AMERICAS

1954 The U.S. Supreme Court, in *Brown* v. *Board of Education,* rules that segregation in public schools is unconstitutional.

1954 U.S. president Eisenhower formulates the domino theory, which asserts that once one country is toppled by communists, others in the area will collapse as well.

1954 Guatemalan president Jacobo Guzman is overthrown in a coup aided by the CIA.

1955 The military seizes control of economically troubled Argentina, forcing President Juan Perón to flee.

1954 The United States sends back to Mexico almost four million illegal immigrants.

1954 Swanson introduces TV dinners.

1954 The first human trials of an oral contraceptive for women begin.

1955 The U.S. Air Force Academy opens in Colorado.

1955 The AFL-CIO labor unions merge, with George Meany as president.

WHAT LIFE WAS LIKE

In TV's Golden Age

Before the baby boom in America, there was the TV boom. Rapid technological advances and higher disposable incomes after World War II led to an explosion in television ownership. In 1950 there were 1.5 million sets in the U.S. The next year, 15 million. By 1960, 85 million. The phenomenon went global just as fast. The Soviets launched Sputnik in 1957 as a volley in the Cold War; in 1964 Japan was using artificial satellites to broadcast the Olympics worldwide. Television was creating a global village that connected cultures in an unprecedented way. The 1950s also saw TV shift from being an extension of radio to creating original formats that endure today: sitcoms like *I Love Lucy* and cop dramas like *Dragnet*. Today virtually every country in the world has developed at least one TV channel.

EUROPE

1953 Nikita Khrushchev is appointed First Secretary of the Central Committee of the Communist Party after Joseph Stalin dies.

1955 The Soviet Union and its satellites form the Warsaw Pact.

1955 Winston Churchill resigns as prime minister of Great Britain.

1953 Heavy flooding in Holland kills 2,000.

1953 Simone de Beauvoir publishes her landmark feminist book, *The Second Sex.*

1953 Bond, James Bond—fictional British spy—undertakes his first mission in print, in Ian Fleming's *Casino Royale.* Bond debuts on the silver screen in 1962 in *Dr. No.*

1955 Commercial TV begins broadcasting in Britain.

MIDDLE EAST & AFRICA

1954 Colonel Gamal Abdel Nasser seizes power in Egypt.

1954 A rebellion against French rule in Algeria begins, which will last eight years.

1955 David Ben-Gurion becomes prime minister of Israel again, reflecting a shift toward confrontation with Israel's Arab neighbors.

1955 The first Sudanese civil war begins, between the new Muslim government and mostly non-Muslim population in the south.

1955 The Baghdad Pact unites Turkey, Iraq, Iran, Pakistan, and Britain against the Soviets.

1950s Saudi oil revenues rise 600 percent; wealth is not doled out systematically.

1953-56 Jews migrate in great numbers from Libya, Morocco, and Tunisia to Israel.

1954 Desert locusts swarm Morocco, destroying $14 million worth of citrus crops in six weeks.

1953-54 Sudan begins the transition to independence when Great Britain and Egypt turn over local governance to the northern (Muslim) Sudanese.

1953 Pro-monarchy forces restore the shah of Iran (Mohammed Reza Pahlavi) to power in a coup supported by the U.S. and Great Britain against prime minister Mohammed Mossadegh, who had nationalized Iran's oil industry and was becoming a Soviet ally.

1953 The Academy of Hebrew Language decides on official terminology and spellings.

1955 Islamic courts are abolished in Egypt.

ASIA & OCEANIA

1953 After further inconclusive fighting, an armistice is signed, ending the Korean War. The boundaries of North and South Korea are drawn along the battle lines of the 38th parallel.

1953 Cambodia gains independence from France.

1954 Vietnamese communists take Dien Bien Phu and occupy Hanoi, forcing a complete French withdrawal from Indochina.

1954 The Southeast Asian Treaty Organization (SEATO) is established to oppose communism in Asia.

1954 Vietnam splits into North and South Vietnam after the communist victory in the Indochina War.

1954 China's Yangtze River overflows, killing 40,000 and forcing 10 million people to evacuate.

1954 Reverend Sun Myung Moon founds the Unification Church in South Korea. His followers are eventually dubbed Moonies.

SCIENCE & TECHNOLOGY

1953 Cigarette smoking is reported to cause lung cancer.

1953 The Redstone missile, the first U.S. intermediate-range ballistic missile (IRBM), is developed by Werner von Braun and other former Nazi scientists.

1954 The U.S. launches the first nuclear-powered submarine, the *Nautilus.*

1954 RCA introduces the first color TVs. NBC begins regular broadcasting in color.

1953 The Soviet Union detonates its first hydrogen bomb.

1955 The British develop an atomic clock.

1955 Two French-made electric locomotives set a world speed record of 205 mph.

Roger Bannister breaks the tape and the four-minute mark at a mile race in Oxford, England.

1955 Tokyo Telecommunications Engineering (Sony) produces the first pocket-size transistor radio.

PEOPLE & SOCIETY

1954 Ernest Hemingway wins the Nobel Prize in Literature.

1955 African American Rosa Parks is arrested after refusing to give up her bus seat to a white person in Montgomery, Alabama. Her arrest sparks a bus boycott led by local minister Martin Luther King, Jr., and sets the American civil rights movement in motion.

1953 British physicist Francis Crick and U.S. biologist James Watson unveil their famous double-helix model of DNA, the material in chromosomes that control heredity.

1954 Britain's Roger Bannister breaks the 4-minute mile barrier, running a mile in 3 minutes 59.4 seconds.

1953 Jomo Kenyatta and five other Kikuyu are convicted for managing Kenya's Mau Mau rebellion.

1953 Ibn Saud, founder of Saudi Arabia, dies. His centralized government, ruling through the Wahhabi sect of Islam, replaced tribal confederations.

1954-62 Frantz Fanon, a French-educated West Indian inspired by the Algerian independence war against France, urges violence against colonial oppressors in his influential book *The Wretched of the Earth.*

1953 Sir Edmund Hillary and Tenzing Norgay become the first people to reach the summit of Mount Everest, the world's tallest mountain.

1954 Ho Chi Minh, addressing French attempts to reoccupy Indochina: "You can kill ten of my men for every one I kill of yours, yet even at those odds, you will lose and I will win."

1955 The Bandung Conference of nonaligned African and Asian nations, designed to promote economic and cultural cooperation and oppose colonialism, takes place in Indonesia.

Hillary and Norgay prepare for their final ascent.

CONQUERING EVEREST

When asked in 1923 why he wanted to climb Mount Everest, British explorer George Mallory coined a new philosophy for any quixotic undertaking: "Because it is there." In truth Mallory was just tired of being asked the question. Climbing the world's tallest mountain was and is considered the summit of physical accomplishment.

Mallory made his attempt in 1924 and never returned. His team came within 1,200 feet of the top, and Mallory and Andrew Irvine climbed on farther before disappearing. In 1952 a Swiss team, aided by Sherpa Tenzing Norgay of Nepal, came within 700 feet of the summit before giving up due to exhaustion. Above 26,000 feet, there is barely enough oxygen to function.

Norgay returned the following year as part of a British expedition with New Zealand explorer Edmund Hillary. As a scrawny child, Hillary had dreamed of adventure, and he later helped to map new routes to Everest from Nepal after the Chinese government closed access to Everest through Tibet. On May 29, 1953, Hillary and Norgay put their feet on the summit, 29,028 feet above sea level. Without the use of the sophisticated climbing equipment and oxygen tanks in use today, they had registered the first confirmed ascent of what Tibetans call the Mother of the Universe.

	POLITICS & POWER	GEOGRAPHY & ENVIRONMENT	CULTURE & RELIGION
THE AMERICAS	**1956 U.S. president Eisenhower** is reelected. **1956 Eisenhower** signs the Federal Aid Highway Act to create the nation's first interstate highway system. **1957 Physician François "Papa Doc" Duvalier** becomes president of Haiti. **1958 The U.S. and Canada** develop NORAD, an early warning radar system to detect missile attacks. **1958 Fidel Castro** launches a revolution against the Batista government of Cuba. Batista flees in 1959; Castro becomes premier of Cuba.	**1956 The green revolution,** a combination of improved agricultural techniques and new plant breeds, allows Mexico to become totally self-sufficient for its wheat supply. The techniques spread worldwide and are credited with saving a billion people from starvation in India and Pakistan. **1959 Pump irrigation** is introduced to the Texas plains and, combined with underground pipes and sprinkler systems, helps produce millions of dollars more in crop value.	**1956 Elvis Presley** releases the first of more than 170 hit singles, "Heartbreak Hotel." **1957 The baby boom** peaks: 4.3 million Americans are born, the most in 30 years. During the 1950s, 29 million babies are born. **1957 Canada** establishes the Canadian Council to Sustain Canadian Culture. **1957 Arkansas governor Orval Faubus** calls out the National Guard to prevent nine African-American students from integrating Little Rock's Central High per a U.S. Supreme Court order. **1958 The Guggenheim Museum,** designed by Frank Lloyd Wright, opens in New York.
EUROPE	**1956 Nikita Khrushchev** to Western ambassadors, "We will bury you." **1956 Soviet premier Nikita Khrushchev** begins "de-Stalinization," releasing millions of political prisoners and liberalizing Soviet politics. Soviet troops, though, invade Hungary and crush an uprising after the satellite tries to withdraw from the Warsaw Pact. **1958 The European Economic Community** (sometimes called the Common Market) comes into being, a bid to give Europe economic leverage equal to the U.S. and Soviet Union.	**1950s Migration** from farms to cities expands at a rapid pace. **1957 Former British colonies** begin to enter the British Commonwealth of Nations.	**1956 American movie star Grace Kelly** weds Prince Rainier of Monaco. **1956 The Italian liner *Andrea Doria*** sinks after colliding with the *Stockholm* off Nantucket Island. **1957 The British** begin allowing women in the House of Lords. **1958 Pope Pius XII** dies; Cardinal Roncalli becomes Pope John XXIII.
MIDDLE EAST & AFRICA	**1956 The second Arab-Israeli war** occurs after Egypt seizes the Suez Canal, part of President Gamal Abdel Nasser's strategy to position the Arab world against the West. Israel invades and Britain and France, with commercial interests in the canal, send troops to the Suez Crisis, but ultimately the UN declares the canal Egyptian property. **1958 Egypt and Syria** join forces to create the United Arab Republic, with Nasser as president. **1958 Iraq's King Faisal** is assassinated by the army. Iraq becomes a republic, withdraws from the Baghdad Pact, and allies with the Soviets.	**1956 Sudan** gains independence from Great Britain; Tunisia and Morocco from France. **1957 Ghana** gains independence from Great Britain. **1958 Madagascar** elects to become an independent republic within the French Community; French West Africa and French Equatorial Africa elect self-government within the French Community.	*Chairman Mao Zedong* 
ASIA & OCEANIA	**1956 Pakistan** becomes an Islamic republic. **1957 North Vietnam** begins guerrilla activity, through the Viet Cong, against South Vietnam.	**1958 An outbreak of cholera** and smallpox in India and East Pakistan (Bangladesh) kills more than 75,000.	**1958 China begins the Great Leap Forward** (1958-1960), a planned, but disastrous, move toward rapid industrial development that leads to mass starvation.

SCIENCE & TECHNOLOGY

1956 FORTRAN, the first computer language, is introduced.

1956 The first large-scale clinical trials (necessary for FDA approval) of oral birth control pills are conducted in Puerto Rico because of restrictive U.S. laws.

1957 Interferons, the body's virus fighters, are discovered.

1958 The U.S. government starts NASA and launches Project Mercury, the country's manned space program.

1956 The first nuclear power plant begins operating, in Great Britain.

1957 The Soviet Union tests the first intercontinental ballistic missile (ICBM). The U.S. tests the ICBM Atlas the following year. The range of the new missiles makes large-scale nuclear war a real possibility.

1957 The Soviet Union launches Sputnik I, the first artificial satellite, setting off a space race with the U.S., which responds with their first satellite, Explorer I, in 1958. Artificial satellites eventually make global communication possible.

Dry your tears, Africa!

Your children come back to you

Out of the storms and squalls of

fruitless journeys. . . .

"DRY YOUR TEARS, AFRICA!"
BY BERNARD DADIE,
IVORY COAST–BORN POET

1956 Tokyo Telecommunications Engineering (Sony) exports its first products when a Canadian retailer decides to sell their transistor radios.

PEOPLE & SOCIETY

1956 Sixteen-year-old Pelé joins Brazil's Santos soccer team.

1957 Canadian leader Lester Pearson wins the Nobel Peace Prize for helping resolve the 1956 Arab-Israeli War.

1957 Martin Luther King, Jr., forms the Southern Christian Leadership Conference (SCLC) to promote nonviolent solutions to segregation.

1958 U.S. engineer Jack Kilby invents the integrated circuit, revolutionizing the electronics industry and laying the groundwork for computer microprocessor chips.

1958 Charles de Gaulle is elected president of France, in large part due to opposition to the Algerian War. In 1959 he is officially declared president of the Fifth Republic of France. He proposes the creation of the French Community, giving French territories the right to choose independence or self-government.

1956 Gamal Abdel Nasser becomes a hero of Arab unity and leader of the Arab world. His book *Philosophy of the Revolution* is translated into many languages.

1957 Kwame Nkrumah leads Ghana to independence through an elected majority rule. He argues for pan-African unity, which he thinks could "stand as an example to a divided world."

1958 Akio Morita and Masaru Ibuka change the name of their company from Tokyo Telecommunications Engineering to Sony.

Elvis Presley on the set of Jailhouse Rock

ROCK-AND-ROLL

Some would argue that the decline of Western civilization can be traced to 1955, the year Bill Haley's "Rock Around the Clock" became rock-and-roll's first national hit. Others would say it was 1954, when Elvis Presley recorded "That's All Right" at Memphis, Tennessee's Sun Records.

In truth, the origin of rock-and-roll—the marching music for rebellious adolescents—is much harder to pinpoint. The term was actually coined by Cleveland disc jockey Alan Freed in 1951 to describe the black rhythm and blues records he was playing. But rock-and-roll as a commercial phenomenon was embodied in the swiveling hips of Elvis Presley, whose ability to combine the rhythms of black gospel, soul, and blues with smoldering sex appeal made him, and rock-and-roll, a worldwide sensation.

Elvis recorded 18 number-one hits, 38 top-10 hits, and 104 top-40 hits until his death in 1977, though Beatlemania had become the new counterculture sensation in the 1960s. As for those who would blame "the King" for pop culture's demise, a 1957 calypso song says it all: "Don't blame it on Elvis, for shakin' his pelvis / Shakin' the pelvis been in style way back since the River Nile."

POLITICS & POWER	GEOGRAPHY & ENVIRONMENT	CULTURE & RELIGION

THE AMERICAS

1959 Fidel Castro installs the first communist regime in the West. The U.S. breaks off diplomatic relations in 1961.

1960 The presidential debate between John F. Kennedy and Richard M. Nixon is broadcast on TV, a first. Kennedy's performance is credited with helping him become the youngest person elected U.S. president.

1961 U.S.-trained Cuban exiles attempt to overthrow Castro in the failed "Bay of Pigs" invasion, a major embarrassment to the Kennedy administration.

1959 Alaska and Hawaii become the 49th and 50th U.S. states.

1959 The St. Lawrence Seaway, a joint U.S.-Canadian venture, is completed, linking the Great Lakes to the Atlantic Ocean.

1960 Students protest segregation in Greensboro, North Carolina, by staging "sit-ins" at whites-only lunch counters.

1960 The U.S. Food and Drug Administration approves Envoid (aka the Pill) as a prescription birth control pill.

1961 President Kennedy establishes the Peace Corps.

1961 Freedom Riders begin organizing to force busing integration.

1961 Canada experiences a boom in car sales, which accelerates suburbanization.

EUROPE

1960 Leonid Brezhnev becomes president of the Soviet Union.

1960 The U.S. is caught spying on the Soviet Union when pilot Gary Powers and his U-2 airplane are shot down in Soviet air space. Powers is later traded back to the U.S. in exchange for captured Soviet spy Rudolf Abel.

1960 The Irish Republican Army (IRA) begins guerrilla fighting against the British to reunite six Northern Ireland counties still under British control despite Ireland becoming a republic in 1949.

1961 Thalidomide, a drug given to prevent morning sickness, is discovered to cause severe birth defects.

Fidel Castro and Ernesto "Che" Guevera in Cuba before the revolution

1960 Cyprus becomes an independent republic.

MIDDLE EAST & AFRICA

1960 The Organization of Petroleum Exporting Countries (OPEC) is founded.

1960 A military coup in Turkey restores secularism and issues a new constitution.

1960 The CIA and KGB battle behind the scenes in the newly independent, mineral-rich Republic of the Congo. CIA-backed Colonel Joseph Mobutu leads a successful coup against KGB-supported prime minister Patrice Lumumba, who is ultimately murdered.

1961 Syria withdraws from the United Arab Republic.

1960 The year of Africa: The Belgian Congo is granted independence and becomes the Republic of the Congo. Nigeria becomes independent from Britain. Somalia is created as a new independent republic from former British and Italian territories. Thirteen former French colonies become independent (Niger, Mauritania, Mali, Senegal, Chad, Ivory Coast, Togo, Benin Bourkina Fasso, Cameroon, Gabon, the Central African Republic, and Madagascar).

1961 Sierra Leone gains independence from Great Britain. South Africa, independent since 1910, withdraws from the British Commonwealth and becomes a republic.

1959 The militant Arab group al-Fatah is established in Kuwait by Yasser Arafat, dedicated to the establishment of a Palestinian state and the destruction of Israel.

1960 Former Gestapo chief Adolf Eichmann is arrested in South America and extradited to Israel, where he is found guilty after a Jerusalem trial in 1961 and hanged in 1962.

1960s Egypt adopts Arab socialism, nationalizing foreign enterprises and reclaiming farmland. The country promises jobs for all university graduates; bureaucracy swells unmanageably.

ASIA & OCEANIA

1959 U.S. noncombat military advisers die in a Viet Cong attack. In 1961 the U.S. agrees to arm and supply South Vietnamese troops.

1959 Tibetans revolt against Chinese control, but China crushes the uprising.

1960 The Sino-Soviet split becomes public, a dispute over philosophical differences regarding communism and the Soviets' involvement in Chinese affairs.

1962 Western Samoa gains independence from New Zealand.

1961 The Museum of the Chinese Revolution opens in Beijing.

SCIENCE & TECHNOLOGY	PEOPLE & SOCIETY
1959 Xerox introduces the first commercial copier. **1959 American Airlines** launches the jet age in the U.S. with the first transcontinental Boeing 707 flight. **1960 U.S. scientists** develop a laser (light amplification by stimulated emission of radiation). **1960 The U.S. Navy bathyscaphe *Trieste*** dives to a record depth of 35,800 feet in the Mariana Trench of the Pacific Ocean. **1960 The pacemaker** is developed.	**1959 Albert Sabin** develops a live-virus polio vaccine that can be taken orally and offers longer immunity than the Salk vaccine. **1959 Lorraine Hansberry's play** *A Raisin in the Sun* opens, the first play by an African-American woman ever to be produced on Broadway. **1961 Ray Kroc,** who opened his first McDonald's franchise in Des Plaines, Illinois, in 1955, officially buys the company from the McDonald brothers. By 1963 more than one billion hamburgers have been sold.
1959 The Soviet Union's unmanned Luna 2 rocket reaches the moon. That same year the U.S. launches into space and safely retrieves two monkeys. **1960 British scientists** invent a jet aircraft that can take off and land vertically. **1961 Yuri Gagarin** of the Soviet Union becomes the first man in space, one month ahead of Alan Shepard of the U.S.	**1959 U.S. vice president Richard Nixon** and Soviet leader Nikita Khrushchev engage in the "kitchen debate" at a U.S. trade show in Moscow. **1961 The Berlin Wall** is constructed to prevent East Berliners from defecting to West Berlin.
1959 Anthropologists Louis and Mary Leakey find the world's earliest known human in a Tanzanian gorge, establishing Africa as the cradle of humanity. **1960 Turkish agricultural output** doubles since 1950; industrial output increases 150 percent; per capita income is up 60 percent.	**1959-1961 Jomo Kenyatta,** imprisoned after the 1953 Mau Mau uprising, is sent into exile by the British. He becomes president of the Kenya African National Union in 1960, and the following year helps negotiate with the British a new constitution for Kenya, which gains its independence in 1963. **1960 Ethiopian Abebe Bikila** becomes the first African to win an Olympic gold medal in track & field. **1960 Population growth** in the Middle East has doubled since 1940; half the population is under 20 years of age.
1960s France tests nuclear weapons at several atolls in the Tuamotu Islands. **1961 The Trans-Siberian Railroad** is electrified.	**1959 Crown prince Akihito** of Japan marries commoner Shoda Michiko, the first time Japanese royalty has married a commoner in 1,500 years. **1960 Demonstrators** take to the streets in Japan to oppose the renewal of the security treaty with the U.S.

SPY GAMES

We caught the American spy—like a thief, red-handed!" bellowed Nikita Khrushchev. The thief was American pilot Gary Powers, and he had indeed been caught red-handed. In his downed Lockheed U-2 plane was a camera with damning evidence of Powers' mission, to spy on the Soviets from above.

The U-2 was the mother of all spy gadgets at the time, a technical marvel of a plane that could fly almost 4,000 miles without refueling and soar above 70,000 feet while still taking detailed surveillance photos. U-2s had been collecting intelligence on Soviet bombers, airfields, and missile development for four years before the 1960 exposure.

Blown covers were an unavoidable risk on the covert side of the Cold War. Powers may have been no James Bond, but the lives of many agents weren't far off from the suave fictional spy, with danger, disguises, high-tech gadgets, and undercover romance all part of the stock-in-trade. Moving world leaders around like pieces of a board game, CIA and KGB agents were involved in revolutions, coups, and election politics in Southeast Asia, Africa, the Middle East, and Latin America in an effort to shape the post–World War II world for or against communism.

The nature of intelligence work tends to make failure much more conspicuous than success, and the CIA has been burned by some high-profile gaffes over the years: The Bay of Pigs fiasco in trying to depose Fidel Castro; the revelation that Aldrich Ames had been a Soviet mole for a decade, selling secrets that led to the killing of numerous secret agents; and more recently, the false intelligence that Iraq possessed weapons of mass destruction, which was used as the basis for the United States' controversial invasion of Iraq.

While the end of the Cold War did not end the need for covert intelligence, it marked the end of an era. The lifting of the Iron Curtain removed a symbolic barrier between good and evil.

POLITICS & POWER	GEOGRAPHY & ENVIRONMENT	CULTURE & RELIGION

THE AMERICAS

1962 The Cuban Missile Crisis: U.S. president John F. Kennedy wins a standoff with Soviet premier Nikita Khrushchev, who reverses plans to install missile bases in Cuba.

1963 U.S. president Kennedy is assassinated November 22 in Dallas, Texas, by Lee Harvey Oswald. Lyndon B. Johnson is sworn in as president, and wins reelection in 1964.

1964 The U.S. Civil Rights Act of 1964 is passed, ending discrimination in public places, guaranteeing equal voting rights, and creating the Equal Employment Opportunity Commission.

1962 Jamaica becomes independent.

Martin Luther King, Jr., delivers his "I Have a Dream" speech at the 1963 March on Washington.

1962 The Wal-Mart discount store is opened by Sam Walton in Bentonville, Arkansas.

1962 Rachel Carson publishes her landmark environmental book, *Silent Spring,* about the dangers of pesticides.

1962 The U.S. Supreme Court rules against compulsory prayer in public schools.

1963 Two hundred thousand freedom marchers descend on Washington, D.C.

1963 Andy Warhol and Jasper Johns are featured in a New York exhibition of pop art.

1964 The Beatles make their U.S. debut on *The Ed Sullivan Show.*

EUROPE

1962 The French colonial empire is virtually nonexistent.

1963 The Profumo crisis rocks Britain's government when British war minister John Profumo admits an affair with 21-year-old Christina Wheeler, who is also involved with a Soviet Navy officer.

1964 Soviet president Leonid Brezhnev becomes Communist Party secretary, replacing Khrushchev, who is forced to resign after the Cuban Missile Crisis.

1963 An undersea volcano erupts off the southern coast of Iceland, creating the new island of Surtsey in a matter of days.

1964 Malta becomes independent.

1962 The Second Vatican Council (1962-65) begins wide-ranging reforms and modernization of Roman Catholic practices, including the end of the Latin Mass.

1963 Pope John XXIII dies, succeeded by Cardinal Montini as Pope Paul VI.

1963 The Beatles release their first album, *Please Please Me.*

MIDDLE EAST & AFRICA

1962 African National Congress (ANC) deputy president Nelson Mandela is arrested for treason for agitating against South Africa's apartheid laws.

1963 The Baath party gains power in Syria with an agenda of Arab nationalism.

1964 King Saud of Saudi Arabia is deposed and replaced by his son, Faisal, who modernizes the country's administration.

1964-65 Civil war erupts in Cyprus between Greeks and Turks.

1965 Israel establishes formal diplomatic relations with Germany.

1962 Algeria becomes independent, ending their eight-year rebellion against France. Uganda and Tanganyika gain independence from Great Britain, as do Rwanda and Burundi from Belgium.

1962 Yemen splits in two after a coup ousts the monarchy. North Yemen is a monarchy; South Yemen a republic.

1964 Kenya becomes an independent republic, with Jomo Kenyatta as president. Zanzibar and Tanganyika unite to form Tanzania. Rhodesia splits, with the north becoming the independent republic of Zambia.

1962 Algerian women march in support of independence during a national referendum.

1962 The Egyptian National Charter proclaims women's equality and grants them the right to vote.

1963 The Organization of African Unity (OAU) is formed.

1964 The Palestine Liberation Organization (PLO) is established under the leadership of Yasser Arafat, head of the Arab guerrilla force al-Fatah.

ASIA & OCEANIA

1962 A U.S. military council is established in South Vietnam.

1963 South Vietnamese president Ngo Dinh Diem is assassinated in a military coup.

1964 North Vietnamese patrol boats allegedly attack U.S. destroyers in the Gulf of Tonkin, causing Congress to allow President Johnson to increase troop levels.

1963 A hurricane and subsequent tsunamis kill 22,000 in East Pakistan (Bangladesh).

1963 Malaysia is formed from the federations of Malaya, Singapore, North Borneo, and Sarawak. Singapore withdraws in 1965.

We choose to go to the moon in this decade and do the other things, not because they are easy, but because they are hard . . . because that challenge is one that we are willing to accept, one we are unwilling to postpone, and one which we intend to win.

PRESIDENT JOHN F. KENNEDY, 1962

SCIENCE & TECHNOLOGY

1962 Telstar, the first telecom satellite, goes into orbit.

1962 John Glenn becomes the first American to orbit the earth.

1963 The measles vaccine is developed.

1963 New subatomic particles called quarks are theorized by U.S. physicists. Strong evidence for quarks is discovered in 1969.

1964 The first maquiladoras, or assembly plants, open in northern Mexico to provide cheap manufacturing labor for U.S. companies.

1963 Russian Valentina Tereshkova becomes the first woman in space.

1963 Philips Company of the Netherlands develops cassette tapes.

1964 The French detonate their first atomic bomb, part of their plan to be independent from U.S. military protection.

1964 Israel directs water from the Sea of Galilee and Jordan River to the coast and northern Negev, a project that "makes the desert bloom."

1964 China explodes its first atomic bomb.

1964 The Tokyo Olympics become the first event relayed throughout the world through a satellite TV feed.

1964 Japan's high-speed commuter train, the New Tokaido Line, begins service.

1964 Sony introduces the first home videotape recorder.

PEOPLE & SOCIETY

1962 Labor leader Cesar Chavez begins organizing California grape pickers and forms the United Food Workers union (UFW).

1963 Betty Friedan publishes *The Feminine Mystique.* Birth control pills, though still illegal in many cases, are in wide use.

1964 Cassius Clay (Muhammad Ali) defeats Sonny Liston for the world heavyweight boxing championship.

1964 Teamsters president Jimmy Hoffa organizes virtually all truck drivers under a single union agreement, creating one of the most powerful unions in U.S. history.

1963 The U.S. and Soviet Union set up a hotline between the White House and the Kremlin.

1962 Nelson Mandela after his trial: "I have cherished the ideal of a democratic and free society in which all persons live together in harmony and with equal opportunity. It is an ideal I hope to live for and to achieve."

1963 The shah of Iran, urged by U.S. president Kennedy to improve his peoples' condition, launches the "white revolution," including land reform and literacy programs. His dictatorial ways, however, bring strong opposition from Ruhollah Khomeini, who is subsequently exiled.

1962 U Thant of Burma (Myanmar) becomes the first Asian elected secretary-general of the UN.

1964 Soka Gakkai, one of the most powerful postwar religious movements in Japan, founds the Clean Government Party and becomes a political force.

President Kennedy as the motorcade departs

THE END OF CAMELOT

Don't let it be forgot / That once there was a spot / For one brief shining moment that was known / As Camelot." Those were the lyrics John F. Kennedy loved from the Broadway musical that came to represent the mythic and tragic nature of his presidency.

Kennedy's November 22, 1963, trip to Texas was to drum up support in a state he had barely won in 1960. The president was to fly into Love Field, ride in a motorcade through downtown Dallas, and give a speech at the Dallas Trade Mart. Dallas police were on high alert because a month earlier Democrat Adlai Stevenson had been assaulted by a Dallas crowd. But the motorcade was virtually without incident before passing the Texas Book Depository, where former Marine marksman Lee Harvey Oswald watched from a sixth-floor window. Oswald fired three shots at Kennedy, hitting him twice, once in the head.

The aftermath produced shocking and indelible images: Oswald being shot dead on live TV by Jack Ruby; young John F. Kennedy, Jr., saluting his father's casket; the still images from the amateur film footage shot by Abraham Zapruder published in *Life* magazine. The assassination of a popular president in the age of television created what one historian called "the greatest simultaneous experience in the history of this people."

1965-1968
TOWARD A NEW WORLD ORDER 1950-PRESENT

POLITICS & POWER	GEOGRAPHY & ENVIRONMENT	CULTURE & RELIGION

THE AMERICAS

1965 The U.S. Congress passes the Voting Rights Act, attacking voting restrictions aimed at African Americans.

1965 U.S. president Johnson announces his Great Society program, creating Medicare and expanding his "war on poverty."

1966 Miranda rights come into being after the U.S. Supreme Court overturns the conviction of a confessed rapist, ruling that he had not been properly informed of his right to counsel and to not testify against himself.

1967 The Quebec sovereignty movement calls for independence for the French-dominated province.

1965 Canada completes the Trans-Canada Highway.

1966 The great Northeast drought (1961-66), the worst in U.S. history, ends.

1966 A series of dams are built along the Missouri River, which generate huge amounts of power but fail to contain flooding.

1965 Martin Luther King, Jr., leads 4,000 people on a march from Selma to Montgomery, Alabama. In New York, Black Muslim leader Malcolm X is assassinated.

1965 The U.S. Supreme Court, citing the right to privacy, strikes down a Connecticut law that prohibits married couples from using birth control pills.

1967 Green Bay beats Kansas City 35-10 in the first Super Bowl.

EUROPE

1967 Colonel George Papadopoulos takes over Greece after a military coup.

1967 The European Economic Community becomes the European Community to reflect its growing political arrangements.

1966 Floods ravage northern Italy, damaging thousands of Renaissance art treasures in Venice and Florence.

1960s Car ownership is democratized as personal income levels rise.

MIDDLE EAST & AFRICA

1966 Dissident army officers topple Ghanaian president Kwame Nkrumah. Declassified U.S. documents suggest CIA involvement in the coup.

1967 The third Arab-Israeli war (the Six-Day War) begins after Egyptian president Nasser begins remilitarizing the Sinai Peninsula. Israel routs the Arab forces of Egypt, Jordan, and Syria, capturing old Jerusalem, the Sinai, the West Bank, and Golan Heights.

1967 The Nigerian civil war (1967-1970) begins over attempts by oil-rich Biafra to secede. The war leads to terrible famine in Biafra.

1965 Gambia becomes independent of France.

1966 Botswana and Lesotho become independent of Great Britain.

1966 The temples and statuary of Abu Simbel in Egypt are moved to save them from the rising waters of the new Aswan High Dam.

1967 The Suez Canal is closed, until 1975.

1967 Both sides in the Nigerian civil war agree to a 48-hour cease-fire so they can watch Pelé play in an exhibition soccer match in Lagos. (*The Times* of London: "How do you spell Pelé? G-O-D")

Brazilian soccer legend Pelé

ASIA & OCEANIA

1965 India and Pakistan fight a second inconclusive war over the disputed Kashmir region.

1965 Singapore withdraws from Malaysia and becomes a republic.

1965 The first U.S. ground troops (3,500 Marines) arrive in Vietnam at Da Nang.

1967 The U.S. begins mining rivers in North Vietnam. By the year's end there are 480,000 U.S. troops in Vietnam.

1965 Cyclones strike East Pakistan (Bangladesh), killing between 12,000 and 20,000 people.

1966 British Guiana becomes the independent nation of Guyana.

1966 Chairman Mao launches China's Cultural Revolution (1966-69), a revolutionary movement by students and workers against bureaucrats in the Chinese Communist Party. Mao's Red Guards begin purging so-called intellectuals and imperialists, who are believed to be opposed to Mao's socialist vision.

SCIENCE & TECHNOLOGY	PEOPLE & SOCIETY
1965 The St. Louis Gateway Arch is completed.	**1967 Thurgood Marshall** becomes the first African American appointed to the U.S. Supreme Court.
1965 The Gemini missions carry the first two-man crews into space and enable the first spacewalk by an American and the first space rendezvous of two manned crafts.	**1967 Revolutionary leader Che Guevera,** who helped bring Castro to power in Cuba, is caught and killed by troops in Bolivia.
1967 The new Apollo I program starts disastrously when a flash fire kills astronauts Virgil Grissom, Ed White, and Roger Chaffee at Cape Kennedy, Florida. As a result the U.S. suspends manned space flights indefinitely.	**1966 Betty Friedan** founds the National Organization of Women (NOW).
	1967 Fifty thousand people protest the Vietnam War at the Lincoln Memorial in Washington, D.C. Students nationwide burn their draft cards; Muhammad Ali is stripped of his boxing title for refusing to join the Army.
1965 Cosmonaut Alexei Leonov is the first person to "walk" in space, spending ten minutes outside Voskhod 2. Later that same year Ed White becomes the first American to walk in space.	**1967 The first automatic teller machine (ATM)** is put in service, at Barclays Bank in London.
1966 The Soviet Union lands the unmanned spacecraft Luna 9 on the moon. The U.S. lands Surveyor I on the moon and transmits TV images of the moon's surface.	
1966 The Soviet Union sends a pair of dogs into orbit aboard Cosmos 110.	
1967 The Soviets are forced to overhaul the Soyuz spacecrafts after cosmonaut Vladimir Kamarov is killed during reentry.	
1967 Dr. Christiaan N. Barnard performs the world's first human heart transplant operation in Cape Town, South Africa. He is assisted by Hamilton Naki, a self-taught black African surgeon, who later receives an honorary degree in medicine.	**1965 Colonel Joseph Mobutu,** who led the CIA-backed overthrow of the government in 1960, seizes control in the Congo.
	1966 Former French army officer Jean-Bedel Bokassa takes over the Central African Republic in a military coup. He declares himself president for life in 1972 and emperor in 1977.
	1967 Loss of the West Bank stimulates the PLO's development into a Palestinian guerrilla army and government-in-exile.
1966 Sony produces the first integrated radio circuit.	**1966 Indira Gandhi,** daughter of Nehru, becomes prime minister of India.
1967 China explodes its first hydrogen bomb.	**1966 Ferdinand Marcos** is elected president of the Philippines.

THE ARAB-ISRAELI WARS

For Jews, the partition resolution passed by the United Nations in 1947 was a godsend. The resolution carved British-controlled Palestine into separate Jewish and Palestinian states, with a third area that included Jerusalem and Bethlehem declared an "international enclave." This was the dream of Zion, a Jewish homeland whose establishment seemed even more urgent in the wake of the Holocaust.

For Palestine's Arab majority, however, the partition was Nakba—disaster. Jews and Arabs both congregated in the streets the day after the resolution passed, the former celebrating, the latter wearing black armbands. Confrontation was inevitable. When Israel formally declared independence on May 14, 1948, it was already engaged in what is now known as the first Arab-Israeli war.

That war, and every conflict since, has been in some sense a challenge and response to Israel's right to exist in what its neighbors consider an Arab land. Egypt under Gamal Abdel Nasser tried in 1956 and again in 1967 to unite Arab forces and wrest land from Israel, with disastrous results. Israel captured old Jerusalem, the Sinai, the West Bank, and the Golan Heights in the Six Day War of 1967 and held the territory in the Yom Kippur War of 1973.

Israel and Egypt made peace in 1978 with the historic Camp David Accords, but conflicts between Israelis and Palestinians persist over territorial rights. Hundred of thousands of Palestinians have been displaced since the first Arab-Israeli war, and Arabs insist on their "right of return." In 1987 the Palestinian *intifada* began with stone-throwing children and evolved into an organized uprising against Israeli rule.

The death of Yasser Arafat, longtime leader of the Palestine Liberation Organization, has given some cause for hope that compromise can be achieved. But for now, a potential melting pot continues to boil.

POLITICS & POWER	GEOGRAPHY & ENVIRONMENT	CULTURE & RELIGION

THE AMERICAS

1968 The U.S. Civil Rights Act of 1968 is passed, outlawing housing discrimination.

1968 The Mexican army massacres student protesters at the Plaza of Three Cultures ten days before the Summer Olympics begin.

1968 The U.S. presidential campaign: President Johnson decides to not seek reelection because of Vietnam; Senator Robert F. Kennedy is assassinated in Los Angeles after winning the California Democratic primary; riots break out at the Democratic Convention in Chicago; Richard M. Nixon, promising to end the Vietnam War, wins the election.

1968 U.S. scientists develop the theory of plate tectonics.

1969 Hurricane Camille strikes the Mississippi Gulf Coast, the strongest hurricane to hit the U.S. since 1935.

1970 Earthquakes, floods, and landslides kill between 50,000-70,000 in Peru.

1970 The Environmental Protection Agency is established. The first Earth Day is celebrated. Greenpeace is founded the next year.

1968 At the Summer Olympics in Mexico City, U.S. sprinters Tommie Smith and John Carlos give the Black Power salute on the medal stand. They are suspended from the team.

1969 More than 300,000 rock-and-roll fans attend the Woodstock Music and Art Fair near Bethel, New York.

1970 Four students at Kent State University in Ohio are killed by National Guardsmen during campus protests against the Vietnam War. The guardsmen are later exonerated.

1970 Pelé leads Brazil to their third World Cup soccer championship.

EUROPE

1968 The Soviet Union invades Czechoslovakia and arrests President Dubček, crushing his Prague Spring ("socialism with a human face"). It is part of the new hard-line Brezhnev Doctrine to quell disloyalty among the satellites.

1969 The Soviets begin Strategic Arms Limitation Talks (SALT) with U.S. president Nixon, seeking détente amid fears of global nuclear war.

1968 Bermuda is granted self-government by Great Britain.

1960s Package tours make air travel to "exotic" lands affordable.

1968 Student rebellions in Paris lead to reform of the French education system.

1968 Pope Paul VI issues an encyclical against all artificial means of contraception. In 1970 he declares that priestly celibacy is fundamental to the Roman Catholic Church.

CONNECTIONS

Meet the Beatles

By the time the Beatles dissolved in 1970, they had become not only the most successful recording group of all time, but also the first to explicitly combine the cultures of East and West in pop music. Guitarist George Harrison began collaborating with Hindustani musician Ravi Shankar and playing the sitar in some recordings. (The two would later join forces to stage the legendary Concert for Bangladesh in 1971.) The "White Album" was written largely in India, and Indian musical influences can be heard in droning bass lines and mantra-like vocals. Many were turned off by the Beatles' interest in the East, especially when John Lennon dismissed Christianity and quipped that the Beatles were "more popular than Jesus." Yet nothing could ultimately dim the popularity or influence of the boys from Liverpool, who to date have sold more than a billion recordings worldwide.

MIDDLE EAST & AFRICA

1968 The Ethiopian Civil War begins over Eritrea's attempt to secede.

1968 Revolution puts the Baath party in control of Iraq with the agenda of Arab socialism.

1970 Clashes between the Jordanian army and PLO guerrillas lead to the PLO's relocation to Lebanon.

1970 Hafez al-Assad is elected president of Syria and moves the country away from socialist principles and dependence on the Soviet Union.

1968 An earthquake in Iran kills 12,000.

1968-1974 Drought in the north African Sahel region kills 500,000.

1968 The island of Mauritius becomes an independent state.

1970 Gambia becomes a republic.

1971 The shah of Iran celebrates 2,500 continuous years of the Iranian monarchy with a lavish, 100-million-dollar event at the ancient Persian capital of Persepolis.

ASIA & OCEANIA

1968 The Tet Offensive: North Vietnam and Viet Cong troops launch a massive attack during the celebration of the Vietnamese New Year, surprising and demoralizing U.S. forces.

1968 U.S. troops massacre 347 men, women, and children in the village of My Lai.

1969 The U.S. begins the policy of Vietnamization, turning more of the war over to the Vietnamese, after U.S. troop levels hit a peak of 543,000.

1970 Congress repeals the Gulf of Tonkin resolution and forbids the use of U.S. troops in Cambodia, where the war has spread.

1970 Cyclones and floods kill 500,000 in East Pakistan (Bangladesh).

1970 Fiji and Tonga gain independence from Britain.

1970 Pope Paul VI escapes an assassination attempt in the Philippines.

SCIENCE & TECHNOLOGY

1969 Apollo 11 lands on the moon. More than 100 million people watch on television around the world as U.S. astronaut Neil Armstrong steps onto the surface.

1969 The microprocessor, a miniature set of integrated circuits, is invented, making the computer revolution possible.

1969 The Advanced Research Projects Agency Network (ARPANET) system goes online. Designed by the U.S. Defense Department, it is a decentralized computer network that connects government agencies, libraries, and universities and is the forerunner of the Internet.

1969 The Soviet Union achieves the first successful docking of two manned crafts (Soyuz 4 and Soyuz 5).

1969 The Concorde, the world's first supersonic jet, makes its maiden flight.

1970 Philips introduces the Video Cassette Recorder.

1968 The Aswan High Dam in Egypt is completed. Funded by Egyptian president Nasser in part by seizing the Suez Canal in 1956, the dam proves controversial environmentally and for submerging most of Nubia's archaeological remains, but allows the reclamation of 650,000 acres of agricultural land and the generation of much-needed electrical power.

1969 Seiko of Japan introduces the first electronic wristwatches.

PEOPLE & SOCIETY

1968 Sirhan Sirhan of Jordan shoots and kills Robert Kennedy in Los Angeles.

1968 Martin Luther King, Jr., is assassinated at the Lorraine Motel in Memphis, Tennessee, by James Earl Ray. Riots erupt across the U.S.

1970s U.S. corporations begin moving to the Sunbelt because of lower taxes, less regulation, and cheaper labor costs.

1970s The Medellin Cartel of drug smugglers in Colombia is built and run by Pablo Escobar. At its height in the 1980s it brings in $60 million per month and is worth an estimated $28 billion.

1968 Physicist Andrei Sakharov, father of the Soviet hydrogen bomb, publishes a paper critical of Soviet totalitarianism.

1969 Writer Alexander Solzhenitsyn is expelled from the Soviet Writers' Union for political heresy. In 1970 he wins the Nobel Prize in literature.

1969 Yasser Arafat is elected chairman of the Executive Committee of the PLO; Mrs. Golda Meir becomes Israel's fourth prime minister.

1969 Muammar al-Qaddafi takes power in Libya with an Islamic socialist doctrine.

1970 Anwar Sadat becomes president of Egypt after the death of Nasser.

Saigon's chief of police executes a Viet Cong prisoner after the Tet Offensive.

Buzz Aldrin in the Sea of Tranquility

ONE GIANT LEAP

The last sentence of a plaque commemorating the Apollo 11 moon landing reads, "We Came in Peace for All Mankind." Yet this awesome achievement was also a victory for the United States in the Cold War battle known as the space race.

When the Soviet Union launched the satellite Sputnik in 1957, it raised the specter of space-based weapons and sent the U.S. scurrying to catch up. The U.S. was humiliated again in 1961 when cosmonaut Yuri Gagarin became the first man in space, a smiling symbol of Soviet supremacy.

Knowing the Soviets had already sent a rocket to the moon, President John F. Kennedy upped the ante in 1962 by promising to put a man on the moon by the end of the decade, which seemed fantastical at the time. The Apollo mission started disastrously in 1967 when Apollo 1 caught fire on the launching pad, killing all three astronauts inside. But by 1968, Apollo 8 had gone so far as to orbit the moon.

On July 20, 1969, Neil Armstrong and Buzz Aldrin piloted the lunar module *Eagle* into the Sea of Tranquility. Armstrong planted his left boot on the moon's surface, a feat the Soviets never duplicated. With one awe-inspiring step of man, the U.S. had won the space race.

*I am writing in a hurry.
I see death coming up the hill.*

A GI's last letter home, 1969

At a Loss in Vietnam

THE THEORY WAS THAT IF YOU LET ONE SMALL COUNTRY FALL TO COMMUNISM, THE rest of the neighborhood would follow, like dominoes. Fear of such a red tide led the United States to look past some hard lessons learned by the Japanese and the French about the tenacity of the Vietnamese. When the French tried to reoccupy Vietnam in 1946, Ho Chi Minh warned them that they could kill ten of his men for every one French casualty and still lose. By 1954 they realized that he was right.

A decade later the U.S. was engaged in what would become the most unpopular war in American history, one that would become shorthand for military futility. Communist North Vietnam had begun guerrilla activity, through the Viet Cong, against noncommunist South Vietnam in 1957. After the deaths of U.S. noncombat advisers in Viet Cong attacks, the U.S. established a military council in South Vietnam in 1962. Then in 1964, a naval attack against U.S. destroyers in the Gulf of Tonkin became the Remember-the-*Maine* provocation for Congress to authorize military action. Thirty-five hundred U.S. Marines landed at Da Nang in 1965; by 1968 almost half a million U.S. troops were on the ground. Ho Chi Minh had his own superpower ally in the Soviet Union, which supplied aid and armaments.

That evidence would later come to light casting doubt on whether the Gulf of Tonkin attack ever happened is emblematic of a war shrouded in secrecy and tainted with deception. In 1969 it was revealed that U.S. troops, a year earlier, had massacred 347 men, women, and children in the village of My Lai. In 1971 the Pentagon Papers were released, exposing a deeper level of involvement in Southeast Asia than had been admitted. Television coverage (a first for a war) broadcast shocking brutality and suffering of both soldiers and civilians.

The sense that their military had lost control and their government was lying drove demonstrators to extremes. Students evaded the draft by leaving the country. Muhammad Ali declared himself a conscientious objector and refused to join the Army. And antiwar protests often became violent, most notably the tragic confrontation at Kent State University in Ohio where four students were killed by National Guardsmen.

Despite eroding support and combat setbacks that ended the presidency of Lyndon Johnson, the U.S. did not withdraw completely until 1973, after secretly trying to extend the war to Cambodia, which was providing supply lines to the Viet Cong. In 1975, with the North Vietnamese occupation of Saigon, the domino had officially fallen, and the U.S. had lost its first war.

A nine-year-old South Vietnamese girl (center) survived an errant napalm attack at Trang Bang by stripping off her burning clothes. Such scenes of civilian misery came to epitomize the Vietnam War.

POLITICS & POWER	GEOGRAPHY & ENVIRONMENT	CULTURE & RELIGION

THE AMERICAS

1971 Former president Juan Perón, in exile since 1955, returns to Argentina and becomes president again in 1973.

1972 The U.S. Congress passes the Equal Employment Opportunity Act, allowing for affirmative action.

1972 D.C. police arrest five men inside the Democratic National Headquarters at the Watergate Hotel.

1972 Richard Nixon is reelected president of the United States.

1973 Marxist Chilean president Salvadore Allende is ousted in a CIA-backed coup.

1972 The pesticide DDT is banned in the U.S. for environmental reasons.

1972 An earthquake in Managua, Nicaragua, kills 10,000.

1973 The Bahamas are granted independence from Great Britain.

1971 Cigarette ads are banned from U.S. TV.

1971 Chilean poet Pablo Neruda, known for his epic historical poems, wins the Nobel Prize in literature.

1972 The U.S. Supreme Court strikes down a Massachusetts law prohibiting the sale of birth control pills to unmarried women.

1973 The U.S. Supreme Court rules in *Roe* v. *Wade* that states may not prohibit abortions during the first sixth months of pregnancy.

1973 Secretariat wins horse racing's Triple Crown.

EUROPE

1972 Britain imposes direct rule on Northern Ireland due to continued violence between Catholics and Protestants. Fourteen unarmed Catholic protesters are gunned down by British police in an incident that comes to be known as Bloody Sunday.

1973 All NATO countries except Portugal deny landing rights to U.S. planes attempting to bring supplies to Israel in the Yom Kippur War, a deliberate show of political independence by the European Community.

1973 Britain, Denmark, and Iceland join the Common Market.

1972 Arab terrorists kill 11 Israeli athletes at the Summer Olympic Games in Munich.

1972 American Bobby Fischer wins the world chess title from Soviet Boris Spassky in a politically charged match in Reykjavik, Iceland.

MIDDLE EAST & AFRICA

1971 President Joseph Mobutu renames the Republic of the Congo "Zaire" in a campaign of pro-African awareness. A year later he renames himself Mobutu Sese Seko.

1972 The first Sudanese civil war ends with the Addis Ababa accords, granting southern Sudan autonomy.

1973 The fourth Arab-Israeli war (the Yom Kippur War) occurs after Egypt launches a surprise attack on Yom Kippur but fails to regain lost territory.

An Israeli tank crew in the Golan Heights during the Yom Kippur War

1972 The Star of Sierra Leone, the largest diamond ever discovered (969.8 carats) is unearthed.

1970s Islam becomes the language of politics throughout the Arab world, replacing secular political discourse.

1973 In retaliation for Western support of Israel, OPEC embargoes oil supplies, precipitating a devastating energy crisis in major industrialized nations, but bringing tremendous wealth to oil-producing countries.

ASIA & OCEANIA

1971 Civil war breaks out in Pakistan, with India supporting East Pakistan.

1971 China attends its first UN meeting as a member after the UN expels Taiwan and formally recognizes the communists as the sole legitimate government of China.

1971 The U.S. turns over all ground troop duties to South Vietnam.

1971 U.S. planes covertly bomb Viet Cong supply routes in Cambodia.

1973 The U.S. and South Vietnam sign a cease-fire agreement with North Vietnam. The last U.S. troops are withdrawn on March 29, 1973.

1972 The U.S. returns Okinawa to Japan.

1972 East Pakistan becomes the sovereign state of Bangladesh.

1972 Ceylon becomes the Republic of Sri Lanka.

1972 The Aboriginal Tent Assembly is established on the parliament steps in Canberra, Australia, to demand sovereignty for the country's indigenous peoples.

SCIENCE & TECHNOLOGY

1971 Texas Instruments introduces the pocket calculator.

1972 The World Trade Center towers are completed, surpassing the Empire State Building as the world's tallest structures (1,368 and 1,362 ft.).

1973 The U.S. launches Skylab, the country's first orbiting work station.

1973-4 U.S. probes Pioneer 11 & 12 transmit the first color photos of Jupiter.

1971 The Soviet Union launches the first manned space station, Salyut 1.

1971 A British engineer develops computerized axial tomography imaging (the CT scan).

1972 Liquid-crystal displays (LCD) are developed by a Swiss lab.

1973 British scientists develop magnetic resonance imaging (MRI).

CONNECTIONS

Rumble in the Jungle

As outspoken as he was talented, Muhammad Ali never shied away from a fight, in the ring or otherwise. His conversion to Islam, his opposition to Vietnam, and his civil rights activism made him both a hero and a villain worldwide, all of which made his 1974 fight with George Foreman in Zaire, billed the "Rumble in the Jungle," far more than a boxing match. Ali was after the title stripped from him for refusing military service. Zaire president Mobutu Sese Seko wanted a stage to show off his wealthy country as a symbol of emerging Africa. Ali later told Newsweek, "[It] was a fight that made the whole country more conscious. I wanted to establish a relationship between American blacks and Africans. The fight was about racial problems, Vietnam. All of that." In the end, Ali pulled off a stunning upset over the younger, more powerful Foreman, using a defensive style dubbed the "rope-a-dope" by the always poetic Ali.

1971 Japan launches the tanker *Nisseki Maru,* the largest ship ever built (372,400 tons).

1971 China launches its first space satellite.

PEOPLE & SOCIETY

1971 Lt. William L. Calley, Jr., is found guilty of premeditated murder in the My Lai massacre. His conviction is later overturned.

1972 Federal Express is started by Fred Smith, who had submitted his idea for an overnight delivery service to one of his business professors at Harvard, who failed him.

1972 American swimmer Mark Spitz captures a record seven gold medals at the Summer Olympics in Munich.

1973 Billie Jean King defeats Bobby Riggs in the "battle of the sexes." King is instrumental in improving tournament conditions and purses for female tennis players.

1970s Charismatic West German chancellor Willi Brandt negotiates treaties with Eastern European states to relax Cold War tensions.

1971 George Harrison and Ravi Shankar organize the Concert for Bangladesh in New York City to raise money and awareness for East Pakistan's independence movement.

1971 Major-General Idi Amin takes control of Uganda and soon becomes one of the world's most notorious dictators, killing or torturing hundreds of thousands. In 1972 he expels all Asians from Uganda, many of whom constituted the business class, plunging his country into economic chaos.

1970s Japanese imports to the U.S. begin to increase dramatically, the beginning of Japan's "economic miracle."

1973 North Vietnam's Le Duc Tho and American Henry Kissinger are awarded the Nobel Peace Prize.

1973 Total combat deaths from the Vietnam War: 184,546 South Vietnamese; 937,562 North Vietnamese/Viet Cong; 415,000 civilians; 45,948 Americans.

WOMEN'S RIGHTS

When New Zealand became the first country in the world to give women the right to vote, in 1893, it didn't exactly launch a revolution for what Simone de Beauvoir called the "second sex." Even after World War II, women who had gone to work while their husbands and fathers were off to war were expected to reassume their traditional roles in the home once the men returned. In some countries, women still did not have the right to vote.

The 1960s brought radical change to the U.S. and elsewhere. In her 1963 book, *The Feminine Mystique*, Betty Friedan gave voice to the lack of fulfillment felt by many housewives. Friedan added political clout to that voice in 1966 by founding the National Organization for Women (NOW), which advocated for women's rights, including their right to a legal abortion.

In the 1970s the women's liberation movement reached its peak. Oral contraception, better known as the Pill, became legal for unmarried women. *Roe* v. *Wade* legalized most abortions in the United States, while legislation legalized abortion in many other countries. Gloria Steinem became the new face of feminism with the founding of *Ms.* magazine in 1972. That same year, Congress passed Title IX—which guaranteed equal opportunity for women to participate in programs, including sports, at federally funded schools—and the Equal Rights Amendment (ERA), which the states later failed to ratify.

Despite some antifeminist backlash since the 1970s, women in industrialized nations continue to make gains in the workforce and politics; in France and India, for instance, women are guaranteed a certain percentage of political offices. Women in developing countries, though, typically face much longer roads to equality.

A woman without a man is like a fish without a bicycle.

GLORIA STEINEM

POLITICS & POWER	GEOGRAPHY & ENVIRONMENT	CULTURE & RELIGION

THE AMERICAS

1974 U.S. president Nixon resigns after additional White House tapes reveal his involvement in covering up the Watergate break-in.

1976 René Levesque's Parti Quebecois wins the provincial elections, setting up a referendum on Quebec secession.

1976 Jimmy Carter is elected president of the U.S., the first Southerner since before the Civil War.

1976-83 Thousands disappear in Argentina's "dirty war," the prolonged use of death squads by military dictators against political opponents after the death of Juan Perón.

1974 Grenada declares independence from Britain.

1975 The U.S. acquires its first territory since 1925 when the people of the northern Mariana Islands in the North Pacific vote to become a U.S. commonwealth.

1976 An American panel warns that chlorofluorocarbons (CFCs), used in aerosol spray cans, damage the ozone layer.

1976 The U.S. Air Force Academy begins admitting women.

1976 The Episcopal Church approves the ordination of women as priests and bishops.

EUROPE

1974 The Greek dictatorship of Papadopoulos is overthrown and elections are held.

1974 IRA terrorists bomb the Tower of London and the British House of Parliament.

1975 King Juan Carlos I becomes the first king of Spain in 44 years after Generalissimo Francisco Franco dies.

1975 Thirty-five European nations, plus the U.S. and Canada, sign the Helsinki Accords, which are designed to increase international cooperation.

1976 Britain suffers its worst drought on record.

1976 Violent earthquakes strike northeastern Italy, as well as eastern Turkey, China, the Philippines, Bali, and Guatemala, killing an estimated 780,000 people in all.

Gymnast Nadia Comaneci of Romania

MIDDLE EAST & AFRICA

1974 Syria and Israel agree to a cease-fire in the Golan Heights.

1974 Cyprus is partitioned into Greek and Turkish sections.

1975 Civil war erupts in Lebanon between Muslim rebels and the Christian government.

1975 The Angolan Civil War (1975-1989) begins between U.S. and communist-backed factions.

1976 Israeli commandos raid the Entebbe airport in Uganda to rescue 103 hostages held by pro-Palestinian hijackers.

1974 A drought-induced famine threatens millions throughout Africa.

1974 Portuguese Guinea declares independence and becomes Guinea-Bissau.

1975 Portugal grants independence to former African colonies Angola, Mozambique, Cape Verde, and Sao Tome and Principe.

1976 Spain relinquishes control of Spanish Sahara, which is divided between Morocco and Mauritania.

1976 The Central African Republic is renamed the Central African Empire by President Bokassa.

Mid-1970s Kurdish separatism and Islamic revivalism is on the rise in Turkey.

1975 Repression by Iran's secret police (SAVAK) intensifies in response to resistance by Marxist and Islamic groups.

1976 Numerous children are killed during a protest in Soweto, a black ghetto of Johannesburg, South Africa, provoking international outrage at apartheid.

ASIA & OCEANIA

1974 Communist and South Vietnamese forces resume fighting. South Vietnam finally surrenders in 1975; Saigon is evacuated.

1975 The communist Khmer Rouge, led by Pol Pot, takes over Cambodia's government. More than two million Cambodians die or are executed in what comes to be known as the killing fields.

1976 Rebels in the Aceh province of Indonesia begin fighting for independence, a struggle ongoing today.

1974 A smallpox epidemic in India kills an estimated 30,000.

1975 Papua New Guinea declares independence from Australia; Suriname becomes independent of the Netherlands.

1975 East Timor is abandoned by Portugal and invaded by Indonesia.

1976 North and South Vietnam are reunited after 22 years of separation as the Socialist Republic of Vietnam. Hanoi is the capital; Saigon is renamed Ho Chi Minh City.

1975-77 Prime minister Indira Gandhi declares a state of emergency to deal with India's overpopulation and sectarian violence. She suspends democratic processes and compels birth control, including involuntary sterilization. She is ultimately voted out of office and arrested on charges of corruption.

SCIENCE & TECHNOLOGY	PEOPLE & SOCIETY
1974 The Sears Tower in Chicago surpasses the World Trade Center towers as the world's tallest building (1,454 ft.).	**1974 Henry Aaron** becomes Major League Baseball's all-time home run king, surpassing Babe Ruth's career total of 714.
1975 The MITS "Altair" is the first desktop microcomputer.	**1974 The "Chicago boys,"** a group of Chilean economists schooled at the University of Chicago, begin a controversial dismantling of Chile's socialist system in favor of free-market privatization under Augusto Pinochet.
1976 Landing vehicles from Viking I and II transmit the first close-up photos of the surface of Mars.	**1975 President Ford** escapes two assassination attempts in California, one by a member of the Manson family.
1976 An unknown illness kills 29 people and affects another 151 who attend an American Legion convention in Philadelphia. The illness, which turns out to be a bacterial infection spread through the air conditioning system, becomes known as Legionnaires' disease.	**1975 Former Teamsters Union president Jimmy Hoffa** disappears forever.

Skulls line a memorial to Pol Pot's reign of terror.

1975 Soyuz 19 links up with Apollo ASTP in the first Soviet-U.S. space linkup.	**1974 Gerry Conlon,** his father, and nine others are arrested and convicted in England for IRA bombings. They are later acquitted after it is proven that their confessions were made under duress and that some of their written statements were altered by the police.
	1976 14-year-old Romanian gymnast Nadia Comaneci wins three gold medals at the Summer Olympics in Montreal. She notches seven perfect scores, the first-ever perfect marks in Olympic gymnastics.

1974 Completion of Syria's Euphrates Dam doubles the area devoted to irrigated agriculture and permits widespread electrification.	**1974 Haile Selassie,** emperor of Ethiopia since 1916, is deposed by Marxists. The new regime's farming controls lead to famine in the 1980s and 1990s.
	1975 King Faisal of Saudi Arabia is assassinated by his nephew.
	1975 Imam Musa al-Sadr of Lebanon founds the Amal (Hope) Party and militia to support disenfranchised Shiite Muslims. In 1978 he disappears in Libya.

1974 India becomes the sixth nation to explode a nuclear device. The following year it launches its first satellite.	**1975 Junko Tabei of Japan** becomes the first woman to climb Mount Everest.
1975 Sony introduces Betamax videotapes. Matsushita/JVC introduce VHS.	**1976 Hua Kuo-feng** becomes premier of the People's Republic of China and chairman of the Chinese Communist Party after the death of Mao Zedong. A coup attempt by Mao's widow and three accomplices (the Gang of Four) is crushed.
ca 1977 Public cell phone testing begins in Japan and the U.S., shifting the communications market away from the place to the person.	**1976 China** launches what Deng Xiaoping calls its Second Revolution, reversing many of Chairman Mao's agricultural policies, such as collective farms. From 1978 to 1984, food production increases 50 percent.

CAMBODIA'S KILLING FIELDS

The Vietnamese claim to have discovered the remains of more than three million people when they invaded neighboring Cambodia to depose the Khmer Rouge government in 1978. Other sources put the figure between one and two million. What is indisputable is that for four years, beginning in 1975, Cambodian premier Pol Pot transformed his country's rice fields and orchards into mass graves.

Cambodia was a hive of violence long before Pol Pot came to power. The country had been a battleground in both the Indochina and Vietnam wars, and the government had been struggling against Khmer Rouge insurgents since 1970. But Pol Pot personified the monstrous dimensions of communist ideology. After leading the Khmer's successful overthrow in 1975, the Paris-educated engineer carried out a radical Maoist program of agrarianism, evacuating cities and forcing people into collective farms. Schools and factories were shut down; skilled workers and "intellectuals" were executed. Others died during forced marches to the countryside, and many more perished from starvation.

Pol Pot continued to lead guerrilla forces in Cambodia's western jungles almost until the end of his life in 1998. The thousands of skulls and bones neatly stacked and displayed around Cambodia are vivid reminders of his brief and terrible reign.

POLITICS & POWER	GEOGRAPHY & ENVIRONMENT	CULTURE & RELIGION

THE AMERICAS

1978 U.S. president Carter brokers the Camp David Accords between Israeli premier Menachem Begin and Egyptian president Anwar Sadat that results in a historic peace treaty.

1978 The FBI's Abscam sting operation begins, resulting in the arrest of seven U.S. congressmen and state and city officials for accepting bribes in exchange for political favors.

1979 Communist Sandinista guerrillas overthrow the government of Nicaragua and install a Marxist regime.

1977 U.S. president Carter and Panama chief Omar Torrijos sign the new Panama Canal treaties, returning the canal to Panama's control.

1978 Residents of Love Canal in New York, near Niagra Falls, are forced to evacuate when it is learned that their houses are built on a toxic-waste landfill.

1979 St. Lucia, St. Vincent, and the Grenadines win independence from Great Britain.

1977 The much-anticipated sci-fi movie *Star Wars* has filmgoers lining up for hours.

1979 Pope John Paul II ends official support for Liberation Theology, a brand of Roman Catholicism popular in Latin America that links Christian theology with political activism, in particular the class struggle of the poor.

1979 *The U.S. Held Hostage* (later *Nightline*) debuts on U.S. television.

1980 Archbishop Oscar Romero of San Salvador is shot to death during mass. A proponent of Liberation Theology, he had been an outspoken critic of human rights violations in El Salvador during the country's civil war.

EUROPE

1979 U.S. president Carter meets with Soviet president Brezhnev in Vienna to sign the SALT-2 arms limitation treaty. The U.S. never ratifies the treaty, however, after the Soviets invade Afghanistan.

1979 Margaret Thatcher becomes prime minister of Great Britain and begins privatizing state-owned companies.

1979 British World War II hero Lord Mountbatten is killed by an IRA bomb.

1977 Bucharest, Romania, is destroyed by an earthquake felt in Moscow and Rome.

1977 Italy ends Roman Catholicism as the state religion.

1978 Cardinal Karol Wojtyla becomes Pope John Paul II, the first non-Italian pope in 456 years. He survives an assassination attempt in 1981.

1980 More than half of married women with children now work outside the home.

MIDDLE EAST & AFRICA

1979 The shah of Iran is forced into exile and replaced by the Ayatollah Khomeini. In retaliation for the U.S. harboring the exiled shah, Iran seizes 66 hostages from the U.S. Embassy, 52 of whom are held for 444 days.

1979 Exiled Ugandans overthrow Idi Amin, sending him into exile in Saudi Arabia.

1979 Emperor Bokassa of the Central African Empire is overthrown in a French-backed coup. He goes into exile, but will return in 1987 and be arrested for torture, murder, and cannibalism.

1979 Southern Rhodesia becomes the independent state of Zimbabwe.

1979 Iran becomes the world's first Islamic republic.

1977 The United Nations issues a mandatory arms embargo on South Africa. It is not uniformly observed by the U.S. and many multinational corporations, and the situation increasingly poses ethical questions for the international community through the 1980s.

1978 Reconciliation with Israel at Camp David isolates Egypt from the Arab world. Opposition groups multiply and OPEC cuts off funding, which, along with an overcommitment to social programs, leads to a fiscal crisis.

ASIA & OCEANIA

1978 China establishes full diplomatic relations with the U.S.

1978 Vietnam invades Cambodia, overthrowing Pol Pot's government.

1979 China invades Vietnam.

1979 The Soviet army invades Afghanistan; U.S. president Carter responds with a grain embargo against the Soviets.

1979 China institutes the one-child-per-family rule to help control its exploding population. Fines, pressure to have an abortion, and even forced sterilization are some of the penalties for subsequent pregnancies.

Mother Teresa with one of her Calcutta orphans

SCIENCE & TECHNOLOGY	PEOPLE & SOCIETY
1977 The Trans-Alaska Pipeline opens, stretching 800 miles from Prudhoe Bay to Valdez. **1977 U.S. scientists** for the first time successfully use drugs to treat a life-threatening viral infection—herpes encephalitis. **1979 Nuclear disaster** is narrowly averted at a reactor on Three Mile Island, Pennsylvania. **1979 U.S. Steel** lays off 13,000 workers and closes 15 plants as technology changes the nation's economy.	**1978 Argentinian mothers (las Madres)** who gather at the Plaza de Mayo in Buenos Aires to protest the disappearance of their children at the hands of the government attract international media attention and spur worldwide demonstrations of solidarity when soccer's World Cup is held in Argentina. **ca 1980 African Americans and Latinos** are twice as likely as other Americans to be living at or below the poverty line. **ca 1980 Violence increases** between African Americans and new immigrant groups such as Koreans and Mexicans in major U.S. cities like New York and Los Angeles.
1977 More than 570 people die in the world's worst aviation disaster to date when a KLM Royal Dutch Airlines Boeing 747 crashes into a Pan Am Boeing 747 on the runway of Los Rodeos Airport in the Canary Islands. **1978 The first "test-tube baby"** is born in England when Lesley Brown gives birth to a girl conceived outside her body.	**1978 Former Italian prime minister Aldo Moro** is kidnapped and murdered by antigovernment Red Brigade terrorists. **1978 Norwegian explorer Thor Heyerdahl** sails on a reed boat *(Tigris)* from Iraq to Djibouti to prove that ancient Indus Valley civilizations could have traded with Mesopotamia. He ends up burning his boat to protest ongoing violence in the Middle East.
1977 Kenyan Wangari Maathai, a U.S.-educated biologist, founds the Green Belt Movement and plants nine tree seeds in the yard of her house, beginning a three-decade-long movement to regain environmental rights.	**1979 Robert Mugabe** leads Southern Rhodesia's (Zimbabwe) successful war of liberation against Britain. Elected prime minister in 1980, Mugabe has been Zimbabwe's only leader since, having evolved into a brutal dictator. As of 2010 Zimbabwe's life expectancy is about 50 years, among the lowest in the world. **1979 Saddam Hussein,** secret police assassin and torturer, becomes president of Iraq and gains U.S. support. **ca 1979 A Western-educated and technocratic generation** comes of age in Middle Eastern politics and begins substituting capitalist economics for socialism.
1978 Japanese imports account for half of the U.S. import car market, following the energy crisis that spikes demand for economy cars. **1978 Konica** introduces the auto-focus camera. **1979 Sony** introduces the Walkman portable cassette player. **1979 A test model** of a Japanese magnetic levitation train hits a record 321.2 mph.	**1977 Japanese baseball player Sadaharu Oh** slugs his 756th home run, passing Henry Aaron as the most prolific home run hitter in the history of professional baseball. **1978 Japanese explorer Naomi Uemura** becomes the first person to complete a solo journey to the North Pole. **1979 The Federate States of Micronesia** enter into a compact of free association with the U.S. **1979 Mother Teresa** wins the Nobel Peace Prize.

REVOLUTION IN IRAN

The discovery of oil in Iran in the early 20th century made the country a focal point of superpower attention. In 1951, when Premier Mussadegh began nationalizing the oil industry and cozying up to the Soviets, Great Britain and the U.S. intervened and helped restore the shah of Iran to power. For the next two decades Iran received economic and military aid in exchange for generous oil arrangements with major Western countries.

The shah's pro-Western policies were denounced by Iran's Islamic clergy, most vocally by exiled cleric Ruhollah Khomeini, who had given himself the title "ayatollah," a nontraditional honorific meaning "sign of God." Khomeini's closest followers considered him the supreme imam, a leader whose authority was infallible because it came directly from God. He used this authority to foment opposition to the secularization of Iran, the shah's autocratic rule, and his ostentatious wealth. (Other opposition groups, ranging from secular liberals to Marxist guerrillas, also actively opposed the shah's policies and corruption.) By January of 1979 Khomeini had chased the shah from the country and declared Iran an Islamic Republic, with the ayatollah as supreme leader.

On November 4, 1979, in retaliation for the U.S. offering asylum to the shah, Iranian militants seized the U.S. Embassy in Tehran, precipitating the worst hostage crisis in American history. Fifty-two hostages were held for 444 days, released only after nearly $8 billion in Iranian assets were unfrozen.

There is no crime America will not commit in order to maintain its political, economic, cultural, and military domination . . . Iran has tried to sever all its relations with this Great Satan.

AYATOLLAH KHOMEINI'S "MESSAGE TO THE PILGRIMS"

POLITICS & POWER	GEOGRAPHY & ENVIRONMENT	CULTURE & RELIGION

THE AMERICAS

1980 Ronald Reagan is elected president of the U.S. and reelected in 1984.

1980 A military junta backed by cocaine barons takes over Bolivia.

1982 Argentina attempts to seize the British-controlled Falkland Islands but is defeated, leading to an overthrow of Argentina's military junta and the restoration of democracy.

1983 The U.S. withdraws from Lebanon after Shiite Muslims bomb the U.S. Embassy in Beirut, killing more than 200 Marines.

1980 More than 120,000 Cubans are allowed to immigrate to the U.S.

1980 Mount St. Helens volcano in Washington State erupts. Most people are evacuated but 36 die. The blast is 500 times more powerful than the atomic bomb dropped on Hiroshima.

1980 CNN becomes the world's first 24-hour news station.

1981 MTV debuts on U.S. television.

1982 Colombian writer Gabriel García Márquez, a leading exponent of magic realism, wins the Nobel Prize in literature.

1982 The Vietnam Wall memorial opens on the Mall in Washington, D.C.

1984 U.S.A. for Africa, a group of top music industry artists, records the song "We Are the World," written by Michael Jackson and Lionel Richie, to aid drought victims in Ethiopia.

EUROPE

1980 Lech Walesa becomes chairman of a new independent trade union (Solidarity) in Poland that demands political reform from the communist government.

1981 Socialist François Mitterand is elected president of France and puts communists in his cabinet.

1983 The U.S. deploys the first cruise missiles to Europe, at the Greenham Common Air Force base, and deploys Pershing missiles in West Germany.

1980 The Summer Olympics in Moscow are boycotted by 50 nations, including the U.S., in protest of the Soviet invasion of Afghanistan.

1984 The Soviet Union and the communist bloc boycott the Summer Olympics in Los Angeles in retaliation for the U.S. boycott in 1980.

Mount St. Helens erupts.

MIDDLE EAST & AFRICA

1980 A U.S. commando raid to free the hostages held in Iran ends in disaster.

1980 Iraq invades Iran, beginning an eight-year-long war; the U.S supports Iraq.

1981 Egyptian president Anwar Sadat is assassinated by Islamic militants and replaced with pragmatist Hosni Mubarak.

1982 Israel invades Lebanon in an attempt to drive out PLO terrorists.

1983 The second Sudanese civil war begins when Sudan's president imposes Islamic Law on the non-Muslim south.

1980 Jerusalem replaces Tel Aviv as the capital of Israel.

1981 Israel annexes the Golan Heights.

1982 Israel returns Sinai to Egypt per the Camp David agreement but intensifies settlement in the West Bank and Gaza.

1983 The death toll from drought in Ethiopia reaches four million.

1984 Upper Volta becomes Burkina Faso.

1980 Islamization of Iranian institutions begins, changing the army, government bureaucracies, educational system, and the legal system.

1982 The political and military organization Hezbollah (Party of God) is founded in Lebanon, with financing from Iran, to oppose the Israeli invasion and occupation of southern Lebanon.

1983 Kenyan writer Ngugi wa Thiong'o publishes *Decolonising the Mind,* arguing that the adoption of colonial language carries ideological implications. He begins to write only in his native Gikuyu language.

ASIA & OCEANIA

1981 Sikhs begin fighting for independence in the Indian Punjab region, where Sikhism originated.

1983 A South Korean airliner is shot down over the Soviet Union on its way from New York to Seoul, killing all 269 on board.

1983 Tamil Tiger rebels begin fighting the Sri Lankan government for the right to create a separate, non-Buddhist state for the ethnic minority Tamils.

1980s Concern over the loss of rain forests in Asia and Brazil becomes a major environmental issue.

1980 Vanatu gains independence from Britain and France.

1983 The population of China reaches one billion.

1984 Brunei becomes an independent sultanate and the 159th member of the UN.

1984 A toxic gas leak from the Union Carbide Plant in Bhopal, India, kills 2,500 and affects thousands more.

1980s Islamic warriors called mujahideen take up arms against the Soviet invasion of Afghanistan with the help of U.S. ground-to-air Stinger missiles, which are used to attack Soviet helicopters.

SCIENCE & TECHNOLOGY	PEOPLE & SOCIETY
1980 Smallpox is eradicated worldwide. **1980 The U.S. Voyager 1 space probe** sends back spectacular photos of Saturn, showing its rings and six new moons. **1981 The first U.S. space shuttle,** *Columbia,* makes it maiden flight. It is the first reusable spacecraft. **1981 Scientists** identify acquired immune deficiency syndrome (AIDS). **1981 IBM** introduces the first home or personal computer (PC). In 1984 Apple launches its Macintosh, the first PC with a graphical interface.	**1980 Former Beatle John Lennon** is shot to death by an obsessed fan. **1981 John Hinckley** attempts to assassinate President Reagan in Washington, D.C. **1981 Sandra Day O'Connor** becomes the U.S. Supreme Court's first female justice. **1981 Bill Gates** devises the Microsoft Disk Operating System (MS-DOS) for IBM. **1983 Barney Clark** of the U.S. dies 112 days after receiving the first artificial heart. **1984 Geraldine Ferraro** becomes the first woman to run on a U.S. presidential ticket.
1980 Robert Ballard of the U.S. and Jean-Louis Michel of France find the *Titanic* 12,000 feet deep in the North Atlantic, where it sank in 1912. **1981 The world's longest single-span bridge** (4,626 ft.) opens in Great Britain, over the Humber Estuary. **1981 The world's fastest train,** the French TGV, begins service between Paris and Lyons. **1982 Soviet spacecrafts Venera 13 and 14** send back the first color photos of Venus.	**1980 Dissident physicist Andrei Sakharov** is exiled by Soviet leader Leonid Brezhnev. **1984 The largest demonstration in French history**—more than a million marchers—forces the government to abandon its challenge to the independence of religious schools.
Writing reflects a community wrestling with its environment to make it yield the means of life. NGUGI WA THIONG'O	**1980s Highly educated Egyptian and Palestinian engineers** and other workers fill jobs in oil-rich countries, making remittances one of the leading sources of foreign exchange after oil. **1980 Middle Eastern welfare states** end and private clinics, hospitals, and social services proliferate, most often run by Islamists. **1984 Bishop Desmond Tutu,** general secretary of the South African Council of Churches, wins the Nobel Peace Prize. **1984 Israel** successfully airlifts and relocates 25,000 Ethiopian Jews from Sudan.
1980 Japan becomes the world leader in manufacturing and a world financial center, with eight of the world's ten largest banks. It also surpasses the U.S. as the world's largest automaker. **1981 High-definition television** (HDTV) is demonstrated in Japan. **1984 Sony and Philips** introduce the first commercial CD players.	**1980 Indira Gandhi** returns to power in India after serving time in jail. In 1984 she is assassinated by her Sikh bodyguards, provoking anti-Sikh riots throughout the country. **1980s Deng Xiaoping** consolidates his power in China as leader of the Communist Party. He strives to improve relations with the West and modernize China, and develops the idea of a "socialist market economy" to improve the economy. **1980s Southeast Asia's "little tigers"** emerge as Hong Kong, Singapore, Taiwan, and South Korea follow Japan's export-driven economic model.

JAPAN'S ECONOMIC MIRACLE

It's hard to imagine that the Japan towering above the industrialized world in the 1980s was the same country as the one that had been in ruins after World War II. The war devastated Japan's industrial sector and destroyed its labor force.

The land of the rising sun would see brighter days, though. The Allies provided massive relief, including food and technical assistance, and during the Korean War, Japan produced billions of dollars worth of supplies for the UN coalition. Before long the country boasted many newly rebuilt plants with state-of-the-art technology. A skilled work force was already in place. Japan embraced free enterprise with a passion and the results were staggering: The country's gross national product (GNP) doubled between 1955-1960, more than doubled between 1960-65, and more than doubled again from 1965-1970.

By 1971 Japan had the world's third-largest GNP after the U.S. and Soviet Union. Businesses were given healthy incentives to invest in capital expansion, and productivity among the Japanese worker was high. Exports were a major key to growth, as Japan began penetrating foreign markets with quality, lower-cost products in the automotive and electronics sectors. The energy crisis of 1973 spurred demand for Japan's economy cars. By 1978 Japanese models accounted for half the U.S. import car market, and Japan surpassed the U.S. as the world's largest automaker in 1980.

Japan's recovery was the model for other free-market Asian success stories, including Taiwan, Hong Kong, Singapore, and South Korea. The flood of Asian imports, as well as heavy Japanese investment in U.S. businesses in the 1980s, sparked fears in the U.S. over lost jobs and foreign influence. By the late 1990s, though, bad loans and weak currencies along the Pacific Rim had led to an economic downturn referred to as the "Asian flu."

POLITICS & POWER	GEOGRAPHY & ENVIRONMENT	CULTURE & RELIGION

THE AMERICAS

1986 The Iran-Contra scandal implicates Reagan aides in a secret plan to divert funds from arms sales to Iran to the anti-communist Contras in Nicaragua. Congress had cut off all Contra aid in 1984.

1987 Costa Rican president Oscar Arias brokers the Arias Peace Plan, an attempt to end political instability in Central America.

1989 U.S. troops invade Panama and arrest Manuel Noriega on drug-trafficking charges.

1989 U.S. president Bush authorizes $300 billion to bail out the scandal-plagued U.S. savings and loan industry.

1987 The last wild California condor is trapped and sent to a zoo for breeding.

1989 The Exxon oil tanker Valdez runs aground in Alaska, causing the world's largest oil spill (11 million gallons).

1989 Millions of TV viewers witness an earthquake strike the Bay Area during a World Series game being played in San Francisco.

1985 *Gringo Viejo,* by Carlos Fuentes, becomes the first American bestseller written by a Mexican author.

1987 At a New York auction, Vincent van Gogh's *Irises* becomes the most expensive piece of art in history, selling for 49 million dollars. Van Gogh's *Portrait of Dr. Gachet* sells for 82.5 million dollars in 1990.

1987 Condom commercials are allowed to run on U.S. television because of AIDS.

1988 The cocaine derivative crack becomes increasingly popular.

EUROPE

1987 New Soviet secretary general Mikhail Gorbachev announces his campaign for glasnost (openness) and perestroika (reconstruction).

1989 East Germany's communist government resigns after thousands of refugees flee to West Germany. A reform government takes power and the Berlin Wall is demolished.

1989 Protesters in Romania overthrow the communist government and hang president Nicolae Ceausescu and his wife.

1989 Dissident Czech playwright Vaclav Havel becomes president of the new, non-communist government of Czechoslovakia.

1987 A Yugoslavian baby boy is declared Earth's five billionth inhabitant by the UN secretary-general.

1988 An earthquake in Armenia kills 80,000.

1988 Archaeologists uncover the original Globe Theater in Southwark, London.

1988 The Soviet Union announces an end to all commercial whaling.

1986 The final supplement (Se-Z) of the Oxford English Dictionary is published, more than a century since the first edition.

1987 U.S. president Reagan visits Berlin to mark the 750th anniversary of the city's founding. Standing before the Berlin Wall, he calls on Soviet leader Gorbachev to "tear down this wall."

1988 A Pan Am 747 explodes over Lockerbie, Scotland, killing all 270 aboard. Libyan-backed terrorists are thought responsible.

1988 McDonald's opens 20 restaurants in Moscow.

MIDDLE EAST & AFRICA

1986 U.S. warplanes bomb Libya in retaliation for Libyan terrorist actions.

1986 South African president P. W. Botha declares a state of emergency after 1.5 million blacks stage a massive labor strike.

1987 The Palestinian *intifada* begins, an organized uprising initially of stone-throwing children against Israeli rule in the West Bank and Gaza Strip. A new militant group, Hamas (Islamic Resistance Movement), is formed, dedicated to the Palestinian cause.

1987 Turkey is rejected for membership in the European Community for not being European enough.

1986 Toxic gas from the volcanic Lake Nyos in Cameroon kills 20,000.

1986 Customs officials in Kenya seize more than half-a-million-dollars worth of poached elephant ivory.

1985-86 Among all girls aged 12 to 18 in Africa, only 46 percent are enrolled in school.

1986 Desmond Tutu becomes the first black archbishop of Cape Town, South Africa.

1988 The Islamic Salvation Front, an activist and political Islamic movement, emerges in Algeria. Their 1990 election win initiates years of political violence and repression.

1989 Iran's Ayatollah Khomeini imposes a *fatwa* (death sentence) on Indian author Salman Rushdie for blasphemy against Islam in his novel *The Satanic Verses.*

ASIA & OCEANIA

1986 Philippines president Ferdinand Marcos flees the country after his reelection is disputed. Challenger Corazon Aquino becomes the new president.

1987 Soviet troops begin withdrawing from Afghanistan, leaving completely by 1989.

1988 Benazir Bhutto becomes prime minister of Pakistan, the first female head of an Islamic nation.

1989 Hirohito, emperor of Japan since 1926, dies, succeeded by Crown Prince Akihito.

1989 China imposes martial law in Lhasa, Tibet.

1989 Pakistan rejoins the British Commonwealth, which it left in 1972.

1989 Great Britain forcibly repatriates the Vietnam boat people from Hong Kong to Vietnam.

1989 Burma is renamed Myanmar after a military takeover. The name is recognized by the UN but not the U.S., Great Britain, or Canada.

1989 The last Vietnamese troops leave Cambodia after 11 years of occupation.

1985 A Japanese jetliner crashes into a Tokyo mountain, killing 520 in the worst single-plane accident to date.

1985 China releases the former Roman Catholic Bishop of Shanghai after 30 years' imprisonment and reopens the Catholic cathedral in Beijing.

1988 Seoul, South Korea, hosts the Summer Olympics, the first without a boycott since 1976.

SCIENCE & TECHNOLOGY	PEOPLE & SOCIETY

1985 Fiber-optic telephone technology is developed, allowing for 300,000 calls to be transmitted at once.

1986 The space shuttle *Challenger* explodes shortly after takeoff, killing all seven crew members, including the first civilian passenger in a spaceship, teacher Christa McAuliffe.

1986 General Motors overtakes Exxon as the largest company in the U.S.

1988 Prozac, a new antidepressant, hits the U.S. market.

1986 Oprah Winfrey's local Chicago talk show debuts nationally. By the mid-90s she is one of the most influential people in America.

1986 Wall Street is rocked by numerous insider trading scandals, which lead to a stock market crash in 1987.

1988 Chico Mendes, a Brazilian rubber tapper who led the fight to stop logging in the Amazon rain forest, is murdered by cattle ranchers opposed to his activism.

1989 General Colin Powell becomes the first African-American chairman of the U.S. Joint Chiefs of Staff. In 2000 he becomes the first black Secretary of State.

1985 The U.K. begins screening blood donations for the AIDS virus.

1986 The world's worst nuclear accident occurs at the Chernobyl Power Station in Kiev, U.S.S.R. Fallout affects all of Europe.

1986 The Soviet Union launches the Mir space station.

AIDS orphans in Kalagala Village, Uganda

1988 Carbon dating shows that the Shroud of Turin, thought to be the burial cloth of Christ, dates only to around 1330 C.E.

1985 British scientist Alec Jeffreys announces genetic fingerprinting, the ability to positively identify an individual based in his DNA. In 1986 Colin Pitchfork becomes the first person convicted with the new technique when his DNA ties him to a rape victim.

1986 Andrei Sakharov's exile is ended by Mikhail Gorbachev, who welcomes the dissident physicist back to Moscow.

1988 Ethnic Albanians begin demonstrating for independence from Serbian rule in Yugoslavia's Kosovo province.

1985 The Third World Conference on Women is held in Nairobi at a critical moment for developing countries, pledging links between equality for women, development, and peace.

1989 F. W. de Klerk succeeds P. W. Botha as president of South Africa.

1985 Hitachi introduces the compact disc read-only memory (CD-ROM).

1985 An Australian baby becomes the first child born from a frozen embryo.

1989 The Dalai Lama wins the Nobel Peace Prize.

1989 Thousands of students occupy Tiananmen Square in Beijing, China, protesting for democracy. After seven weeks the government imposes martial law and uses tanks to clear the square, killing an estimated thousands and damaging Deng Xiaoping's improved relations with the West. Zhau Ziyang is removed as head of China's Communist Party for his sympathetic stance toward the students.

THE GLOBAL AIDS CRISIS

Acquired immune deficiency syndrome (AIDS) was first identified in 1981 and quickly became the most feared and confounding disease on the planet. Caused by an insidious virus (human immunodeficiency virus, or HIV) that destroys the body's infection-fighting T-cells, AIDS leaves one helpless against infections, cancers, and neurological disorders. By the end of 2002, the disease had claimed around 25 million lives.

The virus is transmitted through the direct exchange of body fluids (usually blood or semen) and can be contracted by anyone. Hemophiliacs and others needing transfusions were initially very vulnerable. But the prevalence of AIDS in the gay community in the 1980s made this a medical issue with explosive political dimensions. Gay rights advocates became a vocal minority in the U.S., lobbying for more research funding and sex education. Even notable exceptions like NBA superstar Magic Johnson, who contracted the virus through unprotected heterosexual intercourse, did little to remove the stigma of AIDS as primarily a gay disease.

By the late 1990s, AIDS cases were declining in the U.S. but exploding throughout lesser developed nations. Sub-Saharan Africa, where HIV is thought to have originated in chimpanzee populations, has been hit particularly hard, with some countries showing infection rates of almost 40 percent. The disease here and in Asia has been spread mainly through heterosexual contact and exacerbated by unstable living conditions and poor healthcare.

There is still no cure for HIV, which frustrates researchers by mutating rapidly. Although recent drugs called protease inhibitors have proved effective at interfering with a virus's ability to replicate, they do not eliminate the virus from the body. AIDS continues to be a political hot button with regard to research funding and aid to Africa.

POLITICS & POWER	GEOGRAPHY & ENVIRONMENT	CULTURE & RELIGION

THE AMERICAS

1990 Nicaragua's communist Sandinista government is voted out of power with the election of Violetta Chamorro.

1991 Haitian president Jean Bertrand Aristide is ousted. He returns to power in 1994.

1991 The UN brokers an end to the 10-year-old civil war in El Salvador.

1992 Bill Clinton is elected U.S. president.

1993 A terrorist bomb explodes inside the World Trade Center in New York.

1994 The U.S., Mexico, and Canada sign the North American Free Trade Agreement (NAFTA).

1991 The worst cholera epidemic of the 20th century, thought to be caused by contaminated seafood, breaks out in Peru, affecting nearly 100,000 people.

1992 Hurricane Andrew strikes south Florida, causing 30 billion dollars in property damage, the worst natural disaster in U.S. history.

1990s Wal-Mart launches an aggressive expansion campaign. By mid-decade it is the biggest retailer in the world with 2,400 stores in the U.S. and 137.6 billion dollars in sales.

1991 Michael Jordan leads the Chicago Bulls to the first of six NBA championships.

1991 NBA superstar Magic Johnson announces he is HIV-positive.

1993 AIDS becomes the leading cause of death among U.S men between 25 and 44.

1994 The World Series is canceled for the first time when Major League Baseball players and management fail to settle a strike.

EUROPE

1991 The Baltic states of Latvia, Estonia, and Lithuania and the republics of Georgia, Azerbaijan, Armenia, and Ukraine declare independence from the Soviet Union.

1991 The Warsaw Pact is formally dissolved.

1991 The U.S.S.R. officially ceases to exist on December 9.

1991 Boris Yeltsin is elected president of the Russian Federation.

1992 The Bosnian civil war begins. Serbia undertakes an ethnic cleansing program to remove Bosnian Muslims and Croats from newly independent Bosnia-Herzegovina.

1990 East and West Germany reunify.

1992 Slovenia, Croatia, Macedonia, and Bosnia-Herzegovina secede from Yugoslavia. In 1993 the name Yugoslavia is abolished, leaving the loose commonwealth of Serbia and Montenegro.

1993 The Czech and Slovak Republics (formerly Czechoslovakia) become separate and sovereign countries.

1994 An attempt by the Chechnya region to break away from the Russian government is crushed by the Russian Army.

1992 The U.S. "dream team"—the first Olympic U.S. basketball team featuring NBA professionals—easily wins the gold medal at the summer games in Barcelona, Spain.

1992 Charles and Diana, Prince and Princess of Wales, announce their separation.

1993 New globalism: The European Community becomes the European Union (EU) with the Maastricht Treaty. The U.S. approves NAFTA with Mexico and Canada.

MIDDLE EAST & AFRICA

1990-91 Iraq invades Kuwait; a U.S.-led coalition liberates Kuwait in the Gulf War.

1992 U.S. troops are sent to civil war–torn Somalia to ensure delivery of international food aid.

1994 King Hussein of Jordan and Prime Minister Yitzhak Rabin of Israel sign a declaration ending the conflict between their countries.

1994 Civil war erupts in Rwanda when the Hutu kill more than 500,000 Tutsi. Tutsi forces eventually regain control of the country, forcing two million Hutu to flee. Rwanda becomes synonymous worldwide with genocidal carnage and violence.

1990 Namibia becomes independent.

1991 Iraq deliberately pumps 6-8 million barrels of Kuwaiti oil into the Persian Gulf and also sets fire to oil fields, creating an ecological disaster at the end of the Gulf War.

1992 The Ataturk Dam opens in Turkey, doubling the land area that can be cultivated.

1993 Eritrea becomes the newest African country after its long civil war with Ethiopia.

1994 Rwanda, the most densely populated country in continental Africa before 1994, loses 20 to 40 percent of its population to slaughter or exile.

1990 Nelson Mandela is released from prison after 27 years when South African president F. W. de Klerk declares amnesty for political prisoners and lifts restrictions on the African National Congress. De Klerk begins dismantling apartheid in 1991. In 1994 the first nonracial general election in South African history results in a victory for the African National Congress and makes Nelson Mandela the first black president of South Africa.

1990s Shiite clergyman Hashemi Rafsanjani becomes the leader of Iran after Ayatollah Khomeini's death.

ASIA & OCEANIA

1992 Australia's high court legally recognizes the presence of Aboriginal peoples before European settlement and later recognizes Native Title claims over land in Australia.

1992 Taiwan votes to suspend the ban on trade and social links with the People's Republic of China.

1993 North Korea withdraws from the Nuclear Nonproliferation Treaty.

1991 A cyclone in Bangladesh kills 200,000 people. A later storm surge in the Chittagong delta kills another 125,000.

1991 Mount Pinatubo in the Philippines erupts, spewing the greatest volume of sulfur dioxide ever measured.

1994 Kim Jong Il comes to power in North Korea, replacing his long-ruling father, Kim Il Sung. By 2004 North Korea will have earned the worst score on political and civil liberties from the human rights group Freedom House for 33 years in a row.

SCIENCE & TECHNOLOGY	PEOPLE & SOCIETY
1990 The Hubble Space Telescope is put into operation. It orbits Earth at the edge of the atmosphere, allowing it to take the deepest space pictures ever. In 1994 Hubble finds the first conclusive evidence of Black Holes.	**1990 Peruvian Mario Vargas Llosa**, one of Latin America's leading novelists and essayists, runs for the presidency of Peru, but loses.
1993 The Web browser Mosaic is developed at the University of Illinois. By combining text and images on the page, it rapidly increases the popularity of the World Wide Web.	**1992 Guatemalan Maya Rigoberto Menchu** wins the Nobel Peace Prize for her work trying to hold the army accountable for the killing of Maya natives during the country's civil war.
1993 The U.S. Global Positioning System is completed.	**1993 Toni Morrison** becomes the first African-American woman awarded the Nobel Prize in literature.
1994 The Pan American Health Organization declares the Americas to be free of polio.	**1994 Zapatista rebels** in Mexico protest the country's move toward globalization.

THE END OF APARTHEID

When Nelson Mandela was convicted in 1962 of agitating in opposition to apartheid, he expressed his wish to live to see the day when South Africa would be a "democratic and free society." Miraculously, he not only lived to see that day after 27 years in prison, but became the leader of that society.

Implemented in 1948, apartheid put into law what had already been the unofficial law of the land: racial segregation and the supremacy of whites. Not only were whites to be separated from nonwhites, but nonwhites were to be separated from each other—the nine black African Bantu groups were separated, for example. Large segments of the nonwhite population were forced from cities into rural reservations. Under a euphemistic policy called separate development, the Bantu groups were each granted their own homeland. The reality was that 14 percent of South Africa's land—most of it broken tracts of unarable land—was set aside for 75 percent of the population, while the rest of the country, including the cities and rich mineral areas, was reserved for whites.

1991 British and Australian studies show that passive smoking is a significant cause of lung cancer.	**1990 Helmut Kohl** is elected chancellor of the reunited Germany.
1994 The Channel Tunnel between Britain and France opens.	**1990 Labor leader Lech Walesa** is elected president of Poland.
	1991 British computer scientist Tim Berners-Lee puts the World Wide Web online. Through his invention of HyperText Transfer Protocol (HTTP), Berners-Lee allows documents to be linked together on computers across the Internet.

After generations of black African resistance and decades of international pressure on South Africa, including increasing economic sanctions, the white minority's ability to keep apartheid in place finally eroded. A severe shortage of skilled labor, the fruit of segregationist labor and wage policies, also forced the government to make concessions to blacks.

Oil fires blaze across the Persian Gulf, set by Iraqis in the aftermath of the Gulf War.

1991 The Gulf War becomes the first war in which laser weapons are used extensively.

1993 Israeli prime minister Yitzhak Rabin, former prime minister Shimon Peres, and PLO leader Yasser Arafat negotiate the Oslo Accords, which grant land and authority to Palestinians (including Israel's promise to leave the Gaza Strip and West Bank). Israel, though, fails to withdraw.

1994 Yasser Arafat creates the Palestine National Authority to govern Gaza and Jericho.

By 1991 President F. W. de Klerk had completely repealed all apartheid laws, and the first free elections were held in 1994. The result heard 'round the world was a resounding victory for the African National Congress and new president Nelson Mandela. Finally, in 1996, the Constitution of the Republic of South Africa established a society based on democratic values, social justice, and fundamental human rights.

1994 Construction begins on Three Gorges Dam in China.	**1989-1995 Democratic activist Daw Aung San Suu Kyi** of Myanmar (Burma) holds "gate-side meetings" with supporters from her home, where she is under house arrest. In 1990 she and her party win 80 percent of the vote in the national elections but are not allowed to come to power. In 1991 she wins the Nobel Peace Prize but is not allowed to accept it.

We cannot all live in cities,
  yet nearly all seem determined to do so.

HORACE GREELEY

THE LURE OF CITY LIFE

IT SEEMS ALMOST NATURAL FOR MEXICO CITY TO BE THE PULSATING HIVE THAT IT is. This was, after all, the capital of the Aztec, one of the great civilizations of the Americas. But the Mexico City of today, about 25 million strong, is a recent phenomenon. Just 60 years ago it had only three million people. The dramatic growth of urban populations, especially in developing nations, is one of the defining trends of the post-1950 world.

The industrial revolution caused a quantum leap in urbanization in Europe and America. By 1900 about 14 percent of the world's population lived in cities, and many cities—after thousands of years as unhealthy death traps—featured birthrates in excess of their death rates. Millions more flocked to these cities in search of opportunity and excitement.

By the year 2000, roughly half the human population lived in cities; in North America, more than three-quarters of all people did. Some cities, including Mexico City, grew so large that they were dubbed "mega-cities"—usually defined as cities with more than ten million inhabitants. By 2012, the world had 25 mega-cities, and 5 of them outstripped Mexico City. Tokyo topped the list, followed by Guangzhou, Seoul, Jakarta, and Shanghai, evidence of the pell-mell urbanization of East Asia.

On a national scale, China experienced the largest migration to cities. Hundreds of millions of villagers moved to the cities in the decades after 1980, despite official policies intended to check migration. In 1990, a quarter of the population lived in cities. But by 2013, China had hundreds of cities with more than one million people, and more than half the population was urban. This process, still taking place, is the largest and fastest urbanization in any country in the history of the world.

Unfortunately, rapid urbanization has produced some of the same environmental and social problems experienced in Europe and America during the first decades of industrialization. Pollution and infectious diseases, especially waterborne ones, imperil the health of hundreds of millions of city dwellers. Authorities struggle, often unsuccessfully, to provide water, electricity, sewerage, and police and firefighting services to ever growing cities.

Perhaps a third of all city folk live in informal housing, or slums, surrounded by pollution, disease, and crime. Yet in slums around the world people are energetically striving to better their lot, calculating that their chances of doing so are better there than in the villages that they or their parents left behind.

Smog blankets Beijing. China's premature deaths from air pollution are the highest in the world, owing to rapid growth.

POLITICS & POWER	GEOGRAPHY & ENVIRONMENT	CULTURE & RELIGION

THE AMERICAS

1995 A bomb explodes in the parking garage beneath a federal office building in Oklahoma City, killing 166 and injuring more than 400. Timothy McVeigh and Terry Nichols are arrested.

1996 Bill Clinton is reelected president of the United States. He is impeached by the House in 1998 for perjury and obstruction of justice but acquitted by the Senate in 1999.

1998 U.S. president Clinton and Mexican president Ernesto Zedillo pledge to devise a joint strategy to combat drug trafficking.

1996 The U.S. steps up efforts to restrict illegal immigration from Mexico, hiring more U.S. Border Patrols and installing 40 miles of a 14-foot fence along the border.

1997 Nearly two years of volcanic eruptions on the Caribbean island of Montserrat culminate in a violent pyroclastic flow that virtually destroys the capital of Plymouth.

1998 The weather phenomenon El Niño is blamed for scorching temperatures, drought, and tornadoes across the U.S.

1996 The term soccer moms is used to describe working mothers as a powerful interest group in American politics.

1997 U.S. president Clinton apologizes to 399 African-American men in Alabama who were left untreated for syphilis as part of a government experiment from 1932 to 1972.

1997 U.S. tobacco companies agree to settle claims made against them by former smokers in the amount of 368.5 billion dollars.

1999 A U.S. federal judge rules that software giant Microsoft is a monopoly.

EUROPE

1997 Sinn Fein, the political arm of the Irish Republican Army, wins its first seat in the Irish House of Representatives.

1998 Yugoslavian president Slobodan Milosevic is ordered to withdraw his troops from the province of Kosovo, where Serbians have been on a campaign of ethnic cleansing. In 1999 NATO launches air strikes against Yugoslavia.

1998 Poland, Hungary, and the Czech Republic join NATO.

1999 Russia invades Chechnya, the southern region of the country that tried to break away in separatist fighting in 1994-96.

1996 A volcano erupts beneath the Vatnajökull, a glacier that covers a tenth of Iceland, piercing the glacier and causing floods of melted ice.

1996 The European Commission bans exports of beef from the U.K. because of an outbreak of mad cow disease.

1997 DNA originally extracted from fossils in the Neander Valley in Germany in 1856 supports the theory that modern humans diverged from Neanderthals about 600,000 years ago, arising originally in Africa and replacing Neanderthals, who became extinct.

1997 Diana, Princess of Wales, dies in a car accident in Paris. An estimated two billion people worldwide watch her funeral on TV.

1997 The Roman Catholic Church issues a formal apology for its silence when the French government deported Jews to Nazi death camps during World War II.

1998 Germany announces the establishment of a pension fund to compensate Jewish Holocaust survivors in Central and Eastern Europe.

MIDDLE EAST & AFRICA

1996 PLO leader Yasser Arafat is elected president in the first Palestinian elections.

1996 Israel begins a major offensive against the Lebanese Muslim organization Hezbollah.

1998 Iraq prevents UN weapons inspectors from conducting a search, provoking the U.S. and Great Britain to send naval forces to the Persian Gulf. UN secretary-general Kofi Annan eventually brokers a deal to have the inspectors return and avert a war.

1998 The U.S. launches cruise missiles at terrorist sites in Afghanistan and Sudan in retaliation for two U.S. Embassy bombings in Africa.

1995 Zaire suffers an outbreak of the Ebola virus, which is more lethal than AIDS.

1997 Zaire becomes the Democratic Republic of Congo after Tutsi rebels from Rwanda take the capital and President Mobutu Sese Seko flees.

1997-98 Increased rainfall leads to a sharp rise of malaria and other diseases, including cholera epidemics, in parts of Africa, while available water in Africa's large catchment basins of Niger, Lake Chad, and Senegal decreases by 40 to 60 percent. The instability is thought to be a result of global warming.

1995 Nigeria hangs the writer Ken Saro-Wiwa and eight others for their opposition to environmental damage in the Ogoni region.

1997 Reformist Mohammed Khatami is elected president of Iran. Claiming conservatives have hijacked the revolution, he loosens restrictions and improves civil society, but cannot overthrow the conservatives.

ASIA & OCEANIA

1995 Vietnam resumes diplomatic relations with the U.S. and is the first communist state to be admitted to the Association of South-East Asian Nations.

1996 The Taliban Islamic fundamentalist movement takes over the Afghan capital of Kabul and imposes Islamic law.

1996 Osama bin Laden, founder of the al-Qaeda Islamic terrorist network, moves to Afghanistan after being expelled by Sudan and forges an alliance with the Taliban government.

1997 The British colony of Hong Kong reverts to Chinese control, becoming a Special Administrative Region.

1997 Plantation owners in Indonesia cause the worst forest fires in Southeast Asian history in an attempt to clear farmland. World record levels of atmospheric pollution affect up to 20 million people with throat and respiratory problems. Almost 1.5 million acres of land are consumed.

1999 East Timor votes for independence from Indonesia.

1995 Sarin nerve gas is released into the Tokyo subway system, killing 12 and injuring 5,000. The Aum Shinrikyo religious sect is found responsible.

1997 A state funeral is held in Calcutta, India, for Mother Teresa, the Catholic nun who ministered to that city's poor for 70 years.

1998 The Red Cross estimates that 10,000 children a month are dying in North Korea due to famine caused by poor agricultural practices.

SCIENCE & TECHNOLOGY

1995 The online auction site eBay is founded in California and becomes the fastest-growing company of all time.

1996 IBM's Deep Blue becomes the first computer to beat a world chess champion.

1998 The Google Internet search engine goes online. By 2004 Google is handling almost 80 percent of all Internet search requests.

1998 Viagra, a new pill to cure male impotence, becomes the fastest-selling drug in U.S. history.

1998 U.S. scientists present evidence that the universe is about 15 billion years old.

1995 Russian cosmonaut Valery Poliakov returns to earth after 439 days aboard the Mir space station, the longest stay in space ever.

1995 Great Britain establishes the world's first DNA-based crime database.

1997 British geneticists clone an adult sheep, named Dolly. The news sparks international debate on the future of human cloning.

1998 The U.S. space shuttle *Endeavor* successfully docks with the Russian space station Mir.

1996 The first DVD players and discs are released, in Japan.

1996 The Petronas Towers in Kuala Lumpur, Malaysia, become the world's tallest buildings at 1,483 ft., 29 ft. higher than the Chicago Sears Tower.

1998 The world's largest suspension bridge (2.4 miles long) opens in Japan, linking Kobe and Awaji Island.

1998 India and Pakistan begin testing nuclear weapons, sparking fears of an arms race in southern Asia.

PEOPLE & SOCIETY

1995 Cal Ripken, Jr., of the Baltimore Orioles breaks New York Yankees star Lou Gehrig's 57-year-old record of playing 2,130 consecutive Major League Baseball games.

1995 NFL Hall of Fame running back O. J. Simpson is acquitted of murdering his wife, Nicole Brown Simpson, and Ronald Goldman, in the "trial of the century."

1997 Tiger Woods, 21, becomes the youngest person to win the U.S. Masters golf tournament at Augusta, Georgia.

1999 Jeff Bezos, founder of Amazon.com, is named *Time* magazine's Man of the Year for helping launch the online shopping revolution.

1995 Jacques Chirac becomes president of France, succeeding François Mitterrand.

1995 The World Trade Organization is created to promote economic development worldwide.

1996 Boris Yeltsin becomes the president of Russia, having defeated a communist challenger.

1997 Labor Party leader Tony Blair wins the general election in Great Britain.

1995 The burial ground for hundreds of laborers who constructed the Great Pyramid in Egypt is discovered. Their bones show signs of constant heavy labor.

1995 Israeli prime minister Yitzhak Rabin is assassinated by a Jewish law student in Tel Aviv for ceding land to the Palestinians in the Oslo peace accords.

1996 New Israeli prime minister Benjamin Netanyahu brings the Israeli-Palestinian accord to an end and renews settlements.

Dolly, the first successful clone of an adult animal

1995 Queen Elizabeth II of Britain returns land and money to the Maori tribe of New Zealand as compensation for British aggression in the 1860s.

1996 Japan makes compensation payments to 20,000 women forced to be soldiers' concubines during World War II.

1998 Bad loans, lower exports, and weakened currencies lead to an economic crisis, known as the Asian flu, in Southeast Asia.

Terror's Breeding Ground

The Soviet invasion of Afghanistan in 1979 proved to be a pivotal conflict for the post–Cold War world. Often called the Soviet Union's Vietnam, the decade-long war was seen as a victory for America and the CIA, which had armed and trained the Islamic guerrilla warriors who finally drove the Soviets out in 1989—the same year the Soviet empire began to splinter.

Those Islamic warriors, the *mujahideen,* ultimately toppled the Afghan government and replaced it with one of their own—the Taliban. Part of their funding had come from a wealthy young civil engineer from Saudi Arabia named Osama bin Laden. After being exiled for financing various terrorist operations, bin Laden moved to Afghanistan in 1996 and that same year issued a declaration of war against the U.S.

Under the auspices of the Taliban, Osama bin Laden's al-Qaeda network has been linked to the 1998 bombings of the U.S. Embassies in Kenya and Tanzania, the 2000 attack on the U.S.S. *Cole* in Yemen, and the 2001 attacks on the World Trade Center and the Pentagon. As a result, bin Laden became the world's most wanted man.

The U.S. toppled the Taliban in 2001 but failed to capture bin Laden. Over the next decade, U.S. and NATO forces occupied Afghanistan and supported its government. The Taliban and al-Qaeda found Afghanistan less suitable as a base of operations and increasingly moved between Afghanistan and Pakistan, where bin Laden hid out and where NATO and U.S. ground forces could not go.

At the same time, al-Qaeda decentralized its operations. Bin Laden played a smaller role, and younger figures emerged, mounting terrorist attacks in Europe and Africa and narrowly failing in attempts in the U.S. American counterterror efforts led to the killing of bin Laden in his Pakistan hideout in 2011.

2000-Present

	POLITICS & POWER	GEOGRAPHY & ENVIRONMENT	CULTURE & RELIGION
THE AMERICAS	**2000 Hillary Clinton** becomes the first First Lady elected to public office, winning a U.S. Senate seat in New York. **2000 Vicente Fox** is elected president of Mexico, marking the fall of PRI, Mexico's "official" party since 1929. **2001 Two planes hijacked by terrorists** crash into New York's World Trade Center, destroying both towers and killing nearly 3,000. A third hijacked plane crashes into the Pentagon. A fourth is brought down by passengers. **2008 Barack Obama** is elected the first African-American president of the U.S.	**2005 Hurricane Katrina** strikes the U.S. Gulf Coast in one of the worst natural disasters in the nation's history.	**2000 Scores of dot-com businesses** go belly-up as the 1990s technology boom goes bust. **2002 The Catholic Church** is scandalized by revelations of child molestation by priests and cover-ups by the Church. **2003 The Massachusetts Supreme Court** permits gay marriage. **2004 The Boston Red Sox** overcome sports' most famous curse and win the World Series, their first title since 1918. **2008 Jamaican sprinter Usain Bolt** wins the first of his six Olympic gold medals, shattering world records.
EUROPE	**2000 Vladimir Putin** is elected president of Russia. **2000 Yugoslavian president Slobodan Milosevic** is driven from office. **2004 Rebels** from the breakaway Russian republic of Chechnya seize an elementary school; more than 300 adults and children die. **2007-2012 Europeans** grapple with the effects of worldwide recession.		**2002 Euros**, the currency of the new European Union, begin circulating. **2008 *Mamma Mia!***, the biggest success in British movie box office history, is released. **2010 The Muslim population of Europe** reaches 44 million. *Barack Obama takes the oath of office to become the 44th president of the U.S. and the first African American elected to that office.*
MIDDLE EAST & AFRICA	**2001 Ariel Sharon** becomes prime minister of Israel as violence with Palestinians worsens. **2003 The U.S. invades Iraq** based on intelligence that Saddam Hussein is concealing weapons of mass destruction. Hussein is captured, but WMDs are never found. **2003 Ethnic conflicts** boil over in Sudan as government-backed militia begin a campaign against non-Arab indigenous peoples of the Darfur region. More than 70,000 have been killed and millions more displaced. **2011 Multiple popular uprisings** take place in Arab countries (the Arab Spring).	**2001 The U.S. endorses** the creation of a Palestinian state. **2002 Israel** begins construction of a massive wall called the "security fence" around its settlements in the West Bank. **2003 An earthquake** devastates southeastern Iran, killing more than 40,000. **2004-2005 Six million people** across West Africa's semiarid Sahel region face famine after an invasion of locusts followed by severe drought destroys their crops and grazing land.	**2004-2005 Bowing to international pressure**, Saudi Arabia agrees to hold its first municipal elections in 40 years. Women, though, may not vote or run for office. **2006 Turkish writer Orhan Pamuk** wins the Nobel Prize in literature. **2010 Muslim-Christian religious rioting** in central Nigeria kills more than 200.
ASIA & OCEANIA	**2001 The U.S. bombs Afghanistan** and topples the Taliban government after linking the World Trade Center attacks to Osama bin Laden, leader of the Taliban-supported militant Islamic group al-Qaeda. **2002 The long-standing dispute** between India and Pakistan over the Kashmir region threatens to erupt into nuclear war. **2002 North Korea** admits to having been pursuing nuclear capability in violation of a 1994 pact with the U.S. **2009 The Sri Lankan government** defeats the Tamil Tigers, ending a quarter century of civil war.	**2010 China** becomes the world's largest emitter of carbon dioxide. **2011 A tsunami** causes a nuclear disaster at Fukushima, Japan.	**2000 Chinese writer Ha Jin's** novel *Waiting* wins the U.S. PEN/Faulkner Award for Fiction after winning the 1999 U.S. National Book Award for Fiction. **2008 The Beijing Olympics** are the first ever to be held in China. **2011 New Zealand's national rugby team**, the All Blacks, wins its second World Cup.

SCIENCE & TECHNOLOGY	PEOPLE & SOCIETY
2001 Stem-cell research becomes a political issue in the U.S. as President George W. Bush allows federal funding for research on existing stem-cell lines, but not for creating new ones.	**2000 In the U.S. Census,** citizens are able to claim for the first time more than one racial identity. The percentage of citizens who label themselves "American" rises dramatically.
2003 The U.S. Human Genome Project is completed, identifying and mapping all 20,000-25,000 genes in human DNA.	**2004 Jean Bertrand Aristide** of Haiti is overthrown yet again in a rebellion after becoming president for the third time in 2001.
2003 The _Columbia_ space shuttle explodes over north-central Texas as it returns from a mission.	**2006 The U.S. population** tops 300 million.
2007 Apple releases the first iPhone.	**2012 Three U.S. states** vote to allow same-sex marriage for the first time.
2009 NASA launches the Lunar Reconnaissance Orbiter.	
2004 The world's highest bridge, the Millau Viaduct, which crosses the River Tarn, opens in France's Massif Central region.	**2000 British physician Harold Shipman** is sentenced to life in prison for the murder of at least 15 patients. He is suspected of killing 365, which would make him one of the worst serial killers of all time.
2008 The Large Hadron Collider, the world's largest particle accelerator, opens near Geneva.	**2000s Almost six million refugees** (up from less than a million in the 1980s) struggle to relocate after the collapse of communism and ethnic splintering in Eastern Europe.
2011 Germany announces it will phase out nuclear energy.	**2011 Anders Breivik** perpetrates a mass shooting in Norway, killing 77.
2000s AIDS becomes an epidemic in Africa, particularly sub-Saharan Africa, where in some countries almost 40 percent of the population is HIV-positive.	**2001 Saudi Osama bin Laden** orchestrates the worst terrorist attack ever on U.S. soil.
2003 Libyan dictator Muammar al-Qaddafi agrees to abandon Libya's nuclear weapons program.	**2004 Wangari Maathai,** a Kenyan activist who founded an Africa-wide movement to empower women, confronted corrupt officials, and planted millions of trees in ravaged forestland, receives the Nobel Peace Prize.
2011 Iran's first nuclear power plant, Bushehr 1, officially opens.	**2005 Mahmoud Abbas** succeeds Yasser Arafat as president of the Palestinian Authority.
2012 The Nzema Project, Africa's largest solar energy installation, opens in Ghana.	
2003 The SARS virus (severe acute respiratory syndrome), a lethal pneumonia-like illness, starts in China and spreads to Europe and North America.	**2004 Unocal Corporation of California** agrees to settle landmark human rights lawsuits in Myanmar (Burma). The company will pay damages to Burmese villagers who say the military government used rape, torture, and murder to force them to work on Unocal's pipeline.
2003 China launches Shenzhou 5, their first manned space mission.	**2010 Japan's population growth rate** falls to zero.
2004 It is discovered that the head of Pakistan's nuclear program has been selling nuclear technology to North Korea, Libya, and Iran.	
2011 China's Three Gorges Dam, the biggest power plant ever built, becomes fully operational.	

CLOUD COMPUTING

In the early 2000s, an advance in data-sharing technology called cloud computing altered the way we store and transmit information in the digital age. Cloud computing refers to the storage of data on remote servers over a network, generally the Internet. It is often used as a specific business model: Companies offer several services including data storage, computation, and network security. Consumers pay for access to certain of these benefits. Cloud computing seeks to make information processing as efficient as possible.

With cloud computing people can send much larger and more complex data packages to one another, making cloud computing a special boon to international corporations; programs such as Google Documents operate this way.

NASA has launched a cloud computing platform called Nebula, in which huge amounts of data are stored on the platform, making it easily accessible to worldwide NASA scientists and engineers. This alleviates the need for expensive data centers.

Cloud computing changes everyday life as well. It makes daily weather forecasts more reliable, helps law enforcement agencies crunch numbers on crime statistics in thousands of precincts, and allows health officials to recognize epidemics in their early stages. Governments and, in particular, intelligence services also use cloud computing for storing and analyzing surveillance data concerning the behavior of millions of people.

In some ways, cloud computing resembles the original acquisition of language by our remote ancestors. Before humans had language, their ability to share information and learn from one another was constrained. But with the advent of language, both knowledge and wisdom became more cumulative and social. Useful knowledge rarely vanished with the death of any single individual, because through language our ancestors could share information efficiently and store it in one another's brains.

NATURE STRIKES

O N DECEMBER 26, 2004, IT WAS AS IF A BOMB HAD EXPLODED ON THE OCEAN floor. Or to be more precise, 23,000 atomic bombs, all the size of the one dropped on Hiroshima. Beneath the Indian Ocean, two tectonic plates—the vast, sliding sheets of earth's crust that carry the continents and the oceans—had been rubbing each other the wrong way for 40 million years. The plates had collided, with one being forced under the other, causing the edge of the top plate to bend backward. When the top plate finally sprung free, the result was one of the most massive earthquakes in recorded history.

The mega-atomic force sent billions of tons of water rocketing outward from the epicenter at more than 500 miles per hour. NASA reported that the earthquake actually made the Earth spin faster and wobble in orbit. All anyone noticed, though, were the colossal waves that swamped the shorelines of a dozen countries from Thailand to Africa, leaving almost 300,000 dead and millions homeless.

Less than one year later, on August 29, 2005, disaster struck again on the opposite side of the world. Hurricane Katrina roared into the Gulf of Mexico at a rating of category five—one of the strongest the Gulf had ever seen. By the time it reached the southern coasts of Louisiana and Mississippi it had been downgraded to a category four, but it still became one of the most devastating natural disasters in U.S. history.

The violent surge brought on by Katrina caused the New Orleans levees to burst, and within hours the vibrant city was drowning under nearly six feet of water. More than 1,800 people in Louisiana and elsewhere were killed by the storm and its aftermath, and hundreds of thousands were displaced. More than a decade later, the people of the Gulf Coast were still recovering. Cities and individual homes still bear the damage of catastrophic winds and floods. The struggle to rebuild, both after Katrina and the tsunami, is a reminder of the awesome power of nature and of its tragic consequences.

LEFT: *Fukushima's No. 3 reactor, destroyed by the 2011 tsunami and earthquake that struck Japan*
ABOVE: *Fukushima police in hazmat suits in the aftermath of Japan's 2011 nuclear disaster*

	PREHISTORY	500 B.C.E.	500 C.E.	1000	
THE AMERICAS	**ca 1200 B.C.E.** Olmec civilization is at its peak with a monumental ceremonial complex at San Lorenzo. **ca 1000 B.C.E.** The Cochise culture dominates the area of modern-day New Mexico and Arizona. **ca 700 B.C.E.** Maya begin to organize into 50 separate religious-political entities. **600-500 B.C.E.** Olmec civilization declines.	**ca 400 B.C.E.** Zapotec society develops in Mexico. **ca 250 B.C.E.** Moche society develops in northern coastal Peru while Nazca society develops in southern coastal Peru. **ca 250 C.E.** Maya societies enter into their Classic period, characterized by divine kings ruling over powerful city-states. **ca 450 C.E.** Zapotec and Teotihuacan societies watch over a trade network extending throughout Mesoamerica.	**ca 500** Teotihuacan reaches the height of its influence. **ca 600** The Tiahuanaco Empire rises in southern Peru and Bolivia. **ca 700** The Moche and the Nazca societies collapse. **750** Teotihuacan is sacked and burned by the invading Toltec. **ca 800** A hierarchy of chief-priests leads Caddo groups. **990** The Huari and Tiahuanaco Empires in Peru begin to decline.	**ca 1050** Central Mexican groups invade Maya settlements. **1125** The Toltec Empire begins its decline. **ca 1150** Chimu civilization expands along the coast of Peru. **1428** Itzcoatl forms the Aztec Alliance, bringing his people to the apex of their power. **1440** Aztec ruler Moctezuma I begins conquering tribes outside the Valley of Mexico. **1450** Inca subdue the Chimu.	
EUROPE	**ca 1450 B.C.E.** Mycenaeans on mainland Greece take control of Crete, ending Minoan civilization. **ca 1000 B.C.E.** Proto-Etruscans develop independent city-states in Italy. **800 B.C.E.** Independent city-states, including Sparta and Athens, develop in Greece. **616 B.C.E.** Etruscan Tarquinus Priscus becomes king of Rome. **509 B.C.E.** Romans drive the Etruscans out of Rome and establish the Roman Republic.	**490 B.C.E.** Greeks halt a Persian incursion onto Greek peninsula. **338 B.C.E.** Philip II of Macedon occupies all of Greece. **46 B.C.E.** Caesar becomes dictator-for-life of Rome. His heir, Augustus, becomes the first emperor of Rome. **286 C.E.** Diocletian splits the Roman Empire into eastern and western units. **400s C.E.** Germanic groups and the Huns ravage the deteriorating Roman Empire.	**527-610** Justinian I and Heraclius regain lost territory of the Roman Empire for Byzantium. **711-732** Muslim armies invade Spain from North Africa. **800** Pope Leo III crowns Charlemagne emperor of Rome. **871** Alfred the Great becomes the first king of England. **882** Oleg, uniter of Russia, founds Kiev as his capital. **930** Viking settlers of Iceland form Europe's first parliament.	**1066** William the Conqueror subdues England. **1215** King John of England signs the Magna Carta. **1337-1415** The Hundred Years' War is waged. **1381** Venice defeats rival republic Genoa. **1485** The Tudor dynasty is established in England, ending the Wars of the Roses. **1492** Spanish seize Granada, last Muslim kingdom of Spain.	
MIDDLE EAST & AFRICA	**ca 3200 B.C.E.** Sumer, the first civilization, emerges in Iraq. **2334-2279 B.C.E.** Sargon of Akkad creates the first empire. **1792-1750 B.C.E.** Hammurabi expands the Babylonian Empire. **1490-1436 B.C.E.** Tutmosis III expands the Egyptian Empire. **883-859 B.C.E.** Assyria again rises to power in Mesopotamia. **587 B.C.E.** Nebuchadrezzar II conquers what is left of the kingdom of Israel.	**558-529 B.C.E.** Cyrus the Great expands the Persian Empire. **334 B.C.E.** Alexander the Great invades Persia and carves out an immense empire. **218 B.C.E.** Hannibal marches against Rome. **ca 171 B.C.E.** Mithridates I conquers much of Seleucid Empire. **ca 50 C.E.** The kingdom of Axum is founded in Ethiopia. **224 C.E.** The Parthian Empire is toppled by Sassanid Empire.	**ca 500** The empire of Ghana rises in West Africa. **531** Sassanid king Khosrow I reunites Persia, only to be conquered by Muslims in 651. **661** Muawiyah begins rule of the Umayyad dynasty, whose armies push to the borders of China. **750-754** Abu al-Abbas founds the Abbasid dynasty after overthrowing the Umayyads. **999** Turks conquer northern India and all of Central Asia.	**1025** The Byzantine Empire begins to decline. **1077** The Almoravids invade the kingdom of Ghana in Africa. **1171** Saladin retakes Jerusalem. **1204** Crusaders seize the city of Constantinople. **1380** Tamerlane begins successful campaigns against Persia, Russia, Georgia, and Egypt. **1453** Ottoman Turks take Constantinople. They now rule from Taurus Mountains to the Adriatic.	
ASIA & OCEANIA	**ca 3000-1750** The first dynasties emerge in China. **ca 1500 B.C.E.** Aryan-speaking Indo-Europeans move into the Indus Valley from the north. **1045 B.C.E.** The Shang dynasty is toppled by the Zhou dynasty. **771 B.C.E.** Nomads attack the Zhou, dividing China into eastern Zhou and western Zhou kingdoms. **ca 700** China is torn by a power struggle between rival semi-autonomous states.	**321 B.C.E.** Chandragupta Maurya pushes the borders of his kingdom into northwestern India. **221 B.C.E.** King Zheng of the Qin defeats rival states to become emperor of unified China. **ca 100 C.E.** Funan emerges as a power in Southeast Asia. **220 C.E.** The Han dynasty falls and the three kingdoms of Wei, Wu, and Shu emerge in China. **ca 320 C.E.** Chandra Gupta establishes the Gupta dynasty in India.	**500** Northern Funan falls to the Khmer people of Cambodia. **535** India's Gupta Empire collapses. **712-756** China's Tang dynasty reaches the height of its power. **775** The Srivijaya kingdom extends its domain in Southeast Asia. **ca 800** Jayavarman II unites Khmer states into one kingdom. **985** Chola power reaches its zenith in southern India.	**1086** The "cloistered emperor" system in Japan marks the decline of the Fujiwara family. **1115** Jurchen from Manchuria found China's Jin dynasty. **1200s** States are formed in densely populated Hawaii, Tahiti, and Tonga. **1234-1279** Mongols bring down the Jin dynasty in China; Kublai Khan reunites the country under the Yuan dynasty. **1368** Zhu Yuanzhang founds the Ming dynasty in China.	

1500

1500-1521 Spain conquers vast areas of Latin America, including the Aztec Empire in Mexico.

1532 Francisco Pizarro of Spain conquers the Inca.

1540s Native revolts against the Portuguese in Brazil break out.

1600 Five Algonquin tribes unite to form Powhatan Confederacy.

1619 The first Virginia assembly meets.

1680 The Pueblo Revolt drives Spaniards from New Mexico.

1547 Ivan the Terrible becomes the first tsar of Russia.

1600s European powers expand their colonization efforts.

1600s Religious wars, including the Thirty Years' War, erupt across Europe.

1700s Wars of royal succession engage most of Europe in ongoing conflicts.

1730-1743 Russia, the Holy Roman Empire, and Persia battle the Ottomans.

1501 Ismail Sufan establishes the Safavid Empire in Iran.

1520 Ottoman Sultan Suleyman I expands the empire into the Balkans and Persia.

1530-1540 The Songhai Empire, with its capital at Timbuktu, dominates West Africa.

1593 Ottomans begin the Long War against Austria, losing a last siege against Vienna in 1683.

1623 Queen Nzinga of Ndongo drives away the Portuguese.

1526 Babur invades India and founds the Mughal state.

1550s Warfare rages among the Japanese daimyo lords.

1592-96 Japan attempts to conquer Korea, but fails.

1644-1673 The Ming suffer the War of the Three Feudatories.

1679 Vietnamese and Cambodians go to war.

1690s The Mughal Empire fragments under pressure from Europe and Indian ethnic states.

1750

1775-1783 The American Revolution occurs.

1789 George Washington becomes the first president of the United States.

1820s San Martín and Bolívar lead South American struggles for independence from Spain.

1846-48 The Mexican War results in U.S. possession of California and the Southwest.

1861-65 The American Civil War occurs.

1789 The fall of the Bastille marks the beginning of the French Revolution.

1799-1815 Napoleon seizes power in France and goes on to conquer most of Europe.

1830-1860 Revolutions erupt in France, Germany, Poland, and Italy.

1867 The dual monarchy of Austria-Hungary is formed.

1870-71 The Franco-Prussian War leads to formation of the German Empire.

1750 The kingdom of Darfur expands in East Africa.

1774 Ottomans lose Crimea, Moldavia, and lands around the Black Sea in Russo-Turkish War.

1816 Shaka, ruler of the Zulu kingdom, conquers many peoples of southeastern Africa.

1884 The Berlin Conference divides Africa among European powers.

1899 The Boer War breaks out between Afrikaners and British.

1802 Emperor Gia Long unifies Vietnam.

1818 The Maratha are defeated by the British, who become in effect rulers of India.

1850-1864 Millions die in the Taiping Rebellion, China's—and the world's—bloodiest civil war.

1863 France begins to establish protectorates in Indochina.

1895 The Sino-Japanese War gives Japan dominance over Korea and Taiwan.

1900

1910-11 The Mexican Revolution occurs.

1929 The Partido Revolucionario Institutional (PRI) begins one-party rule in Mexico.

1936 Paraguay installs the Americas' first fascist regime.

1941 Japanese bomb Pearl Harbor, forcing the U.S. into World War II.

1949 NATO is founded as a regional military alliance against Soviet aggression.

1914-18 World War I occurs after the heir to the Austrian throne is assassinated.

1917 The October Revolution is followed by the Russian Civil War, which ends in victory for the Bolsheviks.

1936 The Spanish Civil War begins.

1939 Germany invades Poland; World War II begins. The Allies gain victory in Europe in 1945.

1949 The republic of Ireland is created.

1908 The Young Turk revolution restores the constitution and parliament of the Ottomans.

1922 Egypt declares independence under King Fuad.

1925 Ibn Saud conquers Hijaz and forms Saudi Arabia.

1936 The Great Revolt of the Palestinians begins against Zionist settlement, yet the new state of Israel is created in 1948.

1948 Apartheid is established in South Africa.

1904 The Russo-Japanese War is the first to use trench warfare.

1911 Revolution brings an end to the Manchus in China.

1921 Mongolia becomes the world's second communist state.

1945 The U.S. and the U.S.S.R. divide Korea.

1948 India becomes a republic.

1948 China becomes the communist People's Republic under Mao; Chinese nationalists form a government-in-exile in Taiwan.

1950-Present

1959 Cuba's Castro installs the first communist regime in the West.

1963 U.S. president Kennedy is assassinated in Dallas, Texas.

1974 Watergate forces Nixon to resign the U.S. presidency.

2001 Planes hijacked by al-Qaeda terrorists destroy New York City's World Trade Center.

2008 Barack Obama becomes the first African-American president in the United States.

1964 Khrushchev resigns after the Cuban Missile Crisis.

1968 The Soviet Union invades Czechoslovakia.

1975 The dictatorship of Generalissimo Francisco Franco in Spain ends.

1989 The Berlin Wall is demolished.

1991 The U.S.S.R. officially ceases to exist on December 9.

2002 The European Union's euro begins circulating.

1956-1974 Three Arab-Israeli wars occur, gaining more territory for Israel.

1979 Iran becomes the world's first Islamic republic and seizes hostages from U.S. Embassy.

1994 More than half a million are killed in the Rwandan genocide.

1994 The first nonracial general election in South Africa is won by Nelson Mandela.

2003 The U.S. invades Iraq.

1950-53 The Korean War occurs.

1956-1975 The Vietnam War results in Vietnam's reunification under communist rule.

1979 The Soviets invade Afghanistan.

1989 Thousands of students protest for democracy in Beijing's Tiananmen Square.

2001 U.S. forces oust the Taliban government in Afghanistan, beginning more than a decade of American military action in the region.

	PREHISTORY	500 B.C.E.	500 C.E.	1000	
THE AMERICAS	**ca 10,000 B.C.E.** The last worldwide glaciation ends. **ca 3000 B.C.E.** Mesoamericans begin intensive cultivation of maize, beans, chili peppers, avocados, squash, and gourds. **ca 2500 B.C.E.** Cotton is cultivated in modern-day Peru, as well as potatoes, gourds, and squash. **ca 1500 B.C.E.** Chiefdoms in the lowlands of the Gulf of Mexico produce surplus crops of corn by achieving two crops a year.	**400s B.C.E.** Domestication of beans spreads from Mexico into the North American Southwest. **ca 1 C.E.** Inhabitants of Amazon rain forest utilize a fertile soil called *terra preta* for farming. **200s C.E.** Inhabitants of coastal California plant oak trees to produce acorn crops and ensure a food supply during droughts. **400s C.E.** Scarcity of food in western North America causes many inhabitants to pursue a migratory lifestyle.	**ca 500** Moche society is hit by El Niño droughts and floods. **ca 595** The Joya de Ceren Maya site is buried under ash from the Loma caldera volcano. **ca 800** Increasingly warmer weather and greater rainfall enable Caddo people to develop advanced agriculture. **ca 970-1000** Climate change brings warm, wetter weather to North American plains and allows Cahokia people to accelerate the production of corn.	**ca 1150** Dry coastal Peruvian climate requires elaborate irrigation to support Chimu society. **ca 1275** Droughts hit Mesa Verde pueblo in Colorado, driving the Anasazi away. **ca 1350** The Amazon forms a tropical agricultural zone that supports six million people. **1400s** Shortage of rain stresses resources of the Caddo people. **ca 1450** Droughts and food shortages plague central Mexico.	
EUROPE	**ca 2500 B.C.E.** People in central Europe use slash-and-burn methods to clear forests and make land arable. **ca 1700 B.C.E.** A volcanic eruption on the island of Thera disrupts Minoan civilization. **ca 1400 B.C.E.** The eastern Alps are mined for copper and salt. **1226 B.C.E.** Mount Etna on the island of Sicily erupts. **ca 700 B.C.E.** Etruscans become prosperous because of northern Italy's mineral wealth.	**464 B.C.E.** An earthquake in Sparta kills tens of thousands. **436 B.C.E.** Famine strikes Rome. It is so severe that thousands throw themselves into the Tiber. **225 B.C.E.** The Colossus of Rhodes is toppled by an earthquake. **79 C.E.** Mount Vesuvius erupts, burying Pompeii. **180 C.E.** The population of the Roman Empire declines sharply after a long smallpox epidemic.	**542-594** Plagues strike Europe, halving its population. **ca 760** Muslims introduce cultivation of oranges, lemons, figs, dates, and eggplant in Spain. **ca 800-1000** The population of Europe recovers from the plague and reaches 36 million. **ca 910** Sheep grazing over long distances between summer and winter grounds has ill effects on Spain's environment. **974** England's earliest documented earthquake occurs.	**1000** Frisian dikes are built against floods and invasions. **ca 1160** English fens are drained for farmland. **ca 1315** A little ice age leads to poor harvests and famine across Europe. **1346** An earthquake hits Constantinople, causing the eastern arch of Hagia Sophia to crumble. **1347** The Black Death wreaks havoc in Europe, reappearing in England in 1361.	
MIDDLE EAST & AFRICA	**120,000-90,000 B.C.E.** Heavy rainfall makes the Sahara habitable for humans. Glaciation turns it arid around 75,000. **8000-7700 B.C.E.** Wheat is cultivated in the Fertile Crescent. **ca 3000 B.C.E.** Camels are domesticated in the Middle East. **ca 2000 B.C.E.** Deforestation of the Indus Valley begins. **ca 2000 B.C.E.** Austronesians settle various South Pacific islands, where they introduce yams, taro root, and breadfruit.	**ca 350 B.C.E.** A new strain of wheat is introduced into Egypt, from which bread is produced. **ca 200-100 B.C.E.** Dry episodes in the Sahel region of West Africa shift the climate and population. **125 B.C.E.** A plague of locusts afflicts Roman areas in northern Africa, raising the price of grain. **19 C.E.** An earthquake in Syria kills more than 100,000 people. **ca 224 C.E.** Cultivation of rice, sugarcane, and eggplant is introduced into Iran.	**526** An earthquake in Antioch, Turkey, devastates the area, killing some 250,000 people. **661** Camel herds of the Sahara support nomadic living of people in an inhospitable environment. **ca 700** Umayyads develop desert agriculture in Syria. **ca 800** An earthquake in Egypt destroys Nile port cities. **856** An earthquake devastates Damghan, Persia, killing more than 200,000.	**1033** A severe earthquake occurs in Palestine. **1347** The Black Death reaches Cairo, killing one-third of the population of Egypt. **1488** Bartholomew Dias of Portugal rounds the Cape of Good Hope at the tip of South Africa. **1497** Vasco da Gama of Portugal sails for India via the Cape of Good Hope.	
ASIA & OCEANIA	**ca 10,000 B.C.E.** Rising ocean waters separate Australia and New Guinea, Korea and Japan. **7000-5000 B.C.E.** Rice cultivation is developed in Southeast Asia and southern China. **ca 3000 B.C.E.** People of New Guinea cultivate yams and taro; domesticate pigs and chickens. **ca 1500 B.C.E.** Harappan civilization in the Indus Valley declines, perhaps because of drought. **ca 1500 B.C.E.** The water buffalo is domesticated in China.	**ca 300 B.C.E.** Wet rice cultivation begins in Japan. **ca 140 B.C.E.** Sericulture, the manufacture of silk, spreads from the Yellow River Valley. **ca 100 B.C.E.** Sugar cane is cultivated, based on wild varieties found in the East Indies. **92 C.E.** A cycle of floods and droughts in China is worsened by plagues of locusts. **ca 400 C.E.** Chinese populations decline greatly as diseases find their way along the Silk Road.	**ca 500** The sweet potato is distributed to Pacific islands by Austronesian mariners. **ca 600** Early settlers build the Alekoko fish pond and taro fields on Hawaii. **ca 840** Whereas Asian trade routes connect the Philippines, Indonesia, and New Guinea, the people of the Pacific islands maintain their own trade networks that link many distant groups. **ca 850** Maori sailors discover New Zealand.	**ca 1300** Inhabitants of Hawaii begin the construction of massive fish ponds to ensure regular supplies of favored fishes. **1330s** Bubonic plague (Black Death) originates in Asia. **1420** The Ming capital is moved to Beijing. **1434** The Khmer capital moves from Angkor to Phnom Penh. **1495** The Yellow River is diverted from its course north of the Shandong Peninsula to a new course south of the peninsula.	

1500

1519 Horses are brought to the New World by Hernán Cortés.

ca 1550 Cattle are introduced on the South American pampas.

1612 Tobacco is first grown as a commercial crop.

1660s Domestic stock and crops, not wild game, now provide most of the food in the English colonies.

1680s Disease reduces the Pueblo population from 60,000 to 17,000.

1750

1770 Coffee grown in Venezuela and Cuba becomes a major export crop of the Caribbean along with sugar and cacao.

1790s Sugar and cotton make the lower Mississippi region the heart of the "plantation world."

1869 Railroad cuts in two the buffalo herd of the Great Plains.

1879-1880 Indigenous peoples are driven out of the South American pampas in order to convert more grazing land for cattle.

1900

1905 The National Forest Service is established in the U.S.

1906 An earthquake in San Francisco kills 700 people.

1918 A worldwide influenza epidemic strikes.

1924 Insecticides are used for the first time.

1935 A series of dust storms roars over the U.S. plains.

1936 Lake Mead is created by the completion of Hoover Dam.

1950-Present

1977 Alaskan pipeline opens.

1989 Exxon oil tanker *Valdez* runs aground in Alaska, causing the world's largest oil spill.

1991 20th century's worst cholera epidemic affects nearly 100,000 people in Peru.

2005 Hurricane Katrina, one of the worst natural disasters in U.S. history, devastates the South.

2010 An earthquake in Haiti kills more than 300,000 people.

1500 New World crops and planting methods begin to be exported to Europe.

1509 Constantinople suffers a disastrous earthquake.

1519-1522 Magellan circumnavigates the globe for Portugal.

1546 Flemish geographer Gerardus Mercator describes Earth's magnetic poles.

1680s Crop failures cause severe famines across Europe.

1755 A Lisbon earthquake kills more than 60,000 people.

1760s Turnips, potatoes, and clover are increasingly planted and improve crop yields.

1832 A cholera epidemic kills 31,000 people in Britain.

1845 The Irish potato famine begins.

1849 A cholera epidemic kills about 16,000 in London.

1906 Vesuvius erupts, devastating the town of Ottaiano, Italy.

1908 An earthquake in southern Calabria and Sicily kills 150,000.

1911 Roald Amundsen of Norway becomes the first person to reach the South Pole.

1940 The Lascaux Caves are discovered in France. On their walls are prehistoric paintings dating to approximately 20,000 B.C.

1963 An undersea volcano erupts off the southern coast of Iceland, creating the new island of Surtsey in a matter of days.

1966 Floods ravage northern Italy, damaging thousands of Renaissance art treasures in Venice and Florence.

1976 Britain suffers its worst drought on record.

1986 The world's worst nuclear accident occurs at the Chernobyl Power Station in U.S.S.R.

1560s American crops manioc and peanuts arrive in Africa.

1570s Major plague outbreaks occur in Egypt; plague will recur there periodically until 1865.

1630s African iron smelting deforests vast regions and desiccates the climate.

1713 Smallpox devastates South Africa, opening new land to European settlement.

ca 1750 Planting and exporting of cotton begins in Palestine.

1824-25 Floods devastate Egypt.

1830s The shifting ecology of West Africa brings drier conditions and leads to widespread drought.

1851-1866 Gold, then diamonds, are discovered in southern Africa.

1860-61 Famine leads to bread riots in Iran.

1901 Britain begins oil drilling in Persia.

1908 Four thousand die during famine in the Usoga region of Africa.

1925 Marshes around Haifa, Israel, begin to be drained in the fight against malaria.

1927 Iraq's first oil strike occurs at Kirkuk.

1939 An earthquake in Turkey kills 45,000.

1968-1974 Drought in the Sahel region of northern Africa kills 500,000.

1973 OPEC embargoes oil supplies, causing a worldwide energy crisis.

1977 The last case of smallpox on Earth is reported in Somalia.

2000s AIDS becomes an epidemic in Africa.

2004-05 Six million people across Africa's Sahel region face famine after a locust invasion.

1514 Silver mines open in western Yunnan, China.

1555 An earthquake hits northwest China and kills 830,000.

1573 The Chinese first plant New World crops.

1600 Unrestricted felling of trees denudes Easter Island.

1600 Edo (Tokyo) is made the capital of Japan.

1681 The Chinese increase rice yields to three harvests per year.

1789 Smallpox ravages aborigines of coastal Australia.

1815 The Sumbawa volcano kills more than 50,000 in Indonesia.

1819 The British found Singapore as a free-trade port.

1819 The whaling industry begins in the Pacific islands.

1830s Sugar cultivation begins in Hawaii.

1833 Poor harvests bring famine to Japan.

1900 Famine and bubonic plague in India abate.

1911 Flooding on the Yangtze River kills 100,000 people in China.

1920 An earthquake in Gansu province, China, kills 200,000 people.

1923 Tokyo and Yokohama are destroyed by an earthquake, leaving 120,00 people dead.

1945 Atomic bombs fall on Hiroshima and Nagasaki.

1950 Drought followed by flooding kills 10 million people in northern China.

1970 Cyclones and floods kill 500,000 in East Pakistan (Bangladesh).

2003 The SARS virus spreads from China.

2004 A massive tsunami kills almost 300,000 in Indonesia and South Asia.

2011 A tsunami causes a nuclear disaster at Fukushima, Japan.

CULTURE & RELIGION

THE WORLD AT A GLANCE: PREHISTORY-PRESENT

	PREHISTORY	500 B.C.E.	500 C.E.	1000	
THE AMERICAS	**ca 11,500 B.C.E.** The Clovis culture emerges in North America's Great Plains. **ca 1800 B.C.E.** Andean people of South America build ceremonial pyramids and temples. **ca 1300 B.C.E.** The Olmec practice ritual bloodletting, sculpt colossal stone heads, and develop a lunar calendar. **ca 1100 B.C.E.** The Chavín de Huántar people of the Andes organize a complex society around a religious cult.	**ca 500 B.C.E.** The Paracas of Peru refine traditions that will continue in the Andean regions. **ca 500 B.C.E.** Adena society constructs earthen burial mounds in eastern North America. **ca 100 B.C.E.** Large ceremonial structures are built throughout Mesoamerica and coastal Peru. **ca 100 C.E.** Moche culture is characterized by high-level agriculture and clay pottery. **ca 300 C.E.** Maya societies develop their own system of writing.	**ca 500** Nazca and Moche people continue a rich artistic culture. **ca 540** An elite society in the city-state of Copán fosters literature and architecture. **ca 650** Copán's architecture and cultural life reaches its apogee. The city is replete with ball courts, plazas, temples, and magnificent sculptures. **ca 900** A militaristic tone pervades Toltec cities; sculpted, massive stone warriors line temples and plazas.	**ca 1000** Mandan and Hidatsa make corn central to their origin myth. Women hold special religious prominence due to their role in maintaining cornfields. **ca 1150** The Mixtec perfect the high style of pictographic writing. **ca 1400** The quipu is the numeric device used by the Inca for counting and a mnemonic device for recording oral histories. **1400s** Aztec priests sacrifice tens of thousands of people to the sun each year.	
EUROPE	**32,000-14,000 B.C.E.** Humans express themselves with cave art in southern Europe. **ca 3000 B.C.E.** Passage graves are built throughout England, Ireland, and northern France. **ca 1600 B.C.E.** Stonehenge is used as a religious center. **ca 1400 B.C.E.** Cremation comes into practice, suggesting different ideas about the afterlife. **ca 850 B.C.E.** Homer puts down in written form the *Iliad* and the *Odyssey*.	**ca 387 B.C.E.** Plato founds the Academy, a school of philosophy in Athens. **200s B.C.E.** Three schools of philosophical thought arise in Greece—Epicureanism, skepticism, and Stoicism. **27 B.C.E.** Virgil begins writing the *Aeneid*. **312 C.E.** Emperor Constantine I grants toleration of all religions. **432 C.E.** Patrick, a Christian bishop from Britain, travels to Ireland as a missionary.	**590** Gregory becomes pope and establishes the office as de facto ruler of central Italy. **598** The first English school is founded in Canterbury. **ca 700-850** The Old English poem *Beowulf* is composed. **863** Cyril and Methodius convert the Slavs to Christianity. **976** The Great Mosque of Córdoba is completed, holding 70 libraries, the largest one with 500,000 books.	**1096** The First Crusade begins. **1149** Oxford University is founded, soon followed by Cambridge. **1210s** Francis of Assisi and Dominic found their respective monastic orders. **1233** The Inquisition begins and soon utilizes torture. **1333** Arabic society in Granada reaches a cultural high. **1450** Florence under the Medicis becomes the center of the Renaissance and humanism.	
MIDDLE EAST & AFRICA	**45,000 B.C.E.** The flute, the oldest-known instrument, is used in North Africa. **24,000 B.C.E.** Rock paintings at the Apollo site in Namibia, Africa, can be dated to this period. **2550 B.C.E.** Pharaoh Khufu builds the Great Pyramid at Giza. **ca 2500 B.C.E.** Egyptians begin to mummify their royal dead. **ca 900 B.C.E.** Nok people of Nigeria fashion sculptures of fired clay.	**500-300 B.C.E.** Torah Judaism is developed. **280 B.C.E.** The library of Alexandria is founded. **164 B.C.E.** Judah Maccabee reclaims the Jerusalem temple, inaugurating Hanukkah. **ca 30 C.E.** Jesus of Nazareth is crucified by Roman authorities. **ca 70 C.E.** Work on the Gospels is undertaken. **300s C.E.** Augustine of Hippo writes *Confessions*.	**ca 500** The Sassanid Empire revives Zoroastrianism. **500** Jewish scholars compile the Talmud. **610** Muhammad experiences a spiritual transformation and receives a message from God. **ca 650** Copying the Koran results in ever more artistic forms of calligraphy. **813-833** Greek classics are translated into Arabic at a school in Baghdad.	**1027** Jewish communities organize across North Africa. **1065** The Nizamiyah Madrash, first great school for Muslim learned men, is established. **1090** The Assassins, a clandestine sect of Islam, are known for using murder to eliminate foes. **1118** The Order of the Knights Templar is created to protect the road to Jerusalem. **1180** Moses Maimonides completes Mishnah Torah, his great law code.	
ASIA & OCEANIA	**45,000 B.C.E.** The first rock art in Australia is dated to this time. **ca 18,000 B.C.E.** The first sculptures are crafted in Asia. **ca 12,000-8,000 B.C.E.** Ceramic arts begin in Japan. **ca 1400 B.C.E.** Hindu sages create the Vedas—the earliest Hindu sacred writings. **ca 900-800 B.C.E.** Zhou dynasty craftsmen in China excel at producing artistic bronze wares.	**ca 500 B.C.E.** Jainism and Buddhism begin spreading through northern India. **500s B.C.E.** Lao Zi founds Daoism; Kong Fuzi founds Confucianism. **ca 100 B.C.E.** Buddhism spreads into Central Asia along Silk Road. **ca 400 C.E.** The *Bhagavad Gita* takes on its final form after a number of revisions. **400s C.E.** Hinduism gradually replaces Buddhism as the dominant religious tradition of India.	**ca 500** India's Gupta kings support the arts and poetry, science and mathematics. **500** Trade on the Silk Road continues to connect Asia with Europe. **618-907** The Tang dynasty ushers in a golden age of poetry and culture in China. **645** Buddhism reaches Tibet. **ca 900** The Chola dynasty produces some of the most spectacular bronze works of Indian sculptural art.	**1044** Government edict establishes schools in China to train students for civil service exams. **1091** Building is under way for some 15,000 pagodas, temples, and palaces in Pagan, Burma. **1227** Zen Buddhism is introduced from China to Japan. **1350** Noh theater begins in Japan, theatrical drama in China. **1408** The multivolume encyclopedia *Yongle dadian* is completed in China.	

1500	1750	1900	1950-Present
1553 The University of Mexico is founded. **1636** Harvard College is founded in Massachusetts. **1670s** Missionaries begin losing power over Pueblo peoples, unable to protect them from Apache raids, recurrent drought, or epidemic disease. **1701** Yale University is founded. **1730s** English colonies experience a religious revival: the Great Awakening.	**1750s** African Americans become a central part of the Great Awakening as it sweeps through the Chesapeake region. **1769** The San Diego mission is founded in southern California. **1779** The first school of arts is established in the New World, in Mexico City. **1806** Webster publishes the first American dictionary. **ca 1870** Paiute prophet Wodziwob develops the Ghost Dance.	**1905** The Social Gospel Movement applies Christian progressive ideas to the problems of industrialization. **1916** Jazz sweeps the U.S. **1920s** The Harlem Renaissance sees a flourishing of social thought and artistic achievement among African Americans. **1925** F. Scott Fitzgerald publishes *The Great Gatsby*. **1943** Jackson Pollock has his first one-man show.	**1954** Ernest Hemingway wins the Nobel Prize in literature. **1962** The U.S. Supreme Court rules against compulsory prayer in public schools. **1971** Chilean poet Pablo Neruda wins the Nobel Prize in literature. **1976** The Episcopal Church approves ordination of women as priests. **2002** Revelations of child molestation by priests embroils the Catholic Church in scandal.
1500-1515 Active artists include Botticelli, Cellini, Cranach, Dürer, Grünewald, Leonardo, Michelangelo, Palladio, and Raphael. **1517** Martin Luther instigates the Protestant Reformation. **1605-1612** Miguel de Cervantes Saavedra publishes *Don Quixote* while Shakespeare writes *King Lear, Macbeth, The Winter's Tale,* and *The Tempest*. **1641** A Catholic rebellion erupts in Ireland. Protestants are massacred in Ulster.	**1751** France begins publication of the *Encyclopédie*, a leading volume of the Enlightenment. **1771** *Encyclopedia Britannica* is first published. **ca 1790** The great age of European orchestral music occurs. **1869** Tolstoy publishes *War and Peace*. **1870s** The impressionist school of painting emerges. **1891** Thousands of Jews are forced into Russian ghettos.	**1907** Henri Matisse coins the term cubism. **1922** James Joyce publishes *Ulysses* and T. S. Eliot publishes "The Waste Land," two high points of modernism. **1924** Pablo Picasso begins his abstract period. **1929** The Vatican State is born. **1940** In Warsaw, 350,000 Jews are confined to a ghetto. **1949** George Orwell publishes *Nineteen Eighty-Four*.	**1953** Simone de Beauvoir publishes her landmark feminist book, *The Second Sex*. **1962** The Second Vatican Council begins wide-ranging reforms of Roman Catholic practices. **1968** Pope Paul VI issues an encyclical against all artificial means of contraception. **1978** Cardinal Karol Wojtyla becomes Pope John Paul II. **2010** France bans the burka in public schools.
1515 Ottoman Sultan Selim I declares Sunni Islam the state religion and persecutes Shiites. **1530s** Major Ottoman works on logic, grammar, biography, and religious sciences are written. **1530s** Islamic studies flourish at the university and schools of the Koran in Timbuktu. **1600-1620** Christian Ethiopia suffers attacks from Muslims. **1703** Ottoman Ahmed III opens the empire to Western culture.	**1760-66** Two encyclopedias are written in Iran covering history, geography, science, and earthly and heavenly beings. **1799** The Rosetta Stone is discovered in Egypt, allowing historians to translate ancient Egyptian hieroglyphs. **1840** Bosnian rabbi Judah Alkalai proposes Zionism, the idea of a Jewish homeland. **1881** The first migration of European Jews to Palestine occurs.	**1917** The Balfour Declaration on Palestine pledges British support for the creation of a Jewish homeland, provided that the rights of non-Jewish Palestinians are respected. **1925** Islam is abolished as the state religion in Turkey; modernization begins. **1933** Assyrian Christians are massacred in Iraq. **1940** The Nationalist Islamic Party is founded in Egypt.	**1950** Israel's new "law of return" grants automatic citizenship to any immigrant Jews. **1986** Desmond Tutu becomes the first black archbishop of Cape Town, South Africa. **2002** Boko Haram, an Islamist religious sect, is founded in Nigeria. **2003** Ethnic and religious conflicts boil over in Sudan's Darfur region.
1542 Mughal Emperor Akbar's reforms unify Hindus and Muslims under his rule. **1550s** The Japanese merchant class grows; cities and leisure arts flourish. **1570** The cult of tea reaches its peak of popularity in Japan. **1604** Donglin Academy is founded in China. **1680** Basho, Japanese master of haiku poetry, is at the height of his fame.	**1773** The *Complete Library of the Treasuries* project attempts to compile the literary heritage of China into one collection. **1800s** Christian missionaries gain converts in Pacific islands. **ca 1850** Painter and printmaker Hiroshige flourishes. **1862** A Muslim revolt breaks out in China's northwest. **1870** Anti-missionary sentiments lead to China's Tianjin massacre.	**1906** An All-India Moslem League is founded by Aga Khan. **1912** Rabindranath Tagore translates *Gitanjali* into English. **1913** Rabindranath Tagore wins the Nobel Prize in literature. **1916** China's New Culture movement begins; western-educated Chinese scholars argue for modernization.	**1954** Reverend Sun Myung Moon founds the Unification Church in South Korea. **1958** China begins the Great Leap Forward, followed eight years later by Chairman Mao's Cultural Revolution. **1980s** Islamic warriors called mujahideen take up arms against the Soviet invasion of Afghanistan. **1988** Seoul, South Korea, hosts the Summer Olympics, the first without a boycott since 1976.

SCIENCE & TECHNOLOGY

THE WORLD AT A GLANCE: PREHISTORY-PRESENT

	PREHISTORY	500 B.C.E.	500 C.E.	1000	
THE AMERICAS	**ca 9000 B.C.E.** Flint arrowheads and spear points are made by the Clovis culture. **ca 3000 B.C.E.** Agricultural villages appear in Mesoamerica. **ca 1500 B.C.E.** Metalworking begins in Peru. **ca 800 B.C.E.** The temple at Chavín contains 1,600 feet of internal drainage and ventilation ducts. **ca 800-700 B.C.E.** People of the Bering Strait develop the toggling harpoon to hunt marine life.	**ca 400 B.C.E.** Trephination, a surgical procedure by which sections of the skull are excised, is used in Peru to treat head injuries, migraines, and seizures. **ca 200 B.C.E.** Inhabitants of modern-day Ecuador and Peru develop clay furnaces used to melt gold and silver. **ca 100 B.C.E.** The Moche use bronze to make tools and weapons. **ca 200 C.E.** Hohokam people develop dry farming techniques.	**ca 500** Maya develop advanced astronomical calendars. **ca 550** People in southwest Colorado begin building pit houses. **ca 850** The Caddo use osage orange wood to manufacture quality bows. **ca 900** The Anasazi build a sophisticated road system to integrate all towns in the Chaco Canyon region. **ca 950** The Toltec become skilled in irrigation, tapping the waters of the Tula River.	**1000s** Plains natives use collapsible tepees and sleighlike travois to break camp easily and follow buffalo. **ca 1085** Thule culture develops technologies for making kayaks and whale boats. **ca 1250** Weaving by the Chimu is perfected to 200 waft an inch. **1400s** Inca walls in Cuzco are close-fitted and mortarless, to withstand earthquakes. **ca 1450** The Inca build 20,000 miles of road in the Andes.	
EUROPE	**ca 7000 B.C.E.** Farming tribes spread from Anatolia into Greece. **ca 2000 B.C.E.** Wheeled plows are used in some parts of Europe. **ca 1000 B.C.E.** The use of iron begins in Greece. **ca 800 B.C.E.** Celts of the Hallstatt region adopt iron metallurgy and spread it across Europe. **581-497 B.C.E.** Pythagoras develops basic principles of mathematics.	**ca 500 B.C.E.** Pythagoreans hypothesize from mathematical principles that Earth is a sphere. **ca 400 B.C.E.** Hippocrates begins compiling the Corpus Hippocraticum. **ca 250 B.C.E.** Erasistratus of Chios explains the functions of the heart's valves. **ca 200 B.C.E.** Romans invent concrete and go on to develop immense aqueducts and bridges. **ca 70 C.E.** Vespasian begins construction of the Colosseum.	**537** The Hagia Sophia is completed, the largest Christian church of its time, with a dome spanning 100 feet. **650-850** Benedictine monks clear forests, drain swamps, and employ crop rotation, becoming highly successful farmers. **ca 800** Iron smelting allows Carolingians to produce iron tools, horseshoes, nails, and weapons. **ca 800** The first castles are built in western Europe.	**1098** Nicholas Prevost of Tours writes *Antidotarum*, a collection of 2,650 medical prescriptions. **1125** Alexander Neckam of England writes the earliest account of a mariner's compass. **1202** Fibonacci introduces Arabic numerals in Europe. **1278** Glass mirrors are invented. **1300s** Five hundred cathedrals are built throughout Europe. **1455** Gutenberg invents the modern printing process.	
MIDDLE EAST & AFRICA	**ca 6200 B.C.E.** Copper smelting and textile manufacture begins in Çatal Hüyük, Anatolia. **ca 5000 B.C.E.** Irrigation agriculture begins in the Middle East. **ca 3500 B.C.E.** The potter's wheel and the kiln are invented in Mesopotamia. **ca 1600 B.C.E.** Egyptians write a medical book showing accurate workings of the heart, stomach, bowels, and blood vessels. **ca 1500 B.C.E.** Egyptians invent glassmaking.	**ca 450 B.C.E.** Iron tool technology spreads across Africa. **ca 400 B.C.E.** The *qanat* system of underground canals is further expanded on the Iranian plateau. **ca 300 B.C.E.** Euclid explains geometry in his *Elements*. **297 B.C.E.** Construction begins on the world's first lighthouse, the Pharos of Alexandria. **ca 285 B.C.E.** Herophilus, practicing human dissection, recognizes the brain as the seat of intelligence.	**620** Copper wire is in use in Dambwa, Zambia. **ca 700** Villagers in Kenya produce a version of the world's oldest crucible steel. **ca 750** Ibrahim al-Fazari is the first Muslim to construct an astrolabe. **ca 800** Arab mathematician Muhammad ibn Musa al-Khwarizmi furthers works on algebra. **910** Arab physician al-Razi writes the first account of smallpox and his theory of immunity.	**1000-1040** Metallurgists at West African urban centers cast intricate copper-alloy sculptures. **1071** Constantine the African brings Greek medicine west. **1275-1450** At Zimbabwe, stone walls are built without the use of mortar. **ca 1430** Ottomans become expert cannonmakers. **1470s** A brilliant era in Ottoman mathematics occurs under Ali Kusai and Mulla Lutf.	
ASIA & OCEANIA	**ca 12,000 B.C.E.** Jomon hunter-gatherers in Japan make the first pottery. **ca 10,000 B.C.E.** Agriculture develops in the Yellow River Valley. **ca 8000 B.C.E.** The boomerang is invented in Australia. **ca 4000 B.C.E.** Bronze objects are produced in Thailand, the first use of bronze worldwide. **ca 1400** The Shang dynasty develops a calendar with a 366-day year of 12 lunar months.	**ca 300 B.C.E.** Indian merchants master the art of sailing the Indian Ocean on its seasonal monsoon winds. **ca 200 B.C.E.** The Chinese develop coal as a fuel. **100s B.C.E.** Suits of iron armor are developed by the Chinese. **ca 100 B.C.E.** The use of negative numbers becomes standard for Chinese mathematicians. **105 C.E.** Cai Lun describes the modern method of making paper from hemp, bark, or pulp.	**ca 500** Indian astronomers Varahamihira and Aryabhata discover that the earth turns on its axis. **593** Printing blocks are invented in China. **ca 600-618** Sui emperors in China build the Grand Canal. **634** Chomsongdae Observatory is built in the Korean kingdom of Silla, the oldest known observatory in east Asia. **ca 850** Chinese alchemists create gunpowder.	**ca 1040** Bi Sheng of China invents movable type. **1100s** Easter Island settlers build massive stone monuments. **1151** The Chinese use explosives in warfare. **1428** Ulugh-Beg builds an astronomical observatory at Samarkand. **1450** Defensive walls along the northern frontiers of China are rebuilt to create the Ming era Great Wall.	

1500	1750	1900	1950-PRESENT
1556 A new process for separating silver from raw ore boosts the New World mining industry. **1625-29** Ironworks and printing begin in the English colonies. **1700-1720** Industry develops further in North America, including distilling and gunsmithing. **1723** Indoor plumbing is installed in a house in Newport. **1724** Levees are built along the Mississippi River in Louisiana to protect against damaging floods.	**1794** Eli Whitney patents the cotton gin. **1807** Robert Fulton develops the first practical steamboat. **1825** The Erie Canal is opened. **1852** The elevator is invented. **1869** The U.S. transcontinental railroad is completed. **1876** Alexander Graham Bell patents the telephone. **1878** Thomas Edison invents the incandescent light bulb.	**1903** The Wright brothers fly a powered airplane at Kitty Hawk. **1914** Robert Goddard starts his rocketry experiments. **1914** The Panama Canal opens. **1927** Charles Lindbergh flies nonstop from New York to Paris. **1936** Hoover Dam is completed. **1941** Atomic research begins on the Manhattan Project. **1947** Chuck Yeager breaks the sound barrier.	**1952** Jonas Salk discovers polio vaccine. **1969** Apollo 11 lands men on the moon. **1981** Scientists identify the AIDS virus. **1981** IBM introduces the first personal computer. **1990** Hubble Space Telescope is put into operation. **2003** The U.S. Human Genome Project is completed.
1512 Copernicus postulates a sun-centered universe. **1518** Eyeglasses to aid the shortsighted are developed. **1610** Galileo discovers Jupiter's moons with a telescope. **1619** Harvey describes circulation of the blood. **1666** Newton develops calculus; calculates the moon's orbit. **1735** Linnaeus describes a classification system for plants, animals, and minerals.	**1769** James Watt patents the modern steam engine. **1771** Joseph Priestly discovers that plants release oxygen. **1796** Edward Jenner discovers a smallpox vaccine. **1863** Charles Darwin publishes *The Origin of Species*. **1895** Guglielmo Marconi invents radio telegraphy. **1898** Marie and Pierre Curie discover polonium and radium.	**1900** Sigmund Freud's *Interpretation of Dreams* marks the beginnings of psychoanalysis. **1905** Albert Einstein formulates the special theory of relativity. **1912** *Titanic* sinks on its maiden voyage from England to the U.S. **1913** Niels Bohr formulates his theory of atomic structure. **1928** Alexander Fleming discovers penicillin by chance. **1949** The Soviets create their own atom bomb.	**1953** Watson and Crick unveil their double-helix model of DNA. **1957-1961** The Soviet Union launches the first satellite and puts the first man in space. **1978** The first "test-tube baby" is born in England. **1991** Tim Berners-Lee puts the World Wide Web online. **1997** British geneticists clone an adult sheep named Dolly. **2010** The world's first hydrogen car is introduced in the UK.
1530s African iron and steel is exported to Portugal. **ca 1550** Aqueducts are built to bring water into Istanbul from reservoirs near the Black Sea. **1600s** Increasing use of gunpowder weaponry by the Ottomans renders the cavalry obsolete. **1703** Islamic science is enriched by European instruments such as the telescope.	**ca 1800** West Africans are manufacturing their own gunpowder and expertly repairing imported European weapons. **1816** Wool mills, sugar refineries, glassworks, and other industries are established in Egypt. **1820s** Zulu king Shaka scorns European firearms in favor of the short-handled spear. **1869** The Suez Canal opens. **1878** The world's first oil tanker is launched in the Caspian Sea.	**1911** Istanbul tramways are electrified and public steamship service is started. **1925** Power plants are constructed in Palestine; a hydroelectric station is built on the Jordan River; telephone and electric lines are installed. **1930** South African microbiologist Max Theiler develops a yellow fever vaccine. **1931** Benguella-Katanga, the first trans-African railroad line, is completed.	**1959** Anthropologists Louis and Mary Leakey find the world's earliest known human in a Tanzanian gorge, establishing Africa as the cradle of humanity. **1967** Dr. Christiaan N. Barnard of South Africa performs the world's first human heart transplant operation. **1968** The Aswan High Dam in Egypt is completed. **2011** Iran's first nuclear power plant, Bushehr 1, officially opens.
1520 Chinese begin increasing their use of gunpowder weapons modeled on European designs. **1543** Portuguese reach Japan and introduce firearms there. **1598** The Koreans invent an ironclad ship. **1637** *Tiangong Kaiwu* is published, an encyclopedia of Chinese technology. **1744** Jesuits reform the Chinese calendar and introduce western scientific instruments.	**1750s** Dutch educators spread Western knowledge in Japan. **1805** Japanese doctor Seishu Hanaoka uses general anesthesia for the first time. **1853** India's first railroad and telegraph lines open. **1891** Construction of the Trans-Siberian Railroad begins. **1895** Heavy industry begins to develop in Japan.	**1917** The Trans-Siberian Railroad is completed. **1930** Sir Chandrasekhara Raman of India wins the Nobel Prize in physics for his work on light diffusion and the discovery of the raman effect. **1930** Two halves of the new Sydney Harbor Bridge are joined in Australia.	**1955** Tokyo Telecommunications Engineering (Sony) produces the first pocket-size transistor radio. **1984** Sony and Philips introduce the first commercial CD players. **1994** Construction begins on Three Gorges Dam in China. **1998** India and Pakistan begin testing nuclear weapons. **2004** Taipei 101 becomes the world's tallest skyscraper. **2011** China becomes the world's top filer of patents.

PEOPLE & SOCIETY
THE WORLD AT A GLANCE: PREHISTORY-PRESENT

	PREHISTORY	500 B.C.E.	500 C.E.	1000	
THE AMERICAS	**ca 16,000 B.C.E.** Humans cross the Bering Strait to Alaska. **ca 14,000 B.C.E.** Humans arrive in South America. **ca 3000 B.C.E.** Fishing villages are established in Peru. **ca 1000 B.C.E.** The Adena people form an agricultural society in the Ohio River Valley. **ca 1000 B.C.E.** The Olmec maintain trade relations as far south as modern-day El Salvador.	**400s B.C.E.** Coastal California becomes densely populated. **ca 350 B.C.E.** Origins of the Maya culture are evident. **ca 200 B.C.E.** The Nazca lines begin to appear in Peru. **ca 200 B.C.E.** Hopewell society appears in North America. **ca 100 C.E.** Anasazi settle in southwestern North America. **ca 400 C.E.** Teotihuacan participates in an extensive trade network throughout Mesoamerica.	**ca 500** Maya civilization on the Yucatán Peninsula flourishes. **ca 500** Thule move into Alaska. **ca 650** Hopewell people settle the upper Mississippi River, making it their highway for trade. **ca 700** Mound-building Caddo culture flourishes in Texas and Oklahoma. **ca 800** The Toltec migrate into northern and central Mexico. **ca 850** Anasazi build urban communities in Chaco Canyon.	**ca 1000** Leif Eriksson is believed to have discovered America (Nova Scotia). **ca 1100** The Mississippian settlement of Cahokia is the leading metropolis north of Mexico. **ca 1260** The Chimu of Peru develop an intricate legal code. **1400s** The five nations of Iroquois Indians convene to frame the Great League of Peace. **1492** Christopher Columbus makes landfall in the Caribbean.	
EUROPE	**ca 40,000 B.C.E.** Modern humans arrive in Europe, living alongside Neanderthals. **ca 3000 B.C.E.** Craft specialization and gender division of labor develop in eastern Europe. **ca 2000 B.C.E.** The Minoans on Crete emerge as a civilization. **ca 1000 B.C.E.** A mass migration of Germanic peoples into central Europe begins. **594 B.C.E.** Solon proposes that all free Athenians be allowed to participate in government.	**450 B.C.E.** Rome's first code of law is placed in the forum. **ca 440 B.C.E.** Pericles broadens democracy in Athens and encourages arts and sciences. **342 B.C.E.** Aristotle travels to Macedon to tutor young Alexander the Great. **133-123 B.C.E.** Reforms of the Gracchus brothers are stifled by a corrupt Roman senate. **ca 100 C.E.** Slaves account for a third of the Roman Empire's population.	**500** Angles and Saxons move into the British Isles. **529** Justinian's Code of Civil Law is issued. **530** Frankish tribes overtake Germany and northern France. **600-874** Vikings invade Ireland and England, and settle Iceland. **ca 780** Peasants in Europe begin surrendering land to military leaders in return for protection, becoming serfs. **ca 850** Jews develop Yiddish.	**ca 1100** Annual trade fairs are held just outside town walls and last for days. **1151** The first fire and plague insurance is offered, in Iceland. **1200** Engagement rings become fashionable. **1200s** Venice's Rialto bridge is a bustling center of commerce. **1387** Geoffrey Chaucer writes *The Canterbury Tales*. **1414** The Medicis become official bankers to the papacy.	
MIDDLE EAST & AFRICA	**ca 250,000 B.C.E.** Modern humans emerge in Africa. **ca 100,000 B.C.E.** Modern humans migrate to the Middle East. **ca 3500 B.C.E.** Sumerians invent a form of writing and numbering called cuneiform. Hieroglyphic script appears in Egypt 400 years later. **1792 B.C.E.** Hammurabi compiles his code of laws. **ca 750 B.C.E.** The Phoenician colony of Carthage in North Africa develops into a trade hub.	**ca 300 B.C.E.** Greek colonists bring to the Middle East traditions and laws of the polis. **ca 200 C.E.** Bantu-speaking farmers migrate into much of southern Africa. **ca 200 C.E.** The kingdom of Axum grows into the largest market in sub-Saharan Africa. **ca 20 C.E.** Strabo describes the Arabian Peninsula as a land of fabulous wealth due to the rich spice trade of the Red Sea.	**ca 540** Arabia is peopled by nomadic clans and settled tribes engaged in commerce and trade. **ca 750** African slave trade picks up momentum, along with other trans-Saharan trade. **ca 800** Jewish immigrants settle in North Africa and shift from farming to trade. **ca 800** Jenne-Jeno, in the Niger River delta, becomes a bustling trade center of 10,000. **ca 840** The wealth of the Muslim Empire fuels urbanization.	**ca 1200** In Egypt, Mamluk rule drives Arab nomads south toward Nubia and begins Islamization of the Middle Nile. **1352-53** Geographer Ibn Battuta explores sub-Saharan Africa. **ca 1400** Trade in gold is developed down the Zambezi Valley to the Sofala coast in southeast Africa. **1436-1444** Portuguese navigators explore the west coast of Africa and restart the African slave trade.	
ASIA & OCEANIA	**ca 75,000 B.C.E.** Modern humans arrive in Southeast Asia and China. **ca 60,000 B.C.E.** Modern humans reach New Guinea and Australia by boat. **ca 30,000 B.C.E.** Humans cross a land bridge from Korea to Japan. **ca 3000 B.C.E.** Villages along the Indus River develop into large cities. **ca 1500 B.C.E.** The Lapita exchange network is formed in the Pacific.	**ca 390 B.C.E.** Legalism appears in China. **200s B.C.E.** Trade along the Ganges River flourishes in the hands of private entrepreneurs. **124 B.C.E.** Chinese emperor Han Wudi establishes an imperial university to stock his bureaucracy with educated officeholders. **ca 100 C.E.** Paper becomes the main medium of written communication in China. **ca 500 C.E.** Austronesian mariners settle Easter Island.	**607** King Songstan Gampoh unifies Tibet. **645** Japan institutes the Taika reforms from a Chinese model. **710** Nara is the first urban center in Japan, rapidly gaining a population of 200,000. **960** The Song dynasty reunifies China and ushers in extensive economic and cultural change. **995** Powerful statesman Fujiwara Michinaga exercises nearly complete control over Japan's imperial court.	**ca 1000** Pacific islands experience a rapid population growth. **1023** The first paper money is printed in China. **1100s** Samurai begin to dominate Japanese society. **1206** Genghis Khan becomes leader of the Mongol confederation. **1271** Venetian Marco Polo travels to China. **1404** Japan begins trading with Ming China.	

1500	1750	1900	1950-PRESENT
1509 Slaves are first brought from Africa to America by the Spanish. **1607** The English establish a settlement on the James River. **1647** Massachusetts establishes the first public school system in the colonies. **1673** Boston Post Road links settlements down the East Coast of North America. **1690s** Scarcity of coins encourages American colonies to print paper money and bills of credit.	**1776** The Declaration of Independence is adopted. **1815** The market economy begins to transform U.S. society after the War of 1812. **1820s** After successful independence revolts, most Latin American countries drift into rule by military strongmen. **1838-39** The Cherokee Trail of Tears takes place. **1849** The California gold rush begins.	**1901** J. P. Morgan organizes the U.S. Steel Corporation. **1910s** African Americans migrate in great numbers from the rural South to the industrial North. **1928** Brazil's economy collapses due to overproduction of coffee. **1929** The Wall Street stock market crashes on Black Tuesday. **1935** President Roosevelt signs the U.S. Social Security Act. **1944** Canada institutes the Family Allowance Plan.	**1950s** North America experiences a baby boom. **1955** Rosa Parks's arrest sets the American civil rights movement in motion. **1968** Martin Luther King, Jr., is assassinated in Memphis. **1973** *Roe* v. *Wade* makes abortion a U.S. constitutional right. **1980** CNN becomes the first 24-hour news station. **2004** Facebook is launched.
1506 The first regular newspaper appears, published in Germany. **1589** The French begin using forks as eating implements. **1597-98** Elizabethan Poor Laws are enacted, setting up an early social welfare system in England. **1630** Public advertising of goods is first used in France. **1644** René Descartes writes in *Principia Philosophiae*, "I think, therefore I am."	**1762** Rousseau publishes *The Social Contract.* **1776** Adam Smith publishes *The Wealth of Nations,* the foundation of free-market capitalism. **1789** The Declaration of the Rights of Man and the Citizen is issued in France. **1848** Marx publishes *The Communist Manifesto.* **1870s** Cities improve their water and sewer systems for better public health.	**1909** Men and women older than 70 receive their first old age pensions in London. **1927** Germany's economy collapses on Black Friday. **1929** Stalin's first Five-Year Plan begins. By 1932, famine is widespread in the U.S.S.R. **1936** BBC London inaugurates television service. **1942** Heydrich reveals his "final solution" to exterminate Europe's Jews.	**1950s** Migration from farms to cities expands at a rapid pace. **1967** The first ATM is put in service, in London. **1995** The World Trade Organization is created to promote economic development worldwide. **1990-2010** Millions of refugees relocate after communism's collapse in Eastern Europe. **2011** Europeans take to the streets in opposition to austerity measures.
1506 King Afonso of Kongo introduces European customs. **1560s** The slave trade increases in West Africa. **1579** Ottomans make their first trade agreement with England. **1600s** Muslim empires import guns, powder, and swords from Europe. **1652** Arab traders in East Africa traffic in slaves and spices. **1680s** Masai warriors expand southward in Africa.	**1754-1793** Piracy fuels economic prosperity in Tripoli, Libya. **1760** Boers begin settling the interior of southern Africa. **1787** The first freed slaves from Britain settle in Sierra Leone. **1828** The first Arabic newspaper is published in Egypt. **ca 1840** Zanzibar becomes the commercial center of east Africa. **1870** The transatlantic slave trade between Africa and the Americas comes to an end.	**1905** The Iranian Constitutional Revolution begins with massive popular protests. **1915** Compulsory military service in the African colonies forces thousands of African males to join World War I. **1915** A soaring economic boom in Egypt occurs as resources are devoted to war. An Egyptian business class develops. **1925** Blacks, Indians, and those of mixed race are barred from skilled jobs in South Africa.	**1960s** Egypt adopts Arab socialism, nationalizing foreign enterprises and reclaiming farmland. **1960** OPEC is founded. **1985-86** Among all girls ages 12 to 18 in Africa, only 46 percent are enrolled in school. **1991** Apartheid in South Africa is dismantled. **2011** King Abdullah of Saudi Arabia announces that women will be granted the right to vote in municipal elections.
1550s Mughal emperor Akbar of India reforms taxes and encourages religious toleration. **1600s** European powers skirmish over trade rights in Asia. **1620-1630** Japanese expel foreign traders and their influence. **1668** The English East India Company controls Bombay. **1685** The Chinese open ports to European trade. **1722** Japan's Tokugawa shogunate lifts bans on foreign books.	**1788** A penal colony is set up at Botany Bay, Australia. Free settlers arrive five years later. **1820** Vietnamese emperor Minh Mang models his rule on Chinese laws and institutions. **1853** Commodore Perry sails into Japan's Edo Bay, inspiring the Meiji Restoration in 1868. **1872** Universal military conscription is introduced in Japan. **1893** New Zealand becomes the first country to allow women to vote.	**1905** China abolishes its 1,300-year-old civil service exam system. **1920** Mohandas Gandhi becomes India's leader in its struggle for independence. **1925** Japan introduces general suffrage for men. **1926** Indian women are allowed to run for public office. Untouchables get voting rights in 1932. **1932** Japan begins its conquest of world markets by undercutting prices.	**1953** Hillary and Norgay reach Mount Everest's summit. **1956** Sony exports its first products, to Canada. **1980** Japan surpasses the U.S. as the world's largest automaker. **1983** The population of China reaches one billion. **2010** Japan's population growth rate falls to zero.

Pages 2 & 3 Kenneth Garrett.

Page 5 NASA and The Hubble Heritage Team (STScI/AURA).

Chapter 1: The First Societies Prehistory-500 B.C.E.

14-15, Richard T. Nowitz/NGS Image Collection; 16 & 17, Kenneth Garrett; 18, Iraq Museum, Baghdad, photo by Steve McCurry; 20, Kenneth Garrett; 23, Richard A. Cooke III; 27 (upper), Sisse Brimberg/NGS Image Collection; 27 (lower), Gordon Donkin. By permission of the National Library of Australia; 29, The Bridgeman Art Library/Getty Images; 30, Richard T. Nowitz/NGS Image Collection; 31, Gianni Dagli Orti/CORBIS; 32-33, Oriental Institute, University of Chicago, photo by Victor R. Boswell, Jr.; 33, Georg Gerster/Photo Researchers; 34, Archivo Iconografico, S.A./CORBIS; 35, National Museum of Pakistan, Karachi, photo by James P. Blair; 37, Kevin Schafer/CORBIS; 38 & 39, Kenneth Garrett; 41, Sanxingdui Museum, Guanghan, China, photo by O. Louis Mazzatenta; 43, Kenneth Garrett; 45, Museo Antropología Xalapa/ AFP/Getty Images; 46, Bettmann/ CORBIS; 47, Richard T. Nowitz/CORBIS; 48, Carsten Peter/NGS Image Collection; 49, ©The Trustees of the British Museum, photo by Winfield Parks; 52, Archive Photos/Getty Images; 53, C.M. Dixon/Ancient Art & Architecture Collection; 54, Gianni Dagli Orti/CORBIS; 57, Werner Forman/CORBIS; 59, Araldo de Luca/CORBIS; 60, Sisse Brimberg.

Chapter 2: The Classical Age 500 B.C.E.-500 C.E.

62-63, Museum of Qin Terracotta Warriors and Horses, China, photo by O. Louis Mazzatenta; 65, Bettmann/CORBIS; 67, Hulton Archive/Getty Images; 68, Musée du Louvre, Paris, photo by Jonathan Blair; 71, Dallas and John Heaton/Free Agents Limited/CORBIS; 74, Vanni Archive/CORBIS; 75, Todd Gipstein/NGS Image Collection; 76, Museo Nacional de Antropología, Mexico City, photo by B. Anthony Stewart; 77, Ira Block; 78-79, Georg Gerster/Photo Researchers; 81, Werner Forman/CORBIS; 85, Peter V. Bianchi; 86-87, Michael Yamashita; 88 (upper), Carsten Peter/NGS Image Collection; 88 (lower), Cary Wolinsky; 91 (upper), Bettmann/CORBIS; 91 (lower), Adam Woolfitt/CORBIS; 92 West Semitic Research/Dead Sea Scrolls Foundation/CORBIS; 93, Araldo de Luca/CORBIS; 94, Werner Forman/CORBIS; 95, Nathan Benn/CORBIS; 96, Museo Archeologico Nazionale, Naples, Italy, photo by James L. Stanfield; 96-97, Roger Ressmeyer; 98, Gianni Dagli Orti/CORBIS; 99, Ira Block; 102, Munson-Williams-Proctor Arts Institute, Utica, NY, photo by Otis Imboden; 103, William Albert Allard/NGS Image Collection; 104, Vanni Archive/CORBIS; 105, Arte & Immagini srl/CORBIS; 107, Benoy K. Behl.

Chapter 3: Faith and Power 500-1000

110-111, REZA; 113, Tim Laman/NGS Image Collection; 117, Michael Kirtley and Aubine Kirtley; 119, Paul Chesley; 122 (upper), Chan Chan Museum, Peru, photo by Ira Block; 122 (lower), S. Meltzer/PhotoLink/Getty Images; 123, Richard T. Nowitz/NGS Image Collection; 124, Ohio Historical Society, photo by Richard A. Cooke III; 125 (upper), Michael Yamashita; 125 (lower), Asian Art & Archaeology, Inc./CORBIS; 126-127, Bruce Dale; 128, Kenneth Garrett/NGS Image Collection; 129, James L. Stanfield; 131 (upper), Gianni Dagli Orti/CORBIS; 131 (lower), Sarah Leen; 132, Mansell/Time Life Pictures/Getty Images; 136, ©The Trustees of the British Museum, photo by Otis Imboden; 137, Kenneth Garrett; 139, Museum für Kunst und Gewerbe, Hamburg, photo by James L. Stanfield; 140 (upper), photo by Enrico Ferorelli, computer reconstruction by Doug Stern; 140 (lower), Paul Chesley/NGS Image Collection; 141, Hulton Archive/Getty Images; 145, José F. Poblete/CORBIS; 147, Bettmann/CORBIS; 149, Dewitt Jones/CORBIS; 150, David Muench/CORBIS; 151 (upper), From the collections of the Saint Louis Science Center; 151 (lower), Cahokia Mounds State Historic Site, painting by Lloyd K. Townsend; 154-155, John and Lisa Merrill/CORBIS; 157, Asian Art & Archaeology, Inc./CORBIS.

Chapter 4: Invasions and Advances 1000-1500

158-159, Mongolian Invasion Historical Material Hall, photo by Koji Nakamura; 161, Bibliothèque Nationale de France; 163, National Palace Museum, Taipei, Taiwan, Republic of China; 165, Bettmann/CORBIS; 168, Brian Brake/Photo Researchers; 169, CORBIS; 171, Jed Share/Getty Images; 172, Slim Aarons/ Getty Images; 173, Archivo Iconografico, S.A.; 176 (upper), Bettmann/CORBIS; 176 (lower), Richard Ehrlich/Getty Images; 178-179, Paul Chesley/NGS Image Collection; 181 (both), Bettmann/CORBIS; 182-183, Ira Block; 185, Richard A. Cooke III; 187, Osaka Castle Museum/JNTO, photo by Ira Block; 188, Peter Guttman/CORBIS; 189, Michael Yamashita; 191 (upper), Bruce Dale; 191 (lower), Sandro Vannini/CORBIS; 192-193 (both), James L. Stanfield; 195, Gianni Dagli Orti/CORBIS; 197, Bettmann/CORBIS; 198, Christie's Images/CORBIS; 199, Tor Eigeland; 202, The Gallery Collection/CORBIS; 203 (upper), William Albert Allard/NGS Image Collection; 203 (lower), Bob Sacha.

Chapter 5: Converging Worlds 1500-1750

204-205, Mark R. Godfrey; 206, Hulton Archive/Getty Images; 209, Bettmann/CORBIS; 210, Library of Congress, #LC-USZ62-33994; 211, Hulton Archive/Getty Images; 214, The Bridgeman Art Library/Getty Images; 216-217, Courtesy of the Vatican Museums, photo by Victor R. Boswell, Jr.; 218, Hulton Archive/Getty Images; 220, Stefano Bianchetti/CORBIS; 221, Bettmann/CORBIS; 224, Magyar Nemzeti Muzeum, Budapest, photo by James L. Stanfield; 225, Topkapi Palace Museum, Istanbul, photo by James L. Stanfield; 226, Bettmann/CORBIS; 229, Mansell/Time Life Pictures/Getty Images; 230, Baba Wagué Diakité; 232, Stock Montage/Getty Images; 233 (upper), Bettmann/CORBIS; 233 (lower), Gordon Wiltsie/NGS Image Collection; 235, Edward S. Curtis, courtesy Library of Congress; 236, Bettmann/CORBIS; 237 & 239 (upper), Hulton Archive/Getty Images; 239 (lower), Sakamoto Photo Research Laboratory/CORBIS; 240-241, Michael Lewis/NGS Image Collection; 242, Lester Lefkowitz/CORBIS; 243, Jacob Silberberg/Getty Images; 244, Courtesy of the Observatories of the Carnegie Institution of Washington: 245, National Museum, Lagos, Nigeria, photo by James L. Stanfield; 247, National Geographic photographer William Albert Allard; 248, Bettmann/CORBIS.

Chapter 6: Empires and Revolutions 1750-1900

250-251, Herbert Tauss; 253, Library of Congress; 254, CORBIS; 257, W. & D. Downey/Getty Images; 263 (upper), Hulton Archive/Getty Images; 263 (lower), Bettmann/CORBIS; 264-265, Hulton-Deutsch Collection/CORBIS; 267, Engraving by H.B. Hall after Alonzo Chappel, Library of Congress; 269 (upper), Historical Picture Archive/CORBIS; 269 (lower), Archivo Iconografico, S.A./CORBIS; 270, Hulton Archive/Getty Images; 271 (both) & 272, Bettmann/CORBIS; 273, Art Archive/CORBIS; 274, Hulton Archive/Getty Images; 275, From Nathaniel Isaacs' *Travels and Adventures in Eastern Africa*, 1836; 280, Bettmann/CORBIS; 281, MPI/Getty Images; 282, Bettmann/CORBIS; 285 (upper), National Archives, #16-G-99-1-1; 285 (lower), National Archives, #165-SB-23; 286-287, Library of Congress; 290-291, Library of Congress, #LC-USZC4-4637; 292, National Archives, #111-SC-83726; 293 (upper), Hulton Archive/Getty Images; 293 (lower), Museum of the City of New York/Getty Images; 294 & 295, Hulton Archive/Getty Images.

Chapter 7: Global Conflict 1900-1950

296-297, Peter Stackpole/Time Life Pictures/Getty Images; 299, Bettmann/CORBIS; 303, National Archives, #238-NT-282; 304, W. Eugene Smith/Time Life Pictures/Getty Images; 309, Fox Photos/Getty Images; 311 (upper), ©2006 Estate of Pablo Picasso/Artists Rights Society (ARS), New York, Digital image ©The Museum of Modern Art/Licensed by SCALA/Art Resource, NY; 311 (lower), Topical Press Agency/Getty Images; 312, Underwood & Underwood/CORBIS; 314, Courtesy Imperial War Museum, Neg. #Q2041; 314-315, Courtesy Imperial War Museum, Neg. #Q5100; 317, CORBIS; 319, Frank Driggs Collection/ Getty Images; 320, Mansell/Time Life Pictures/Getty Images; 322 & 323, Bettmann/CORBIS; 324, AP/Wide World Photos; 325, H.S. Wong, National Archives, #208-AA-132N(2); 326, AP/Wide World Photos; 327 & 328, Bettmann/CORBIS; 329, National Archives, #80-G-19948; 330, National Archives, #242-EAPC-6-M713a; 333, National Archives, #80-G-205473; 334, National Archives, #208-NP-6XXX-1; 335, National Archives, #111-SC-189-099; 336-337, National Archives, #26-G-2343; 338, Keystone/Getty Images; 339, National Archives, #208-N-43888; 340, National Archives, #111-SC-204811; 340-341 & 343, Margaret Bourke-White/Time Life Pictures/Getty Images.

Chapter 8: Toward a New World Order 1950-Present

344-345, Alexandra Avakian/Woodfin Camp/Time Life Pictures/Getty Images; 347, AFP/Getty Images; 348, Larry Burrows/Time Life Pictures/Getty Images; 351, Peter Magubane; 352, Jean-Philippe Arles/Reuters/CORBIS; 353, Carlos Cazalis/CORBIS; 356, Bettmann/CORBIS; 359 (upper), Hulton Archive/Getty Images; 359 (lower), Keystone/Getty Images; 360, Bettmann/CORBIS; 361, Frank Driggs Collection/Getty Images; 362 & 364, Hulton Archive/Getty Images; 365, Bettmann/CORBIS; 366, AFP/Getty Images; 369 (upper), NASA; 369 (lower), Eddie Adams, AP/Wide World Photos; 370-371, Huynh Cong ("Nick") Ut, AP/Wide World Photos; 372, Henri Bureau/CORBIS SYGMA; 374, Bettmann/CORBIS; 375, Gina Martin/NGS Image Collection; 376, Bettmann/CORBIS; 378, Roger Werth/Woodfin Camp/Time Life Pictures/Getty Images; 381, Karen Kasmauski; 383, Steve McCurry; 384-385, chuyu/iStockphoto; 387, Najlah Feanny/CORBIS SABA; 388, AP Photo/Jae C. Hong; 390-391, Issei Kato/AFP/Getty Images; 391, Rex Features via AP Images.

Appendix: The World at a Glance Prehistory-Present

392-393, NASA.

General Reference

Barnavi, Eli, ed. *A Historical Atlas of the Jewish People*. New York: Alfred A. Knopf, 1992.

Bentley, Jerry H., and Herbert F. Ziegler. *Traditions and Encounters: A Global Perspective on the Past*. Boston: McGraw-Hill, 2000.

Bellwood, Peter. *The Polynesians: Prehistory of an Island People*, rev. ed. London: Thames and Hudson, 1987.

Blainey, Geoffrey. *Triumph of the Nomads: A History of Aboriginal Australia*. Melbourne: Macmillan, 1975.

Bukdall, Jørgen, and others, eds. *Scandinavia Past and Present*. 3 vols. Copenhagen: Arnkron, 1959.

Calloway, Colin G. *One Vast Winter Count: The Native American West Before Lewis and Clark*. Lincoln: University of Nebraska Press, 2003.

Daniels, Patricia S., and Stephen G. Hyslop. *National Geographic Almanac of World History*. Washington, D.C.: National Geographic Society, 2003.

Goucher, Candice L, Charles A. LeGuin, and Linda A. Walton. *In the Balance: Themes in Global History*. New York: McGraw-Hill, 1998.

Grove, Noel. *Atlas of World History*. Washington D.C.: National Geographic Society, 1997.

Grun, Bernard. Based on Werner Stein's *Kultur Fahrplan*. *The Timetables of History,* 3rd rev. ed. New York: Simon & Schuster /Touchstone Books, 1991.

Hall, John Whitney, and John Grayson Kirk, eds. *History of the World: Earliest Times to the Present Day*. North Dighton, Mass.: World Publications, 2002.

Howe, K.R. *Where the Waves Fall: A New South Sea Island History from First Settlement to Colonial Rule*. Honolulu, 1984.

Mancall, Peter C., and James H. Merrell, eds. *American Encounters: Natives and Newcomers From European Contact to Indian Removal, 1500-1850*. London: Routledge, 2000.

Meade, Teresa A., and Merry E. Wiesner-Hanks, eds. *A Companion to Gender History*. London: Blackwells, 2004.

McKay, John, Bennett D. Hill, and John Buckler. *A History of Western Society,* 7th ed. Boston: Houghton Mifflin, 2002.

McNeill, J.R., and William H. McNeill. *The Human Web: A Bird's-Eye View of World History*. New York: W.W. Norton, 2003

O'Brien, Patrick K., ed. *Oxford Atlas of World History*. New York: Oxford University Press, 2002.

Waldam, Carl. *Atlas of the North American Indian*. New York: Facts on File, 1985.

Chapter 1: The First Societies Prehistory-500 B.C.E.

Gero, J.M., and M.W. Conkey, eds. *Engendering Archeology: Women and Prehistory*. Oxford, England: Basil Blackwell, 1991.

Goucher, Candice L., and Linda A. Walton. *Bridging World History* (26-part video series and interactive Web site). Annenberg and the Corporation for Public Broadcasting, 2004. (Used also for Chapters 7 and 8.)

Haywood, John, with Thomas Freeman, Paul Garwood, and Judith Toms. *Historical Atlas of the Ancient World*. Abingdon, Oxfordshire, England: Metro Books, 2001.

Kuhrt, Amelie. *The Ancient Near East: c. 3000-330 B.C.* 2 vols. London: Routledge, 1995.

Lemonick, Michael D. "Hobbits of the South Pacific," *Time* (November 8, 2004).

Time-Life Books. *The First Americans*. Alexandria, Va.: Time-Life Books, 1992.

Time-Life Books. *What Life Was Like on the Banks of the Nile: Egypt 3000-30 B.C.* Alexandria, Va.: Time-Life Books, 1996.

Thurstan, Shaw, and others. *The Archaeology of Africa: Food, Metals and Towns*. London: Routledge, 1993. (Used also for Chapters 2 and 3.)

Sasson, Jack M., ed. *Civilizations of the Ancient Near East*. 4 vols. New York: Scribner, 1995.

Scarre, Christopher, and Brian M. Fagan. *Ancient Civilizations*. New York: Longman, 1997. (Used also for Chapters 2, 3, and 4.)

Wells, Spencer. *The Journey of Man: A Genetic Odyssey*. Princeton: Princeton University Press, 2002.

Chapter 2: The Classical Age 500 B.C.E.-500 C.E.

Ball, Warwick. *Rome in the East: The Transformation of an Empire*. London: Routledge, 2000.

Edwards, Mike. "Han," *National Geographic* (February 2004).

Freeman, Charles. *Egypt, Greece and Rome: Civilizations of the Ancient Mediterranean*. New York: Oxford University Press, 1996. (Used also for Chapter 3.)

Gore, Rick. "The Dead Do Tell Tales at Vesuvius," *National Geographic* (May 1984).

Gwin, Peter. "Peruvian Temple of Doom," *National Geographic* (July 2004).

Hessler, Peter. "Rising to Life: Treasures of Ancient China," *National Geographic* (October 2001).

Hitchcock, Susan Tyler. *Geography of Religion*. Washington, D.C.: National Geographic Society, 2004.

Mellersh, H.E.L. *Chronology of World History: Prehistory-A.D. 1491: The Ancient and Medieval World*. Vol. 1. Santa Barbara, Calif.: ABC-Clio, 1999.

Miller, Barbara Stoler, trans. *Bhagavad-Gita: Krishna's Counsel in Time of War*. New York: Bantam Books, 1986.

Moffett, Samuel H. *History of Christianity in Asia*, 2nd ed. Maryknoll, New York: Orbis Books, 1998.

Paxton, John, and Edward W. Knappman, eds. *The Wilson Calendar of World History*. New York: H.W. Wilson, 1999.

Time-Life Books. *What Life Was Like When Rome Ruled the World: The Roman Empire 100 B.C.-A.D. 200*. Alexandria, Va.: Time-Life Books, 1997.

Washington, Peter, ed. *The Roman Poets*. New York: Alfred A. Knopf, 1997.

Chapter 3: Faith and Power 500-1000

Abun-Nasr, and Jamil M. *A History of the Maghrib in the Islamic Period*. Cambridge: Cambridge University Press, 1987. (Used also for Chapters 4-8.)

Hitti, Philip. *History of the Arabs, 10th ed.* New York: St. Martin's Press, 1970. (Used also for Chapters 4-6.)

Hodgson, Marshall G.S. *The Venture of Islam: Conscience and History in a World Civilization*. 3 vols. Chicago: University of Chicago Press, 1974. (Used also for Chapters 4-8.)

Hourani, Albert H. *A History of the Arab Peoples*. Cambridge: Harvard University Press, 1991. (Used also for Chapters 4-8.)

Iliffe, John. *Africans: The History of a Continent*. Cambridge: Cambridge University Press, 1995.

Stillman, Norman A. *The Jews of Arab Lands: A History and Source Book*. Philadelphia: Jewish Publication Society of America, 1979. (Used also for Chapters 4-6.)

Wiesner, Merry E. *Women and Gender in Early Modern Europe,* 2nd ed. Cambridge: Cambridge University Press, 2000. (Used also for Chapter 4.)

Time-Life Books. *What Life Was Like in the Lands of the Prophet*. Alexandria, Va.: Time-Life Books, 1999.

Chapter 4: Invasions and Advances 1000-1500

Bromer, Jerome, ed. *Chronicle of the World*. New York: Simon & Schuster /Prentice Hall/ Ecam, 1990.

Canby, Thomas Y. "The Anasazi Riddles in the Ruins," *National Geographic* (November 1982).

Edwards, Mike. "The Adventures of Marco Polo, Part I," *National Geographic* (May 2001).

Edwards, Mike. "Marco Polo in China, Part II," *National Geographic* (June 2001).

Edwards, Mike. "Marco Polo: Journey Home, Part III," *National Geographic* (July 2001).

Kopper, Philip, and the Editors of Smithsonian Books. *The Smithsonian Book of North American Indians Before the Coming of the Europeans*. Washington, D.C.: Smithsonian Institution, 1986.

Montes, Auguste F. Molina. "The Building of Tenochtitlan," *National Geographic* (December 1980).

Reader's Digest. *Everyday Life Through the Ages*. New York: The Reader's Digest Association, 1992.

Regan, Geoffrey. *Lionhearts: Richard I, Saladin and the Era of the Third Crusade*. New York: Walker, 1998.

Reps, Paul, and Nyogen Senzaki, transcribers. *Zen Flesh Zen Bones: A Collection of Zen and Pre-Zen Writings*. Boston: Tuttle Publishing, 1998.

Teeple, John B. *Timelines of World History*. New York: Dorling Kindersley, 2002.

Von der Porten, Edward. "The Hanseatic League: Europe's First Common Market," *National Geographic* (October 1994).

White, Peter. "The Temples of Angkor: Ancient Glory in Stone," *National Geographic* (May 1982).

Chapter 5: Converging Worlds 1500-1750

Aronson, Marc. *Witch-Hunt: Mysteries of the Salem Witch Trials*. New York: Atheneum, 2003.

Barwise, J.M., and N.J. White. *A Traveler's History of Southeast Asia*. New York: Interlink Books, 2002.

Boorstin, Daniel. *The Discoverers*. New York: Random House, 1983.

Chasteen, John Charles. *Born in Blood and Fire: A Concise History of Latin America*. New York: W.W. Norton, 2001.

Crosby, Alfred W. *The Columbian Exchange*. Westport, Conn.: Greenwood Press, 1972.

Diagram Group. *Peoples of Central Africa*. New York: Facts on File, 1997.

Diagram Group. *Peoples of East Africa*. New York: Facts on File, 1997.

Gernet, Jacques, translated by J.R. Foster and Charles Hartman. *A History of Chinese Civilization*. Cambridge: Cambridge University Press, 1996.

Gombrich, E.H. *The Story of Art*. London: Phaidon Press, 1966.

Goodwin, Jason. *Lords of the Horizons: A History of the Ottoman Empire*. New York: Henry Holt, 1998.

Hazen-Hammond, Susan. *Timelines of Native American History*. New York: The Berkley Publishing Group, 1996.

Johnston, Robert D. *The Making of America*. Washington, D.C.: National Geographic Society, 2002.

Josephy, Alvin M., Jr. *500 Nations: An Illustrated History of North American Indians*. New York: Alfred Knopf, 1994.

Kamen, Henry. *The Spanish Inquisition: A Historical Revision*. New Haven, Conn.: Yale University Press, 1997.

Keen, Benjamin, and Keith Haynes. *A History of Latin America.* Boston: Houghton Mifflin Company, 2000.

Kirchner, Walther. *Russian History.* New York: Harper Collins Publishers, 1991.

Mann, Charles C. "1491," *The Atlantic,* Vol. 289, No. 3 (March 2002).

Metcalf, Barbara D, and Thomas R. Metcalf. *A Concise History of India.* Cambridge: Cambridge University Press, 2002.

Nardo, Don. *Traditional Japan.* San Diego, Calif.: Lucent Books, 1995.

Ochoa, George. *Atlas of Hispanic-American History.* New York: Checkmark Books, 2001.

Paludan, Ann. *Chronicle of the Chinese Emperors.* London: Thames and Hudson, 1998.

Patnaik, Naveen. *A Second Paradise: Indian Courtly Life: 1590-1947.* Garden City, N.Y.: Doubleday, 1985.

Reader, John. *Africa: A Biography of the Continent.* New York: Alfred A. Knopf, 1998

Rothfarb, Ed. *In the Land of the Taj Mahal: The World of the Fabulous Mughals.* New York: Henry Holt, 1998.

Shaw, Stanford J., and Ezel Kural. *History of the Ottoman Empire and Modern Turkey.* 2 vols. Cambridge: Cambridge University Press, 1976-77. (Used also for Chapters 6-8.)

Shillington, Kevin. *History of Africa.* New York: Macmillan, 1989.

Chapter 6: Empires and Revolutions 1750-1900

Brinkley, Alan. *American History: A Survey.* Boston: McGraw-Hill, 1999.

Cribb, John, Mary Beth Klee, and John Holdren (eds). *The Human Odyssey: The Modern World.* McLean, Va.: K12 Inc., 2005.

Farrington, Karen. *Historical Atlas of Empires.* New York: Checkmark Books, 2002.

McCarthy, Justin. *The Ottoman Peoples and the End of Empire.* New York: Arnold/Oxford, 2001.

Time-Life Books. *What Life Was Like in Europe's Romantic Era: Europe, A.D. 1789-1848.* Alexandria, Va.: Time-Life Books, 2000.

Time-Life Books. *What Life Was Like During the Age of Reason: France, A.D. 1660-1800.* Alexandria, Va.: Time-Life Books, 1999.

Ward, Geoffrey C. *The Civil War: An Illustrated History.* New York: Knopf, 1990.

Yapp, Malcolm. *The Making of the Modern Near East: 1792-1923.* London: Longman, 1987.

Chapter 7: Global Conflict 1900-1950

Barry, John M. *The Great Influenza: The Epic Story of the Deadliest Plague in History.* New York: Penguin Books, 2005.

Gilbert, Martin. *The First World War: A Complete History.* New York: Henry Holt, 1994.

Kagan, Neil, ed. *Great Photographs of World War II.* Birmingham, Ala.: Oxmoor House Press, 2003.

Keegan, John. *An Illustrated History of the First World War.* New York: Alfred A. Knopf/ Borzoi Books, 2001.

Laqueur, Walter, ed. *The Holocaust Encyclopedia.* New Haven: Yale University Press, 2001.

National Geographic Society. *National Geographic Eyewitness to the 20th Century.* Washington, D.C.: National Geographic Society, 1999. (Used also for Chapter 8.)

Time-Life Books. *The American Story: World War II.* Alexandria, Va.: Time Life, 1997.

Winter, J.M. *The Experience of World War I.* New York: Oxford University Press, 1989.

Winter, Jay and Blaine Baggett. *The Great War and the Shaping of the 20th Century.* New York: Penguin Books, 1996.

Chapter 8: Toward a New World Order 1950-Present

Howe, Marvine. *Turkey Today: A Nation Divided over Islam's Revival.* Boulder: Westview Press, 2000.

Milestones of the 20th Century. Danbury, Conn.: Grolier, 1999.

Nova, "Wave That Shook the World." PBS, NOVA/WGBH, and Channel 4 Television.

Parfit, Michael. "Mexico City: Pushing the Limits." *National Geographic,* August 1996.

Time-Life Books. *Our American Century: Events That Shaped the Century.* Alexandria, Va.: Time-Life Books, 1998.

Time-Life Books. *Secrets of the Century: Inside the CIA.* Alexandria, Va.: Time-Life Books, 2000.

Tucker, Neely. "Anatomy of a Cataclysm: Science of the Tsunami." *The Washington Post,* March 29, 2005.

Wetterau, Bruce. *The New York Public Library Book of Chronologies.* New York: Prentice Hall Press, 1990.

Williams, Neville. Chronology of World History. *1901-1998: The Modern World.* Vol. 4. Oxford, England: Helicon Publishing, 1999.

LIST OF MAPS

ABOUT THE CONTRIBUTORS

EDITOR

NEIL KAGAN heads Kagan & Associates, Inc., an editorial company specializing in creating innovative illustrated books. Over his 30-year career, the former publisher/managing editor and director of New Product Development for Time-Life Books created numerous book series, including the award-winning Voices of the Civil War, What Life Was Like, and the Time Life Student Library. As an accomplished photographer and creative director, Kagan brings a strong vision to designing illustrated history books.

CONTRIBUTING AUTHORS

ROBIN CURRIE, born in Belfast, is an 11-year-veteran of Time-Life Books, where he worked as a text editor on the company's history series. He has written and edited for a number of publishing organizations, including National Geographic, the Smithsonian, McGraw Hill, K12 Inc., the Nature Conservancy, National Endowment for the Humanities, and America Online.

STEPHEN G. HYSLOP is a writer and editor of books on American and world history, including *National Geographic Almanac of World History* (with Patricia S. Daniels). He served as editor at Time-Life Books for the history series Time Frame, What Life Was Like, and American Indians. He is a contributing writer for the History Channel Magazine and the author of *Bound for Santa Fe: The Road to New Mexico and the American Conquest* (2002).

KARIN KINNEY is a writer and editor in Washington, D.C. She has edited a number of books for the National Geographic Society, including *Mystery of the Ancient Seafarers*, *Geography of Religion,* and *Mother, Daughter, Sister, Bride*. She also served as editorial director for Time-Life for Children, editing such series as Understanding Science and Nature and the Time Life Student Library.

JOCELYN G. LINDSAY holds a history degree from the College of Wooster. As a professional researcher and writer, she has contributed to many history and science series at Time-Life Books and the National Geographic Society. Her freelance writing includes journal articles, fiction for children and adults, and poetry.

J. R. McNEILL is a professor of history and University Professor at Georgetown University. His most recent books include *Something New Under the Sun: An Environmental History of the Twentieth-Century World* (2000), *The Human Web: A Bird's-Eye View of World History* (co-written with W. H. McNeill in 2003), and *Mosquito Empires: Ecology and War in the Greater Caribbean, 1620-1914* (2010).

DAN O'TOOLE has contributed to a number of National Geographic books, including *Encyclopedia of Space*, *Geography of Religion*, and *Historical Atlas of the United States*. He is also an aspiring archaeologist and has worked at sites in both the United States and Italy. He is a graduate of Georgetown University, where he earned a degree in classical languages and archaeology.

TRUDY WALKER PEARSON is a 24-year veteran of Time-Life Books, where she worked on a number of history series, including What Life Was Like and American Indians. Currently a freelancer, she has helped to create museum exhibits and was illustrations editor for *Trail to Wounded Knee,* a National Geographic Society publication.

BARRY WOLVERTON has spent the past 15 years writing and editing books, documentary television scripts, and interactive content for the Library of Congress, Discovery Channel and Discovery Education, Time-Life Books, Time Warner, Prentice Hall, and U.S. News Online. His credits include numerous episodes of the Emmy-nominated children's show *Assignment Discovery.* He is also an award-winning screenwriter and is currently working on a children's novel.

BOARD OF ADVISERS

JERRY H. BENTLEY is professor of history at the University of Hawaii and editor of the *Journal of World History*. His early publications focused on the religious, moral, and political thought of Renaissance humanists. More recently his research has concentrated on the history of cross-cultural interactions. His recent publications include *Old World Encounters: Cross-Cultural Contacts and Exchanges in Pre-Modern Times* (1993), *Shapes of World History in Twentieth-Century Scholarship* (1996), and (with Herbert F. Ziegler) *Traditions and Encounters: A Global Perspective on the Past* (2000, 2003).

LINDA T. DARLING is associate professor of history at the University of Arizona, where she teaches Ottoman, Middle Eastern, and world history. She is the author of *Revenue-Raising and Legitimacy: Tax Collection and Finance Administration in the Ottoman Empire, 1560-1660* (1996) and is currently working on her second book, *Justice and Power in the Middle East.*

EDWARD J. DAVIES teaches world history and the United States in world history at the University of Utah. He has served on the executive council of the World History Association. Presently, he is completing two manuscripts: "The United States in World History" and "Romancing the Swastika: The American Encounter with the Russo-German War, 1945-2000."

PATRICIA LOPES DON is an assistant professor of world, colonial Latin American, and early modern European history at San Jose State University. Her main research interests are the encounters between Europe and the Americas in the early Atlantic world, particularly the Spanish Empire in the 16th century. Professor Don is currently working on a manuscript entitled "Bonfires of Culture: Franciscans, Indians and the Inquisition in Early Mexico, 1536-1543."

MERRY WIESNER-HANKS is professor of history and director of the Center for Women's Studies at the University of Wisconsin-Milwaukee and is co-editor of the *Sixteenth Century Journal*. She has been awarded Fulbright and Guggenheim Fellowships for her research and is the author or editor of 18 books, including *Women and Gender in Early Modern Europe* (2000), and (with Susan Karant-Nunn), *Luther's Writings on Women: A Sourcebook* (2003). Recently, she created a book for young adults, *An Age of Voyages, 1350-1600.*

CANDICE GOUCHER is professor of history and director of undergraduate studies, Washington State University, Vancouver. She has directed archaeological projects in West Africa, the Caribbean, and the Indian Ocean and has authored numerous articles and books, including (with Linda A. Walton) *In the Balance: Themes in Global History* (1998). She was co-lead scholar on *Bridging World History*, a 26-part multimedia world history curriculum, and has produced an award-winning documentary film, *Blooms of Banjeli.*

LINDA A. WALTON is professor of history and international studies and chair of the history department at Portland State University. She has conducted research in Japan, Taiwan, and the People's Republic of China, and is the author of a book, book chapters, and articles on the social and intellectual history of middle period China (11th-14th centuries). She is co-author of *In the Balance: Themes in Global History* (1998) and one of two lead scholars for *Bridging World History*, a 26-part multimedia world history curriculum.

NATIONAL GEOGRAPHIC CONCISE HISTORY OF THE WORLD
Edited by Neil Kagan
Foreword by Jerry H. Bentley and J. R. McNeill

PUBLISHED BY THE NATIONAL GEOGRAPHIC SOCIETY

John M. Fahey, Jr. *President and Chief Executive Officer*
Gilbert M. Grosvenor *Chairman of the Board*
Nina D. Hoffman *Executive Vice President*

PREPARED BY THE BOOK DIVISION

Kevin Mulroy *Senior Vice President and Publisher*
Kristin Hanneman *Illustrations Director*
Marianne R. Koszorus *Design Director*
Carl Mehler *Director of Maps*
Barbara Brownell Grogan *Executive Editor*

PRODUCED BY KAGAN & ASSOCIATES, INC., FALLS CHURCH, VIRGINIA

Neil Kagan *President and Editor-in-Chief*
Sharyn Kagan *Vice President and Director of Administration*

STAFF FOR THIS BOOK

Stephen G. Hyslop *Text Editor, Introductions*
Barry Wolverton *Text Editor, Time Lines*
Neil Kagan *Illustrations Editor*
Carol Farrar Norton *Art Director*
Robin Currie *Contributing Authors*
Stephen G. Hyslop
Karin Kinney
Jocelyn G. Lindsay
Dan O'Toole
Trudy Walker Pearson
Barry Wolverton
Mary Beth Oelkers-Keegan *Associate Editor/Copy Editor*

NATIONAL GEOGRAPHIC STAFF FOR THIS BOOK

Dan O'Toole *Project and Illustrations Coordinator*
Stacy Gold *Photo Research Editor*
Matt Chwastyk *Map Production*
Thomas L. Gray
Martin S. Walz
Meredith Wilcox *Illustrations Specialist*
Gary Colbert *Production Director*
Lewis R. Bassford *Production Project Manager*
Michael Greninger *Editorial Assistants*
Emily McCarthy

MANUFACTURING AND QUALITY CONTROL

Christopher A. Liedel *Chief Financial Officer*
Phillip L. Schlosser *Managing Director*
John T. Dunn *Technical Director*
Mary Clare Tracy *Manager*

STAFF FOR 2013 EDITION

Gail Spilsbury *Project Editor, Text Editor*
J. R. McNeill *Writer*
Nancy Marion *Photo Editor*
Marshall Kiker *Associate Managing Editor*
Judith Klein *Production Editor*
Lisa A. Walker *Production Project Manager*
Katie Olsen *Production Design Assistant*
Robert L. Barr *Manufacturing Manager*

CELEBRATING
‹125›
YEARS

The National Geographic Society is one of the world's largest nonprofit scientific and educational organizations. Founded in 1888 to "increase and diffuse geographic knowledge," the Society's mission is to inspire people to care about the planet. It reaches more than 400 million people worldwide each month through its official journal, *National Geographic,* and other magazines; National Geographic Channel; television documentaries; music; radio; films; books; DVDs; maps; exhibitions; live events; school publishing programs; interactive media; and merchandise. National Geographic has funded more than 10,000 scientific research, conservation and exploration projects and supports an education program promoting geographic literacy. For more information, visit www.nationalgeographic.com.

For more information, please call 1-800-NGS LINE (647-5463) or write to the following address:

National Geographic Society
1145 17th Street N.W.
Washington, D.C. 20036-4688 U.S.A.

For information about special discounts for bulk purchases, please contact National Geographic Books Special Sales: ngspecsales@ngs.org

For rights or permissions inquiries, please contact National Geographic Books Subsidiary Rights: ngbookrights@ngs.org

ISBN: 978-1-4262-1178-2

The Library of Congress has cataloged the 2006 edition as follows:

National Geographic concise history of the world: an illustrated time line / edited by Neil Kagan.
   p. cm.
   Includes bibliographical references and index.
   ISBN 0-7922-8364-3 (hc)
   1. Chronology, Historical. I. Title: Concise history of the world. I. Kagan, Neil.

   D11.D37 2005
   909'.02—dc22

ACKNOWLEDGMENTS

There are many people to thank for making this book a reality—Barbara Brownell Grogan and Kevin Mulroy of the National Geographic Book Division for their support and guidance; Art Director Carol Norton for her incredibly elegant and imaginative design; Stacy Gold from the National Geographic Image Collection for her monumental photo research effort and her keen eye for great photographs; Carl Mehler for his direction and care in putting together the maps; and Dan O'Toole for his valuable assistance in the day-to-day coordination of this project and his enthusiasm for all things ancient and modern. I would also like to thank Georgetown University Professor John Voll for suggesting world historian Jerry Bentley as "the best person in the country" to head up our Board of Advisers, and Jerry for accepting the challenge and for putting together a world-class team of advisers to help us create a totally new and unique global history. I want to give special thanks to all of our authors and editors—Stephen G. Hyslop, Karin Kinney, Dan O'Toole, Trudy Walker Pearson, Jocelyn G. Lindsay, Robin Currie, Mary Beth Oelkers-Keegan, and Barry Wolverton—for their endless creativity, hard work, and perseverance. And finally, I would like to thank my family, Sharyn, Lisa, and Josh, who gave me the encouragement to try to piece together this complex history of the world.   *—Neil Kagan*

Printed in the United States of America
13/CK-CML/1